Table of Contents

National Goals and Research for People with Intellectual and Developmental Disabilities

Editors
K. Charlie Lakin and Ann P. Turnbull

THE ARC OF THE U.S.
AMERICAN ASSOCIATION ON MENTAL RETARDATION
2005

Published by
American Association on Mental Retardation
444 North Capitol Street, N.W., Suite 846
Washington, DC 20001-1512

Library of Congress Cataloging-in-Publication Data
National goals and research for persons with intellectual and developmental disabilities / editors, K. Charlie Lakin and Ann P. Turnbull.
    p. ; cm.
    Based on a conference entitled Keeping the Promises: National Goals, State of Knowledge, and Research Agenda for Persons with Intellectual and Developmental Disabilities held in early 2003 in Washington, DC
    Includes bibliographical references.
    ISBN 0-940898-90-X
    1. People with mental disabilities-Services for-United States-Congresses. 2. Developmentally disabled—Services for—United States—Congresses. 3. People with mental disabilities—Research—United States—Congresses. 4. Developmentally disabled—Research—United States—Congresses. [DNLM: 1. Disabled Persons—United States—Congresses. 2. Mental Health Services—organization & administration—United States—Congresses. 3. Education, Special—United States—Congresses. 4. Employment, Supported—United States—Congresses. 5. Health Policy—United States—Congresses. 6. Health Services Research—United States—Congresses. [WA 305 N277 2005]
    I. Lakin, K. Charlie. II. Turnbull, Ann P., 1947– III. American Association on Mental Retardation.
HV3006.A3N35   2005
362.196'8'00973—dc22
                                             2005019408

The creation of each chapter in this book was truly a group effort, which grew out of presentations and discussions that took place at the 2003 conference entitled "Keeping the Promises: National Goals, State of Knowledge and Research Agenda for Persons with Intellectual and Developmental Disabilities." Therefore, both the coauthors and those who contributed substantially to the discussion are listed for each chapter. For purposes of citing these papers, the coauthors (named first in capital and small capital letters) may be listed and the other contributors (all names following "with") may be excluded.

Figures

Tables

Acknowledgments

In 2003 more than 200 national experts participated in a conference entitled "Keeping the Promises: National Goals, State of Knowledge, and Research Agenda for Persons with Intellectual and Developmental Disabilities" (National Goals Conference). This volume is the product of the collective knowledge and wisdom of these leaders and scholars in the field of disabilities. In its pages, they identify and describe what this nation knows and needs to learn to align the reality of persons with intellectual and developmental disabilities with public policy—the clear and unambiguous promises made to them in our national legislation, court decisions, promises of our President, and other sources of national policy. Many organizations and individuals contributed to the process and products described in this volume. Without question the National Goals Conference would not have been possible without the support of our sponsoring organizations. Of special note in that regard was the initial commitment to convene such a conference and the generous support of it by The Arc of the United States Research Fund and The Arc of Washington Research Trust Fund, without which we could not have undertaken the conference and subsequently this publication.

Generous financial support was also provided by 10 separate federal agencies. Sponsoring agencies from the U.S. Department of Health and Human Services include: the Office of the Assistant Secretary of Planning and Evaluation; Administration on Developmental Disabilities; Social Security Administration, Office of Disability; Centers for Disease Control and Prevention, National Center on Birth Defects and Developmental Disabilities; National Institute on Child Health and Human Development; the Centers for Medicare and Medicaid Services; and the President's Committee for People with Intellectual Disabilities. Two agencies from the U.S. Department of Education also helped to sponsor the conference: the National Institute on Disability and Rehabilitation Research and the Office of Special Education and Rehabilitation Services. Of course, sponsorship of the National Goals Conference in no way signifies that these agencies endorse the contents and conclusions contained in this volume, nor do the contents and conclusions represent the official position of the sponsoring agencies.

Leading private professional and advocacy organizations from around the nation also contributed important financial and staff support. In addition to The Arc of the United States, these organizations include: American Association on Mental Retardation; American Network of Community Options and Resources; Association of University Centers on Disability; CARF—the Commission on Accreditation of Rehabilitation Facilities; the Council on Quality and Leadership; the Joseph P. Kennedy, Jr. Foundation;

the National Association of State Directors of Developmental Disabilities Services; and the National Down Syndrome Society.

Academic organizations providing significant financial support for the program include: Beach Center on Disability, University of Kansas; Coleman Institute for Cognitive Disabilities, University of Colorado; Institute for Community Inclusion, University of Massachusetts Boston; Institute on Community Integration, University of Minnesota; Research and Training Center on Community Living, University of Minnesota; and the University of Maine Center for Community Inclusion and Disability Studies.

The participation of a number of invitees was supported by the universities and agencies that employ them. The organizations providing this support to their staff and to this program include: AbleLink Technologies; Human Services Research Institute; Center on Human Policy, Syracuse University; Nathan and Toby Starr Center for Mental Retardation, Brandeis University; The Rehabilitation Research and Training Center on Aging with Developmental Disabilities, University of Illinois at Chicago; Indiana Institute on Disability and Community, University of Indiana; Rehabilitation Research and Training Center, Virginia Commonwealth University; the Rose F. Kennedy University Center for Excellence in Developmental Disabilities, The Albert Einstein College of Medicine of Yeshiva University; Center for Disabilities and Development, University of Iowa; Institute on Disabilities, Temple University; Center on Aging and Aged, Indiana University; California Department of Rehabilitation; Frank Porter Graham Child Development Institute, University of North Carolina at Chapel Hill; Department of Special Education, University of Utah; and the Elizabeth M. Boggs Center on Developmental Disabilities, University of Medicine and Dentistry of New Jersey (UMDNJ), Robert Wood Johnson Medical School, Department of Pediatrics.

We are terribly grateful to Darcy Littlefield of The Arc of the United States, who organized and managed the logistics of the National Goals Conference, including travel, hotel, logistical, and luncheon arrangements for 200 participants working in 12 separate topical working groups. She was amazingly effective, unflappable, and charming in all aspects of this challenge. John Westerman of the University of Minnesota developed and managed a very useful National Goals Conference Web site (http://rtc.umn.edu/goals) as a means of supporting communication within the individual topical working groups and for all participants.

We deeply appreciate the efforts of our topical group leaders, whose organizational and intellectual efforts led to the papers contained in this volume. Our topical groups leaders were: David Braddock, Ph.D., David Coulter, M.D., James Gardner, Ph.D., Susan Hasazi, Ph.D., Tamar Heller, Ph.D., Mary Louise Hemmeter, Ph.D., Robert Horner, Ph.D., Margaret McLaughlin, Ph.D., Laurie Powers, Ph.D., Ann P. Turnbull, Ed.D., Rud Turnbull, J.D., Steven Warren, Ph.D., and Paul Wehman, Ph.D. The Arc Research and Dissemination Committee members deserve much credit for their support and contributions to this effort. They are: Sharon Davis, Ph.D., Mike Hardman, Ph.D., Bill Kiernan, Ph.D., Lyle Lehman, Ph.D., Pat Levitt, Ph.D., Duane Superneau, M.D., and Steve Warren, Ph.D. of The Arc. We are grateful for the excellent editorial assistance authors received from Joyce Lipman and Ray Pence in preparing manuscripts for publication. We deeply appreciate the willingness, energy, and skill of Ann Turnbull in working with authors to develop high quality chapters that convey our national goals, state of knowledge, and needed future directions in research to the benefit of persons with intellectual and developmental disabilities, their families and communities.

In addition to the many contributors and sponsors, we want to thank our friends at AAMR, Doreen Croser, executive director, and Bruce Applegren and Anu Prabhala of the Office of Publications, for their unfailing encouragement and efforts to publish this book. Also, with Scribe editing and producing the book, especially Mark Fretz and Jennifer Boeree, the project was in the best of hands.

Of course, the products of the National Goals Conference would not have been possible without the national experts who participated in the conference. We are grateful for the commitments made by each of the individual participants, whose names and contact information are contained in the List of Participants.

Space does not permit recognition of all the many people who contributed to this project. It was truly a project of our "field" and we hope that it will be viewed as a contribution to the field in its commitments to increased independence, inclusion, opportunity, and self-determination of Americans with intellectual and developmental disabilities.

Steven M. Eidelman, Executive Director
K. Charlie Lakin, Chair, Research and Dissemination Committee
The Arc of the United States

Foreword

The sociocultural history of the United States in the twentieth century was marked by three great movements that extended the rights of citizenship to three groups not originally envisioned by the founding fathers: (1) extending full suffrage to women; (2) enforcing civil rights for African-Americans by ending segregation; and (3) mainstreaming into society persons with intellectual or physical disabilities. These three changes dramatically altered virtually every aspect of life in this country, with ramifications that continue to evolve.

Identifying the landmarks that actually implemented the change is fairly easy for the first two: the Nineteenth Amendment to the Constitution, ratified in 1920, forbade denying the right to vote because of gender, and the Supreme Court decision on segregation in 1954 followed by the civil rights laws enacted by the Congress in the 1960s are clear milestones. Tracing touchstone governmental actions for the broadened inclusion in society of persons with intellectual or physical disabilities is more difficult, because the events were spread over a longer period of time and took a variety of forms, ranging from Congressional legislation (Developmental Disabilities Assistance and Bill of Rights Act, Individuals with Disabilities Education Act, Americans with Disabilities Act), to state and Supreme Court decisions, Executive Orders, and Presidential programs, such as the New Freedom Initiative. Less well known among the key Congressional actions in this area are the pieces of legislation passed during the Kennedy administration years at the President's request, that which provided for research and training in mental retardation. This legislation began the change process and laid the foundation for what followed.

The Kennedy-era legislation established three new federal programs. First was a new Institute at the National Institutes of Health, the National Institute of Child Health and Human Development, to provide research funding with a developmental emphasis on the causes and treatments of mental retardation. Second, to facilitate this research, Congress provided funds to support construction of 12 new Mental Retardation Research Centers, located not at residential institutions but at major universities and medical schools, to get this research and its subjects into the academic mainstream of research. Third, to train and upgrade the personnel providing care for persons with mental retardation, and do research on improvements in care, funds were provided to construct University Affiliated Facilities on campuses around the country.

It is impossible to overestimate the impact of this legislation. It promoted mental retardation to a fully recognized and respected field of scientific study, attracting skilled researchers and funds. It demonstrated that affected persons could be brought out of residential institutions and cared for like persons with any other condition. From this effort came the discoveries that contributed the knowledge base for the transformation. More than in any other field, measures were developed and introduced to prevent mental retardation—PKU, congenital hypothyroidism, congenital rubella, measles encephalitis, Hemophilus influenzae type b meningitis, Rh hemolytic disease, and several other conditions disappeared as causes of mental retardation (now commonly called intellectual disability) in the United States. Other research documented the adverse consequences of residential institutional placement for children and adults with intellectual disability, along with the benefits of new effective teaching and management techniques that made it feasible to place children with intellectual or physical challenges in regular or special classes in school and in community-based living settings and employment. Without the scientific base to bolster the case, the pleas of advocates for change might still be going unheeded.

The impact of these changes in all three areas on citizens of the United States today is similar, particularly among younger generations. They shake their heads in amazement and disbelief that in this country there was a time, not long ago, when women could not vote, African-Americans had to go to schools, and eat at restaurants, and sleep in hotels, and play on sports teams all of which were separate from the population at large, and children with severe intellectual or physical disabilities were denied access to public school education and the opportunity to live in the community.

We in the United States are not yet where we want to be in any of these three areas, which is why the national goal-setting conference was held, that which occasioned this book. Being able to vote has not eliminated the "glass ceiling" or produced equal pay for equal work for women. Racism persists in many forms, often subtle but occasionally public and violent. Similarly, even though most residential institutions for people with mental retardation have closed, opportunities for such people for education and community living remain limited. Positive signs of progress continue to surface, such as the participation in the national goals conference of the people who will be most affected by the outcomes, but there is a long way yet to go.

The chronicles in this book describe what remains to be done for the intellectual disability community if America's promise to them is to be kept. It is likely to shake readers out of any complacency they have, based on the notion that we have already gone as far as we need to in achieving that promise, while at the same time showing how the promise could be kept and the goals achieved.

All those who have labored to get this far are counting on the torch being passed once again to those willing to carry it for the next part of the yet-uncompleted journey.

Duane Alexander, M.D., Director
National Institute of Child Health and Human Development
National Institutes of Health
U.S. Department of Health and Human Services

National Goals Conference Participants

John Agosta
Vice President
Human Services Research Institute

Duane Alexander
Director
National Institute of Child Health and
  Human Development
National Institutes of Health

Barbara Altman
Special Assistant for Disability Statistics
Department of Health and Human Services
National Center for Health Statistics

Edward Ansello
Director
Virginia Center on Aging
Virginia Commonwealth University

Sally Atwater
Executive Director
President's Committee for People with
  Intellectual Disabilities
Administration for Children and Families
U.S. Department of Health and Human
  Services

Ansley Bacon
Executive Director
Westchester Institute for Human
  Development
Westchester Medical Center
New York Medical College

Donald Bailey
Director
Frank P. Graham Child Development Institute
University of North Carolina at Chapel Hill

Linda Bambara
Professor, Special Education
College of Education
Lehigh University

Paul Bates
Professor, Educational Psychology and Special
  Education
Southern Illinois University, Carbondale

Mark Batshaw
Professor and Chair
Department of Pediatrics
George Washington University

Joan Beasley
Consultant
Chestnut Hill, MA

Katherine Belknap
Project Director
ABLEDATA

Rodney Bell
Principal Consultant
ASSET Consulting

Forrest Bennett
Professor, Pediatrics
University of Washington

Michael Benz
Professor, Special Education
University of Oregon

Arnold Birenbaum
Associate Director, Rose F. Kennedy Center
Professor of Pediatrics, Albert Einstein College
  of Medicine

Jan Blacher
Professor
School of Education
University of California, Riverside

Jacquelyn Blaney
Director
Independent Living, Inc.

Cathy Bodine
Assistant Professor and Project Director
Physical Medicine and Rehabilitation
Assistive Technology Partners
University of Colorado Health Sciences
  Center

Gail Bottoms
Consumer Leadership Trainer
People First of Georgia

Coleen Boyle
Associate Director for Science and Public
  Health
National Center on Birth Defects and
  Developmental Disabilities
Centers for Disease Control and Prevention

David Braddock
Executive Director
Coleman Institute for Cognitive Disabilities
University of Colorado System

Mac Brantley
Deputy Director of Communications
The Arc of the United States

Lynn Breedlove
Executive Director
Wisconsin Coalition for Advocacy

Diane Bricker
Former Director, Early Intervention Program
Professor Emerita, Early Intervention
College of Education
University of Oregon, Eugene

Carrie Brown
President
Innovative Human Services, Inc.

Fredda Brown
Professor, Educational and Community
  Programs
City University of New York, Queens College

Diane Nelson Bryen
Executive Director
Professor of CITE (Curriculum, Instruction
  and Technology in Education)
Institute on Disabilities
Temple University

Thomas Buckley
Executive Director
UPARC

Larry Burt
Deputy Director
National Center on Birth Defects and
  Developmental Disabilities
Centers for Disease Control and Prevention
Division of Human Development and
  Disability

Brian Burwell
Vice President
MEDSTAT

Stan Butkus
State Director
South Carolina Department of Disabilities
  and Special Needs

Amanda Cade
Deputy Director
National Quality Review Team
The Council on Quality and Leadership

Michael Callahan
Consultant/President
Marc Gold and Associates/Employment
  for All

Tina Campanella
Executive Director
Quality Trust for Individuals with Disabilities

Vincent Campbell
Health Scientist
National Center on Birth Defects and
  Developmental Disabilities
Centers for Disease Control and Prevention

Edward Carr
Leading Professor
Department of Psychology
State University of New York at Stony Brook

Mary Cerreto
Director
Center on Self-Determination and Health
Boston University Medical Center

Michael Chapman
Chesapeake Management Consulting

Robert Clabby
Administrator
Division of Developmental Disabilities
Wyoming Department of Health

Brian Cobb
Professor
School of Education
Colorado State University, Fort Collins

Robin Cooper
Director of Technical Assistance
NASDDDS, Inc.

Stephen Corbin
Dean
Special Olympics University
Special Olympics, Inc.

Jose Cordero
Director
National Center on Birth Defects and
 Developmental Disabilities
Centers for Disease Control and Prevention

Diane Coughlin
Director
Maryland Department of Health and Mental
 Hygiene
Developmental Disabilities Administration

David L. Coulter
Professor
Department of Neurology
Children's Hospital, Boston

Allen Crocker
Program Director
Institute for Community Inclusion
University of Massachusetts, Boston

Doreen Croser
Executive Director
American Association on Mental Retardation

Ric Crowley
President
MACROW Associates

Scott Danforth
Associate Professor, Chair
Division of Teaching and Learning
College of Education
University of Missouri, St. Louis

Philip Davidson
Chief
Strong Center for Developmental Disabilities
Department of Pediatrics
University of Rochester Medical Center

Daniel Davies
President and Founder
AbleLink Technologies, Inc.

Sharon Davis
Director
Professional and Family Services
The Arc of the United States

Sharman Davis-Barrett
Co-Director
Technical Assistance Alliance for Parent
 Centers
PACER Center

Curtis Decker
Executive Director
National Association of Protection and
 Advocacy Systems, Inc.

Kay DeGarmo
Administrator/Prevention Specialist
Center for Disabilities and Development
Prevention of Disability Policy Council
University of Iowa Health Care

Frank DeRuyter
Chief
Division of Speech Pathology and Audiology
Department of Surgery
Duke University Medical Center

Lizanne DeStefano
Associate Dean for Research and Director
Bureau of Educational Research
University of Illinois at Urbana-Champaign

Robert Dinerstein
Professor of Law
Washington College of Law
American University

Nancy DiVenere
Executive Director
Parent to Parent of Vermont

Fred Dominguez
Chief Community Resources Development
  Section
Community Resources Development Section
Department of Rehabilitation-California

Robin Doyle
Social Insurance Specialist
ODP, ODEP, CPT
Social Security Administration

Sharon Duffy
Professor of Education and Associate Dean
Graduate School of Education
University of California, Riverside

Glen Dunlap
Professor
Department of Child and Family Studies
Louis de la Parte Florida Mental Health
  Institute
Division of Applied Research and Educational
  Support (DARES)
University of South Florida

Dale Dutton
Consultant
Noble Solutions, Inc.

Steven Eidelman
Executive Director
The Arc of the United States

Elizabeth Erwin
Coordinator and Associate Professor
Special Education, Educational and
  Community Programs
City University of New York, Queens College

Alan Factor
Associate Director for Training and
  Dissemination
Rehabilitation Research and Training Center
  on Aging with Developmental Disabilities
University of Illinois at Chicago

Anne Farrell
Director, Early Childhood Services
Westchester Institute for Human
  Development
Westchester Medical Center
New York Medical College

Celia Feinstein
Associate Director
Institute on Disabilities
Temple University

Rebecca Fewell
Consultant
Nashville, TN

Cathy Ficker-Terrill
President and CEO
Ray Graham Association

Chester Finn
Self-Advocate
New York State Office of Mental Retardation
 and Developmental Disabilities (OMRDD)
Chair, Self-Advocates Becoming Empowered
 (SABE)

Robert Fletcher
Executive Director
National Association for the Dually Diagnosed

Marty Ford
Director of Legal Advocacy
The Arc of the United States

Annie Forts
Self Advocate and Motivational Speaker
"UP" Syndrome Fund, Inc.

Lise Fox
Director, Division of Applied Research and
 Educational Support (DARES)
Research Professor, Department of Child and
 Family Studies
Louis de la Parte Florida Mental Health
 Institute
University of South Florida

Susan Fox
Director, Real Choice Systems Change Project
Institute on Disability
University of New Hampshire

Marian Frattarola-Saulino
CEO, Community Interactions, Inc.

Glenn Fujiura
Associate Professor and Director of Graduate
 Studies, DHD
Center Director, Center on Epidemiology and
 Demography of Disability
Department of Disability and Human
 Development
University of Illinois at Chicago

Suellen Galbraith
Director of Public Policy
American Network of Community Options
 and Resources (ANCOR)

James Gardner
President and CEO
The Council on Quality and Leadership

Alan Gartner
Chief of Staff to the Deputy Mayor for Policy
Equal Employment Opportunity Office
Department of Citywide Administrative
 Services, New York City

William Gaventa
Director of Community and Congregational
 Supports
Elizabeth M. Boggs Center on Developmental
 Disabilities
Associate Professor, University of Medicine
 and Dentistry of New Jersey
Robert Wood Johnson Medical School, New
 Brunswick

Bob Gettings
Executive Director
National Association of State Directors of
 Developmental Disabilities Services

Lawrence Gloeckler
Deputy Commissioner
New York State Education Department

Amy Goldman
Associate Director
Institute on Disabilities
Temple University

Gary Goldstein
President
Kennedy Krieger Institute

Rick Greene
Program Specialist
U.S. Administration on Aging

Cary Griffin
Senior Partner
Griffin-Hammis Associates, LLC

Teresa Grossi
Director
Center on Community Living and Careers
Indiana Institute on Disability and
  Community
Indiana University, Bloomington

Randi Hagerman
Professor, Pediatrics
School of Medicine
University of California, Davis Health System
Medical Director, U.C. Davis M.I.N.D.
  Institute

Jim Halle
Professor
Department of Special Education
University of Illinois at Urbana-Champaign

Thomas Hamilton
Director, Survey and Certification Group
Centers for Medicare and Medicaid Services
U.S. Department of Health and Human
  Services

James Hanson
Chief, Mental Retardation and Developmental
  Disabilities Branch
National Institute of Child Health and
  Human Development
National Institutes of Health

Dennis Harkins
Consultant
A Simpler Way

James Harris
Professor of Psychiatry and Pediatrics
Johns Hopkins University

Amy Harris-Solomon
Director
McWhorter Family Children's Center
Easter Seals, Tennessee

Debra Hart
Coordinator of School and Community
  Projects
Institute for Community Inclusion
University of Massachusetts, Boston

Jason Hartle
Arc of Carroll County
Westminster, MD

Susan Hasazi
Professor
Education Department
University of Vermont, Burlington

Barbara Hawkins
Professor and Director
Smith Research Center, School of Education
Indiana University Center on Aging and Aged
Indiana University, Bloomington

Mike Head
Project Manager
Michigan's Self-Determination Initiative
Michigan Department of Community Health

Tamar Heller
Professor and Director
Institute of Disability and Human
  Development
University of Illinois at Chicago

Mary Louise Hemmeter
Associate Professor
Department of Special Education
University of Illinois at Urbana-Champaign

Amy Hewitt
Director, Interdisciplinary Training
Research Associate
Research and Training Center on Community
  Living
University of Minnesota, Minneapolis

Martha Hodgesmith
Director, Community Supports and Services
Health Care Policy Division
Kansas Department of Social and
  Rehabilitation Services

Mike Hoenig
Director, IDEAS
Center for Disabilities and Development
University of Iowa Health Care

Steve Holmes
Administrative Director
Self-Advocacy Association of New York
  State, Inc.

Robert Horner
Professor, Special Education
College of Education
University of Oregon, Eugene

Marilou Hyson
Senior Advisor for Research and Professional
  Practice
National Association for the Education of
  Young Children

Matthew Janicki
Director for Technical Assistance
Rehabilitation Research and Training Center
  on Aging with Developmental Disabilities
University of Illinois at Chicago

George Jesien
Executive Director
Association of University Centers on
  Disabilities

Elbert Johns
President
The ArcLink, Inc.

David Johnson
Director
Institute on Community Integration
University of Minnesota, Minneapolis

Larry Jones
Law Offices of Larry A. Jones, Seattle

John Jordan
Chair, Minnesota Region 10 Quality
Assurance Commission
Houston, MN

Lynda Kahn
Executive Director
Division of Developmental Disabilities
Department of Mental Health, Retardation
  and Hospitals, Rhode Island

David Keer
Program Manager
Department of Education Organizational
  Structure and Offices
National Institute on Disability and
  Rehabilitation Research
Office of Special Education and Rehabilitative
  Services
U.S. Department of Education

William Kiernan
Director
Institute for Community Inclusion
University of Massachusetts, Boston

Gloria Krahn
Director
Oregon Institute on Disability and
  Development
Oregon Health and Sciences University,
  Portland

Marty Wyngaarden Krauss
John Stein Professor of Disability Research
The Heller School for Social Policy and
  Management
Brandeis University

John Kregel
Chairman, Department of Special Education
  and Disability Policy and Research
Director, VCU Rehabilitation Research and
  Training Center on Workplace Supports
Virginia Commonwealth University,
  Richmond

K. Charlie Lakin
Director
Research and Training Center on Community
 Living
University of Minnesota, Minneapolis

Sheryl Larson
Research Associate
Research and Training Center on Community
 Living
University of Minnesota, Minneapolis

Lewis Leavitt
Professor of Pediatrics
Waisman Center
University of Wisconsin-Madison

Stephanie Lee
Director
Office of Special Education and Rehabilitative
 Services
Office of Special Education Programs
U.S. Department of Education

Lyle Lehman
Professor Emeritus
Special Education
State University of New York, Geneseo

Barbara LeRoy
Director
Developmental Disabilities Institute
Wayne State University, Detroit

Deborah Leuchovius
Project Coordinator, Technical Assistance
Transition and the Rehabilitation Act
 (TATRA) Project
PACER Center

Dorothy Kerzner Lipsky
Professor
Graduate School
City University of New York

Ethan Long
Program Director
Association of University Centers on
 Disabilities

John Luna
Director of Vocational Services
Career Design and Development
Employment and Vocational Services
Dallas Metrocare Services

Myra Madnick
Executive Director
National Down Syndrome Society

David Mank
Professor, School of Education
Executive Director, Indiana Institute on
 Disability and Community
Indiana University, Bloomington

Paul Marchand
Assistant Executive Director for Policy and
 Advocacy
The Arc/UCPA Disability Policy Collaborative

D.J. Markey
Co-Director
Pyramid Parent Training, New Orleans

Ursula Markey
Co-Director
Pyramid Parent Training, New Orleans

Philip McCallion
Director
Center for Excellence in Aging Services
School of Social Welfare
State University of New York at Albany

Katherine McCary
Vice President in Human Resources
Manager of Accessing Community Talent
 (ACT)
SunTrust Banks, Inc.

Catherine McClain
Director
Center for Development and Disability
University of New Mexico Health Sciences
 Center

Suzanne McDermott
Professor
Department of Family and Preventive
  Medicine
University of South Carolina School of
  Medicine, Columbia

John McDonnell
Professor
Department of Special Education
University of Utah, Salt Lake City

Ken McGill
Associate Commissioner
Office of Employment Support Programs
Social Security Administration

Patricia McGill-Smith
Senior Advisor
National Down Syndrome Society

Margaret McLaughlin
Professor
Department of Special Education
University of Maryland, College Park

Elise McMillan
Director of Community Outreach, Core
  Assistant Director
Vanderbilt Kennedy Center for Research on
  Human Development
Vanderbilt University

Merle McPherson
Director
Division of Services for Children with Special
  Health Needs
Maternal and Child Health Bureau
U.S. Department of Health and Human
  Services

Joe Meadours
Director of Consumer Empowerment
State of Alabama Department of Mental
  Health and Mental Retardation

Richard Melia
Director
Research Sciences Division
National Institute of Disability and
  Rehabilitation Research
Department of Education Organizational
  Structure and Offices
Office of Special Education and Rehabilitative
  Services
U.S. Department of Education

Dennis Mithaug
Professor
Department of Health and Behavior Studies
Teacher's College, Columbia University

Teresa Moore
Consultant
Moore Advocacy Consulting

Gerry Morrissey
Commissioner
Department of Mental Retardation
Commonwealth of Massachusetts

Patricia Morrissey
Commissioner
Administration on Children and Families
Administration on Developmental Disabilities
U.S. Department of Health and Human
  Services

Chas Moseley
Director of Special Projects
National Association of State Directors of
  Developmental Disabilities Services

Ray Murphy
Parent Advisor
Rehabilitation Research and Training Center
  on Aging with Developmental Disabilities
University of Illinois at Chicago

Wendy Nehring
Acting Associate Dean for Educational
  Services and Professor
Southern Illinois University, Edwardsville

Tia Nelis
Self-Advocacy Specialist
Institute on Disability and Human
Development
University of Illinois at Chicago

Jan Nisbet
Director
Institute on Disability
University of New Hampshire

Liz Obermayer
Quality Consultant
The Council on Quality and Leadership

David O'Hara
Associate Director
Westchester Institute for Human
Development
Westchester Medical Center
New York Medical College

Tom O'Neill
Vice President
Admetco, Inc.

Fred Orelove
Professor, Special Education and Disability
Policy
Executive Director, Partnership for People
with Disabilities
Virginia Commonwealth University,
Richmond

David Patterson
President and Senior Scientist
Eleanor Roosevelt Institute
University of Denver

Ruth Perou
Child Development Studies Team Leader
Centers for Disease Control and Prevention
Division of Human Development and
Disability

Missy Perrott
Living Free Campaign Coordinator
The Arc of Maryland

Renee Pietrangelo
CEO
American Network of Community Options
and Resources (ANCOR)

Clifford Poetz
Community Liaison
Research and Training Center on Community
Living
University of Minnesota, Minneapolis

Mark Polit
Executive Director
California Alliance for Inclusive Communities

Laurie Powers
Co-Director
National Center on Self-Determination and
21st Century Leadership
Regional Research Institute for Human
Services
Graduate School of Social Work
Portland State University

Chris Privett
Director of Communications
The Arc of the United States

Siegfried Pueschel
Professor Emeritus, Pediatrics
Brown University

Tim Quinn
Executive Director
The Arc, Northern Chesapeake Region

Rick Rader
Director
Morton J. Kent Habilitation Center

Sharon Ramey
Director
Center for Health and Education
Susan H. Mayer Professor for Child and
Family Studies
Georgetown University

Olivia Raynor
Co-Director
Tarjan Center for Developmental Disabilities
University Center for Excellence for
  Developmental Disabilities
Neuropsychiatric Institute and Hospital
University of California, Los Angeles

Joe Reichle
Professor
Department of Communication Disorders
University of Minnesota, Minneapolis

James Rimmer
Professor
Department of Disability and Human
  Development
University of Illinois at Chicago

Mary Rizzolo
Associate Director
Institute on Disability and Human
  Development
University of Illinois at Chicago

Pat Rogan
Associate Professor, Special Education
Indiana Institute on Disability and Community
Indiana University-Purdue University,
  Indianapolis

Mary Ann Romski
Professor
Department of Communication
Georgia State University, Atlanta

John Rose
Vice President
Risk Management
Irwin Siegel Agency

Beth Rous
Community Education Director
Interdisciplinary Human Development
  Institute
University of Kentucky, Lexington

Leslie Rubin
Director
Developmental Pediatrics
Department of Pediatrics
Emory University School of Medicine

Nancy Safer
Executive Director
Council for Exceptional Children

Wayne Sailor
Professor, Special Education
Co-Associate Director, Beach Center on
  Disability
University of Kansas, Lawrence

Rosa Santos
Assistant Professor
Department of Special Education
University of Illinois at Urbana-Champaign

Paul Saulino
CFO
Community Interactions, Inc.

Liz Savage
Director
Housing and Health Care Policy
The Arc of the United States

Robert Schalock
Schalock and Associates
Chewelah, WA

Ilene Schwartz
Professor, Faculty Advisor
Director, Project DATA (Developmentally
  Appropriate Treatment for Autism)
Experimental Education Unit
University of Washington

Marsha Seltzer
Professor and Director
Waisman Center
University of Wisconsin-Madison

John Shea
Partner
Allen, Shea, and Associates

Lorraine Sheehan
Deputy Director for Public Policy
Maryland Disability Law Center

Bobby Silverstein
Director
Center for the Study and Advancement of
  Disability Policy

Rune Simeonsson
Professor, School of Education
Research Fellow, Frank P. Graham Child
  Development Institute
University of North Carolina at Chapel Hill

Marlene Simon
Associate Division Director
Office of Special Education and Rehabilitative
  Services
Office of Special Education Programs
U.S. Department of Education

George Singer
Professor
Givertz Graduate School of Education
University of California, Santa Barbara

Gary Smith
Senior Project Director
Human Services Research Institute

Michael Smull
Support Development Associate
Annapolis, MD

Martha Snell
Professor
Curry School of Education
Department of Curriculum, Instruction, and
  Special Education
University of Virginia, Charlottesville

Patricia Snyder
Associate Dean for Research and Graduate
  Studies
School of Allied Health Professions
Louisiana State University Health Sciences
  Center, New Orleans

Lon Solomon
Senior Pastor
McLean Bible Church

Leslie Soodak
Associate Professor, School of Education
Pace University, Pleasantville

Deborah Spitalnik
Executive Director
Elizabeth M. Boggs Center on Developmental
  Disabilities
Professor of Pediatrics
Robert Wood Johnson Medical School, New
  Brunswick

Karen Staley
Past President
The Arc of the United States

Glen Stanton
Deputy Director
Disabled and Elderly Health Programs Group
Centers for Medicare and Medicaid Services

Bob Stodden
Director
Center on Disability Studies
University of Hawaii at Manoa

Sue Swenson
Associate Director
The Arc of the United States

Steve Taylor
Co-Director
Center on Disability Studies, Law, and
  Human Policy
Syracuse University

Nancy Thaler
Deputy Secretary for Mental Retardation
Pennsylvania Department of Public Welfare

Colleen Thoma
Assistant Professor
Special Education and Disability Policy
Virginia Commonwealth University,
  Richmond

Ann Thomas
Past President
People First of Ohio

Travis Thompson
Executive Program Director
Minnesota Autism Center
Professor of Pediatrics, University of
  Minnesota School of Medicine

Martha Thurlow
Director
National Center on Educational Outcomes
University of Minnesota, Minneapolis

Roger Titgemeyer
Director, Special Schools and Programs
Division of Special Education Services
Orange County Department of Education

John Trach
Associate Professor
Department of Special Education
University of Illinois at Urbana-Champaign

Ann P. Turnbull
Professor, Special Education
Co-Director, Beach Center on Disability
University of Kansas, Lawrence

Rud Turnbull
Professor, Special Education
Co-Director, Beach Center on Disability
University of Kansas, Lawrence

Lawrence Velasco
Chief Executive Officer
Colorado Bluesky Enterprise, Inc.

David Wacker
Professor of Pediatric Psychology
Center for Disabilities and Development
University of Iowa Health Care

Hill Walker
Director, Center on Human Development
College of Education
University of Oregon, Eugene

Royal Walker, Jr.
Associate Director
Institute for Disability Studies
University of Southern Mississippi, Jackson

Joey Wallace
Policy Analyst/Funding Specialist
Leader, Adult Team
Partnership For People With Disabilities
Virginia Commonwealth University,
  Richmond

Nancy Ward
Self Advocacy Coordinator
Oklahoma People First

Steven Warren
Director, Life Span Institute
University of Kansas, Lawrence

Paul Wehman
Professor, Teacher Education
Director, Rehabilitation Research and Training
  Center
Virginia Commonwealth University,
  Richmond

Michael Wehmeyer
Director, Kansas University Center on
  Developmental Disabilities
Associate Professor, Department of Special
  Education
University of Kansas, Lawrence

Nancy Weiss
Executive Director, TASH

Michael West
Research Associate
Research and Training Center
Virginia Commonwealth University,
  Richmond

Barbara Wheeler
Director
Center for Disability Studies and Community
 Inclusion
Associate Professor of Clinical Pediatrics
University of Southern California Keck School
 of Medicine

Sheryl White-Scott
Director
St. Charles Developmental Disabilities Program
St. Vincent Catholic Medical Centers

Madeleine Will
Chair
President's Committee for Persons with
 Intellectual Disabilities

Betty Williams
President
Self-Advocates Becoming Empowered (SABE)
Region 5

Valerie Williams
Director, Center for Interdisciplinary Learning
 and Leadership
Associate Dean for Faculty Affairs, College of
 Medicine
University of Oklahoma Health Sciences
 Center, Oklahoma City

Mary Woolley
President
Research! America

Tracy Wright
Ask Me! Southern Regional Coordinator
The Arc of Maryland

Lucille Zeph
Director
Center for Community Inclusion and
 Disability Studies
University of Maine, Orono

CHAPTER 1

Introduction: Keeping Promises to Americans With Intellectual and Developmental Disabilities

K. CHARLIE LAKIN

This book is a follow-up to a unique conference held in early 2003 that brought together national leaders in research, public policy, advocacy, and service delivery related to the well-being of Americans with intellectual and developmental disabilities. The conference was entitled, "Keeping the Promises: National Goals, State of Knowledge and Research Agenda for Persons with Intellectual and Developmental Disabilities." The participants were committed to three core propositions:

1. High-quality research is essential to setting and achieving national goals for persons with intellectual and developmental disabilities.
2. High-quality research is defined by gathering valid, useful information about important topics.
3. Important national topics are established in promises the United States has made to its citizens with intellectual and developmental disabilities in its laws, regulations, administrative priorities, judicial decisions, and other statements of national purpose.

The United States has made many important promises to its citizens with intellectual and developmental disabilities. These promises are found in the Developmental Disabilities Assistance and Bill of Rights Act, the Americans with Disabilities Act (ADA), the decisions of the Supreme Court and other federal courts, the Individuals with Disabilities Education Act (IDEA), the Rehabilitation Act of 1973, President Bush's New Freedom Initiative, and other laws, rules, decisions, and findings. These expressions of national commitment to people with intellectual and developmental disabilities are fundamental to the well-being of those individuals. Therefore, the nation must carefully attend to how its investments in gathering, sharing, and using information can contribute to more effective and efficient promise-keeping.

1

The United States has made remarkable promises to people with intellectual and developmental disabilities and their families in its laws, rules, decisions, and administrative policies. There have always been those who doubted that the promises could be kept or suspected that the promises were made without full commitment to keeping them. For the most part, however, those on the "receiving end" of the promises have taken their nation's commitments seriously. These people expect results when their country guarantees them "access to needed community services, individualized supports, and other forms of assistance that promote self-determination, independence, productivity, and integration and inclusion in all facets of community life" (as in the Developmental Disabilities Assistance and Bill of Rights Act). Since their country recognizes "the right of individuals to live independently, enjoy self-determination, make choices, contribute to society, pursue meaningful careers and enjoy full inclusion and integration in the economic, political, social, cultural and educational mainstream of American society" (Rehabilitation Act of 1973 as amended, 29 U.S.C. 794), they expect that they indeed will control their own lives. They expect that when their President issues an Executive Order stating that "The United States is committed to community-based alternatives for individuals with disabilities and recognizes that such services advance the best interests of the United States" (as in Executive Order 13217 of June 18, 2001), all U.S. citizens will benefit.

The justice of America's promises to citizens with intellectual and developmental disabilities does not mean the promises are easily kept. Many of the promises demand the nation as a whole, or particular regions, overcome generations of discrimination, prejudice, and segregation. Living up to these promises requires commitment, knowledge, and the capacity to change society and its institutions. Research has played, and continues to play, a major role in setting and meeting national goals for disability rights. From Walter Fernald's (1919) early follow-up studies revealing that persons released from state institutions fared better than most people (including Dr. Fernald) expected, to recent studies illustrating the capacity of people with intellectual and developmental disabilities and their communities to work together for the benefit of all, research has helped build a better society. As society solves old problems only to discover new ones, research agendas must be reviewed periodically to ensure they address important issues, focus on useful and valid information, and provide results that benefit as many people as possible. Such commitments are not easy to sustain. Research enterprises often have been arrogantly separated from their responsibilities to the well-being of human beings in the name of "science." We must review the nature of research enterprises to ensure they help us honor national commitments.

In 2003, a remarkable conference on responsible research took place in Washington, DC. The conference was notable not just because half of the 250 invited participants were among the most prominent researchers in the fields of intellectual and developmental disability. The rest of the participants needed exemplary research for their work as national and state leaders in public policy, health and social service delivery, and advocacy. These individuals met to review national goals for people with intellectual and developmental disabilities and to explore the role of research in achieving them. Participants were sponsored by more than forty organizations that included nine federal agencies (see the acknowledgments for a list of the sponsors). Along with national leaders in research and in policy and program management, family and self-advocacy leaders with intellectual and developmental disabilities were well represented. All sponsoring organizations took part in nominating the leaders in research, policy, health and social service, and advocacy who were invited to participate, and other invited participants.

Twelve topical groups conducted the conference's primary work. These groups were established to represent the life-span from youth to maturity and diverse social roles from learning and development to work and community life. All participants were assigned to a topical group based on their expertise. The twelve chapters in this book address those topical areas.

THE IMPORTANCE OF NATIONAL GOALS

The United States has made important commitments to people with intellectual and developmental disabilities in federal laws and regulations, court decisions, national policy initiatives, reports of national panels such as the Healthy People 2010 Objectives, and elsewhere. These national goals serve two purposes. First, they guarantee people with intellectual and developmental disabilities opportunities to participate fully in the life of the nation and its communities. Second, the goals establish intended outcomes of public policies and programs. A synthesis of these national goals articulates a clear national purpose:

- Increasing self-determination and personal control in decisions affecting people with intellectual and developmental disabilities and their families
- Providing opportunities to people with intellectual and developmental disabilities to live and participate in their own communities
- Improving quality of life for individuals and families as they define it for themselves
- Supporting families as the most important and permanent unit of development, protection, and lifelong assistance to persons with intellectual and developmental disabilities
- Investing in each individual's developmental potential and capacity to contribute in age-related roles as productive, respected community members
- Assuring access to sufficient, high-quality health and social supports to protect each person's health, safety, rights, and well-being

These goals, along with other goals for major life areas such as education and work for persons with special needs (e.g., accommodations through technology or access to behavioral and/or mental health therapies) were addressed in each topical area. Group members defined the current knowledge base and identified directions for future goal-oriented research.

THE VALUE OF—AND VALUES FOR—RESEARCH TO SUPPORT NATIONAL GOALS

Research plays a central role in defining and achieving national goals for people with intellectual and developmental disabilities and their families. To be useful, this research must provide accessible, relevant information to people with disabilities and their families, professionals, the general public, and public officials. To do so, research must be comprehensible and accessible to a wide audience, not just to "experts." Research results also must reach policymakers and civic and corporate leaders who make connections between public investment and public and private outcomes. Such connections are increasingly important because demand for publicly funded human and social services is outstripping available funding. Conference participants noted that case studies have been more useful than central tendency and population statistics in illustrating the nature and potential of these connections. These case studies describe what might be emulated and encourage emulation. Discussions about the relative benefits of various approaches to research and of the dangers of *a priori* assumptions about scientific validity without regard to the information needed and its context(s). P. B. Medawar (1977), Nobel laureate in medicine in 1960, provided this perspective:

> If a broad line of demarcation is drawn between the natural sciences and what can only be described as the unnatural sciences, it will be recognized as a distinguishing mark of the latter that their practitioners try most painstakingly to imitate what they believe—quite wrongly, alas for them—to be the distinctive manner and observances of the natural sciences. Among these are: (a) the belief that measurement and numeration are intrinsically praiseworthy activities (the worship, indeed, of what Ernst Gombrich calls idola quantitatis); (b) the whole discredited farrago of inductivism—especially the belief that facts are prior to ideas and that sufficiently voluminous compilation of facts can be processed by a calculus of discovery in such a way as to yield general principles and natural-seeming laws; (c) another distinguishing mark of unnatural scientists is the faith in the efficacy of statistical formulas, particularly if processed by a computer.... (p. 13)

Still, conference participants recognized that use of a wide range of research methods has helped achieve national goals for persons with intellectual and developmental disabilities.

Public commitment to research must reinforce public commitments in policies, programs, and services. Little research deals with the use of billions of dollars of public funding that is reserved for persons with intellectual and developmental disabilities. Although controlled research can be difficult to conduct within the ideals of scientific research design, generating useful, valid information that supports individual rights to choose "treatment groups" is both possible and effective. This "applied research" is crucial to the future of Americans with intellectual and developmental disabilities.

Research must adhere to principles in order to help meet national goals for persons with intellectual and developmental disabilities. Some of the most important principles are listed here:

- Research must have direct or indirect applications to daily needs of individuals with intellectual and developmental disabilities and their families and to their ability to live in their own communities.
- Research must foster public awareness and support for policies, programs, and services that contribute to achieving national goals.

- Research must contribute to quality of life outcomes for people with intellectual and developmental disabilities and their families.
- Research must consider cost-effectiveness when evaluating how to use public resources.
- Research must "scale up" exemplary practices to study issues that emerge when effective policies and practices expand beyond their pilot sites.
- Research must consider what support people with intellectual and developmental disabilities and their families need for managing their own lives and services.
- When developing goals and interpreting results, researchers must incorporate perspectives and needs of people who may be affected.
- Research must consider cultural, ethnic, racial, and other differences that affect access to and benefits from programs and services.
- Research must monitor progress of each state in achieving national goals so that lack of progress can be identified and addressed.
- Research must incorporate multiple quantitative and qualitative methodologies appropriate to research questions.
- Research must monitor the extent to which systems, programs, and professional practices reflect and advance the nation's goals.

THE ROLE OF THE FEDERAL GOVERNMENT

Numerous federal government agencies are involved in defining and financing research. These agencies shape and monitor how individuals with intellectual and developmental disabilities and their families receive educational, social, vocational, and other support. Although it is axiomatic that such functions must be part of research policy, procedures for allocating research resources are often isolated from consideration of goals and financial resources of public policy. Research often seems to be appreciated more as an independent activity than as a service to public purposes. To the extent that research enjoys such independence, it is less valuable than those who pay for it have a right to expect. Similarly, government agencies often operate research programs with limited knowledge of and coordination with other research funding programs. Given the limited resources available for research, consistent interagency coordination and collaboration is vital. Coordination between and within agencies and around national themes (such as those defined in this book) helps ensure the best use of research funding. Although there are interagency groups within the federal government, cross-agency integration of research planning and support is rare. This needs to change.

Efforts to implement effective, coordinated programs of publicly funded research also must include appropriate representation from all stakeholders. In 1993, the National Institute on Disability and Rehabilitation Research (NIDRR) issued guidelines for Constituency-Oriented Research and Dissemination (Fenton, Batavia, & Roody, 1993). The guidelines are quite helpful in determining topics, research questions, methods, findings, and uses. Much of the constituency-oriented research approach is derived from the Participatory Action Research (PAR) described by Whyte (1991). PAR is a problem-solving research model designed to form research teams whose members represent those with knowledge of problems and stakes in solving them.

"Constituency-oriented" or PAR approaches include in the research teams not just academic researchers, but also advocates, administrators, teachers, direct support professionals, people with disabilities, family members, and others. Such approaches are probably more important in establishing research priorities than at any other point in the research process. The more federal agencies assure major stakeholder representation in research planning and prioritizing, the more valuable that research is likely to be. Our national research enterprises should visibly and effectively identify and respond to national needs through collaboration with stakeholders in funded research. Examples of ways to strengthen a national research agenda include the following:

- Setting cross-agency research priorities so that pooled funding will generate sufficient resources to address cross-agency concerns and responsibilities
- Sharing information about research needs and findings across agencies
- Reducing duplication of effort and gaps in research that result from limited communication across and within agencies
- Encouraging and coordinating use of multiple research methods to evaluate policies, programs, and services
- Funding joint research and demonstration activities that respond to shared interests and commitments related to national goals
- Funding joint efforts to "scale up" exemplary projects for new sites
- Issuing joint statements about effective policy, program, and service approaches to achieve national goals
- Promoting the value of PAR, which involves partnerships among researchers, family members, practitioners, and policy-makers to design, implement, and interpret research data within federal agencies and federally funded organizations
- Providing sufficient funding for objective and well-designed evaluations of programs that offer significant policy innovations of potential national significance

States and local entities also have stakes in shaping research agendas suited to achieving national goals. Research is most useful when it is relevant to state and local situations (e.g., resource constraints, caregiver capabilities, and service provider capacities). State and local entities are laboratories for testing new approaches to services and policies. Federal agencies must work closely with states and other entities to ensure that research is appropriate to systems for people with intellectual and developmental disabilities and their families. Examples of local and state systems include schools, health care, social services, state developmental disability programs, and vocational rehabilitation. Families should also be included as systems.

State and local entities must use data collection and objective analysis to reform practices and to share what they learn with others. Monitoring and achieving national goals for people with intellectual and developmental disabilities can occur only when states and other entities evaluate their abilities to achieve the same goals. State and local entities can improve the national research agenda by taking the following actions:

- Participating actively in setting priorities for federal research programs
- Proposing outcome-based research, evaluation, and demonstration projects for federal funding

- Establishing collaborative relationships with applied researchers to use state and local programs as national research laboratories
- Requesting federal agency support for ongoing coordinated research involving multiple states or local entities
- Advocating for federal research that helps achieve the national goals that further define state and local program goals

RESEARCH CHALLENGES IN THE ACHIEVEMENT OF NATIONAL GOALS

Mary Woolley, President, Research! America provided her perspectives in a presentation during the 2003 conference:

> It's a fact that research changes the history of health and well-being. Things that we regard as common sense today were not always so: consider the use of seat belts, putting babies and toddlers in infant seats, practicing safe sex, checking the blood supply for toxic agents, getting flu shots—the list goes on. The fact is that today's common sense is based on research conducted over the years. Research will lead us to tomorrow's common sense. (2003, p. 15)

Research's primary goal should be to help achieve national goals, but this is not always the case. There is much valuable information that can be used for this purpose, but there also are many barriers between generating information and applying it. Overcoming these barriers involves (a) improving links between established knowledge and public policy, (b) assuring relevance of research for all stakeholders, (c) putting research information into effective, common practice, and (d) improving ways to share information with its potential beneficiaries.

Improving Links Between Current Knowledge and Public Policy

Millions of people with intellectual and developmental disabilities are affected by expenditures and expectations related to public policy. There is no lack of information about what works well, what types of services and supports individuals and families want most, and how to structure delivery systems for effective supports. However, sharing research information in ways that influence policy is difficult.

Ursula and D. J. Markey (2003), parent leaders from New Orleans, made the following comment during conference discussions:

> All across America, there are thousands of families who never get information, training, or support in making research-based best practices work in their lives. These families are referred to as the "traditionally underserved." They are families who have become isolated for a number of reasons, including poverty, racism, discrimination, cultural and language differences, geographic location, and socio-economic factors. These are our families. Many of our families do not even realize the potential that research holds for improving their lives. Others do understand but they are also aware of the huge disconnect between science and solutions for them. They have lost hope for a promising future for their family member with a disability despite the help that research may be able to provide. (2003, p. 8)

Research funding agencies and researchers must work as closely as possible with public and private agencies and organizations that advocate for, support, and are responsible for achieving national goals. These include advocacy, administrative, trade, and professional organizations. Achieving such goals requires increased inter- and intra-agency commitment and cooperation to identify and promote research aimed at achieving national goals. Funding agencies need to ensure that research priorities include practical perspectives of people who do and do not experience the consequences of national goals, related policy, programs, and services in their daily lives. This requires more and better investment in the accessibility of research activities to those with limited experience or background in research, but whose experiences make them indispensable to gathering and sharing information. A diverse group of participants, including people with disabilities, their families, and other personnel (e.g., teachers, direct support staff, regulators, trainers, service administrators, and legislators) should obtain, analyze, and critique products of public research. Such activity needs to include, at a minimum, research summaries that are timely, concrete, and accessible to general audiences. Those who set research policies and priorities must report information from stakeholders outside the research process in a systematic manner. For the most part, such efforts are obvious and indispensable components of a commitment to align research funding with achievement of national goals.

Increasing Commitment to Research by Increasing its Relevance

Wooley (2003) offered this assessment of the current state of the public's role in research:

> Public interest in health and quality of life has never been greater.... Public opinion polls...not only show very strong public interest, but also show strong public support to pay for more research.... We also know from public opinion research...that public commitment to those who have been historically underserved by research—including those with intellectual and developmental disabilities—has never been greater. Again, this is because research is moving more rapidly than ever and the possibilities are tantalizing. It is also because civil society is becoming more civil: more willing to acknowledge that fairness has not always been practiced even as it has long been preached. (p. 11)

Ironically, in spite of this optimism there are few objective reasons to conclude that research is valued as a means to improving the lives of people with disabilities. There may be public support for the idea that research is a beneficial activity in general, but most stakeholders perceive disability research as an activity with more relevance to academia than to real life and real people. This perception is especially common in regard to research with a foundation in what Medawar (1977) calls the "unnatural sciences" and with methodological ties to education, psychology, sociology, and economics. Such research often seems conducted by researchers for their benefit and according to their rules. Of course, limited advocacy for disability research and its stagnant funding, even as the number of Americans with disabilities and the specific promises to them grow, is a product of the limited constituency and passion for research within potential stakeholder groups.

Clearly, research dominated by the interests and perspectives of researchers will lack the support, prominence, and direction to contribute to the well-being of people with intellectual and developmental disabilities, their families, and the nation. Moreover, current proposals to limit funding for services for persons with disabilities will also affect disability-related research negatively. These effects are apparent in decreasing support for research and dissemination in programs such as the Projects of National Significance of the Administration on Developmental Disabilities and the Rehabilitation Research and Training Centers of the National Institute of Disability and Rehabilitative Research. In sum, funding for research relative to public investment in disability services is decreasing even though the public supports national goals for people with disabilities and related research. Robert Gettings (2003), Executive Director of the National Association of State Directors of Developmental Disabilities Services, observes that

> collectively, the states expend over $32 billion annually on providing long-term services and supports to individuals with cognitive, intellectual and other developmental disabilities. This figure does not include the billions of additional dollars the federal government, the states and localities spend on special education and vocational rehabilitation services for this population. And yet, as a nation, we invest only a tiny fraction of this amount in expanding our knowledge base regarding the most effective approaches to assisting individuals with lifelong disabilities to live meaningful and productive lives. (Gettings, 2003, p. 9)

Research will be integral to the realization of goals the United States has set for its citizens with intellectual and developmental disabilities so long as all people with a stake in those goals participate in, use, and advocate for research. This requires attitudinal and procedural changes, to ensure that as many stakeholders as possible participate in establishing research priorities, questions, approaches, and uses. Research needs to be coordinated across agencies to give comprehensive attention to essential components of well-being and full citizenship for persons with disabilities. Furthermore, there need to be more training and support initiatives to include those people with disabilities, family members, experts, and stakeholders who do not currently participate in research. Reinforcement and reaffirmation of commitments to and expectations for participatory action research and constituency-oriented approaches will reach those that research affects the most. Funding agencies must recognize that this type of research model will require more financial support; but in return such agencies will benefit from increased advocacy for their own funding. Finally, it is important that higher standards for national research agendas be met not only in federally funded studies, but also in national statistical programs that federal agencies conduct.

Improving Translation of Research Into Guides for Effective Practice

Those involved in research as a public investment are responsible for producing outcomes that benefit society. We lack evaluation and monitoring of the impact of current funded research on federal and state responses to the needs of people with intellectual and developmental disabilities. Knowledge of the effects of research can be improved through stronger ties between national goals and research priorities, and between research results and those responsible for implementing and advocating for validated procedures. Raising expectations for research is crucial and requires more visibility and better dissemination. We need researchers, research agencies, advocacy organizations, and public and private service agencies to better explain how information will strengthen policies, programs, and services.

The public is entitled to access to useful research, which means that publication of research in professional journals, while essential, does not fulfill the researcher's responsibilities. Indeed, many practitioners rarely look to professional journals for useful assistance. There is a need for clear, concise, easily understood, and widely available publications from consumer, family, and trade organizations; training programs; general media; and accessible Web sites. Achieving broad distribution that reaches target audiences is not solely the researcher's duty, however. The traditional view that researchers are responsible only for information gathering and that practitioners, advocates, family members, and policymakers are the ones who apply research in real life is obsolete. Instead, research is a collaborative enterprise in which all research stakeholders are responsible for providing information to those who need and use it.

Bridging the translation gap between research-generated knowledge and the daily lives of potential end users requires systematic program and product development. We need to create and evaluate "research-to-practice" sessions to present and discuss research findings with practical applications at conferences and meetings of advocates and self-advocates, families, professionals, policymakers, and their staffs. Such forums must explore the implications and implementation of research results within programs, services, and individual interventions. In doing so, researchers working alone usually will have less impressive results than a broader group of experts on the topic will achieve. Advocacy and trade publications for health, advocacy, direct support, and other professionals need to attend more "translation of research" features that show how research information can be made available to the widest possible audience. Accountability in research entails responsibility to foster the sharing of research across the full range of stakeholders through publications, Web sites, and training programs. There also must be greater attention to and investment in demonstration and evaluation projects that use research-to-practice interventions to achieve efficacy in "real world" programs and systems. We have learned repeatedly that results of intervention research involving human subjects and those who intervene— whether they are longitudinal single-subject, clinical trial, or other approaches—differ substantially and produce varying results depending on circumstances and people. The ultimate tests of policy, program, and service interventions take place in the everyday settings where individuals with disabilities, family members, direct support professionals, teachers, and others live.

Improving Ways to Share Information With All Who Need It

Information is central to modern life. Information shapes decisions, raises expectations, empowers, and stimulates creativity. Information can also identify benefits and risks in the choices people make. Unfortunately, there are significant obstacles to turning research results into information that is widely accessible. One problem involves time: more than a year typically passes between development and publication of research articles. A more serious problem is reliance on research journals as primary instruments in disseminating research. Such publications reach only a small number of those who need information, and that information is usually expressed in the language of experts and professionals.

Investment must be made in research dissemination. The only reason for carrying out research is to share what is learned. Too often, research funding ends with the study and before findings are provided to those who will find them useful. Too often researchers justify limited information-sharing efforts by noting that non-academic publications are little valued within academia. Such sentiments reduce research to an activity existing only to give researchers something to do to benefit their careers.

Inadequate effort to share information with all interested audiences reduces research benefits, undermines contributions to national goals for persons with intellectual and developmental disabilities, and detracts from the role of research in the disability community. To improve information-sharing, those who provide funding must set standards to ensure that information reaches multiple audiences in appropriate ways. Such standards should also address needs for sufficient time, creativity, and resources for dissemination and for appropriate funding for all persons and agencies that take part in dissemination. The language in which research information is summarized must also be a priority. It requires attention to culturally and linguistically diverse audiences and much greater sophistication in providing information in ways that can be used by larger numbers of persons with intellectual and developmental disabilities.

EMERGING ISSUES THAT WILL SHAPE RESEARCH GOALS AND ACTIVITIES

The ideals and accomplishments that have shaped national goals for persons with intellectual and developmental disabilities constitute a foundation for future progress. That foundation also illustrates the rapidly changing nature and commitments of U.S. society. Three areas of social change and expectation will be particularly important to shaping national goals and related research: self-determination and empowerment, demographics, and technological advances.

Self-Determination and Self-Advocacy

Today federal policy emphasizes self-determination and self-advocacy (e.g., the Developmental Disabilities Assistance and Bill of Rights Act of 2000). Within the states, thousands of individuals and families have been provided the opportunity and have accepted the responsibility, through "consumer-directed support" options, to arrange services to meet their own specific needs. More than 1,000 self-advocacy groups exist nationwide so that people with disabilities can speak out on important issues in their lives. Nevertheless, broad-based systemic change that fosters self-determination, self-advocacy, and social freedom is limited. Most laws and judicial decisions recognize these concepts but do not provide for their enforcement. More than 100,000 people with intellectual and developmental disabilities remain institutionalized in the United States (Prouty & Lakin, 2004). Many others, while not institutionalized according to common definitions, have little control over where, with whom, and how they live in their communities. Large numbers of these people want opportunities to contribute to their communities through useful part-time employment. Tens of thousands of individuals and families have no access to basic services that would offer, at the least, a modicum of control over their lives.

The concepts of self-determination, empowerment, and self-advocacy have widespread support from people with disabilities, service providers, advocates, professionals, and policymakers. However, the realities that people with intellectual and developmental disabilities and their families face suggest that there are fewer choices and less control than national goals promise. Research has a crucial role in helping the nation address the gap between such promises and the realities of people's lives.

Self-determination is an important principle, but relatively little is known about its implementation for individuals and groups. As service systems shift to consumer and family control, traditional public responsibilities change. This shift has raised questions about who will fulfill these new public responsibilities in areas such as individual health, safety and well-being, service financing, and standards for professionals and direct support workers. A self-determination approach is expected to increase the use of generic community services, but little is known about how this will affect access to and quality of services that respond to unique personal needs. As public commitments to self-determination increase and more individuals and families choose to manage their own services, there will be a greater need for information about how to help them do so effectively. Approaches to self-determination through consumer-directed supports are gaining visibility, but there is limited information about reactions to their different uses and the effects of limitations placed on them. In sum, there is insufficient knowledge of what resources and supports will be required for effective participation of people with intellectual and developmental disabilities in self-determination policy, research, and service delivery activities.

Demographic Changes

Changing demographics complicate the pursuit of national goals for people with intellectual and developmental disabilities in many ways. Survival rates of low and very low birth weight children suggest increasing demands for services that are already in short supply. Increased longevity among people with intellectual and developmental disabilities increases the average number of service years that people will need. Aging parents who have supported their adult children at home for decades reach the point at which they can no longer do so. Rising numbers of people with intellectual and developmental disabilities are facing age-related impairments that make it difficult for family members to provide them with help and social supports.

The changing racial and ethnic composition of the United States is another key factor in the fulfillment of national goals. Birth rates within some minority groups exceed those of Anglo-Americans, and immigration rates continue to rise. These trends bring shifts in preferences for approaches to support people with intellectual and developmental disabilities. Achieving national goals for supporting people through ethnically, linguistically, and personally preferred responses requires new levels of flexibility and an unprecedented degree of variety in service delivery.

U.S. demographic trends show a growing population of older citizens who are increasingly dependent on public services. As more and more baby boomers reach retirement age, the numbers and proportions of elderly people in the U.S. will reach historic highs. Increasing numbers of elderly citizens will put unprecedented pressures on publicly funded programs for social, health, mental health, housing, and income maintenance services. As a group, elderly citizens will have great political influence when advocating for programs that meet their needs. The effects of this advocacy on resources for persons with intellectual and developmental disabilities are unknown. Research must determine and explain the magnitude and implications of these demographic shifts.

The country's changing ethnic and racial composition challenges service provision for individuals and families in ways that reflect perceptions, preferences, and needs of people from various cultures and communities. The challenges of these demographic shifts drive efforts to recruit researchers who represent the changing face of the United States and have the unique abilities and the skills necessary to reach communities that have been left out.

Advances in Technology

The promise of technology has never been greater and its impact will be enormous. The challenge is to harness technology's great potential, while also anticipating its impact. Technological advances create new opportunities to assist people with disabilities in their daily activities. Medical technology can increase their longevity. Internet technology makes information more readily and quickly available. Internet-based distance learning has the potential to make training and education available and affordable to nearly everyone, anywhere, at any time.

Advances in technology bring concerns along with progress. With the Internet's status as a dominant resource for information of all sorts, those who lack Internet access risk isolation. Technological advances must be integrated into daily life for as many U.S. citizens as possible and adapted to the needs and wants of people with intellectual and developmental disabilities. To do so requires sensitivity to gaps in technology, to presumptions about access to technology and information, and to opportunities that derive from access.

Clearly, technology has the potential to improve the lives of people with intellectual and developmental disabilities. Hand-held devices can help people navigate the demands of their day and the paths of their communities. People without conventional reading and writing skills can use e-mail and other computer programs. The list of technological applications that respond to the challenges of intellectual and developmental disabilities grows longer each day; however, developing and adapting such technology for the needs of its intended customers may require more than marketplace incentives. Research has a role not only in technology development, but also in defining technology-related needs and outcomes for people with disabilities.

With these broad considerations in mind, the following chapters focus on twelve topical areas that address what we currently know and what we must learn to better achieve national goals related to citizens with intellectual and developmental disabilities. Research is an essential part of this process and one that requires the utmost attention and the highest expectations from all of us.

CHAPTER 2

Young Children with, or at Risk for, Developmental Disabilities

MARY LOUISE HEMMETER, ROSA SANTOS, PATRICIA SNYDER,
MARILOU HYSON, AMY HARRIS-SOLOMON, DONALD BAILEY,
ANNE FARRELL, DIANE BRICKER, AND REBECCA FEWELL
with
George Jesien, Merle McPherson, Ruth Perou, Sharon Ramey,
Beth Rous, Rune Simeonsson, Nancy Thaler, and Tracy Wright

REAL LIVES

Leah and Kenya were the best of friends for years. They were both diagnosed with spastic quadriplegic cerebral palsy at approximately one year of age and had very similar abilities. They attended an inclusive early intervention program together from the time they were one year old until they reached kindergarten age. The early intervention services were provided on site for both children through staff employed at the center. Therapy services were provided off site for Leah at nearby clinic settings. Occasionally, the therapist visited the classroom to consult with the teacher. The ongoing communication and coordination of services was facilitated primarily by the parent; however, the classroom teacher was the designated service coordinator. Kenya received no regular therapy (except when she went along with Leah and her mother) because her mother—single and living in public housing—had no means of transportation and was unable to take her other three children with her to therapy while maintaining a job to support her family. The two girls, although initially very similar in development and abilities, increasingly began to show marked differences in their developmental skills over the next few years.

At age three, the transition to preschool services (Part B) from early intervention (Part C) was a relatively smooth one for Leah and Kenya as they continued through the same university-based program. Although the preschool special education program provided services and contracted for a portion of the educational day for both Leah and Kenya, Leah was able to remain in the classroom full time because her parents were employees of the university and therefore able to access the "typical" child care for the extended day. This was not an option for Kenya, whose mother was not a university employee and who could not afford the costs of child care anywhere else. The early intervention services had included a five-day-a-week, six-hour-a-day program for Kenya, along with transportation to and from the school. Kenya's mother was forced to quit working as Kenya's school days were reduced to three half-days. Leah continued to show progress in all developmental areas; she received an augmentative communication device to assist in her communication, a wheelchair, a walker, and canes for mobility. She attended social functions with her classroom peers, continued with private therapies as well as therapy provided through the school system, and had teachers and parents who advocated for her needs every step of the way. Kenya, on the other hand, went through preschool without any assistive technology, even though her skills and ability to progress paralleled Leah's.

These girls, who started out life with a similar diagnosis as well as prognosis, showed very different progress by the time they went to kindergarten. Leah actually began kindergarten a year early through the gifted program and started in her neighborhood school with all the supports in place. Kenya began kindergarten in a segregated special education classroom for children with severe needs. One has to wonder, had Kenya been afforded the same opportunities and level of support that Leah received, would they still be in school together, being the best of friends, laughing together, and holding hands as they walk down the halls of school?

INTRODUCTION

Each member of our workgroup has had experiences with young children with disabilities and their families that are similar to those described in the vignette. These experiences, some positive and some negative, as well as our knowledge about research on effective practices and our understanding of both the letter and spirit of the laws related to the provision of services for young children, guided our considerations about potential national goals related to young children and their families. This chapter focuses on young children with, or at risk for, developmental disabilities, from birth to five years of age, and their families.

Services for our youngest citizens are defined by a unique set of characteristics that are foundational to and influence the development of our national goals. These characteristics relate to the critical role of the family in the lives of young children; differences and discontinuity of services across the age range; the nature and type of services and service delivery models available for young children and their families; and the training requirements and experiences of professionals working with young children and their families. First, contemporary theories share the fundamental assumption that child development and learning are shaped through continuous interaction between biology and experience (National Research Council and Institute of Medicine, 2000). In the lives of young children, critical experiences occur in the context of families and through interactions with primary caregivers. Thus, the recognized primacy of the family in the lives of young children informs the design and delivery of services and supports for young children and their families and must help inform our national goals and the related research agenda. Second, systems and legal requirements for services for young children are not consistent across the birth to five years age range. There are different legal requirements for children in the birth to three years age range and the three to five year age range. For example, services for children under the age of three can be coordinated by a lead agency other than the state department of education, whereas services for children ages three to five years must be coordinated by a state's department of education. Moreover, services for children under the age of three are guided by an individualized family services plan (IFSP), whereas services for children ages three to five are guided by an individualized education plan (IEP). Second, unlike services for school age children, there is no primary service delivery system for children with, or at risk for, disabilities under kindergarten age. Young children are served in a variety of settings (e.g., home, school, child care center) administered by different agencies, including public schools, Head Start, child care, mental health agencies, and others. Further complicating the diversity of services is the difference in requirements for personnel credentialing and training, which can range from a high school degree and no training to a bachelor's degree, certification, and more. Unlike public schools, in which the primary service provider is from the education profession, early childhood service providers may be from education, psychology, mental health, or other related services. These characteristics present both challenges to and opportunities for high-quality, coordinated, community-based services for young children and their families, and as such, were critical considerations in identifying our national goals for this population.

GOALS AND SOURCES

The work of our group was driven by an overarching commitment to ensuring that all young children with, or at risk for, developmental disabilities and their families have access to high-quality services and programs in natural environments and that these services and programs address the unique needs of each child and involve their families in ways that are meaningful to and valued by each family. Because many children with disabilities spend significant amounts of time in a variety of community-based services, in order to meet our goals, we focused on ensuring quality in all early childhood service delivery systems. To address this overarching commitment, we identified four goals:

1. Children with, or at risk for, developmental disabilities will be identified as early as possible so that they can have access to quality services.
2. Measurable, cost-effective, and sound intervention features, strategies, and content that advance the developmental trajectories of children and support their health, well-being, and community participation will be identified.
3. Families will be able to make informed decisions and effectively partner with professionals to achieve positive outcomes.
4. Children and families will have access to a community-based, coordinated system of evidence-based services provided by supportive and skilled personnel who value individual and cultural differences resulting in continuity of supports, community inclusion, and measurable benefits for children and their families.

Our workgroup considered two primary sources of information in the development of our goals. First, we considered federal legislation in terms of what services and supports are mandated for children and families. Second, we considered ongoing research and policy initiatives that not only influence the provision of services, but also help define the quality of services. Each of these two sets of sources will be described here briefly and referenced throughout this chapter.

Services for young children with, or at risk for, disabilities have been available for over three decades. The Head Start Act, which was signed into law in the 1960s, represented the first large-scale federal program for children who are at risk. Its influence on services for children with identified disabilities was strengthened with the passage of the Economic Opportunity Act in the early 1970s, which required Head Start programs to reserve 10% of their slots for children with disabilities. Also, in the late 1960s, the Handicapped Children's Early Education Program was created to provide federal assistance to develop model programs for young children with disabilities. The passage of the Education for All Handicapped Children Act in 1975 provided incentives for states to deliver services to preschool children with disabilities. However, it was the amendments to the Education for All Handicapped Children Act in 1986 that mandated services for children with disabilities ages three to five and created a program for states to provide early intervention services to children ages birth to three years. This legislation created what is known today as the preschool program (§ 619) and the Part C program for infants and toddlers. However, the services provided to these two age groups were quite different; the preschool program followed the provisions for school-age children, including the use of IEPs, whereas the Part C program included the use of IFSPs in place of IEPs. The use of IFSPs was only one of the many differences in the two programs. Another significant difference was the identification of the lead agency for services for infants and toddlers. The preschool program was to be implemented by state departments of education, but states had the authority to identify a different lead agency for the Part C programs. In 1990, Public Law 99-457 was amended and became known as the Individuals with Disabilities Education Act (IDEA). Although IDEA continued to be reauthorized as recently as November of 2004, the most significant reauthorization in terms of the provision of services for young children was made in 1986.

Our group also considered recent and ongoing research to be a primary source for our national goals. Although it is beyond the scope of this chapter to review all of the research, major research will be cited throughout. Two recent initiatives resulted in recommendations that were key to the development of our national goals. First, over the last several years, the National Research Council of the National Academy of Sciences formed several committees to engage in a discussion and review of what we know as the field of early childhood education and development. These committees conducted comprehensive reviews of the scientific literature and developed recommendations for our field in terms of service delivery, research, and personnel development (National Research Council and Institute of Medicine, 2000; National Research Council, 2001a). Second, recent publications by the National Association for the Education of Young Children (NAEYC) (Bredekamp & Copple, 1997) and the Council for Exceptional Children's

Division for Early Childhood (DEC) (Sandall, Hemmeter, Smith, & McLean, 2005) provided guidance to our group in terms of recommended practices for the field.

Review of Knowledge and Recommendations

Proposed National Goal A: Children with, or at risk for, developmental disabilities will be identified as early as possible so that they can have access to quality services

Overview of the Knowledge Base

Early childhood services are built on the assumption that earlier is better in terms of providing services and supports. In fact, the legislation that established the Part C program was developed in response to the research on the importance of beginning services early in order to prevent disabilities or to minimize the impact of the disability on the child's development. However, for children to benefit from these services, they must be identified and determined to be eligible as early as possible. By third grade more than 11% of the school-aged population are receiving special education or related services. In contrast, relatively few children are served during the early childhood years. Part C serves about 2.2% of the population of children, and the preschool program serves about 5%. Thus, approximately 15% of the children who are eligible for school-aged special education services are provided infant and toddler services, and about 44% are provided preschool services. Based on these statistics, it is likely that a large number of young children are eligible for services but do not receive them. The primary reasons for this relate to definition and eligibility issues and strategies and processes for identifying children who might be eligible for services.

States vary widely in the identification of children who qualify for services and the receipt of these services. For example, at the infant-toddler level, Alabama, Georgia, Nevada, and South Carolina serve less than 1.2% of the population, whereas Hawaii, Massachusetts, and New York serve more than 4% of the population. At the preschool level, California, the District of Columbia, Hawaii, and Texas serve less than 4% of the population, whereas Arkansas, Kentucky, Maine, West Virginia, and Wyoming serve more than 8% of the population.

One of the primary reasons for this variation in the percentage of children served relates to state differences in eligibility criteria. A major challenge to states offering Part C services is the determination of eligibility definitions and criteria. Eligibility criteria obviously influence the number of children served, the types of services provided, and ultimately the cost of services to states. State eligibility criteria vary in the extent of the delay, the areas in which the delay is manifested, the method used to determine the delay, or the number of areas in which a delay is observed (Danaher & Armijo, 2004). Furthermore, states have the discretion to provide services to children who are at risk for experiencing developmental delays. If states choose to serve at-risk children, they must define the risk factors and the criteria and procedures for identifying those children. States vary greatly in the criteria they use to determine if a child is at risk. Finally, many states have chosen not to serve children considered to be at risk. In fact, in 2002, only nine states were serving children identified as at-risk. The consequence of variation in definitions is that a substantial number of children who are eligible for services in one state are not eligible in another.

Further complicating the process of determining eligibility is the insufficient number of instruments that are available for determining if a child has a developmental delay. Instrumentation is an issue in general in the field of special education, but the issue is even more pervasive in the developmental testing of young children in particular. Although predictive validity obviously is a key attribute of an evaluation tool for young children, there is a lack of tools that meet the standard of acceptable reliability and validity.

Procedural issues related to evaluation, eligibility determination, referral for services, and IFSP planning can also be barriers to children receiving services early. State regulations dictate the timelines for the process of evaluation to the beginning of service delivery, and there is evidence that this process often takes longer than it should. A study based on interviews with a nationally representative sample of over 3,000 parents of young children with disabilities who were receiving early intervention services found a significant length of time between diagnosis and referral for services (Bailey, Hebbeler, Scarborough, Spiker, & Mallik, 2004). The average length of time between diagnosis and referral for services was 5.2 months, and the average was significantly longer for children with developmental delays compared to children with established conditions or children identified as at-risk. In addition, there was an almost eight-month lag between when the concerns were first noted and when the IFSP was developed. To address this and similar issues, a committee of the American Academy of Pediatrics recommended that pediatricians move from surveillance (i.e., watching a child during routine visits over time) to a more systematic process of screening infants and toddlers (Committee on Children with Disabilities, 2001).

Finally, issues related to cultural and linguistic diversity also can be barriers to early identification for services. Although it is beyond the scope of this chapter to address these issues in detail, we will describe a few of the issues that affect access to services for children from culturally and linguistically diverse families. First, families differ on what they view as a disability or risk factor (Skinner, Rodriquez, & Bailey, 1999). A family's view of what constitutes a disability may be impacted by their religious beliefs, as well as other cultural factors. Second, the extent to which families are referred to services may differ across families because of issues such as language (Kochanek & Buka, 1998). Further, accessing families from culturally and linguistically diverse backgrounds may be difficult (Barrera, 2000). Third, tools typically used to assess and evaluate children and determine eligibility may not be appropriate for, or accessible to, families from different ethnic and linguistic backgrounds. The use of these tools with children from culturally and linguistically diverse backgrounds may lead to over- or under-identification of children and families in need of services. With the exception of a few tools, most are not normed on diverse populations, and yet, they are used with diverse populations. Although there is a great deal of information in the field on recommended practices for assessment and evaluation with families from culturally and linguistically diverse backgrounds (e.g., Sandall, et al., 2005; McLean, 1999), there is evidence that these practices are not being implemented adequately and the impact is that children from diverse backgrounds may not be receiving the services they need.

Recommendations for Research

In the coming decade, debates will continue concerning the desirability and efficacy of earlier identification of children who are at risk for, or have, disabilities. Clearly, factors such as rapid changes in the technology for screening genetic disorders; the development of new clinical screening tools; evidence that early expression of behavior disorders is highly predictive of later social and behavioral problems; research documenting the validity of parental concerns about early development; emerging guidelines urging pediatricians to incorporate systematic developmental screening in routine pediatric practice for all children; and the cumulative evidence for the efficacy of early intervention all point to a push toward earlier identification. This movement needs to be informed by systematic research. Furthermore, these factors exist in an increasingly diverse society, and research is needed to assure culturally appropriate and effective child find, screening, and evaluation activities. To this end, Wolery and Bailey (2002) suggest five questions that need to be studied to improve early identification practices:

1. Why are some children identified earlier than others? Although part of this variation is certainly due to variation in state eligibility requirements, it is likely that other factors are relevant, such as variation in local practice, unresponsive health care professionals, lack of diagnostic expertise, and lack of appropriate clinical guidelines and screening measures.

2. What is the relative efficacy of various multi-disciplinary, community-based models for early identification of children with disabilities? Studies should include information about enhancing the role of pediatricians and other health care professionals and models for responding more rapidly to parent concerns. The mandated child find components of IDEA should be examined to compare and contrast the efficacy and implementation of various child find models.

3. What are the earliest presenting signs of selected categories of disability? There is wide variation in the age of diagnosis of children with disabilities such as fragile X syndrome, autism, behavioral and emotional disabilities, and learning disabilities. We need to know how (and even if) these disorders are expressed during the early childhood years.

4. What tools could improve the accuracy and efficiency of screening? Screening practice relies on appropriate screening tools. Newer and more precise tools need to be developed and validated drawing on research about the variability in presenting signs of selected categories of disability.

5. Do unintended negative consequences occur as a result of earlier identification, and how can these consequences be avoided? For example, genetic screening could have unanticipated consequences for some families. Identifying a child as at-risk for behavior problems or a learning disability could create a negative expectation for future performance. Furthermore, the possibility of racial or ethnic discrimination in the implementation of screening and early identification programs needs to be studied, and models must be developed to assure that early identification is viewed as fair and positive for all participants. (pp. 90–91)

Proposed National Goal B: Measurable, cost-effective, and sound intervention features, strategies, and content that advance the developmental trajectories of children and support their health, well-being, and community participation will be identified

Overview of the Knowledge Base

This goal addresses the need to identify and make explicit intervention features, strategies, and content that advance the developmental trajectories of children and support their health, well-being, and community participation. As we indicated earlier, support for families is a critical foundation for services for young children. Outcomes related to families should meet the same criteria discussed in this goal and will be addressed in more detail in Goal C, which is devoted entirely to working with and providing support to families. Goal B includes the need for research on interventions and strategies that are defined and implemented with fidelity (LeLaurin & Wolery, 1992). This goal ensures that we can answer questions concerning which specific intervention features, strategies, and content delivered when, where, how often, and with what intensity are responsible for child change. In addition, this goal requires methodologically appropriate research that offers precise descriptions of the functional abilities and ecocultural characteristics of children and families to determine which well-defined interventions are efficacious for children with certain types of disabilities, for children of different ages, and for children from different family and cultural backgrounds (Wolery & Bailey, 2002). To evaluate whether developmental trajectories are advanced as a result of well-defined and implemented interventions, the goal also addresses the need to develop psychometrically sound measures of important child outcomes by those with the technical expertise to "do the job well" (Shonkoff, 2002, p. 105). Finally, this goal acknowledges that scientifically valid interventions should not only advance children's developmental trajectories over time, but also should support functional outcomes related to their health, well-being, and community participation (Frey, Brown, Rooney, & Braun, 2003).

Those involved in the field of early intervention/early childhood special education have attempted to document intervention impact on children's development for over 30 years. Efforts to establish intervention impact have been hindered by several barriers and technical challenges (e.g., measurement challenges; difficulty implementing rigorous group experimental design research in policy contexts that mandate individualization of child interventions; attention to global program features without careful examination and parsing of intervention efforts into definable features, strategies, and content). Despite these and other methodological and technical challenges, as Guralnick (2002) noted, "the knowledge base with respect to the developmental science of normative development, the developmental science of risk and disability, and intervention science is considerable" (p. 101). The current status of the knowledge base is due, in part, to the growing emphasis on integration of research from fields such as neurobiology, psychology, anthropology, sociology, education, rehabilitation science, human ecology, and medicine.

The seminal work *From Neurons to Neighborhoods: The Science of Early Childhood Development* (National Research Council and Institute of Medicine, 2000) reflects the work of a prestigious interdisciplinary committee that reviewed and integrated a substantial amount of empirical research related to early development. This group acknowledged that there is a *single* science of early childhood development rather than different sciences related to early care and education, poverty, disability, mental health, and child maltreatment (Shonkoff, n.d.). Based on a review of existing evidence, the group offered several broad-based conclusions about what we know or have learned from empirical research in relation to the science of early childhood development. Table 2-1 shows the major conclusions of the committee.

Related to the committee's conclusion that early development can be altered by effective interventions, a number of published reviews of empirical research have addressed issues related to whether early intervention is effective for young children with disabilities or those at risk for disabilities (e.g., Casto & Mastropieri, 1986; Dunst & Rheingrover, 1981; Farran, 1990, 2000; Guralnick, 1997). Empirical findings accumulated over the

---

Table 2-1
Major Conclusions Described in *From Neurons to Neighborhoods: The Science of Early Childhood Development*

- Human development is shaped by a dynamic and continuous interaction between biology and experience.
- Culture influences every aspect of human development and is reflected in childrearing beliefs and practices designed to promote healthy adaptation.
- The growth of self-regulation is a cornerstone of early childhood development that cuts across all domains of behavior.
- Children are active participants in their own development, reflecting the intrinsic human drive to explore and master one's environment.
- Human relationships, and the effects of relationships on other relationships, are the building blocks of healthy development.
- The broad range of individual differences among young children often makes it difficult to distinguish normal variation and maturational delays from transient disorders and persistent impairments.
- The development of children unfolds along individual pathways whose trajectories are characterized by continuities and discontinuities, as well as by a series of significant transitions.
- Human development is shaped by the ongoing interplay among sources of vulnerability (risk) and sources of resilience (protection).
- The timing of early experiences can matter, but, more often than not, the developing child remains vulnerable to risks and open to protective influences throughout the early years of life and into adulthood.
- The course of development can be altered in early childhood by effective interventions that change the balance between risk and protection, thereby shifting the odds in favor of more adaptive outcomes.

Note: From National Research Council and Institute of Medicine. (2000). From neurons to neighborhoods: The science of early childhood development. Committee on Integrating the Science of Early Childhood Development. J. P. Shonkoff & D. A. Phillips (Eds.). Board on Children, Youth, and Families, Commission on Behavioral and Social Sciences and Education. Washington, DC: National Academy Press. Copyright 2000 by the National Academy Press. Adapted with permission.

past 30 years permit us to move beyond questions related to whether intervention should be provided or whether intervention is effective, to questions related to which specific and well-defined interventions, services, and supports are most effective for which children and families under what circumstances (e.g., Wolery & Bailey, 2002; Guralnick, 1997).

The need to define and deliver scientifically valid interventions and to examine their differential effects on individual children, as well as groups of children, not only has become an important research agenda, but also has become intertwined with national policies related to accountability for program results. Implementation of the *No Child Left Behind Act of 2001*; the report issued by the President's Commission on Special Education, *A New Era: Revitalizing Special Education for Children and their Families* (Office of Special Education and Rehabilitative Services, 2002); and other early childhood accountability systems implemented nationally (e.g., Good Start, Grow Smart, n.d.; Head Start Performance Standards on Services for Children with Disabilities, 2001) and in individual states (Harbin, Rous, & McLean, 2004) have propelled current knowledge about measurable, cost-effective, and educationally sound intervention features, strategies, and content into the national spotlight. Several national committees, established to investigate evidence, develop policy, and make recommendations for future research, have reviewed the existing empirical literature to examine the impacts of different intervention curricula and strategies on children's development and have noted important variances (National Research Council, 2001a; National Research Council, 2001b). These committees have uniformly endorsed the use of "scientifically valid" curricula and strategies for children with and without disabilities. Currently, researchers and policymakers are debating what types and levels of empirical evidence are needed to characterize an intervention feature or strategy as scientifically valid, particularly for young children with disabilities and their families (e.g., Dunst, Trivette, & Cutspec, 2002; Odom & Strain, 2002; Snyder, Thompson, McLean, & Smith, 2002; National Research Council, 2002b).

In part to address the need for the identification of scientifically valid intervention features or strategies, the Division for Early Childhood (DEC) of the Council for Exceptional Children conducted a systematic review and evaluation of nine years of early intervention/early childhood special education empirical research (1990 through 1998) published in 48 refereed journals (see Smith, McLean, Sandall, Snyder, & Broudy, 2004) to inform the promulgation of recommended practices for the field. In all, 1,018 empirical research studies were reviewed and coded to evaluate scientific credibility.

Researchers associated with DEC's Recommended Practices project found the efficacy of various intervention practices designed to impact child and family outcomes were differentially supported by research studies that spanned a continuum of scientific credibility and by the number of studies that supported each practice. In addition, three major types of research methods differentially supported practices (e.g., group quantitative, single-subject, qualitative). For example, child-focused and family-based practices were primarily supported by group quantitative and single-subject experimental designs. Results of the DEC project, which includes descriptions of the numbers of studies associated with particular intervention practices, suggest that convincing evidence in support of some intervention practices is accumulating, despite the fact that designs often characterized as most rigorous were not used. Odom and Strain (2002), for example, found strong single-case experimental design evidence to support the efficacy of several child-focused intervention strategies such as the use of systematic naturalistic teaching procedures including models, expansions, incidental teaching, mand-model procedures, and naturalistic time delay. These authors noted that the effects of the treatment strategies were replicated an average of 5.5 times per study, and most treatment strategies were implemented with a high degree of fidelity. As the DEC project demonstrated, in order to inform the identification of measurable, cost-effective, and educationally sound intervention features, strategies, and content that advance the developmental trajectories of children and their families and support their health, well-being, and community participation, scientific evidence must accumulate across studies. Findings from a single study must be synthesized and integrated with knowledge generated from other studies addressing similar questions.

When describing the status of the knowledge base in early intervention/early childhood special education, particularly related to effective intervention practices and outcomes, Carta (2002) noted that "research findings have given early intervention enough of a start for it to work" (p. 102). Comparing the use of the knowledge base to inform intervention practices to a young bicycle rider pedaling without training wheels for the first few times, she asserted that, although research to date has provided a foundation on which practices have been built, practice is moving forward somewhat shakily and has a ways to go before it will be able to operate efficiently. Additional empirical work will be necessary to accomplish Goal B. To do so will require "new insights and strategies that offer greater possibilities for more successful implementation" (Shonkoff, 2002, p. 106).

Recommendations for Research

In their testimony before the President's Commission on Special Education, Wolery and Bailey (2002) offered recommendations regarding five areas that they asserted deserved special attention in relation to an early intervention/early childhood special education research agenda for the next decade. Several research questions these authors suggested be addressed relate specifically to Goal B. First, Wolery and Bailey (2002) suggested the need for studies to examine the relative efficacy of different types of treatment. They asserted that questions of efficacy need to move beyond treatment versus no-treatment questions to those that examine which interventions are most efficacious for which children and families under which circumstances. These types of "aptitude/attribute by treatment interaction" (ATI) studies (Cronbach, 1957; 1975) will help advance our understanding about which intervention procedures and content advance the developmental trajectories of which children and which children benefit (or do not benefit) from specified procedures and content. Second, they proposed studies to evaluate differential impacts on child outcomes based on planned variations in frequency and intensity of treatment. As these authors noted, special attention should be given to identifying those amounts below which treatment is determined to be ineffective and those amounts above which additional intervention has marginal benefit, permitting evaluation of the cost-effectiveness of various interventions. Third, Wolery and Bailey (2002) asserted that data are needed on the quality of treatment provided in relation to outcomes achieved. "Components of quality will need to be defined, validated, and measured, and the effects of varying levels of quality need to be assessed" (p. 92). Fourth, these authors acknowledged the importance of examining mediating and moderating factors that influence intervention efficacy.

Regarding the identification of measurable, cost-effective, and educationally sound intervention features, strategies, and content, Wolery and Bailey (2002) proposed that new models and treatment practices need to be developed and validated in selected areas (e.g., intervention approaches for children with autism or behavioral challenges, interventions related to peer-related social competence). They suggested that additional studies are needed to evaluate promising models for preventing and treating behavior challenges and for promoting infant mental health. Finally, given the growing emphasis on embedded intervention approaches in early intervention/early childhood special education, these authors and others (e.g., Hemmeter, 2000) have suggested that additional research is needed to understand impacts and outcomes of these approaches, including examination concerning whether or not embedding intervention into children's ongoing activities in the settings where they spend time results in sufficient learning opportunities to advance their developmental trajectories.

To answer research questions related to whether or not intervention features, strategies, and content advance the developmental trajectories of children and their families and support their health, well-being, and community participation, challenges associated with developing psychometrically sound measures must be addressed in future research. Research related to improving measurement of outcomes in early intervention is critical in order to move the science of early intervention forward (Carta, 2002; Early Childhood Outcomes Center, 2004; Snyder, et al., 2002). As Shonkoff (2002) noted, the creation and use of these measures will require substantial commitment of funds dedicated specifically to this purpose and must involve those who have the needed technical measurement expertise. Homegrown measures, or measures developed primarily to distinguish between children who are developing typically and those who are not, must not continue to be the primary dependent measures in early intervention/early childhood special education research (Snyder, et al., 2002). Many available measurement tools mark progress or change for individual children, but they are not designed to monitor the rate of progress or change, an important dimension related to evaluating developmental trajectories over time (McConnell, 2000). Those with substantive expertise in the field and consumers who can help identify which child outcomes are most important to evaluate should be linked with technical measurement experts to produce a new genre of measures that produce reliable, sensitive, and valid data. As Carta (2002, p. 103) noted, "A field with an over-reliance on measures that are insensitive or invalid for many of its participants cannot ascertain precisely when interventions are working."

Finally, the field must come to general consensus about which child and family outcomes, beyond those focused on traditional child developmental domains, are important (i.e., what dependent variables should be operationalized) and how to measure these dependent variables most effectively and efficiently. Early proposals have been put forth regarding the utility of adopting an outcome system that emphasizes not only functional abilities (e.g., gross motor skills, social skills, literacy levels), but also the ability to engage in age- and developmentally appropriate activities (with or without accommodations) and opportunities to participate as an active member in community-based (natural) contexts

(Frey, et al., 2003). The International Classification of Functioning, Disability, and Health (World Health Organization, 2001b) has been proposed as one framework that might guide the systematic study of child and family outcomes, programs and services, and disability policy (Frey, et al., 2003; Pledger, 2003). The utility of this framework, methodologies for measuring intermediate care facility (ICF) outcomes, and the relationships between interventions and ICF outcomes should be an important focus of the research agenda in the next decade (cf. Tate & Pledger, 2003). In addition, the work of the Early Childhood Outcomes Center (http://www.fpg.unc.edu/~eco/), funded by the Office of Special Education Programs, U.S. Department of Education, should help inform the development and continuous refinement of a model for implementing a comprehensive outcomes system useful for program improvement and accountability in early intervention/early childhood special education, particularly in relation to the portrayal of aggregated outcomes for those young children and their families who participate in federally funded early intervention/early childhood special education programs.

Proposed National Goal C: Families will be able to make informed decisions and effectively partner with professionals to achieve positive outcomes

Overview of the Knowledge Base

Goal C focuses on the importance of supporting families in making informed decisions about services for their children and their families in collaboration with skilled and culturally competent professionals. To make informed decisions, families must be aware of the range of service options available (Turnbull, Turbiville, & Turnbull, 2000). It is also critical that families have access to the evidence-based information, materials, and supports necessary to make decisions that meet their individual needs. Information regarding the efficacy of various strategies and settings to support children's developmental outcomes and family outcomes should be clear, reliable, and valid. Families must also have a variety of options for ways to be involved in services for their children, and those options should reflect the diversity of families in terms of their backgrounds, needs, and access to resources (Hanson & Carta, 1995). To achieve these goals, it is important to have skilled and culturally competent professionals who not only support families in making decisions, but also collaborate with them to create options and build the knowledge base for effective services for young children and their families. Professionals should be able to collaborate with families as partners, sharing information that enables families to understand and access services designed to support their children's development.

The two components of this goal—the ability to make informed decisions and to collaborate with professionals—are tightly linked to the quality of the relationship between families and professionals. In the last 50 years, we have witnessed the evolution of relationships between professionals and families of children with disabilities (Erwin, Soodak, Winton, & Turnbull, 2001; Turnbull, et al., 2000). Although the field of early intervention and early childhood special education (EI/ECSE) is relatively young, it has been deeply affected by these changes. Services for young children with disabilities and their families have evolved from those that viewed children and families as passive recipients of services, to those that recognized children and families as the center of services, to those that valued families as empowered collaborators in supporting children's development

(Turnbull, et al., 2000). Changes in family-professional relationships reflect the growing recognition of the critical contribution of families in the design, implementation, and evaluation of early childhood services (Erwin, et al., 2001; National Research Council and Institute of Medicine, 2000; Sandall, et al., 2005; Soodak & Erwin, 2000). However, we need to gain further understanding of how this effective family-professional collaboration is reflected and supported in research and practice (Bailey, 2001; Eiserman, Weber, & McCoun, 1995; Erwin, et al., 2001).

Finally, although the cost-effectiveness of EI/ECSE has not been explored fully, the relative benefits of family-professional collaboration in designing, implementing, and evaluating EI/ECSE services is presumed to have long-term effects on the child and the family's quality of life, including health and well-being and the full inclusion of children with disabilities into community life (Barnett, 2000; Eiserman, et al., 1995; Dunst, Trivette, & Deal, 1988; National Research Council and Institute of Medicine, 2000). A series of studies conducted by Dunst and his colleagues found that a family's ability to access social support and resources within (intra-) and outside (extra-) of the family nucleus related positively to the quality of that family's functioning and their satisfaction with those services (Dunst, et al., 1988). Eiserman and his colleagues also found no relative difference, in terms of cost, between home-based and clinically based EI services. They note that "parents in both intervention groups preferred direct involvement and responsibility in addressing their child's developmental needs…" (p. 40). They further noted that data from their study support the notion that providing choices to families is preferable to providing families with only one type of intervention choice. Nonetheless, additional studies are needed to further illuminate variables that are cost-effective and produce long-term effects.

Families as Informed Decisionmakers

The extent to which families are able to make informed decisions is crucial to the success of EI/ECSE. Bailey (2001) noted that "families are the ultimate decisionmakers and long term care providers for their children, [thus] services should be organized in ways that enable families to feel and be competent in advocating for services" (p. 1). This is important in several ways. The first consideration emerges from a values perspective: informed families are paramount in a service system that values individuality, dignity, and adaptation and considers the child within the context of his family and his community, which may include individuals beyond the nucleus (Hanson & Lynch, 2004; Kalyanpur & Harry, 1999). Programs and services that reflect family concerns and priorities, which in turn reflect the process of family-professional collaboration, are a measure of the quality of EI/ECSE. True collaboration requires equality. This does not mean equal expertise, but rather it implies that the family and professionals have complementary, equivalent contributions in designing, implementing, and evaluating services. Turnbull, et al. (2000) described a collaborative family-professional relationship that thrives and builds on each other's strengths.

A second and related values issue is the clear preference of families to be involved and informed and to influence policy and practice (Winton & DiVenere, 1995). Families expend enormous emotional, temporal, and economic resources on the care of their children (Park, Turnbull, & Turnbull, 2002; Soodak & Erwin, 2000). Their desire to be informed is evidenced by the burgeoning popular literature on parenting children with disabilities, the explosion of advocacy, self-help, and support groups (both face-to-face and "virtual" support on the Internet), and the popularity of print and Internet-based materials on specific disabilities and cutting-edge interventions. Meeting family information needs is a pivotal component of a service system in a society that values self-sufficiency and inclusion for individuals with disabilities.

Supportive, Culturally Competent Personnel

A key component to effective family-professional collaboration is the preparation, support, and experience of professionals who are supportive of families from a variety of diverse cultural, ethnic, and linguistic backgrounds (Capone & Divenere, 1996; Dunst, et al., 1988; Harry, Rueda, & Kalyanpur, 1999; Sileo & Prater, 1998). There appears to be a consensus among researchers that effective family-professional collaboration is a critical skill that needs to be addressed both at the preservice and in-service levels. Although virtually all EI/ECSE providers have exposure to tenets of family-professional collaboration, practice nonetheless poses challenges to professionals across disciplines. Providers acquire training through traditional pedagogic models. In many cases, a medical model is used (e.g., therapists, mental health providers), which rarely addresses communication skills or learning first-hand from families about the importance of family-professional collaboration (Capone & Divenere, 1996; Winton & DiVenere, 1995).

Moreover, there are attitudinal, perceptual, and cultural and linguistic barriers to effective communication and collaboration between families and professionals (Barrera, Corso, & Macpherson, 2003; Kalyanpur & Harry, 1999; Sileo & Prater, 1998). Factors such as contrasting beliefs, practices, and values present real challenges to building collaborative relationships between families and professionals. They impact various aspects of EI/ECSE services in a way that could become detrimental to a child's development. According to Chen, McLean, Corso, and Bruns (2005) in extreme cases, differing expectations, roles, values, and world views contribute to the under-utilization of EI/ECSE services by families from diverse cultural, ethnic, and linguistic backgrounds.

Several strategies and guidelines for promoting effective family-professional collaboration have been recommended for those who provide personnel training (Capone, & Divenere, 1996; Winton & DiVenere, 1995; Winton, 2000; Winton, McCollum, & Catlett, 1997). For example, the Division for Early Childhood of the Council for Exceptional Children recently published its recommended practices, which are firmly rooted in the belief that families are critical and central to effective EI/ECSE services (Sandall, et al., 2005). However, further understanding of components within personnel development models that are effective in promoting family-professional collaboration is needed.

Recommendations for Research

Despite the clear acceptance of meaningful family participation in EI/ECSE services and the existence of many exemplary programs, there remains a gap between research, values, and practice (National Research Council, 2001a; Turnbull, et al., 2000; Winton, 2000; Winton, et al., 1997). Overburdened providers, personnel shortages, demands for immediate services, and the associated pressures present barriers to effective EI/ECSE services that reflect true family-professional collaboration. Too often, these pressures result in services that do not reflect the dynamic interplay among developmental domains, the child, the family, and the community. Thus, the following future research activities are recommended to address these gaps.

1. Evaluate the efficacy of elements that contribute to effective family-professional collaboration.
   a. The relationship between informed family choice, family satisfaction with services, and development of meaningful outcomes for children and families
   b. The families' understanding of children's development and their ability to navigate early intervention/early childhood special education services
   c. The replicable professional development models that promote effective family-professional collaborations, within and across disciplines
2. Document the benefits of meaningful family participation on quality of life, including the health and well-being of individual children and families and the impact on the community.
3. Develop, evaluate, and disseminate guidelines for families as they consider choices for early intervention/early childhood special education services, including assessment and intervention.
4. Evaluate the extent to which families develop the ability and confidence to make decisions regarding assessment, intervention, and the evaluation of progress for their children and family.
5. Support the development of reliable, valid information to guide family decisions about early intervention/early childhood special education services (e.g., relative efficacy of various interventions, intensity, contexts, and goals).
6. Address barriers that hinder the promotion of effective family-professional collaboration in direct service and personnel development programs (e.g., personnel shortages, demand for services, lack of training, competing policies and regulations, and many others) so that quality assurance can become a clear priority.

Proposed National Goal D: Children and families will have access to a community-based, coordinated system of evidence-based services provided by supportive and skilled personnel who value individual and cultural differences resulting in continuity of supports, community inclusion, and measurable benefits for children and their families

Overview of the Knowledge Base

The language of Goal D ties together several themes that were articulated in Goals A through C. Goal A focused on early identification of children in need of services. Goal B emphasized that once children are identified as having or being at risk for disabilities and developmental delays, we also need to identify those interventions that are most likely to be effective in promoting children's positive development and community inclusion. Goal C focused on ensuring that families will be able to make informed decisions and work with others on behalf of their young children. Although identifying the children, finding the right interventions, and informing families are necessary features, they are not sufficient. Goal D articulates the need for a well-integrated, community-focused, comprehensive array of services provided by personnel (teachers and other professionals) who have the supportive attitudes and specific competencies that benefit young children and their families. Ultimately, the keys to success in achieving all four of these goals are in the hands of those who work directly with young children and their families within a coordinated system of services and supports.

Because young children with disabilities are, and should be, thoroughly integrated into the fabric of their communities, much of what we know about systems of high-quality services and the characteristics of effective teachers and other personnel is drawn from the broader body of research in early childhood care and education. This research identifies the characteristics needed by adults who aim to significantly influence young children's developmental trajectories. Unfortunately, the research also documents the gap between what is needed and what is currently available in early childhood education programs, as well as gaps in preservice and in-service professional preparation. Finally, the research uncovers the flaws in the current delivery systems for services for all young children and the ways in which those flaws affect young children with disabilities who participate in those systems every day.

Characteristics of Well-Prepared Teachers of Young Children and of the Programs That Prepare Them

Research has consistently identified early childhood teachers' education and training as critical components of program quality and has predicted the kinds of experiences and interactions that are associated with positive child outcomes, including outcomes for young children with disabilities. Both college degrees and recent specialized preparation in child development and early education have been found to contribute to teachers' effectiveness, although the reasons for the associations between teacher qualifications and child outcomes are not yet well understood (National Research Council, 2001a; National Research Council and Institute of Medicine, 2000).

In its standards for early childhood professional preparation, the National Association for the Education of Young Children has set forth evidence-based expectations for what well-prepared practitioners should know and be able to do in five areas: promoting child development and learning; supporting families and communities through respectful, knowledgeable, and culturally sensitive relationships; observing, documenting, and assessing young children's learning and development; teaching in ways that blend positive teacher-child relationships, an array of effective and individualized teaching strategies, sound content knowledge, and the ability to create effective curriculum for all children; and becoming a reflective, collaborative, and ethically grounded professional (Hyson, 2003). These standards are relevant to the preparation of professionals who work with all children, with and without disabilities, including children from diverse cultural and linguistic backgrounds. For those who are preparing to become early interventionists or early childhood special educators, the Council for Exceptional Children and its Division for Early Childhood have developed similar well-aligned standards. Unified or "blended" programs—those that prepare professionals both in general and early childhood special education—are expected to address both sets of standards in an integrated way (Sandall, et al., 2005).

Gaps Between Research and Reality in Teachers' Characteristics and Preparation

Unfortunately, research also shows extensive gaps between the standards recommended by these national reports and current levels of professional education and training for the early care and education work force. Because young children with disabilities are served in natural environments within community settings, much of their time is spent with staff that frequently lack the formal education and training described above. Although some settings, such as state-funded prekindergarten programs and public school early childhood special education services, typically require bachelor's degrees and teacher certification, community child care classrooms are often led by teachers who hold only a high school diploma and have few if any required hours of specialized training. State requirements for teachers working in licensed child care centers range from a bachelor's degree to a GED, with most at the lower end of the educational continuum. Even when states require degreed, certified teachers (as in many state prekindergarten or early intervention initiatives), state licensure requirements, the definition of "early childhood educator," and the age range of "early childhood" vary greatly.

Requiring college degrees for all early childhood teachers is a worthwhile goal. However, the content of higher education programs often falls short of what is needed for teachers to promote positive development for all children. Reforms of teacher education, including early childhood professional preparation, have often focused exclusively on content and skill development in academic domains such as literacy and mathematics. Important as these domains may be, the result has sometimes been to decrease time available to develop skills in other essential areas (e.g., addressing challenging behaviors, promoting social and emotional competence, implementing effective assessment practices for young children with disabilities and young English language learners, creating partnerships with families, or working with other professionals). These topics are important for all early childhood professionals, but they gain even greater urgency as more and more young children with disabilities and developmental delays are included in early childhood programs (Early & Winton, 2001).

Just as the achievement of Goal D requires changes in the preparation of general early childhood educators, it also requires a reexamination of the preparation of early childhood special educators. What is the role of the special educator or early interventionist in a more inclusive and community-based system of services within natural environments? Roles are shifting: "regular" teachers in child care, prekindergarten, and other programs must meet the needs of all children, including many with significant disabilities and developmental delays, ensure that those children have access to the general curriculum, and individualize curriculum, teaching strategies, and assessment. In the future, early childhood special educators may need to take on a more indirect and supportive role, but one that is essential to an inclusive system of services. New collaborative and interdisciplinary models of professional development hold promise (Buysse, Wesley, & Able-Boone, 2001; Miller, Fader, & Vincent, 2000).

Fragmented and Underfunded Systems of Services and Supports

Finally, every discussion of the condition of U.S. early childhood education characterizes it as a "non-system," or, at best, a fragmented collection of funding streams and delivery systems (e.g., family child care, community child care centers, state-funded public school prekindergarten, kith and kin care, etc.) with widely varying expectations for teacher qualifications, ongoing professional development, curriculum, and assessment and accountability. Each and every one of these subsystems includes young children with, or at risk for, disabilities and developmental delays. At present, the likelihood that young children with disabilities and their families will experience positive outcomes is largely dependent on the community educational contexts and other settings in which children spend their days (National Research Council and Institute of Medicine, 2000).

For all children, but especially young children with disabilities, the high rate of teacher turnover (averaging 30% nationally) further contributes to fragmentation in ways that directly affect the system's ability to provide consistent and effective developmental services. Salaries and working conditions in child care and other early education programs are a significant contributor to staff turnover, which in turn diminishes program quality and undermines the quality of the entire service delivery system.

National and international reports, with varying levels of attention to young children with disabilities, have proposed strategies to organize and fund a far more coordinated system than presently exists in the U.S. Despite these recommendations, at present the U.S. early childhood care and education system lags far behind other countries in coordination, integration, public will, and funding (Committee for Economic Development, 2002; Organization for Economic Cooperation and Development, 2001). Dramatic changes are needed in coordination and financing if young children with disabilities are to participate in and fully benefit from the system.

Recommendations for Research

Although Goal D is well supported by research, many questions still need to be answered if we are to ensure that every child with, or at risk for, disabilities has access to a community-based, coordinated system of evidence-based services provided by supportive, skilled, and culturally competent personnel. Following are some key questions that future research must address:

1. What are the early care and education arrangements for young children with disabilities; how do those arrangements vary by poverty, culture and community, and other contextual factors; and what are the effects of those variations on children's experiences and developmental outcomes?

2. What models of early childhood professional preparation are most effective in developing practitioners who can promote the positive development and learning of young children with disabilities in inclusive, community-based settings?

3. What approaches are most effective in recruiting and retaining well-prepared, culturally and linguistically diverse professionals to work in community settings that serve young children with disabilities?

4. What are the most effective professional relationships among early childhood educators, early childhood special educators, and others who interact with young children with disabilities and their families in community settings, and what conditions promote those positive relationships?

5. What public policies are most effective in promoting full participation of young children with disabilities in high-quality early childhood education and other community settings?

USING KNOWLEDGE TO SHARE OUR NATIONAL GOALS

We have devoted the majority of this chapter to a review of the existing research related to our national goals, as well as a discussion of the content and type of research that is needed to advance our field in terms of providing high-quality services to young children and their families. These discussions clearly demonstrate that we have a significant knowledge base related to effective services. However, as demonstrated through the literature reviews, there is a significant gap between what we know about effective services and what is actually being implemented in the field. Many members of this workgroup have spent a significant portion of their careers trying not only to conduct methodologically sound research, but also to disseminate it in a way that makes it useful to our consumers, including family members, practitioners, administrators, researchers, policy makers, and in-service and preservice training providers. Given changes in demographics, advancements in technology, and increasingly complex demands on families, we must continue to strive to find ways to disseminate research in such a way that it is usable to our consumers, time-efficient, and comprehensive. Based on our collective work toward this end and research about utilization of knowledge, we suggest the following critical activities to ensure that information is developed, packaged, and disseminated in a way that is useful to all of our consumers:

1. Include consumers as active participants in all aspects of research endeavors (Schiller & Malouf, 2000). It will be important to go beyond including consumers on advisory boards or asking consumers for feedback on products once developed. Although these are important steps, past experience suggests they are not adequate for ensuring the development of useful materials and products. We suggest an action research approach that involves consumers in the identification of important research questions, implementation of research in a way that addresses and is respectful of the needs of consumers, and development of information and products based on the research findings that will increase the likelihood of use by relevant consumers.

2. Work with faculty at institutions of higher education (IHE) to develop materials that will be effective in preparing teachers, but which also will be sensitive to the challenges facing personnel preparation programs. Increasingly, IHEs are challenged by declining budgets, growing expectations for accountability, changing requirements associated with state certification guidelines, more diverse students, and a rapidly growing knowledge base related to effective practices. At the same time, IHE programs provide the most comprehensive context for preparing teachers. It is critical that researchers consider the challenges mentioned above when developing materials and products (e.g., textbooks, technology applications, training modules) for use in IHEs. For example, in a recent survey of early childhood higher education programs (Hemmeter, Santos, & Ostrosky,

2004), faculty identified preparing students to work with challenging behaviors as a high-priority training need. At the same time, they identified a lack of expertise by faculty and lack of room in the curriculum as barriers to more effectively addressing this topic. When given choices about the types of materials that would be most useful, they rated "materials for an entire course" lower than supplementary materials that could be embedded into multiple courses.

3. Ensure that our knowledge links research-based practices to training requirements and credentials across early childhood delivery systems. As indicated, there is great variability in the types of training requirements and credentials for personnel in different early childhood settings. Teachers in child care settings might be required to have only a high school degree and to get minimal in-service training, whereas teachers in public school settings typically are required to have certification. Regardless of training requirements, one strategy for increasing the likelihood that information will be used by consumers is to link what we know about effective practices to training requirements, certification standards, and learning outcomes for children.

4. Provide ongoing support and technical assistance to those who are implementing research-based practices. We know that the dissemination of information through products and materials, as well as training, is only one step in supporting the use of the information in applied settings. There is a growing knowledge base of effective strategies for providing ongoing support and technical assistance. The challenges of implementing these strategies are complicated significantly by issues of early childhood service delivery systems. First, administrators who are often in the position to provide some level of training and ongoing support may not have the training they need, either in content or process, to support direct service providers. An important strategy for addressing this issue is to ensure that administrators' credentials, where available, include knowledge and skills related to both content and strategies for providing ongoing support and training. Second, unlike school systems, many early childhood service delivery systems do not have staff that are responsible for providing training and support to teachers; thus we must continue to pursue alternative and effective ways for providing ongoing support and training to teachers. We must ensure that those who are available to provide support and training have access to evidence-based practices and information in formats that will help them support teachers in using these practices.

Anticipating the Changes of the Future

In this chapter, we have identified effective practices, developed a research agenda, and discussed challenges and strategies related to using the information produced through research. The field of early childhood special education has come a long way in a very short period of time. We are both lucky and challenged by the ever-growing emphasis on the importance of the early years in supporting children's development and preventing the emergence or escalation of developmental problems. Because of the rapidly expanding nature of our field, it is critical that we pause to consider the types of changes and impacts that are likely to affect our field in the near future. The changes and impacts that follow are only a few of the contextual issues that our field must address, but they provide a tremendous opportunity for expanding the effectiveness of services for young children with, or at risk for, disabilities and their families. In order to achieve our goals, we must address the following:

1. The increasing focus on the importance of the early childhood years is resulting in an increase in federal and state support for early childhood programs, along with a growing demand for accountability within these programs. Over the last ten years, there has been a tremendous increase in the commitment at both the state and federal levels to early childhood programming. Evidence of this commitment has been seen at the federal level by such programs as Early Head Start and at the state level by the growing number of states who are investing in some form of preschool program for children at risk for school failure. At the same time, this increase in commitment has been accompanied by a demand for accountability by these programs. This demand is evidenced by, for example, the implementation of the National Reporting System in Head Start and the inclusion of preschoolers in state accountability systems. Experts in early childhood education and development are challenging the developmental appropriateness of some approaches to including young children in these accountability systems. However, it is clear that this trend will continue, and it will be important for the field of early childhood special education to identify effective ways for assessing children on goals and outcomes, identified by local, state, or federal programs, that are developmentally appropriate and that provide reliable and valid information.

2. The financial situation facing our nation and states is challenging the value our society places on social service systems relative to other costly government programs and priorities. Although early childhood and school readiness are often at the forefront of policy makers' attention, ongoing and, in many respects, worsening budget problems, as well as the focus on other national and world crises, are clearly affecting the early childhood service delivery system in significant ways. The field of early childhood education and development must commit to working together to ensure high-quality programs for all children, regardless of setting, and refrain from competing for money in a way that will have a detrimental affect on any segment of our service delivery system. We must not put one program at risk in order to advocate for another. Head Start, Early Head Start, early intervention, public school early childhood programs, and child care are all critical and closely related components of our system. We must continue to find ways to work together to ensure high-quality, coordinated, community based, accessible services that are responsive to the differing needs of the families and children served by those programs.

3. As we have pointed out elsewhere in this chapter, the population of children and families being served in early childhood programs is increasingly diverse. The system must address this issue in a way that is sensitive to the diverse needs of all

children and families. We must prepare professionals to be responsive to the individualized needs of children and families, and we must prepare professionals who reflect the diversity of the families we serve. Finally, we must make services accessible and affordable to all families.

Enhancing Real Lives

Leah, now 11 years old and a year ahead of peers her age in school, excels in school, is incredibly active in community activities, and is the recipient of numerous awards for her academic and community accomplishments. Let's consider her progress in the context of our national goals. Why has she been so successful? First, she was identified early, began services quickly, and received all early intervention services identified by her team. Second, Leah had access to high-quality, community-based, coordinated services. She received most of her services in inclusive settings and participated in community activities much like her older sibling. In addition, she had medical procedures and surgeries that enhanced her physical development. Third, her parents were able to be involved, informed, and supported by the early intervention service delivery systems. Finally, Leah was fortunate to receive many of her services from highly skilled and qualified professionals.

As positive as Leah's experiences were, it was not always easy for her or her parents. In order to stay in her high-quality inclusive child care program, she had to go elsewhere for her therapy services. Although there was some interaction between the two settings, her parents provided a great deal of the coordination. When Leah entered the public school system, her family faced obstacles in terms of keeping her in an inclusive setting and ensuring the supports were there for her to be successful in that inclusive setting. Her parents had to fight for what they believed was best for Leah, and there were many obstacles they had to overcome.

Leah was fortunate, and her success to date demonstrates that. She had the benefit of parents who were educators and knew how to challenge the system when they did not feel that her needs were being met appropriately. Not all children are as fortunate as Leah, and that is what our group considered as we developed our national goals. We want all children to receive the services Leah received and to have the positive outcomes that Leah accomplished. And we want a system that makes it easier for all children and families to access and benefit from services. Public Law 99-457 began as a vision of high-quality services for our youngest citizens with disabilities and their families. The national goals described in this chapter are designed to ensure that that vision becomes a reality for all children and families.

CHAPTER 3

Effective Education in the Least Restrictive Setting

MARGARET MCLAUGHLIN, JAN BLACHER, SHARON DUFFY,
MICHAEL HARDMAN, JOHN MCDONNELL, JAN NISBET, NANCY SAFER,
AND MARTHA SNELL
with
Sally Atwater, Scot Danforth, Alan Gartner, Jason Hartle,
Dorothy Kerzner Lipsky, Fred Orelove, Ilene Schwartz,
Eunice Kennedy Shriver, Marlene Simon, Karen Staley,
and Lucille Zeph

REAL LIVES

Anna, a Student at Wilson Elementary School

By the time Anna was seven years old, she had been in two different schools, both located several miles from her home. Anna, who was identified at 18 months as having significant developmental delays, first received services through a center-based program at a special school exclusively for students with disabilities. She remained in the special school through her preschool years and, at age five, was transferred to a self-contained special education class at Wilson Elementary School, about 15 miles from her home. The school district buses all students with mental retardation to two central locations, one of which is Wilson.

Anna's parents are concerned about the two-hour round trip bus ride each day and the fact that she has very limited interaction with school peers without disabilities. In addition, Anna's parents question why her special education teacher at Wilson Elementary is given responsibility for teaching students with intellectual and developmental disabilities without being fully licensed to do so. After two years with Anna at Wilson, they have asked the district to establish an inclusive education program that would accommodate her needs at Bay Hill Elementary, their local neighborhood school.

The school district has considered the request from Anna's parents but they are not willing to set up an inclusive program at Bay Hill. District personnel indicate that Anna's current program at Wilson is the least restrictive environment based on her IEP goals and objectives. Anna's IEP focuses on specialized and intensive instruction in reading and math, as well as support in managing her time and developing appropriate social and personal care skills. Instruction in these content areas is not available at Bay Hill Elementary.

Robert, a Student at River View High School

Robert is an 18-year-old student with Down syndrome who attends River View High School. His verbal communication is limited to two- or three-word phrases, but he is able to write his name and has a functional sight-word vocabulary of about two dozen words (e.g., exit, restrooms, danger). Robert is friendly and well-liked by his classmates and teachers. He requires extensive support to participate in home, school, and community activities. Although Robert goes to River View High, he spends most of his day in a self-contained special education class with eight other students with intellectual and developmental disabilities. He and his classmates are taught by Ms. Somers, the special education teacher, and Marissa, a paraprofessional.

Robert has very limited contact with peers without disabilities. Upon arriving at school on a special bus, he goes straight to his locker, located right outside the special education classroom. During the morning session, he has one-to-one and small group instruction on basic skills such as counting coins, telling time, and learning to identify international symbols. During lunch, he sits with Marissa and his special education classmates at a table in the school cafeteria.

After lunch, the special education students head to the gym for their afternoon physical education (PE) class, where the high school PE teacher teaches them sports skills. Robert doesn't dress for PE or shower afterward because a male paraprofessional isn't available for help in the boy's locker room. Following PE, Ms. Somers reviews some of the functional reading and math skills that the students have been trying to master throughout the school year. On Tuesdays and Thursdays, Ms. Somers leads an art activity or allows free time for the students to play a game or watch a video. At 2:30, Robert takes the special bus home.

INTRODUCTION

Today, education is perhaps the most important function of state and local governments.... It is the very foundation of good citizenship. Today it is a principal instrument in awakening the child to cultural values, in preparing him for later professional training, in helping him to adjust normally to his environment. In these days, it is doubtful that any child may reasonably be expected to succeed in life if he is denied the opportunity of an education. Such opportunity, where the state has undertaken to provide it, is a right which must be made available to all on equal terms.

—Chief Justice Warren, writing for the majority
in Brown v. Board of Education, (1954)

Although written almost a half century ago, the words of Justice Warren remain compelling and meaningful today. As U.S. schools move into an era of greater accountability and higher expectations for student learning, it is imperative that all students benefit from these reforms and that resources directed to achieving the goals of those reforms "be made available to all on equal terms" (*Brown v. Board of Education*, 1954).

This chapter will present the findings and deliberations of a group of professionals, parents, and self-advocates reflecting on what it means to have an effective education in the least restrictive setting. This chapter will present the national goals for the education of students with intellectual and developmental disabilities as specified by the expert panel. It will also present the policy base for these goals, provide a review of current knowledge, and recommend ways to increase our existing knowledge base and refine our educational policy and practices. Finally, in speculating about what the future may hold for individuals with intellectual and developmental disabilities, this chapter identifies the challenges that confront educators, families, and students as they seek an effective education in the least restrictive setting.

Definitions

In their discussion of effective education in the least restrictive setting, the expert panel first sought definitions to common terms:

1. Effective education
2. Special education
3. Related services
4. Least restrictive environment (LRE)
5. Inclusive education

The following definitions served as the foundation of discussions and recommendations for the panel.

What Is an Effective Education?

An effective education is defined in terms of the curriculum and instructional activities delivered within public education systems to children and adolescents with intellectual and developmental disabilities between the ages of 3–21. Both the curriculum and the instructional activities must prepare these students for valued post-school outcomes including employment, community integration and living, continued education and training, and participation in a democratic society. This definition is consistent with the findings section of the Individuals with Disabilities Education Improvement Act of 2004 (IDEA 2004), which states, in part, that

> disability is a natural part of the human experience and in no way diminishes the right of individuals to participate in or contribute to society. Improving educational results for children with disabilities is an essential element of our national policy of ensuring equality of opportunity, full participation, independent living, and economic self-sufficiency for individuals with disabilities.
>
> Since the enactment and implementation of the Education for All Handicapped Children Act of 1975, this title has been successful in ensuring children with disabilities and the families of such children access to a free appropriate public education and in improving educational results for children with

disabilities. However, the implementation of this title has been impeded by low expectations and an insufficient focus on applying replicable research on proven methods of teaching and learning for children with disabilities.

Almost 30 years of research and experience has demonstrated that the education of children with disabilities can be made more effective by having high expectations for such children and ensuring their access to the general education curriculum in the regular classroom, to the maximum extent possible, in order to meet developmental goals and, to the maximum extent possible, the challenging expectations that have been established for all children. (IDEA 2004, Part A, § 601(c))

What Is Special Education?

As defined within the IDEA, special education means

(A) instruction conducted in the classroom, in the home, in hospitals and institutions, and in other settings; and (B) instruction in physical education, provided at public expense, under public supervision and direction and without charge; designed to meet the standards of the state educational agency (SEA), including an appropriate preschool, elementary, or secondary education; and developed in conformity with a student's individualized education program (IEP). (IDEA 2004, Part A, § 602, 29)

What Are Related Services?

As defined within IDEA, related services include

transportation, and such developmental, corrective, and other supportive services (including speech-language pathology and audiology services, interpreting services, psychological services, physical and occupational therapy, recreation, including therapeutic recreation, social work services, school nurse services designed to enable a child with a disability to receive a free appropriate public education as described in the individualized education program of the child, counseling services, including rehabilitation counseling, orientation and mobility services, and medical services, except that such medical services shall be for diagnostic and evaluation purposes only) as may be required to assist a child with a disability to benefit from special education, and includes the early identification and assessment of disabling conditions in children. (IDEA 2004, Part A, § 602)

What Is the Least Restrictive Environment?

The IDEA includes the following language regarding what constitutes the least restrictive environment:

IN GENERAL—To the maximum extent appropriate, children with disabilities, including children in public or private institutions or other care facilities, are educated with children who are not disabled, and special education classes, separate schooling, or other removal of children with disabilities from the regular educational environment occurs only when the nature or severity of the disability of a child is such that education in regular classes with the use of supplementary aids and services cannot be achieved satisfactorily. (IDEA 2004, § 612(a)(5))

The overall goal of the IDEA is to provide an appropriate education to each student with a disability and to do so to the greatest extent possible in general education classrooms alongside classmates who do not have disabilities.

What Is Inclusive Education?

The term inclusive education does not appear in the IDEA. The term has had multiple uses, but according to Lipsky and Gartner (1996)

> inclusive education is the provision of services to students with disabilities, including those with severe impairments, in their neighborhood school, in age-appropriate classes, with the necessary support services and supplementary aids (for the child and teacher), both to assure the child's success—academic, behavioral, and social—and to prepare the child to participate as a full and contributing member of society. (p. 763)

In developing this chapter, we determined that inclusive education means that all students are educated in their neighborhood schools in general education homerooms and classes with students with disabilities assuming a natural proportion (~10%) in relation to the population. All students must also participate in both social and instructional activities with flexible and individualized decisions guiding that participation. Table 3-1 presents one overarching national goal and three supporting goals that can be used to guide new policies that promote inclusive and effective education for students with intellectual and developmental disabilities.

Table 3-1
National Goal and Supporting Goals

All children and adolescents with intellectual and developmental disabilities will receive an individually referenced, culturally relevant, effective education that is provided in the least restrictive setting (i.e., education in the general education school and classroom) and leads to post-school outcomes.

Supporting Goals:
1. Parents and families, and youth with intellectual and developmental disabilities themselves, when appropriate, will be full partners in determining what constitutes an effective education, as well as what constitutes the least restrictive setting.
2. Accountability standards and procedures will be sufficient to ensure that each child or youth with intellectual and developmental disabilities receives an effective education within the least restrictive setting.
3. Children and adolescents with intellectual and developmental disabilities will have access to sufficient human and fiscal resources, supports, and services required for them to be effectively educated in the least restrictive setting.

GOALS AND SOURCES

Policy Sources and Legal Foundations That Support the National Goal

The national goals identified here pertain to the education of children with intellectual and developmental disabilities and are articulated primarily within the IDEA 2004. The provisions of this act are grounded in judicial decisions, as well as state constitutional law. The IDEA policy goals are also supported by other important pieces of federal legislation—Title IV and VI of the Civil Rights Act of 1964 and the 1965 Elementary and Secondary Education Act (ESEA). The former extended the guarantees of the Fourteenth Amendment. ESEA provided the basic policy framework for federal educational policy that was carried forward in the No Child Left Behind Act (NCLBA), the 2001 reauthorization of ESEA.

In addition, both Section 504 of the 1973 Vocational Rehabilitation Act and the Americans with Disabilities Act of 1990 (ADA) address discrimination against persons with disabilities in educational settings and establish the right to reasonable accommodations in those settings. However, the guarantees and definitions of what constitutes both an "effective education" as well as the "least restrictive setting" are set down primarily in the IDEA and ESEA.

The IDEA brings together two long-standing national goals. The first goal is to provide each child and adolescent with a disability with an "appropriate" education, which requires an individually designed educational program of "special education and related services." The second major national goal is to educate children and adolescents with disabilities in regular classrooms to the greatest extent possible. Thus, the overall national promise is to educate each student with a disability in the least restrictive and most educationally appropriate environment. What constitutes an "appropriate" or "effective" education, as well as what defines the "least restrictive environment or setting," has been the subject of separate policy interpretations and implementation.

What Constitutes an Effective Education?

The cornerstone of federal special education law is the individual student's entitlement to a "free appropriate public education" (FAPE). Specifically, the term "free appropriate public education" means

> special education and related services that (A) have been provided at public expense, under public supervision and direction, and without charge; (B) meet the standards of the State educational agency; (C) include an appropriate preschool, elementary school, or secondary school education in the State involved; and (D) are provided in conformity with the individualized education program required under § 614(d). (IDEA 2004, Part A, § 602, 9)

Under current law, the term "individualized education program" or "IEP" means a written statement for each child with a disability that is developed, reviewed, and revised in accordance with procedures set forth in law (IDEA 2004, § 614(d)) and that includes:

(I) a statement of the child's present levels of academic achievement and functional performance, including—

  (aa) how the child's disability affects the child's involvement and progress in the general education curriculum;

      (bb) for preschool children, as appropriate, how the disability affects the child's participation in appropriate activities; and

      (cc) for children with disabilities who take alternate assessments aligned to alternate achievement standards, a description of benchmarks or short-term objectives;

(II) a statement of measurable annual goals, including academic and functional goals, designed to—

      (aa) meet the child's needs that result from the child's disability to enable the child to be involved in, and make progress in, the general education curriculum; and

      (bb) meet each of the child's other educational needs that result from the child's disability;

(III) a description of how the child's progress toward meeting the annual goals described in subclause (II) will be measured and when periodic reports on the progress the child is making toward meeting the annual goals (such as through the use of quarterly or other periodic reports, concurrent with the issuance of report cards) will be provided;

(IV) a statement of the special education and related services and supplementary aids and services, based on peer-reviewed research to the extent practicable, to be provided to the child, or on behalf of the child, and a statement of the program modifications or supports for school personnel that will be provided for the child—

      (aa) to advance appropriately toward attaining the annual goals;

      (bb) to be involved in, and make progress in, the general education curriculum in accordance with subclause (I) and to participate in extracurricular and other nonacademic activities; and

      (cc) to be educated and participate with other children with disabilities and nondisabled children in the activities described in this subparagraph;

(V) an explanation of the extent, if any, to which the child will not participate with nondisabled children in the regular class and in the activities described in subclause (IV)(cc);

(VI) (aa) a statement of any individual appropriate accommodations that are necessary to measure the academic achievement and functional performance of the child on State and districtwide assessments consistent with § 612(a)(16)(A); and

      (bb) if the IEP team determines that the child shall take an alternate assessment on a particular State or districtwide assessment of student achievement, a statement of why—

            (AA) the child cannot participate in the regular assessment; and

            (BB) the particular alternate assessment selected is appropriate for the child.

At the time of passage of Education for All Handicapped Children Act in 1975, Congress clearly indicated that the requirement for individualized programs was essential to achieving the ambitious goals of the legislation (Ballard & Zettel, 1977; Levine & Wexler, 1981). Furthermore, the term "appropriate" came to mean that it was suitable for the individual student (Zettel, 1982). However, although recent reauthorizations have maintained the individually referenced nature of the IEP, there are increasing requirements to consider a child's educational program in the least restrictive environment as it supports the child's progress in the general education curriculum.

The Supreme Court has played a significant role in determining what constitutes an "appropriate" education for students with disabilities. In *Board of Education of Hendrick Hudson Central School District v. Rowley* (1982), the Court held that an "appropriate" education is one that is provided at public expense, meets the state's educational standards, approximates the grade levels used in the state's regular education, comports with the child's IEP, and is reasonably calculated to enable the child to achieve passing marks and advance from grade to grade.

The act establishes a "floor of educational opportunity" (Data Research, 1997, p. 7), and individual states have been given the authority to make the more substantive decisions of what constitutes an appropriate education. Most legal interpretations of the "appropriate" provision suggest that a child's education is considered appropriate if it is designed to conform with the procedures specified in law and if the child is receiving some benefit or making progress on individual goals based on some judgment of their capabilities (McDonnell, McLaughlin, & Morison, 1997; Smith & Brownell, 1995). However, the IDEA 1997 amendments began to focus on the need to ensure better educational outcomes for students who receive special education services and began to establish a link between IDEA and general education curriculum and standards. As noted earlier, the findings excerpted from the IDEA 2004 further challenge states to turn their focus to what students with disabilities are learning.

The IDEA 1997 amendments established for the first time the importance of "results" and "outcomes" and linked these to concepts of "appropriate" and "effective" education. The 2004 reauthorization reinforced and expanded this commitment. However, it is the NCLBA, the 2001 amendments to the ESEA, that have solidified this link to an "effective" educational standard.

No Child Left Behind Act: State Standards, Accountability, and "Appropriate Education"
The 2001 NCLBA builds on ESEA reauthorizations in requiring that states (a) establish challenging standards in (at least) reading, math, and science and annually assess the performance of *all* students in grades 3–8, (b) disaggregate assessment results by student subgroups (including students with disabilities), and (c) institute an ambitious accountability system based on student results.

Under NCLBA, states must assess at least 95% of all students and students in each of five target groups, including students with disabilities. In addition, states must publicly report disaggregated subgroup performance as long as student confidentiality is maintained. However, schools are only accountable for groups that are large enough to allow statistically valid and reliable conclusions to be made regarding adequate yearly progress (AYP). The minimum number for subgroup accountability is determined by each state.

States must set separate annual statewide progress objectives in mathematics and reading/language arts, ensuring that all groups of students remain on a trajectory toward proficiency by 2013–2014. Recognizing that grade-level assessments would not be appropriate for some students with disabilities, especially those with severe impairments, the NCLBA regulations give states and school districts the flexibility to measure the achievement of students with the most significant cognitive disabilities against alternate achievement standards and to count the "proficient" scores of these students *with the most significant cognitive disabilities,* as defined by the state, who take assessments based on alternate achievement standards (§ 200.1(d)), as proficient in the calculation of AYP (§ 200.13(c)(1)(i)). However, to ensure that alternate achievement standards are not used as a loophole to evade accountability for large numbers of students with disabilities, the number of proficient scores on alternate achievement standards at the LEA and state levels must not exceed a small percentage (now 3%) of all students in reading/language arts and in mathematics (McLaughlin & Nagle, 2004). The regulations define an alternate achievement standard as an expectation of performance that differs in complexity from a grade-level achievement standard. The final regulations make clear that alternate achievement standards are appropriate for only a small percentage of students with disabilities, including those with significant cognitive disabilities. Individual states are allowed to define their alternate achievement standards, but they must be aligned with the state's academic content standards, promote access to the general curriculum, and reflect professional judgment of the highest achievement standards possible (§ 200.1(d)). Thus, the emerging national "goal" of an effective education for all students is one that is standards-driven and based on attainment of prescribed content or knowledge (McLaughlin & Nagle, 2004).

What Constitutes the Least Restrictive Setting?

The IDEA states that education should occur in the most appropriate, least restrictive environment (LRE), which means that, *as much as possible,* students with disabilities should be educated in the same environment as students without disabilities. The law recognizes that supplementary aids, supports, and services may be needed to achieve this goal. This LRE requirement is essentially unchanged from its original statement in the Education for All Handicapped Children Act. However, since 1975 numerous due process and federal district court cases have arisen concerning the interpretation of this requirement.

Case Law on LRE

According to Douvanis and Hulsey (2002), the Education for All Handicapped Children Act did not define LRE, an omission that allowed for different interpretations by different courts. Some see LRE as a relative term determined by the needs of the child (i.e., what is *least restrictive* for one child is restrictive for another).

"The law continues to express a preference rather than a mandate for placement of students with disabilities in the regular classroom" (Bateman & Linden, 1998, p. 13). Yet case law supports *both* inclusive placements and restrictive placements. The IEP team plays a major role in determining LRE. The role of the team is to craft priority goals and objectives first, then determine which placement or combination of placements will result in progress toward those outcomes. The Fourth Circuit of Appeals stated, "Under IDEA, mainstreaming (another term for LRE) is a policy to be pursued so long as it is consistent with the Act's primary goal of providing disabled students with an appropriate education. Where necessary for educational reasons, mainstreaming students assumes a subordinate role in formulating an educational program" (*Hartmann v. Loudoun County Board of Education*, 1997).

Case law pertaining to LRE is complicated and often contradictory. Because the Supreme Court has refused to hear the appeals of cases that relate specifically to LRE, local and regional interpretation remains the rule of law.

Courts frequently establish tests to address issues related to LRE. In *Roncker v. Walter* (1983), the court developed the following two-part test to guide the appropriate placement for a student with a disability:

1. Can the educational services that make the segregated setting superior be feasibly provided in a nonsegregated setting? (If so, the segregated placement is inappropriate.)
2. Is the student being mainstreamed to the maximum extent appropriate?

Similar tests were applied in *Daniel R.R. v. State Board of Education* (1989). In *Greer v. Rome City School District* (1991), the court stated that schools must first consider the least restrictive setting prior to making a placement in a segregated program. In *Oberti v. Board of Education of the Borough of Clementon School District* (1993), the court held that inclusion was a "right," not a privilege. This was the first time that the word "inclusion," rather than "mainstreaming," was used in relation to IDEA.

In *Sacramento v. Rachel* (1994), the court ruled that, in determining the appropriate placement, educators must compare the educational benefits of the general education classroom with supplemental aids and services to the educational benefits of the special classroom. Schools must also consider the nonacademic benefits of interaction with nondisabled students and evaluate the effect of the student's presence on the teacher and on other students.

Several court decisions have eroded the progress toward inclusive placements. In *Light v. Parkway* (1994), the court held that "a student who is violent, dangerous, and disruptive of the education of others is never properly placed in a regular classroom setting." The court further argued that for some students, regular education, even with supplemental aids and services, may never be appropriate. In *Clyde K. v. Puyallup School District* (1997), the court found for one student who had not made progress that "a mainstream placement is no longer appropriate."

In *Hartmann v. Loudoun County Board of Education* (1997), the court stated that mainstreaming is not required when a student with a disability will not receive an educational benefit from it, and any marginal benefit from mainstreaming would be outweighed by benefits that could only be obtained in a separate educational setting.

Likewise, *Doe v. Arlington County* (1999) continued with this line of reasoning, concluding that if a child has not benefited educationally in a regular educational setting, separate placement is more appropriate.

REVIEW OF KNOWLEDGE AND RECOMMENDATIONS

In the previous section, we established the basic legal foundations for the national goal. In this section, we provide an overview of the research related to the national goal and selected supporting goals for effective education of students in the least restrictive setting.

Overarching Goal: Children and adolescents with intellectual and developmental disabilities will receive an appropriate individually referenced education that is provided in the general education school and classroom and leads to valued post-school outcomes

Effective Education

The knowledge base relative to what constitutes an "effective" education for children with intellectual and developmental disabilities is extensive. Moreover, it is confounded by changing policies about the purpose of education as well as our collective experience educating children and adolescents with intellectual and developmental disabilities. The "effectiveness" research can fit into three rather large and somewhat overlapping areas: medical- or treatment-oriented research, instructional design, and the search for the optimal environment. We will not review the extant research in all of these areas; rather, we will cite only some illustrative studies. However, it is important to note that research within each of the broad areas has focused on improving an individual's overall functioning in domains critical to daily living.

Medically oriented research, conducted mostly in institutions or similar segregated settings, has focused on the physical aspects of mental retardation and developmental disabilities and the differential response to treatments designed to improve specific physical, sensory, or cognitive functions or ameliorate the effects of losses in these areas.

A second productive area of research has focused on identifying interventions and conditions that help people acquire specific skills. Basic behaviorally based interventions and research designs have created the foundation of much of this instructional research. Studies using applied behavioral analysis (ABA) abound in the research related to education of students with intellectual and developmental disabilities, and they have provided considerable information about effective instruction for these and other students with disabilities. Three research-based principles have emerged: individualization, instructional intensity, and explicit instruction (McDonnell, et al., 1997; McLaughlin, Fuchs, & Hardman, 2000). These instructional principles are not placement-specific; they describe how effective instruction occurs, not where instruction takes place.

A third area of research has focused on the effects of specific environments on the development of children and adolescents with intellectual and developmental disabilities. The most important concept to emerge from this line of research is "the criterion of ultimate functioning" (Brown, Nietupski, & Hamre-Nietupski, 1976). As described by Brown, Nietupski, and Hamre-Nietupski, the criterion refers to a dynamic, personalized cluster of skills and abilities that each person must possess in order to function as productively and independently as possible in integrated adult community environments. The criterion of ultimate functioning was used as a rationale for the movement of students with significant intellectual and developmental disabilities from segregated schools to classrooms in regular schools. The criterion asserts that the ultimate goal of education for children and adolescents with these disabilities should be to prepare them to function as adults in complex heterogeneous community settings.

The "life skills/adult outcomes approach" to instructional programming for students with mild intellectual disabilities is consistent with the criterion of ultimate functioning. Patton, Cronin, Polloway, Hutchison, and Robinson (1989) described the life skills approach as the curricular option best suited to meet the needs of students with mild intellectual disabilities because it is sensitive to the students' need to move toward important adult outcomes and emphasizes topics that are meaningful and motivating to these students. However, this line of research posited a separate or differentiated curriculum from that offered in general education classrooms.

More recently, education of individuals with significant intellectual and developmental disabilities has emphasized building a supportive environment through natural supports rather than teaching the explicit skills stressed in the criterion of ultimate functioning and life skills approach to curricula.

> Natural supports are resources and strategies provided by people or equipment in a given environment that (a) potentially lead to desired personal and performance outcomes, (b) are typically available and culturally appropriate in the respective environments, and (c) are supported by resources from within the environment, facilitated by the degree necessary by human service coordination. (American Association on Mental Retardation, 2002, p. 152)

Related to the concept of natural supports is person-centered planning. Several models of person-centered planning have been described in the literature, including lifestyle planning (O'Brien, 1987a), the McGill Action Planning System (MAPS) (Vandercook, York, & Forest, 1989), personal futures planning (Mount & Zwernick, 1988), the Team Environmental Assessment Mapping System (TEAMS) (Campbell, Campbell, & Brady, 1998), and Big Picture Planning (McDonnell, Mathot-Buckner, & Ferguson, 1992). The key feature of each model is a planning process directed by students and their families. The planning process is focused on identifying quality-of-life outcomes (e.g., satisfaction with friendships and social relationships, ability to make choices) and long-term goals such as employment, living arrangements, and financial security.

The planning process culminates in the identification of the activities and resources necessary for each student to achieve his or her outcomes. To date, little research exists on the efficacy of either person-centered planning or natural supports in terms of achieving desired outcomes.

Research Related to Education in the LRE

The most recent data reported by the U.S. Department of Education (2002) indicate that, in the 1999–2000 school year, 95% of students with disabilities were educated in regular school buildings and in regular classrooms for 80% or more of the school day. Only 3% of all students with disabilities were educated in separate public or private schools. Placement differs by disability category and age. For example, only 17% of the students categorized as having mental retardation are in the general education classroom for 80% of the day, and 51% of this group of students categorized as having mental retardation is educated outside general education classrooms more than 60% of the school day.

According to the same state-reported data, whether a student with disabilities is educated in general education classrooms also depends on where he or she lives. For example, a student in Connecticut is more likely to be educated in a restrictive setting than a student in Vermont, regardless of disability (U.S. Department of Education, 2002).

Benefits of Inclusive Education

The growing body of research on the benefits of inclusive versus separate or self-contained placements includes multiple methodologies, age groups, and settings. For example, Moore (1998) summarized the research on educating students with disabilities in general education classrooms. Overall, some evidence exists that communication and social and behavioral skill acquisition is superior in inclusive classes or schools (Casey, Jones, Kugler, & Watkins, 1988; Cole & Meyer, 1991; Laws, Byrne, & Buckley, 2000; Fisher & Meyer, 2002; Guralnick & Groom, 1988; Hunt, Farron-Davis, Beckstead, Curtis, & Goetz, 1994; Saint-Laurent & Lessard, 1991).

Several researchers have documented positive social, communication, and academic outcomes (Fisher & Meyer, 2002; Kishi & Meyer, 1994; Helmstetter, Curry, Brennan, & Sampson-Saul, 1998; Peck, Donaldsson, & Pezzoli, 1990). In a meta-analysis of the impact of setting on learning, Baker, Wang, and Walberg (1994, 1995) found a small-to-moderate beneficial effect of inclusive education on the academic and social outcomes of special needs students. A small number of studies have validated the negative impact of placement in regular education when individualized supports are not provided (Baines, Baines, & Masterson, 1994; Zigmond & Baker, 1995). No studies to date have found a negative impact of inclusive practices on students without disabilities, and Fisher and Meyer (2002) specifically argue that academic performance of nondisabled students is at least as good in inclusive classrooms as in comparison classes.

Many researchers have identified key factors that appear to influence whether or not inclusion is successful; however, how success is measured differs across studies. Eight of the more frequently cited factors identified include (a) schools/classrooms that value and support inclusion and diversity, (b) teachers with positive attitudes, (c) parents and families who provide support, (d) teachers who plan together through collaborative teaming, (e) classrooms that encourage both social and instructional inclusion, (f) teachers who use adaptations so students can learn in general education classes, (g) peer support, and (h) paraprofessionals who foster, rather than prevent, peer interactions (see McGregor & Vogelsberg, 1998).

Supporting Goal A: To allow parents, families, and youth with intellectual and developmental disabilities, when appropriate, to be full partners in determining what constitutes an effective education as well as the least restrictive setting

Family participation in every phase of IDEA services is mandated. To be effective advocates, families must learn to navigate in a complex, confusing, and seemingly contradictory maze of laws, rules, and practice. A vast and varied literature exists on the involvement of parents and families with their children who have intellectual or developmental disabilities. We highlight a few key points here in order to place our recommendations in historical perspective.

Historical Perspective

Parents were originally excluded from any involvement with their children who had intellectual disabilities. Indeed, within the American Association on Mental Retardation (AAMR) research archives, the first major interest in parents as a focus of study dates to 1939 (Blacher & Baker, 2002).

Research interest in parents as "subjects" grew continually throughout the 1950s and 1960s, and by the 1970s, parents and parent involvement were considered "de rigeur" for developing appropriate education programs for children and adolescents with special needs. This is due, in part, because the spirit and letter of the federal legislation passed in 1975 (and all of its subsequent amendments) mandated that parents should be substantively involved.

In reality, however, involvement of parents is often superficial. Harry, Allen, and McLaughlin (1995a) described this difficulty in their study of involvement of African-American parents. The authors underscored the point that the formal conference setting is the main vehicle used to involve parents, albeit often unsuccessfully, in special education. Ironically, a solid database supports the involvement of parents in teaching and schooling (Baker, 1989; Turnbull & Turnbull, 2000). Research suggests that involvement of parents is highest at critical transition points (e.g., entering kindergarten and leaving high school) (Blacher, 2001; Pianta & Cox, 1999; Pianta, Kraft-Sayre, Rimm-Kaufman, Gercke, & Higgins, 2001).

Researchers and professionals know much more about the amount, type, continuity, and importance of parent involvement when children are in the early childhood years (see Bailey, 2002) rather than in the higher grades, in part because much more research has focused on this point of the life-span. Although often mandated, involvement does seem to decrease over time. Even at the point of transition to kindergarten, parents reported feeling more involved and more supported when their children were in early intervention or preschool programs than during this important transition (Hamblin-Wilson & Thurman, 1990).

Fortunately, early involvement by parents offers collateral benefits. For example, one study indicated that parent involvement in preschool and kindergarten led to better reading scores by eighth grade, better overall achievement and lack of grade retention, and fewer placements in special education (Miedel & Reynolds, 1999). When it is time to leave high school altogether, parent involvement appears to make the transition process easier (Blacher, 2001). Studies of parents and transition clearly suggest that parents of young adults with severe disabilities are highly involved (Geenen, Powers, Lopez-Vasquez, 2001; Kraemer & Blacher, 2001).

Schools have had less success with parents from culturally and linguistically diverse backgrounds. A research study that focused on African-Americans uncovered a trend of a high and consistent rate of parent involvement early on with a decline in participation after the transition to kindergarten; participation seemed to be inhibited by school factors (Harry, et al., 1995a). Schools also have much to learn about how to involve non-English speaking parents. For instance, a growing series of articles suggests that Latino families need more tools to guide them through the special education maze (Lian & Fantanez-Phelan, 2001; Shapiro, Monzo, Rueda, Gomez, & Blacher, 2004). Sometimes the benefits of parents' hands-on involvement and awareness of their child's own strengths extend well beyond child gains. For example, research has demonstrated collateral improvements in parental well-being, such as lower rates of depression, less stress, and fewer reported parent and family problems (Baker, 1989; Baker, Landen, & Kashima, 1991).

The Roles of Parents

Basically, parents have assumed three roles: patients, teachers, and advocates (Blacher & Baker, 2002). Although the early view of "parents as patients" was patronizing, it did lead to sensitivity to parents' thoughts and feelings—an essential backdrop for providing the family support and involvement that later defined effective education. "Parents as teachers" is emphasized less these days, unless one's child has severe behavioral challenges (e.g., autism spectrum disorder or other behavioral phenotypes). In these cases, parents often learn the principles of applied behavior analysis in order to assure that their child's IEP (or home program, if they have one) contains an appropriate behavior-management plan.

The current prevalent role of "parents as advocates" refers to efforts by parents to secure family supports and appropriate education for their children. Despite the progress made in the years since the passage of IDEA, students with disabilities and their families frequently must fight to ensure that the goals of the Act are honored. An increasingly adversarial relationship has developed between local school officials and parents of children and adolescents with disabilities (Blacher, 2002; Mulick & Butter, 2002).

Supporting Goal B: To provide sufficient accountability standards and procedures to ensure that each child or youth with intellectual and developmental disabilities receives an effective education within the least restrictive setting

When the 1975 Education for All Handicapped Children Act was passed, lawmakers chose a procedural approach to ensuring that each child with a disability received a free, appropriate public education. These procedures included the individualized educational planning process; procedural safeguards, including parental notice and involvement; and due process. The underlying assumption of this approach was that, if all of these procedures were in place, the IEP team, including the child's parents, would develop an appropriate educational plan for the child. The plan would include annual goals and short-term objectives, as well as the requisite services that would be provided. The Act required states, under the General Supervision provisions, to monitor local education agencies to ensure that all necessary procedures were followed. In addition, the secretary would review the policies and practices of state education agencies to ensure that the proscribed procedures were in place and report the outcomes of those reviews. The IDEA 1997 amendments included a new provision requiring states to establish performance goals and indicators for children with disabilities and to report on the progress toward meeting those goals biennially. The IDEA 2004 links the performance goals and indicators more closely to NCLBA. Specifically, states are required to

> establish goals for the performance of children with disabilities in their state that are the same as the State's definition of adequate yearly progress, including the State's objectives for progress by children with disabilities, under § 1111(b)(2)(C) of the Elementary and Secondary Education Act of 1965; address graduation rates and dropout rates, as well as such other factors as the State may determine; are consistent, to the extent appropriate, with any other goals and standards for children established by the State. (IDEA 2004, Part B, § 612(D))

States must report annually on their progress toward meeting the goals.

According to U.S. Department of Education (2001) reports, between 1994 and 1998 every state was out of compliance with IDEA requirements to some degree. In addition, states and districts cited the enormous amount of paperwork associated with compliance monitoring, and families expressed frustration that the paperwork is often a meaningless activity unrelated to the quality of education provided (President's Commission on Excellence in Special Education, 2002). As a result of these concerns, as well as the movement to focus on outcomes or results, the Office of Special Education Programs within the U.S. Department of Education has taken specific actions to improve accountability through a process referred to as Continuous Improvement and Focused Monitoring System (CIFMS) (S. S. Lee, personal communication, April 6, 2004). The CIFMS is a four-part accountability strategy meant to (a) verify the effectiveness and accuracy of each state's monitoring, data collection, and assessment systems, (b) identify, based on data, those states at high risk for compliance, financial, and/or management failure, (c) support each state in assessing their performance and compliance and in planning, implementing, and evaluating improvement strategies, and (d) focus OSEP's intervention on states with low performance in critical performance areas. Performance data include LRE data, as well as assessment results, graduation and dropout rates, and other important compliance indicators (http://www.ed.gov/policy/speced/guid/idea/monitor/index.html, retrieved, January 10, 2005).

Both the OSEP data-based monitoring, as well as the emphasis on student performance under NCLBA, are providing greater transparency and accountability for all students, including those with intellectual disabilities. The IDEA and NCLBA have great promise for ensuring that each student with a disability, including those with intellectual and developmental disabilities, receives an effective education. Nonetheless, there are a number of unresolved issues that complicate the implementation of these laws (McLaughlin & Embler, in press). Among these are issues surrounding the meaning of alternate achievement standards and the quality and meaningfulness of alternate assessments.

Supporting Goal C: To allow children and adolescents with intellectual and developmental disabilities access to sufficient human and fiscal resources, supports, and services required for them to be effectively educated in the least restrictive setting
A well-qualified teacher is the most critical resource for educating students with intellectual and developmental disabilities. Indeed, the teacher is the foundation of the promise to educate these students in the least restrictive setting. Yet, in spite of the commitment to ensure that every student has access to a qualified professional, there has been, and continues to be, a severe shortage of qualified special education teachers and related services personnel to meet the educational needs of students with intellectual and developmental disabilities in America's schools.

The importance of every child's having access to a well-prepared, qualified teacher has been well documented in the literature. Research on student learning increasingly suggests that the quality of a student's teacher is the essential factor in improving performance (Darling-Hammond & Young, 2002; Wenglinsky, 2000). The National Commission on Teaching and America's Future (1996) suggests that the school reform movement has ignored the obvious: What teachers know and can do makes the crucial difference in what children learn. New courses, tests and curriculum reforms can be important starting points, but they are meaningless if teachers cannot use them well.... Student learning in this country will improve only when we focus our efforts on improving teaching. (p. 7)

Clearly, good teaching has never been more important than it is today. The obvious corollary is that good teacher education also has never been more important. The NCLBA recognized the importance of having qualified personnel and required all new Title I teachers to meet the highly qualified teacher requirements by 2002–2003. Additionally, a state's Title I plan must include measurable objectives to ensure that all teachers providing instruction in "core subjects" (e.g., English, math, science, social studies, foreign languages, art) meet the definition of "highly qualified" by the end of the 2005–2006 school year. Teachers are not considered to be qualified if they have provisional, temporary, or emergency certification (U.S. Department of Education, 2002).

Qualifications for current teachers are also specified in the law. They must hold at least a bachelors' degree and be held to the same standard as new elementary and secondary teachers. They may, however, demonstrate their competence in the teaching of academic subjects based on a "High Objective Uniform State Standard of Evaluation" (HOUSSE).

Clarification on the issue of highly qualified special education teachers came through the NCLBA Final Regulations (34 CFR Part 200, December 2, 2002). The federal regulations stated that all teachers of core subjects must be highly qualified by 2005–2006. The regulations further indicated that any teacher, general or special, providing instruction to students with disabilities in core subjects must be trained according to the same standards for content knowledge as other teachers.

This definition was adopted for special education teachers in IDEA 2004, which states that the term "highly qualified" has the same meaning when applied to elementary, middle, and secondary teachers in NCLBA (IDEA 2004, § 602(10)(A)). This means that new and veteran special education teachers at the elementary level must have subject knowledge and teaching skills in reading, writing, mathematics, and other areas of the basic elementary curriculum. New and veteran middle and secondary level special education teachers must have subject knowledge and teaching skills in the academic subjects they teach.

Specifically, IDEA 2004 requires that special education teachers must hold a bachelors degree and "obtain full State certification as a special education teacher (including certification obtained through alternative routes to certification) or pass the State special education teacher licensing examination (IDEA 2004, § 602(10)(A))...." Under IDEA 2004, just as in the state's Title I law, elementary and secondary teachers are not qualified if they have provisional, temporary, or emergency certification.

In addition, special education teachers who are teaching core academic subjects "exclusively to children who are assessed against alternate achievement standards" must meet the same requirements as highly qualified general elementary teachers unless the instruction is "above the elementary level" (IDEA 2004, § 602(10)(A)). In that case, the special education teacher must have subject matter knowledge appropriate to middle or secondary level instruction.

New and veteran special education teachers who teach two or more subjects at the middle or secondary level must also meet the applicable requirements in NCLBA. New special education teachers who teach multiple subjects must be highly qualified in one subject area (e.g., mathematics, arts, science) and will have two years from the date of employment to demonstrate competence in the additional core academic subjects they teach by passing a state's approved evaluation standards, or HOUSSE, or by meeting NCLBA-defined content requirements. Veteran special education teachers at the middle or secondary level who teach multiple subjects must also demonstrate competence in all core academic subjects they teach by passing a state's HOUSSE or meeting NCLBA content requirements; however, they are not provided the two-year grace period to demonstrate competence. Finally the conference report for IDEA 2004 (H. Rep. No 108-77, November 17, 2004, p. 171) clarifies that Congress intends that special education teachers in consultative roles be considered highly qualified if such individuals meet all other applicable requirements under § 602.

As we move into this new era of federally defined "highly qualified" special education teachers, there still remains a paucity of research on the qualities that produce good teachers. Research is needed to examine the models and measures that define beginning teacher quality and produce student results. Brownell, Ross, Colon, and McCallum (2002) suggested the need to establish a more definitive link between what special education teachers do and how much their students learn.

Given that students with intellectual and developmental disabilities are characterized by an extremely broad range of education needs, teachers must have knowledge and expertise that goes well beyond what is typically provided in many special education pre-service programs (Baumgart & Ferguson, 1991; Fox & Williams, 1992; McDonnell, Hardman, & McDonnell, 2003). Many states require beginning teachers to provide educational services to students with moderate to profound intellectual disabilities, multiple disabilities, autism, and other health impairments.

The roles for these teachers have become more challenging in the last ten years due to a greater emphasis on including this group of students in general education classes and curricula (Ford, Davern, & Schnorr, 2001; Meyer, Peck, & Brown, 1991; National Association of State Boards of Education, 1992; The Arc, 1998; Association of Persons with Severe Handicaps, 2000). These teachers must not only be prepared to meet the unique educational needs of these students, but also to do so within typical schools and classrooms.

Since its inception, IDEA has called attention to the need for quality teachers in order to provide an effective education in the least restrictive environment. The act has continuously addressed the critical role the federal government must play in acquiring and relaying to teachers and related services personnel significant knowledge derived from educational research. States have had to demonstrate that they will adopt promising practices, materials, and technology. In addition, institutions of higher education (IHEs) and school districts within a state have undertaken activities to improve and reform their existing programs to prepare teachers and related services personnel to work collaboratively in general education settings. With the passage of IDEA 2004 and the highly qualified standard for special education teachers, states and IHEs must work together more closely to incorporate evidence-based knowledge and practices into the preparation of new and veteran teachers so those teachers will have the skills they need to improve educational results for children with disabilities.

Although the federal government has a strong commitment to ensuring that there is a qualified teacher for every student with a disability, severe shortages continue across the country. The Council for Exceptional Children (2001) reports that more than 30,000 teachers without appropriate licenses are teaching students with disabilities in the United States. Based on a 16:1 student-to-teacher ratio in special education (Smith, Pion, Tyler, Sindelar, & Rosenberg, 2001), these numbers translate to approximately 480,000 students receiving their education from unqualified personnel. The problem is further compounded by the fact that IHEs are only able to prepare about half the number of teachers needed to fill vacancies in local school districts. As such, the U.S. Department of Labor estimates that public schools will need more than 200,000 newly qualified teachers through 2006 (Council for Exceptional Children, 2000).

USING KNOWLEDGE TO SHAPE OUR NATIONAL AGENDA

Although an abundance of research exists related to our central goal of providing effective education to children and adolescents with intellectual and developmental disabilities, the knowledge base has significant gaps. Table 3-2 includes our recommendations regarding the knowledge that is needed to meet the four goals.

In large part, our recommendations for research result from the changing educational context. As schools move into an era of increased accountability for performance of students, including those with intellectual and developmental disabilities, their educational practices need to be grounded in the language of standards. The ante has gone up in terms of what needs to be learned and who needs to learn it. However, as of yet, no consensus has been reached regarding how to connect the academic general education standards to the skills and knowledge that lead to meaningful post-school outcomes for students with intellectual and developmental disabilities.

Perhaps educators' most urgent research question is how to meaningfully include individuals with intellectual and developmental disabilities within the new state and federal requirements set forth in NCLBA and to insure progress in the general education curriculum within a fully inclusive educational context. To meet this goal, researchers need to address five major questions:

1. How can we create learning environments that support a broad range of learner needs?
2. What are the impacts of a standards-driven curriculum on valued post-school outcomes?
3. Which educational experiences and curricular focuses lead to the student's attainment of meaningful post-school outcomes?
4. How can we obtain valid and reliable indicators of the performance of individuals with intellectual and developmental disabilities to ensure accountability for learning?

Table 3-2

Research Questions to be Answered to Achieve the National Goals

- To what extent and under what conditions will valued post-school outcomes result if all students with intellectual or developmental disabilities (i.e., across the spectrum of needs, cultural and linguistic groups, and families at risk) achieve state standards postschool?
- What educational practices, including teacher expectations, curricula and instruction, and settings, are associated with positive academic and/or post-school achievement for persons with intellectual and developmental disabilities?
- What are the conditions (e.g., instructional techniques, curricula, supplemental supports, school organization, staffing, class size, technology, experiences) under which all students with intellectual and developmental disabilities can participate in instructional and other school activities and can achieve state standards?
- What are the characteristics and rigor of alternate standards developed for students who cannot (due to the severity of their intellectual disability) achieve state standards? Are these alternate standards comparable across the 50 states?
- What are the most effective strategies to support parent and caregiver involvement in the education of children?
- How are schools meeting the needs of culturally diverse families and what are the most successful strategies for increasing the involvement of these families in their children's schooling?
- What are the most effective practices and models to prepare and retain adequate numbers of personnel who meet the "highly qualified" standard (including special and regular educators and paraprofessionals), as well as administrators and related services professionals to support all students with intellectual and developmental disabilities in the achievement of high standards and valued post-school outcomes?

5. What are the specific knowledge and skills that beginning teachers need to effectively meet the needs of students with intellectual and developmental disabilities?

How Can We Create Learning Environments That Support a Broad Range of Learner Needs?

Information from research on a number of specific topics can lead to classrooms that fully accommodate and support every student. Implicit in the question is the need to push the limits of technology in the universal design of curricula and instructional environments. To date, the research related to universal design has centered primarily on students without intellectual disabilities. However, O'Neill and Dalton (2002) are exploring how the principles of universal curricular design can support learning of basic literacy skills among students with mild to moderate intellectual disabilities. This line of research needs to be rapidly expanded, both in terms of the effects on individual performance, as well as on self-esteem and self-determination.

What Are the Impacts of a Standards-Driven Curriculum on Valued Post-School Outcomes?

The tension between having an individually referenced educational plan and one that is linked to, or driven by, standards is greatest for students with the most heterogeneous support needs. A committee of the National Research Council (McDonnell, et al., 1997) explored these tensions and concluded that individual educational programs and standards could be complementary and actually could create opportunities and higher expectations for many students with disabilities.

However, the impacts of a uniform set of curricular standards on individuals with intellectual and developmental disabilities are untested and unknown. Although standards raise the bar and create higher expectations for all students, content standards that may be unattainable or irrelevant to the life goals of individuals may result in lost opportunities. For example, only 14% of students designated as having mental retardation graduated with the standard high school diploma during the 1999–2000 school year. The remaining 86% received "certificates of completion" or "IEP diplomas," representing the largest group of students with disabilities who received such diplomas (U.S. Department of Education, 2002). These nonstandard diplomas provide little useful information to parents, employers, or students regarding the recipient's accomplishments and skills. In the new assessment climate, it is likely that even fewer students with intellectual and developmental disabilities will receive a standard high school diploma.

In addition, no one knows if the key effective elements for teaching discrete functional skills to students with intellectual and developmental disabilities will also help them attain more complex content knowledge. Most of the research on instructional strategies has focused only on the functional skills.

Which Educational Experiences and Curricular Focuses Lead to the Student's Attainment of Meaningful Post-school Outcomes?

To do their job, schools need *scientifically valid* research on what educational experiences and interventions predict the outcomes considered necessary for students with intellectual and developmental disabilities to receive an effective education. We assume universal acceptance of the idea that "effective" means that students exit the public school only after completing their education and then enter into employment or postsecondary training. Researchers need to include children and adolescents with intellectual and developmental disabilities in samples that examine effective literacy interventions and in similar research that seeks more efficient and effective curricula and pedagogy.

In addition, new knowledge about how people learn is shaping curricula and pedagogy in schools (National Research Council, 2001). This research is also providing a rich understanding of how individuals adapt to and negotiate their environments. Similar research is needed to expand our understanding of how children and adolescents with intellectual and developmental disabilities do or do not differ from other learners in important areas such as memory and reasoning, and learning higher order skills.

How Can We Obtain Valid and Reliable Indicators of the Performance of Individuals with Intellectual and Developmental Disabilities to Ensure Accountability for Learning?

Assessing students with intellectual and developmental disabilities is among the greatest challenges facing special education today given the demand for universal accountability. Many students with intellectual and developmental disabilities are expected to be assessed, with or without accommodations, on the same state standards as all other students; whereas some will be assessed using an alternate assessment and their performance will be measured against alternate achievement standards. The NCLBA also requires that a representative sample of each state's school population participate in the National Assessment of Educational Progress (NAEP) in order to have an "independent" measure of student progress and performance. Scores of students with disabilities participating in an alternate assessment will not, however, be able to be compared to the NAEP, and thus there will be no way to judge the rigor of a specific state standard and assessment. These requirements signal the need for research on how best to create meaningful accountability for individuals with intellectual and developmental disabilities.

What Are the Specific Knowledge and Skills That Beginning Teachers Need to Effectively Meet the Needs of Students with Intellectual and Developmental Disabilities?

In spite of a significant research base on effective practices for teaching students with intellectual and developmental disabilities (c.f., Browder, 2001; Snell & Brown, 2000), researchers have put forth surprisingly little effort in defining the specific knowledge base that beginning teachers must have to effectively serve this group of students. Although CEC has developed 10 content standards described as essential for newly prepared special education teachers, no evidence proves that if teachers meet these standards, their students will get a better education.

The Association for Persons with Severe Handicaps (TASH) (2002) has also identified specific areas of knowledge and expertise essential for teachers working with students with severe intellectual and developmental disabilities. The TASH standards are based on the assumption that all students should be educated in general education classes and should participate in the general education curriculum. TASH has yet to articulate the specific competencies that each standard should include, and we do not know how the competencies will relate to the "highly qualified" standards.

Little, if any, consensus exists about what beginning teachers of students with intellectual and developmental disabilities should know and be able to do. The specific knowledge, skills, and expertise that this group of teachers is expected to demonstrate before entering the profession vary significantly from state to state. Unfortunately, attention to the preparation of teachers of students with intellectual and developmental disabilities has been conspicuously absent from the dialogue about teacher education reform (Blanton, Griffin, Winn, & Pugach, 1997; Ford, et al., 2001; Ryndak & Kennedy, 2000). Although there is a robust research literature on recommended educational practices for students with intellectual and developmental disabilities, little research has examined effective ways to prepare new teachers to implement these practices or effective ways to evaluate their competence (Baumgart & Ferguson, 1991; Kaiser & McWhorter, 1990; Ryndak & Kennedy, 2000).

Currently, the most widely used evaluation model for determining teacher competence in intellectual and developmental disabilities consists of a set of performance-based standards developed by the CEC. A second source for determining teacher competence in this area is the Interstate New Teacher Assessment and Support Consortium's (INTASC) ten core principles for licensing special education teachers. The CEC and INTASC models meet the criteria for credibility (stakeholders' validation) and practicality (costs and training requirements). However, they fail to meet criteria related to utility (used by other researchers), generality (full range of contexts related to roles or teacher assignments), comprehensiveness (richness and breadth), or soundness (reliability and validity). Thus, strong evaluation instruments that will measure the criteria or standards are yet to be developed.

Anticipating the Changes of the Future

The education of all children and adolescents with disabilities is at a pivotal crossroads. The ever-increasing emphasis on standards and the notion that "all" (but some very small number of students) must achieve at the same level on the same content is a lofty goal. Some will say that the goal is unattainable; yet the overall policy framework demanding higher levels of student achievement of common content standards is deeply rooted in current educational policy. We assume that this framework will continue to drive both policy and practices within America's schools for some time. Within that context we see a number of critical challenges ahead for how to meet our goal of effectively educating students with intellectual and developmental disabilities.

Perhaps the most central challenge is to align the construct of an "effective" education with the construct of an "appropriate" education. Effectiveness is based on student performance on specific assessments and the outcomes of schooling. To ensure that an "appropriate" education is also an "effective" education, educators must know that the current standards that are driving curriculum and instruction in today's schools address the important knowledge and skills proven to lead to the types of educational outcomes that students with intellectual and developmental disabilities and their families want.

The assumption that access to the general education curriculum is the desired goal of education is not without challenges. Some argue that the general education curriculum is almost always appropriate when meaningful modifications are made (Brown, Udvari-Solner, Temple, Kluth, Suomi, & Ross, 2000), whereas others maintain that a more "functional curriculum" that focuses on teaching individual students everyday living and employment skills will best meet the future needs of students who are not likely to master the general education curriculum. Thus, standards pertaining to what to teach are as important as where a student is taught.

Evidence is emerging that our schools may be making progress in improving outcomes for some of these students. Data from the National Longitudinal Transition Study 2 indicated that youth with mental retardation were the only group among students with disabilities to experience a significant decrease in the dropout rate and to see an increase in the holding of work-study jobs (Wagner, Cameto, & Newman, 2003). However, these youths were the only young people among all other categories of disability to not experience a significant increase in earning more than minimum wage.

Educators need research to guide them in developing standards, and they also need improved assessment techniques to validly and reliably assess each student's progress toward the standards as the student moves through the school years. The results of these assessments must also be reported in the aggregate. An additional looming policy challenge lies in defining the "exclusionary" group of students who, under NCLBA, may be held to alternate achievement standards. As of April 2005, that group was expanded from 1 to 3%. In a letter to the U.S. Department of Education signed by The Arc, UCP, and AAMR, the 1% of the population of students who may be held to alternate standards was estimated to include about 600,000 students with intellectual disabilities, whereas the best estimates of the number of students with the "most significant" intellectual disabilities is approximately 100,000 (Cleveland, Triest, & Luckasson, May 19, 2003). The change in policy means that some number of students with mild and moderate intellectual disabilities may now be held to different standards for achievement based on IEP team decisions. The potential for these students to be held to less rigorous or meaningful standards and curriculum is a major policy concern.

Finally, to achieve the goal of educating all students with intellectual and developmental disabilities in general education classrooms, researchers and educators must examine conditions under which these students can be fully included and receive the effective education described above.

As special educators reflect on the evolution of education for children and adolescents with intellectual and developmental disabilities, they can acknowledge that they have made some progress toward our national goal of having both an effective and inclusive education. However, the progress has been neither swift nor even. Research has yielded knowledge about the conditions that appear to support inclusive education. It has also given teachers some models for effective instruction as well as preparation of professionals for inclusive education. Educators also know more about the experiences and supports that lead to employability and community integration. Yet we have far to go. The new emphasis on educational standards and accountability provides the impetus to bind the entitlement to an "effective" education to that of an "inclusive" one. Researchers must embrace this goal and develop an agenda to realize it.

ENHANCING REAL LIVES

If the gaps eventually closed between existing policy and the knowledge base in the field, educational programs for students like Anna and Robert from our opening vignettes would be substantially enhanced. Anna would be enrolled in a second grade class in her neighborhood elementary school. She would have an IEP designed to promote achievement in as many of the second grade academic standards as appropriate. The IEP would also focus on helping her develop the communication, social, motor, and daily living skills necessary for her to function successfully in school, home, and community settings. The curriculum and school-wide assessment system would incorporate the principles of universal design and would be structured to accommodate the needs of all students in the school. The day-to-day process of schooling would be driven by the assumption that all students can meet high expectations and will achieve with adequate support.

Anna's general education teacher would have the knowledge and skills to differentiate instruction for all students in the class. The teacher would be able to design lessons so that the content matched each student's skills level and unique learning needs. Research-validated instructional strategies would maximize learning for all students, allowing them to achieve at their own pace. The special education teachers and related services personnel would know how to adapt curriculum and instructional activities for Anna to help her meet IEP goals within the general education class and the school. She would receive "transparent" services and supports in the general education class. As a result, Anna's school day would look very much like that of her peers without disabilities.

Robert's educational program would be designed to maximize his inclusion and participation in the community after graduation and to prepare him for adult roles and responsibilities. His IEP would focus on outcomes such as getting a job, learning to use the bus and train system, going out with his friends, and taking care of his apartment. Rather than attending River View High School, he would take courses at the local community college and would have a job. He would receive instruction in a variety of community settings to help him learn the skills necessary to go to the movies, use the bank, and go to his favorite restaurants. Although the special education teachers and related services personnel would provide direct training in these settings, these services would build on the natural supports provided by Robert's friends, family, teachers, coworkers, and other community members.

The school district would have formal systems in place to coordinate Robert's transition from school to adult and community service programs. They would have well-established collaborative relationships with adult services, including vocational rehabilitation, mental retardation/developmental disabilities, and other community agencies. Counselors and case workers from these agencies would attend the annual IEP meeting to work with Robert and his family in arranging participation in valued service programs following graduation. The school and community service agencies would work together to ensure that Robert's life in the community was not disrupted when he left school at age 22.

CHAPTER 4

Transitions From Home and School to the Roles and Supports of Adulthood

---

Susan Hasazi, David Johnson, Martha Thurlow, Brian Cobb,
John Trach, Bob Stodden, Deborah Leuchovius, Debra Hart,
Michael Benz, Lizanne DeStefano, and Teresa Grossi
with
Stephanie Lee, Lyle Lehman, Joe Meadours, Gerry Morrissey,
Sue Swenson, Nancy Weiss, and Madeleine Will

REAL LIVES

Matthew Boardman, who has Down syndrome, is the 24-year-old only son of Jane and Robert Boardman. When Matthew was born, Jane and Robert were primarily concerned about his physical health and wanted to ensure that he received the best possible care for his congenital heart condition. Once his medical status was stabilized through surgery, they began to explore preschool opportunities and identify other families in their neighborhood who had children Matthew's age.

Their vision for Matthew included a rich life surrounded by a loving extended family, friends with and without disabilities, teachers who recognized and valued his attributes, and opportunities for him to make important choices about the way he wanted to live his life. Unfortunately, the school district in which the Boardmans lived operated a preschool program that was available only to children with disabilities. After a year of advocacy, the school district agreed to pay for Matthew to attend a preschool in a nearby community that included students with and without disabilities. Matthew thrived in this program and to this day maintains friendships with children he met as a toddler in his inclusive preschool.

Following preschool, Jane and Robert decided to move to a community that was committed to inclusive education. They purchased a home in a neighborhood with young families such as themselves, and Matthew made many new friends. He completed his entire education in this school district and attended general education classes throughout his career. He was also involved in many co-curricular activities such as basketball, soccer, and the band, where he played the drums. He also worked at the snack bar during baseball seasons. In addition, he earned a Black Belt in Karate and became a co-instructor for the elementary-level classes. While Matthew was in high school, he participated in a variety of career development opportunities to help him decide what kind of job he might pursue following graduation.

* * *

Amanda Chavez is the 20-year-old daughter of Louisa Chavez. Amanda and Louisa live in a large city where Amanda attended school until she was 18 years old. During high school, Amanda attended a regional career and technology center, and during her junior and senior years, she was enrolled in a human services child care program. She had a great deal of experience taking care of her many cousins who lived in the neighborhood and thought that working in a child care center after graduation would be a great choice for her. Louisa was enthusiastic about Amanda's choice, but worried that Amanda needed additional skills, experience, and supervision to do the job well. Amanda and Louisa approached the teachers at the career and technology center and asked if they would be willing to hire her as a teacher's assistant for a year so that Amanda could receive more training and supervision. The teachers agreed and Amanda was thrilled to begin her new job. She traveled to and from the center every day using the city bus system and ate lunch each day with the teaching staff.

INTRODUCTION

During the past 25 years, federal legislation has been enacted to support the full participation of youth with disabilities in education, post-secondary education programs, employment, and other aspects of community living. The Education for All Handicapped Children Act; the Vocational Act Amendments of 1976; the Vocational Rehabilitation Act of 1973, with its accompanying § 504 provisions; and the Comprehensive Employment and Training Act of 1973 created important education, training, and employment opportunities for youth with disabilities.

By the mid-1980s, the U.S. Department of Education's Office of Special Education and Rehabilitative Services (OSERS) stressed the importance of improving transition services nationally. In 1983, OSERS identified the transition from school to work as one of the major federal priorities of special education programs nationwide. Much of the rationale for issuing this priority was based on the recognition that many young adults with disabilities were exiting high school unprepared for adult life.

Follow-up studies of former special education students conducted during the early 1980s consistently documented the limited outcomes achieved by young adults with disabilities as they left school and attempted to access employment, post-secondary education programs, and adult community services (Halpern, 1985; Hasazi, Gordon, & Roe, 1985; Mithaug, Horiuchi, & Fanning, 1985). Predominant themes emerging from the findings of these and other studies included lower than desired academic achievement levels; high dropout rates; substantial levels of unemployment and underemployment, economic instability and dependence; social isolation; and low levels of participation in post-secondary education and training programs.

Based upon these study findings and in response to increased pressures from parents, professionals, and advocacy groups, OSERS initiated significant research and demonstration activities specifically focused on the transition from school to adult life. These research and demonstration grant programs resulted in advances in interagency cooperation and planning, access to post-secondary education and training, supported employment, transition planning, student and parental involvement in school and post-school decisionmaking, and development of adult living skills. These varied approaches and strategies established a foundation upon which state and local agencies, in partnership with community service agencies, parents, and students, have based the development of their transition programs and services.

In 1990, Congress enacted the Individuals with Disabilities Education Act (IDEA). For the first time since the passage of the Education of the Handicapped Act of 1975, specific provisions were put into place requiring local education agencies to address the school to adult life transition needs of youth with disabilities. IDEA specifically stressed the critical importance of engaging families, outside community service agencies, and other public and private entities in discussions and decisions concerning the school and post-school needs of students with disabilities and their families.

The definition of transition services in IDEA 1997 emphasized the importance of achieving a wide range of school and post-school results and addressed the transition from a systems perspective. In this legislation, the term "transition services" means

> a coordinated set of activities for a student, designed within an outcome-oriented process that promotes movement from school to post-school activities, including post-secondary education, vocational training, integrated employment (including supported employment), continuing and adult education, adult services, independent living, or community participation. (§ 300.29)

As noted in the 1997 statute, the "coordinated set of activities" must be based upon the student's individual needs and take into account the student's preferences and interests. It must include instruction and community experiences. Looking to the future, schools must help the student develop employment and other post-school adult living objectives and, if appropriate, acquire adult living skills. A functional vocational evaluation may also be necessary. IDEA and the final regulations published later in 1992 continue to serve as the essential federal policy framework for addressing the transition of youth with disabilities.

The IDEA 1997 reauthorization required that students gain greater access to the general education curriculum and assessment systems. IDEA 1997 also expanded transition requirements that the individualized education program (IEP) include, at age 14 or earlier, a statement of transition service needs that focused on the student's courses of study (e.g., participation in advanced placement courses or vocational education programs). According to IDEA 1997, the IEP also needed to include, beginning at age 16 or younger, a statement of necessary transition services and interagency responsibilities or any needed linkages.

The earlier provisions of IDEA 1990 concerning the definition of "transition services" and the specification of what a "coordinated set of activities" should entail carried forward into the IDEA 1997 reauthorization. What emerged based on these federal legislative developments was a coherent policy framework intended to guide state and local actions on behalf of young people with disabilities and their families as they prepared for and eventually left their public schools to enter adult life.

The current challenge is to integrate and align the transition service requirements with other IDEA 1997 and IDEA 2004 requirements that give students with disabilities greater access to the general education curriculum and assessment systems and that stress high academic achievement and the inclusion of students with disabilities in state and local standards-based accountability systems. Furthermore, discussions will also continue to focus on effective strategies and interventions that help students develop other essential adult life skills through vocational education, training and adult living skills, community participation, and other methods. The culmination of federal policy, research and demonstration, and state and local initiatives since 1975 have all focused on improving school and post-school results for youth with disabilities and their families. This results-based policy ideology will no doubt continue to be a major influence on both special education and general education throughout the current decade.

The National Commitment to Transition and Associated Goals

The goals identified and addressed in this chapter reflect the expressed national commitment that youth and young adults with intellectual and developmental disabilities (ID/DD) will be educated and supported to develop the skills and experience the opportunities to realize personal goals and choices about how to lead lives as productive, integrated, and empowered members of their communities and society. The origins of our national goals for transition of youth with ID/DD into adult roles are conveyed in eight major pieces of federal legislation.

Sources of National Goals in Federal Legislation

Given the complexity and long-term nature of transition, it is evident that families, schools, adult service providers, state agencies, and post-secondary institutions cannot carry the entire burden of fiscal, programmatic, and planning responsibility. Over the past two decades, Congress has enacted a broad range of federal legislation to make available an array of programs and services designed to support young people with disabilities in their transition from school to post-secondary education, employment, and community living. The following briefly summarizes several of these major legislative developments.

Rehabilitation Act of 1973, With Subsequent Amendments (Rehab Act)

The Rehab Act provides comprehensive services to all individuals with a disability, regardless of the severity of the disability, and outlaws discrimination against citizens with disabilities. Section 504 of the Rehab Act specifically prohibits discrimination in employment on the basis of disability. It also focuses on adults and youth transitioning into employment settings and ensures the development and implementation of a comprehensive and coordinated program of vocational assistance for individuals with disabilities, thereby supporting independent living and maximizing employability and integration into the community.

Technology-Related Assistance for Individuals With Disabilities Act of 1988 (Tech Act)

The Tech Act assists states in developing comprehensive programs for technology related assistance and promotes the availability of technology for individuals with disabilities and their families.

Americans With Disabilities Act of 1990 (ADA)

The ADA guarantees equal opportunity and civil rights for all individuals with disabilities. The ADA mandates "reasonable accommodations" for individuals with disabilities in areas including employment, access to public facilities, transportation, telecommunications, and government services.

Carl D. Perkins Vocational and Applied Technology Education Act of 1990

The Perkins Act requires states to ensure that special population students have equal access to vocational education and that localities ensure the full participation of these students in programs that are approved using Perkins money. States receiving federal vocational education money must fund, develop, and carry out activities and programs to eliminate gender bias, stereotyping, and discrimination in vocational education. The Act includes a wide range of programs and services, such as vocational education classes and work-study for students in high schools, as well as access to post-secondary technical education programs.

Goals 2000: Education America Act of 1994

Goals 2000 established a new framework for the federal government to provide assistance to states for the reform of educational programs. It encourages the establishment of high standards for all children, including children with disabilities, and specifies eight national education goals.

Workforce Investment Act of 1998 (WIA)

WIA creates a comprehensive job training system that consolidates a variety of federally funded programs into a streamlined process that allows individuals to easily access job training and employment services. As outlined in § 106 of WIA, states and localities are required to develop and implement workforce investment systems that fully include and accommodate the needs of individuals with disabilities.

Ticket to Work and Work Incentives Improvement Act of 1999

The Ticket to Work program makes it possible for individuals with disabilities to join the workforce without fear of losing their Medicare or Medicaid coverage. The legislation creates two new options for states. First, it creates a new Medicaid buy-in demonstration to help people whose disability is not yet so severe that they cannot work. Second, it extends Medicare coverage for an additional four and one-half years for people in the disability insurance system who return to work.

No Child Left Behind Act of 2001 (NCLB)

NCLB redefines the federal goal in K–12 education as closing the achievement gap between disadvantaged and minority students and their peers. It is based upon four basic principles: stronger accountability for results, increased flexibility and control, expanded options for parents, and an emphasis on proven teaching methods. The law specifically addresses the importance of structuring implementation to include every child. To achieve this outcome, young adults and their families must have access to highly trained educators and human services professionals who are able to collaborate with families, multiple agencies, and post-secondary higher education and training institutions.

THE NATIONAL GOALS

Together, these and related commitments constitute the eight national goals in supporting the transition of youth with ID/DD into adult roles. These goals provide a framework for this chapter's analysis of the state knowledge base and the research, demonstration, dissemination, and policy reform needed to build and maintain a comprehensive system to promote personal aspirations, skill acquisition, and increased opportunities for our youth with ID/DD and other disabilities. Table 4-1 presents these goals.

Table 4-1
Eight National Goals for Achieving Effective Transitions for Youth with Disabilities to Productive, Integrated, Independent, and Empowered Adult Roles

1. To promote the student's self-determination and self-advocacy
2. To ensure that students have access to the general standards-based curriculum
3. To increase the graduation rate of students with disabilities
4. To ensure access to and full participation in post-secondary education and employment
5. To increase parent participation and involvement
6. To improve collaboration and links between systems to support student achievement of meaningful school and post-school outcomes
7. To ensure availability of a qualified workforce
8. To ensure that students have full, active participation in all aspects of community life, including social, recreational, and leisure opportunities

---

REVIEW OF KNOWLEDGE AND RECOMMENDATIONS

In this section we briefly review the literature related to each of the eight national goals. We then include the set of research questions associated with each goal that we believe is essential to improve the post-school satisfaction and achievements of young adults with intellectual and developmental disabilities.

Goal A: To promote the student's self-determination and self-advocacy
Overview of the Knowledge Base

Starting with the 1990 reauthorization of IDEA, transition services were required to be based on students' needs and take into account students' interests and preferences. The IDEA 1997 amendments further supported student participation in transition planning by requiring that all students with disabilities age 14 and older be invited to their IEP meetings when transition goals were discussed. For student participation in transition planning to be successful, students had to attend meetings and have the skills and opportunity to advocate effectively for themselves. The current consensus among parents, educators, and researchers is that we need to actively promote student self-determination, self-advocacy, and student-centered planning.

Recent studies have shown that many students do, in fact, attend their IEP meetings; however, a significant number do not actively participate (Hasazi, Furney, & DeStefano, 1999; Johnson & Sharpe, 2000). Whether nonparticipating students are not being extended opportunities for involvement or have not acquired the skills related to self-determination is not entirely clear. Evidence shows, however, that helping students acquire and exercise self-determination skills leads to more positive educational and employment outcomes (Agran, 1997; Algozzine, Browder, Karvonen, Test, & Wood, 2001; Field, Martin, Miller, Ward, & Wehmeyer, 1998; Serna & Lau-Smith, 1995; Wehmeyer & Schwartz, 1998; Wehmeyer, Agran, & Hughes, 1998; Wehmeyer, Palmer, Agran, Mithaug, & Martin, 2000).

For example, Wehmeyer and Schwartz (1997) found that one year after graduation, students with learning disabilities who received self-determination training were more likely to achieve positive adult outcomes, including being employed at a higher rate and earning more per hour, when compared to peers who did not receive training. Additional research supports this relationship between self-determination and positive educational outcomes (e.g., Perlmutter & Monty, 1997).

Researchers are just beginning to study how self-determination skills are cultivated. Izzo and Lamb (2002) offer a number of suggestions in that regard, from empowering parents as partners in promoting self-determination and career development skills to specific student training in self-determination skills. Children typically begin developing these skills at an early age through naturally occurring opportunities to make choices. When explicit training in self-determination skills should begin has not been empirically determined, but many educators, parents, students, and researchers argue that it should begin before, and intensify during, the student's high school years (Sands & Wehmeyer, 1996; Wood & Test, 2001). Among the skills identified as important are self-advocacy, social, and organizational skills; community and peer connections; conflict-resolution; career skill building and career development; and computer/technological competency (Martin & Marshall, 1996; Wehmeyer, Kelchner, & Richards, 1996).

Exemplary school-based self-determination programs appear to have a common element: the presence of a qualified instructor with the knowledge and commitment to ensure that self-determination practices are implemented (Wood & Test, 2001). Strong administrative support also appears to be important in developing a commitment to policies and practices that encourage self-determination programs school-wide (Wood & Test, 2001). Families play a critical role in supporting their young adults in developing self-determination skills through providing increased opportunities for them to make their own decisions related to housing options, employment, and recreational activities. Most importantly, families should prepare themselves to accept their children in new adult roles and allow their adult sons and daughters to take active roles in the decisions that will determine their futures, even if it means allowing them to make mistakes (Beach Center, 1998).

Recommendations for Research

Although the need for, and value of, student participation and involvement in the IEP and transition process seem clear, many important questions related to self-advocacy and student-centered planning remain. These questions include the following:

1. How do self-determination and self-advocacy skills develop over the life-span?
2. What factors differentiate between students who attend/participate in IEP and transition processes and students who do not do so?
3. How can student attendance and participation in IEP and transition processes be increased?
4. What specific skills do students need to advocate effectively on their own behalf, and how can these skills best be developed?
5. What school characteristics and practices are associated with more effective student self-determination and self-advocacy?
6. What features of families (e.g., cultural values, beliefs and expectations, socio-economic conditions, family interactions) affect the development of self-determination skills?

Goal B: To ensure that students have access to the general standards-based curriculum

Overview of the Knowledge Base

The standards-based reform movement was stimulated by the publication of the National Commission on Excellence in Education's *A Nation at Risk* in 1983. By the year 2000, most states had adopted standards defining the curriculum for all students. According to Nolet and McLaughlin (2000), IDEA 1997 was "intended to ensure that students with disabilities have access to challenging curriculum and that their educational programs are based on high expectations that acknowledge each student's potential and ultimate contribution to society" (p. 2). Within the educational context of the late 1990s and early 2000, this has meant that all students with disabilities, regardless of the nature of their disability, were required to have access to standards-based education. Research on this important topic is still in its infancy.

The standards-based requirements of IDEA 1997 were based, in part, on research findings indicating a lack of educational success (or a lack of information about educational success) on the part of many students with disabilities (e.g., McGrew, Thurlow, & Spiegel, 1993; Shriner, Gilman, Thurlow, & Ysseldyke, 1994/95). Additional research has revealed that students with disabilities very often have been provided with an inappropriately watered-down curriculum (Gersten, 1998) or one undifferentiated for students with disabilities (McIntosh, Vaughn, Schumm, Haager, & Lee, 1993).

States' experience with the assessment requirements of IDEA 1997 has highlighted the need for students with disabilities to access the general curriculum. States have often had to adjust traditional standardized assessments to enable many students with disabilities to participate in them. Without accommodations, adaptations, modifications, and other adjustments to existing assessments, many students with disabilities could not demonstrate their knowledge and skills on the same standards used by other students (Thurlow, Elliott, & Ysseldyke, 1998).

The need for adjustments in assessment practices has underscored the related needs for accommodations and differentiation in the curriculum and instruction to which students have been exposed. For example, an analysis of the IEPs of students with disabilities in relation to national and state mathematics standards has shown little relationship between IEP goals and objectives and the standards toward which general education students were working (Shriner, Kim, Thurlow, & Ysseldyke, 1993). The need for states to develop alternate assessment methods has led them to examine more carefully their standards, especially for students with significant cognitive disabilities.

The development of alternate assessment methods has spurred research on their technical characteristics (Kleinert & Kearns, 2001) and has helped to improve instruction and access to the general curriculum for students with disabilities (Browder, 2001). A number of researchers have investigated whether or not students with significant cognitive disabilities maintain improved standards-based educational outcomes following graduation from high school into post-school training or work environments (Kleinert, Kearns, Costello, Nowak-Drabik, Garrett, Horvath, et al., 1999; Kleinert, Kennedy, & Kearns, 1999).

As states have adopted accountability requirements, educators have been seeking information regarding the best ways to ensure that students with disabilities have access to the general education curriculum based on agreed-upon content standards. Appropriate instructional accommodations are a key element for enhancing instructional outcomes (Elliott & Thurlow, 2000), but researchers also have identified other important factors, including the specification of curriculum domains, time allocation, and decisions about what to include or exclude (Nolet & McLaughlin, 2000).

Specifying the curriculum in a subject matter domain requires cataloging the information included in the domain (facts, concepts, principles, and procedures) and setting priorities with respect to outcomes. Allocation of time for instruction should be based on the priorities that have been established. Decisions about what to include or exclude in curriculum should allow for adequate scope of coverage while maintaining enough depth to ensure that students are learning the material. Universal design is another means of ensuring access to the general curriculum (Orkwis & McLane, 1998). When applied to assessment, universal design can help ensure that tests are usable by the greatest number of students possible (Thompson, Johnstone, & Thurlow, 2002).

Finally, a number of researchers have investigated various approaches designed to increase access to the general curriculum and to standards-based instruction for students with disabilities. Several approaches demonstrate that access to the general education curriculum can result in positive outcomes for students with disabilities. These approaches include various forms of differentiated instruction (Tomlinson, 1999), effective instructional techniques (Kame'enui & Carnine, 1998), strategy instruction (Deshler, Schumaker, Lenz, Bulgren, Hock, Knight, et al., 2001), textbook organization (Crawford & Carnine, 2000; Harniss, Dickson, Kinder, & Hollenbeck, 2001), and technology use (Rose & Meyer, 2000).

Recommendations for Research

Although federal legislation has established expectations for the engagement of students with ID/DD with standards-based curriculum, there is relatively little information access to such curriculum and the types and effects of accommodations to support access. Related research questions include the following:

1. What does access to the curriculum entail for students with intellectual disabilities?
2. What are the differences in academic, behavioral, and functional performances between students with intellectual disabilities who have greater access to the general education curriculum and those who have less access to the general curriculum?
3. What accommodations significantly increase access to the general education curriculum for students with significant intellectual disabilities?
4. What adjustments to IEPs have promoted access to the general education curriculum for students with intellectual disabilities?
5. What instructional interventions (e.g., differentiated instruction, technology use) are effective for improving the academic outcomes of students with intellectual disabilities?

Goal C: To increase the graduation rate of students with disabilities

Overview of the Knowledge Base

Students with disabilities are at greater risk than other students for dropping out of school, and this is one of the most serious and pervasive problems facing special education programs nationally. During the 1999–2000 school year, only 57% of youth with disabilities graduated with a regular diploma (U.S. Department of Education, 2001). In spite of some improvement in the overall graduation rate of students with disabilities in the United States during the last decade, the dropout rate for students with disabilities remains twice that of students without disabilities (Blackorby & Wagner, 1996; Pasternack, 2002). Further, certain students with disabilities are at increased risk for dropping out based upon gender, ethnicity, and socioeconomic status.

Dropping out of school has serious implications for social stability and economic development. Youth who drop out generally experience negative outcomes—unemployment, underemployment, incarceration, and other difficulties. School dropouts, for example, report unemployment rates as much as 40% higher than youth completing school. Arrest rates are alarming for youth with disabilities who drop out of school—73% for students with emotional/behavioral disabilities and 62% for students with learning disabilities. In 1997, 68% of state prison inmates had not completed high school (U.S. Department of Justice, 2003). The social and economic costs of incarceration have been well documented and affect every level of society. Further, the rising importance of postsecondary education to careers that provide a livable wage means that students who drop out of school have significantly diminished employment prospects.

At present, concerns about the dropout problem are increasing because of state and local special education agencies' experiences with high-stakes accountability in the context of standards-based reform and associated assessments of students' performance

(Thurlow, Sinclair, & Johnson, 2002). Large numbers of students are not faring well on these assessments. Failure can have significant consequences for them, such as determining whether or not they are promoted from one grade to the next or graduate from high school with either a standard diploma or alternative credential (Thurlow & Johnson, 2000). For these reasons, students who experience failure or who see little chance of passing these tests may decide not to stay in school.

Dropout prevention programs have been implemented and evaluated for decades in the United States, but the empirical base of well-researched programs is scant. Few well-done evaluations of dropout prevention programs specifically targeted to students with disabilities exist. Perhaps the best-researched program at the secondary level for students with disabilities at risk of dropping out is Check and Connect (Christenson, 2002; Sinclair, Christenson, Evelo, & Hurley, 1999). Using randomized assignments with experimental and control groups, the program has obtained significant positive results by using a number of core elements: (a) student monitors/advocates who build a trusting relationship, monitor the student on risk indicators, and help problem-solve difficult issues between the student and the school; (b) student engagement with the school; (c) flexibility by school administrative personnel with staffing patterns and punitive disciplinary practices; and (d) relevancy in the high school curriculum.

The empirical literature on dropout prevention programs for at-risk students (including, but not restricted to, students with disabilities) is somewhat broader in scope but still lacking in high-quality research designs. Lehr, Hansen, Sinclair, and Christenson (2002) performed a meta-analysis of dropout studies published between 1980 and 2001. Only 45 research studies were included in the final integrative review; less than 20% employed randomized assignment procedures, and none were true experiments. Nonetheless, their findings were quite consistent with well-researched components of the Check and Connect model and were equally consistent with a number of other sources of empirical information. Lehr, Johnson, Bremer, Cosio, & Thompson (2004) reviewed research on the outcomes of various dropout intervention programs. After reviewing more than 300 documents, they identified just 11 programs meeting their criteria for demonstrated effectiveness.

Two of the most consistent components of secondary dropout prevention programs are work-based learning and attention to personal development and self-esteem building (Dynarski & Gleason, 2002; Farrell, 1990; Orr, 1987; Smink, 2002). Equally important, however, is tailoring these and other intervention components to the particular context of school environment (Lehr, et al., 2002; Lehr, et al., 2004).

Finally, early intervention also appears to be a powerful component of a school district's menu of services for dropout prevention. In a remarkable experimental study that involved 22 years of longitudinal data collection, Schweinhart and Weikart (1998) documented impressive outcomes of their High/Scope Perry preschool study of three- and four-year-olds who were at risk of school failure. Similarly, Chambers, Abrami, Massue, and Morrison (1998) reported outstanding gains in academic outcomes in their elementary-level Success for All program (Slavin, Madden, Karweit, Dolan, & Wasik, 1992) in Montreal, Quebec.

Recommendations for Research

The existing research is clear: students with disabilities are at increased risk of dropping out of school and may face increased challenges in that regard given standards-based reforms. Researchers especially need to assess the effectiveness of dropout prevention programs and the impact of new accountability initiatives. Studies addressing these general issues would benefit from greater use of longitudinal research strategies. In that context, researchers need to consider the following suggestions:

1. Develop an evidence base around dropout prevention for youth with disabilities that examines models in relation to the incentives and methods needed for them to be fully implemented within state and local school district programs.
2. Demonstrate and validate the efficacy of dropout prevention programs with particularly high-risk groups of students (e.g., students with emotional/behavioral disabilities, minority students, students living in poverty).
3. Find out how new accountability initiatives (e.g., high-stakes testing, stiffer graduation requirements, varied diploma options) have affected the exit status and school completion of youth with disabilities. No studies to date have examined the relationship between school policies and practices, the relationship between "high-stakes" assessment practices and graduation requirements, or other school- and community-level influences on dropout rates for students with disabilities.
4. Understand how contextual variables associated with home, school, community, and peers interact with the ways in which students exit from school.

Goal D: To ensure access to, and full participation in, post-secondary education and employment

Overview of the Knowledge Base

Young adults with disabilities still face significant difficulties in securing jobs and participating in post-secondary education. However, the passage of recent federal legislation (Americans with Disabilities Act 1990 and IDEA 1997) has produced an expanding social awareness of the accessibility and disability issues facing youth with disabilities as they seek access to post-secondary education, lifelong learning, and employment (Benz, Doren, & Yovanoff, 1998; Horn & Berktold, 1999; Johnson, Stodden, Emanuel, Leucking, & Mack, 2002).

In spite of the many challenges, students have had some important gains, particularly in access to higher education. Since 1990, 90% more colleges/universities, community colleges, and vocational and technical education centers are offering opportunities for persons with disabilities to continue their education (Pierangelo & Crane, 1997). Information from the National Longitudinal Transition Study illustrates that, of those who graduated, only 19% of students with disabilities, in contrast to 56% of students without disabilities, attended a post-secondary school within the first two years of leaving high school (Blackorby & Wagner, 1996). Importantly, the number of youth in post-secondary schools who report a disability has increased dramatically, climbing from 2.6% in 1978, to 9.2% in 1994, to nearly 19% in 1996 (Blackorby & Wagner, 1996; Gajar, 1992; Wagner & Blackorby, 1996).

More recent data in a publication of the National Organization on Disability (2000) reports that as many as 17% of all students attending higher education programs in the United States are identified as having a disability. However, few higher education programs serve students with intellectual and developmental disabilities (Hart, 2002).

Further, difficulties experienced by young people with disabilities in completing high school or receiving a post-secondary education credential also influence adult employment opportunities (Benz, et al., 1998; Blackorby & Wagner, 1996; Gilson, 1996). Only 15.6% of persons with disabilities with less than a high school diploma participate in the labor force. The rate doubles, however, to 30.2% for those who have completed high school and triples to 45.1% for those with some post-secondary education (Reskin & Roos, 1990; Yelin & Katz, 1994).

Another pressing societal challenge is the high overall unemployment rate among adults with disabilities in the United States. Although employment has improved somewhat over the past 14-year period for people with disabilities, employment is still an area with the widest gulf between all people with disabilities and the rest of the population. Only 32% of persons with disabilities aged 18 to 64 work full or part time, compared to 81% of the nondisabled population—a 49% gap (National Organization on Disability, 2000). According to a study by the National Organization on Disability (2000), employment prospects for 18- to 29-year-olds are the most promising. Among this cohort, 50% of those with disabilities who are able to work are working, compared to 72% of their nondisabled counterparts.

Related to the future workplace participation of youth with disabilities is the need to involve these young people in state and local workforce development initiatives, such as the Workforce Investment Act of 1998 (WIA). WIA services for youth include the following:

1. Establishment of local youth councils
2. Youth Opportunity grants that promote employment and training
3. Comprehensive career development services based on individual assessment and planning
4. Youth connections and access to the One-Stop Career Center System
5. Performance accountability focused on employment

Although access to WIA services could provide additional supports to youth with intellectual and developmental disabilities, lack of program capacity and expertise appears to have limited these young adults' access to services (U.S. Government Accounting Office, 2003). Vocational rehabilitation agencies have enhanced their involvement with transition of youth, who currently represent 13.5% of their client population (Hayward & Schmidt-Davis, 2000). Overall, nearly two-thirds (63%) of transition-age youth who were vocational rehabilitation clients achieved an employment outcome as a result of the services they received (Hayward & Schmidt-Davis, 2000). At the same time, state vocational rehabilitation agencies are struggling to provide the resources to this large and growing population, many of whom have not had community-based work experiences while in high school (SPeNSE, 2002).

The National Center for the Study of Post-secondary Educational Supports (NCSPES) at the University of Hawaii has conducted an extensive program of research focused upon the access, participation, and success of youth with disabilities in post-secondary education and subsequent employment. NCSPES has studied these issues within four areas of intervention:

- The process and content of preparation received by students with disabilities in high school under IDEA. Findings indicate that students need to understand themselves and their disability in relation to needed services and supports and be able to describe their needs and advocate for themselves in various post-school educational and employment settings (Izzo & Lamb, 2002; National Center for the Study of Post-secondary Educational Supports, 2000b; Stodden & Conway, 2003; Stodden & Jones, 2002).

- The manner in which services and supports, including the use of technology, are made available and provided to students with disabilities in post-secondary programs. Findings indicate the need for a minimal standard of post-secondary support provision and new models of support provision that are personally responsive, flexible, and individualized, as well as coordinated with instruction and integrated with the overall support needs of the student (National Center for the Study of Post-secondary Educational Supports, 2000a; Stodden & Dowrick, 2000a; Stodden & Conway, 2003).

- The coordination and management of educational supports and services with the many other services and supports required by most students with disabilities in post-secondary education. Most students with disabilities have a range of health, human service, transportation, and fiscal needs beyond the educational supports typically provided in post-secondary programs. A significant number of students with disabilities in post-secondary education require either assistance with case management or the skills, knowledge, and time to manage their own services and supports (National Center for the Study of Post-secondary Educational Supports, 2000b; Stodden & Dowrick, 2000b; Stodden & Jones, 2002).

- Transition or transfer of educational supports from post-secondary settings to subsequent employment settings. Many students with disabilities completing post-secondary education have difficulty finding subsequent employment in the profession for which they have prepared. Few post-secondary institutions facilitate or provide assistance with the transfer of supports to the workplace (National Center for the Study of Post-secondary Educational Supports, 2000b).

Estimates of the employment rate of persons with disabilities vary, depending upon factors such as the method of data collection used, and the definition of disability. Data from the Bureau of Labor Statistics (BLS) indicate that in 2002, an estimated 30.9% of civilian non-institutionalized people with a disability in the United States, aged 18 to 24, were employed, compared to 84.7% of those without a disability (Houtenville, 2004). This statistic indicates that many adults with disabilities face significant barriers to participation in the workforce. The BLS estimate is based on the Current Population Survey (CPS), which is a monthly survey conducted by the Bureau of the Census. For purposes of the CPS, persons with a disability are those who have a health problem or disability that prevents them from working or limits the kind or amount of work they can do.

Another pressing challenge is the lack of participation of youth with disabilities in state and local work force development initiatives, such as the Workforce Investment Act (WIA) of 1998. Participation in WIA programs offers expanded opportunities for community-based work experiences and access to employment training services and career supports (Luecking & Crane, 2002). It is critically important to ensure that initiatives such as WIA's youth employment programs are fully accessible to individuals with disabilities as they pursue post-secondary education and employment opportunities. By design, WIA programs further promote cross-agency approaches to serving youth, leading to strong coordination and collaboration of services.

Recommendations for Research

Research needs to address many issues to expand the knowledge base related to positive post-school outcomes in employment and post-secondary education. Although the data on students across disabilities attending post-secondary institutions has improved over the past several years, the number of students with intellectual and developmental disabilities attending post-secondary educational programs remains extremely low. Research must be conducted on the following questions:

1. What kinds of work experiences during high school have a positive effect on post-school employment outcomes?
2. How can youth with intellectual and developmental disabilities be included in services and training opportunities provided through the Workforce Investment Act youth program and the Ticket to Work?
3. How can employers and school personnel collaborate effectively to enhance career development opportunities and post-school employment outcomes for youth and young adults with disabilities?
4. What kinds of model federal and state policy frameworks will promote positive post-secondary education and employment outcomes?
5. What are the range, variation, and outcomes of post-secondary education programs, policies, and practices for young adults with intellectual and developmental disabilities?
6. To what degree are youth and young adults with intellectual and developmental disabilities receiving appropriate and effective services and supports from state vocational rehabilitation and workforce development agencies?
7. What are the barriers and supports related to successful post-secondary education experiences and outcomes?
8. Would differential financial incentives encourage post-secondary institutions to revise their admissions and/or support policies for young adults with disabilities?

Goal E: To increase parent participation and involvement

Overview of the Knowledge Base

Parent participation in IEP meetings has been required since the passage of the Education of All Handicapped Children Act in 1975. That law, later refined in IDEA 1990 and its 1997 amendments, as well as the Rehabilitation Act and its recent amendments, has promoted the participation of parents in developing and implementing transition and vocational plans and services.

A substantial number of studies have detailed how much participating parents contribute to the IEP process. For example, family involvement in program design, planning, and implementation has been shown to be a significant factor contributing to positive youth outcomes (Catalano, Berglund, Ryan, Lonczak, & Hawkins, 1998). Similarly, parent participation and leadership in transition planning have been linked to successful transitions for youth with disabilities, as well as the implementation of transition policy (DeStefano, Heck, Hasazi, & Furney, 1999; Furney, Hasazi, & DeStefano, 1997; Hasazi, et al., 1999; Kohler, 1993; Taymans, Corbey, & Dodge, 1995).

Work readiness and employment also benefit from family participation (Timmons, Schuster, & Moloney, 2001; Twenty-Sixth Institute on Rehabilitation Issues, 2000; Way & Rossmann, 1996). For instance, family members serve as systems advocates, role models, teachers, service coordinators, and job developers (Lankard, 1993) and often play a significant role in finding and helping to support and maintain employment for their sons and daughters with disabilities (Crudden, McBroom, Skinner, & Moore, 1998; Twenty-Sixth Institute on Rehabilitation Issues, 2000). Students themselves report the need for their families to guide and support them as they plan for the future (Morningstar, Turnbull, & Turnbull, 1995).

In spite of the demonstrated importance of family participation, special education and vocational rehabilitation professionals have under-used families as resources (Czerlinsky & Chandler, 1993; DeFur & Taymans, 1995; Marrone, Helm, & Van Gelder, 1997; Salembier & Furney, 1997). Parent centers report that families of young adults with disabilities are deeply frustrated by the lack of coordinated, individualized services for high school students and the scarcity of resources, programs, and opportunities for young adults once they graduate. Although parents and professionals are working to forge new collaborative relationships, they still need to build the level of trust and collaboration between them (Guy, Goldberg, McDonald, & Flom, 1997). Although increasingly students are able to advocate for their own choices during transition planning, family advocates continue to play a significant role as youth are developing their self-advocacy skills. Parents continue to do so even after their children have reached the age of majority (National Transition Alliance, 1996).

Family relationships and support may be especially important among youth from diverse cultural communities (Hosak & Malkmus, 1992; Irvin, Thorin, & Singer, 1993; Leung, 1992; Ong, 1993), who are among the most under-employed of all young people with disabilities (National Council on Disability, 2000). At the same time, many acknowledge that the participation of parents from diverse multicultural and economic backgrounds has been difficult to achieve in both special education and rehabilitation systems (Johnson, et al., 2002). Tailoring training to the cultural traditions of families improves recruitment and enhances outcomes (Kumpfer & Alvarado, 1998). For example, parents from culturally and racially diverse populations often prefer one-on-one meetings to more traditional training formats such as workshops (Minnesota Department of Children, Families and Learning, 1998; National Center for the Dissemination of Disability Research, 1999).

Recommendations for Research

Although the research literature supports the importance of parent participation in developing and implementing educational, transitional, and vocational services, a number of important questions remain regarding how best to engage and train family members, especially those from culturally diverse and economically disadvantaged backgrounds. To that end, we recommend research on the following questions:

1. What are the key strengths of families that engender self-determination and self-advocacy, and how can professionals help families develop and nurture these qualities?
2. How does the medical model of disability that parents are exposed to when their children are young (e.g., ones that stress "overcoming" disability through medical interventions and education) impact a parent's ability to foresee and prepare for the lifelong nature of significant physical and intellectual disabilities?
3. What kinds of training programs are effective in building parent/professional partnerships, developing self-determination skills, and/or improving educational and employment outcomes for youth with disabilities?
4. At what point is it helpful for parents of children with disabilities to become acquainted with adults who have disabilities, and what is the best way to make that happen?
5. What strategies are most effective in establishing the trust and enlisting the participation of diverse cultural groups in the transition process?

Goal F: To improve collaboration and links between systems to support student achievement of meaningful school and post-school outcomes

Overview of the Knowledge Base

Helping youth with disabilities successfully negotiate the transition from school to work, post-secondary education, and community life requires innovative, effective, and enduring partnerships among a variety of key stakeholders. The importance of stakeholder collaboration and systems linkages to support student achievement and post-school outcomes was recognized in early analyses of transition concepts and challenges (e.g., Halpern, 1985; Will, 1984) and remains critical (e.g., Hasazi, et al., 1999; Johnson, et al., 2002).

The continuing national attention to stakeholder collaboration and systems linkages is due in part to research that documented that students and families were not receiving the information and assistance necessary to support successful transition to work, post-secondary education, and community life. A study of school exit patterns in eight states documented that 80% of all youth with disabilities exiting high school in the 1994–1995 school year required further case management to achieve their employment, continuing education, and independent living goals (U.S. Department of Education, 1996). More recently, in a survey of parents conducted by the National Down Syndrome Society (2002), a majority of respondents indicated the need for more information and assistance with employment and independent living and better collaboration with community resources as essential for improving the post-school outcomes of young adults with Down syndrome.

Several factors have been identified as barriers to effective collaboration, including a lack of the following:

1. Shared knowledge and vision by students, parents, teachers, and human services professionals and agencies
2. Shared information across school and community agencies and coordinated assessment and planning processes
3. Meaningful roles for students and parents in the transition decision-making process, including respect for students' emerging need for independence and self-determination and parental encouragement and support for their children's decisions
4. Meaningful information on anticipated post-school services needed by students and follow-up data on students leaving school
5. Effective practices for establishing and using state and local interagency teams as a means for capacity-building in transition collaboration and systems linkages (e.g., Benz, Johnson, Mikkelsen, & Lindstrom, 1995; Furney, et al., 1997; Hasazi, et al., 1999; Johnson, Bruininks, & Thurlow, 1987; Johnson & Sharpe, 2000; Johnson, et al., 2002)

These barriers to more effective collaboration are not insurmountable. Indeed, not only can stakeholders address them, but research suggests that systems can also work more effectively together to support students in the achievement of meaningful secondary and post-school outcomes and to improve them by:

1. Using written interagency agreements that structure collaborative transition services
2. Establishing key positions funded jointly by schools and adult agencies to deliver direct services to students
3. Developing and delivering interagency and cross-agency training;
4. Using interagency planning teams to foster and monitor capacity building efforts in transition
5. Providing a secondary curriculum that helps students identify and reach transition goals and prepares youth for success in work, post-secondary, and community living environments (e.g., Benz, Lindstrom, & Latta, 1999; Benz, Lindstrom, & Yovanoff, 2000; Furney, et al., 1997; Hasazi, et al., 1999; Johnson, et al., 2002).

Promising collaboration strategies have been proposed to link secondary systems with employers and community employment services funded under the Workforce Investment Act (e.g., Luecking & Certo, 2002; Mooney & Crane, 2002) and post-secondary education opportunities (e.g., Stodden, Whelley, Chang, & Harding, 2001; Stodden & Jones, 2002).

Recommendations for Research

The remaining challenge is to use what research reveals about effective collaboration strategies in constructing effective collaboration practices in schools and communities throughout the country. To make this happen, educators and human service professionals will need to continue examining the use of legislation and policy as instruments of change and improvement and replicate existing evidence-based collaboration models (Benz, et al., 2000; Hasazi, et al., 1999; Johnson, et al., 2002). Specifically, researchers need to:

1. Develop and validate a research-based, coherent federal interagency policy framework that supports collaboration and a systems view of needs assessment, service delivery, and outcome attainment

2. Conduct research on factors needed to manage and sustain effective interagency collaboration (e.g., cross training, discipline, definitional differences, competing goals)

3. Validate effective interagency strategies at the state and local levels that lead to desired outcomes, including family and consumer participation and satisfaction;

4. Examine alternatives to interagency collaborative agreements that are person-centered, needs-based, and outcomes-oriented

5. Develop methods and systems for determining the anticipated service needs of youth with disabilities and using this information in systems planning.

Goal G: To ensure availability of a qualified workforce

Overview of the Knowledge Base

The school and human service systems cannot achieve the goals outlined in this chapter without the ability to find appropriately trained professionals, including general and special education teachers; paraprofessionals; related services personnel, such as rehabilitation counselors; and community support professionals. Unfortunately, the data show both an inadequate supply of such professionals, as well as some significant deficiencies in their training.

With regard to the availability of personnel, we summarize here the results of a few recent studies to illustrate the scope of the problem. In 1999–2000, more than 12,000 openings for special education teachers were left vacant or filled by substitutes, and an additional 31,000 special education teachers were not fully certified for their positions (U.S. Department of Education, 1999). Furthermore, the state-federal system of rehabilitation is in the midst of what may be the largest turnover and retirement of counselors in its history (Bishop & Crystal, 2002; Dew & Peters, 2002; Muzzio, 2000), with projections as high as 30%–40% in some states (Institute on Rehabilitation Issues, 2001).

Significant worker shortages and the associated factors of compensation, recruitment, training, support, and supervision have become increasingly prominent issues within the adult service-delivery system for individuals with intellectual and developmental disabilities (Larson, Lakin, & Hewitt, 2002). In the past quarter-century, staff turnover rates have consistently averaged between 43%–70% in community residences alone (Larson, Lakin, & Bruininks, 1998).

Personnel shortages are compounded by inadequacies in the training of many professionals to address specific student needs associated with transition issues. Miller, Lombard, and Hazelkorn (2000) reported, for instance, that few special education teachers have received training on the methods, materials, and strategies to develop meaningful IEPs and to provide effective transition planning and programming for students with disabilities. For example, the vast majority of special education teachers underutilized community work-experience programs or coordinated referrals to adult service providers (i.e., 31% and 43% of teachers respectively) (SPeNSE, 2002).

Miller, et al. (2000) found that nearly eight out of ten teachers (79%) in their national study received five hours or less of in-service training to help students with disabilities take part in their districts' school-to-work programs. Further, slightly less than half (49%) indicated that they received no in-service training related to inclusionary practices for students with disabilities. Although an increasing number of paraprofessionals are helping deliver special education services, they participate in professional development programs an average of just 37 hours annually (U.S. Department of Education, 2001).

The school and adult service systems must develop several strategies to address this concern regarding the availability of a qualified workforce to meet the secondary education and transition needs of youth with disabilities. First, state and local education agencies need to focus on the shortages of personnel specifically responsible for transition at the high school level and beyond. If they cannot recruit individuals with specific knowledge and skills related to transition, they will jeopardize the post-school success of students with disabilities. Thus, all these agencies need to encourage institutions of higher education to increase the emphasis they place on such training within their preservice education programs for educators, related services personnel, rehabilitation counselors, and human services professionals.

Second, special education, vocational rehabilitation, and human services personnel must possess the unique skills and competencies to address transition service needs of youth with intellectual and developmental disabilities. State and local agencies must work closely with institutions of higher education to commit the resources necessary to ensure that current and future professionals have the skills and competencies necessary to fully address the transition service needs of youth with disabilities. These efforts must include cross-training of professionals, alignment of information for a common understanding, an emphasis on interprofessional collaboration, and a commitment to securing outcomes.

Third, researchers and schools need to examine carefully the roles that general education teachers can and must play in relation to supporting a student's transition to adult life. General education teachers must have the appropriate training and supports to address the transitional needs of students and better prepare them for post-secondary education, employment, and community living. Finally, paraprofessionals and direct support staff must receive sufficient and appropriate introductory and ongoing training. These personnel provide vital support to general and special education teachers, as well as to students who are placed into community work, residential, and adult-living skill-development experiences following high school.

Recommendations for Research

This nation faces enormous challenges in providing sufficient numbers of well-qualified professional and paraprofessional education and human services personnel to meet the school and community life support needs of youth and young adults with ID/DD. Without a more effective response to the current and growing crisis in personnel recruitment training and retention, many of the national goals for personas with ID/DD will not be met. Among the questions requiring well-researched answers are:

1. What national, state, and local strategies (e.g., professional development opportunities, tuition incentives, recruitment methods) do we need to create to ensure that an adequate supply of fully certified and licensed special education teachers are available to address the secondary education and transition needs of youth with disabilities and their families?

2. How can institutions of higher education work collaboratively with state education agencies to develop high-quality professional development programs leading to the full certification of special education teachers who are not fully certified for their positions?

3. What new certifications and/or licensures with a specific focus on secondary education and transition services for youth with disabilities do state education agencies need to develop and adopt?

4. What strategies (e.g., policies, cross-training, school restructuring, financial incentives) do schools need to develop and implement so that general and special educators will better collaborate to address the secondary education and transition needs of youth with disabilities?

5. As the role of paraprofessionals and related services staff continues to increase nationally, what type and level of training programs do state education agencies and local school districts need to make available to ensure that these personnel have the knowledge, skills, and competencies necessary to address the secondary education and transition needs of youth with disabilities?

6. What strategies (e.g., recruitment, financial incentives) do school and adult service systems need to create to effectively recruit and retain special education, vocational rehabilitation, and human services personnel representing diverse, multicultural perspectives?

7. With the anticipated large turnover and retirement of vocational rehabilitation counselors over the next several years, what recruitment strategies (e.g., professional development opportunities, tuition incentives) will effectively address the projected national shortage of rehabilitation counselors?

8. What type and level of professional development programs will ensure that direct support professionals, frontline supervisors, and other human services personnel possess the knowledge and skills necessary to address the school and post-school needs of youth with disabilities as they make the transition to adult life?

Goal H: To ensure that students have full, active participation in all aspects of community life, including social, recreational, and leisure opportunities

Overview of the Knowledge Base

Along with work, post-secondary education, and community living, the sphere of social, leisure, and recreational activity has long been identified as a critical area of life (Ochocka & Lord, 1998; Schalock & Alonso, 2002; Schleien, Ray, & Green, 1997; Wilcox & Bellamy, 1982) in which students with disabilities need instruction during their young adult years. Federal legislation, including ADA § 2, the President's New Freedom Initiative, the Olmstead decision, IDEA 1997, and the No Child Left Behind Act, contains provisions that underscore the need for full participation of youth with disabilities in community life, including social, recreational, and leisure options.

In spite of these considerations, non-work-related outcomes, such as recreation and relationships, have received little attention in IEP and transition processes. Although many people agree that engaging in activities with friends is at least as important as making beds or balancing checkbooks, the curriculum in special education for students with intellectual disabilities has focused primarily on these latter types of functional skills in the transitional years (Amado, Conklin, & Wells, 1990; Schleien, Hornfeldt, & McAvoy, 1994; Schleien, et al. 2002).

A growing body of research supports the proposition that success in most areas of life is highly related to positive relationships and productive use of free time (Gottlieb, 1998; Logan, Jacobs, Gast, Streu, Daino, & Skala, 1998; Malmgren, Edgar, & Neel, 1998; Schalock, 1996; Wehmeyer & Schwartz, 1998). In that regard, a number of studies have shown that leisure education, constructive use of leisure time, and inclusive recreation are directly related to the success of individuals with disabilities in achieving their transitional goals of having friends and participating in community life (Gottleib, 1998; Mahon, Mactavish, & Bockstael, 2000; McGrew, Bruininks, Thurlow, & Lewis, 1992). Similarly, social relationships or social inclusion are among the first or second most important factors identified by individuals with disabilities as contributing to their quality of life (Abery, 1997; Schalock, 1996; Schalock & Alonso, 2002). Parents of individuals with disabilities often rate friendship and social relationship development as having greater importance than education in functional life skills (Hamre-Nietupski, Nietupski, & Strathe, 1992; Thorin & Irvin, 1992).

Unfortunately, most adult services providers and school personnel are focused primarily on practical skills and pay little attention to the social aspects of community participation for young adults with disabilities (Gallivan-Fenlon, 1994; Komissar, Hart, & Friedlander, 1996). However, with careful transition planning beginning at an early age, students with disabilities can have greater opportunities for developing peer relationships and natural supports (e.g., friends) in order to participate in community activities throughout their lives (Butterworth, Hagner, & Helm, 2000; Schleien, et al., 1997).

Nationally, examples abound of promising practices to assist youth with disabilities in becoming valued members of their communities. These examples include, but are not limited to, Best Buddies, Citizen Advocacy organizations, the National Service Inclusion Project, and a planning process called Whole Life Planning (Butterworth & Hagner, 1993). Teachers and advocates for youth, as well as the youth themselves, need planning strategies that increase opportunities for relationships among individuals of varying abilities to develop and continue (Schleien, Green, & Stone, 2002). The young people need social networks that will last beyond high school and enable them to participate in the more frequently used but less formalized settings of adult recreation (e.g., night clubs, concerts, movies, restaurants, health clubs, dating) (Bedini, Bullock, & Driscoll, 1993; Komissar, Hart, Friedlander, Paiewonsky, & Tufts, 1997).

Recommendations for Research

Overall, research is scarce on the development and role of social networks for transition-aged youth with disabilities. What research does exist highlights the importance of formal and informal social connections in ensuring meaningful and successful participation in secondary education, post-secondary education, and employment options for youth as they begin to experience adult life.

To enhance opportunities for young adults with intellectual and developmental disabilities, researchers need to identify the following:

1. Social skills needed to participate in the social aspects of work, post-secondary education, and other community options
2. Strategies that infuse social skills instruction into naturally occurring settings
3. Approaches that allow families to become more involved in helping children acquire social skills early in life
4. Interventions used by other disciplines (e.g., leisure studies, therapeutic recreation, self-determination, sociology) to study and promote friendships and social connections

USING KNOWLEDGE TO SHAPE OUR NATIONAL AGENDA

Over the past 20 years, the knowledge base related to the transition of youth with intellectual and developmental disabilities has expanded regarding systems, curricula, instruction, and policy interventions. In spite of the knowledge acquired through research studies, the findings generally have not been adopted by professionals in education, rehabilitation, or developmental disabilities. As such, researchers need to ensure that the information derived from their studies becomes accessible to a variety of constituencies and that additional research addresses emerging areas of need, including the following:

1. Researchers need to compile effective anti-dropout interventions and make them available for use by professionals and families to increase the likelihood that students with disabilities remain engaged in school. Students with disabilities, including those with intellectual and developmental disabilities, are dropping out of school at alarming rates. These students are more likely to remain unemployed, work in low paying jobs without benefits, and have fewer opportunities for additional education and training. However, several large-scale interventions have been effective in preventing students with disabilities from prematurely leaving school.
2. Researchers must synthesize and disseminate the current knowledge related to effective interagency collaboration in transition. With growing caseloads across human services and employment agencies, it is critical that processes and

procedures be efficient, responsible, and effective. Researchers need to validate model interagency collaboration practices and develop performance standards to help state, regional, and local agencies develop and measure effective interagency processes and outcomes related to transition.

3. Researchers need to provide information on how committed, sustained, and knowledgeable leadership enhances the likelihood of effective transition services in schools and human services agencies. At the same time, the longevity of principals, special education administrators, and vocational and developmental disabilities administrators is declining with many inexperienced and minimally trained professionals assuming these roles. Federal agencies must sponsor interagency leadership training programs to encourage the development of leaders skilled and knowledgeable in systems change, community engagement, and collaboration related to transition process.

4. Researchers also need to provide data about how to coordinate different agencies and federal programs. Over the past several years, legislation such as IDEA (1997), Vocational Rehabilitation (1998), Ticket to Work (1999), and the WIA (1998) have provided policy initiatives for including youth and adults with disabilities in a variety of training programs designed to better prepare them for employment opportunities. It is well known that the vast majority of individuals with disabilities want to work, but many lack the resources or skills to obtain employment. The human services system needs to coordinate and streamline the processes across these federal programs and increase work incentives to enhance the participation of young adults with intellectual and developmental disabilities.

5. Researchers need to catalogue, validate, and distribute the existing curriculum developed through federal initiatives to enable young adults with disabilities to make choices about their future. A variety of self-advocacy curricula have developed through federally supported initiatives over the past decade, some of which have been empirically validated. Young adults with disabilities must acquire the skills and knowledge related to self-advocacy and determination so they can communicate their aspirations and preferences as required in various elements of federal legislation.

Anticipating the Changes of the Future

People with intellectual disabilities have made noteworthy gains in recent years. According to the National Longitudinal Transition Study 2 (NLTS2) (Wagner, Cameto, & Newman, 2003), youth with intellectual and developmental disabilities have experienced the only significant decrease in the dropout rate when compared to youth in other disability categories. However, NLTS2 findings also revealed that people with intellectual and developmental disabilities were the least likely of all individuals with disabilities to be paid more than minimum wage. For people with intellectual disabilities to reach a more level playing field in the education, employment, and independent living arenas, we believe that the research community must address at least five related issues:

1. **Declining employment opportunities due to automation and technology.** In the past 25 years, globalization and technology have drastically changed the types

of jobs available and how individuals enter and progress through the workforce. High-wage/low-skill jobs are scarce, which has resulted in dead-end work for people who do not have the skills required for career advancement. All people, including people with intellectual disabilities, need the skills for initial job entry and the continual upgrading of their skills in relation to new workplace requirements and demands. This skill-building is essential to prevent individuals from being trapped in entry-level positions. Some of the critical skills and competencies identified for entering and advancing in today's job market are (a) resources (the employee identifies, organizes, plans, and uses resources effectively), (b) interpersonal skills (the employee works with others), (c) information (the employee acquires and uses information), (d) systems (the employee understands complex interrelationships), and (e) technology skills (the employee works with a variety of technology) (U.S. Department of Labor, 1991).

2. **Low-paying jobs without benefits that lead to a life of poverty.** Because the United States exists within a global community in which skill levels are continually increasing, the majority of jobs in today's market require at least a high school diploma and some post-secondary education and training. Positions that require no formal education are often low-paying and offer no benefits. Youth who drop out of school experience unemployment rates as much as 40% higher than youth who have completed school. According to a 2001 U.S. Department of Education study, youth with mental retardation were the least likely to graduate with a high school diploma of any youth with disabilities.

3. **Effects of standards on school completion and type of diploma received.** Under the Title I requirements of the No Child Left Behind Act (NCLB), schools are identified as needing improvement if their overall performance does not increase yearly or if any of a number of subgroups does not make adequate yearly progress. Students with disabilities are included as one of the subgroups in NCLB's accountability systems. Researchers and other key stakeholders have voiced concerns regarding whether these new accountability systems may compel students with disabilities to seek alternative programs or to drop out of school altogether. States are also experimenting with different types of diploma options. Questions regarding the rigor and value of these alternative diplomas remain unanswered. In the years ahead, researchers need to study carefully both the intended and unintended consequences of systems based on standards, performance, and accountability to monitor their impact on students with intellectual disabilities.

4. **Increased risk of involvement in the juvenile justice system.** School failure, along with poorly developed social skills and limited school and community supports, significantly increases risks for arrest and incarceration (Rutherford, Nelson, & Wolford, 1986). Youth who acquire literacy and other academic skills are better prepared for life; these skills also greatly reduce their likelihood of involvement with the juvenile justice system. Research indicates that 30%–50% of youth in the juvenile justice system have disabilities. Emotional behavior disorders (EBD), attention deficit hyperactivity disorder (ADHD), learning

disabilities (LD), and mild mental retardation (MR) are the most frequently represented disability categories in the juvenile justice system.

5. **Limited access to post-secondary education.** Post-secondary education has long been the key to career advancement and increased earning potential for many nondisabled youth. Since 1990, the number of students with disabilities entering colleges and universities has increased significantly (Pierangelo & Crane, 1997); however, this trend has not extended to youth with intellectual disabilities. In recent years, through supported education and other models, youth with intellectual disabilities have begun to seek opportunities to attend post-secondary programs.

These five issues create significant challenges for people with intellectual disabilities to access education and employment opportunities. Researchers must continue to explore innovative models that promote meaningful access for all individuals in challenging economic times.

ENHANCING REAL LIVES

As the time came closer for Matthew Boardman to transition from high school to community life, Jane and Robert became increasingly involved in statewide policy efforts to expand family- and consumer-directed services. They had learned through their years of advocacy for inclusive schools that policy and innovative practices were most often initiated by families and people with disabilities. The Boardmans advocated with the high school for the development of a collaborative employment program between the school and the local employment agency responsible for serving adults with intellectual and developmental disabilities. Both the school and the agency agreed to the plan to enable Matthew to begin his work experiences during his senior year. Doing so ensured that he would be able to access Medicaid dollars to support his employment training following graduation. It was the Boardmans' goal first to find Matthew a job he liked with help from the regional employment service and then gradually assume the responsibilities for hiring and supervising a job coach.

Matthew was excited about anything involving sports, so he and an employment specialist visited a sports equipment and clothing store and decided this was his dream come true. He has been working in this store for two years and considers this job "his career." He has built friendships with co-workers, most of whom are close to his age, and he has acquired more advanced skills, such as electronically coding and searching for merchandise. Although the agency employment specialists who supported Matthew in his job were helpful, they usually stayed for only three to four months. This was frustrating to Matthew and his family, and Jane, Robert, and Matthew decided that they wanted to develop more self-directed supports over which they had more control.

Because of Jane's interest in and commitment to developing this approach as a policy alternative, she was invited to serve on a statewide committee responsible for writing guidelines for self-directed supports. Jane served as the co-chair for the committee, and over a two-year period, the group developed a set of policies and best practices that are being implemented throughout the state.

From a personal perspective, the Boardman family was thrilled to be able to hire Frank, their own employment specialist, who has been working with Matthew for over a year. Frank receives ongoing professional development from a regional employment services agency and is connected to a network of employment specialists throughout the region. Frank works for Matthew four-and-a-half days a week and meets with the Boardman family two to three days a week. Because Matthew's employment situation is stable, and he is now working more hours, Matthew is beginning to think about moving into his own apartment with a friend during the next year. The biggest challenge for Matthew is locating a place that will accept pets, since he and his dog are inseparable.

The dreams that Jane and Robert had for Matthew 23 years ago are being realized. Matthew has acquired the skills and aspirations to live like most of his colleagues—working in a job he chooses, spending time with his large family and network of friends, playing baseball once a week with a neighborhood team, and living in a place of his choice. When he has time, Matthew is happy to share his experiences at state and national meetings. He wants his audiences to understand that, although he talks things over with his family, "it is me who decides about my life."

* * *

Amanda began her work at the career center with great enthusiasm, especially because she admired the teachers and knew some of the children. The teachers, aware of her aspirations and skills, were able to organize her responsibilities so that she could be successful. Over time, they provided her with responsibilities that were more challenging, as well as specific feedback on her work.

Although Amanda performed her work to the satisfaction of the teachers, several parents of children in the preschool raised issues about Amanda's competence. Assured of her skills and relationships with the children, the teachers invited three of the parents to visit in the classroom at different times. The teachers had informed Amanda before the visits that parents were coming to observe the classroom and watch how they all worked with the children. Two of the parents were totally satisfied with what they had observed, and one remained skeptical, not because of Amanda's performance, but because of her "label." The teachers were delighted with the outcome and were even more determined that Amanda have the opportunity to pursue her dreams. They vowed to eradicate labels from their vocabulary!

During the year Amanda served as a teacher's aide, she asked about going to college to learn even more. Louisa and Amanda met with the teachers, and they discussed the possibility of Amanda's taking a course at the local community college in teaching young children. Because she was an employee of the career center, she was eligible for reduced tuition, which was necessary for her enrollment.

Louisa was concerned about how difficult the course might be and wondered about the availability of support services. The teachers made several calls and discovered that a homework and support center was open before and after class and the tutors had experience with students with disabilities. Amanda decided that she would like to try the class, which was held two times a week in the late afternoon. The teachers recommended that Louisa and Amanda contact their local vocational rehabilitation office to help support her tuition and travel. With all that was going on in her life, Amanda decided that work and college were enough challenges for one year. She wanted to stay in the neighborhood with her many cousins and live with Louisa at least until she finished college!

CHAPTER 5

Positive Support for Behavioral, Mental Health, Communication, and Crisis Needs

ROBERT HORNER, GLEN DUNLAP, JOAN BEASLEY, LISE FOX,
LINDA BAMBARA, FREDDA BROWN, STAN BUTKUS, EDWARD CARR,
CHESTER FINN, ROBERT FLETCHER, SUSAN FOX, JIM HALLE,
JAMES HARRIS, THOMAS INSEL, ETHAN LONG,
PATRICIA MCGILL-SMITH, WAYNE SAILOR, ROGER TITGEMEYER,
LAWRENCE VELASCO, DAVID WACKER, AND HILL WALKER

REAL LIVES

Darin is 11 years old and has autism, mental retardation, and mental health problems. He lives in a world where he is "locked out" from others. His autism makes it difficult to communicate with others, and his mental retardation limits his understanding. His mental health problems make his mood either very high or very low. When his teachers and mother ask him to act in certain ways, Darin does not respond in a socially acceptable manner. He shouts loudly, shoves people, and even attacks them. It seems that Darin's behavior reflects his desire to escape demands or places that he does not like.

Darin qualifies for special education, which entitles him to receive a "free appropriate public education" with the related services he needs to function in school. To address his communication, behavior, education, and safety needs, his school organized a team of experts to evaluate why Darin acts the way he does. The team included doctors, teachers, psychologists, and his mother. They met to decide what "function" his behavior served: What is Darin trying to tell us by acting as he does? What and who makes him aggressive?

With good answers to those questions, Darin's team designed a plan around his abilities, disabilities, strengths, and needs by using a process called "person-centered planning." The team developed ways for him to communicate what he wants. Darin now carries a notebook to point to pictures to express his needs and moods (e.g., a picture of food to indicate he is hungry, a glass to say he is thirsty, a smiling face to say he is happy). To give him a predictable routine, the team developed a calendar that has pictures to show how he will spend part of each day. The doctor prescribed medication to stabilize Darin's high and low moods. His teachers and mother started using sign language rather than asking him to speak and write, and they learned how to reward his good behavior and ignore or redirect unacceptable behavior. His classmates also have learned some of his communication techniques. Currently, the team observes and records Darin and others around him so that they can change, if necessary, how they teach and interact with him. These accommodations are essential features of positive behavioral support designed to improve Darin's behavior and increase his ability to participate in family, school, and community life.

Research on positive behavioral support and bipolar disorders have allowed Darin to attend a community school and live with his family rather than in an institutional setting. Communication strategies for people with autism have been developed and refined over the past several decades, providing readily used communications systems so that young people like Darin are no longer locked out from peers and the world around them.

INTRODUCTION

This chapter will outline the rationale and content for a national research agenda to promote positive support for behavioral, mental health, communication, and crisis needs for individuals with developmental disabilities. This research agenda focuses on the development and delivery of technology to prevent and reduce problems of behavioral adaptation and the disruptions these problems can cause in the lives of individuals with disabilities and their families.

The chapter is a contribution from the subgroup on Positive Support established by The Arc's National Goals, State of Knowledge, and National Research Agenda directed by Charlie Lakin and Steven Eidelman. The chapter builds upon results and guidance from (a) The Arc's National Goals conference, held January 6–8, 2003, (b) the NIH Emotional and Behavioral Health Report, issued 2001, (c) the Mental Health, Schools, and Families Working Together concept paper, issued 2002, and (d) current research reports. We hope that, with this chapter as a guide, researchers will create an integrated program to increase the conceptual knowledge, practical intervention procedures, and feasible systems of support needed to reduce the impact of problem behaviors on the lives of individuals with disabilities and their families.

Positive Behavioral and Mental Health Supports

The goal of positive support is to prevent or minimize problem behaviors and the barriers that problem behaviors impose on the overall quality of life of individuals with disabilities and their families. By "problem behaviors" we mean any behaviors or behavior patterns, both externalizing and internalizing (Sovner, 1986; Walker, Colvin, & Ramsey, 1995), that serve as obstacles to achieving self-determined social, educational, employment, or health goals. Problem behaviors include response categories such as aggression, self-injury, bullying, disruption, depression, vandalism, withdrawal, nonresponsiveness, and defiance.

Problem behaviors develop through an array of etiologies. Some people acquire and maintain problem behaviors when they are exposed to dysfunctional environments (Carr, 1977; Carr, Levin, McConnachie, Carlson, Kemp, & Smith, 1994; Iwata, Dorsey, Slifer, Bauman, & Richman, 1982; Iwata, Pace, Dorsey, Zarcone, Vollmer, Smith, et al. 1994; Koegel, Koegel, & Dunlap, 1996). Specific physiological disabilities also increase risk for learning, developing, or evoking problem behaviors (Durand, 1990; Koegel & Koegel, 1995). Mental disorders may elicit or encourage problem behaviors (Emerson, Moss, & Kiernan, 1999; Fletcher, 1993).

Any national research agenda must acknowledge both the impact of problem behaviors on the broad lifestyle of an individual with disabilities and the variety of ways problem behaviors can become part of an individual's repertoire. Today, problem behaviors remain the most common reason individuals with disabilities are excluded from typical home, school, work, and community settings (Reichle & Wacker, 1993; Schalock, Baker, & Croser, 2002). If we are to attain the goal of a society that not only includes but embraces individuals with disabilities, then a practical and integrated approach for addressing problem behaviors is essential.

The need exists for a comprehensive and focused research agenda addressing how to prevent, remediate, and control problem behaviors. This agenda should emphasize *positive support* for behavioral, mental health, communication, and crisis needs and build from the most current knowledge related to complex behavior support needs. "Positive support" emphasizes *prevention* as well as remediation of problem behaviors (Walker, Horner, Sugai, Bullis, Sprague, Bricker, et al., 1996) and development of the emotional and coping competencies that minimize problem behaviors. It also stresses commitment to improved quality of life as well as reduction of dangerous, destructive, and harmful behaviors (Beasley & Kroll, 2002; Carr, Dunlap, Horner, Koegel, Turnbull, Sailor, et al., 2002).

The present chapter provides the rationale and focus for the needed research agenda. We first review the existing national mandates that call for developing a practical technology of positive support. We then propose a comprehensive research agenda based on four key goals: (a) assessment and monitoring; (b) access to positive behavior supports; (c) comprehensive systems of care and crisis intervention; and (d) development and support of personnel who can deliver positive support practices.

Existing Mandates for a National Research Agenda on Positive Supports

The national policy agenda mandates implicitly and, in many cases, explicitly that the service system develop effective positive supports to meet the behavioral, mental health, and communication needs of individuals with developmental disabilities. We in this field can reach these goals only with the help of a coordinated research initiative. A number of legislative, legal, and policy sources identify goals and mandates that provide the foundation for such a vigorous, focused program of applied research. These sources uniformly assert values and objectives for access to, and participation in, the mainstream of community life. To ensure that everyone can participate, regardless of challenges, support personnel must promote behavioral adaptation in typical community contexts.

Recent policy sources that are most relevant to the behavioral, communication, and mental health needs of individuals with developmental disabilities appear in documents related to community living and education. The New Freedom Initiative focuses on ensuring that community opportunities are available to all and that pertinent, reasonable supports are available to guarantee access to these opportunities. The initiative includes an explicit goal of "Promoting Full Access to Community Life," which includes four elements. One of the elements emphasizes a commitment to community-based care and, in particular, a swift implementation of the Olmstead decision. This pivotal legal decision, rendered by the U.S. Supreme Court (*Supreme Court v. L.C.*, 527 U.S. 581, 1999), mandated that states provide residents with developmental disabilities with the most integrated, noninstitutional settings appropriate to meet the needs of the individual. This mandate clearly requires the human service system to develop and implement effective positive supports that help people establish and maintain the adaptive behavioral repertoires they need to fully access the breadth of community activities.

The most prominent policy documents in education are similarly emphatic about the need for positive behavioral, mental health, and communication supports. No Child Left Behind requires that all children, including those with developmental disabilities, receive a free and appropriate education. Following from this position, the President's Commission on Excellence in Special Education identifies themes consistent with the need to implement early and inclusive supports to "embrace a model of prevention, not a model of failure." Most explicitly, the 1997 amendments to the federal Individuals with Disabilities Education Act (IDEA) (and revisions under consideration as this is written) require that schools consider and use functional behavioral assessments and positive behavioral interventions and supports whenever a student's behavior impedes learning and, in particular, whenever the school is considering a change of educational placement for students with disabilities and problem behaviors.

The need for a clear research agenda on this issue also appears in such authoritative documents as the Surgeon General's 2002 report *Closing the Gap: A National Blueprint* (U.S. Public Health Service) and the November 2001 research recommendations of the NIH on the Emotional and Behavioral Health of Persons with Mental Retardation/Developmental Disabilities. Furthermore, the official positions of numerous national professional and advocacy organizations all feature explicit goals of increased activity in positive behavior and emotional supports. Organizations with clear statements include the American Association on Mental Retardation (AAMR), the National Association of School Psychologists (NASP), the American Psychological Association (APA), the Association for Persons with Severe Handicaps (TASH), and the Council for Exceptional Children (CEC). In each case, policy makes it clear that affiliated professionals will follow conventional professional practice only if they implement the assessment, design, practices, and ongoing evaluation of support outcomes associated with positive behavior support.

Summary of Existing Knowledge

Prevalence of Problem Behaviors and Mental Disorders

Due to the large number of individuals with developmental disabilities who experience problem behaviors, the need for a national research agenda on positive supports is great. Of special concern is the need to recognize the number of these individuals who also experience mental disorders. Individuals with developmental disabilities experience the same range of psychiatric disorders experienced by people without disabilities and may actually be at greater risk for developing a psychiatric syndrome (Campbell & Malone, 1991; Charlot, Arbend, Silka, Kuropatkin, Garcia, Bolduc, et al., 2002; Phillips & Williams, 1975; Rojahn, Borthwick-Duffy, & Jacobson, 1993). Known risk factors include central nervous system compromise, deficits in communication abilities, victimization, lack of varied social experiences, dysfunctional learning histories, and limited social supports (Charlot, et al., 2002; Dosen, 1993; Sovner, 1986; Sovner & Hurley, 1982).

Although methodological limitations and cross-study differences make estimates difficult, there is some consensus (Hurley, 1996) that the rate of problem behaviors and/or mental disorders among individuals with developmental disabilities is alarmingly high. In a comprehensive review of over 30 prevalence studies, Reiss (1994) concluded that as many as 35% of people with mental retardation have behavioral or mental disorders, totaling as many as one to two million Americans. It is important to note, however, that such estimates are still a best guess (Borthwick, 1988; Reiss, 1994). Many believe that dual diagnoses remain underdetected and that research is still needed to adequately describe and classify the co-occurrence of problem behaviors, mental disorders, and developmental disabilities (Cantwell, 1996).

Functional Assessment and Positive Behavior Support

One of the most noteworthy developments in the past two decades for assessing and treating problem behaviors has been positive behavior support (Horner, 1990, 2000; Koegel, et al., 1996). Positive behavior support is the reengineering of environments to reduce problem behaviors while improving the social, educational, employment, and leisure quality of life (Carr, et al., 2002; Sugai, Horner, Dunlap, Hieneman, Lewis, Nelson, et al., 2000). Positive behavior support merges a technology derived largely from applied behavior analysis with person-centered values that assert the primacy of personal dignity, autonomy, and opportunity to participate in the mainstream of community life. When applied at the individual level, positive behavior support is a process of setting goals, assessing function, and developing and carrying out multicomponent support plans. These plans are based on assessment data and the characteristics of the settings in which they will be implemented (Bambara & Kern, 2005; Janney, Snell, & Elliot, 2000; Lucyshyn, Dunlap, & Albin, 2002).

Hundreds of studies, largely using case study and single-subject experimental designs, have examined the efficacy and critical parameters of positive behavior support. In addition, comprehensive reviews and meta-analyses (e.g., Carr, Horner, Turnbull, Marquis, Magito McLaughlin, McAtee, et al., 1999) have demonstrated that positive behavior support is an effective approach for decreasing and preventing problem behaviors.

Two major aspects of positive behavior support deserve comment. The first, functional assessment, is the process used to collect and synthesize information to define the problem behaviors, determine what maintains it, and describe the environmental context associated with high and low rates of the behavior (Carr, et al., 1994; Durand, 1990; O'Neill, Horner, Albin, Sprague, Storey, & Newton, 1997). Numerous investigations have proven the value of functional assessment for analysis and intervention in a variety of problem behaviors (e.g., Repp & Horner, 1999).

For instance, research has shown conclusively that many problem behaviors are maintained by social consequences, such as gaining access to reinforcing objects, activities, and social contacts or avoiding aversive objects, activities, stimuli, and social contacts (Donnellan, Mirenda, Mesaros, & Fassbender, 1984; Durand, 1990). In an early, classic example, Iwata, et al. (1994) documented that of 152 individuals with developmental disabilities and self-injurious behavior (SIB), nearly 70% engaged in SIB that was maintained by access to, or escape from, socially controlled events. Understanding the relationship between problem behaviors and communication has led to the development of powerful intervention strategies, such as functional communication training (e.g., Carr & Durand, 1985).

The second major aspect of positive behavior support is the array of intervention procedures that constitute the behavior support plan. Each plan is derived from the process of individual functional assessments and is created to follow logically from the assessment data and to fit the social, physical, and personal characteristics of the setting. Among the multiple components included in the plan are, typically, procedures to:

1. Redesign the environment so that environmental events evoke desirable rather than problem behaviors;
2. Teach new skills;
3. Prevent delivery of rewards following problem behaviors;
4. Ensure that rewards follow desired behaviors; and
5. Ensure the safety of all individuals involved (Horner & Carr, 1997).

Numerous experiments have demonstrated the benefits of these components in reducing problem behaviors and increasing alternative and lifestyle competencies (e.g., Carr, et al., 1999; Lucyshyn, et al., 2002; Luiselli & Cameron, 1998).

Although positive behavior support offers useful knowledge for addressing the challenges of behavioral adaptation experienced by many individuals with developmental disabilities, it remains a relatively new approach. Future research must answer key questions, such as the extent to which (and the mechanisms by which) the approach can produce sustainable outcomes and whether or not the assessment and intervention strategies can be replicated in the full range of diverse communities. Researchers also need to verify that positive behavior support can help individuals with developmental disabilities cope with the range of circumstances they will encounter in the community.

Knowledge Related to a System of Care

More knowledge is available on specific assessment and intervention practices than the *systems* needed for efficient access to effective services and supports. It is clear that, for the most part, the community service system has not adequately addressed the needs of people with developmental disabilities, problem behaviors, and/or mental illness/mental retardation (MI/MR) (Fletcher, 1993; Jacobson, 1996; Smull, 1988). The reports of the President's Commission on Mental Health (1978;1988) detailed the problems associated with poor behavioral and mental health service delivery and described a fragmented service delivery system in which people with developmental disabilities, problem behaviors, and/or mental disorders frequently fell through the cracks. According to the 1978 report, people with these disorders were "neglected by both the mental health and mental retardation service systems" (p. 2007). Ten years later, the 1988 commission report was unable to cite significant improvements in service delivery.

In February 2002, in *A Report of the Surgeon General's Conference on Health Disparities and Mental Retardation* (U.S. Public Health Service, 2002), David Satcher described mental health care services to people with mental retardation as a pressing unmet health need and disparity. The "national blueprint" prescribed in Satcher's report included steps to evaluate systems and services on local, state, and national levels.

In an effort to fill in the gaps in the community service systems, model programs have been established in selected locations. Early evidence from these programs has shown some reduced reliance on expensive alternatives to community care, such as psychiatric hospitalizations, restrictive and sometimes punitive actions, and institutionalization (Hanson & Wieseler, 2002). Most of the model programs employ an interdisciplinary or multimodal approach (Gardner, 1998; Griffiths & Gardner, 2002a, 2002b) that includes consultation, psychiatric treatment and assessment, and positive behavior support planning in addition to crisis prevention and intervention services (Beasley & Kroll, 2002).

Some of the approaches that show promise include the Rochester model (Davidson, Cain, Sloane-Reeves, Giesow, Quijano, & Houser, 1996), the START model in Massachusetts (Beasley & Kroll, 2002), the Minnesota Special Services Program (Rudolph, Lakin, Oslund, & Larson, 1998), the Case Management Mental Health Network (Patterson, Higgins, & Dyck, 1995), the Cambridge regional community support team (Colond & Weisler, 1995), and the Vermont Crisis Intervention Network (Resources for Community Living, 1997). Encouraging findings include significant reductions in the use of emergency (crisis) services for problem behaviors and less recidivism.

Although the preliminary results from these model programs are encouraging, research is needed to assess the generality and replicability of individual program findings. Research also must evaluate the effects of such community models on community participation and quality of life outcomes. Such an emphasis would contribute to improved state and local policies to better serve individuals with mental retardation, challenging behaviors, and mental health needs.

A RESEARCH AGENDA ADDRESSING CURRENT NATIONAL MANDATES

A research agenda responding to the current need to understand, identify, prevent, and remediate problem behaviors and mental disorders should be multifaceted. Among the major limitations in the available research on problem behaviors and mental disorder are the inadequate integration of behavioral, medical, mental health, and psychological variables that affect the lives of individuals with developmental disabilities. To address this limitation, we propose research on the following four major goals: (a) assessment and monitoring; (b) access to effective, evidence-based positive support; (c) comprehensive systems of care and crisis intervention; and (d) appropriately trained personnel.

Assessment and Monitoring

Goal A: To provide individuals with intellectual and developmental disabilities and problem behaviors and/or mental disorders with ongoing access to appropriate assessment that (a) guides support practices and (b) includes person-centered planning, mental health/medical evaluations, and functional behavioral assessment

Assessment and monitoring of problem behaviors, behavioral adaptation, and quality of life are crucial for developing and maintaining appropriate, effective community supports. The assessment process includes identifying, describing, diagnosing, analyzing, and assessing all relevant areas of community functioning. As supports and services are implemented, ongoing assessment and program monitoring remain critical. Although progress has been made in differential diagnosis methods (Lowry, 1998; Sovner, 1986) and functional assessment (Repp & Horner, 1999), no one has conducted research on a comprehensive approach. We propose four major questions for the research agenda under the goal of assessment and monitoring.

What Constitutes Appropriate Assent and Consent?

The first question pertains to the procedures and ethics of securing informed agreement of an individual with developmental disabilities to participate in behavioral and mental health services. Research needs to focus on self-determination; techniques to enhance decision-making capacities; and involvement of families, friends, consultants, advocates, and service providers. In addition, epidemiological studies are necessary on practices for sharing information and soliciting the active involvement of participants.

What are the Appropriate Instruments and Procedures Needed to Diagnose and Formulate Treatment?

This second question addresses the major, fundamental, and complex determinants involved in understanding and treating problem behaviors and other mental health challenges. Researchers need to investigate intensively how to develop, identify, validate, and use instruments that effectively guide behavioral and mental health professionals to optimal support practices. Some have argued that problem behaviors can be understood best in the context of an assessment of multiple medical, psychiatric, psychological, and environmental conditions (Gardner, 2002; Gardner & Cole, 1987). Therefore, accurate psychiatric assessment and monitoring of treatment effects are crucial to serving individuals with mental retardation and complex behavioral presentations (Sovner & Hurley, 1990).

The challenges of assessment begin with an appreciation that neuropsychiatric disorders in people with mental retardation are both misdiagnosed and underdiagnosed (Emerson, et al., 1999; Lowry & Charlot, 1992; Marcos, Gil, & Vasquez, 1986; Reiss, 1990). People with developmental disabilities continue to receive antipsychotic medications at high rates, in some cases without having any psychiatric diagnosis on record (Jacobson & Ackerman, 1988; Kalachnik, 1999). Clearly, an overarching concern is to improve the accuracy of psychiatric diagnoses among people with disabilities (Singh, Sood, Somenkler, & Ellis, 1998).

Although the challenges of diagnosing mental disorders in individuals with developmental disabilities are apparent (Charlot, 2002), there has been progress in the methods of differential diagnosis and the articulation of conceptual guidelines. For instance, Sovner's (1986) analysis of the effects of mental retardation has been helpful in distinguishing the effects of mental disorder from other phenomena associated with mental retardation. In addition, diagnostic inventories (e.g., the Aberrant Behavior Checklist [Aman & Singh, 1986], the Reiss Screen, the Psychopathology Instrument for Mentally Retarded Adults) have been developed to assist the process of diagnosing mental health problems in people with developmental disabilities. Nevertheless, further work in this area is essential. In particular, studies must assess the validity and reliability of adaptations to standard diagnostic and assessment tools and the extent to which use of these tools and strategies leads to appropriate intervention protocols.

Studies must continue to focus on the process of functional assessment (Dunlap & Kincaid, 2001) in order to ensure its applicability to the complete range of behavioral and mental health challenges (Nelson, Roberts, Mathur, & Rutherford, 1999) and to evaluate its contributions to sustainable behavior support associated with meaningful lifestyle change. In this respect, it is urgent that researchers examine the processes of functional assessment in the larger context of strengths-based assessments and person-centered planning (Kincaid & Fox, 2002).

Finally, the research agenda should also encourage studies to examine procedures for longitudinal monitoring of the impact of support plans and their relationship to diagnosis and assessment. In particular, it is crucial to study strategies for monitoring the impact on self-determination, normalization, community integration, and the implementation of transition plans.

What Strategies are Most Effective for Assessing and Monitoring the Efficacy of Treatment Over Time?

The third key research question under the assessment goal asks whether researchers and support personnel know how to sustain effects and interventions. It also highlights the need to develop and evaluate valid strategies for assessing long-term outcomes. This topic has not been the subject of much research to date, but it is assuming prominence as the field turns to the need for durable lifestyle enhancements. Future investigations should evaluate variables related to maintenance, access to ongoing support, and the relation of treatment integrity to long-term effectiveness. Researchers need to use parametric analyses of treatment protocols to determine the conditions under which evidence-based interventions yield short- and long-term effects across multiple complex community environments.

What are the Perceptions of Labels and Diagnoses by Persons with Disabilities, Their Families, Their Service Providers, and Policy Makers?

A final question related to the broad goal of assessment involves the effects of labels and diagnoses on the perceptions of key constituents and stakeholders. In particular, research must assess attitudes and situational reactions of various constituents to labels and diagnoses. Such studies should also investigate the collateral effects of disability labels and clinical diagnoses. Research should identify pathways to overcoming the stigma of labels, particularly as it relates to self-determination.

Access to Effective, Evidence-Based Positive Support

Goal B: To provide individuals with developmental disabilities with access to effective, positive, and evidence-based behavioral, mental health, medical, and social supports to (a) prevent and reduce problem behaviors or mental disorders, (b) support social resilience, and (c) promote desired lifestyle outcomes

Among the most important advances in developmental disabilities over the past 15 years is a practical technology of positive support (Bambara & Kern, 2005; Carr, et al., 1999; Koegel, et al., 1996). Research is needed to bring this technology to fruition, expand the array of contexts and conditions in which the technology can be effective, and make positive support technology available on a national scale. To meet this goal, The Arc's National Goals Conference committee focused on two major directions for research. These directions are based on an assumption that mutual responsibility exists between individuals without disabilities and individuals with disabilities and problem behaviors. All members of society share a responsibility to minimize factors that evoke, exacerbate, and maintain serious problem behavior, and individuals bear personal responsibility for acquiring the competencies necessary to reduce problem behaviors.

What are the problem contexts and personal competencies associated with problem behaviors, and what interventions will be most effective in addressing these contexts and competencies?

To recognize the obligation of society as a whole, one must take into account the full array of physical, medical, mental health, and social factors that contribute to problem behaviors. Research must address those factors that initiate, exacerbate, and maintain problem behaviors. This large set of variables recognizes that positive support is focused as much on designing effective environments as on developing effective personal competencies. To date, research on positive support has addressed remediation strategies once problem behaviors are identified as a major challenge. Although a strong technology is necessary to address problem behaviors, it is equally important to identify the environmental, medical, and personal conditions that place an individual at greater risk for acquiring problem behaviors. The obligation of society is to organize contexts that promote and support positive behaviors.

What are the supportive contexts and personal competencies that prevent problem behaviors from emerging?

The personal obligation of all individuals (with and without disabilities) focuses on developing skills that make problem behaviors irrelevant or inefficient. Central to needed research is the role of teaching/instruction as a behavioral intervention tool. The generalized and durable reduction of problem behaviors often will involve not simply focusing on eliminating undesirable behaviors, but also actively strengthening socially valued skills that make problem behaviors irrelevant or inefficient. Building effective verbal or augmentative communication skills, for example, has been shown to reduce problem behaviors caused by frustration from an inability to communicate (Carr, et al., 1994; Durand, 1990). Moreover, recent research suggests that investing in teaching new skills (e.g., providing enhanced capacity) produces more durable and generalized reductions in problem behaviors (Durand, 1999; Schindler & Horner, 2005).

The need for research that addresses access to positive behavior support extends across the life-span (young children, school-age children, young adults, adults), across the spectrum of mental health disorders (e.g., obsessive-compulsive disorder, depression, anxiety disorders, bipolar disorder), and across home, school, workplace, and community contexts.

System of Care Variables, Crisis Prevention, and Support

Goal C: To allow individuals with developmental disabilities to receive effective and sustained positive behavioral and mental health supports across their life-span through established systems of care based on progressive policy, sound organization, and quality assurance

Individuals with disabilities who are affected by problem behaviors and/or mental disorders need access to a system of care that can address their diverse and complex individual needs. This must be done in a manner that is comprehensive, community-based, efficient, and effective. Despite substantial research on effective prevention and intervention approaches and many demonstration models, access to comprehensive services within a system of care remains elusive for many individuals. Services are typically fragmented and include restrictive enrollment criteria. They also are contingent on the severity of problem behaviors or the perception of service need, and they deliver treatment within restrictive settings.

A "system of care" describes the provision of community-based services and programs and the processes and structures to ensure that these services are comprehensive, cohesive, and coordinated. Services within a system of care are diverse. They address positive behavior support, mental health, physical health, substance abuse, family support, shelter, and vocational, recreational, advocacy, and case-management needs. All services, according to the system's core values, must be person-centered, community-based, comprehensive, culturally competent, and accountable. A system of care implies that multiple agencies and programs work together, forming a network to achieve service integration and coordination. The components of this system are interrelated, with the effectiveness of one dependent on the availability of the others. Thus, in a system of care, individuals with disabilities and problem behaviors and/or mental health disorders and their caregivers have access to a multitude of interventions and supports necessary to meet their dynamic and complex needs.

The research agenda is focused on three areas: service use, design of effective crisis prevention and intervention supports, and identification of necessary service system elements. We recommend that this research agenda be conducted as a multisite, multicollaborator initiative. Research conducted across diverse communities by multiple researchers offers rich possibilities of thorough investigations that address complex questions and results with greater generality. The following questions and descriptions offer more information on those research areas and variables for consideration.

How are Services Used by Individuals With Developmental Disabilities Who Are Affected by Problem Behaviors and/or Mental Disorders Across the Life-Span?

Services include the processes of identification, screening, referral, assessment, and entry into effective comprehensive interventions and supports. Research must focus on the use of services for and by individuals with developmental disabilities affected by problem behaviors and/or mental disorders across the life-span, including all processes of those services. To date, researchers know little about the pathways to accessing services, the experiences of individuals as they seek services, and the efficiency and validity of screening and assessment processes.

Research conducted in this area should examine service use across multiple local, regional, and state locations so it truly examines the national scope of issues and practices. These investigations must also access multiple data sources, including descriptive statistics and consumer perspectives and exemplars. Important areas include what eases and what blocks service access, what works and what challenges the screening and assessment processes, and how services are integrated and individualized within the system of care.

What Are the Characteristics of an Effective Crisis Prevention and Intervention Service System for Individuals With Developmental Disabilities Who Have Problem Behaviors and/or Mental Health Challenges?

Many individuals with disabilities and problem behaviors and/or mental disorders experience times in their lives that can be perceived as crises. Crises for an individual with behavior challenges may include episodes of behavior that are dangerous to the individual or others or circumstances (e.g., homelessness, illness, disruption in services, incarceration) that compromise the ability of the person to receive needed supports. Few systems of care offer effective and comprehensive crisis supports within the community.

Systems of crisis care can be both reactive and preventive, addressing challenges in managing unpredictable and disruptive behaviors (Reiss, 1994; Sovner, 1986), helping individuals avoid acute mental health episodes and psychiatric hospitalizations (Beasley, Kroll, & Sovner, 1992), and providing access to appropriate ongoing behavioral and mental health services as needed (Fletcher, 1993; Mechanic, 1989). Program components addressing the various challenges include comprehensive treatment planning, diagnostic assistance, functional assessment, family systems consultation, interdisciplinary planning and training, and follow-up monitoring incorporating all aspects of the system.

A key feature of this crisis system is the integration of components with careful coordination linking programs, professionals, and caregivers. Thus, focused research must delineate and evaluate the mechanisms of collaboration, in particular how these mechanisms address the support needs of individuals with developmental disabilities and crisis management.

In general, researchers need to define the necessary service elements of an effective crisis prevention and intervention service system of care. Data of interest will be measures of planned and unplanned service contacts over time, inquiry focused on the experiences of individuals over time, outcomes associated with crisis intervention, and the relationship of crisis management to other services within a system of care.

What Are the Essential Core Elements for Developing an Effective, Comprehensive System of Care Across the Life-Span of Individuals With Developmental Disabilities and Problem Behaviors and/or Mental Health Challenges?

Researchers need to identify necessary core elements for developing an effective, comprehensive system of care across the life-span. Developing a system of care will involve weaving together multiple programs and services into a comprehensive and coherent system that meets the diverse needs of individuals with developmental disabilities and problem behaviors/or mental health disorders. Investigations should examine the role of each discipline, agency, or service provider within the system of care (e.g., developmental disabilities, mental health, social services, medicine, criminal justice, education) and identify the elements that promote cross-system and cross-agency collaboration and integration. In addition, research should examine factors related to access to services, including eligibility criteria, demographic characteristics of individuals served by the system, and blending of funding streams to ensure access. Research should investigate factors related to sustained and effective comprehensive supports, including the costs of establishing and maintaining a system of care. Most important, research should examine the outcomes for individuals who access services from a system of care, including long-term quality-of-life outcomes.

Appropriately Trained Personnel

Goal D: To provide to self-advocates, families, employment settings, and local communities a sufficient cadre of leadership, direct support, and coordination personnel trained in the theory, practices, and systems of positive behavior and mental health supports

This goal asserts that efforts to meet the behavior support needs of individuals with developmental disabilities must include increasing well-trained personnel at all levels throughout relevant systems of care. For a community to possess such capacities, personnel in all of the intersecting disciplines must receive pertinent and effective training. These disciplines include education, psychology, medicine, social work, counseling, speech/language therapy, additional therapies (e.g., physical, occupational), behavior analysis, and positive behavior support. Furthermore, training must be coordinated across disciplines and service systems. To achieve this goal, we propose a research agenda focusing on a number of interrelated key questions. Two of the most prominent questions are delineated below. The first critical research question addresses the essential skills and knowledge required for a team to function effectively in the context of a comprehensive, local system of care; the second focuses on the systems needed to provide durable supports to ensure that assessment and treatment produce desired long-term gains.

What Are the Competencies and Knowledge Foundations Needed Within a Team to Improve (a) Diagnosis, Assessment, and Access to Appropriate Services; (b) High-Quality Implementation of sucpport and Treatment Plans; and (c) Sustained Achievement of Lifestyle Outcomes and Reduction of Problem Behaviors?

Competencies are the practical skills and knowledge of pertinent facts and theoretical frameworks. The term "knowledge foundations" refers to needed information about the person, the person's preferences and individual history, and the contexts in which the person functions.

Ample evidence shows that competence in functional assessment of problem behaviors can be instrumental in helping a team design more effective intervention plans (Repp & Horner, 1999). Similarly, family involvement in developing and carrying out treatment plans can lead to improved maintenance and generalization of effects (Lucyshyn, et al., 2002). However, the full complement of essential skills and knowledge foundations has neither been delineated nor empirically validated.

Furthermore, the manner in which skills and knowledge blend in the context of a local team has not been researched adequately. These substantial, far-reaching issues require solid evidence if the human service system is to establish comprehensive local capacity in the form of a cadre of trained personnel. The answers to these questions will lead to more effective, more integrated, and more efficient training programs.

To function effectively on behalf of individuals with developmental disabilities and behavioral/mental health challenges, teams require core competencies shared by all members. They also need specific and specialized competencies among experts in particular disciplines. Research in response to this question will need to identify and distinguish competencies that must be present in all local teams at all times versus those that should be accessible to teams but maintained for particular systems operations deployed for relatively intensive (e.g., crisis) circumstances. Examples of core competencies may include relational interactions, family functioning, collaborative teaming, and the processes of positive behavior support. Specific competencies may include neuropsychological assessment, biomedical evaluation, clinical diagnosis, and intensive functional analysis. The research agenda will need to categorize these competencies empirically and analyze how competencies can be incorporated across systems and disciplines. The agenda will also need to examine the composition of teams and focus on how to incorporate the functional contributions and perspectives from professional, family, and paraprofessional team members.

What Agencies and/or Individuals in a System of Care Have an Impact, Indirectly and Directly, on the Sustained Achievement of Lifestyle Outcomes and Reduction of Problem Behaviors Across the Life-Span?
This question relates directly to the first. Only knowledgeable personnel can deal with the legislation, policy, funding, and administration critical to sustaining support programs. The competence of these individuals will be instrumental in the development and implementation of the system's operations.

The necessary research requires analyses to identify entities whose influence can be associated with successfully maintaining effective support plans and interventions. The focus of the research, both within and across systems, should include the roles of administrators and managers, agency boards of directors, school boards, and oversight groups, such as human rights committees and peer review and professional standards committees. This list can be expanded to include county commissioners and state legislators.

Using Knowledge to Shape Our National Agenda

The charge of the topical group on Positive Support for Behavioral, Mental Health, Communication, and Crisis Needs was to consider existing knowledge and policy, to articulate national goals, and to delineate a relevant research agenda designed to help achieve those goals. Our work yielded four major goals: to design an assessment and monitoring program; to provide access to effective community-based supports; to construct a functional system of care; and to build a cadre of competent personnel at all levels of policy, administration, and service delivery. The recommended research agenda previously described comprises a range of questions that need to be answered in order to progress toward achieving these goals. We constructed the questions to be ambitious yet feasible. We purposefully oriented them to produce new knowledge that will clearly benefit the lives of individuals with developmental disabilities who also have problem behaviors and/or mental health challenges.

We have not suggested methodologies to accompany the research agenda. Rather, we believe that the different questions will call for a range of quantitative and qualitative designs to acquire the most relevant, valid, and usable information. However, regardless of the optimal methods selected to address a particular question, we urge researchers to apply the very highest standards of methodological rigor and establish a preference for designs that employ multiple collaborators working from multiple community sites. Though they are more costly than single-investigator, limited-research endeavors, such large-scale efforts have the potential to produce knowledge with high levels of validity, reliability, and generality. Such characteristics increase the likelihood that the data produced will have an impact on policy, practice, and the lives of individuals with disabilities.

CHAPTER 6

Comprehensive Health Supports and Health Promotion

DAVID L. COULTER
with
Ansley Bacon, Arnold Birenbaum, Vincent Campbell, Mary Cerreto,
Stephen Corbin, Allen Crocker, Gloria Krahn, Catherine McClain,
Suzanne McDermott, Wendy Nehring, Renee Pietrangelo,
Rick Rader, Deborah Spitalnik, and Sheryl White-Scott

REAL LIVES

Drew's mother Angela was 25 years old when she became pregnant. Angela had a difficult personal history that included physical and sexual abuse when she was a teenager. She ran away from home when she was 16 years old and lived on the street for a few years. She became addicted to heroin and entered a drug treatment program when she was 20, but relapsed a year later. During the years before she became pregnant with Drew, she lived with a number of different men and had children with them; all her children were removed by the Department of Social Services. She managed to stop taking drugs, but could not stop drinking or smoking cigarettes. She had been binge drinking about once a week when she found out she was two months pregnant with Drew.

At that point, she was determined to change her life and sought treatment for her alcoholism. Her adherence to the program was uneven during the pregnancy, and she had a few relapses before she finally committed to a spiritually based 12-step program. She then stayed clean and sober, took prenatal vitamins, and kept her prenatal visits with the obstetrician during the last two months of the pregnancy.

Drew was born at full term but weighed only 5 pounds, 2 ounces at birth. The delivering obstetrician immediately noticed that the baby had a number of problems and transferred Drew to the Neonatal Intensive Care Unit. The pediatricians there recognized that Drew had the facial features of fetal alcohol syndrome. When Drew showed signs of cardiac problems, the pediatricians obtained cardiologic evaluation that showed the presence of serious congenital heart disease. Drew underwent cardiac surgery at two weeks of age that partially corrected the abnormality, but further surgery was anticipated when he got older. Drew gradually gained weight and was ready for discharge at two months of age.

During all of this time, Angela made daily visits to the hospital and stayed in contact with her social worker. She had found an apartment and was receiving financial support from several social service agencies. After considerable discussion between Angela and the doctors, nurses, and social worker, the decision was made to discharge Drew to his mother. Plans were made for frequent visits from the social worker and a visiting nurse, and Drew was referred to the local early intervention program.

Drew and Angela did well for about six months, so the visiting nurse felt she could cut back to monthly monitoring visits. Soon after that, the Department of Social Services transferred the social worker assigned to the case, and the new social worker's caseload was too great to allow frequent visits. On her own, Angela took Drew to all of his doctor visits and made sure he got all of his immunizations. When Drew was 15 months old, his mother moved in with her new boyfriend Joey, who lived in a nearby town. Unfortunately, Joey soon became abusive toward Angela and would beat her up when he was drunk.

After a while, Angela started drinking again. She did not enroll Drew in the early intervention program in the town where she and Joey were living and missed several appointments with the doctors at the hospital where Drew was born. Finally, when Drew was 28 months old, his mother left Joey and went to live in a shelter with Drew. During the next six months, she and Drew lived at the shelter while she completed treatment for alcoholism, took parenting classes, and went through a job training program. During this time, Drew received medical care from the free clinic at the shelter, but he did not receive early intervention services because he was not considered to have a stable address by the local service provider.

When Drew was three years old, Angela graduated from the job training program and landed a job as a secretarial assistant at the local women's clinic. She was determined to make it and felt she had a lot of support from the staff at the clinic. She was also determined to keep Drew with her, since he was the only child she still had. She began to talk to other women at the clinic who had been through similar problems and helped start a women's support group there. With her income from the job she was able to get an apartment nearby.

She realized that Drew needed help and talked to the doctors at the clinic, who referred her to an excellent pediatrician in the community who accepted Medicaid. The pediatrician referred Drew to the developmental assessment clinic at the hospital, where they identified significant delays in cognitive, language, and gross and fine motor development. He was referred to the cardiologist for further management of his congenital heart disease and to the local public school system for enrollment in special education. Angela and Drew were finally safe, secure, stable, and surrounded by caring friends and professionals who could give them the support they needed.

INTRODUCTION: A NEW WAY OF THINKING ABOUT INTELLECTUAL DISABILITY AND HEALTH

The medical model is dead. It had been lingering on life support for a long time, but it was finally pronounced dead in Chicago at the 2003 Annual Meeting of the American Association on Mental Retardation (AAMR) (Coulter, 2003a). That symbolic end to an outmoded way of thinking about the role of health for persons with intellectual disabilities reflected the development of a vigorous new way of thinking that is the basis for this report. This new way of thinking applies the fundamental principles of normalization, self-determination, and the functional basis of disability to a vision of community-based health supports and services and health promotion activities (Coulter, 2003b).

What was the medical model? Allen Crocker has identified a number of aspects of the medical model of disability (Crocker, 1999), which are summarized in the sections that follow.

Medicalization of Disability

What was called mental deficiency or mental retardation was seen as a problem located within the individual, rather than within society or the environment. Mental abilities were deficient or underdeveloped as a result of some physical, neurological, or genetic disease or disorder. As such, the retardation was an innate trait that one was (usually) born with and that was life-long. Society considered the individual sick, diseased, abnormal, or inferior to others who did not have this trait. Because the problem was located within the body (specifically within the brain), diagnosis and treatment of the problem involved a medical approach. Early medical approaches emphasized "hygiene" and efforts to prevent the occurrence of the medical disease or disorder that would otherwise result in mental retardation. Later medical approaches to treatment emphasized progressive improvement of the disease or disorder along a continuum that would eventually restore the individual to a more "normal" state.

Unequal Roles

The medical model of disability meant that individuals with mental deficiency or mental retardation were patients who were cared for by doctors and nurses. This way of thinking led to a form of medical paternalism in which the doctor had the knowledge and the power to determine what was best for the patient. Power was unidirectional, and the doctor saw no need to seek or respect the patient's perspective about treatment.

Medical Control

In the medical model, doctors and nurses remained in charge and controlled all aspects of the patient's life, including residential settings and social opportunities. People with mental deficiency or mental retardation lived in hospitals or neurological institutes. For many years, these places were usually controlled by doctors (typically psychiatrists) and were divided into wards controlled by nurses.

Differential Treatment

"Patients" received health care within the institutions from doctors who worked for the institution. These doctors often considered themselves to be working primarily for the benefit of the institution rather than for the patient. Because the institution budget limited medical treatment options, doctors often based their treatment decisions on what was best for the budget rather than what was best for the patient. Institutional doctors who also had private practices outside the institution might then prescribe different treatments for patients living in the institution than they would for patients living in the community.

New Perspectives of Intellectual Impairment

In 1992 the AAMR radically redefined mental retardation as a state of functioning rather than as an innate trait (Luckasson, Coulter, Polloway, Reiss, Schalock, Snell, et al., 1992). This state of functioning was based on the way limitations in intellectual functioning and adaptive skills interact with the demands and constraints of the social environment. Although medical conditions might predispose an individual to limitations in functioning, mental retardation was now identified with these limitations rather than with the predisposing medical condition. The medical model began to disappear. In its place, the supports paradigm emphasized that appropriate and timely supports could help people function more effectively in the community. Supports were chosen by the team to respect the wishes and goals of the individual and family.

The World Health Organization's (WHO) 2001 publication of the International Classification on Functioning further emphasized this new way of thinking (2001a). In this model, three interactions affect the way a person functions: (a) impairments in body structure and functioning (anatomy and physiology); (b) limitations in performing desired (self-chosen) activities; and (c) restrictions on participating in a full social life. Thus the World Health Organization now defines disability as a problem in functioning. In 2002 the AAMR redefined mental retardation as a disability that represents the expression of limitations in intellectual functioning within a social context (Luckasson, Borthwick-Duffy, Buntinx, Coulter, Craig, Reeve, et al., 2002).

The old terms "mental deficiency" and "mental retardation" were based on the medical model, which viewed these conditions as innate traits. The new way of thinking recognizes that those terms describe individuals who have a problem in functioning or a disability related to intellectual limitations. The term "intellectual disability" is a better description for individuals who have this problem in functioning and will be used throughout the rest of this chapter.

This new way of thinking about intellectual disability requires a new way of thinking about health. The community health supports model developed to replace the medical model represents a vision of what health should become for individuals with intellectual disabilities. It incorporates the functional model developed by the AAMR, the supports paradigm, and the WHO International Classification of Functioning. The defining statement of the community health supports model says, "a support activity fosters physical, mental, social and/or spiritual well-being (health) when it helps the individual to manage physical impairments in order to perform self-chosen activities that promote participation in desired social roles within the community of choice" (Coulter, 2003a).

In comparison to the medical model, this new model recognizes that disability is a problem in functioning and not an innate trait, disease, or brain disorder. In this new model, individuals with intellectual disabilities control their destiny, and power is shared between health providers, individuals with intellectual disabilities, and their families. Health supports and services should be provided in community settings, not in the segregated or residential settings that characterized the medical model. They should be designed to help individuals function within those community settings. The community health supports model requires that individuals with intellectual disabilities receive the same type and quality of health services and supports as everyone else. This new model provides a benchmark for measuring progress in health services and policy and offers a vision of what health should become for individuals with intellectual disabilities. It is the vision upon which the goals and recommendations of this chapter are based.

Goals and Sources

Overview

Goals are statements about what one hopes to accomplish in the future that are grounded in certain basic principles or assumptions that reflect the state of current knowledge. These principles derive from research, knowledge, experience, teaching, and public policy and represent the general consensus about current thinking in the area of health for persons with intellectual disabilities. Taken together, the principles enumerated in the pages that follow describe this current consensus and form the basis for the community health supports model. The goals that follow then represent what is needed to achieve this vision in the future.

Principles

Eight basic principles must guide health support and health promotion for persons with intellectual and developmental disabilities if our supports are to be true to our expressed national goals. These principles are described as follows:

1. **Persons with intellectual disabilities are valued as much as all other persons.** Health care is delivered without discrimination based upon the presence or absence of disability. This also means that the presence of a disability should not determine whether or not health care providers decide to offer life-sustaining treatment or attempt resuscitation. They should never apply the practices of euthanasia and physician-assisted suicide to persons with intellectual disabilities.

2. **Health care is culturally competent, universally accessible, and delivered within the communities in which persons with intellectual disabilities live.** Within the WHO model of functioning (which is incorporated in the community health supports model), these cultural and community aspects of health represent the personal and environmental factors that influence the way a person functions. Personal factors include age, race, gender, educational background, fitness, lifestyle, habits, coping style, social background, and past and current experiences. Environmental factors include the physical, social, and attitudinal environments in which people live and conduct their lives. This principle states that health services delivery respects all of these contextual factors that influence individual functioning.

3. **Health care respects the values, contributions, and gifts of persons with intellectual disabilities.** The repudiated medical model identified these persons

as deficient, abnormal, or inferior. The accumulated wisdom and experience of many professionals in pastoral ministry with persons with intellectual disabilities has shown that this attitude is wrong. A substantial literature (not cited here) and at least one professional journal (the Journal of Religion, Disability and Health) have documented these gifts and contributions extensively. The community health supports model recognizes persons with intellectual disabilities as valued members of society and respects the gifts and contributions they bring to the life of the community.

4. **Health care decisions are based upon the choices of persons with intellectual disabilities, and the decision-making process is shared between these persons, their families, and health care providers.** The community health supports model incorporates the principle of self-determination and recognizes that the power of decisionmaking must be shared between all persons who are involved in the process and who have a stake in the health outcome.

5. **Health care includes the comprehensive range of primary care and specialized services available in outpatient, inpatient, and community settings.** These services include emergency treatment and treatment for acute health conditions, as well as long-term health maintenance and health promotion activities. The community health services model incorporates the principle of normalization, which states that whatever health services are normally available for other persons in society should also be available for persons with intellectual disabilities.

6. **Health care encompasses the full range of health services and supports required to meet the generic and specific needs of persons with intellectual disabilities.** The previous principle emphasized that we all should have access to the same health services. This principle emphasizes that these health services should address all of the needs of people with intellectual disabilities. Some of the areas of greatest need currently include mental health, vision, and oral/dental health.

7. **Health care financing promotes full, active community participation and is not restricted on the basis of intellectual disability.** Financing should not be available only in restricted settings such as nursing homes or institutions. Health care financing should pay for the services and supports people need to live active lives within the community.

8. **Health services research is relevant throughout the entire life-span of people with intellectual disabilities and addresses life stage transitions from youth, to adulthood, to old age.** Research should be integrated across systems such as health, education, and employment services to promote health in all settings across the life-span. This principle emphasizes that research is relevant for persons at all ages, but also recognizes that the current state of knowledge is limited for adults and seniors.

National Goals

Contemporary policy and social principles have established seven basic areas and goals for health supports for persons with intellectual and developmental disabilities. These derive from legislation, judicial decisions, administrative directives, and other sources of national policy and principle. These areas and goals include quality (Goal A), financing (Goal B), self-determination (Goal C), training (Goal D), wellness (Goal E), knowledge (Goal F), and mental health (Goal G). The specific goals are as follows:

A. To allow people with intellectual disabilities to have access to high-quality health care that is universally available, appropriate, timely, comprehensive, and provided within the communities in which they live

B. To make sure that people with intellectual disabilities will receive affordable health care that promotes community inclusion

C. To promote partnerships between people with intellectual disabilities and their families and health care providers; so they may access and use health information to make well-informed, freely chosen decisions about their own health goals, services, and health promotion activities

D. To ensure that people with intellectual disabilities are treated with respect by health care providers who are well trained in providing health services and supports for adults and children with intellectual disabilities

E. To help people with intellectual disabilities participate in the full range of health promotion and wellness activities available to other children and adults in the community (including, but not limited to, activities that promote physical fitness, emotional well-being, social and environmental health, and spiritual growth)

F. To identify, evaluate, and expand knowledge about the health status of individuals with intellectual disabilities across the life-span

G. To allow people with intellectual disabilities access to comprehensive mental health, behavioral, and other allied services and supports to meet their needs within the community

The Sources of National Goals

In recent years, a great deal of national attention has been given to the quality and accessibility of health supports and health promotion for persons with intellectual and developmental disabilities in the United States. Perhaps the most visible source for the national goals described above is the 2002 report of the Surgeon General's Conference (U.S. Public Health Service, 2002). This conference and its subsequent report was the culmination of a year-long process undertaken by U.S. Surgeon General David Satcher. Dr. Satcher began this process after receiving a comprehensive report on the health status and needs of individuals with mental retardation that was commissioned and published by the Special Olympics (Horowitz, Kerker, Owens, & Zigler, 2000).

The report was presented at a meeting of the Senate Appropriations Subcommittee called by Senator Ted Stevens of Alaska in March 2001. Dr. Satcher conducted a series of "listening sessions" in October 2001 at four nationwide sites in which people with intellectual disabilities and their families were invited to present testimony about their experiences, ideas, and concerns regarding health care. Additional comments and suggestions (8,500) were also received electronically at a special Web site set up for this purpose. Dr. Satcher then convened a two-day working session in Washington, DC, in

December 2001, during which eight panels of invited experts reviewed the evidence and made recommendations that included nearly 50 issue areas and 200 action steps. All of this information was then considered carefully and distilled into the final report published in February 2002.

This final report, entitled "Closing the Gap: A National Blueprint to Improve the Health of Persons with Mental Retardation," included six goals and 31 action steps needed to achieve these goals. Within each action step, the blueprint also identified a number of potential strategies. This was a practical report; it did not reflect an overarching model or vision of what health should be, but it is entirely consistent with the community health supports model. Many of the individuals involved in developing this chapter's national goals also participated in the Surgeon General's Conference, so these goals are also consistent with the Surgeon General's report.

A related conference held at the National Institutes of Health in November 2001, immediately prior to the Surgeon General's Conference, reviewed the mental health needs of persons with intellectual disabilities and made recommendations for research, services, and policy in this area. The report of this conference (National Institutes of Health, 2001) also served as an important source for the national goals in this chapter.

An important general source for goals and recommendations concerning all aspects of health is *Healthy People 2010* (U.S. Public Health Service, 2001). Chapter six of this report identifies 13 objectives related to disability and secondary conditions, many of which are relevant for individuals with intellectual disabilities. These objectives are particularly important because they are focused federal policy, and relate directly to identifying and achieving national goals.

The report of the Tampa Scientific Conference on Intellectual Disability, Aging, and Health (Davidson, Heller, Janicki, & Hyer, 2003) provided an additional source for specific goals regarding aging with intellectual disabilities. This report relates to national goals regarding health across the life-span.

REVIEW OF KNOWLEDGE AND RECOMMENDATIONS

Goal A: To allow people with intellectual disabilities to have access to high-quality health care that is universally available, appropriate, timely, comprehensive, and provided within the communities in which they live

Overview of the Knowledge Base

Knowledge about the health status of people with intellectual disabilities was reviewed comprehensively by Horowitz, Kerker, Myer, and Zigler (2000). This report reviewed 513 publications and analyzed the data for physical health conditions, mental health disorders, ocular impairments, oral/dental problems, and use of health services. In general, the data demonstrate that people with intellectual disabilities remain at high risk for a number of serious health conditions and often experience preventable secondary conditions. Mental health services are limited in some instances, but excessive in others. Doctors often prescribe medications even though very little data exist regarding safety and efficacy for persons with intellectual disabilities. The quality of these health services is often fragmentary, restricted, or poor.

Recommendations for Research

The concept of a "medical home" was developed by the American Academy of Pediatrics to describe a place where health care providers are able to meet all of the support needs of children with complex medical problems and their families (American Academy of Pediatrics, 2001). Directors of public agencies responsible for adults with developmental disabilities have said that a similar concept applied to their clients would be the single most important element in assuring the clients delivery of quality health services to their clients. It is important to expand the medical home model and put it into practice across the life-span and to spend substantial time evaluating and continuing to improve this approach.

The work group shared the strong concern expressed by self-advocates about the issue of limitation in care and the subtle or overt practice of euthanasia against persons with disabilities. We recommend a study to examine the current frequency, causal attributions, and nature of such practices. These data would then be useful for developing strategies to oppose these practices and to promote high-quality health services for all persons with disabilities.

There is a lack of sufficient scientific evidence to develop well-informed practice guidelines and standards of care for persons with intellectual disabilities (see Goal F). As new data emerge and adequate guidelines are developed, the disability community will need to study and validate them. In particular, studies are needed to assess the impact of these standards and guidelines on utilization of health services and achievement of high-quality health outcomes.

Goal B: To make sure that people with intellectual disabilities will receive affordable health care that promotes community inclusion

Overview of the Knowledge Base

Most individuals with intellectual disabilities receive health care financing through public agencies such as Medicaid. The adequacy of this public financing varies greatly from state to state, however. In some states, adequate public financing is only available in restricted settings, such as institutions or nursing homes. Many community-based health care providers are unwilling to care for persons with intellectual disabilities due to inadequate reimbursement from Medicaid and other public sources. Moreover, health coverage often varies based on the disability label, even though service needs are similar. Some individuals with intellectual disabilities have private health care financing, but very little data exist on the adequacy of coverage by these plans.

An issue of particular importance for self-advocates is the limited availability of private health insurance through the workplace, because their low-level jobs often do not provide adequate health benefits. Thus they may be forced to choose between working and not receiving health insurance coverage, or not working and relying on Medicaid.

There is grave concern about the future of Medicaid as the primary source of health care financing for persons with intellectual disabilities. Ongoing proposals to alter the regulatory structure of Medicaid, as well as pressure to reduce rapidly expanding Medicaid budgets, could have severe consequences for persons with intellectual disabilities (Birenbaum, 2003).

Recommendations for Research

Studies are neeeded to assess the impact of state funding variations and different models of public and private health care financing on key health and functional outcomes for people with intellectual disabilities. We also recommend studies to assess the impact of differences in specific benefits and services covered by these plans. We also need to know whether such coverage would be sufficient in plans to provide universal health care.

Medicaid will likely remain the most important payer for health services for people with intellectual disabilities in the near future; thus we recommend studies to determine how dependence on Medicaid as a payer affects access to care and quality of care and what specific factors contribute to limitations in access and quality. Based on these studies, we also recommend health policy analyses to improve the role of Medicaid in assuring high-quality health care.

In view of the serious threats to Medicaid noted above, we recommend careful study of any proposed changes in Medicaid and appropriate advocacy to support responsible public policy.

Goal C: To promote partnerships between people with intellectual disabilities and their families and health care providers; so they may access and use health information to make well-informed, freely chosen decisions about their own health goals, services, and health promotion activities

Overview of the Knowledge Base

Although the literature on self-determination is extensive, until recently few studies looked at how to facilitate the application of self-determination to health care. Self-determination in health care was mentioned briefly in the tenth edition of the AAMR's classification manual (Luckasson, et al., 2002, p. 181). The Center on Self-determination and Health Care for Persons with Disabilities at Boston University has just begun to collect data on this topic. Anecdotal evidence suggests that well-informed consumers generally receive higher quality health care and are more satisfied with the care they receive. Application of information technology for persons with intellectual disabilities is just beginning, however. A number of studies are currently underway to develop methods to help these consumers access usable health information on the Internet.

Recommendations for Research

Studies are needed to identify strategies that will effectively increase the knowledge and participation of people with intellectual disabilities in their own health promotion activities and health services. Self-determination in the health arena will require new ways, including the Internet, to disseminate usable health information that is accessible to all. We recommend studies to assess whether providing this user-friendly health information will lead to better health care choices and outcomes. We also recommend studies to assess the impact of "parent-to-parent" programs that introduce parents of a child with a genetic disorder to parents of children who have the same or similar disorders.

Self-advocates must be involved in designing, implementing, and analyzing research on the health of people with intellectual disabilities. Current increased attention to issues of informed consent, privacy, and protection of private health information in research may create barriers to achieving this standard. In particular, most states currently lack statutory language to permit surrogates (guardians) to consent to research involving adults with significant intellectual limitations. It is important that ethical and policy analyses determine the best way to protect the privacy, rights, health, and safety of persons with intellectual disabilities involved in health research.

Goal D: To ensure that people with intellectual disabilities are treated with respect by health care providers who are well trained in providing health services and supports for adults and children with intellectual disabilities

Overview of the Knowledge Base

The Surgeon General's report (U.S. Public Health Service, 2002) found that, in general, training of all physicians and other health care providers is grossly inadequate. The limited training they receive most often applies only to children and youth. Moreover, most health care providers receive virtually no training regarding health assessment and treatment of adults with intellectual disabilities. This grim situation may change soon. The only major textbook devoted specifically to health care for persons with intellectual disabilities (Rubin & Crocker, 1989) is currently undergoing extensive revision, and a new edition is expected in 2005.

A new curriculum for training family medicine physicians in the care of adults with developmental disabilities, sponsored by the Society of Teachers of Family Medicine, is also due out in 2005. New curricula are also being developed to train nurses and dentists (Nehring, 2005). Nonetheless, meaningful change will come slowly as newly trained providers enter the health care workforce. Continuing education training for health care providers already in the workforce will remain a problem, since available data suggest that most current continuing education programs do not alter providers' practices significantly.

Recommendations for Research

The first step in addressing the training issues is to assess the current situation. Studies are needed that determine how much training on health services for people with disabilities is conducted currently across the country and what is being taught and in what context (i.e., didactic activities versus direct experience). Additional studies need to evaluate the effectiveness of these training programs in improving the knowledge, attitudes, and behavior of those who provide health services to individuals with intellectual disabilities across the life-span. We also recommend similar studies to assess current continuing education activities and to develop improved methods for educating health care providers already in the workforce.

One element of such studies is to analyze whether providing training in working with individuals with intellectual disabilities makes a difference. Thus we recommend studies to determine whether the health care provided by health professionals specifically trained to work with people with intellectual disabilities and their families differs significantly from the health care provided by those who have not received such training. We are particularly concerned with the perspective of those who receive care.

Goal E: To help people with intellectual disabilities participate in the full range of health promotion and wellness activities available to other children and adults in the community (including, but not limited to, activities that promote physical fitness, emotional well-being, social and environmental health, and spiritual growth)

Overview of the Knowledge Base

Health promotion and wellness activities are well developed and accepted for the general population, but very little data exist regarding their application for persons with intellectual disabilities. The Special Olympics report (Horowitz, et al., 2000) reviewed some of these data, especially regarding vision and oral/dental health promotion. The Web site (http://www.ncpad.org) of the National Center for Physical Activity and Disability, located at the University of Illinois in Chicago, is an excellent source of data on physical health promotion for persons with intellectual disabilities. The AAMR is developing evidence-based health promotion guidelines for persons with intellectual disabilities, and a report covering 15 topic areas for health promotion is set for release in 2005.

Recommendations for Research

There is considerable interest in improving health promotion in order to enhance the health of the general public. The work group recommends applying this public health model to research on health and wellness for people with intellectual disabilities. Thus new studies must develop more evidence-based guidelines for health promotion and assess their effectiveness in improving health outcomes. There is also considerable interest in complementary and alternative medicine practices, many of which have little scientific validation. We recommend well-designed scientific studies to determine whether or not these practices are safe and effective in improving the health and well-being of people with intellectual disabilities.

The National Center on Birth Defects and Developmental Disabilities (http://www.cdc.gov/ncbddd), a new center opened in 2000 within the Centers for Disease Control and Prevention, is emerging as an important sponsor of clinical studies on health promotion for persons with developmental disabilities. We recommend substantially increased funding for the center for work in this area.

Goal F: To identify, evaluate, and expand knowledge about the health status of individuals with intellectual disabilities across the life-span

Overview of the Knowledge Base

Much of the information reviewed under Goal A is also relevant here. In addition, the report of the Tampa Scientific Conference on Intellectual Disability, Aging, and Health (Davidson, et al., 2003) provides information about the state of knowledge regarding aging with intellectual disabilities.

Recommendations for Research

Many researchers have expressed concern that the National Institutes of Health (NIH) is unwilling to fund clinical studies regarding treatment for people with intellectual disabilities. It is important that the NIH reverse this policy and enhance funding for clinical studies. Clinical trials involving new and existing drugs and treatments must include people with intellectual disabilities.

In addition, we recommend studies to correct the imbalance of health knowledge across the life-span. Much more research is needed on the health status of adults and individuals aging with developmental disabilities. This research needs to include strategies to provide sensitive, ethical, and humane palliative care at the end of life.

Goal G: To allow people with intellectual disabilities access to comprehensive mental health, behavioral, and other allied services and supports to meet their needs within the community

Overview of the Knowledge Base

The National Institutes of Health report summarized the status of current knowledge on emotional and behavioral health for persons with intellectual disabilities (National Institutes of Health, 2001); the Special Olympics report (Horowitz, et al., 2000, Chapter 3) and the AAMR manual (Luckasson, et al., 2002, Chapter 10) also reviewed these issues. Consensus-based recommendations for treatment of mental health disorders, including the use of medication, are available (Reiss & Aman, 1998; Rush & Frances, 2000). These reports confront the issue of diagnostic overshadowing, in which the diagnosis of mental retardation overshadows and obscures the coexisting diagnosis of a mental health disorder. Thus the reported prevalence of these disorders may be low.

Nonetheless, the data suggest that mental health disorders are common and that, in general, individuals with intellectual disabilities have the same types of mental health disorders as the general population. Certain rare genetic disorders appear to carry a higher risk for mental health disorders, however. Individuals with Down syndrome have a particular risk for Alzheimer disease and dementia as they age. Other behavioral phenotypes (specific mental and behavioral disorders that occur more commonly in some genetic disorders) have been identified for a few conditions, including Williams syndrome, fragile X syndrome, Angelman syndrome, Prader-Willi syndrome, Smith-Magenis syndrome, velocardiofacial syndrome, and Rubinstein-Taybi syndrome (Dykens, Hodapp, & Finucane, 2000).

Recommendations for Research

We endorse all of the recommendations of the National Institutes of Health conference (National Institutes of Health, 2001); however, the full text of these 49 separate recommendations is beyond the scope of this chapter. These recommendations cover research on the epidemiology of mental and behavioral disorders, diagnostic assessment, and treatment interventions for people with intellectual disabilities. Additional recommendations cover research designs, research training, and ethical considerations in research with people with intellectual disabilities.

USING KNOWLEDGE TO SHAPE OUR NATIONAL AGENDA

It is important that research is relevant to those who have a stake in the process and outcome, particularly researchers and individuals with intellectual disabilities and their families. Researchers need to be able to participate in determining current funding priorities. They also need to learn how to use existing research knowledge to address policy issues and impact the decisions of policy makers. This will likely require new ways of "packaging" research knowledge so that it is more understandable and usable. Researchers need to help private foundations expand their areas of interest and funding priorities to include disability-related topics. For example, foundations interested in aging could fund studies of aging and disability, or those interested in poverty and health disparities could fund studies of poverty, health, and disability.

Research findings need to be disseminated in ways and venues that are accessible to people with disabilities, their families, and their support staff. Participatory action research methods (described in other chapters) can be used to assist people with intellectual disabilities in participating effectively in all aspects of health care research. When they are aware of existing research and research needs and have a stake in the process, self-advocates and their families can be effective partners in advocating for improved research funding and better targeted research policies.

Many stakeholders are interested in accessing usable health information and research results. We recommend that a Web site be developed that would focus on health and disability, similar to http://www.ncpad.org and http://www.qualitymall.org. The Web site would need to be funded adequately as a "clearing house" for usable health information. It should be relevant and accessible to multiple audiences, including self-advocates, their families, and their support staff. The site could also link to other research networks, such as the Centers for Disease Control, the Association of University Centers on Disability, and the Mental Retardation Research Centers.

Self-advocates want to learn how to become better trained in achieving optimal health outcomes for themselves. It is important to support their goals to develop and evaluate self-advocate training in how to make the most of their health and wellness experiences and how to help health care providers provide quality care. We also support their interest in receiving training as recipients of public or private fellowships on health and disability policy. Well-informed and committed stakeholders can work together to assure that existing public laws and policies (such as the Americans with Disabilities Act) are fully implemented to improve the quality of health care for all people with disabilities.

We believe that many programs and health service providers deserve recognition for excellence in health care for persons with intellectual disabilities. We recommend developing strategies to identify and recognize excellence in health practice and health promotion programs that provide high-quality services and supports for people with intellectual disabilities.

Anticipating the Changes of the Future

Globalization means that information is readily available from all over the world and can be shared easily. The worldwide availability of information on the Internet has made global information-sharing much easier, although the quality of this information is highly variable. Ready access to electronic information will help some people learn more about health, but other people with intellectual disabilities who do not have Internet access or skills may become isolated and deprived. Data obtained in one country may well be applicable to consumers in another country. One example is the widespread translation into many languages of the AAMR's definition and classification manual (Luckasson, et al., 2002). The 2004 12th World Congress of the International Association for the Scientific Study of Intellectual Disability also promoted global information exchange. Some research may be performed more effectively in one country rather than another, perhaps because unique databases are available or because researchers do not have to contend with certain locally prevalent research problems. Researchers could then develop international networks to pursue projects of mutual interest.

The impact of new genetic knowledge will undoubtedly have a major impact in the future. The Human Genome Project is just the beginning and will be followed by accelerating research into the genetic basis of health, functioning, and disability. One area of impact concerns the ethical use of this new information; genetic research findings may be used to devalue the lives of persons with disabilities and reduce their social and psychological status. The "cult of perfection" describes efforts to use genetic knowledge to eliminate human imperfections, which could then be used to eliminate persons with such conditions through subtle and overt euthanasia practices. On the other hand, evolutionary theory recognizes that variability in the gene pool is necessary for natural selection to improve the species, so the cult of perfection could prove to be counterproductive in the long run.

Advances in genetic knowledge undoubtedly will lead to new methods for screening and testing for genetic disorders. These methods will allow more individuals to know if they are at risk for having a child with a genetic disorder and to receive appropriate preconception counseling even before they decide whether or not to have a child. Expanded prenatal genetic testing will allow individuals more opportunities to exercise reproductive choice regarding the birth of a child who has been identified as having a genetic disorder. Comprehensive universal newborn screening for treatable genetic disorders will identify more infants who can be treated before they develop any disabilities. New diagnostic genetic testing will identify more individuals who have genetic disorders that predispose them to treatable secondary conditions so that further disability can be prevented.

Genomics is the study of genetically based risks for specific health conditions. Although genetics identifies absolute risks for some disorders (e.g., if you have the gene for Huntington disease, you will develop the condition), genomics identifies relative risks for disorders that are only partly genetically determined. Thus genomic data may indicate that an individual has a much higher risk for heart disease or a much lower risk for cancer. Knowing the relative risk means that patients could undertake health promotion activities to reduce the nongenetically determined risk (e.g., by quitting smoking or losing weight). Genomics will likely revolutionize the system of health care financing, which is based on the principle of aggregate risk. Everyone pays into the system because no one knows for sure who will get sick. If genomics identifies some people who are very likely to get sick and some who are not, those who are not at high risk will be unwilling to pay into the system since they will not receive any benefit. Voluntary (private) health insurance systems will then collapse, and a new system will need to emerge. This situation could result in universal health coverage financed by the national government, which is charged with protecting the health of all of its citizens.

The impact of new technology is reviewed elsewhere, but assistive technologies will likely help individuals with intellectual disabilities use health information to promote health and wellness.

CONCLUSION

The story of Drew and Angela at the beginning of this chapter illustrates that health is multifactorial and involves physical, emotional, social, environmental, and spiritual well-being. It also illustrates that enhancing the health of children with intellectual disabilities requires enhancing the health of their families, and enhancing children's quality of life requires enhancing the quality of life of their families. Drew and Angela needed a complex array of medical, behavioral, social, environmental, and spiritual health supports to finally achieve a personally satisfying quality of life.

The health and disability communities need a new way of thinking about health and disability. Otherwise, they will not be able to understand the research and policy changes needed to assure that these health supports are available for all persons with intellectual disabilities and their families. The community health supports model has replaced the medical model, which is no longer appropriate. This new model incorporates the principles of self-determination and normalization and the functional understanding of disability. It is based on a number of key principles and assumptions described above. Moreover, it is defined by the understanding that a support activity fosters physical, mental, emotional, social, environmental and/or spiritual well-being (health) when it helps the individual to manage physical impairments in order to perform self-chosen activities that promote participation in desired social roles within the community of choice.

Recently, the European Association of Intellectual Disability Medicine (http://www.mamh.net) released a report of a conference, held in conjunction with the European Year of People with Disabilities 2003, entitled "The European Manifesto: Basic Standards of Health Care for People with Intellectual Disabilities" (European Association of Intellectual Disability Medicine, 2003). The standards listed in this report are similar to the principles and national goals listed in this chapter. The report thus further validates the new way of thinking described in this chapter and provides an exciting opportunity for international cooperation in enhancing health and wellness for all persons with intellectual disabilities worldwide.

This new way of thinking leads directly to our national goals. These are the goals that will realize the vision expressed by the community health supports model. Achieving these goals will require much new research, including (but not limited to) the studies recommended in this chapter. New practice and policy initiatives will also be needed to implement research findings and enhance all aspects of health for persons with intellectual disabilities. In a rapidly changing and increasingly global world of knowledge, everyone involved will need continued vigilance and dedication to assure that all people with intellectual disabilities achieve optimally healthy and personally satisfying lives.

CHAPTER 7

Biomedical Research for Primary and Secondary Prevention

STEVEN WARREN, MARK BATSHAW, FORREST BENNETT,
RANDI HAGERMAN, AND MARSHA SELTZER
with
Duane Alexander, Barbara Altman, Coleen Boyle, Jose Cordero,
Sharon Davis, Kay DeGarmo, James Hanson, Lewis Leavitt,
Elise McMillan, David Patterson, Siegfried Pueschel, John Rose,
Travis Thompson, and Mary Woolley

REAL LIVES

It is the year 2050. Kevin is now 12 years old. He was born with Down syndrome. He is in sixth grade and attends his local public school. His academic performance and participation in extracurricular activities are just below age level for typical children. Like many kids, he occasionally receives some individual tutoring. He is an aspiring artist and plays trombone in the school band. His health status is good, and his life expectancy is estimated to be 77 years. He plans to marry and have his own family some day and, like his friends, is starting to think about various career options.

Kevin was identified with Down syndrome in utero and received treatment for a heart condition prior to birth. Since shortly after birth, he has taken several drugs designed to stimulate neurocognitive growth and development in general and working memory specifically. During his first year of life, he also benefited from a neurovocal therapy that stimulated optimal oral-motor development. As a result, he spoke his first clear words at 18 months of age. Later in adulthood, he will begin taking a drug designed to prevent the onset of Alzheimer's disease. His Down syndrome has been treated since before birth by an interdisciplinary team that still closely monitors his growth and development and has individualized his treatment and education in response to his specific needs as well as those of his family and siblings. There is no question that he has Down syndrome, just as there is no question that he has brown hair. However, advances in biomedical research and clinical and educational practice have minimized the impact of this syndrome on his health status, development, and day-to-day quality of life.

Had Kevin been 12 years old 100 years earlier, in 1950, his life expectancy would have been less than 25 years. He might well have died as an infant due to his congenital heart condition. His level of mental retardation would likely have been severe, his oral-motor development disordered, and his education minimal. He might well have spent much of his life living in a large institution.

If Kevin were 12 years old in 2005, his life expectancy, general health status, educational potential, and the overall likelihood that he would live a long life of reasonable quality would be substantially better than the bleak picture in 1950. For example, the heart problem he was born with might have been addressed in the first year of his life, and his life expectancy would have increased to almost 50 years, double what was in 1950. He would probably live at home and might have some reading skills. Nevertheless, to achieve the quality of life envisioned for the Kevin in 2050, much remains to be accomplished.

INTRODUCTION

We live in extraordinary times. The combination of science, democracy, and capitalism has turned on the engines of human creative activity in a way never before seen in history. One effect of this is the continuing advances in the life sciences, which promise to revolutionize health care and quality of life. We can see numerous signs of these advances; increasing life-spans in the developed countries and increasingly effective treatments for a wide variety of disorders and disabilities are just two indicators. To what extent will this knowledge ultimately benefit the Kevins of this world and other individuals with intellectual and developmental disabilities? Although the potential is great, we have no guarantees that the life of the Kevin described in our 2050 vignette can or will be achieved.

This chapter reports the findings and recommendations of the Task Group on Biomedical Research on Primary and Secondary Prevention of Intellectual and Developmental Disabilities. Our task group reached consensus on four broad national goals for this area. For each goal we also generated a large number of specific recommendations that, if followed, we believe ultimately will result in our reaching the proposed goals. We have offered 50 such recommendations.

In this chapter we first describe the process we followed in generating these goals. Next, we present and briefly discuss each goal, then offer the specific recommendations that accompany that goal. This section forms the bulk of our report. We conclude the chapter with a discussion of four questions of central importance to this effort:

1. What outcomes should we expect if these goals are achieved?
2. What conditions are necessary to achieve these goals?
3. How can we improve the link between research in this domain and practice that affects people's lives?
4. What potential threats hamper progress and limit the potential impact of research in this area?

Although this chapter is focused primarily on biomedical research, the perspective that informs our recommendations might best be described as "bio-behavioral" (Warren, 2002). It is increasingly evident to biological and behavioral scientists that human beings are inherently attuned to and affected by their environment. Consequently, as important as they are, inherited genetic factors often account for only part of the variance in human behavior. Thus, to fully understand human development and behavior, scientists must analyze the functional interactions between biology, environment, and behavior (Strohman, 2002; Reiss & Neiderhauser, 2000; Rutter, 2002). Further progress in preventing or treating many complex disorders (and many intellectual and developmental disabilities are clearly the outgrowth of complex disorders, of which autism is a prime example) will require interdisciplinary collaborations of biomedical and behavioral scientists working from this bio-behavioral perspective.

GOALS AND SOURCES

The Process

Our group began working together in November 2002. Like the nine other task groups who participated in the overall effort to craft a research agenda for intellectual and developmental disabilities, we held face-to-face meetings in January 2003 in Washington, D.C. At the conclusion of that meeting, the five individuals identified as the authors of the chapter agreed to refine the work of the larger task group into this chapter.

Of the 10 task groups who participated in this overall goal-setting exercise, our work scope was among the most challenging because of the vast area of research to be covered. Biomedical research relevant to primary and secondary prevention covers a broad domain of inquiry involving a large number of disciplines and dozens of fertile research topics. The complexity and potential of these areas, to say nothing of the rapidly changing landscape within many of them, meant that to encompass them accurately into a report of this nature would be difficult, at best, and perhaps sheer folly. Furthermore, like the other task groups, we agreed to use an approach that might best be characterized as a "shotgun technique." The formula for this technique is to charge a representative group of experts with the generation of goals and recommendations, give them a few months to organize those goals and recommendations electronically, hold one face-to-face meeting, request a final report, and hope for the best.

Having agreed to this charge, we set out to do the best we could. Daunting as it was, our task was aided in several ways:

1. Our distinguished group consisted of many strong senior scientists and national leaders, as well as parents and advocates. The group possessed both a breadth and depth informed by an extraordinary degree of "real world" experience. Importantly, all members set aside their own personal agendas, rolled up their sleeves, and went to work on the task at hand.

2. We used electronic communication extensively before our meeting in Washington. Individual members initially nominated both national goals and specific research recommendations. A long list of "candidates" for these goals and recommendations was assembled, then vetted to the group, revised, and

sent out for more feedback. We also solicited input from a large number of scientists, practitioners, advocates, and parents outside the committee.

3. When we met in Washington, we worked to build consensus by limiting our-
    selves to just four broad goals while allowing the breadth, depth, and potential
    of each area to be conveyed through a large number of specific recommenda-
    tions. This required all of us to compromise and work for consensus, which we
    did remarkably well.

4. After our meeting in Washington, a small but representative group took over the
    task of putting our findings and recommendations together into this and related
    documents. These five team members serve as the authors of this chapter in
    recognition of our extended efforts. However, the goals and recommendations
    are the work of many. They reflect the combined experiences of all those who
    partook in this endeavor, their deep scientific and clinical knowledge, and their
    commitment to improving the quality of life of individuals with intellectual and
    developmental disabilities. They also reflect the countless others who have built
    and are building the knowledge base which holds so much promise for the future
    for people like Kevin.

REVIEW OF KNOWLEDGE AND RECOMMENDATIONS

**National Goal A: To use new scientific techniques emerging from genetics, neuro-
biology, molecular biology, imaging, toxicology, behavioral/cognitive sciences, and
related fields to identify specific mechanisms that interfere with development
throughout the life-span and lead to intellectual and developmental disabilities**

Experts now recognize that, in many cases, mental retardation and other developmental
disabilities have their origin in errors (genetic or environmental) that affect specific
aspects of brain development; for example, neuronal migration in the case of learning disabilities and neurotransmitter receptor development in attention deficit hyperactivity
disorder (ADHD) (Galaburda, 1991; Swanson, Flodman, Kennedy, Spence, Moyzis,
Schuck, et al., 2000). Among conditions causing severe mental retardation, over two-
thirds are thought to have their origin in abnormalities in early brain development
(Laxova, Ridler, & Bowen-Bravery, 1977).

It is clear that our knowledge of the neuropathology of developmental disabilities is
limited. When, for example, scientists study the brains of 10%–20% of individuals with
severe mental retardation of unknown origin using standard neuropathology, they can
find no signs of abnormality. In fact, the majority of brains of these individuals show only
mild, nonspecific changes that correlate poorly with the degree of mental retardation
(Kaufmann & Galaburda, 1989; Volpe, 2001).

In spite of these limitations, scientists now have insights into some of the mechanisms
of embryogenesis:

1. Evidence shows that the same teratogen (i.e., poison) can cause different anom-
    alies at varying points in embryonic development. The classic example of this is
    the effect of thalidomide on limb development (Newman, 1986). If a pregnant
    woman takes thalidomide between 21-24 days of gestation, only the upper

extremities will show phocomelia; between 24-35 days, both upper and lower limbs are affected; and after 35 days, there is no teratogenic effect.

2. Different insults can cause the same anomaly if they occur at the same time in development. Intrauterine infections, whatever their cause, when occurring at the same point in gestation, lead to microcephaly and virtually indistinguishable brain anomalies (Epps, Pittelkow, & Su, 1995).

3. A teratogen often has a dose effect. Following the atomic bomb blasts in Hiroshima and Nagasaki, there was a correlation between the distance from the bomb's epicenter and the degree of microcephaly in children born to women exposed during pregnancy (Wood, Johnson, & Omori, 1967).

4. A genetic predisposition can interact with a teratogen that affects fetal outcome. A genetic deficiency of the mitochondrial detoxifying enzyme epoxide hydrolase explains why fetal hydantoin syndrome occurs only in a minority of women who receive the anti-epileptic drug diphenhydramine (Dilantin) during the first trimester of pregnancy (Buehler, Bick, & Delimont, 1993).

5. Environment affects gene expression. Meninogomyelocele, a neural tube defect, has a genetic predisposition; that is, it is more common in individuals of Irish descent. However, if a pregnant woman does not take enough folic acid, she seems to have a greater chance of a neural tube defect regardless of her ancestry. This increase suggests an interaction between genetics and environment (Manning, Madsen, & Jennings, 2000; Northrup & Volcik, 2000; Trembath, Sherbondy, Vandyke, Shaw, Todoroff, Lammer, et al., 1999; Watkins, 1998).

Since the early 1980s, the applications of new molecular biological approaches to the fundamental questions of ontogenesis has improved our understanding of embryology. The programming of the central nervous system is now known to involve a process of induction, and central nervous system maturation has been defined in terms of genetic, molecular, autocrine, paracrine, and endocrine influences. In addition, several receptors, signaling molecules, and genes have been identified. Furthermore, it is now documented that the same genetic transcripts that play a crucial role in fetal development also maintain the different types of neurons (i.e., brain cells) in the adult brain (Morrison, 2001; Nieto, Schuurmans, Britz, & Guillemot, 2001; Sarnat, 1998). The integration of previous embryological knowledge with this new molecular information provides a clearer understanding not only of maturational changes that occur in brain development, but also of how and why such changes take place (Sanes, Reh, & Harris, 2000).

As an example of this new knowledge, a number of syndromes thought to involve complex chromosomal abnormalities have been found instead to be caused by single gene mutations involving induction. Rubinstein-Taybi syndrome, a disorder marked clinically by broad thumbs and toes, characteristic faces, and mental retardation, has been shown to result from a mutation in the gene encoding for the transcriptional co-activator CREB-binding protein (CBP), an important factor in controlling gene expression during early embryogenesis (Kaufmann & Worley, 1999; Petrij, Giles, Dauwerse, Saris, Hennekam, Masuno, et al., 1995).

As scientists learn more about the way the brain develops and how genetic/environmental influences affect its normal development, a window of opportunity opens for using new technology to understand the ontogeny of intellectual and developmental disabilities. From this technology may come new strategies for prevention and treatment. Goal A addresses this opportunity. We propose 16 specific recommendations to support this goal. These are divided below into recommendations regarding neurobiological, genetic, and environmental factors.

Specific Issues and Recommendations: Neurobiological Factors

1. The innovative technologies involved in genomics, proteomics, and bioinformatics have great potential to inform basic knowledge about the underlying causes of intellectual and developmental disabilities.

    Recommendation. Establish a national data warehouse and tissue bank on normal and abnormal tissue, mRNA, DNA, and proteins relevant to intellectual and developmental disabilities, and support research efforts using these tools.

2. New methods in cellular imaging, gene expression tracing, and cell manipulation have given us a clearer picture of how the human brain is constituted from conception to early childhood. Studies of the specific stimuli that sustain brain development can help us understand how genes, environment, and/or drugs can modify the brain and help us develop specific therapies to correct mechanisms that may not be working properly. For example, glial cells may represent as much as 90% of the cells in the human brain, yet their roles and functions are poorly understood.

    Recommendation. Create a research initiative to determine the roles played by various neural cells in the expression of intellectual and developmental disabilities.

3. Stem cell research provides a new methodology to uncover genetic and cellular processes in nervous system development. Such work has already identified differential gene expression in Down syndrome nerve cells (Bahn, Mimmack, Ryan, Caldwell, Jauniaux, Starkey, et al., 2002). This research has therapeutic implications, since stem cells ultimately may provide the means to correct aberrant cellular and metabolic processes that cause intellectual and developmental disabilities.

    Recommendation. Create research initiatives on embryogenesis and early neural development of specific disorders (e.g., fragile X syndrome) using stem cell methodologies.

4. Traumatic brain injury, through intentional or unintentional injury to the susceptible brain, is a significant cause of disabilities in childhood. It is now clear that, in addition to physical trauma, excitotoxicity plays a major role. Understanding the cellular mechanisms of traumatic brain injury may inform diagnosis and treatment. This work may also impact on hypoxic/ischemic brain injury in premature infants.

    Recommendation. Increase funding for clinical and basic science research into acquired brain injury in childhood.

5. Evidence reveals that alterations in metabolic processes—for example, energy metabolism and oxidative stress—play a significant role in cognitive development as well as in cognitive deterioration during aging in some persons with intellectual disabilities (e.g., Down syndrome). These metabolic processes influence cell processes, such as cell signaling, gene expression, apoptosis (programmed cell death), and susceptibility to environmental insults.

   Recommendation. Continually pursue efforts to apply therapeutic interventions to these processes.

Specific Issues and Recommendations: Genetic Factors

6. Single gene disorders (e.g., fragile X syndrome) provide an ideal starting place for better understanding of brain function and the role of genes.

   Recommendation. Enhance supports for the study of single gene disorders associated with intellectual disabilities.

7. Many disorders causing intellectual and developmental disabilities represent contiguous gene disorders or disorders that involve alterations in multiple genes. New methodologies, such as the use of fluorescent in situ hybridization (FISH) and single nucleotide polymorphisms (SNPs), offer the opportunity to explore these conditions.

   Recommendation. Support the planned haplotype program that will identify the complete complement of SNPs in the human genome.

8. Epigenetics (the study of the impact of environment on gene regulation) has emerged as an important field for understanding a number of disorders, including Rett syndrome, Prader-Willi/Angelman syndromes, and possibly autism.

   Recommendation. Investigate this phenomenon, since it may lead to innovative treatment approaches involving environmental/nutritional manipulation. Studying these models also will improve our understanding of how genes are turned on and off during the life cycle.

9. Some developmental disabilities occur disproportionately in one sex or the other (e.g., autism), yet the mechanisms responsible for these effects are unclear. In addition, the phenotypic characteristics of some developmental disabilities appear to vary with the sex of the affected person.

   Recommendation. Determine the roles played by sex chromosomes and hormones on brain and behavioral development and on mechanisms of differential expression of disabilities among males and females.

10. Genetically engineered mouse models (e.g., transgenic, knock-in, knock-out) represent an important tool for understanding the effects of genetic disorders and for creating potential treatments for a wide range of disorders.

    Recommendation. Expand support for the creation of genetically engineered mouse models of specific disorders (e.g., Prader-Willi syndrome, DiGeorge syndrome, Williams syndrome) as well as for sharing and distributing existing and new animals across labs.

Specific Issues and Recommendations: Environmental Factors

11. Some intellectual and developmental disabilities may result from the interaction of a "triggering event" (e.g., a toxin) with a genetic vulnerability.

    Recommendation. Accelerate animal models and human research on the impact of environmental toxins, substance abuse, viruses, prematurity, low birth weight, diet, and hypoxia on early brain development and maintenance of brain function. Research should particularly emphasize the identification of genetically vulnerable groups. We also recommend support for the proposed National Children's Study (a longitudinal study of environmental effects on child health and human development of 100,000 participants). This study will take a major step toward answering questions about these issues.

12. Behavior and development result from complex gene-brain-environment interactions over time.

    Recommendation. Support longitudinal bio-behavioral studies that combine measures of brain functioning, gene expression, and behavior in humans and in animal models of specific disorders (e.g., fragile X syndrome, Down syndrome).

13. New methods in cellular imaging, gene expression tracing, and cell manipulation have given us a clearer picture of how the human brain is constituted from conception to early childhood.

    Recommendation. Support studies of the specific stimuli that sustain brain development. These studies can help us understand how genes, environment, and drugs can modify the brain and aid in the development of specific therapies to correct mechanisms that may not be working properly.

14. Recent work has shown that experiences (e.g., activity, learning, sensory experiences) influence the developing nervous system at the level of genes, nerve cell structure, and interaction.

    Recommendation. Study experience-dependent nervous system development to help inform educational and environmental interventions for therapy. Neurobehavioral studies need to clarify these issues.

15. Many intellectual and developmental disabilities share intriguing areas of overlapping etiology that may hold a key to better understanding the nature of such disorders.

    Recommendation. Support research aimed at understanding the extent of, and reason for, areas of overlapping etiology shared by two or more specific disabilities (e.g., autism and fragile X syndrome).

16. It is clear that environmental factors in the mother can influence the fetus in many ways and cause developmental disabilities. These environmental factors include maternal exposure to infectious agents (e.g., HIV, bacterial infections), alcohol and other drugs of abuse (e.g., cocaine), and pharmaceutical agents (e.g., valproate, retinoic acid).

    Recommendation. Continue pharmacogenetic studies—studies of individual genetic variation in the way people metabolize medications—to understand why certain women have increased susceptibility to these agents and to develop prevention strategies.

National Goal B: To use new research on screening and diagnosis of intellectual and developmental disabilities to maximize opportunities for effective prevention and intervention

Early intervention for children at risk for intellectual and developmental disabilities to optimize long-term outcomes is an important goal. Its success depends, in part, upon identifying these conditions as early as possible. In turn, early identification requires effective population screening methodologies and improved diagnostic capabilities. To both prevent and lessen the effects of developmental disabilities, researchers must develop new, emerging screening and diagnosis techniques and medical personnel must implement them.

The era of universal newborn screening was launched in the 1960s with the Guthrie test to detect elevated phenylalanine levels in spots of blood obtained before babies went home from the nursery (Guthrie & Susi, 1963). For the first time, doctors could accurately identify a metabolic disorder (e.g., phenylketonuria) with a consistent outcome of mental retardation before signs and symptoms of harm appeared; thus, they could intervene early and effectively with an elimination diet. Subsequent follow-up studies confirmed that this intervention prevented mental retardation (Dobson, Williamson, Azen, & Koch, 1977). Since this breakthrough, newborn screening has detected, and thus prevented or ameliorated, an increasing number of other conditions causing intellectual disabilities (e.g., congenital hypothyroidism, galactosemia, homocystinuria) (O'Brien & McCabe, 1981).

Technologies currently being developed will allow the simultaneous identification of hundreds of adverse conditions from small amounts of newborn blood. The ethical, population-wide application of these techniques, with their incredibly increased diagnostic capabilities, is a complex topic requiring multidisciplinary consideration. Although countless families and individuals already have benefited from mandated newborn screening programs, what should be the response to the possibility of identifying serious conditions early if no effective intervention currently exists?

Even prior to broad newborn screening, prenatal diagnosis and treatment opportunities, such as improved radiographic and laboratory techniques, will provide increasing diagnostic accuracy for concerned parents. Likewise, fetal medical and surgical interventions will be available to ameliorate a growing number of conditions associated with intellectual and developmental disabilities.

The ability to determine a specific etiologic diagnosis for children with intellectual disabilities has increased with improved clinical, neuroimaging, biochemical, cytogenetic, and molecular approaches (Shevell, Ashwal, Donley, Flint Gingold, Hirtz, et al., 2003). Nevertheless, in a substantial number of cases, no unifying diagnosis can be made, even following extensive evaluation. This is unfortunate for a number of reasons. First, parents may desperately search for a genetic cause of their child's disabilities so they can better understand the condition and stop blaming themselves or others for the disability. Second, a specific diagnosis often leads to clearer recognition of associated health, developmental, and behavioral problems. Finally, accurate diagnosis creates the possibility of preventing recurrences.

For these reasons, the need will continue for improved, accessible postnatal diagnosis of disorders that may lead to intellectual and developmental disabilities, as will the need to improve the diagnostic specificity for developmental-behavioral disorders such as autism, ADHD, and other learning disorders. These prevalent developmental-behavioral diagnoses are all currently defined by ever-broadening spectrums of dysfunction that threaten to dilute the original intent of these concepts. The development of precise biological markers for these disorders will be a major contribution to our understanding of their prevalence, epidemiology, natural history, and treatment. It should also create the opportunity for much earlier identification and intervention.

Widespread application of routine, periodic developmental screening for developmental delay in primary child health care remains an elusive goal (Bennett, Nickel, Squires, & Woodward, 1997). Even though screening recommendations have been published for more than 35 years, the continued lack of reliable, valid, and practical developmental and behavioral screening instruments has been a major barrier to their implementation. Providers may miss important opportunities for the early identification and diagnostic assessment of children with globally delayed development. Similarly, timely ameliorative intervention opportunities may be lost. After all these years, researchers are still searching for more "user-friendly" tools that will be consistently employed in a variety of community settings.

At this time, screening, diagnostic, and treatment capabilities are expanding. The approach to conditions associated with intellectual and developmental disabilities will become more precise prenatally, neonatally, and postnatally. Goal B addresses these opportunities with seven specific recommendations.

Specific Issues and Recommendations

1. Tandem mass spectrometry and microchip assays provide for the possibility of newborn screening for hundreds of conditions simultaneously from cord or newborn blood spots. These technologies, combined with new knowledge in genomics and proteomics, will allow for enhanced identification of newborns with conditions associated with developmental disabilities.

   Recommendation. Further develop and test emerging technologies to determine their feasibility, social acceptance, yield, and cost-effectiveness to substantially increase the number of conditions routinely screened for in newborns. At the same time, comprehensively address bioethical issues associated with screening efforts for conditions for which no known cure exists.

2. Enhanced newborn screening capabilities will provide the basis for expanded research on the early development and treatment of specific disorders (e.g., fragile X and other X-linked disorders).

   Recommendation. Support research on the early development and treatment of specific disorders that can be identified as a result of expanded newborn screening capabilities.

3. There is increasing potential for fetal therapies to prevent or ameliorate conditions associated with developmental disabilities (e.g., disorders of the aorta associated with Down syndrome).

Recommendation. Accelerate research to promote earlier, safer, and more reliable prenatal diagnosis and treatment.

4. The specific etiology of many intellectual and developmental disabilities remains unclear.

   Recommendation. Accelerate research in improved cytogenetic and molecular techniques for postnatal diagnosis of intellectual and developmental disabilities.

5. Lack of clear biological markers for many common developmental disorders (e.g., ADHD, autism, learning disabilities) continues to undermine the reliability of early screening and diagnosis.

   Recommendation. Further enhance research to identify biological markers for these disorders.

6. Lack of reliable and valid developmental and behavioral screening tools remains a major hurdle to the early identification of children with developmental delay.

   Recommendation. Expand research to develop practical screening tools for use in a variety of community settings (e.g., primary care, child care, school).

7. Population-based newborn and developmental screening will provide new collaborative epidemiological research opportunities.

   Recommendation. Establish a national and international epidemiologic database on developmental disabilities to foster collaborative research on the causes and treatments of these disorders.

National Goal C: To use new genetic, pharmacological, metabolic, bioengineering, behavioral, and educational approaches to treat or cure intellectual and developmental disabilities throughout the life-span

We are in an age in which molecular interventions for genetic conditions can help fulfill the promise of the human genome project. As human and other animal genomes have been sequenced, scientists are beginning to understand the functions of the estimated 10,000 plus genes that impact the brain and the nature of the mutations in these genes. Hundreds of molecular intervention studies or gene therapy trials have taken place, some demonstrating sustained corrections, such as X-linked severe combined immunodeficiency with *ex vivo* gene therapy (Hacein-Bey-Abina, Le Deist, Carlier, Bouneaud, Hue, De Villartay, et al., 2002). However, serious side effects have plagued many of these efforts. A particularly challenging task is placing the corrected gene or protein into the neurons of the central nervous system.

Nevertheless, scientists are making progress, and efforts will continue until they yield consistent success (Pfeifer & Verma, 2001). Research is progressing in fetal gene therapy, in which molecular lesions are corrected in utero, a process that has the potential to completely eliminate cognitive deficits as the brain is developing (Tarantal, O'Rourke, Case, Newbound, Li, Lee, et al., 2001). Gene transfer in immunologically immature fetuses also has the benefit of avoiding the cellular immune responses that can shorten the effectiveness of treatment. Further research in gene therapy and protein replacement trials is essential; it holds the promise of ultimately curing or ameliorating many intellectual and developmental disabilities.

Stem cell research has made remarkable gains in the last few years. Stem cells have been harvested from several tissues and can give rise to differentiated cells of tissues and organs unlike those in which they reside. For example, it is possible to harvest neural stem cells from bone marrow, and neural stem cells can be converted into blood cells (Vescovi, Galli, & Gritti, 2001). Stem cell populations expand remarkably with the use of growth factors and can subsequently differentiate into neurons or glial cells. Stem cells also have the ability to go to damaged areas of the brain for regenerative purposes. Stem cell therapy research holds enormous promise for the treatment of developmental disorders, and research in this area must be supported (Weissman, Anderson, & Gage, 2001).

Molecular research advances have led to a greater understanding of pharmacogenomics, the study of individual genetic variation in the way people metabolize medications. Research in this area will lead to the ability to find the most efficacious drug with the fewest side effects for each individual (Weinshilboum, 2003). Molecular pharming, the use of genetically modified plants and animals as vehicles for producing valuable proteins, will also expand with research and provide the proteins needed for therapy (Worton, 2001).

A remarkable secondary gain of molecular studies is the discovery of commonality in the pathways of protein-protein subcellular interactions. For instance, some of the X-linked mental retardation-related proteins interact significantly, either directly or indirectly, with the FMR1 protein that is deficient in those with fragile X syndrome (Bardoni, Castets, Huot, Schenck, Adinolfi, Corbin, et al, 2002). Downstream effects of a mutation may also lead to new possibilities of pharmacological interventions, such as the reduction of AMPA receptors in some types of autism and in fragile X syndrome. Development of medications that directly affect cognition by enhancing long-term potentiation (LTP) or alleviating long-term depression (LTD) via glutamate pathways are a result of the impact of neurobiology and molecular genetics on pharmacology. New experimental ampakine medications, which may enhance excitatory communication in the brain leading to improved memory and learning, now are being studied in autism and fragile X syndrome and hold the promise of not only ameliorating developmental disorders, but also enhancing memory in aging individuals.

Scientists are also realizing that so-called "single gene disorders" may actually involve many genes, particularly if the missing protein impacts other genes, proteins, or messages in a central way. The MECP2 gene (deficient in patients with Rhett syndrome), for example, is involved in silencing multiple genes. The treatment of Rhett syndrome, fragile X syndrome, and other single gene disorders may be far more complicated than originally expected because many gene systems are involved. Genomics—research into these complicated gene system interactions—will lead to better treatments.

In the past, simple interventions, such as dietary restrictions of phenylalanine in individuals with phenylketonuria (PKU), have led to the prevention of mental retardation. Research into molecular pathways hopefully will lead to new keys to interventions that may be more feasible to implement. More complicated dietary interventions, such as the ketogenic diet for those with poorly controlled epilepsy, also require further research.

The molecular age also has brought a renewed appreciation for the effects of environment on gene expression and brain development. Animal studies have shown that rats affected by fetal alcohol syndrome can have remarkable improvements in brain structure with an intensive trial of motor therapy that stimulates new synaptic connections between neurons (Klintsova, Goodlett, & Greenough, 2000). Animal studies allow researchers to look directly at the effects of various types of treatment on the brain; these studies are particularly important in gene therapy and molecular intervention research.

Although the promise of molecular intervention and stem cell therapy could eventually lead to cures for many disorders associated with intellectual and developmental disabilities, many of the medications available today have not been studied in individuals with these disabilities, particularly in aging patients. For researchers to find out if these medications will help this population, individuals with intellectual and developmental disabilities will have to take part in controlled trials of new pharmacological agents. The recently published controlled trial of risperidone in children with autism (McCracken & RUPP, 2002), one of the few examples of such research, has had a remarkable effect on clinical practice. In clinical work, multiple interventions are carried out at once. Studies need to examine how combined therapies, such as behavioral interventions in addition to medication, can work together to produce a desired effect.

With new imaging techniques, such as functional magnetic resonance imaging (FMRI), magnetic resonance spectroscopy (MRS), and positron emission tomography (PET) scanning, the methodologies now exist to actively study the effects of interventions on the brain. In addition, electrophysiological techniques, such as event-related potentials (ERP), can be performed on infants or even in utero. The use of these techniques in treatment studies is just beginning and must be expanded to better assess the efficacy of our interventions (Strauss, Unis, Cowan, Dawson, & Dager, 2002).

The focus of many treatment studies is medication, but other treatments are extremely important for individuals with intellectual and developmental disabilities. Well-controlled trials of multi-component treatments are needed, particularly in motor, language, behavioral, and educational interventions. These trials are important not only in childhood, but throughout the life-span. Adults and aging individuals are often excluded from intervention trials, but treatment can have a sustained effect on vocational abilities and mental and physical health throughout the life-span. The use of computer technology, for instance, has been remarkable in the augmentative communication field, but it can also improve the abilities of those with developmental disabilities in the areas of learning, literacy, academics, vocation, and even behavior (Hagerman, 1999). Because stakeholders are just beginning to appreciate the therapeutic potential of computer technology, researchers must expand this area of inquiry.

Goal C addresses these and related issues through 15 specific recommendations. These recommendations are organized into four groups: molecular genetics, pharmacology and nutrition, behavior and education, and integration of technologies.

Specific Issues and Recommendations: Molecular Genetics

1. Molecular genetic interventions hold great potential for preventing and treating developmental disabilities.

   Recommendation. Pursue both gene and protein therapy for genetic disorders.

2. As the functions and actions of specific genes become clear, scientists will become more aware of commonalities in molecular dysfunction causing a variety of intellectual and developmental disabilities.

    Recommendation. Accelerate studies that investigate mechanisms and commonalities of gene action and ways to modify these actions for therapeutic purposes.

3. Intriguing evidence shows that the environment affects specific gene expression in animals and humans.

    Recommendation. Support an expanded agenda of basic and applied research on how environmental effects and interventions alter gene expression and how this impacts development and behavior.

4. Growth factors play an important role in cell development and functioning that may have implications for developmental disabilities.

    Recommendation. Expand research on the neuroprotective effects of growth factors, or neuropeptides, on cellular developments and other aspects of neurobiology.

5. Stem cells may have unique potential for both primary and secondary prevention and treatment of intellectual and developmental disabilities.

    Recommendation. Accelerate research initiatives on potential stem cell therapies for developmental disabilities.

Specific Issues and Recommendations: Pharmacology and Nutrition

6. Many pharmacological agents, although routinely used, have never been appropriately tested in individuals with developmental disabilities.

    Recommendation. Support controlled trials of currently available pharmacological agents to prevent or treat medical and mental health problems associated with specific intellectual and developmental disabilities.

7. New pharmacological agents hold the potential for mitigating many primary and secondary effects associated with developmental disabilities.

    Recommendation. Support the development and testing of new pharmacological agents aimed at enhancing memory, cognition, language, emotion, and behavior throughout the life-span.

8. Nutritional and metabolic interventions, including specific vitamins, have been shown to ameliorate some intellectual and developmental disabilities.

    Recommendation. Support an expanded research agenda focusing on the impact of nutritional supplements on the development of specific disorders and the remediation of some or all of the primary and secondary conditions associated with these disorders.

Specific Issues and Recommendations: Behavior and Education

9. Despite the long-acknowledged potential of early intervention and later school-based treatment to prevent or minimize the effects of intellectual and developmental disabilities, few well-controlled clinical trials have been conducted to test promising approaches.

Recommendation. Support clinical trials and longitudinal follow-up of early family-based and environmental interventions on the development and behavior of infants and children at risk for developmental disabilities. Support and expand well-controlled trials of school-based treatments using a variety of approaches, including speech and language, occupational therapy, physical therapy, psychological, and educational interventions.

10. Behavioral and psychiatric disorders are still the primary limiting aspects of daily functioning for many individuals with intellectual and developmental disabilities. Few well-validated diagnostic instruments exist for mental health disorders in people with developmental disabilities.

    Recommendation. Expand well-designed basic and clinical research on diagnosis and the use of new technologies to treat these problems at whatever point they occur in the life-span.

11. Biotechnology holds promise for substantially enhancing development in a number of domains.

    Recommendation. Expand the use of biotechnology, including computers, to improve cognition, sensory, motor, learning, language, vocational, and adaptive skills, in individuals with intellectual and developmental disabilities.

Specific Issues and Recommendations: Integration of Technologies

12. New brain imaging technologies hold great promise for knowledge of brain functioning.

    Recommendation. Support research on the use of imaging and electrophysiological technologies (e.g., FMRI, Magnetoencephalography (MEG), ERP, PET scan) to guide and evaluate the effects of interventions.

13. Multiple interventions are often used simultaneously in individuals with intellectual and developmental disabilities.

    Recommendation. Expand research on the synergistic effects of two or more simultaneous treatments in individuals with developmental disabilities.

14. Advances in the knowledge base of early development provide the basis for ameliorating various abnormalities before they precipitate disabling conditions.

    Recommendation. Support the development of therapies to ameliorate identified abnormalities (or the risk of such abnormalities) prior to conception, in utero, and in early childhood.

15. All too often consumers and family members have no voice in how studies are designed and conducted.

    Recommendation. Engage consumers and family members in the design, ethical issues, informed consent, implementation, and evaluation of interventions.

National Goal D: To provide new screening, diagnosis, and treatment approaches without disparities in access or quality for individuals with intellectual and developmental disabilities throughout the life-span

As evident in the discussion of national goals A through C, many of the causes of intellectual and developmental disabilities remain poorly understood. Moreover, many challenges remain in developing effective screening, diagnosis, and treatment for many developmental disorders. In addition to such challenges in knowledge and practice, fundamental problems affecting individuals with developmental disabilities and their families include the following:

- Difficulties and delays in obtaining accurate diagnoses
- Limited access to preventive interventions and effective treatments
- Differential patterns of age-related health problems relative to the general population
- Risk of secondary conditions
- Barriers to accessing high-quality health care services

These difficulties result in a pattern of health disparities for persons with intellectual and developmental disabilities that may derive from individual characteristics, such as race, gender, and socioeconomic status, as well as policy considerations, such as state-to-state variation in eligibility for services.

In the United States, 85% of individuals with serious intellectual and developmental disabilities of all ages live with family members, as compared with 41% in the general population (Larson, Lakin, Anderson, & Kwak, 2001). Thus, in most cases, parents (and at later stages of the life-span, adult siblings) serve as the intermediators between individuals with developmental disabilities and the diagnostic and health care systems.

Parents of children with intellectual and developmental disabilities often experience a "diagnostic odyssey" in their attempts to identify the cause of their child's delayed development. Whereas some causes of developmental disorders are diagnosed easily at birth (e.g., Down syndrome), in other disorders, especially rare disorders or those with only behavioral diagnostic markers (e.g., autism), it may take years to obtain an accurate diagnosis. This is particularly problematic in geographic areas not served by a major medical center and where expertise in developmental disabilities may be lacking.

Much remains unknown about the effectiveness of treatments and preventive interventions for individuals with intellectual and developmental disabilities. However, even in instances in which good data are available regarding effective treatments, access to such interventions remains uneven. For example, a recent National Research Council report concluded that solid evidence proves the effectiveness of early intensive intervention services for children with autism spectrum disorders (Lord & McGee, 2001). However, few young children with autism have access to the recommended level of 25 hours per week of intervention, 12 months per year. The report also documented the uneven implementation of early intervention and other state-of-the-art services for children with autism, due in part to intrastate and interstate variation in funding levels and adherence to federal policies.

Research has documented that many people with developmental disabilities have complex health care needs that are often addressed inadequately (Horwitz, Kerker, Owens, & Zigler, 2000). Indeed, although the life expectancy of individuals with moderate to severe mental retardation is now nearly 20 years longer than it was as recently as 1970 (Braddock, 1999), it is still an average of 10 to 20 years shorter than that of the general population (Janicki, Dalton, Henderson, & Davidson, 1999). Those with severe or profound mental retardation and those with Down syndrome have a shorter average life expectancy than those with mild or moderate mental retardation and those whose retardation is due to conditions other than Down syndrome.

Longer life expectancy brings increased risk of age-related health conditions experienced by the general population. However, basic information is lacking on how the phenotypes of various conditions may change across the life-span, particularly with respect to distinct patterns of vulnerability (and resilience) to age-related health conditions. Researchers have reason to expect such differences because of the known neurological, endocrine, and metabolic disorders associated with intellectual and developmental disabilities that can affect multiple organ systems across the life-span (Kapell, Nightingale, Rodriguez, Lee, Zigman, & Schupf, 1998).

Among developmental disorders, scientists and professionals know the most about individuals with Down syndrome. Individuals with this disorder are also at risk for elevated rates of respiratory and cardiac conditions (Kapell, et al., 1998), leukemia (Hasle, Clemmensen, & Mikkelsen, 2000), obesity (Fujiura, Fitzsimons, Marks, & Chicoine, 1997), thyroid disease (Pueschel, 1990), orthopedic anomalies (Pueschel, 1998), depression (Burt & Alyward, 1999), and dementia (Zigman, Schupf, Sersen, & Silverman, 1996). However, they have lower rates of solid tumors (Hasle, et al., 2000) than individuals with other types of mental retardation and lower rates of hypertension than the general population (Kapell, et al., 1998). Women with Down syndrome and fragile X syndrome have earlier onset of menopause than women in the general population (Walsh, Heller, Schupf, & Lantman-de Valk, 2000).

Experts know much less about the age-related health problems and health care needs of individuals with other intellectual and developmental disabilities; determining these needs should be a high research priority. Evidence has revealed later-life complications suffered by individuals with neural tube defects, such as shunt failure and neurogenic scoliosis (Henderson, 2002). Adults with Williams syndrome have smaller brains and show age-associated declines in episodic and working memory starting around age 50 (Brown, 2002). Because of prolonged use of anticonvulsant medications, the bones of people with epilepsy lose mineral content. These people can also experience functional and cognitive declines due to intractable seizures (Henderson, 2002). Research is needed on the way that PKU manifests itself over a lifetime, especially as the person ages (NIH Consensus Statement, 2001).

On the other hand, evidence shows an abatement of some of the symptoms of autism in adulthood as compared with childhood (Seltzer, Krauss, Shattuck, Orsmond, Swe, & Lord, 2003). Unlike the knowledge base about the life-span manifestations of Down syndrome, few studies support these indications of the age-related course of other specific disorders. Those that do exist often used small and nonrepresentative samples; thus, a great deal more research is necessary.

Persons with developmental disabilities also are at increased risk for preventable health problems and death due to poor health behaviors. Many adults with intellectual and developmental disabilities lack preventive health care, particularly those living alone or with family (Lewis, Lewis, Leake, King, & Lindemann, 2002). Evidence also shows poorer levels of physical fitness as compared with the general population (Pitetti &

Campbell, 1991) and, among residents of group homes, elevated rates of smoking (Rimmer, Braddock, & Fujiura, 1994). Rates of death due to unintentional injury are higher than in the population at large (Baird & Sadovnick, 1988; Dupont, Vaeth, & Videveck, 1987).

Although only a few studies have addressed access to health care and health care use by persons with developmental disabilities, the available evidence suggests that such individuals have less access and experience more barriers than the general population. Barriers include reliance on Medicaid and managed care with inadequate levels of reimbursement, difficulties in recognizing and reporting health problems that need care and in adhering to prescribed medical regimens, and inadequately trained health care professionals. They also lack continuity of care, because this population more often has no regular source of care (Horowitz, Kerker, Owens, & Zigler, 2000; Walsh & Kastner, 1999).

In addition to the barriers to health care experienced by all persons with disabilities, evidence shows increased health disparities associated with race, poverty, and socioeconomic status. Within the population with developmental disabilities, nonwhite persons have substantially lower life expectancies than whites (Skinner, 2002). Fujiura's (2000) research has demonstrated, however, that although people with disabilities experience racial and ethnic disparities in access to health care services, it is the poverty associated with race and ethnicity that has the greatest effect. Indeed, people living below the poverty line show an 86% increase in the risk of all types of disability, including intellectual and developmental disabilities.

In summary, researchers must ensure that the knowledge base about the causes of intellectual and developmental disabilities and knowledge about screening, diagnosis, and treatment approaches is translated into improved care without disparities for people throughout the life-span. Goal D addresses this need through 12 specific recommendations.

Specific Issues and Recommendations

1. Evidence shows that individuals with developmental disabilities have more limited access to high-quality medical care and treatment options than the general population.

   Recommendation. Support research to determine the causes of health disparities across specific developmental disabilities and within subgroups of this population to develop mechanisms for addressing current gaps and disparities.

2. The differential rates of intellectual and developmental disabilities across and within states may contribute to health disparities and raise important questions about the definitions, causes, and effects of such disorders.

   Recommendation. Establish common definitional and diagnostic standards to enhance uniform access to treatments and services.

3. If the National Institutes of Health began to require the inclusion of individuals with intellectual and developmental disabilities in clinical trials, this action could have a very positive impact on the health care and treatment of these individuals. The NIH should exclude individuals with developmental disabilities only when a strong clinical and/or scientific rationale exists.

   Recommendation. The NIH should consider requiring that all clinical research includes individuals with developmental disabilities, just as it currently requires the inclusion of children, women, and minorities, unless a valid clinical or scientific reason exists for their specific exclusion.

4. Developmental disabilities are often accompanied by potentially devastating secondary conditions (e.g., violent behavior, communication deficits, depression, mood disorders, chronic pain) that may complicate diagnosis and intervention and compromise health, learning, and overall quality of life.

    Recommendation. Expand research on the prevalence, neurobiology, and course of secondary impairments associated with intellectual and developmental disabilities to develop effective treatments and services.

5. Little research addresses the role of gender in developmental disabilities, despite evidence of gender effects associated with a variety of specific disorders.

    Recommendation. Expand research on differential causes, diagnosis, and treatment of developmental disabilities in females and males.

6. The role of ethnicity and minority status in research on intellectual and developmental disabilities is unclear. Some disorders are associated with population subgroups for genetic reasons (e.g., Tay-Sachs). In other cases, overrepresentation or underrepresentation may result from diagnostic bias and/or differential exposure to environmental risk and toxins (e.g., mild mental retardation).

    Recommendation. Support research on differential causes, diagnosis, and treatment of intellectual and developmental disabilities in individuals from distinct ethnic groups and underrepresented minority groups.

7. Little longitudinal research explores how the phenotypes associated with specific developmental disabilities may change across the life-span, particularly during old age.

    Recommendation. Support research on the life course trajectories of the phenotypes of specific intellectual and developmental disabilities (e.g., autism, fragile X syndrome, Williams syndrome).

8. Individuals with developmental disabilities now generally live far longer than they did just 30 years ago. Scientists know very little about the occurrence of age-related conditions (e.g., Alzheimer's disease, cardiovascular disease, obesity, diabetes, cancer) for these individuals.

    Recommendation. Support multimodal longitudinal research on the occurrence, course, and treatment of such conditions associated with specific intellectual and developmental disabilities.

9. There is often a long lag between discoveries in the laboratory and their translation into clinical practice.

    Recommendation. Support research to identify effective incentives for researchers and practitioners to enhance the translation of research results into practice.

10. Research results often do not translate into practice because of caps on payments and reimbursements from private insurance carriers and federal and state agencies for clinical services to individuals with developmental disabilities.

    Recommendation. Support research to identify strategies for reducing these barriers to effective practice.

11. Individuals with intellectual and developmental disabilities and their families have an increasingly large role in coordinating the health care they now receive, but often lack the knowledge and connections necessary to handle the task well. **Recommendation.** Enhance the knowledge to which families and consumers have access, and foster better communication among health care professionals, therapists, educators, families, and consumers.

12. The rapid growth of knowledge about the genetic basis of specific intellectual and developmental disabilities poses substantial challenges for the delivery of high-quality health care as well as for the widespread implementation of screening, prevention, and treatment programs. However, knowledge of developmental disabilities among physicians and other health care personnel remains limited. **Recommendation.** Expand efforts to teach the clinical aspects of intellectual and developmental disabilities as a standard part of training for physicians, nurses, genetic counselors, and allied health professionals. Provide continuing education to the medical community to assure the availability of reliable, up-to-date treatment, information, and counseling.

Using Knowledge to Shape Our National Agenda
Will Achieving These Goals Really Make a Difference?

If researchers and health practitioners meet, or even partially achieve, the four national goals proposed, what tangible difference will this success make for individuals with intellectual and developmental disabilities and their families? We believe success in achieving these goals can lead to the following five broad benefits for these individuals, their families, and the larger society, each building on the ones before:

1. Improved clinical and therapeutic practices
2. Improved development, learning, health, and overall quality of life for these individuals
3. Enhanced quality of life for family members and other caregivers
4. Over time, less serious primary and secondary conditions for affected individuals
5. Fewer long-term costs for families and society at large

It is important to realize that progress in achieving these national goals will be uneven, particularly for some specific disabilities; that is, new knowledge and technology will surely impact some disabilities in major ways and lead to increasingly effective intervention and prevention, while progress will proceed more slowly for other disorders. We must remember that intellectual and developmental disabilities have hundreds of specific causes. Fortunately, progress in one disorder can often have unexpected benefits for other disorders that may result from similar causal mechanisms; thus, progress in treating Huntington's disease could have substantial implications for fragile X syndrome, because both conditions result from a similar genetic mechanism (i.e, triplet repeat expansion), although the genes themselves are different as are their effects.

This fact can also make it difficult to judge the relevance of different types of research to intellectual and developmental disabilities. Basic research on the genetic mechanisms conducted with relatively primitive organisms has already generated results of enormous relevance to human genetics. In sum, progress will continue along multiple paths, some of which may be short and straight, while many will be long, circuitous, and bumpy.

What Will It Take to Achieve These Goals?

To achieve these goals will require nothing more than endless amounts of patience and persistence combined with money, creativity, and serendipity. Of course, vision is essential, and leadership helps. More specifically, four conditions seem important. First, governments and foundations cannot avoid the necessity of providing substantial, long-term financial support. Private enterprise can also play an important role. The mapping of the human genome went much faster and at a lower cost than anticipated. An upstart company named Celera entered the contest with the claim that it could do the whole project in a fraction of the time and money it would take traditional research enterprises. Then Celera did just that. But more often than not, progress takes longer than expected. Scientists are a long way from solving the secrets of human biology. Fortunately, the enormous progress of the last 100 years suggests that they can solve them, at least eventually. But they clearly will need continuing support to do so.

Second, support for both basic and applied research needs to be complemented by support for "translational" research. Translational research focuses directly on the issue of how to turn knowledge generated in the lab, even in well-controlled clinical trials with humans, into actual, effective practice. Currently, the gap between what is possible and what can be realistically and routinely offered to individuals in clinical settings appears to be widening. Additional focus on, and support for, efforts aimed at bridging the bench-to-bedside gap could have a high payoff for enhanced health and well-being.

Third, the complexity inherent in many disorders makes it clear that substantial progress will ultimately depend on extraordinary levels of collaboration across disciplines. Incentives in support of this difficult work are necessary at many levels, and Ph.D. training programs in the behavioral and biological sciences need to focus more on preparing young scientists for this emerging model of science. Otherwise, progress in many complex disorders may be hampered by what is, in effect, a cultural problem—the inability of scientific teams to organize themselves and their rewards in ways that support high levels of collaboration and cooperation instead of competition and insulation.

Fourth, the National Institutes of Health could increase the relevance of much of their clinical research for individuals with intellectual and developmental disabilities by requiring their participation, except as justified by strong clinical or scientific reasons, as it has that of women, children, and minorities. This requirement could be a remarkably cost-effective way to spread the value of this clinical research to individuals who may benefit enormously from new therapies or be subject to problematic side effects not observed in the general population. This recommendation was offered in Goal D, but we restate it here because of the broad impact its implementation could potentially have on the prevention and treatment of intellectual and developmental disabilities.

Ensuring That Knowledge Informs Policy

Ensuring that knowledge generated by biomedical research on primary and secondary prevention informs policy requires the same actions as ensuring that biomedical research, in general, informs policy. Thus, the entire biomedical and behavioral research enterprise should make common effort in this cause. Three general recommendations apply to this endeavor. First, think of the impact that research in this area could have if the broad class of policy makers had to identify the empirical bases upon which health care policies and practices are based. As with education, this requirement would enable the human service system to more speedily apply new knowledge in practice and remove ineffective and unsound practices. Unfortunately, identifying the potential value of this collaboration and making it happen are two entirely different things.

Second, sustained, widespread efforts to translate research findings into everyday language and to make findings easily accessible to policy makers, practitioners, and the general public must remain a priority for the foreseeable future. This is difficult work since the complexity of science and technology is only increasing. Nevertheless, this translation can and must be done to ensure sustained support for this work. If biomedical science loses touch with those who make it possible through the provision of necessary resources, then its future will be tenuous at best.

Third, the general lack of understanding of the scientific method and how "progress" occurs may continue to hamper the potential impact of new scientific breakthroughs. Scientific advances often undermine older practices and beliefs. Consequently, what appears to be a "fact" today may be discarded knowledge tomorrow. Furthermore, the probabilistic nature of most scientific knowledge remains poorly understood in general and dissatisfies those who want sure answers. Ultimately these are problems the field of education must combat with a greater degree of scientific training in elementary and secondary schools.

Anticipating the Changes of the Future

This domain for biomedical research relevant to primary and secondary prevention is broad, and research is proceeding rapidly on many dimensions. Identifying emerging trends and concepts can be a hazardous undertaking because scientists temporarily can easily miss something important. Thus, we will limit our discussion to three very general areas of concern that could broadly impact the potential of biomedical research. Two of these could impact long-term funding and commitment for this research, and the third could be a potential wild card that might have either positive or negative effects or both.

The first area of concern is a potential backlash against biomedical research for ethical and/or cultural reasons. The present high-stakes debates over the future of therapeutic cloning and stem cell research are excellent examples. Both hold great promise for improving the treatment of many intellectual and developmental disabilities; yet each is the focus of a complicated and often misleading debate. For example, efforts to outlaw all forms of cloning have made inroads, in part, because of a lack of understanding of the differences between therapeutic and reproductive cloning. Very few scientists support reproductive human cloning. However, therapeutic cloning is an entirely different matter. Likewise, embryonic stem cells hold extraordinary potential both for gaining a greater understanding of how development occurs and for helping the body heal and recover from various insults and disorders.

Another likely debate on the horizon is whether or not medical personnel should routinely screen at birth (or before) for disorders for which no proven effective medical treatment exists. For example, at present no genetically based cure exists for fragile X syndrome. Nevertheless, doctors could screen for this disorder at birth and provide optimal early intervention, family support services, reproductive counseling, and health services, all of which could substantially improve the outcome for the children with fragile X and their families (Bailey, Skinner, & Warren, in press). Should this screening take place? This complicated debate and others (Alper, Ard, Asch, Beckwith, Conrad, & Gellar, 2002) no doubt lie directly ahead.

A second area of concern is the potential in the United States for increasing difficulties with the financing of health care that will lead to a functional rationing of such services. Although excellent health care services for those who can afford them may remain readily available, services for those who are uninsured, poor, or disabled could be increasingly difficult to obtain beyond a very basic level. Such health disparities were the focus of the 2002 Report of the Surgeon General's Conference on Health Disparities and Mental Retardation. Our concern about this is substantial enough to make it the subject of one of our four national goals.

Our final concern is one that could have both positive and negative results. Presumably in the near future, the rapid commercialization of genetic technologies will lead to individuals being able to discover their genetic propensities for a long list of disorders and diseases (Ard & Zucker, 2002). For example, if someone learns of a certain probability of developing some form of cancer, the person might be able to lower that probability through a lifestyle change (e.g., by avoiding certain foods or engaging in certain practices, or not). What effects will the availability of this knowledge have on society? Such knowledge could lead to improved quality of life for some people or to certain reproductive decisions for others. The point is that the availability of personal genomic knowledge ultimately could impact the way society views such information and, thus, the way it views biomedical research in primary and secondary prevention.

ENHANCING REAL LIVES

Let's get back to where we started—with Kevin, a 12-year-old boy with Down syndrome who, less than 50 years from now, could live a life we can only dream of today. Could this really happen? Absolutely. Will this happen, and will it happen broadly for individuals with intellectual and developmental disabilities due to a wide range of causes and consequences? That, of course, remains to be seen. But there is one thing we do know: it cannot happen unless we remain steadfast in our drive to achieve the four national goals proposed in this chapter.

CHAPTER 8

Employment and Productive Life Roles[1]

PAUL WEHMAN, DAVID MANK, PAT ROGAN, JOHN LUNA,
JOHN KREGEL, WILLIAM KIERNAN, CARY GRIFFIN, AND
COLLEEN THOMA
with
Paul Bates, Larry Burt, Michael Callahan, Robert Clabby,
Robin Cooper, Fred Dominguez, Robin Doyle, Dale Dutton,
Barbara LeRoy, Katherine McCary, Ken McGill, Allyson Merkle,
Liz Obermayer, Lorraine Sheehan, and Michael West

INTRODUCTION

In the early 1980s, initial published reports began to appear on supported employment as a means to assist people with significant disabilities to become competitively employed. In the past 20 years, we have learned a great deal about what does and does not work in promoting competitive employment outcomes (Mank, Cioffi, & Yovanoff, 1997, 2000; Wehman, 2001; Wehman, Revell, Brooke, & Inge, in press). We also know that competitive employment may not be for everyone in the traditional sense; that is, there are self-employment arrangements (e.g., Griffin & Hammis, 2003) that can be highly effective or a variety of customized employment alternatives that give greater control to the worker with disabilities to design his or her own job (Callahan, 2002).

With each of these alternatives, however, we have learned that there are many challenging implementation issues, as well as persistent philosophical differences, that have created major barriers to full implementation. We have seen more people leaving institutions (Hayden & Abery, 1994; Racino, 2002), the closing of state institutions (Stancliffe & Lakin, 1999), the downsizing of sheltered workshops, and the selective reallocation of funds targeted for segregated programs to integrated programs (Rogan, Held, & Rinne, 2001). Nonetheless, despite a more significant voice given to people with disabilities via the statutes and the advocacy movement (Wehmeyer & Lawrence, 1995; Wehmeyer, Gragoudas, & Shogren, in press), lack of person-centered planning approaches (Everson

1. This chapter was developed in conjunction with the Employment Team appointed by The Arc of the United States. It was partially supported by NIDRR Project # H133B9800036.

& Reid, 1999) and individual client control over resources continues to impede true freedom of choice. We have seen changes in the way that individuals with intellectual disabilities are classified by the American Association on Mental Retardation (Luckasson, Coulter, Polloway, Reiss, Schalock, Snell, et al., 1992; American Association on Mental Retardation, 2002). We are moving away from intelligent quotient labels derived from tests toward a description of the supports, in terms of both level and intensity, that are required by persons with intellectual disabilities (American Association on Mental Retardation, 2002).

The past two decades have seen programs that define themselves in a context of supports, including supported employment, demystify disability. Indeed, this is their greatest contribution (e.g., Smith, Spring 2002). Too often in our society, perceptions related to disability are immediately linked to descriptors such as handicapped, impaired, unable, dependent, and less qualified. The gift of supported employment, natural supports, workplace supports, and so on is that a focus is placed upon the *abilities* of individuals with disabilities to be valued and productive in the workplace. Individual employment in the community reduces the impact of disability, even if it is only during the eight hours that the individual is at work. Once that individual departs the workplace, she or he may well be forced into "reattaching" their physical disability or mental retardation label because needed supports are not present at home or in other places in the community (Smith, Spring 2002).

For example, consider Lisa, a woman with a significant intellectual disability and also a physical disability. Lisa has very limited speech and requires some personal assistance services throughout the day. When Lisa works in the electronics department at the Target department store placing security scanners on the CDs, she earns $8.40 an hour, receives health benefits, and participates in the profit sharing plan. With supports at work, Lisa reduces or neutralizes the effects of her disability label. In fact, she is not disabled at all during the work day. In the eyes of her coworkers and manager, she is not disabled; they depend on her to complete her work assignments. However, once her work shift ends, she is dependent on and at the mercy of the local transit system that serves people with physical disabilities. Once Lisa leaves Target, she must again "reattach" her label and be dependent. The more the concept of support can permeate not only the human service system, but also communities and society as a whole, the more individuals with disabilities will become infused into the mainstream of daily life in the community.

When we review the progress made in promoting quality employment and career advancement over the last two decades, we must always return to our core values. These core values have not only defined competitive employment, they have also created the substantial spillover effect of supports equaling reduction of disability. The concept of true independence rarely exists; we are all interdependent (Condeluci, 1991). We may all feel that we are completely independent at one time or another in our lives, but invariably we will need others to help combat the physical, emotional, and intellectual disabilities that crowd into our lives. Understanding that we are all interdependent helps pave the way for understanding the role and impact of supports in designing systems aimed at elevating people to a higher level of functioning.

The core values that permeate excellent competitive employment outcomes are inclusion; informed choice; a career path; parity in wages, hours of employment, and benefits; parity in work style options and choices; and the opportunity to be employed in the quickest, most efficient manner possible (Wehman, Revell, & Brooke, 2003). These core values are in stark opposition to the opportunities available to an individual with a significant disability who is limited to participating in segregated day programs and living in a nursing home or other congregate setting. The core values are critical as we move forward and provide a context for the goals in this chapter.

Current Status of Employment Outcomes for Persons With Intellectual Disabilities[2]

Unfortunately, as noted, many individuals with intellectual disabilities are either unemployed or "underemployed" in stereotypical jobs with low wages, no benefits, and no opportunity for career advancement. Many people with significant disabilities and high support needs are placed in "Special Minimum Wage" programs under § 14(c) of the Fair Labor Standard Act, earning less than minimum wage with little hope of advancing to competitive employment. McGaughey, Kiernan, McNally, Gilmore, and Keith (1994) reported that as few as 18% of all individuals with developmental disabilities in adult day programs were actually participating in integrated employment. This is despite growth of persons in supported employment from 9,800 in 1986 to 140,000 in 1995 (Wehman, Revell, & Kregel, 1998) and now over 300,000 (Braddock, Rizzolo, & Hemp, 2004).

A recent U.S. General Accounting Office report estimated that 424,000 employees are working under § 14(c), with approximately 95% of this number in sheltered workshops (2001). Both research and practice demonstrate that individuals who are viewed as "unemployable" can be successful in jobs earning minimum wage or above, that include benefits and opportunities for career advancement. However, the system remains virtually unchanged.

What Progress Has Been Made?

Customized employment strategies, such as supported employment, supported entrepreneurship, coworker supports, job restructuring, workplace accommodations, and federal legislation, have helped foster the integrated employment outcomes for persons with developmental disabilities. In addition, policy shifts have expanded opportunities for integrated employment (see Wehman, et al., in press).

The purpose of the Vocational Rehabilitation (VR) program as stated in the Rehabilitation Act of 1973, as amended, is to enable individuals with a disability to achieve employment in an integrated setting (Federal Register, 2001). In response to this priority, first highlighted in the 1992 amendments, the 1990s was marked by a decline in sheltered workshop placements. Nationally in the 1990 fiscal year (FY), VR agencies placed 11,605 individuals in sheltered workshops. In FY 1998, the number of sheltered workshop VR case closures dropped 34%. In contrast, the number of individuals "closed"

---

2. The authors acknowledge the effort of John Butterworth and Sheila Fesko in completing part of this section.

in integrated work settings rose steadily during the 1990s. VR closed approximately 9,528 individuals in supported employment in FY 1991, 13,950 individuals in FY 1994, and 23,056 individuals in FY 1998 (Gilmore & Butterworth, 2001).

Unfortunately, Gilmore and Butterworth (2001) found in the *same time period* that the number of individuals entering nonintegrated employment (including facility-based and nonwork) also greatly expanded. Despite the Americans with Disabilities Act (ADA) and other federal initiatives, competitive employment *still is not the first choice* for the majority of individuals with disabilities (Wehman, et al., 2003).

What Barriers Have Inhibited Change?

Some aspects of the adult disability service system have limited providers' success in evolving their programs from the past, when individuals with disabilities needed care, to the present, when individuals choose the needed supports to care for themselves. One example is § 14(c) of the Fair Labor Standards Act. This regulation allows employers to pay subminimum wages if the individual has a disability that limits productivity. Originally intended to create employment opportunities, § 14(c) has resulted in the perpetuation of poverty, reliance on public support, and segregation for workers with disabilities.

The U.S. General Accounting Office (GAO) reports that approximately 84% of the employers that pay special (sub)minimum wage are work centers established to provide employment supports and services to individuals with disabilities (2001). This report also finds that sheltered workshops hold up to 95% of title 14(c) certificates. Table 8-1 shows a breakdown by type of provider and the number of people served by these providers. Although segregated day services may be well-intentioned, they are inconsistent with the core values of community inclusion that underlie recent disability legislation (Wehman, 2001).

Table 8-1
Holders of Title 14c Certificates

Type of Employer	People		Centers	
	N	%	N	%
Work centers (sheltered workshops)	400,440	94.5	4,724	84.2
Businesses	1,549	0.4	506	9
Hospital or other residential care facilities	19,307	4.6	294	5.2
Schools	2,290	0.5	88	1.6

Recent studies conducted on title 14(c) certificate holders focused primarily on sheltered workshops, or facility-based work centers (e.g., Morris, Ritchie, & Clay, 2002). GAO reported that 46% of funding for these centers is from state and county agencies. Currently, state departments of mental retardation are major funders of these work centers (Gilmore & Butterworth, 2001).

Movement from Segregated to Integrated Employment Outcomes

Although it seems contradictory to highlight the growth of integrated employment and the policies that hinder it, this dichotomy pervades employment of people with disabilities. Mank (1994) refers to this as the "underachievement of supported employment." Increased wages are an important impetus for the movement from sheltered to integrated employment. The average wage for individuals closed in sheltered employment by VR in FY 1998 was $2.54 per hour and $64.51 per week. The corresponding wages for individuals closed by VR in supported employment during the same time period was $5.88 per hour and $142.93 per week. These wage differences are consistent across various disability groupings (Gilmore & Butterworth, 2001).

Over the last decade, the ADA has aided growth of competitive employment (Wehman, 1993, 2001). Based on this legislation, the Supreme Court upheld the Olmstead case (*Olmstead v. L.C., et al., 1999*; Legal Information Institute, 2002), a landmark community integration decision. However, the actual growth in competitive employment is relatively small compared to the array of nonintegrated programs serving people with disabilities. For example, Gilmore and Butterworth (2001) found that in FY 1999, state MR/DD agencies served just over 300,000 individuals in facility-based work and nonwork services, including 140,000 in sheltered workshops that did not involve any community-based services. This is corroborated by even larger numbers in the study by Braddock, et al. (2004).

Medicaid, a significant source of funds for state MR/DD agencies, has been changing its regulation to allow more people access to community employment through Home and Community Based (HCB) waiver funds. Gilmore and Butterworth (2001) found that over 40 states list supported employment as part of the range of services covered by the HCB waiver. However, West, Hill, Revell, Smith, Kregel, and Campbell (2002) reported that in FY 1999, only approximately 15% of the more than 130,000 on the waiver for day habilitation services participated in supported employment. The rest were in a variety of settings that were not work-focused and frequently not integrated.

National Goals for Employment and Productive Participation

The legislation governing and providing financing for services to persons with ID/DD in the United States lays out a very clear national commitment. This legislation directs those engaged in teaching and supporting persons with ID/DD to establish competitive, integrated employment opportunities that incorporate community businesses through public-private partnerships to provide the jobs, job training, wages, and benefits needed by individuals to establish and advance in careers of their own choosing that provide them with integrated and valued productive roles within our society. A few of the important pieces of legislation, which as a body articulate this national purpose, are noted below.

The Rehabilitation Act

The Rehabilitation Act (Rehab Act) of 1973 and subsequent amendments work cooperatively with local education authorities to serve youth with disabilities during their transition from secondary education to adult life; it is the primary employment support resource for adults with a disabilities. The Rehabilitation Act Amendments of 1998 provide federal dollars, matched by state dollars, to all 50 states to give people with disabilities the opportunity to obtain employment and independent living assistance as needed. The amendments also provide new opportunities for people with disabilities to gain access to vocational rehabilitation services and to choose the specific services needed for them to achieve their individualized employment goal. For example, the amendments require that a trial work experience in the most community-integrated setting possible be made available to certain individuals with significant disabilities to help identify the services and supports necessary for them to achieve an employment outcome. Also, recipients of vocational rehabilitation services have control over the contents of their individualized plans for employment (IPEs) and have information made available so they may make informed choices about specific services they will receive.

The Developmental Disabilities Assistance and Bill of Rights Act

In the Developmental Disabilities Assistance and Bill of Rights Act (DD Act) of 2000, Congress observed that national policy for people with disabilities should be characterized by independence, productivity, and integration. This built on the 1984 Amendment which for the first time has focused on employment as an important hallmark of ID/DD services.

The Americans With Disabilities Act

The intent of the ADA of 1990 is to end discrimination toward people with disabilities throughout society. ADA was a logical outgrowth of the DD Act and reflects the rights of persons with disabilities to be in the community. This act was followed exactly one year later by a comprehensive set of regulations that provided for accessibility, nondiscrimination, and greater access to workplaces, community facilities, public transportation, and telecommunications. The law went on to state that individuals with disabilities continually encounter various forms of discrimination, including outright intentional exclusion; the discriminatory effects of architectural, transportation, and communication barriers; overprotective rules and policies; failure to make modifications to existing facilities and practices; exclusionary qualification standards and criteria; segregation; and relegation to lesser services, programs, activities, benefits, jobs, or other opportunities.

As noted earlier, the ADA and its subsequent interpretation by the U.S. Supreme Court in *Olmstead v. L.C., et al.* (1999) makes it clear that discrimination against persons with disabilities is illegal. The Olmsted decision embraced not only the importance of community inclusion, but also productive activity and employment.

The Workforce Investment Act of 1998

In the Workforce Investment Act of 1998 (WIA), Congress established a requirement that states and localities fully include and provide for appropriate accommodation for persons with disabilities. WIA is the first major reform of the nation's job training system since 1982. WIA, which supersedes the Job Training Partnership Act (1982) of 1981, includes the following key components:

- Streamlining services through a one-stop service delivery system
- Empowering job seekers through information and access to training resources through individual training accounts

- Providing universal access to core services
- Ensuring a strong role for local workforce investment boards and the private sector in the workforce investment system
- Improving youth programs

With the passage of WIA, local service delivery areas across the country are teaming with other employment and workforce development partners to establish a One-Stop Career Center System.

Ticket to Work and Workforce Incentives Improvement Act of 1999

The Ticket to Work and Work Incentives Improvement Act (TWWIIA) of 1999 is designed to ensure that many of the country's nine million disabled adults receiving Medicare and Medicaid keep their benefits after they obtain remunerative jobs. Until the law went into effect, many people with disabilities were faced with losing federal benefits needed to cover their medical costs if they went to work. Some feared that, by taking any jobs that paid even a minimal income, they would be cut off from access to these benefits, which are vital to maintaining their lives.

With the passage of the TWWIIA, a dramatic new era of work opportunities for persons with disabilities has been ushered in. Often people with disabilities have been determined ineligible for Medicaid and Medicare if they work, thus putting thousands of individuals in the position of having to choose between health care coverage and work. When Congress passed the TWWIIA, people with disabilities were able to join the workforce without fear of losing their Medicare or Medicaid coverage.

Individuals With Disabilities Education Act

The Individuals with Disabilities Education Act (IDEA) of 1990, 1997, and 2004 established clear expectations that the secondary school programs of adolescents with disabilities, including those with substantial disabilities would include the explicit statement that special education and related services are intended to prepare students for employment and independent living; this makes it clear that educators, parents and students must consider adult outcomes as they plan for students' school experiences. A key element of IDEA related to employment is in § 300.29:

As used in this part, transition services means a coordinated set of activities for a student with a disability that

(1) Is designed within an outcome oriented process, that promotes movement from school to post-school activities, including post-secondary education, vocational training, integrated employment (including supported employment), continuing and adult education, adult services, independent living, or community participation;

(2) Is based on the individual student's needs, taking into account the student's preferences and interests

(3) Includes:
- Instruction
- Related services
- Community experiences

- The development of employment and other post-school adult living objectives
- If appropriate, acquisition of daily living skills and functional vocational evaluation

Transition services for students with disabilities may be special education, if provided as specially designed instruction, or related services, if required to assist a student with a disability to benefit from special education.

At a minimum, the IEP team should address each of the areas including instruction, community experiences, and development of employment and other post-school adult living objectives. In many cases, each of these areas, and possibly some others, will be included in students' IEPs; however, transition services may be provided by the education agency or, as outlined in § 300.348 of the IDEA regulations, by agencies outside the school.

GOALS AND SOURCES

The laws reviewed in his chapter provide a crucial and clearly stated foundation by the U.S. Congress on the policies that should be in place for persons with ID/DD. The expectations of these seminal and exemplary pieces of legislation as a body establish seven national goals in the area of employment and productive life roles for persons with ID/DD. Beneath each goal are two research questions that are important to expand the knowledge base and to help practitioners be more effective. These seven goals include the following:

1. Develop and expand quality competitive employment opportunities
   - How can Medicaid dollars be more directly focused on competitive employment outcomes?
   - How can states be motivated to establish integrated employment as the first service choice?
2. Convert segregated day programs to integrated competitive employment and real career opportunities
   - How can greater employment choices be established throughout communities?
   - How can segregated programs be motivated to redirect the use of their funds from day programs to integrated employment programs?
3. Expand the role of business coalitions and public/private partnerships to support integrated employment
   - What is the effect of public/private employment partnerships on long-term job tenure and earnings?
   - What is the best way to expand the role of business in integrated employment efforts and especially in on-site training activities?
4. Effectively implement the Ticket to Work and Work Incentive Program
   - How can employment networks be motivated to participate more fully in the Ticket to Work implementation?
   - How much are benefit counseling resources being utilized by individuals with ID/DD and their families?

5. Implement the requirements of the ADA, its specifications in the Olmstead decision and the Workforce Investment Act
   - What progress has been made in implementing the Olmsted decision, especially as it relates to productive activities such as integrated employment?
   - How accessible and user-friendly are one-stop centers for individuals with ID/DD?
6. Expand the use of business ownership as an employment option
   - How can persons with disabilities gain access to service delivery funds to help establish their own businesses?
   - How can federal and state economic development agencies be motivated to extend resources to persons with disabilities?
7. Implement effective person-centered transition planning and effective curriculum practices in high schools
   - How can dual enrollment programs be expanded to include more students with ID/DD in college programs?
   - How can more students with disabilities be empowered to take greater control over their IEPs?

What follows are seven national goals that came from the work of the National Goals Conference of 2003. The major recommendations from this work are listed at the end of this chapter.

National Goal A: To develop and expand quality competitive employment opportunities

Goals and Sources

The goals of employment for people with severe disabilities are simply stated: to earn an income in typical and integrated settings with individualized supports for each person and with opportunities for career advancement over time. Competitive employment for people with severe disabilities requires the intersection of work for real income, integrated settings, and individualized supports for ongoing employment.

Work for Real Income

Income for employment directly translates into improved quality of life. Public benefits may account for basic housing, sustenance, and health, but only discretionary income—almost always as the result of employment—can provide opportunities for meaningful and ongoing community participation. Employment in this context is meant to include competitive employment, customized employment, self-employment, and other integrated work alternatives.

Integrated Settings

Work for real income calls for employment in typical, integrated, and business settings where people without disabilities are employed. Integrated settings, in which people with disabilities work beside employees without disabilities, provide several benefits not possible in segregated settings. First, people with disabilities who work in typical integrated settings have been shown to have far greater opportunities to develop relationships with people without disabilities both on and off the job. Second, typical, integrated businesses provide far more access to a greater variety of work. Sheltered settings typically have notable limits in the variety of service or manufacturing work. Third, typical business settings—large medium, or small—provide the fundamental context for employment in the United States. If income and employment are a goal for people with disabilities, then employment must first be sought out in the places where the rest of Americans work.

Individualized Supports

For the past 20 years, it has been clear that people with severe disabilities could work if provided opportunities for support and supervision in segregated settings. Competitive employment, historically, was thought to mean the end to the added value of supports, instruction, and supervision. Supported employment calls for the use of human resources found in segregated settings to provide or create employment supports in typical, integrated environments. Although all employees receive some kind of employment or personal supports at work, the notion of specifically creating such supports in integrated settings made it possible to imagine real jobs for people with severe disabilities in the wide range of businesses in any community.

Review of Knowledge

These goals—earned income, integrated employment settings, and individualized supports, all leading to career opportunities—result from a great deal of knowledge developed over several decades about the employment of people with disabilities and the employment of people with severe disabilities. The following seven points highlight what is already known.

1. People with severe disabilities can work. Over the last 30 years, society's beliefs about people with significant disabilities have changed dramatically. In the 1960s, people with developmental disabilities were assumed to be incompetent in nearly every way. Those who did not live with their families lived in large institutions. In 1960, as many as 200,000 people with intellectual disabilities lived in state institutions nationwide. Today, fewer than 40,000 people live in such state institutions. In large part, this change has come about as we have discovered that many people with intellectual disabilities can learn the skills needed for day-to-day life in the community.

2. Support can be provided in integrated work settings. Across the country, state agencies have adjusted to the realization that people with intellectual disabilities can, and want to, work. Historically, services funded by state mental retardation agencies were services provided in quite segregated settings, both residential settings and day service settings. These services were designed as "treatment." Over time, these agencies have widely expanded services that place more and more in integrated community settings. By providing supports and assistance to individuals in community settings, the agencies have allowed individuals to participate more fully in all manner of community activities. Rehabilitation agencies have undergone major changes in the last 15 years in the interest of the community employment of people with intellectual disabilities. Historically, state VR agencies served a small percentage of people with intellectual disabilities. One major factor in this had been a belief that people were often unemployable

because they may need some level of ongoing support to stay employed and that such support needed to be provided in segregated settings.

3. Wages and integration are better in community jobs. The early demonstrations of supported employment showed the possibilities of improved wages and real integration in supported employment. The twenty-year history has shown that these demonstrations could grow dramatically in numbers in communities in every state and across the world. Wages for those in supported employment clearly exceed the wages of individuals with similar disability labels still in segregated settings, (Wehman, 2001).

4. New strategies are emerging for quality employment. In addition to the early development of supported employment in the 1980s and the improvements emerging with the advent of natural supports in work settings, new methods of quality employment have emerged as the notion of employment of people with severe disabilities has evolved. Self-employment, business ownership, customized employment, transition from school to work, and other concepts have extended the outcomes and the choices of people with disabilities relative to employment, integration, and career development.

5. Self-determination presents new opportunities for quality employment. Person-centered planning and self-determination have emerged as promising approaches to ensuring that people with disabilities and their personal allies control decisions, choices, and resources. The self-determination movement focused first on where and how people live. More recently, these same notions are being applied to employment and career development, in addition to other parts of life.

6. Policy and funding changes can increase the expansion of supported employment. In the last 10 to 15 years, policy and funding changes have led to increases in integrated employment for people with disabilities. VR no longer accepts segregated work as an employment outcome and Medicaid waivers are implemented in some states in ways that allow use of the funds for employment only if that employment is in integrated settings. Some states provide greater funding for integrated employment than for segregated employment. Changes in the Social Security Act are reducing the disincentives for people with disabilities to go to work. Transition from school to work provisions in special education and rehabilitation emphasize integrated employment. Such policy and funding changes provide incentives to expand competitive and integrated employment over other kinds of day service options. Although a great deal of funding and policy continues to support segregation over integration in day services and employment, it is also clear that policy and funding changes have had an impact on increasing meaningful employment opportunities for people with disabilities.

7. Increases in employment and earned income reduce reliance on subsidies to people with disabilities. The cost of services and the cost of an individual's reliance on public income and benefits is a great concern for people with disabilities, their families, and society. Employment and earned income for people with disabilities directly reduces the need for social security income, food stamps, and other types of state and federal subsidies to individuals. For some

people, employment results in no need for public benefits. For many other people with disabilities, employment can result in less reliance on subsidies from state or federal sources.

Vision for Implementation

The following are statements of vision that relate to the overall goal of quality, competitive and integrated employment for people with disabilities.

1. **Consumer engagement.** People with disabilities and their personal allies create and control the options, choices, and resources in the pursuit of quality, competitive, and integrated employment and careers over time.
2. **Service delivery practices.** Services and supports resulting in quality employment are provided in ways that encourage self-determination, high wages, and career development.
3. **Resource allocation.** Resources invested for quality employment emphasize personal budgets. Funding policy emphasizes quality employment with individual supports in integrated settings.
4. **Service assessment.** Services are evaluated on the outcome of clear increases in access to quality, competitive, supported, and integrated employment. Improvements are assessed based on wages, integration, variety in jobs, and career development.
5. **Personnel development.** The human resources that help people with disabilities find and keep jobs have the skills and the support to produce expanding employment opportunities and to implement innovations in employment support as they emerge.

National Goal B: To convert segregated day programs to integrated competitive employment and real career opportunities

Goals and Sources

Sheltered facilities for adults with disabilities are one of the last bastions in our society of mass segregation of a group of individuals based solely on their characteristics. Under the rubric of "needs," "treatment," and/or "rehabilitation," people assigned to sheltered facilities become what Glasser (1978) termed "prisoners of benevolence," (p. 106) because they are deprived of the right to pursue meaningful work opportunities of their choice (Murphy & Rogan, 1995). Segregated facilities have expanded as the primary day service option for adults with disabilities since the 1960s. Workshops and day activity centers claim to address three major needs: shelter, vocational readiness, and choice. The most frequently cited reason for why people are kept in segregated day services is that they are deemed not ready to leave; that is, some believe that people need to be taught work or social skills in artificial, simulated environments to prepare for the real world of work.

The Movement Toward Community

We are fortunate to have strong disability-related legislation in the United States that promotes and protects the civil rights of Americans with disabilities. For example, the Rehabilitation Act Amendments of 1998, Title IV of Pub. L. 105-220 (Workforce Investment Act of 1998) stipulates that the intended outcome of vocational rehabilitation services is employment. Section 102 of the amendments of the act includes the term "presumption of benefit," which means that all individuals can benefit from VR services unless the state unit can demonstrate, by clear and convincing evidence, that an individual is incapable of benefiting in terms of an employment outcome due to the severity of the individual's disability. This policy change is empirically supported by the work of Kregel and Dean (2002), which compared the relative efficacy of economic benefits of supported employment over sheltered employment.

Many national organizations have responded positively to federal and state initiatives to provide integrated employment services. As a result, in the past decade nearly 30,000 people considered unemployable are now working and earning more money than in any other vocational option (Wehman, et al., 1998). Research has shown that quality of life outcomes are better for those in supported employment compared to their counterparts in segregated day services (Gilmore & Butterworth, 1996; McCaughrin, Ellis, Rusch, & Heal, 1993; Wehman, et al., 1998). A growing number of organizations have completely shifted from facility-based to community-based services and supports. These organizations have demonstrated that the provision of "services without walls" is not only possible but results in better outcomes for both individuals and the organization itself.

Review of Knowledge

The process of organizational change, often referred to as *conversion*, is complex. Among its many challenging facets, organizational change involves a period of simultaneously operating dual systems (the old and the new), changing staff attitudes and skills, marketing a new organizational image, interfacing with businesses, and shifting fiscal structures and priorities. It also involves helping people with disabilities to develop self-determination as well as employment and career opportunities in the pursuit of their dreams.

Conversion Studies

Researchers are now beginning to discover why some organizations have chosen to undertake the changeover process, why only some succeed, what barriers they encounter, what strategies are most successful in helping them make the change, and what outcomes they achieve.

Murphy and Rogan (1995) described the experiences of four organizations that had completed the conversion process. Although each of the four organizations experienced unique barriers to changeover, common barriers included the following:

- Funding
- Lack of staff competence
- Organizational structures and personnel roles that impeded a focus on employment and community services
- Negative attitudes among various stakeholders
- Lack of transportation
- Difficulty in finding quality jobs, especially for people with the most significant disabilities

This study identified multiple strategies considered key to the success of conversion efforts. Organizations reported the importance of first articulating a clear vision; involving key stakeholders from the start; using individualized, person-centered planning approaches; and training and hiring quality staff. Then they moved on to securing high-quality jobs, ending facility admissions, accessing external consultants to help guide the change, and working to flatten the organizational structure, with most staff providing direct services. At the same time, they worked on changing the agency's image through marketing, building business partnerships, divesting of buildings and equipment, and pursuing flexible funding and alternative sources of funds.

Albin, Rhodes, and Mank (1994) studied the changeover process and consequent outcomes of eight organizations that had either converted or were in the conversion process. The decisions to change were primarily driven by values. As in the Murphy and Rogan (1995) study, a major barrier was the difficulty of trying to operate two programs at the same time. Finding adequate resources and working through conflicting values also presented challenges. The majority of respondents said that trying to negotiate contradicting policies was a barrier, as well as the lack of staff with needed skills. Negative attitudes regarding the abilities of the people being served and the unfriendly nature of the funding systems were also stated as primary obstacles to changeover.

Among the numerous factors these organizations attributed to their success, all reported leadership as the single most important element. Incentive funding also sparked change. Other successful strategies included sharing decisionmaking, connecting with others undergoing changeover, adopting and abiding by a vision of community, and listening to and acting on the desires of people with disabilities and their families. In-depth case studies of six organizations that have undertaken organizational change revealed similar themes to previous studies (Butterworth & Fesko, 1998). For these organizations, organizational changes led to confusion about roles and responsibilities. Some staff said that it was difficult to determine how to move from "taking care of" individuals with disabilities to supporting them to become more self-determined. Facilitating inclusion at work and in the community was mentioned as an ongoing challenge for staff.

Rogan, Held, and Rinne (1999) conducted a national study to identify organizations that had undertaken the changeover process, to find out how they implemented the process, and to determine the outcome they achieved. The researchers identified 146 organizations throughout the United States that had either completed the changeover effort or were in the process of conversion. Of the 146 surveys sent, 49 (33.6%) were returned and 41 were used for data analysis. Of the 41 agencies, 12 (29.3%) had converted, while the remaining 29 (70.7%) were in various stages of the process.

Visions for Implementation

The following visions for implementation describe the different issues which must be recognized and overcome. They include:

1. **Overcoming Negative Attitudes.** Agencies addressed negative attitudes among various stakeholders by providing a great deal of information and training and arranging discussion sessions, including parent-to-parent meetings and consumer-to-consumer meetings. Demonstrations of success and showcasing success stories have helped to shift attitudes. Person-centered planning approaches have helped families and individuals design desired services and supports,

thereby easing fears. Agency staff worked first with supportive families. Individuals with disabilities were invited to participate in job clubs, job shadowing, job try-outs, volunteer work, and other community activities.

2. **Creating Funding Alternatives.** Strategies for addressing funding issues included developing better working relationships with funding agencies and policy makers, advocating for increased funding, negotiating alternative funding mechanisms, cutting expenses, redirecting excess earnings to community-based services, and demonstrating success and earning funding agency support.

3. **Managing Regulatory Barriers.** Changing state regulations involved ongoing discussions with policy makers and legislators. Partnering with other agencies with similar interests was also helpful in building a lobbying effort. Some organizations were able to negotiate waivers of problematic regulations.

4. **Developing More Expertise.** Training, attendance at conferences, membership in professional organizations, and networking with other agencies were all used to build expertise within these organizations. For some, experience in the field, along with "figuring it out as you go," proved helpful. Finally, hiring staff with desired skills and increasing participatory management were successful strategies.

5. **Developing New Leadership.** To address a lack of leadership, organizations hired new leaders, brought in expert consultants, and formed change management teams to guide changeover activities. Agencies also partnered with and/or visited organizations that were further along in the conversion process. To support staff development and collaboration, some agencies reorganized staff into teams and provided cross training in order to learn about each other's areas of expertise.

National Goal C: To expand the role of business coalitions, and public/private business partnerships

Goals and Sources

The U.S. Department of Labor , Bureau of Census (2004), reported that the U.S. unemployment rate was 5.6% in December 2004. On the other hand, the unemployment rate for persons clinically diagnosed as having a mental illness is 85%. This is significant because the majority of people who are considered disabled and receiving government assistance (e.g., Supplemental Security Income (SSI)) fall into the categories of (a) psychiatrically disabled (36%) or (b) intellectually disabled (25%) (U.S. Social Security Administration, Office of Policy, 2001).

Review of Knowledge

Striking progress and true change have transpired over the last two decades regarding the employability of people with significant disabilities—those who were once thought unable, unqualified, and uninterested in participating in the nation's competitive labor market. A number of corporate initiatives have emerged, such as activities undertaken by Universal Studios, Hollywood (Weiner & Zivolich, 1998); MBNA; and Prudential Insurance Company (Miano, Nalven, & Hoff, 1996), in which business and industry have assumed the lead role in employing and supporting individuals with significant disabilities. Even prior to the passage of ADA, a number of businesses recognized the economic benefits of early return-to-work and disability management (DM) programs for their employees who were injured or became disabled while employed (see McMahon, Wehman, Brooke, Habeck, Green, & Fraser, 2004).

A substantial body of research has emerged over the past three decades regarding beliefs and practices of employers, supervisors, and coworkers with regards to individuals with significant disabilities, including mental retardation. What does this research tell us about increasing employment opportunities for members of this population?

First, the research indicates that some negative attitudes about workers with disabilities continue to persist, although less than many have thought (Unger, 2002a). Employers may not hire a person with a disability due to liability issues or the anticipated cost of making accommodations, despite much evidence to the contrary (Blanck, 1998; Olson, Cioffi, Yovanoff, & Mank, 2000). Many employers express concern regarding absenteeism, work rate and quality, and ability to integrate into the workplace culture (Johnson, Greenwood, & Schriner, 1988). Some studies have found that attitudes are generally more negative toward individuals with mental illness and mental retardation than for other types of disability groups (McFarlin, Song, & Sonntag, 1991). As Unger (2002a) notes, these findings have been contradicted by other, typically more recent, studies that have indicated more favorable views of employees with disabilities in these same areas (McFarlin, et al., 1991; Nietupski, Hamre-Nietupski, VanderHart, & Fishback, 1996).

Interrelated with negative attitudes is the lack of information being delivered to businesses regarding hiring and retaining workers with disabilities. For example, Livermore, Stapleton, Nowak, Wittenburg, and Eiseman (2000) found that many employers believe that the cost of providing accommodations is unfeasible, despite evidence to the contrary (Job Accommodation Network, 1995). Most employers in this study also stated that the perceptions and attitudes of co-workers and supervisors constitute the primary barrier to employment.

The research also suggests that negative attitudes about workers with significant disabilities can be mitigated with experience. For example, two studies of small and large employers in New York state (Levy, Jessop, Rimmerman, & Levy, 1992; Levy, Jessop, Rimmerman, Francis, & Levy, 1993) found that employers with prior experience employing individuals with significant disabilities had more favorable attitudes toward them. Unger (2002b) conducted surveys of front-line supervisors in 35 companies, with each company returning an average of nearly six surveys. A key finding from the survey was that personal experience with disability, such as having a relative or friend with disabilities, was strongly correlated with positive views of work performance of employees with disabilities.

Visions for Implementation

The visions for implementation listed below are associated with quality implementation:

1. **Utilization of Tax Incentives.** There is a strong need to better advertise tax incentives for businesses so they will be encouraged to hire individuals with disabilities.
2. **Overcoming Federal Disincentives.** Medicaid and other federal programs must remove employment disincentives.

3. **Establishing Improved Public Relations.** Major national advertising and public relations campaigns regarding the benefits of employing individuals with intellectual disabilities are essential to change attitudes.

4. **Expanding Marketing Strategies.** Development and empirical validation of new business-to-business marketing strategies will help implement these new practices.

National Goal D: To fully implement the Ticket to Work and Work Incentive Program

Goals and Sources

The Ticket to Work (TTW) program provides a ticket to eligible Social Security Administration (SSA) beneficiaries that can be used to obtain VR or employment services through an employment network (EN). An EN is any qualified entity that has entered into an agreement with SSA to assume responsibility for coordinating and delivering employment services to beneficiaries who assign their tickets to the EN. Both public and private providers can enroll as ENs. Individuals between the ages of 18 and 64 who are currently receiving either Disability Insurance or Supplemental Security Income disability benefits are eligible to participate in the TTW program.

Employment networks may choose to be paid under one of two payment systems: (a) an outcome payment system or (b) an outcome-milestone payment system. Under the *outcome payment system*, SSA will make up to 60 monthly payments to the EN for each beneficiary. Monthly payments are equivalent to 40% of the Payment Calculation Base (PCB)—the prior calendar year's national average monthly DI or SSI disability payment amount. In 2002, monthly outcome payments were $317 for DI and $191 for SSI. Under the *outcome-milestone payment system*, SSA will pay the EN for up to four milestones achieved by a beneficiary who has assigned his or her ticket to the EN. In addition to the milestone payments, monthly outcome payments can be paid to the EN during the outcome payment period.

The ticket payment system has two important implications for the participation of individuals with intellectual disabilities. First, the ticket payment system is based on the possibility of potential savings to SSA that may result from an individual's no longer receiving SSI or Social Security Disability Insurance (SSDI) cash benefits. Second, payments received by ENs electing the milestone-outcome system are significantly lower than those provided through the outcome system. Some suggest that since many ENs will likely view persons with intellectual disabilities as challenging to serve, these ENs would probably prefer to serve them under the milestone-outcome system. If reimbursement under the milestone-outcome system is significantly less, it may reduce the willingness of ENs to accept tickets from beneficiaries with intellectual disabilities.

Expanded Health Care Coverage

The Ticket to Work and Work Incentives Improvement Act (TWWIIA) attempts to expand public health insurance for people with disabilities in a number of ways:

1. Section 201 allows states the option to liberalize income, asset, and resource limitations for workers with disabilities who buy into Medicaid. States can also continue to offer the Medicaid Buy-in to workers with disabilities, even if they are no longer eligible for DI or SSI because of medical improvement.

2. Section 202 extends the Medicare Extended Period of Eligibility (EPE) from four to eight-and-a-half years.
3. Section 203 establishes Medicaid Infrastructure Grants intended to provide assistance to states in the development of Medicaid Buy-in programs. To qualify for such grants, states must offer, or be in the process of establishing, personal assistance services capable of supporting full-time competitive employment.

Benefits Planning and Assistance

Authorized by § 121 of the TWWIIA, 116 Benefits Planning, Assistance and Outreach (BPAO) programs are providing services to SSA beneficiaries in all 50 states and five territories. Collectively, the 116 BPAO projects employ over 400 benefit specialists and have served over 40,000 individuals since implementation in early 2001. The purpose of the BPAO initiative is to provide SSA disability beneficiaries with accurate and timely information about SSA work incentives and other federal efforts to remove regulatory and programmatic barriers to employment for persons with disabilities. Trained benefits specialists in local BPAO programs work with individual beneficiaries to explain the myriad of regulations, provisions, work incentives, and special programs that complicate an individual's decision to enter or reenter the workforce.

Review of Knowledge

Little is known about the participation of individuals with intellectual disabilities in the Ticket to Work or Medicaid buy-in programs. These initiatives have only recently begun to enroll beneficiaries in the majority of states, and little formal evaluation data exists at this time. However, considerable information is available on individuals accessing the SSA benefits planning, assistance, and outreach programs. Data from this program provide useful information on the types of individuals seeking employment as well as their ability to access health care and employment services through the ticket.

The Benefits Assistance Resource Center at Virginia Commonwealth University maintains a uniform data management system that allows BPAO contractors to submit, revise, and aggregate information on their clientele via Web-based forms. The National BPAO Data System collects information on areas such as type of disability, current benefits received, current employment status, reasons for contacting the BPAO, types of services delivered, and work incentives.

Of the 34,725 beneficiaries served by the BPAO program through September 30, 2002, 3,665 reported having an intellectual disability as their primary disability. It is evident that, although beneficiaries with intellectual disabilities were very similar to other beneficiaries in many ways, they also differed in a number of important variables that illustrate the unique needs of persons with intellectual disabilities who attempt to obtain or maintain employment.

In terms of current SSA benefits status, approximately 50% of beneficiaries with intellectual disabilities received SSI, whereas less than one third received SSDI. Nearly 60% of beneficiaries with intellectual disabilities receiving intensive benefit support were employed either full or part time, and another third were actively seeking employment. This is in sharp contrast to those without intellectual disabilities receiving intensive benefit support. As with the beneficiaries with intellectual disabilities, just over 5% of these beneficiaries were employed full time. However, less than one third of beneficiaries without intellectual disabilities were currently employed, whereas 60% were seeking employment. In both groups, it is clear that the majority of beneficiaries receiving intensive benefit support were either employed or in the process of seeking employment.

In summary, four key differences emerged between those BPAO participants with intellectual disabilities and those without intellectual disabilities:

- **Beneficiaries with intellectual disabilities were more likely to be youth.** Indeed, more than a quarter of these individuals were under the age of 22, while less than 7% of beneficiaries without intellectual disabilities fell within this age range.
- **Individuals with intellectual disabilities served by the BPAO program were more likely to be SSI beneficiaries.** The data reveals that half of all BPAO participants with intellectual disabilities and less than one third of all participants without cognitive disorders were current SSI beneficiaries.
- **Beneficiaries with intellectual disabilities were more likely to be employed part time.** More than 50% of beneficiaries with intellectual disabilities receiving intensive benefit support and almost 30% of those receiving Information and Referral/Problem Solving.
- **Beneficiaries with intellectual disabilities were less likely to use the Ticket to Work program.** These individuals were half as likely as beneficiaries without intellectual disabilities to indicate Ticket Communication from SSA as a reason for requesting BPAO services. Beneficiaries with intellectual disabilities were also less likely to indicate that they intended to utilize the Ticket to Work Program in seeking a new or supplemental job.

Vision for Implementation

There are five issues which need to be considered as we move to the implementatin stage:

1. **Improve Reimbursements Regulations.** Modify the Ticket to Work program so that ENs receive reimbursement for partial cash benefit reductions for individuals who are SSI or SSDI beneficiaries.
2. **Expand Provider Incentives.** Modify the payment structure for the Ticket to Work program to provide greater incentive for providers to serve individuals with intellectual disabilities.
3. **Expand Technical Assistance.** Provide technical assistance to ENs to enable them to adequately meet the needs of beneficiaries with disabilities attempting to assign their tickets.
5. **Expand Availability.** Ensure that the Medicaid Buy-in program is available in all states.

National Goal E: To enhance the roles of Olmstead and Workforce Investment Act in Integrated Employment

Goals and Sources

In recent years the federal government has increased its interest in streamlining the range of employment programs. With the passage of the Workforce Investment Act (WIA) of 1998 and the establishment of the One-Stop Career Center System, the emphasis on a less complex and more customer-focused employment and training system has emerged. This legislation provides states with an opportunity to develop a consolidated workforce investment plan that will respond to the needs of job seekers as well as employers. WIA is designed to create a single access system with a "no wrong door" strategy, such that any individual who is interested may seek employment. The level of services will vary, depending upon both the needs of the individual and the capacity of the job seeker to self-direct his or her job search efforts. The potential for developing a uniquely focused employment plan through the use of an Individual Training Account (ITA) reflects the strong role that individuals with disabilities may play in the job preparation and job seeking processes.

Additionally, although not a legislative initiative, the Olmstead decision rendered in 1999 interpreted Title II of the ADA and its implementing regulation, which obliges states to administer their services, programs, and activities "in the most integrated setting appropriate to the needs of qualified individuals with disabilities" (28 CFR 35.130 (d)). This ruling, although initially directed at the provision of community living services, also calls into question the use of nonwork or sheltered work settings when integrated employment options are available. In ruling in the case of *Olmstead v. L.C., et al.* (1999), the Supreme Court affirmed the right of individuals with disabilities to receive public benefit and services in the most integrated setting appropriate to their needs.

The U.S. Department of Health and Human Services (2001), in response to Executive Order 13217, Community-Based Alternatives for Individuals with Disabilities, noted a number of avenues that the U.S. Department of Labor can use to foster integrated employment for individuals with disabilities, who have typically been relegated to nonwork, or segregated settings. This report calls for increases in the following:

1. Access to mainstream workforce programs, increased choices for securing employment and related supports, increased capacity and availability of "customized" employment services, and expanded opportunities for self-employment and micro-enterprise (businesses employing one to five workers) development for people with disabilities

2. Availability of high-quality personal care staff and community workers, including the availability of incentives for hiring, retention, career advancement, and training opportunities for these individuals

3. Leveraging of technology focused on fostering and increasing telecommuting work opportunities and employment in technology-related industries

4. Innovative and strategic partnerships between the federal government and employers, people with disabilities, family members, providers, community organizations, and others in the private sector, including foundations and faith-based organizations

5. Hiring of people with disabilities in the federal workforce, with leadership by example through DOL's commitment to hiring people with disabilities

Review of Knowledge

National data on employment of adults with disabilities remain troubling. In 1997, males without disabilities were reported to have a labor force participation rate of 95.2%, whereas men with disabilities reported a rate of 35.5%. For women with and without disabilities similar disparities are noted, with a labor force participation rate of 80.7% for women without disabilities and 31.9% for women with disabilities. Using a broad definition of disability, the 2000 U.S. Census reported the incidence of disability to be 19.2% in the overall population between the ages of 21 and 64. This percentage rises to 41.9% in those over 65 years of age. This same report notes that 56.6% of those who report having a disability are employed, in comparison to the 77.2% employment rate for those not reporting a disability (U.S. Bureau of the Census, 2000). It is clear that regardless of the perspective, definition, or severity, those individuals who report a disability are more often unemployed (Houtenville, 2001).

Service Systems

These general trends are echoed in the employment outcomes for individuals with significant disabilities. An ongoing data collection effort of the Institute for Community Inclusion reported that only 25% of adults supported by state Mental Retardation and Developmental Disabilities agencies are in real work settings, and the remainder are split between sheltered employment and nonwork programs. This same ongoing data analysis compared trends from FY 1988 through FY 1999. Some clear trends include the following:

- **MR/DD agencies significantly expanded their capacity to provide day and employment services, supporting almost 470,000 individuals in FY 1999.** This represents an increase of 71%, or 195,000 individuals, from FY 1988.
- **Integrated employment expanded steadily.** The number of people in integrated employment increased by over 200%, from 32,391 in 1988 to 107,820 in 1999.
- **Agencies maintained dual systems.** Despite the significant growth in integrated employment, the data show continuing growth in the number of individuals supported in facility-based and nonwork services. The number of individuals in facility-based and nonwork services increased during this period from 241,883 in FY 1988 to an estimated 362,022 in FY 1999.
- **Individuals became increasingly likely to use multiple services or settings.** In FY 1996 and FY 1999, reports showed increasing numbers of individuals who had begun receiving multiple services simultaneously, dividing their time between a community job and other service options. This is a significant change from FY 1988, when most individuals were in a clearly designated service category.

The investment in employment opportunities by state Mental Health (MH) agencies is even more limited. In FY 1993, only 25 out of 38 state mental health agencies could identify or estimate the number of individuals receiving vocational services, and the agencies reported that less than 1% of individuals supported were in integrated employment. More recently, a 1999 National Association of State Mental Health Program Directors (NASMHPD) survey found that most states could not specify their expenditures on employment supports, which indicates that employment remains a low priority.

Wages

Wages are paid to individuals with disabilities in both segregated and integrated settings. In the sheltered workshops (i.e., segregated settings) the wage payment is typically determined

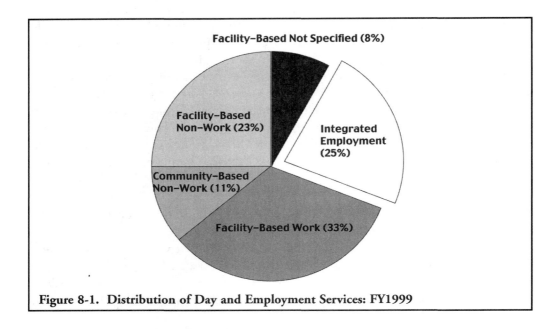

Figure 8-1. Distribution of Day and Employment Services: FY1999

by the wage payment. The average wage payment, when viewed as an hourly wage, is usually quite low. Individuals in sheltered employment earn minimal wages, averaging only $2.46/hour for individuals recently closed by state VR agencies. The lowest sheltered wages—$52/week—were earned by individuals with mental retardation; the average wage of across all disability groups was $64/week. Overall, wages in sheltered employment are one third to one quarter of those in competitive employment, even after accounting for severity of disability (Gilmore & Butterworth, 2001).

Settings

Sheltered employment and nonwork services continue to be the dominant model for day and employment services (Braddock, et al., 2004). An estimated 7,000 community rehabilitation providers (CRPs) in the United States support over 1,000,000 individuals with significant disabilities (McGaughey, Kiernan, McNally, Gilmore, & Keith, 1994). The state and federal Departments of Labor provide certificates to many of these programs that allow wages based on rates of productivity, with most individuals in these settings earning considerably less than the minimum wage. A September 2001 GAO report noted the need for significant revisions in how the U.S. Department of Labor, Wage, and Hour Division monitors and implements this program.

The current system of service reflects a lack of clear commitment to integrated employment as the outcome of first preference for all individuals with disabilities, including those with intellectual and other developmental disabilities. The challenge is to identify effective practices for accessing, maintaining, and advancing employment for individuals with disabilities in the coming decade.

Vision for Implementation

Many strategies exist for securing integrated, competitive employment for people with disabilities, especially people who might have been considered "nonfeasible" for employment and people who have been segregated in institutions, nursing homes, and day activity programs. These strategies include the following:

1. **Consumer engagement.** The challenge for consumer engagement lies in providing accurate information about opportunities and redirecting our message of dependence to one of support and assistance.

2. **Service delivery practices.** Current practices, as noted, are at best fragmented and at times oppositional. We must develop a more uniform approach to supporting individuals with disabilities in their quest for jobs. The principles expressed in the Workforce Investment Act, if adhered to, will go a long way toward streamlining the areas of job access.

3. **Resource allocation and expenditures.** Current allocations for support of individuals with disabilities are delivered by multiple agencies and often are not coordinated. Attempts to have resources follow the individual have been effective within single agencies, but support across agencies for an individual is a rare phenomenon. The individual job seeker needs more effective cross-agency support.

4. **Service assessment.** A shared perspective on the mission and focus of the various agencies is essential for moving service assessment across agencies. Without a national employment plan or emphasis, agencies will find it difficult to develop shared data collection systems and shared program evaluation strategies. Many continue to discuss the goal of developing common data sets for planning, program evaluation, operations, or some other reason.

5. **Personnel development.** Most community-based organizations face the challenge of securing and supporting a qualified workforce. Agencies clearly need to deal with a shortage of trained staff at many levels. They also need to consider what types of support an individuals with disabilities may need or want and where those supports will be coming from. The need for training of professionals and direct support personnel in human services continues. Over the past decade, government and service systems have come to recognize the important role that direct support professionals play.

National Goal F: To expand the use of business ownership as a viable model of employment

Goals and Sources/Validation

The self-employment rate in America is growing at over 20% annually; an estimated 20 million Americans own home-based businesses (Griffin & Hammis, 2003). Between 1990 and 1994, microenterprises generated 43% of all new U.S. jobs, and in the past decade, 60% of microenterprises were owned by women. All of these businesses created more jobs than the entire Fortune 500 combined (Sirolli, 1999; Forrester, 1996; Access to Credit, 1998; Friedman, 1996). This cultural and economic shift, which appears to be largely unaffected by the state of the economy, presents another promising career option to individuals with significant disabilities (Griffin, 1999a; Griffin, 1999b; Arnold, 1998; Taylor & Wacker, 1997; Hammis & Griffin, 2002).

Approximately 2.5% of VR closures (5,000 people) are for self-employment, and the numbers are growing daily (Arnold, 1998). Numerous agencies such as Vocational Rehabilitation, Developmental Disabilities, and Mental Health in various states—including Montana, Colorado, Kentucky, Tennessee, Maryland, New Jersey, North Carolina, South Dakota, New York, California, and Washington—are exploring policy and funding mechanisms to increase self-employment opportunities. The newly created Office of Disability and Economic Policy (ODEP) at the U.S. Department of Labor is encouraging small business ownership through their guiding legislation, the Workforce Investment Act of 1998, and is funding special projects and training programs for individuals with disabilities. The Rehabilitation Services Administration (RSA), within the U.S. Department of Education, is promoting self-employment as a reasonable outcome for state Vocational Rehabilitation agencies and is demonstrating various aspects of entrepreneurial ventures through training and grant programs.

Self-employment is not for everyone, but it may be an excellent prospect for many unemployed or underemployed persons with intellectual disabilities. It is a personal choice that should be balanced by a variety of life circumstances, including financial position and funding, availability and quality of business and personal supports, and the viability of the business idea.

Review of Knowledge

Self-employment potentially provides a number of advantages over wage employment, including the following:

1. With over 80% of men and 54% of women with disabilities unemployed in the United States, the risk of attempting small business ownership is minimal compared to the possibilities of success (U.S. Bureau of the Census, 2001).

2. Self-employment offers the only substantial options available under our Social Security and Medicaid/Medicare systems to accumulate personal wealth and manage income in a way that is predictable and personally adjustable (Griffin & Hammis, 2003; Hammis & Griffin, 2002). Almost without exception, people with disabilities in the U.S. receive Supplemental Security Income (SSI) and/or Social Security Disability Insurance (SSDI) and Medicaid or Medicare benefits. Under Medicaid and SSI regulations, an individual beneficiary cannot accumulate more than $2000 in cash, unless the cash resources are sheltered in an irrevocable trust managed by someone else or in a Plan for Achieving Self Support (PASS). However, a business owner on SSDI, SSI, Medicaid, or Medicare can have unlimited funds in a small business checking account for legitimate operating expenses as defined by the IRS and SSA rules as Property Essential for Self Support (PESS). A small business owner can accumulate operating cash and other business capital resources and accumulate unlimited net worth in the business.

3. Because of Social Security benefits, self-employed people with disabilities can have a financial cushion and income for survival during the business start-up phase and often throughout the life of the entire business.

4. Self-employed people with disabilities may have access to alternate sources of capital to build their businesses. Conventional small business loans for business start-ups are sometimes difficult to acquire, often carry high interest rates, and load people with anxiety-causing debt. Banks prefer not to make small business loans unless substantial collateral is available.

5. Self-employment works for people labeled with significant disabilities. To many, self-employment appears beyond the reach of people with such labels. Understanding the individual in his or her home, community, and day-to-day context of living reveals opportunities for self-employment. Business ownership comes through a discovery process that lines up personal attributes, supports, dreams, talents, resources, and the marketplace. Indeed, the model used in supported employment may be utilized for self-employment. VR may provide time-limited startup services (e.g., business plans, equipment purchase, training) with continued support for the business operation provided by day program (or residential) support monies after VR closure.

6. Although over 350,000 individuals traditionally served by community rehabilitation programs (CRPs) are now wage-earners through supported employment, almost 400,000 people remain in day programs that need new avenues to address community employment (Braddock, et al., 2004). Self-employment offers people career advancement through increased wages and integration with suppliers, customers, and mentors.

Vision for Implementation

The vision for implementation includes the following:

1. **Consumer engagement.** Individuals with disabilities can and must be given the opportunity to develop and implement their own small businesses.

2. **Better service delivery practices.** Local programs and funding agencies in the community must be willing and able to help individuals with disabilities start their businesses and work through obstacles.

3. **Resource allocations and expenditures.** Persons with disabilities must have funds available for developing and implementing business plans.

4. **Service assessment.** Funders and other community agencies should know how to assess the economic opportunities, markets, and obstacles in new small business planning.

5. **Personnel development.** Training institutes, seminars, and online courses, plus technical assistance, are critical to providing persons with disabilities with the knowledge to start their businesses.

National Goal G: To implement person-centered transition planning and effective curriculum practices throughout high school

Goals and Sources

Approximately one decade after the Education for All Handicapped Children Act was passed, a series of post-school follow-up studies were undertaken and information was published on the outcomes experienced by the first generation of graduates

(Wehman, in press). Although many individuals with disabilities were succeeding, far too many individuals experienced post-school outcomes that were less than desired. Specifically, these follow-up studies revealed high levels of unemployment and underemployment, low engagement levels in post-secondary education opportunities, and relatively little movement toward more independent community living possibilities (Hasazi, Gordon, Roe, 1985; Mithaug, Horiuchi, & Fanning, 1985). In effect, the life experiences of many individuals did not mirror the optimism that had accompanied educational entitlement legislation. Wehman (2002), through his testimony to the President's Committee on Excellence in Special Education, noted that something was obviously missing from the educational experience and post-school circumstances of students with intellectual disabilities. These reflections and policy analyses led to the conclusion that the traditional process for developing a student's individualized education program (IEP) focused too much on student deficits and too little on successful transitions from high school to adult life.

In addition to poor employment outcomes, the literature reported sobering post-secondary education outcomes (e.g., Getzel & Wehman, in press). Level of education clearly relates to successful adult employment outcomes for adults with disabilities (e.g., Benz, Doren, & Yovanoff, 1998; Blackorby & Wagner, 1996; Gilson, 1996; Reis, Neu, & McGuire, 1997).

Early and comprehensive transition planning, with a strong emphasis on student self-determination throughout the process, remains the key for students with disabilities who attain successful employment-related post-secondary education (e.g., Thoma, Rogan, & Baker, 2001). In fact, there are two themes that emerge from literature describing best practices in transition planning: preparing stronger individuals and creating receptive systems. Stronger individuals are those who have skills and knowledge to succeed in employment settings or in post-secondary education that prepares them for employment. These skills and knowledge include, but are not limited to, the following:

- Basic skills such as reading, math, and writing to succeed in the workplace and/or post-secondary education environment
- Self-determination skills, including self-advocacy skills and an awareness of the impact of one's disability (e.g., Agran, 1997; Thoma, et al., 2001; Wehmeyer, et al., in press)
- Career awareness (e.g., Callahan & Garner, 1997; Parker & Schaller, 1996)
- Technology skills (e.g., Fichten, Barile, & Asuncion, 1999)
- Knowledge of the laws and of the rights one has under these laws (e.g., Frank & Wade, 1993; Wehmeyer, 2001)
- Experience interacting with peers without disabilities, which is especially important for post-secondary education success (e.g., U.S. Department of Education, 1995)
- Work-related knowledge and skills, including time management, conflict management, feedback, and an understanding of the unwritten rules of the workplace (e.g., Wehman, et al., in press).

Creating receptive systems is an equally important step in developing effective transition planning, but it is more often overlooked. Special education has a long history of focusing on changing the individual, but the individual also must learn to function in a series of different environments. Abery and Stancliffe (1996) proposed an ecological approach to fostering student self-determination in transition planning, and this approach remains relevant for this second component of effective transition planning. The ecological model, based on the work of Bronfenbrenner (1979), reminds us that there are many forces that impact transition planning beyond the day-to-day interactions that occur at the microsystem—or one-on-one interaction—level.

Review of Knowledge

Over the past 25 years, there have been many changes in program planning practices involving individuals with disabilities. In 2002, transition planning was institutionalized as part of the IEP process. In many cases, transition planning has proven to be a powerful tool for assisting students and families in clarifying their vision for the future, identifying barriers that impede progress and frustrate initiatives, and expanding opportunities and supports needed to achieve a more desirable future. Unfortunately, in too many cases, transition planning has simply meant additional documentation on the IEP rather than substantive change in planning, curriculum, and outcomes.

For example, Grigal, Test, Beattie, and Wood (1997) evaluated the transition components of 94 high school students and found that the majority of the transition requirements were included, but many of the "best practice" elements of transition planning were lacking. Thoma, et al. (2001) compared the transition plans for eight individuals with disabilities and found that, although these written plans reflected the obtained outcomes, these outcomes did not match students' preferences and interests for their adult lives. If school and adult service systems wish to optimize, rather than institutionalize, the promise of transition planning, they must ensure that several foundation principles of effective transition planning are in place. These foundational principles include (a) expanded partnerships, (b) person-centered transition planning, (c) relevant curriculum experiences, (d) student self-determination, and (e) seamless transition to desired post-school employment and/or post-secondary education.

1. **Expanded partnerships.** In virtually all conceptualizations of effective transition planning, dynamic partnerships involving students, families, educators, rehabilitation counselors, and others are considered to be foundational practices (Kohler, 1993). Federal transition legislation makes it very clear that post-school service agencies must act as collaborative partners with students, their families, and school resources. However, the composition of most IEP transition teams does not represent these broad-based partnerships. Although federal law requires student attendance at IEP meetings that include transition planning, many students still fail to attend their own meetings. Similarly, parents choose not to attend these meetings in spite of federal mandates that, as part of the IEP process, require that schools notify parents and advise them of their rights.

2. **Person-centered transition planning.** Person-centered transition planning practices have proven effective in identifying a student's vision for his or her future beyond high school and the experiences needed to realize that vision. Person-centered transition planning is a strengths-based process for identifying a student's preferences and interests in the context of clarifying that student's vision for the future (Wehman, Everson, & Reid, 2001). According to Storms, O'Leary, and Williams (2000), a student's desired post-school goals or vision for the future is the first step in the transition planning process.

3. **Relevant curriculum experiences.** A student's curriculum should match his or her own vision for the future. Students need consistency and congruence between what they want to do when they leave high school and what they are doing in high school. Their dreams and aspirations for the future must be matched with rich and varied experiences that allow them to determine whether their transition goals are right for them. In general, secondary curriculum needs to value doing real things in real places. If students want to work in the community, they need community-based work experience in career areas that match their interests.

4. **Student self-determination.** Self-determination and self-advocacy are perhaps the most basic and fundamental of all the foundational pieces of effective transition planning. Everyone involved must respect the self-determination capability of individuals with disabilities and make every attempt to expand opportunities for individuals to exercise control over transition planning. Basically, people will make decisions based on what is right for them. By enriching a student's experiences, schools contribute to his or her understanding of what works for him or her in the workplace, the classroom, and community life.

5. **Seamless transition to desired post-school employment and/or post-secondary education.** Finally, the outcomes attained by participants in the process must determine whether the transition was successful. When students cross the stage at graduation, this matriculation should result in a continuation of, and/or expanded opportunities for, community inclusion rather than the end of such opportunities. If graduation is to be a relatively seamless transition to desired post-school outcomes, a student's transition plan must be built around that individual's desired future, and personalized post-school supports (if needed) must be secured through collaborative partnerships. The transition planning process has been most successful when students' curriculum experiences match their desired outcomes and they are given increasing responsibility for all decisions that impact their lives beyond high school.

Transition planning requires a futuristic orientation to planning, an optimistic attitude regarding individual possibilities, and a deterministic approach to securing needed experiences and supports for the student to succeed beyond high school. In effect, these five foundational principles embody that kind of approach to assisting persons with mental retardation in the move from public school to post-school employment and/or post-secondary education.

Vision for Implementation

These five points summarize the vision for implementation:

1. **Universal student direction.** Student self-determination must be a cornerstone of any transition planning, not an added feature for some.
2. **Preparation for transition.** Schools must prepare students for the transition to employment and/or employment-related post-secondary education opportunities.
3. **Informed decisions.** Students and families must receive relevant information to make informed decisions about their visions for life after high school.
4. **Skill instruction.** Special educators must be prepared to teach self-determination skills to students with disabilities and to facilitate students' use of these skills during the transition planning process.
5. **Appropriate assessments.** In transition planning, special educators must use appropriate career education assessment and development processes.

Conclusion

One major recommendation derives from each of the seven national employment outcome goals reviewed in this chapter. These specific yet broad-based recommendations emerge as a blueprint for policy and practice changes in the years ahead for both state and federal government. The need for such recommendations is well documented by the literature review and source validations. The recommendations intersect in the sense that they cannot be implemented in isolation. What this review suggests is that all stakeholders desperately need a well-connected employment policy that flows from school to college to adulthood with funding and financing that is supportive, not isolated and disconnected. An ideal system will include the following:

1. People with intellectual and developmental disabilities will have access to adequately supported competitive employment, customized employment, self-employment, or other integrated work to permit their inclusion and productivity and to increase their economic freedom.
2. Students will be involved in multiple paid integrated work experiences before leaving high school and will leave high school with a job or other work-related vocational plans.
3. All federal and state funding programs, including Medicaid, will support integrated employment and full-day programs in the community.
4. Students will have the option to control direct access to the service delivery funds and select individualized programs consistent with their choice.
5. Backed by policy, funding that emphasizes personal control of employment support resources will continue to grow and will be available to all.
6. To increase employment and career opportunities, supported employment practitioners must regard potential employees as partners and customers).
7. Individuals will have full and equal access to specialized and generic resources that provide job training and job placement/support as needed to support employment outcomes.

8. Relevant federal agencies, such as the Small Business Administration, will support business ownership as a viable employment option.

Remember Lisa from the beginning of this chapter? It is clear that the tens of thousands of persons like her would be much better off if these recommendations could be put into place. Agencies such as the Department of Labor, Department of Education, and Social Security Administration mostly communicate with each other and legislatively integrate their policies to support Lisa, not to confuse her or her family. Ultimately, one can only ask: Should there be one law and only one law which governs *all* policies? Should all policies and practices come through one regulatory body with decentralized offices in the states and localities? How can these populations and their families, who are among the least empowered and most vulnerable, navigate a system that is so complex and confusing?

As we move into the next millennium, these are the hard questions that we must answer and resolve.

CHAPTER 9

Access and Support for Community Lives, Homes, and Social Roles

K. Charlie Lakin, James Gardner, Sheryl Larson, and
Barbara Wheeler
with
Jacquelyn Blaney, Brian Burwell, Amanda Cade, Tina Campanella,
Celia Feinstein, Cathy Ficker-Terrill, Marty Ford, Suellen Galbraith,
William Gaventa, Robert Gettings, Thomas Hamilton, Larry James,
John Jordan, Mark Polit, Tim Quinn, Glen Stanton, Steve Taylor, and
Ann Thomas

REAL LIVES

Inside and Out

By Russell Daniels

I was 12 years old when I was sent to a state school. When I left there I was 28 years old. I'm 50 years old now. I went in April of '58. It was a rainy day. I went to the institution because I had problems with going to school and stuff like that. You know, when you don't like school that's what happens. And that's one reason why I had to go to the institution, because I was a problem child. Everybody, you know, sometimes gets in trouble and they don't like to go to school and stuff like that.

I wasn't allowed to see my family the first day. They give you a week without seeing them. After a while they start letting you have visitors. In those days they let you go out for the day but when you came back you would be searched. You couldn't have money, watches, rings, or anything. They'd take everything away because that was the rules and regulations.

I'm really proud to be out and I never want to go back to any institution at all. It was terrible.... "Do this, and do that. Sit down and don't say a word." So, when I got about 17, something like that, I took off. Packed up my lunch and took off and went into the woods and went on the highway and started walking. Then I got picked up by the police.

I wanted to leave because I didn't like it after that first time. I didn't like it at all. I was scared, and didn't know anybody, and all that. But after a while I got used to it. I got friendly with everybody. Yeah, it was all right then. Yet, I wasn't given any choices.

During the day they put you in a room with a bunch of other people and they'd stay there. After I got used to being there I went to school and I had a job. I used to help clean the place up and do dishes and set tables. They didn't pay you. That was a job, and that's what you had to do. For fun they would have movies and dances and stuff like that.

You'd have to get up at six in the morning, get dressed, make sure everybody else is up, make your bed, and then everybody went downstairs in the day hall. They are ready to go down for breakfast at seven o'clock. We all had to be in line. The second shift comes in, they go outdoors and play, you know, play baseball or something like that, lunch-time was about noon, and then they come in about five o'clock. Everybody comes in, washes their face and hands, line up and get a tray and get their food in line and sit down. At night they watched TV until nine, which was bedtime. Everything shut off, the lights off and that's it.

Now, I live like a king. I'm happy I do what I want, go where I want, I can come back when I want. Nobody tells me, "You can't go here, you can't go there." 'Cause that's annoying. I live by myself. I pay my own rent. I pay my bills. I work at the Senior Center. I have been working there for about three years. I'm a janitor. I clean up the place and lock up and help the elderly people out. You know, help them down stairs and stuff. I love it. And they all love me. (Daniels, 1996)

Dare to Dream

By Michael Maloney

Today, I'm moving into my new apartment. As we pack boxes, my thoughts return to 1989—the year I dared to dream.

In 1989, when I was 29 years old, I started looking for an affordable apartment. It was time to move out of my parents' home. I am a person with many abilities who needs daily supports. My social worker told me the only housing choice that would meet my needs was a nursing home. Of course, it was not my first choice. However, moving there was going to get me out of my parents' home, so I moved and continued to dream of living in a home of my own.

While I was in the nursing home, I met people who helped me learn more about the disabilities services system. Before the Medicaid waiver, choices were extremely limited. Once I got on the waiver list and selected a support coordinator, I moved into a group home. The group home was not what I wanted, but it was a step closer to my own apartment. With help from my friends and support coordinator, I left the group home and moved to a facility with individual apartments. But I was not allowed to choose my roommate.

Now, after 10 years, I'm moving into an apartment of my choosing, with a roommate of my choice, close to public transportation, and near a college campus, where I plan to continue my education—another dream of mine. (Malony, 1999)

INTRODUCTION

This chapter addresses national commitments to ensure physical and social inclusion and full community citizenship for people with intellectual and developmental disabilities (ID/DD). We identify commitments to community supports that respond to individual needs and preferences in the context of healthy, safe, and integrated lifestyles and the challenges in maintaining them.

Background

Since 1967, and especially since 1977, a major shift has occurred in locations where persons with ID/DD receive residential and related supports. In June 1977, an estimated 207,356 (83.7%) of the 247,780 persons with ID/DD receiving residential services lived in public and private institutional settings with 16 or more residents. Twenty-six years later, just 72,474 (18%) of the estimated 402,281 persons receiving residential services lived in institutional settings. During this same period, the number of residents in "community" settings with 15 or fewer residents increased from 40,424 persons to an estimated 329,804 persons, with about 90% of the increase occurring in settings with six or fewer residents. In addition, the number of persons with ID/DD living in nursing facilities and public psychiatric units decreased by about 22,000 persons between 1977 and 2003 (Prouty, Smith, & Lakin, 2004).

National expectations and commitments regarding access and support for community living are about much more than moving people out of institutions and into community housing. These broader commitments are often expressed through the concept of *supported community living* (Bradley, Ashbaugh, & Blaney, 1994; Lakin & Smull, 1995; Taylor, Racino, Knoll, & Lutfiyya, 1987a). The goals of supported community living include the following:

- People will have "real homes" in places where they control their own front doors and will choose their homes and the people with whom they live.
- People will have a choice of settings for everyday living, which will involve selecting services and supports for those settings; people will not be compelled to choose certain living sites because assistance is located only in those sites.
- People will be assisted in defining the lifestyles they want and supported in achieving them. People will receive help in developing and expressing lifestyle preferences.
- People will be able to choose and participate in employment, volunteer work, and activities that contribute to their community and the sense of personal value and well-being.
- People will have service providers who are sensitive to and respectful of people's homes and the rights and courtesies to which their residents are entitled.
- People will choose and control their services and supports and those who provide them.
- Quality assurance efforts will focus on improving quality of life and desired personal outcomes within the context of protecting basic health and safety.

GOALS AND SOURCES

Access to and support for community lives have changed rapidly during recent decades. These changes have brought new opportunities and challenges in providing access to integrated, satisfying community lives. Publicly and visibly, the U.S. government has set national goals that promise places for persons with ID/DD in communities where they were born or that they choose. The Center for Disease Control and Prevention's (CDC) Healthy People 2010 report explains the importance of these goals:

> Institutionalization and other forms of congregate care are inconsistent with positive public health policy and practice. They diminish people's opportunities to realize essential features of human well-being: choice, control, ability to establish and pursue personal goals, family and community interaction, privacy, freedom of association and the respect of others. (National Center on Birth Defects and Developmental Disabilities, 2003, p. 181)

Goals that promise access to and support for integrated community lives for people with ID/DD are found in numerous legislative, judicial, and administrative sources. These goals can be grouped into five national commitments:

A. To allow people with ID/DD to live in and participate fully in their communities
B. To ensure that people with ID/DD will have satisfying lives and valued social roles
C. To help people with ID/DD and their families choose supports they need and control how resources are used to provide them
D. To provide people with ID/DD with stable, skilled support providers when needed
E. To provide people with ID/DD with health, safety, and support to manage life's risks

Goal A: To allow people with ID/DD to live in and participate fully in their communities

The national commitment to ensuring physical access to, and participation in, community life is evident in many national laws and directives. The following are key cases.

Americans with Disabilities Act (ADA) and the Supreme Court's Interpretation in Olmstead

In *Olmstead v. L.C., et al.* (527 U.S. 581 [1999]), the U.S. Supreme Court ruled that Title II of the ADA requires states to provide services, programs, and activities that are developed for people with disabilities in the "most integrated setting appropriate" (527 U.S. 581 [1999]). The court also concluded that states are obligated to place qualified people with disabilities in community settings, provided that (a) treatment professionals determine that community placement is appropriate, (b) the individuals themselves do not oppose appropriate community placement, and (c) the state in which the person lives can reasonably accommodate community placement, taking into account available resources and the needs of others with disabilities.

The Presidential Executive Order and the New Freedom Initiative

On June 18, 2001, President George W. Bush signed an Executive Order that committed the Executive Branch of the U.S. government to the Olmstead assertion that "unjustified isolation or segregation of qualified individuals with disabilities through institutionalization is a form of disability-based discrimination prohibited by Title II of the ADA of 1990 (ADA)" (42 USC 12101). The president's order stated that the nation "is committed to community-based alternatives for individuals with disabilities and recognizes that such services advance the best interests of Americans" (Bush, 2001, p. 1). The order also called on federal departments to (a) "work with States to help them assess their compliance with the Olmstead decision and the ADA," (b) "provide technical guidance and work cooperatively with States to achieve the goals of Title II of the ADA," (c) "ensure that existing Federal resources are used in the most effective manner to support the goals of the ADA," (d) "evaluate the policies, programs, statutes, and regulations of their respective agencies to determine whether any should be revised or modified to improve the availability of community-based services," and (e) "focus on identifying affected populations, improving the flow of information about supports in the community, and removing barriers that impede opportunities for community placement" (Bush, 2001, p. 2).

Healthy People 2010 Objectives

The Healthy People 2010 project is guided by the CDC to establish and monitor national objectives to improve the health of U.S. citizens. Project objectives include a health agenda based on disability and secondary conditions. Among the agenda's goals are two that address community support specifically: "Objective 6.7a. Reduce the number of adults aged 18-64 years in congregate care facilities by 50% [and] Objective 6.7b. Reduce to zero the number of children aged 17 years and younger living in congregate care facilities." Congregate care refers to "settings in which children and adults live in a group of four or more persons with disabilities in order to receive needed supports and services" (National Center on Birth Defects and Developmental Disabilities [NCBDDD], 2003, p. 181).

The Developmental Disabilities Assistance and Bill of Rights Act 2000

In the Developmental Disabilities Assistance and Bill of Rights Act of 2000 (DD Act), Congress found that disability "does not diminish the right of individuals with developmental disabilities to live independently, to exert control and choice over their own lives" (§ 101(a)(1)) and that

> the goals of the Nation properly include the goal of providing individuals with developmental disabilities with the information, skills, opportunities, and support to…live in homes and communities in which such individuals can exercise their full rights and responsibilities as citizens. (§ 101(a)(16)(B))

Congress also recognized the national interest of helping people "achieve full integration and inclusion in society in an individual manner, consistent with the unique strengths, resources, priorities, concerns, abilities and capabilities of each individual" (§ 101(a)(16)(E)).

Goal B: To ensure that people with ID/DD will have satisfying lives and valued social roles

The national commitment to the welfare of persons with ID/DD recognizes life satisfaction and valued social roles. Objective 6.6 of Healthy People 2010 encourages us to "increase the proportion of adults with disabilities reporting satisfaction with life" (National Center on Birth Defects and Developmental Disabilities, 2003, p. 175).

Developmental Disabilities Assistance and Bill of Rights Act of 2000

In the DD Act, Congress identified "the right of individuals with developmental disabilities…to fully participate in and contribute to their communities through full integration and inclusion in the economic, political, social, cultural and educational mainstream of United States society" (§ 101(a)(1)). The Act also states that "the goals of the Nation properly include providing individuals with developmental disabilities with the information, skills, opportunities and support to…have interdependent friendships and relationships with other persons" (§ 101(a)(16)(E)). Regarding programs the act authorizes, Congress mandates that "individuals with developmental disabilities have access to opportunities and necessary support to be included in community life, have interdependent relationships…access to and use of recreational, leisure, and social opportunities to enrich their participation in community life" (§ 101(c)(8)&(12)).

The Rehabilitation Act

The findings of the Rehabilitation Act of 1973 (as amended) include the affirmation that disability

> in no way diminishes the right of individuals to a) live independently; b) enjoy self-determination; c) make choices; d) contribute to society; e) pursue meaningful careers; and f) enjoy full inclusion and integration in the economic, political, social, cultural, and educational mainstream of American society. (29 USC 701(a)(2))

Furthermore, according to the act, "the goals of the Nation properly include the goal of providing individuals with disabilities with the tools necessary to…a) make informed choices and decisions; and b) achieve equality of opportunity, full inclusion and integration in society, employment, independent living, and economic and social self-sufficiency" (29 USC 701(a)(2)).

Goal C: To help people with ID/DD and their families choose supports they need and control how resources are used to provide them

National goals envision a society in which people with ID/DD and family members (when appropriate) will control services they need and the resources for purchasing them. As noted, the Rehabilitation Act sets a goal of "providing individuals with disabilities the tools necessary to make informed choices and decisions" (29 USC 701(a)(2)). Other sources for national commitments to enhanced choices of, and control over, services include the following legislation.

Developmental Disabilities Assistance and Bill of Rights Act of 2000

In the DD Act, Congress stated that

> services, supports and other assistance should be provided in a manner that demonstrates respect for individual dignity, personal preferences, and cultural differences…[and that] specific efforts must be made to ensure that individuals with developmental disabilities from racial and ethnic minority backgrounds and

their families enjoy increased and meaningful opportunities to access and use community services, individualized supports, and other forms of assistance. (§ 101(c)(4))

The New Freedom Initiative

The New Freedom Initiative is based on President Bush's belief that "the United States is committed to community-based alternatives" and that "the United States seeks to ensure that America's community-based programs effectively foster independence and participation" (Bush, Executive Order 13217, p. 1). To continue fostering independence and participation, the Secretary of Health and Human Services announced an "Independence Plus" waiver program in May 2002. Independence Plus facilitates state requests for programs in which people with disabilities and family members have more authority "to decide how to best plan, obtain, and sustain community-based services, placing control into the hands of people using the services" (Thompson, 2002, p. 1). This option is based on experiences with state "Self-Determination" and "Cash and Counseling" demonstrations funded by the Robert Wood Johnson Foundation (Conroy & Yuskauskas, 1996).

Goal D: To provide people with ID/DD with stable, skilled support providers when needed

Secretary of Labor Elaine Chao noted that "direct support workers...are critical to the success of the New Freedom Initiative...[and] the cornerstone of America's long-term care system." Chao added that "the [nation's] fundamental, long-term challenge is to develop a committed, stable pool of workers who are willing and able to provide quality care" (2002). Laws and Congressional resolutions reinforce the need for sufficient size and quality of the direct support workforce.

The Developmental Disabilities Assistance and Bill of Rights Act

In the DD Act of 2000, Congress found that

> as increasing numbers of individuals with developmental disabilities are living, learning, working, and participating in all aspects of community life, there is an increasing need for a well-trained work force...to provide the services, supports and other forms of direct assistance required to enable the individuals to carry out those activities. (§ 101(a) (14))

Congress also found that "direct support workers, especially young adults, have played essential roles in providing the support needed by individuals with developmental disabilities, and expanding community options for those individuals," but expressed concern about a shrinking labor pool of young adults, more community services demands, stagnant wages, and inadequate training and professional advancement (§ 301(1)).

Congressional Joint Resolutions and Report Language

In 2003, Direct Support Professional Recognition Resolutions were passed in Congress. These resolutions noted that

> private providers and the individuals for whom they provide supports and services are in jeopardy as a result of the growing crisis in recruiting and retaining a

direct support workforce, which impedes the availability of a stable, quality, direct support workforce. (U.S. Senate, 2003)

The resolutions also found that "workforce shortage is the most significant barrier to implementing the Olmstead decision and undermines the expansion of community integration as called for by President Bush's New Freedom Initiative, placing the community infrastructure at risk" (U.S. Senate, 2003, p. 513062). In conclusion, Congress stated:

> It is the sense of the Congress that the Federal Government and States should make it a priority to ensure a stable, quality direct support workforce for individuals with mental retardation, or other developmental disabilities that advances our Nation's commitment to community integration for such individuals and to personal security for them and their families. (p. 513062)

The resolution was further reinforced by both the House and Senate Fiscal Year (FY) 2005 Appropriations Bills for the Labor, Health and Human Services, and Education (H. Rept 108-636; and S. Rept 108-345), which recognized problems in "recruiting and retaining quality direct support professionals to serve people with mental retardation and other developmental disabilities living in the community," and by legislation introduced in the House in March 2005 ("Direct Support Professional Fairness and Security Act of 2005," text available at http://thomas.loc.gov by indicating H.R.1264).

Goal E: To provide people with ID/DD with health, safety, and support to manage life's risks

People with ID/DD are generally recognized in national policies and programs as being among the nation's most vulnerable citizens. Along with goals to ensure access to community living, homes, and social roles, there is a pledge to ensure that health and safety are monitored and supported. Laws and acts related to this national goal include the following:

Developmental Disabilities Assistance and Bill of Rights Act of 2000

The DD Act (42 U.S.C. § 15002(23)(A)(B)(C)) notes that "individuals with developmental disabilities are at greater risk than the general population of abuse, neglect, financial and sexual exploitations, and the violation of their legal and human rights" (§ 101(a)(5)). The law provides for "quality assurance activities," and for

> advocacy, capacity building, and systemic change activities...that result in systems of quality assurance and consumer protestation that include monitoring of services, supports and assistance provide[d]...that ensures the individual will not experience abuse, neglect, sexual or financial exploitation, or violation of legal or human rights. (§ 102(23))

Medicaid Law

Section 1905(d) of the Social Security Act established federal cost-sharing for residential programs (Intermediate Care Facilities for Persons with Mental Retardation—ICFs/MR) providing "active treatment" for persons with ID/DD in settings of four or more residents. Conditions of participation include standards for health, safety, and individual rights that states monitor and that are subject to a federal "look behind." Medicaid §

1915(c) of the Social Security Act gave states the opportunity to provide alternative home and community-based services (HCBS) to persons otherwise eligible for ICF/MR admission. Under this program, the states, rather than complying with uniform federal standards, must define, monitor, and improve protection of the health and welfare of service recipients. State systems must be described in applications to provide HCBS and approved by the federal government. States are accountable to the federal government for assurances they make in applications.

Other Laws Protecting Health and Safety

The Civil Rights of Institutionalized Persons Act (CIPA), 42 U.S.C. § 1997 et seq., authorizes the Attorney General to investigate and take legal action in respect to conditions of confinement in public (but not private) residential facilities. These investigations focus on residents' constitutional rights to safety, medical and mental health care, habilitation, freedom from unreasonable restraints, and education. The Crime Victims with Disabilities Awareness Act (P. L.105-301) and the Violence Against Women Act 2000, Chapter I Subtitle B (Protection Against Violence and Abuse for Women with Disabilities) address the need for more research and protection for people with ID/DD, particularly women. Section 613 of the Omnibus Crime Control and Safe Streets Act (OCCSSA) of 1968 (42 U.S.C. 378gg(b)) also recognizes "domestic violence, and the forms of violence and abuse particularly suffered by women with disabilities." Sections 614 (Public Health and Human Services Act), 615 (Family Violence Prevention and Services Act), and 616 (Violence Against Women Act) have been amended to include persons with disabilities.

REVIEW OF KNOWLEDGE AND RECOMMENDATIONS

U.S. citizens still have much to learn about the status and required conditions for achieving national goals. There is a need for research that monitors and improves national, state, and local performance in five national goals areas.

Goal A: To allow people with ID/DD to live in and participate fully in their communities

Current Status of the Movement to Community Access and Support

Support for citizens with ID/DD in community settings has increased markedly during the last 20 years. Table 9-1 illustrates this progress, which includes significant decreases in public, private, and nursing home institution populations. There have also been dramatic increases in the numbers of people receiving residential support in community settings, especially in settings with three or fewer residents (Prouty, Smith, & Lakin, 2004).

The significance of these changes is reinforced by trends in the closings of institutions. There was an average of 0.6 closures per year between 1960 and 1979; an average of 4.3 closures per year between 1980 and 1990; and an average of 8.3 closures per year between 1991 and 2003. Despite this progress, an estimated 72,474 persons remained in public and private institutions for persons with ID/DD, and 35,005 persons with ID/DD were in nursing facilities in June 2003.

The shift from institutional to community supports during the past quarter century was due in large part to expansion of, and changes in, federal-state partnerships involving

Table 9-1

People with Intellectual and Developmental Disabilities Living in Residential Settings of Different Sizes on June 30, 1982 and June 30, 2003

	Nursing Facilities	16+ Residents /State	16+ Residents /Nonstate	7-15 Residents	4-6 Residents	1-3 Residents
■ 1982	40,538	122,750	57,396	30,515	17,486	15,702
▨ 2003	35,005	42,835	29,639	54,346	94,459	177,260

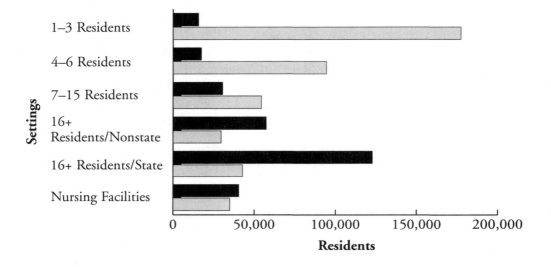

Source: Prouty, Smith, & Lakin, 2004

Medicaid. Prior to 1982, Medicaid's long-term care programs for people with ID/DD financed institutional services almost exclusively. In June 1982, Medicaid's long-term care program for people with ID/DD provided for only 11,095 persons in community residential settings and 171,508 persons in institutions. Medicaid programs supported only 17.6% of all 63,073 community residential service recipients. In June 2003, Medicaid financed services for an estimated 338,807 out of 402,281 total residential service recipients and an estimated 272,180 out of 329,807 community residential service recipients (82.5%). Medicaid Home and Community-Based Services (HCBS) programs also financed vocational assistance, personal assistance, service coordination, respite care, and other services for about 171,000 people living with parents or other relatives in 2003 (Prouty, Smith, & Lakin, 2004).

Interstate Variability Within Current Trends

National trends in institutional depopulation mask major differences among states. In 2000, 57.2% of all state institution residents lived in the one-third (17) of all states that were the slowest in depopulating their state institutions. Nine years earlier, in 1991, these same 17 states had housed only 43.9% of all state institution residents (Lakin, Smith, Prouty, & Polister, 2001). Because these slower-moving states now house the substantial majority of state institution residents, the future of the national commitment to deinstitutionalization is now largely in their hands.

Access to and support for community life also varies from state to state in the number and proportion of people waiting for services. In 2003, it was estimated that a total of 75,300 people with ID/DD were waiting for community residential supports (excluding those in institutions). Of 35 reporting states, 11 would have needed to increase the total number of people receiving residential services by more than 25% to serve those waiting, whereas 12 states had waiting lists of less than 5% of the number of people currently receiving residential services (Prouty, Smith, & Lakin, 2004). Development and access to community services has been historically left to the discretion of states. Statistics such as these suggest that unless national goals include substantial inducements not presently perceived by a number of states, the achievement of the national goals will remain largely within states that have already made community living a state goal.

Cost-Effectiveness and Service Access

With substantial growing, and often unmet, demand for community supports, the cost-effectiveness of services is of considerable relevance. The ability to finance the demand for community supports is a challenge to state budgets, which face major growth restrictions. It has often been assumed that resources committed to the care of people in institutions would move with them to community settings through deinstitutionalization, but many "fixed costs" remain in institutions even as populations decline. As average daily state developmental disabilities institution populations decreased from 151,532 to 43,289 between 1977 and 2003, the cost per person for operating institutions increased from $48,921 per year (constant 2003 dollars) to $131,123 per year (Prouty, Smith, & Lakin, 2004). Thus, decreasing state institution populations by 71.4% yielded real dollar savings of 23.4%. In FY 2002, 22% of all ID/DD service system funding was spent on the 5% of all residential and family support recipients who lived in public institutions (Rizzolo, Hemp, Braddock, & Pomeranz-Essley, 2004).

There are a number of differences between institutional and community services, such as case mix, or the relative intensity and/or specialization of the services and supports needed by recipients, and the comprehensiveness of services that programs offer. Critical reviews of literature and cost comparison studies' efforts to control for common limitations have addressed methodological considerations in cost comparisons (Lewis & Bruininks, 1994; Walsh, Kastner, & Green, 2003). Several of the latter efforts have gathered generally comparable cost information for public institutions and small community facilities that include similar service packages: full-time staffed residential care, day programs, case management, transportation, and medical services (Ashbaugh & Allard, 1984; Bensberg & Smith, 1984; Campbell & Smith, 1989; Jones, Conroy, Feinstein, &

Lemanowicz, 1983; Knobbe, Carey, Rhodes, & Horner, 1995; Schalack & Fredericks, 1990; Stancliffe & Lakin, 1998; Touche Ross & Co., 1980). Each study found that costs of comparable comprehensive service packages were more similar than typically reported. This can be attributed to the fact that institution expenditures usually included more services and that institution residents were typically people who were in need of more assistance. As a group, these studies found that comprehensive community services averaged about 85% of the costs of institutional programs, with a range of 72% to 95%. Critiques of this research suggest that public institutions are not inherently more expensive; rather, institutions are more expensive because direct support staff earn, on average, about 34% more than private community employees (Polister, Lakin, & Prouty, 2003) because they are highly regulated and professionalized and because policy decisions that have led to depopulation have also challenged institutions to operate efficiently at a point below their design capacity (Stancliffe, Lakin, Shea, Prouty, & Coucouvanis, 2005). By contrast, in Britain, where wages are more nearly equal and public institutions operate closer to designed capacity, institutions may be less expensive (Emerson, Robertson, Gregory, Kessissoglou, Hatton, Hallam, et. al, 2000). The United States and Britain do appear to share more positive outcomes associated with various options available in communities (Emerson, Robertson, Hatton, Knapp, Walsh, & Hallam, 2005; Stancliffe & Lakin, 2005).

Despite complexities and ambiguities, continued attention to costs within different service models is crucial because of challenges that states face in funding current services while also responding to those waiting for services. The need for such research will be reinforced by increased attention to reducing Medicaid costs (or at least reducing Medicaid cost increases) and by the problems states face in raising their required contributions to Medicaid's federal-state cost share.

From the early 1990s through 2005 states were particularly successful in claiming Medicaid cost share for services that states had once financed. State dollars were replaced by federal dollars and reinvested as the state cost share for new services, which were co-financed with federal cost shares. Between FY 1991 and FY 2000, federal contributions for community services for persons with ID/DD increased 227% in real 2000 dollars (an increase of $7.36 billion), compared with substantial but much lower real dollar increases of 46.4% in state expenditures for community services (an increase of about $3.65 billion). Between FY 1991 and FY 2000, inflation-controlled state and federal service expenditures for all ID/DD services increased 45% ($20.34 billion to about $29.5 billion). Over the same period, total state expenditures (in real 2000 dollars) increased from $12.7 billion to $14.72 billion (15.9%), whereas total federal expenditures increased from $7.64 billion to $14.78 billion (93.5%) (Braddock, et al., 2002; Prouty, Smith, & Lakin, 2003).

This recent period of success in maximizing the federal cost share has left most states needing to raise additional revenues for further service expansion. But with most states facing revenue difficulties and with new Medicaid service development now more likely to require new state revenues, research on costs and cost-effectiveness of different service models will be essential. These efforts will have important consequences for future community services.

People Living with Families

At any one time, less than 20% of all persons identified as having ID/DD and about one-third of adults (18 and older) receive residential services outside their family homes (Jaskulski, Lakin, & Zierman, 1995; Larson, Lakin, Anderson, Kwak, Lee, & Anderson, 2001). Without question, the system of community support is dependent on sustaining high levels of family support for members with ID/DD. Ironically, most social policy and resources that support community access for persons with ID/DD have focused on people living outside of their family homes.

There is a limited body of research on long-term experiences and outcomes in the following areas:

1. Families as primary care providers for adults with ID/DD (Krauss & Seltzer, 1993; Parish, Seltzer, Greenberg, & Floyd, 2004)
2. Lifestyle, autonomy, and development of persons with ID/DD who live with their families well into adulthood (Seltzer, 1985)
3. Contributions that adult children make to their families (Heller & Factor, 1993b)
4. Need for, and contributions of, family supports to the well-being of family members with ID/DD (Hoyert & Seltzer, 1992)
5. Variation in needs for, and contributions of, family supports across family life cycles (Roberto, 1993; Smith, Tobin, & Fullmer, 1995)
6. Cost benefits of family supports in home and community services programs (Hewitt, Larson, & Lakin, 2000; Lewis & Johnson, 2005)
7. General family quality of life (Poston, Turnbull, Park, Mannan, Marquis, & Wang, 2003)

Nevertheless, the body of research on adults with ID/DD who live with family members (with or without support services) is quite small given the size of this population, the benefits of family care to long-term support systems generally, and related effects of family care on families themselves. Although data collection was limited to families with children, the National Health Interview Survey—Disability Supplement showed that 53% of families with school-age children with ID/DD reported one or more of the following consequences: (a) unemployment or underemployment; (b) changing or reducing work schedules; (c) quitting or changing jobs; (d) changing sleep patterns; and (e) severe financial problems. This compares with 23% of families with children with disabilities but not ID/DDs (Anderson, Larson, Lakin, & Kwak, 2002).

Other researchers have identified similar effects on family economic life and the strain this may place on families as they approach mid-life with lower income, savings, and retirement benefits levels (Parish, et al., 2004). In the past decade, policy makers have acknowledged the importance of specific supports for families with members with ID/DD living at home. In 2002, states spent an estimated $1.38 billion dollars to help families of persons with ID/DD: $86 million in cash subsidies and an estimated $1.29 billion in direct family support services. This $1.38 billion represented a 31% increase from two years earlier (Rizzolo, Hemp, Braddock, & Pomeranz-Essley, 2004) and did not include Supplemental Security Income (SSI), the single most important family support system. Nationally, about 253,400 children with ID/DD received SSI payments in December 2001, as did approximately 830,600 adults with ID/DD. These benefits of about $6.4 billion went primarily to persons with ID/DD living with family members or in their own homes (Social Security Administration, 2001).

Permanency Planning

One Healthy People 2010 objective is to "reduce to zero the number of children [with disabilities] in congregate care." Efforts to provide children the opportunity for the normal, permanent, developmental experience of family life are often referred to as *permanency planning*. In order of priority, permanency planning encourages the following: (a) support and training to a natural family to assist with raising a child; (b) temporary out-of-home placement with support in preparing for family reunification; (c) if reunification is not in the child's best interest, parental release and adoption of the child; (d) family foster care; and (e) the least restrictive nonfamily placement with movement to a stable, permanent home a soon as possible. When coupled with special education services, SSI for low income families, state family subsidy programs, respite care, personal care and other support services, and consumer-directed supports, permanency planning reduces congregate care of children and youth with ID/DD. Nationally, the number of children and youth (ages birth to 21 years) in residential care decreased from 90,200 in 1977 to an estimated 25,800 in 1997. In 1977, children and youth made up 37% of out-of-home residential service recipients; by 1997, the rate dropped to 8% (Lakin, Anderson, & Prouty, 1998). Family support has provided the assistance envisioned in permanency planning, with its evaluations supporting efficacy of both cash subsidy and family support service approaches (Freedman, Griffiths, Krauss, & Seltzer, 1999; Zimmerman, 1984).

Providing Community Access for People With Severe Disabilities

Although access to community services started improving by the late 1960s in most states, only recently has it improved for people with severe cognitive impairments. Between 1967 and 1977, total state institution populations decreased by 48,000 persons, and the number of state institution residents with profound ID/DD actually increased by 20,000. Since then, this population's numbers have decreased by more than 41,000, including a decline of 23,700 in the years between June 1991 and June 2002 (Prouty, Smith, & Lakin, 2003). But documentation of outcomes of community life for this population has not kept pace. Most studies of community living outcomes have included relatively limited samples of individuals with more severe limitations and have rarely made specific analyses of outcomes and unmet support needs of individuals with severe ID/DD (Kim, Larson, & Lakin, 2001). There is a need for development and evaluation of outcome instruments that measure desired outcomes for people with severe ID/DD. These efforts must respond to (a) the challenges of individuals to understand and/or communicate verbally about key indicators of community life outcomes, (b) the validity of using proxy responses for those who cannot, and (c) the need for instruments that capture developmental change in increments smaller than those of traditional adaptive behavior measures used in most research studies (Stancliffe, Hayden, Larson, & Lakin, 2002).

Research Recommendations

Several research commitments and priorities are important to ensure that Americans with ID/DD live, and participate fully, in their communities:

- Identify, analyze, and describe key elements of successful efforts to overcome barriers to people participating in community life in transportation, social networks, jobs, volunteer activities, emergency supports, communications, and other areas.
- Continually monitor and publicize the extent to which the nation and individual states are providing and planning services and supports to assure every person's right to live and participate in the community.
- Monitor the extent to which national promises are kept to different degrees in different states and for different groups of people; develop and evaluate information, training, technical assistance, and incentive initiatives to prompt states and groups who are falling behind to use information and experiences form others to achieve improved responses.
- Attend to community outcome experiences and needs of subgroups of persons with ID/DD, especially those with severe intellectual, communication, physical, health, and behavioral impairments.
- Evaluate efforts to improve cost-effectiveness of service and supports with respect to management/direction approaches (i.e., consumer-directed approaches), rate setting systems (e.g., individual budgets based on assessed needs), and service alternatives (e.g., family support) that yield high service quality and affordability.
- Use research to address the needs of the majority of persons with ID/DD who live with family members and to support the needs, expectations, and challenges of sustaining "family care" as a major element in the "long-term care system," while addressing the outcomes and needs of family members with ID/DD.

Goal B: To ensure that people with ID/DD will have satisfying lives and valued social roles

As people with ID/DD have increased their community presence and participation, they have taken on new roles (e.g., as shoppers, volunteers, employees). These roles involve participating in community life and contributing to the community.

Community Resource Use

There has been extensive research comparing lifestyles of persons living in communities with those living in institutional settings. This research is impressive for the magnitude and consistency of its findings that favor outcomes of community living (Conroy, 1998; Conroy & Bradley, 1985; Conroy, Spreat, Yuskauskas, & Elks, 2003; Felce, de Kock, & Repp, 1986; Horner, Stoner, & Ferguson, 1988; O'Neil, Brown, Gordon, Schonhorn, & Green, 1981; Stancliffe & Lakin, 1998). The only study to compare levels of community participation among random samples of persons with ID/DD in community service settings and members of the general population (336 and 100 persons, respectively) found the former to have slightly higher levels of community resource use than the latter (Hill, Lakin, Bruininks, Amado, Anderson, & Copher, 1989). Despite these indicators of positive aspects of community life, others have observed that many people with ID/DD living in communities participate in their communities less than might be expected or desired (Abery & Fahnestock, 1994; Crapps, Langion, & Swaim, 1985). In 1990, among 13,000 persons with ID/DD and family members participating in the National Consumer Survey, the most frequently reported support needs were social and recreational services and transportation. One-third of all respondents reported unmet needs for recreational and leisure services (Temple University Developmental Disabilities Center, 1990). In the National Health Interview Survey on Disability, 27% of adults with ID/DD living with family members or in their own homes reportedly wanted to take part in more social and recreational activities (Larson, et al., 2001).

Recreation and Leisure Participation

Leisure, recreation, and other community activities are important for engaging persons with ID/DD in social relationships and valued roles (Ittenbach, Larson, Speigel, Abery, & Prouty, 1993). Major barriers to social and recreational integration have been identified, including a lack of companions, friends, and advocates; finances; transportation; activities; needed support; skills development; and, assistance with challenging behaviors (Temple University Developmental Disabilities Center, 1990; Ittenbach, Abery, Larson, Speigel, & Prouty, 1994). Research on use of community resources and recreation and leisure participation found that severity of intellectual impairment and challenging behavior are predictive of low levels of participation in community activities (Bell, Schoenrock, & Bensberg, 1981; Dalgleish, 1983; Lakin, Burwell, Hayden, & Jackson, 1992). Overcoming these barriers requires systematic support to improve skills, identification of resources and support to use them, and development of new resources (Ittenbach, et al., 1994).

Community Participation Support and the Americans With Disabilities Act

The ADA and the subsequent Olmstead decision recognized the interests of persons with disabilities in avoiding segregation and their rights to accommodations to avoid segregation. Most individuals with ID/DD, especially those with functional disability in areas such as verbal language, judgment, memory, interpersonal interactions, and reading and writing, require very different accommodations from persons with physical or sensory disabilities. ADA Title II and Title III forbid discrimination in government-operated programs and in "public accommodations," prohibit denial of services or benefits on the basis of disability, and require equal opportunity for persons with disabilities to participate in, or benefit from, a service or activity that is offered to the general public. The effectiveness of the ADA for people with ID/DD is linked to appropriate accommodations for functional disabilities, to socioeconomic roles that establish familiarity and reduce stereotypes, and to primary consumers' ability to learn about their rights and advocate for themselves.

Ethnically and Racially Sensitive Participation

Human service systems respond to persons with ID/DD as genderless, raceless, classless, and without culture (Traustadottir, Lutfiyya, & Shoultz, 1994). Social responses to persons with ID/DD have often assumed that clinical conditions and service needs have much more relevance to the individual than do social and cultural aspects of the individual's life and environment. In the past decade, there has been greater recognition of social and cultural circumstances for people with ID/DD. Professionals and service providers increasingly recognize community as something complex and meaningful, not just an alternative to an institution. Efforts have been made to move beyond providing services in the community to supporting people's membership in sociocultural communities within a multicultural society (Hutchinson, 1990; Taylor, Bogdan, & Racino, 1991). Growing attention to social and cultural contexts of the lives of persons with ID/DD has led to terms of awareness and skills such as "cultural competence" and "cross-cultural competence" (Cross, 1988; Lynch & Hanson, 1992). These and related terms reflect the responsibility to accommodate and respect the real communities of people and their importance.

Sensitivity to the rights, needs, and desires of persons with ID/DD from minority communities remains a significant challenge. There is substantial evidence of differential access. Minorities are often overrepresented in segregated special education and institutional human services (Mercer, 1973; Oswald, Coutinho, Best, & Singh, 1999), but underrepresented in some of the more desirable, flexible programs of home and community supports, including the Medicaid HCBS program (Hewitt, et al., 2000). Several factors contribute to these differences: (a) less community service development in states and communities with higher proportions of minority citizens; (b) minority community members not supported to develop human service agencies; (c) less information about community services and supports for people of color; (d) skeptical attitudes toward public agencies among some minority community members; and (e) lack of harmony between middle-class Euro-American service approaches (i.e., concentration on services provided out-of-home) and cultures of some minority communities, especially those valuing in-family and extended family support (Harry, 1992; Hewitt, et al., 2000; O'Connor, 1993). Successful efforts to serve individuals from minority communities and cultures require more than professional sensitivity. Major reforms in service system design, regulations, resource use, and minority business development are required for equal access and quality of human services in communities outside the dominant culture.

Social Relationships With Other Community Members
Much attention has been paid to people's support networks (Abery & Fahnestock, 1994; Bott, 1971; Center on Human Policy, 2002; Rosen & Burchard, 1990). Social networks are groups of people who provide reciprocal support and friendship. Many compelling arguments have been made about the importance of social relationships for people with ID/DD (Bogdan, 1995; Bogdan & Taylor, 2001; O'Brien, 1987b; Strully & Strully, 1985; Taylor, Biklin, & Knoll, 1987). Efforts to support persons with ID/DD are often not sufficiently responsive to their social needs. Qualitative and follow-up research studies document that physical integration in community settings does not guarantee social and interpersonal relationships with others (Abery & Fahnestock, 1994; Bercovici, 1983; Bruininks, Thurlow, Lewis, & Larson, 1988; Rosen & Burchard, 1990; Stancliffe & Lakin, 1998).

Limited community participation and social isolation are common themes in the lives of many adolescents, young adults, and adults with disabilities, especially those receiving home and community service (Abery & Fahnestock, 1994; Bogdan & Taylor, 1987a, 1987b; Burchard, Hasazi, Gordon, & Yoe, 1991; Crapps, et al., 1985; Ittenbach, et al.,

1994; Young, Sigafoos, Suttee, Ashman, & Grevell, 1998). These findings show that development and maintenance of social relationships are challenges in supporting the community lives of persons with ID/DD. The most common friendships (between 43% and 85% of all friendships) for persons with ID/DD are with other persons with disabilities in service settings (Abery & Fahnestock, 1994; Hill, et al., 1989; Malin, 1982; Willer & Intagliata, 1984). Horner, et al. (1988) analyzed social networks of 67 people in community settings and found, on average, that participants had 12.3 socially important people in their lives on average and 5.5 of them were paid providers, 2.4 were family, 3.9 were friends from service settings, and just 0.45 were neighbors.

Hayden, Lakin, Hill, Bruininks, and Chen (1992) found that 60% of the people in community residential settings lacked even one nondisabled friend. Hewitt, et al. (2000) found that, of those Minnesotans receiving support through the Medicaid waiver program, 25% could not identify a "best friend" or regular friends, including other persons with disabilities. Reports from the Council on Quality and Leadership (2000) on personal outcomes of personal living in community homes showed that friendship and social roles are consistently absent. When friendships and benefactors were present, they tended to be individuals who provided professional services to individuals at some point in the past (Abery & Fahnestock, 1994; Newton, Olson, & Horner, 1995).

Social Relationships of People Living With Family Members

Considering that many more adults with ID/DD live with their families than in residential settings (Larson, et al., 2001), it is surprising that the literature on the lives of persons with ID/DD in out-of-home residential settings is much larger. The nature of the variables included in research on persons with ID/DD in residential settings often makes it inapplicable to people living with their families (e.g., independent variables such as size of residential setting and distance from family home, and dependent variables such as frequency of family visits). Krauss and Erickson (1988) noted that the size, composition, and functional roles of informal support networks for persons who live with their families differed markedly and consistently from those of persons living outside family homes. This study also noted that adults with ID/DD living in their family homes tended to have smaller social networks and spent most of their leisure time with family members.

A descriptive study of social networks of more than 400 adults with ID/DD living at home noted diversity in social situations but also identified challenges to inclusion. Males and persons with severe mental retardation were at higher risk for social isolation (Krauss, Seltzer, & Goodman, 1992). Adults living at home tended to have had social networks in which family members prevailed. Nearly half had no friends (peers) in their social networks. Paid professionals were seldom viewed as having social relationships and roles in the lives of people living at home. Families had little formal (paid) support for activities that might extend social support, and the lives of adults living at home were dependent on the social relationships of their parents. In contrast, social networks of persons in community residential settings are made up mostly of fellow residents with ID/DD. Social activities usually involve, and are dependent on, paid caregivers, but persons living in community residential settings engage in a relatively higher number of community activities (Hayden, et al., 1992). Individuals in host ("foster") family situations tend to have social network patterns more similar to those of people living with their own families than in community residential settings (Hill, et al., 1989).

Research on parent attitudes and experiences provides many suggestions from families about how family involvement can be supported and sustained while people are moved from institutions to communities (Larson & Lakin, 1991). Parents suggest responding directly to perceptions and concerns about program change; facilitating participation of the individual and family in decisionmaking; arranging opportunities to learn about and visit potential home and work sites and service providers; offering choices for consumers and families in selecting homes, jobs, and service providers; and maintaining communication and promoting family participation between community service providers and family members after placement.

Relationships With Family of People Living Outside the Family

Although most people in residential service settings maintain contacts with family members, the levels of contact and involvement are limited (Blacher, Baker, & Feinfeld, 1999; Conroy, et al., 2003; Lowe & de Paiva, 1991; Seltzer, Krauss, Hong, & Orsmond, 2001). Family engagement is limited among persons who have been institutionalized; most do not have monthly or more frequent contact with family members after moving to a community setting (56%–70%) (Evans, Todd, Beyer, Felce, & Perry, 1994; Feinstein, Lemanowicz, & Conroy, 1988; Stancliffe & Lakin, 1998). Several variables influence relationships between persons in community living arrangements and their family members. Stoneman and Crapps (1990) found that when variables such as having living parents and the age of the person were controlled, the level of parental involvement in the placement process and the encouragement of parents by the provider agency accounted for significant variability.

Direct comparisons of family involvement in the lives of people living in group homes with fewer versus more residents have found that people living with fewer residents have more family involvement (Feinstein, et al., 1988; Hill, et al., 1989). Factors associated with family engagement include living near one's family, living in smaller homes, and relative youth of parents (Booth, Simons, & Booth, 1990; Felce, Lunt, & Kushlick, 1980; Raynes, Sumpton, & Flynn, 1987). However, Seltzer, Krauss, Hong, and Orsmond (2001) note substantial engagement of older parents in their adult child's life after leaving home. Efforts to support constructive family involvement in the lives of persons with ID/DD who are living away from their families should be a priority in the future (Seltzer, et al., 2001). Efforts to adopt "outcome-based performance measures" as a basis for quality assurance (Council on Quality and Leadership, 2000), person-centered planning (Holburn & Vietze, 2002), individually managed service budgets (Moseley, Gettings, & Cooper, 2003), consumer-controlled housing (Fields, Lakin, Seltzer, Backman, Sprague, Hinze, et al., 2000) and other innovations may benefit from participation by family members.

Support for Social Engagement

The problem of social isolation of people with ID/DD is complex. Considerable research has focused on social skill "deficiencies" of individuals in relation to social engagement (Craig & McCarver, 1984; Hayden, et al., 1992; Holman & Bruininks, 1985). Studies have examined the contextual nature of relationships and interventions to increase social interaction in given environments (Chadsey, Linneman, Rusch, & Camera, 1997; Hunt, Farron-Davis, Wren, Hirose-Hatae, & Goetz, 1997). Social interaction of persons in communities was affected both by individual and environmental characteristics (Willer & Intagliata, 1980). Social interactions were much more frequent among persons living in homes where practical social skills were taught (Felce, Lowe, & Jones, 2002) and where there were fewer residents (Emerson, et al., 2001), but differences cannot be consistently identified below six residents (Felce & Emerson, 2005). Social networks are often most developed among people who share networks with support providers, whether regular staff, host families, or their own families (Hayden, et al., 1992; Hill, et al., 1989; Krauss & Erickson, 1988). The extent to which these are individually satisfying networks of people with shared interests has not been addressed.

The most powerful factor in establishing friendships is regular, ongoing social contact (Abery & Fahnestock, 1994; Amado, 1993). Friendships are more likely when and where people have access to, and participate in, recurring activities that result in more social interaction. Many authors have documented opportunities for people with ID/DD to join community associations and groups and their results (Gretz & Ploof, 1999; Harlan-Simmons, Holtz, Todd, & Mooney, 2001; Reidy, 1993; Taylor, Bogdan, & Lutfiyya, 1995). Faith communities are identified as productive sites for such regular involvement (Gaventa, et al., 2002), but studies report limited engagement with typical ("generic") community agencies and organizations (e.g., community education, social clubs, recreational resources) and few efforts by existing community agencies to reach out to reduce social isolation (Bruininks & Lakin, 1985; Bruininks, et al., 1988; Certo, Schleien, & Hunter, 1983; Halpern, Close, & Nelson, 1986).

Few service provider agencies appear to organize programs around social and emotional attachments and connections that constitute "community" as a sense of belonging (Walker, 1999). Many demonstrations and qualitative studies of "natural experiments" have revealed many ways of expanding networks of valued relationships through community leisure/recreation programs and agencies, churches, community arts groups, and neighborhood organizations. The efforts led to establishment of the Community Builder Award by the American Network of Community Options and Resources Foundation and the Full Community Inclusion Award by the American Association on Mental Retardation. However, there have been no case studies or dissemination to encourage replication of successful efforts.

Person-centered planning, in which individuals in a support network create a vision of what the person wants and needs and then develop an action plan, assists development and expands social networks (Abery, McBride, Pierport, & Snow, 1998; Everson & Zhang, 2000; Holburn & Vietze, 2002). Social inclusion facilitators with knowledge of, and connections to, the community have been recruited and trained to help the individual make connections with others in the community (Abery & Fahnestock, 1994). These and other strategies look to the community for these natural sources of relationships and (a) promote continued use of the family social network after an individual leaves home, (b) recognize the value of friends and neighbors and taking them into consideration in lifestyle and support planning, (c) involve persons with ID/DD in organizations that are sources of friendship (e.g., churches, recreation organizations, Boy or Girl Scouts, other civic organizations), (d) seek commitments to inclusion from communities and community organizations, and (e) support people in real roles in real community settings (e.g., work settings). Despite evidence that some environments and commitments foster social relationships better than others and despite stable relationships between persons with and without developmental disabilities, few community service programs have integrated strategies for positive social relationships.

Research Recommendations

A number of research commitments and priorities are important to the goal of ensuring positive social roles for people with ID/DD. These include the following:

- Identify similarities and/or differences in definitions, measurement, and effectiveness of instruments in assessing quality of life and life satisfaction among people with ID/DD, the general population, and people with different types and/or degrees of ID/DD.
- Identify, analyze, and describe the factors, experiences, and circumstances most associated with life satisfaction and the effective means of providing access to them.
- Identify and describe community support activities and programs that enable people with ID/DD to participate and have valued social roles.
- Develop and refine survey practices to obtain reliable and stable responses to quality of supports and quality of life from persons with significant intellectual and communication impairments.

Goal C: To help people with ID/DD and their families choose supports they need and control how resources are used to provide them

Personal autonomy—including decisionmaking, personal choice, self-advocacy, self-determination, and self-expression—is a right and expectation for most adults in the United States. Autonomy has only recently been recognized as a goal for persons with ID/DD, but it has long been identified as a key component of independent living (Budde & Bachelder, 1986). Self-determination includes attitudes and abilities that help people define their goals so they may take the initiative to reach those goals (Ward, 1988).

Increased opportunities to develop and use skills required for personal autonomy are urgently needed for persons with ID/DD (Guess, Benson, & Siegel-Causey, 1985; National Conference on Self-Determination, 1989; Wehmeyer & Stancliffe, 2003). As families, community support providers, and others improve in their ability to reinforce community participation by people with ID/DD (including those with severe and profound intellectual disabilities), they are challenged to foster self-expression and choice-making. Responding to such challenges is part of their responsibility to contribute to the well-being of community members with ID/DD.

Environments vary in how they facilitate and encourage personal autonomy. Community living settings are superior to institutional living in supporting autonomy and encourage people to make decisions, manage their own affairs, and be involved in decisions affecting them (Rotegard, Hill, & Bruininks, 1982; Seltzer, 1981; Stancliffe & Lakin,

1998). Within community settings, the capacity to make choices is consistently associated with settings with relatively few residents, although the association sometimes is confounded by factors related to administrative structures (e.g., ICF-MR versus HCBS financing in Conroy, 1996; Stancliffe & Lakin, 1998) or by the characteristics of individuals (Stancliffe, Abery, & Smith, 2000). Although there is a tendency for greater autonomy, independence, and choice to be associated with smaller community homes, community living by no means assures universal or sufficient self-determination outcomes for all persons with ID/DD (Kishi, Teelucksingh, Zollers, Park-Lee, & Meyer, 1988; Wehmeyer & Metzler, 1995).

Development of Personal Autonomy

Personal autonomy in choice-making involves "the act of an individual's selection of a preferred alternative from among several familiar options" (Shevin & Klein, 1984) and requires skills in communication and in choice-making. The choice-making process includes a number of distinct steps: being aware of preferences, knowing that choices among preferences exist, recognizing decision-making opportunities, defining choices or decisions, setting personal outcome standards or goals, generating alternative choices, evaluating alternatives, and choosing alternatives suited to individual goals (Abery, 1994).

Researchers who have examined choice-making by persons with severe or profound intellectual disabilities have found that when individuals are free to make choices, their observed behavior often does not reflect their known preferences (Shevin & Klein, 1984). Mithaug and Hanawalt (1978) noted factors that limit choice among persons with severe ID/DD: ambiguity in situations in which persons have opportunities to choose, limited abilities to respond in an interpretable manner, and task avoidance behaviors developed as a result of situational ambiguity and communication difficulties. The "acquiescence" that has long been evident in research and evaluation studies with subjects with ID/DD is a recognized result of the difficulty persons with ID/DD have in expressing their personal independence and preferences over desires to be "right" or compliant (Finlay & Lyons, 2002; Sigelman, Schoenrock, Winer, Spanhel, Hromas, Martin, et al., 1981). Despite difficulties with appropriate supports, the large majority of persons with ID/DD can learn skills and attitudes critical to self-determination (Abery, 1994; Wehmeyer, Agren, & Hughes, 1998). Training adults with ID/DD in assertiveness and decision-making can influence their skills in personal autonomy (Foxx, Faw, Taylor, Davis, & Fulta, 1993; Tymchuk, Andron, & Rahbar, 1988).

Several researchers have developed and field-tested educational programs to enhance the self-determination of adolescents and adults with various disabilities, including ID/DD (Hoffman & Field, 1995; Ludi & Martin, 1995; Martin & Marshall, 1995; Serna & Lau-Smith, 1995; Wehmeyer, Agran, & Hughes, 1998). Outcome data from these efforts are generally encouraging and suggest that effective development of personal autonomy skills and orientations involves direct instruction in choicemaking, assertiveness, decisionmaking, and expression of preferences; systematic integration of choicemaking, decisionmaking, and self-expression in daily life; capitalizing on natural opportunities; and provision of opportunities to make choices and experience their results. More demonstration and evaluation of methods for increasing skills and orientation toward autonomy, self-expression, and accountability are needed, especially for people who have had few opportunities for expressing individuality (e.g., people institutionalized in restricted settings, people who have relatively less ability to communicate, people with severe cognitive limitations).

Environmental Support for Personal Autonomy

Environments that provide few choices or those in which "well-meaning" caretakers dominate often inhibit expression of preference. Even when people with ID/DD express preferences, support providers are not always attentive. For example, in a school for students with severe cognitive impairments, teachers responded to an average of only 7% to 15% of student-initiated expressions of preferences or choice-making behaviors (Houghton, Bronicki, & Guess, 1987). Factors associated with community services, such as staff presence and the number of individuals served, affect self-determination (Stancliffe, 1997). Controlling for disability level and decision-making skills, the fewer hours that staff members spend in a community setting and the smaller the number of persons for whom staff members are responsible, the greater the opportunities for self-determination (Stancliffe, 1991; Stancliffe, Abery, & Smith, 2000). The very presence of staff can inhibit residents from taking personal control. Although it would be simplistic and even dangerous to propose reducing support to increase self-determination, such findings remind us that opportunities for self-determination are available in the absence of authority figures.

Levels of self-determination are affected by skills of staff and family members in providing supports necessary for the exercise of personal control. Direct support staff and family members need training to recognize preferences among persons with severe/profound disabilities, to identify areas of life in which informed decisions and choices can be made, and to support collaborative decisionmaking. Because such training is often unavailable, individuals with ID/DD lack opportunities to control basic aspects of their lives.

Empowerment Through Organized Self-Advocacy

Self-advocacy groups are an exception to the general lack of attention to independence, preference, and self-determination for persons with ID/DD disabilities. A survey by Longhurst (1994) of 271 active self-advocacy groups in 43 states and the District of Columbia found the following time allocations:

- 38.2% to individual self advocacy (rights, decisionmaking, advocating for individual rights)
- 24.4% to recreational activities (social events, learning about relationships)
- 15.1% to group advocacy (community education, contacting political leaders, advocating for all persons with disabilities)
- 14.8% to self-help activities (improving self-respect, fighting against labeling, helping others)
- 7.6% on group development activities (attending conferences, fundraising, recruiting members, selecting advisors)

Of the 6,309 members within the 271 groups in Longhurst's study, approximately 80% of reporting self-advocates indicated ID as their primary disability. An earlier study found that members of 98 self-advocacy groups were diagnosed with mild (45%), moderate (42%), and severe (12%) intellectual disabilities (Browning, Thorin, & Rhoades, 1984).

Self-advocacy promotes pride, enhances recognition of civil rights, and fosters policy and program involvement among persons with ID/DD. As a result, the number of self-advocacy groups grew from fewer than 400 in 1990 to more than 1,000 in 1996, with groups meeting in every U.S. state (Hayden & Senese, 1996). Increasing numbers of such groups, their growing membership, and the support of self-advocates to allow those with ID/DD to play significant roles in local, state, and federal policy are an indication of the national commitment to self-determination and empowerment of persons with ID/DD. Perhaps because self-advocacy is considered more important as a concept and movement than as an intervention, there has been little attention to its effects on participants.

Legal and Regulatory Barriers to Personal Autonomy

As attention to promoting personal autonomy through direct support has increased, the legal and regulatory framework promoting that concept has changed more slowly. Persons with ID/DD are often kept from making decisions because they are thought to be legally incapable of doing so competently, even when this conclusion responds to lack of capacity within one area, such as financial management (Flower, 1994; Stancliffe, 1994). The result has been widespread use of plenary (i.e., all-encompassing) guardianship orders that often are lifelong and take all legal decision-making authority away from the individual. The civil rights of persons with ID/DD lost because of such orders may include rights to vote, marry, hold a drivers license, or make independent decisions regarding health care, living arrangements, employment, and even who will provide the most intimate care for them. Despite evidence that many persons with ID/DD are competent to make life decisions (Lindsey, 1994), plenary guardianship orders remain the norm in many parts of the United States. Such legally determined overprotection substantially diminishes personal autonomy. Guardianship reforms that use individually tailored, time-limited orders, which are reviewed regularly to ensure they fit the person's current capacities and circumstances, would aid the cause of self-determination, as would clearer legal criteria of competence (Flower, 1994). Many persons with ID/DD need some level of protection, but often there is an imbalance of legal or regulatory requirements and the individual rights to personal autonomy. Implementation of more balanced and individualized protections with the least restriction on personal autonomy is crucial for tens of thousands of persons restrained by guardianship.

Controlling Resources for Needed Support

Programs to provide cash to families for costs and assistance in supporting family members with ID/DD began in 1974 with Supplemental Security Income (SSI) payments to households with limited financial resources. These payments were extended through family subsidy programs to other families in the early 1980s. There has been little research on effectiveness of family cash subsidies. Zimmerman (1984) found that 97% of 38 families thought the Minnesota cash subsidy was helpful in caring for their children with severe ID/DD at home. Meyers and Marcenko (1989) evaluated the effects of a cash subsidy program on 81 randomly selected Michigan families and found that the measured family stress was lowered, life satisfaction of parents increased, and the proportion of mothers who anticipated placing their child out of her or his home in the future became smaller (dropping from 32% to 19%). Heller, Ruch-Ross, and Kopnick (1995) also found that families receiving cash subsidies reported fewer anticipated placements than did families not selected to receive the subsidy (13% compared to 26%), as well as higher levels of community participation, better reported relationships with family members, and fewer reported unmet service needs.

Family subsidies have been a catalyst for individual budgets that give persons with ID/DD and their family members maximum control and flexibility in using resources allocated for individual services (i.e., purchasing what the individual needs to achieve the lifestyle desired). Such initiatives were nurtured by Robert Wood Johnson Foundation's Self-Determination project grants and are now provided in consumer-directed support models. Evaluations of these programs (Conroy, Fullerton, Brown, & Garrow, 2002; Conroy & Yuskauskas, 1996) have identified improved outcomes in integration, friendships, health outcomes, and achievement of personal goals. Of course, because consumer-directed supports are voluntary programs, individuals and families who engage in them are likely to benefit. Understanding benefits, demands, and needed supports of participation in self-determination approaches to service financing will greatly assist other individuals and families in decisionmaking.

Outcome-Based Quality Assurance

Program regulations can contribute to fewer personal choices and less self-determination for service recipients. This is particularly true of highly regulated programs in which staff performance is governed by compliance to uniform standards of "quality." Conroy (1996) reported substantial, statistically significant lower levels of choice among community ICF-MR residents than among a matched group of residents who used less-regulated (and smaller) Medicaid Home and Community Based Services funded living arrangements. According to Conroy, ICF-MR regulations can constrain staff members' responses to residents' self-determination (e.g., requiring that a nutritionist/dietician make dietary plans, thus limiting people's own choices of food) (1996).

As commitment to viewing quality in human services from the perspective of quality of life for individual service recipients has increased (Bradley & Kimmich, 2003; Lakin, Prouty, & Smith, 1993), several states have reviewed traditional quality assurance (Gardner & Nudler, 1998). Common elements have emerged: a culture of quality rather than simple regulatory compliance; consumer-centered development, value-driven standards; decentralized authority and responsibility for quality; multi-stakeholder monitoring; choice and flexibility in producing quality technical assistance before sanctions; and assessment based on consumers' quality of life (Bradley & Kimmich, 2003; Lakin, Prouty, & Smith, 1993). In many states, there are efforts to develop, implement, and evaluate alternative quality assurance systems based on individual outcomes and performance-based assessment (e.g., Pennsylvania, Massachusetts, Minnesota, and Utah as described in the 1996 Community Services Reporter and http://www.qualitymall.org). These efforts seek full alignment of quality assurance definitions and assessments with commitments to honor individual preference, choice, and control. They also promise to achieve better definitions of quality as experienced by individual service recipients while still offering the safety and health protection expected from publicly funded programs. They are, for the most part, shield systems that have not been well evaluated.

Research Recommendations

Several research commitments and priorities will be important to permitting people with ID/DD to have greater control over their lives and to gain choice in their supports and how resources are used to support them.

- Develop and evaluate methodologies to better assess and understand the preferences and choices of people with the most severe disabilities.
- Evaluate the effects of people exercising control over the purchase of services or the choices they make and the outcomes they experience in service selection, community participation, and quality of life; determine how the effects differ for persons in traditional community services.
- Assess public perceptions related to public support of consumer-controlled funding, the uses of that funding, and the basic standards and principles governing public support.
- Examine and describe changes in financing practices at federal and/or state levels that would support increased choice and control, and expanded connections.
- Examine and describe support practices, learning experiences, social engagements, and experiences that contribute to increased self-determination attitudes, skills, and outcomes.
- Evaluate alternatives to traditional regulatory practices and legal statuses (especially in quality assurance, case management, and guardianship) and their effects on self-determination and choice.

Goal D: To provide people with ID/DD with stable, skilled support providers when needed

The decentralization of community support services has increased challenges for recruiting, training, and retaining direct support professionals. Increasing use of in-home services, semi-independent living arrangements, supported living arrangements, and small group homes requires new skills from workers who now have far less direct supervision and contact with other workers than in congregate care settings. This shift has produced roles with great autonomy and responsibility. This increased responsibility is given primarily to direct support professionals, only about 30% of whom have college degrees in a discipline relevant to their task (Larson, Hewitt, & Knoblauch, 2005). Despite the need for service workers to prepare for their roles, scheduling and arranging for training is difficult because direct service professionals do not work in centralized locations. Therefore, greater attention and resources will be needed in years to come. Also, personnel issues are far more complex than just training. It will be necessary to recruit people who can acquire the needed skills, who will respect people who are dependent on their assistance, and who can find satisfaction and value in their work. Once they are hired and trained, it will be important to retain these individuals so that their skills and their familiarity with the individuals they serve can grow and continue to contribute to the well-being of people with ID/DD.

High Levels of Staff Turnover

There has been growing concern about personnel problems in community services. During the past quarter century, staff turnover rates have consistently averaged between 40% to 70% in community residential settings, with the average across 18 recent studies being 53% (i.e., American Network of Community Options and Resources, 2001; Braddock & Mitchell, 1992; George & Baumeister, 1981; Lakin, Bruininks, Hill, & Hauber, 1982; Larson & Lakin, 1992; Larson, Lakin, & Bruininks, 1998; Larson, et al., 2005), significantly higher than in public institutions, which had a 2002 turnover rate of 28% (Larson, Coucouvanis, & Prouty, 2003), and in other occupations (Price, 1977).

Growing Challenges in Recruitment

The increasing problem of recruitment exacerbates the problem of high turnover rates among current employees. Low birth rates in the 1960s and the 1970s led to labor shortages that will continue through 2010. The occupations that suffer most from labor shortages are those that pay the least, demand the most, and draw personnel primarily from the young adult population. These occupations obviously include direct support. In this traditionally female-dominated profession, problems have worsened as new and better paying occupations are more available to women. Competition also is growing among service providers for persons with ID/DD in the community and for service providers for children, persons with mental health needs, and persons who are aging (Larson, et al., 1998). For example, the number of people in the United States aged 85 and older (the group most likely to require supports to remain in their homes) is projected to nearly double from 3.02 million in 1990 to an estimated 5.79 million by 2010 (U.S. Census Bureau, 2001). The Bureau of Labor and Statistics projected that the number of personal and home care aides will increase 62% between 2000 and 2010 (Bureau of Labor Statistics, 2001). This means that the demand for persons in direct support roles will increase dramatically, while traditional pools of new workers (at least those aged 20 to 44 years) will decline.

These conditions will pose major challenges in staff recruitment, causing employers to draw more heavily from nontraditional employment pools and stimulating more attention to staff retention. Pay and benefits will need to grow, but given the likelihood of slow or no growth in funding, there must be more attention to increased productivity: specifically, reducing personal use of direct support units and their costs. Community service systems have barely touched issues of productivity, nor has there been adequate development and testing in human services of alternative approaches to compensation (e.g., state-supported tuition credits at public colleges, group purchasing pools for health insurance). Increased opportunities for professional growth and advancement are also needed.

Issues of Compensation

The relationship between adequate compensation (pay and benefits of cash value) and staff turnover, vacancies, and recruitment is well established. When compensation is higher, staff turnover rates are lower. This relationship is well documented in the general personnel literature (Price, 1977) and within the developmental disabilities literature (Braddock & Mitchell, 1992; Hewitt, et al., 2000; Lakin & Bruininks, 1981; Lakin & Larson, 1992; Larson, Lakin, & Bruininks, 1998, Larson, Hewitt, & Lakin, 2004).

Deviations from the consistency of these findings appear only to occur when the rates of compensation within a study fall within relatively narrow bands. In other words, small changes in compensation do not consistently affect turnover. When substantial differences exist in compensation rates, they are consistently predictive of staff turnover. Nationwide in public institutions in 2002, the average hourly wage for direct support workers was $12.33 per hour, and the average turnover rate was 28% (Larson, et al., 2003). In private community settings within 37 states reporting such data between 1998 and 2002, the average hourly wage was $8.68 with turnover rates reported in the range of 40%–70% (Polister, et al., 2003). In comparing these statistics there is essential consistency in the nature of the public and private work roles; the primary varying factor is compensation.

Effects of Workforce Crisis

Lower compensation for direct support professionals (DSPs) is also associated with higher proportions vacancies in staff positions (Hewitt, et al., 2000). Failure to find people to fill vacancies caused by staff turnover is an increasingly common phenomenon. Understaffed programs are unable to meet the basic needs of the people they support. Staff members work increasing amounts of voluntary or involuntary overtime, often to the point of exhaustion. To avoid regulations related to staffing levels, organizations are compelled to hire people they would not have otherwise hired, leaving people with disabilities vulnerable to abuse and neglect. Regulatory agencies and newspapers around the United States have recognized this fact in numerous reports and exposés (e.g., Boo, 1999; Corcoran & Fahy, 2000). Vacancies are also causing families with members with developmental disabilities in the family home to do without the level of family support services that are written into service plans and without which they are susceptible to stress, income and job loss, abusive relationships, and decisions to place their family member outside the family home (Hewitt, et al., 2000).

There are also relationships between turnover, vacancies, and staff compensation and quality of life of people with ID/DD (Larson, et al., 2004). The human cost of repeated early turnover is significant to people being supported because they lose contact with persons on whom they depend. Longer-term DSPs and supervisors become less willing to invest in development of new staff members as expectations for return on that investment diminish. People receiving supports become more vulnerable because new DSPs do not always know the unique needs and preferences of the individuals they support.

In a Minnesota study examining the impact of inadequate staff compensation, high turnover, and vacancy rates, individual quality of life of persons with ID/DD, as reported by 486 case managers, was significantly lower for persons in settings that paid lower wages (Hewitt, et al., 2000). Fifty percent of people whose family member received supported living services identified staff turnover as a problem for that family member. Staffing issues were particularly troublesome for families receiving home supports or respite services. Only 46% of families reported receiving the total number of hours of allocated respite services, and 56% stated that home supports were available when needed—in large part because direct support professionals were not available to provide supports. Interviews with 82 individuals with ID/DD revealed that those receiving supports from direct support professionals who were paid relatively lower salaries reported significantly fewer opportunities to participate in community activities (Hewitt, et al., 2000).

Response to Workforce Challenges

DSPs leave not only because of wages, but also because they do not get along with coworkers or their supervisors, or because they are dissatisfied with how their organization treats them (Larson, et al., 1998). DSPs who leave often report lower satisfaction with morale, opportunities for ongoing development, recognition for accomplishments, and feedback and evaluation of performance, as well as with rate of pay, benefits, and paid time off (Larson, et al., 1998; Lakin & Bruininks, 1981). New research is offering new ways to address workforce challenges. New hires who hear about the job from an inside source or who have had a realistic job preview are less likely to quit prematurely (Larson, et al., 1998). Initiatives to help organizations train and support supervisors and to improve personnel practices helped to address workforce challenges (Larson, Lakin, & Hewitt, 2002). These initiatives included the following:

- Recruitment and selection (inside recruitment sources, agency marketing, structured interviews, realistic job previews)
- Orientation and training (worker-centered orientations, structured coworker support, competency-based training, mentoring programs)
- Supervision/management (recruitment and retention outcome evaluation, support and training of supervisors, team-building, participatory management planning)
- Recognition (networking, enhancement of opportunities for workers, formal and informal recognitions of staff) (Larson & Hewitt, 2005)

Demonstration projects integrating these strategies have documented success. An effort by 13 organizations in Minnesota documented an average 33% reduction in turnover of DSPs over 24 months (Hewitt, Larson, Sauer, Anderson, & O'Nell, 2001). A similar two-year project with 15 organizations in Kansas resulted in decreases in DSP turnover from 58% to 49% and decreases in frontline supervisor turnover from 23% to 16% (Hewitt & Larson, 2004). Continued efforts to document effects of such interventions are important for developing the knowledge base on how organizations can approach challenges. As individuals with ID/DD and their families are empowered through consumer-directed supports to select, hire, train, and supervise their own support staff, they too will benefit from assistance in integrating effective personal support and management strategies.

Competency-Based Training

Challenges in training and supporting the DSP workforce have a knowledge base as a resource. There is a large body of literature in industrial/organizational psychology on training and support for employees. Professional associations on training, development, and human resource management have identified and provided access to effective practices. Administrators, trainers, and supervisors of DSPs often lack knowledge and mastery of this information. In 1987, the Administration on Developmental Disabilities began funding

University Centers on Excellence in Developmental Disabilities Services (UCEDDS) for training initiatives in areas of critical shortage and importance, including direct support. The monies provided to UCEDDS specifically for training initiatives under this program were recently rolled into UCEDDS core budgets without regard to continuation of training obligations. So, while the U.S. Congress and Executive Branch have recognized the crisis in direct support, federal targeted commitments to preparing direct support workforces have decreased.

Training required for, and delivered in, community agencies is typically defined by topic and hours of instruction. Most training requirements are met through time spent in topical presentations rather than through demonstrated competence in relevant skills (O'Nell & Hewitt, 2005). Despite limitations of such approaches in developing practical skills, organizations report problems in getting direct support professionals to attend "required" training (Larson, et al., 1998; Larson, et al., 2002). As gaps between employee skills and job demands grow, the threat to people receiving supports in terms of health, safety, and well-being also grows.

Competency-based training, which includes job analysis, assessment of initial skill, setting expectations for learning, selection of the best format and curricula to deliver training, provision of a setting in which skills can be transferred to on-the-job performance, and post-training evaluation of on-the-job competence, is a preferred training model (O'Nell & Hewitt, 2005). Nationally validated competencies have been created for human services workers (Taylor, Bradley, & Warren, 1996) and for frontline supervisors (Hewitt, Larson, O'Nell, Sauer, & Sedlezky, 1998). Training based on these competencies has been implemented in the District of Columbia and states such as Pennsylvania, Wyoming, Virginia, Kansas, Minnesota, New York, and Tennessee using the College of Direct Support (http://www.collegeofdirectsupport.com) or the College of Frontline Supervision (http://rtc.umn.edu/cfs/main/) online training curricula and in other states (e.g., Ohio, Illinois, Massachusetts) using different curricula.

The 2003 Joint Congressional "Direct Support Professional Recognition Resolution" states that "community inclusion and enhanced lives for individuals with mental retardation and developmental disabilities is at serious risk" and that "the Federal government and the States should make it a priority to ensure a stable quality direct support workforce that advances our Nation's commitment to community integration" (U.S. Senate, 2003, 513062). Greater attention to establishing, implementing, and evaluating knowledge-based recruitment, retention, and training of DSPs is a significant part of the needed response.

Research Recommendations

Several research commitments and priorities are important in assuring that people with ID/DD have access to qualified, stable support providers. Recommendations include the following:

- Identify, describe, and test interventions to improve aspects of workplace culture and organization that lead to a more satisfied and stable workforce.
- Identify and describe characteristics of staff knowledge, attitudes, and skills associated with quality of life and satisfaction with service outcomes.

- Develop and evaluate practices for training and supporting direct support professionals and supervisors to fulfill responsibilities of their roles in a decentralized service system.
- Identify and describe effects of systematic efforts to improve working conditions, compensation, recruitment, training, and other inventions on stability and performance of direct support professionals.

Goal E: To provide people with ID/DD with health, safety, and support to manage life's risks

In the last decade, three areas have been relevant to the health and safety of individuals with ID/DD. First is the trend toward deinstitutionalization and support for community living. Second is recognition that self-determination and personal choice have brought new freedom—but also risks—to people who are choosing their living arrangements and their coworkers, friends, and relationships. Third is the growing awareness due to research, program review, and media stories that community life alone will not prevent abuse, neglect, and other dangers. There must be serious attention to minimizing risks and ensuring appropriate responses to victims or to those in danger of abuse, neglect, and exploitation.

Protections for persons with ID/DD involve different systems and approaches depending on whether or not individuals are participants in formal publicly financed service programs. For persons receiving publicly financed services, there are formal quality assurance (QA) systems made up of licensing, regulatory, or other standards as well as persons in the designated roles of monitoring quality of services, personal well-being, and individual rights. For persons with ID/DD who live outside publicly financed and regulated service systems all or part of the time, protection and information about individual health, safety, and well-being are less available.

Quality Assurance

Integrated community living poses risks. The potential for harm is evident in reports of federal agencies (Health Care Financing Administration, 1998), in the statistics gathered in "vulnerable adult" reporting systems (Larson, et al., 2001), and in newspaper accounts (Boo, 1999; McEnroe, 2002). A primary challenge in providing QA for community services is the rapid growth of those services and even greater growth in the number of settings in which service recipients are found. In 1982, there were about 15,000 residential settings for persons with ID/DD; by 2002, people with ID/DD receiving residential services lived in more than 125,000 different locations (Prouty, Smith, & Lakin, 2003). States have not expanded quality assurance systems commensurate with this growth. Even if the states had, they would have needed to adjust to new expectations. What was considered quality in community services in 1982, or even in 1992, does not meet current standards or national goals. Today, quality includes dimensions of quality of life in addition to protection of health and safety. The proper response to risks that persons receiving community supports face, and to past failures to address those risks, is to evaluate assessment and improvement approaches that support valued outcomes while also safeguarding basic health and safety.

Evolving approaches to quality assessment and improvement reflect changing social expectations for persons with ID/DD. Borrowing terminology that Donobedian (1966) applied to health care systems, approaches have shifted from a focus on structures and processes of service delivery to a focus on outcomes. This shift is congruent with the World Health Organization's International Classification of Functioning, Disability and Health (2001a). Consistent with assessments of personal outcomes, the focus on valued personal outcomes as the basis of QA has begun to shift the focus of QA from attention to professional standards to attention to universal human desires (e.g., safety, health, participation, freedom of choice) with the assumption that the assessments will be useful in improving desired personal outcomes. Quality evaluators must understand each individual's life outcomes and needs and stimulate improvement (e.g., in living circumstances, relationships, service provisions). Shifts in focus from the treatment to the treated have been developed in accreditation systems (Council on Quality and Leadership, 1993), in programs such as the National Core Indicators (Taub, Smith, & Bradley, 2003), and in state quality assessment systems (Feinstein & Caruso, 2003).

Despite a greater emphasis on systems of outcome assessment and improvement, such systems remain inconsistently applied across the service system for several reasons: (a) the required allocations of time of skilled personnel for their application as compared with traditional QA; (b) the greater complexity in maintaining even rudimentary QA because of the rapid growth and dispersal of community service settings; (c) resistance to their application because of the greater difficulty in achieving outcomes than in implementing processes; (d) general resistance to change; and (e) difficulty in establishing infrastructures to use "outcome" data to support improvements on individual, organizational, state, or national levels (Kimmich, 2003; Lakin, Prouty, & Smith, 1993). Despite these challenges, there is no turning back in the struggle to make personal outcomes the foundation of quality assessment and improvement. Nor is there any lack of commitment to the belief that people can have positive outcomes in health and safety while also enjoying positive outcomes in the lifestyles they desire.

The Medicaid HCBS program was established 20 years ago to permit states to provide community services to prevent or reduce the risk of institutionalization. As a federal program, HCBS has charged states with developing their own programs of community quality assurance to protect the safety and well-being of service recipients. The federal government responsibility is to approve state service programs of quality assurance and to determine that states are implementing what was approved. Today, with more than 400,000 total HCBS recipients, the HCBS program is the primary national program financing community services. Over the past decade, there have been reminders of the gap between these ideals and daily applications of community quality assurance. A March 19, 1993, House hearing called by Rep. (now Senator) Ron Wyden of Oregon to examine quality of community services concluded that "State public officials charged with their oversight had little or no knowledge of the conditions with their homes...or at best found out only after terrible events had occurred" (Wyden, 1993, p. 64). Rep. Wyden concluded the hearing by noting that "we must consider how to build better quality assurance systems" (Wyden, 1993, p. 57).

The Wyden hearing led to press exposure of inadequate, life-threatening, sometimes lethal lack of quality in community services in the late 1990s and early 2000s. In June 2003, the GAO issued a report on quality assurance that recommended the federal government (a) establish detailed criteria for necessary components of quality assurance systems, (b) require states to submit specific information about quality assurance approaches, (c) ensure that states provide sufficient, timely information in annual reports on efforts to monitor quality, (d) develop guidance for federal reviews of state programs, and (e) ensure allocation of sufficient resources for reviews of quality and hold federal regional offices accountable.

Such commitments may be useful, but there is very little information to guide decisions about designs, procedures, instrumentation, and use of quality assurance activities. Requiring more or different models of quality assurance in the face of obvious shortcomings is justifiable, but it is unlikely to produce positive results until there are evidence-based concepts for effective models of quality assurance.

Abuse of Citizens With ID/DD

Although it is evident that abuse and neglect deserve much greater attention, information on abuse and neglect of people with ID/DD, particularly those outside the formal service system, is rarely collected systematically. Information on abuse and neglect is based primarily on anecdotal evidence, data from convenience samples, and the best information available in program evaluations. There is little empirical research about the nature, frequency, severity, and life consequences of physical and sexual abuse of people with ID/DD (Baladerian, 1997; Petersilia, 2001). There is more information on children than adults and more information on women than men, but there are only a few studies that address abuse and neglect of persons with ID/DD specifically. Studies from the United States, Canada, Australia, and Britain consistently find higher rates of violence and abuse against people with ID/DD than against members of the general population (Wilson & Brewer, 1992). People with disabilities are more likely to experience abuse for a longer time (Schaller & Fieberg, 1998), be victims of multiple abuse episodes (Nosek, 1996), experience more severe abuse, and be victims of a larger number of predators than are nondisabled persons (Nosek, 1996).

Sexual Abuse

Sexual assault affects many people directly and indirectly, and it may be severe in personal, social, and economic terms. The National Violence Against Women Survey found that one of six American women and one of 33 American men have been victims of a completed or attempted sexual assault. Although most studies agree that persons with ID/DD are at greater risk of sexual assault than their counterparts in the general population (Edgerton, 1981; Halpern, et al., 1986; Johnson, Andrew, & Topp, 1998; Wilson & Brewer, 1992; Sobsey & Doe, 1991; Senn, 1988), specific findings on prevalence rates are mixed. Exceedingly high rates were reported by Baladerian (1985), Hard (1986), Ryerson (1984), Stomsness (1993), and Summers (1987), who suggest that more than 70% of people with ID/DD aged 18 and younger have been sexually abused. Similarly, Wilson and Brewer (1992) and Kempton and Stanfield (1998) estimated that people with ID/DD are three to four times more likely to be sexually abused than their peers without ID/DD. Sobsey (1994) has stated that if criteria for sexual abuse were restricted to more severe offenses and to repeated victimization, the risk for people with ID could be five or more times greater than risks for nondisabled people.

More moderate estimates include those by Senn (1988), who summarized a number of studies indicating that 39%–68% of girls and 16%–30% of boys with ID/DD were likely to be sexually abused before the age of 18. A Canadian survey of 245 women with disabilities (Ridington, 1989) found that 40% had experienced sexual abuse, and 12% had been raped. Another Canadian study confirmed that 40% of women with disabilities have been assaulted, raped, or abused (Roeher Institute, 1994). Not only is sexual abuse common, it is usually part of a pattern. A study of 166 abuse cases (82% female, 70% persons with ID, ages 18 months to 57 years), found that 79% of the individuals interviewed had been victimized more than once, 83% of women with ID had been sexually assaulted, and nearly half of the members of that group were assaulted 10 or more times (Sobsey & Doe, 1991).

Vulnerability to Abuse

Individuals with ID/DD are vulnerable to abuse for many reasons including, but not limited to, the following: inability to escape an abusive situation because of mobility impairments and/or cognitive disabilities; communication or physical impairments that limit their ability to defend themselves from a perpetrator and disclose abuse (Brantlinger, 1985; Edmondson, 1988; Petersilia, 2001; Sobsey & Varnhage, 1991); dependence on others for essential, intimate caregiving; exposure to large numbers of care providers; limited social contacts outside abusive relationships; low self-esteem (Lumley & Miltenberger, 1997; Sobsey, 1994; Tharinger, Horton, & Millea, 1990); stereotypes of vulnerability (Nosek, 1996); difficulty defending themselves and getting assistance (Petersilia, 2001; Petersilia, Foote, & Crowell, 2001); limited ability to recognize danger (Petersilia, 2001); limited sex education and knowledge of appropriate sexual behavior and potential abuse (Chenoweth, 1996; Sobsey, 1994; Tharinger, et al., 1990); and effects of compliance training, especially when caregivers are also perpetrators (Sobsey, 1994; Tharinger, Horton, & Millea, 1993).

People who support individuals with disabilities are often the same people who victimize them (Curry & Powers, 1999; Petersilia, 2001; Young, Nosek, Howland, Chanpong, & Rintala 1997). Sobsey and Doe (1991) reported that in 96% of verified abuse cases, victims knew the perpetrators; 44% of the perpetrators were service providers. Sobsey and Doe (1991) estimated that risk of abuse increases by 78% due to exposure of the "disability service system" alone. In a study of abuse by attendants and health care providers, Young, et al. (1997) found that women with disabilities reported excessively high incidence of abuse from direct support providers. Petersilia, Foote, and Crowell (1991) reported that 26% of perpetrators were paid caregivers providing services related to their victims' disabilities, 17% were natural family members, 14% were neighbors or acquaintances, 11% were other service providers, and 8% were disabled peers. Turk and Brown (1992) found that 48% of offenses took place in the homes of victims, 10% occurred in perpetrators' homes, 14% in day/leisure facilities, 12% in public places, and 16% in vehicles or various unspecified locations. These figures highlight the boldness of offenders.

People with ID/DD frequently are not the focus of vigilance by a network of caring social supporters and often are isolated in their living arrangements and routine daily activities (i.e., employment, civic engagement, leisure). This contributes to their vulnerability and to a belief among predators that they will not be caught. People with ID/DD who live alone or with other disabled individuals are often at the most risk of abuse (Wilson & Brewer, 1992).

Underreporting Within the Justice System

Despite the high rate of reported abuse, there is still significant underreporting of crime against people with disabilities. The importance of people with disabilities in the criminal justice system is minimal and gives potential offenders the impression that criminal activity will go unpunished. The general population reported only 37% of all crimes to the police (Petersilia, Foote, & Crowell, 2001). The percentage of those reporting stigmatized crimes such as sexual assault is lower still and even lower for victims with disabilities (Petersilia, et al., 2001). Ridington (1989) reported that less than half of sexually abused women reported the incidents. In Stomsness' (1993) and Sobsey's (1994) studies, approximately 39% of identified incidents were never reported.

Studies suggest that the unresponsive criminal justice system is a reason for underreporting of crimes against people with disabilities. According to Sobsey's (1994) study of the 61% reported cases, 37% resulted in no conviction. Turk and Brown (1992) reported similar findings: 48% of offenders received no punishment for their actions. Of 13 abused victims who did report, Stomsness (1993) found that only two cases (15%) resulted in some kind of legal action.

Literature on criminal offenders and crime victims with ID/DD argue that these people constitute a special population when interactions with criminal justice systems are warranted. People may not understand their rights, but pretend to do so. They also may not comprehend commands and questions, may be overwhelmed by police presence, say what they think others want to hear, have difficulty describing facts or details of the incident (verbally and with assistance), and be confused about who is responsible for a crime (Davis, 1995).

Although crimes against persons with ID/DD are a national problem, public records and national crime surveillance do not adequately capture data on the presence of developmental disability among victims. Large population-based studies do not provide additional clarity because public records usually do not indicate whether victims have disabilities (Curry, Hassouneh-Phillips, & Johnston-Silverberg, 2001). National surveys of victimization in the U.S. typically have excluded people with disabilities from their samples. Until very recently, the two national crime statistics survey systems in the U.S.—the Uniform Crime Reports (UCR) of the Federal Bureau of Investigation (FBI) and the National Crime Victimization Survey (NCVS) of the Bureau of Justice Statistics—did not identify respondents with disabilities (Petersilia, et al., 2001).

The NCVS has recently been modified to include questions about disabilities of victims, but even with inclusion of disability data on these national surveys, the estimates of prevalence will continue to be inaccurate due to underreporting of abuse and neglect (Petersilia, et al., 2001). One of the major challenges facing all institutions responsible for the well-being of persons with ID/DD, whether the institutions are specialized or generic, is building infrastructures with expectations, monitoring systems, data collection, and response systems to assure that the many benefits afforded to people with ID/DD through community living can be enjoyed without fear of injury, abuse, or neglect. These are substantial challenges, ones for which available evidence is disconcerting. Too little is known and too little effort is invested in learning how well this society is serving those who need protection and how that protection can be improved. This is a basic aspect of the promises of access and support, and it deserved much more attention.

Research Recommendations

Commitments and priorities that will help ensure that people with ID/DD are healthy, safe, and supported in managing life's risks include the following:

- Establish and employ data collection methodologies to improve basic knowledge of the extent and nature of abuse, neglect, and exploitation within service settings, individual homes, and families and between caregivers and persons with disabilities and between persons with disabilities.
- Document differences in abuse, neglect, and exploitation among persons with different characteristics and circumstances and the factors associated with the different rates.
- Identify efforts to address abuse, neglect, and exploitation and identify successful efforts (or successful aspects of efforts).
- Evaluate and describe outcomes of traditional and alternative quality assurance systems for protecting health, safety, and exposure to risk.
- Describe essential features of, and expectations for, adequate systems of planning and monitoring to protect individual health, safety, and well-being.

CONCLUSION

As more people with ID/DD use opportunities to choose services and service providers, traditional community service agencies and organizations will need to redesign service models to fit those who were assigned to programs. Responding to this new way of doing business will challenge government and private organizations. Learning and communicating about efforts to achieve such transformations and factors that influence success are crucial. These challenges bring information gatherers and users closer together. As full partners in the evolution of support programs, people with disabilities and family members will be more involved in all aspects of research: identifying questions, collecting and responding to data and other information, and analyzing findings. Accommodating these new roles and expectations will bring needed changes to traditional research standards and practices.

Public support for services for people with ID/DD has become far more visible and threatened in recent periods of federal and state budget austerity. It will be increasingly important for information about benefits of community supports to reach the public through popular media as well as through academic journals. But research that contributes to efficient, cost-effective delivery of essential supports will be increasingly important.

Successful support of, and access to, community living for people with ID/DD ultimately depends upon a knowledgeable, well-trained community labor force. There is still a national crisis in ensuring a workforce of sufficient size and quality to meet current demands and future needs. Research must contribute to recruiting, training, and retaining a workforce that will help keep promises to persons with ID/DD. Above all, research that monitors achievement of national goals for all people with ID/DD is essential. Despite remarkable progress, these goals remain unmet.

CHAPTER 10

Support of Families and Family Life Across the Life-span

Ann P. Turnbull, Rud Turnbull, John Agosta, Elizabeth Erwin,
Glenn Fujiura, George Singer, and Leslie Soodak
with
Lynn Breedlove, Diane Coughlin, Bob Day, Steven Eidelman,
Annie Forts, Marty Wyngaarden Krauss, Myra Madnick,
Paul Marchand, D.J. Markey, Ursula Markey, and Richard Melia

REAL LIVES

Jerome Davis is the 15-year-old son of Elizabeth and Charles Davis, African-American citizens who live in the inner city of a major metropolis. Jerome has autism. His father, Charles, works in an automobile manufacturing plant. His mother, Elizabeth, used to work in the family's church as secretary and financial officer, but she has had to leave her job to care for Jerome and the family's new grandson, the child of Jerome's older sister and her husband, both of whom work. The Davis' income places them just above the federal poverty level, and Charles' employer-sponsored health insurance program has exclusion provisions that bar reimbursement for many of Jerome's therapies.

Jerome's disability and the failure of his school to implement positive behavior support in his IEP are contributing to his problem behavior and causing him to be increasingly placed out of the general education program at school. At his many IEP conferences and at other meetings with his teachers, Elizabeth is often confused by the technical terms the teachers use. When she asks why Jerome continues to be suspended or "asked to go home," the faculty tell her they are doing their best.

Having attended some local parent-support programs to learn what Jerome's rights are and what resources may be available to his family, Jerome's sister Danielle says his teachers are not using the best possible techniques for working with him. She wants to come to the school meetings despite the fact that his teachers say she is not allowed to be there. She also is upset that her parents are paying a private therapist to do what the schools are required to do—to assess why Jerome behaves the way he does and to intervene so he will not be sent to the "alternative education" program far from his home school. Danielle continues to raise fundamental questions: "What will become of my brother once he leaves high school? Where will he work and live? Does anyone here plan for his future, or do we just take him back home like some baby, which he won't be?"

* * *

Moira Manley is the 39-year old daughter of Jessie and Peter Manley. Jessie has never worked outside the family home; she recently has experienced several small strokes. Peter practiced law in a large mid-eastern city until his retirement at the age of 70; he recently has been diagnosed with a brain tumor. Jessie and Peter have two other children—Devvie, 26, and Sallie, 32. Moira experiences both a significant intellectual disability and rapid-cycling bipolar disorder. Her family is relatively well-to-do, in large part because her parents and their ancestors have been financially cautious and because Peter earned a good living as a litigator.

For the past four years, Moira, her parents, and her brother and sister have been anticipating her parents' health challenges and debating where Moira will live after they die. No one, certainly not Moira, wants her to remain in her parents' large home. A small condo or cooperative apartment seems more suitable to her needs and capacities. Because Peter's family has lived in the community for several generations and because Moira's siblings and cousins also live there, everyone in her family—parents, brother and sister, and cousins—believes she should remain in their home community; indeed, each of them expects her siblings and cousins to provide her with jobs and extensive and varied support for her lifetime. Moreover, Moira is an especially headstrong person; she is determined to live on her own and makes her needs and wishes known through her words and even more often by her problem behavior.

Some of Moira's family members, her psychiatrist, and the director and front-line staff at the local adult services agency strongly believe that she is not competent to look after her needs (as her parents have done all of her life). They also secretly believe that Moira's family will continue to "control" her, in part for their own convenience. They want to petition a court to have Moira adjudicated incompetent, and they want an "independent" or "disinterested" person from outside the Manley family to be appointed as her personal and financial guardian. What will happen to Moira, they ask, after Jessie and Peter die? What if the most reliable of her siblings or cousins leave the community or become unable or unwilling to provide services and supports? They argue that their agency is the only reliable source of services and supports; besides, its staff, not the family, know what is best for a person "like Moira," who has a dual diagnosis. It's time, they say, for the family to "get a break and take a break" from looking after Moira.

INTRODUCTION

This chapter focuses on families of individuals with disabilities across the life-span. Its theme is simple: leave no family behind. To that end, we first define "family"; then we explain the factors we have taken into account in reviewing the knowledge base and recommending future research directions.

Definitions

During our deliberations concerning the nature of family support, we generally relied on two definitions of "family." One is the typical legal definition: those who are related by blood or marriage or by legal adoption or foster-parent relationship. That definition limits the individuals who benefit from public funding; it also establishes legal accountability for the care of individuals who are minors or meet the legal standard for "incompetency." Curiously, federal statutes in the disability field do not define "family"; state statutes define "family" in various ways and for various purposes. The legal definition applies to both the Davis and Manley families.

A second definition is the functional one: A family includes the people who think of themselves as part of a family, whether they are related by blood or marriage, and who support and care for each other on a regular basis (Poston, Turnbull, Park, Mannan, Marquis, & Wang, 2003). This definition (a) recognizes that families are highly idiosyncratic and have unique ways of characterizing themselves, determining membership, carrying out their functions, and evolving over the life-span (Turnbull, Turnbull, Erwin, & Soodak, 2006) and (b) enlarges the family to include those who provide respite caregiving, such as long-time but unmarried partners.

Multiple Perspectives on Family Life

Three perspectives on family life are important to consider in reviewing and then reframing a research agenda: (a) family systems, (b) life-span considerations, and (c) cultural and linguistic diversity.

Family Systems

A family systems approach recognizes that whatever happens to any one member of a family happens to all of them in one way or another (Turnbull, et al., 2006; Whitechurch & Constantine, 1993). Within the Manley family, for example, whatever happens to Moira clearly affects her brother and sister as well as her parents. A leading family therapist describes the impact of family members on each other as analogous to a mobile:

> In a mobile all the pieces, no matter what size or shape, can be grouped together and balanced by shortening or lengthening the strings attached or rearranging the distance between the pieces. So it is with the family. None of the family members is identical to any others; they are all different and at different levels of growth. As in a mobile, you can't arrange one without thinking of the other. (Satir, 1972, pp. 119-120)

Accordingly, a family systems approach concerns itself with the quality of life of all members of the family, not just the individual with the disability. This approach identifies the whole family as the focus of policy, the beneficiary of services, and the focus of research. There is not a single member of the vignette families who is not affected by disability in one way or another.

Related to a family systems orientation is family centeredness—one of the core concepts of disability policy, especially at the early childhood life-span stage (Turnbull,

Beegle, & Stowe, 2001). The core concept of family centeredness means that (a) families should be included in decisionmaking at family, agency, and systems levels; (b) services should be individualized and appropriate for the whole family and not just for the individual with a disability; (c) families' priorities should guide goals and services; and (d) families' choices should be respected (Allen & Petr, 1996; Turnbull, Beegle, & Stowe, 2001).

Life-Span Considerations

Family life cycle theory holds that families move through a series of predictable stages during the family's life-span and that transitional phases occur between those stages. The exact number of life cycle stages varies according to different theorists (Carter & McGoldrick, 1999), but for this report we characterize life cycle stages as prenatal and early childhood, elementary/secondary/transition to adulthood years (the Davis family), young/middle adulthood years, and elderly years (the Manley family). Typically the life cycle stage of the family is determined by the age of their oldest child (Terkelson, 1980). Transitions are the periods between discrete stages during which the family adopts and must adapt to new interactions, roles, and challenges associated with the next life cycle stage (Rodgers & White, 1993).

Cultural and Linguistic Diversity

Approximately one-fourth (27%) of the population of the United States is characterized by ethnic/racial diversity (Deardorff & Hollman, 1997). National experts emphasize that "race and ethnicity continue to be salient predictors of well-being in American society" (National Research Council, 2001b).

- African-American students are more than twice as likely to be identified as having mental retardation than Euro-American students. African-American students account for 17% of the general student population, but they account for 33% of the population of the students identified as having mental retardation (National Research Council, 2002a).

- Poverty among African-Americans is three times as high as among Euro-Americans (Blank, 2001).

- A higher disability rate among children is associated with households characterized by poverty and single-parent status (Fujiura & Yamaki, 2000; National Research Council, 2002a).

- Low income is associated with higher rates of exposure to dangerous toxins, poor nutrition, less stimulating home and child-care environments, and lower birth rate (National Research Council, 2002a).

- Schools with more children from low income and racially/ethnically diverse backgrounds experience significant disadvantages as compared to schools with higher concentration of children from middle and upper income backgrounds who are not characterized by racial and ethnic diversity (National Research Council, 2002a).

GOALS AND SOURCES

The Overarching Goal and Five Associated Goals

Before describing the overarching goal and its five associated goals, we need to point out that the family traditionally has been the core unit of American society (*Troxel v. Granville*, 2000). As the Supreme Court has stated, "the history and culture of Western civilization reflect a strong tradition of parental care for the nurture and upbringing of their children. This primary role of parents in the upbringing of their children is now established beyond debate as an enduring American tradition" (*Wisconsin v. Yoder*, 1972). The biological bond of sanguinity explains the history and culture; it also justifies the goals. The legal bonds of matrimony do, too. The common law upon which our national legal principles are based has long asserted the "family as foundation" principle. The common law doctrine of *parens patriae* both enables the state to act to enhance families' quality of life and also limits state intervention. The federal and state constitutions codify the *parens patriae* doctrine in their respective general welfare clauses. Because the family represents the core unit of society, coercive intrusions into the family's traditional roles have been justified only when the family is unable or unwilling to protect its vulnerable members, particularly children and those with disabilities.

We turn now to the goals. After carefully analyzing the family- and disability-related statutes enacted by Congress and decisions issued by the U.S. Supreme Court, we find a single overarching goal and five associated goals (Turnbull, Beegle, & Stowe, 2001; Turnbull, Wilcox, Stowe, & Umbarger, 2001). The overarching goal is to enhance families' quality of life. The associated goals support this goal and set out various means for achieving the associated, and thereby the overarching, goal. Table 10-1 sets out the goals, and Table 10-2 is a matrix that connects the goals to key federal statutes and judicial decisions.

Table 10-1

Overarching Goal and Five Associated Goals to "Leave No Family Behind"

- *Overarching goal:* To support the caregiving efforts and enhance the quality of life of all families so that families will remain the core unit of American society
- *Goal A:* To ensure family-professional partnerships in research, policy-making, and the planning and delivery of supports and services so that families will control their own destinies with due regard to the autonomy of adult family members with disabilities to control their own lives
- *Goal B:* To ensure that families fully participate in communities of their choice through comprehensive, inclusive, neighborhood-based, and culturally responsive supports and services
- *Goal C:* To ensure that services and supports for all families are available, accessible, appropriate, affordable, and accountable
- *Goal D:* To ensure that sufficient public and private funding will be available to implement these goals and that all families will participate in directing the use of public funds authorized and appropriated for their benefits
- *Goal E:* To ensure that families and professionals have full access to state-of-the-art knowledge and best practices and that they will collaborate in using knowledge and practices

---

Table 10-2
Matrix of Goals, Statutes, and Cases

	Individuals with Disabilities Education Act	Family Education Rights and Privacy Act	Developmental Disabilities and Bill of Rights Act	Title V, Social Security	Title XVI, Social Security	Title XVIII, Social Security	Title XIX, Social Security	Title XX, Social Security	Title XXI, Social Security	Katie Beckett	Child Health Act	Health Insurance Portability and Accountability Act	Emergency Medical Treatment and Active Labor Act	Family and Medical Leave Act	Indian Child Welfare Act	Technology Assistance Act
Overarching Goal: To enhance quality of life of all families	◆		◆	◆	◆	◆	◆	◆	◆	◆	◆		◆	◆	◆	◆
Goal A: To partner for control of destiny	◆	◆	◆		◆		◆						◆			
Goal B: To fully participate in communities of choice	◆		◆	◆	◆			◆		◆	◆					
Goal C: To receive services and supports	◆	◆	◆	◆	◆	◆	◆	◆	◆	◆	◆	◆				◆
Goal D: To receive and direct funding						◆		◆								
Goal E: To use knowledge and best practices	◆			◆												◆

Although not all of the statutes explicitly adopt these goals in the language we use here, their underlying statements of purpose and policy justify the expression of goals in the terms we use; moreover, the cases cited in Table 10-2 similarly justify our terms.

REVIEW OF KNOWLEDGE AND RECOMMENDATIONS

In this section we provide a condensed review of literature related to the overarching goal and the five associated goals; space limitations prohibit us from providing a more extensive review. Table 10-3 includes the key research studies and syntheses related to each of

Table 10-3
Illustrative Literature Review

Authors/Date/Sample	Illustrative Instruments	Key Findings
Overarching Goal: To Enhance Quality of Life of All Families		
1. Essex, et al., 1999 • 133 married mothers (mean age 68) and fathers (mean age 70) of adults with MR • 99% Euro-American mothers, 97% Euro-American fathers • Lower middle to middle class income range	• Center for Epidemiologic Studies Depression Scale (Radloff, 1977) • Burden interview (Zarit, Reever, & Bach-Peterson, 1980) • Multidimensional Coping Inventory (Carver, Scheier, & Weintraub, 1989)	• The average scores for mothers and fathers place them substantially out of the range for clinical depression. • Mothers who used problem-focused coping and who did not use emotion-focused coping had decreasing levels of psychological distress. • Neither problem-focused nor emotion-focused coping strategies buffered the stresses of caregiving for fathers. • Mothers of sons or daughters with greater behavior problems reported an increase in their level of burden during this study. • Fathers had increasing depressive symptoms over time when their son or daughter was older and had more severe limitations.
2. Hayden & Heller, 1997 • 105 caregivers (87% mothers, 7% fathers) with a mean age of 58 • Sample not described in terms of race/ethnicity or income • Subjects divided into two groups of caregivers—55 or younger and 56 or older • About one-half of younger group and two-thirds of older group had high school education or less	• Family Crisis Oriented Personal Evaluation Scales (McCubbin, Olson, & Larsen, 1981) • Personal Burden for Respondent Subscale of the Questionnaire on Resources and Stress-Short Form (Holroyd, 1987)	• No differences were seen in the number of support services received by older and younger caregivers. • Younger caregivers reported significantly more unmet service needs and rated significantly more of them as a critical or emergency need. • Older caregivers perceived the family member with MR as less of a burden than younger caregivers.

Table 10-3 (continued)
Illustrative Literature Review

Authors/Date/Sample	Illustrative Instruments	Key Findings
3. Krauss, et al., 1996 • 140 adult siblings of a brother or sister with MR still living in parental home • Sample not described in terms of race/ethnicity or income • Subjects divided into two groups based on perception of best future living arrangement and expectation for living arrangement	Mail questionnaire including questions on: • Siblings' characteristics (e.g., birth order, marital status) • Demographics, characteristics of brother or sister with MR (e.g., gender, number of behavior problems) • Mother's characteristics (e.g., age, health status)	• No significant differences were found between groups on key characteristics of siblings or mothers' characteristics. • A higher proportion of those who anticipated co-residence were sisters. • Siblings were more likely to plan to co-reside with sisters who had less severe retardation.
4. Singer, et al., 1999 • 128 parents (72 in control group, 56 in treatment group) • 91% Euro-American, 5.5% African-American, 3.5% Latino • 39% with incomes below $25,000, 17% with incomes over $50,000 • 70% married, 40% single	Subscales of the Kansas Inventory of Parental Perceptions (Behr, Murphy, & Summers, 1991) • Family Empowerment Scale (Koren, DeChillo, & Friesen, 1992) • Parent Coping Efficacy Scale (Blanchard, Powers, Ginsberg, Marquis, & Singer, 1996) • Semi-structured interviews	Parent-to-Parent programs had a statistically significant impact on the following: • Attitudes important for the parents to adapt mentally to disability • Parents' progress in getting help for their problems • Coping skills • 89% of the participants in the treatment group rated the program as helpful
5. Park, et al., 2003 • 1,197 individuals from 459 families from 13 states • Approximately half Euro-American; the rest distributed across all racial/ethnic groups • About one-fourth with income below $24,999; about one-third with income over $50,000 • All with a family member with a disability 21 years or younger	Interview protocol developed by authors included nine domains of family quality of life with four conceptual measures: • Attainment (getting, having, or accomplishing something that the family wants) • Opportunities (options that are available within their environments that are relevant to their needs) • Family initiative (taking advantage of opportunities) • Overall satisfaction with family life	• Overall life satisfaction of families was fairly high. • Families reported relatively low satisfaction with the support they received from other people and from disability services. • Family relationships, spiritual/cultural beliefs, and careers appeared to be positive contributors to family quality of life. • Many families reported they did not spend a lot of leisure time together and were moderately dissatisfied with this situation.

Authors/Date/Sample	Illustrative Instruments	Key Findings
Goal A: To Partner for Control of Destiny		
7. Turnbull, Turbiville & Turnbull, 2000 • Historical and conceptual review of the research literature		• Professional dominance characterized early views of families as being "sick." • A parent training emphasis stressed parents as professional's agents. • Family-centered models emphasized family choice and family strengths. • Collective empowerment enabled mutual control of resources to achieve shared goals.
8. McBride, et al., 1993 • Interviews of 15 mothers and 15 professionals • 13 families Euro-American, 1 Hispanic, and 1 interracial	• Qualitative interviewing methods and analysis	• Although professionals held family-centered beliefs, their practices were still child-focused. • Families were provided limited decisionmaking roles. • Parents believed that the early intervention programs strengthened their families.
9. Harry, et al., 1999 • Case studies of African-American, Latino, Palestinian-American, and Asian-American families ranging in socioeconomic status (SES) from lower to middle class	• Participant observation and interview	• Parents were deeply committed to their children and viewed them positively. • Organizational and professional practices discouraged and disempowered low income and ethnic minority parents. • Large systems such as Social Security and the public schools could be unresponsive and inflexible.

Table 10-3 (continued)
Illustrative Literature Review

Authors/Date/Sample	Illustrative Instruments	Key Findings
10. Harry, et al., 1995 • 12 low-income African-American mothers of school-aged children with disabilities	• Participant observation	• Parents initially wanted to be active partners with school professionals. • Detrimental professional attitudes and practices discouraged parents and left them feeling unheard. • Organizational inflexibility prevented family control of placement decisions.
11. Romer & Umbreit, 1998 • 3 service coordinators • 9 families: 4 Hispanic, 4 Euro-American, and 1 African-American	• Author-developed instrument	• A widely used family-centered training program did not change case coordinators' practices. • When family-centered practices were implemented, families were satisfied with services. • Organizational variables impeded partnerships.
12. Everson & Zhang, 2000 • 9 individuals active in person-centered planning circles for individuals with intellectual disabilities	• Focus group interviews	• Person-centered planning groups produced positive outcomes. • Obstacles to person-centered planning included difficulties in getting and keeping the planning teams together. • It was challenging to encourage focus persons to participate.

Authors/Date/Sample	Illustrative Instruments	Key Findings
Goal B: To Fully Participate in Communities of Choice		
13. Kraemer & Blacher, 2001 • 52 families (88% mothers) with children with severe mental retardation (between 20 and 24 years old) • 77% Euro-American, 10% Latino, 8% African-American, 6% other • 68% married, 25% divorced • 63% employed, 27% housewives, 10% unemployed • 61% with incomes over $50,000, 34% with incomes between $15,000–$ 49,000, 4% with incomes under $15,000	• Face-to-face and phone interviews • Family Data Sheet designed to provide demographic information • Vineland Adaptive Behavior Scales (Sparrow, Balla, & Cicchetti, 1984) • Scales of Independent Behavior-Revised, Problem Behavior Scale (Bruininks, Woodcock, Weatherman, & Hill, 1996) • Transition Experiences Survey examining current and previous involvement in programming related to transition • Parent Involvement in Transition Planning designed to assess parents' level of involvement in transition planning	• Although more than half the parents were aware that their child had a transition plan, one-third of parents did not know if the child had plan or the child did not have one. • There seemed to be a lack of available options for young adults with severe MR after leaving school; many were in segregated settings. • The majority of parents did not want their child to move out of the family home after school; 88% of the students who left high school were still living at home. • Parents had more interest in vocational and social issues than community living.

14. Romer, et al., 2002
• Surveyed 312 families who participated in the state of Washington's Family Support Opportunities program
• Approximately 75% of the families Euro-American, almost equal number of additional families African-American, Asian, Latino/Hispanic, and American Native/Pacific Islander
• 53 families indicated that they had used a community guide
	• Mail survey assessing:
	  - Family needs for services and supports
	  - Effectiveness of program
	  - Impact of the program on their family
	• Face-to-face interviews
		• 44% of families were very satisfied, and 26% were very dissatisfied with the program.
		• Community guides' success in making resource connections was a critical factor in determining families' satisfaction.
		• Families having a positive experience described community guides as those who were knowledgeable, persistent, and efficient; who could communicate; and who allowed families to decide their own needs.

Table 10-3 (continued)
Illustrative Literature Review

Authors/Date/Sample	Illustrative Instruments	Key Findings
15. Erwin, et al., 2001 • Analysis and synthesis of research on families and early childhood inclusion since the 1980s		• Both early and later studies suggested that, with quality instruction and support, inclusion benefits children with social challenges. • Significant progress has been made in designing and implementing family-centered approaches. • Parents want to be involved in their child's education but do not want responsibility for ensuring its success.
16. Duhaney & Salend, 2000 • Reviewed 17 studies of parents' perceptions of and experiences in inclusive and integrated educational settings • 17 studies included mothers of children with disabilities • 15 studies included parents of children with and without disabilities • Parents representing children age 6 weeks to 35 years		• Most parents of children with disabilities supported inclusion as they felt it promoted their child's social acceptance and development. • Some parents of children with disabilities expressed concern about the lack of qualified personnel and support services, particularly for their children in early childhood settings. • Parents of children without disabilities were generally positive, though some expressed concern about the instructional effectiveness and lack of qualified teachers.

Authors/Date/Sample	Illustrative Instruments	Key Findings
17. Soodak & Erwin, 2000 • 10 mothers of young children (age 4 to 8) with significant disabilities being educated in inclusive settings • 6 of the mothers Euro-American, 3 Latino or Spanish, 1 African-American • 7 in two-parent families, 3 in single parent families • Socioeconomic status (self-characterized): 5 middle, 3 middle-high, 1 low-middle	• Face-to-face personal interviews consisting of open-ended questions regarding perceptions and experiences in their child's inclusive education	• Parents' participation in their child's inclusive education was influenced by the school's beliefs about inclusion, receptivity to parents, and willingness to change. • Parent-professional partnerships worked best when characterized by trust, a shared vision about children and schooling, and open communication. • Parents agreed that the experience of accessing quality inclusive education for their children was emotionally and financially draining for themselves and their families, and many expected their struggle to continue.
18. Pretti- Frontczak, Gialloutakis, Janas, & Hayes, 2002 • Case report describing the outcomes associated with a graduate early childhood teacher preparation program that adopted a family-centered preservice curriculum	• Course evaluations • Interviews • Journal entries • Self-assessment inventory	• Graduate students reported high satisfaction after participating in courses co-taught by a faculty member and a parent. • Students' self-reported capacity to implement family-centered practices increased across time.

Table 10-3 (continued)
Illustrative Literature Review

Authors/Date/Sample	Illustrative Instruments	Key Findings
Goal C: To Receive Services and Supports		
19. Wang, et al., 2004 • 78 parents • 53% African-American • 33% Caucasian • 3% Hispanic • 11% other and missing data • 32% low income • 24% middle income • 25% high income • 24% missing income data	• Qualitative semistructured interviews of focus groups made up of 6-12 parents from three regions of the U.S.	• Parents viewed advocacy as an obligation. • Advocacy improved services. • Advocacy enhanced coping. • Advocacy was stressful. • Views were mediated by the degree of partnership with professionals and the quality of the child's education.
20. Bailey, Skinner, Correa, Arcia, Reyes-Blanes, Rodriquez, et al., 1999 • Interviewds with 200 Latino parents - 50 Mexican couples - 50 Puerto Rican couples - Mean age 30.3 years	• Face-to-face interviews for needs assessment • Categories that guided interviews: - Family and social support - Information - Finances - Explaining to others - Child care - Professional support	• Parents' needs were similar to those in the majority population as assessed in an earlier study. • Families had more unmet needs than those in the previous sample. • Families received more support from other family members than from formal support services. • English language proficiency predicted both needs and amount of received support.

Authors/Date/Sample	Illustrative Instruments	Key Findings
21. Westling, 1996 • Review of 25 studies assessing needs and preferences of parents of children with moderate/severe disabilities • Hispanic and African-American parents in several studies	• Narrative review of the literature and summaries in table form	• The studies produced multiple findings. • Parents had high levels of satisfaction with special education. • The majority preferred neighborhood schools. • Parents concerns about inclusion were resolved favorably with experience. • Scheduling problems caused low levels of participation by Hispanic families. • Families were dissatisfied with the adult service system. • Parents preferred functional skills instruction and focus on friendship.
22. Denney, et al., 2001 • 6 families whose infants were being treated in a neonatal intensive care unit (NICU) • Parents were recent Mexican immigrants who primarily spoke Spanish • Parents ranged in age from 30-40 years	• Semi-structured interviews conducted in Spanish in the NICU • Review of medical records providing descriptive information about the infants. • Demographic questionnaire assessing income, education, years since immigration, and English language proficiency	• Parents' cultural beliefs about dietary requirements clashed with hospital practices. • Parents' beliefs about infant care also differed from hospital practice. • Hospital staff members did not understand a cultural system of beliefs concerning the role of heat and cold in newborn care. • NICU clerks and family members, rather than nurses and physicians, were the main source of information for parents. • Language barriers prevented parents from obtaining needed information.

Table 10-3 (continued)
Illustrative Literature Review

Authors/Date/Sample	Illustrative Instruments	Key Findings
23. Zoints, et al., 2003 • 24 African-American parents • Parents' income status upper middle class, middle class, poverty level • Children ranged in age from 7-21 • Children's labels included mental retardation (8), autism (5), and emotional disorders (11)	• In depth face-to-face interviews • Open-ended questions about parents' perceptions of impact of ethnicity on special education services, overall satisfaction with special education and community services, and extent to which they believed the first two questions were interrelated	Six themes emerged: • Parents reported disrespect for parents and children by school personnel. • Parents perceived negativity toward their children and themselves. Schools blamed parents for children's problems. • Parents wanted personnel to have a greater understanding of cultural differences, which would allow personnel to distinguish culturally different behavior from inappropriate behavior. • Parents wanted school personnel to have better training. • Parents were open to collaborative partnerships if available.
24. Ainbinder, et al. (1998) • 24 parents who received Parent to Parent support (23 mothers, 1 father) • 83% white Euro-American, 17% African-American • Average age 37 (range 22-51) • Average age of children 7 years • Disability labels including developmental disabilities, learning disabilities, health impairments, sensory impairments	• Telephone interviews • Semi-structured interviews • Open-ended question asking parents to describe their experiences with Parent to Parent programs	• Parents reported that Parent to Parent programs became reliable allies. • Reliable alliances consisted for four major components: - Parents were highly believable sources of informational and emotional support because of shared experiences. - Help-seeking parents learned information and skills by comparing experiences. - The availability of support via telephone at flexible hours aided the success of Parent to Parent programs. - Parents perceived support to be mutual.

Authors/Date/Sample	Illustrative Instruments	Key Findings
25. Johnson & Duffet, 2002 • 510 parents of children served in special education • Random sample based on random-digit-dialing technology • Two analytic categories created based on severity of children's disabilities (mild and severe).	• Telephone interviews using public opinion survey methods to ask multiple questions	• 55% believed schools took the right approach in identifying children's needs. • 29% felt the school dragged its feet. • More than one in four African-American parents feared that race was a factor in labeling children with disabilities. • 70% believed that parents were not provided adequate information about available services. • 84% believed special educators care about their children. • Depending on the question, 15%–30% of parents were dissatisfied and 16% considered suing their public school.
Goal D: To Receive and Direct Funding Studies assessing needs and uses of family-directed funding		
26. Heller, et al., 1998; Herman, 1991; Herman & Hazel, 1991; Agosta, et al., 1992; Melda & Agosta, 1994a, 1994b, 1995a, 1995b; Meyers & Marcenko, 1989; Zimmerman, 1984. • Evaluations of state-based family support programs serving persons with ID • Programs located in IL (n=166), LA (n=485), MI (n=2,968); reimbursement-based support programs in RI (n=27), SD (n=99), UT (n=545)	• Program evaluation questionnaire covering basic demographics, effect of disability on family, needs, future plans, use and impact of support, and satisfaction (RI) • Supplemental interviews (IL, SD)	• Families reported significant opportunity costs in terms of deferred parent employment. • Families used subsidy funds primarily for clothing, transportation, respite, and medical expenses. Education-related expenses were common among families with minor children. • Families reported cash supports very helpful in improving family life; low-income families were more likely to use funds for basic needs. • The most common support services accessed are respite services.

Table 10-3 (continued)
Illustrative Literature Review

Authors/Date/Sample	Illustrative Instruments	Key Findings (continued)
		• Study showed mixed findings on the influence of programs on family intent to continue home care (note that all evaluations queried intent rather than actual outcomes over time).
27. Brown & Foster, 2000; Conroy & Yuskauskas, 1996; Foster, et al., 2002. Evaluations of Robert Wood Johnson Foundation Self-Determination programs in 19 states, including • AR (n=200), FL (n=231), NH (n=38), NJ (n=240) • Persons with ID (NH), elderly and nonelderly with disabilities (AR, FL, NJ)	• Life quality and choice-making protocols, adaptive behavior, satisfaction, costs, services and supports (NH) • Telephone interviews with service recipient or guardian covering life quality, health and function, use of caregivers, expenditures, and program satisfaction (AR, FL, NJ)	• The majority of the non-DD recipients used funds to hire caregivers and to purchase personal care supplies. • The vast majority were very satisfied with the program and reported improvements in quality of life. • Respondents reported a better fit between needs and services under a self-determination model. • The Conroy & Yuskauskas (1996) report suggests a decrease in per-person expenditures after beginning a cash program.
Studies assessing how family-directed funding fits into the larger system of services financing		
28. Parish, Pomeranz, & Braddock, 2003 ; Braddock, et al., 2002. • All state (and DC) MRDD agencies • Agency line-appropriation programs providing for vouchers, direct cash payments to families, reimbursement, or direct payments to service providers identified by the state as "family support"	• Two categories of funding support: cash subsidy and all other forms of support services identified by the state as "family support" • Inflation-adjusted total spending per state fiscal year	• Nationally, family support spending comprised 3.6% of total MRDD public spending in fiscal year 2000. • Average spending per family in 2000 was $2,722; subsidy payments averaged $2,674. • Total national spending has increased 85% between 1996 and 2000, serving 385,414 families in 2000. • 19 states had cash subsidy programs in 2000.

Authors/Date/Sample	Illustrative Instruments	Key Findings
Systems level studies evaluating the relationship of family- or self-directed programs to traditional systems		
29. Bradley, et al., 2001 • 19 states participating in the 1997-2000 Robert Wood Johnson National Self-Determination program • Emphasis on developing new models of individual control over services and funding, but family-oriented implementation common • Projects ranged from broad, system-level reforms to small localized pilot efforts	• In the evaluation of the financial management of the demonstration projects, site-visits to selected (n=7) states, using informant interviews, telephone follow-up and review of documents • Focus on program management methods, the degree to which self-determination models forced changes in funding regulations, effects on overhead costs, and impact on management information systems	• Consumer control models stimulated changes from standardized payment rates to variable pricing and individualized rates. • Variable and individualized rates required modification of information systems. • Financial intermediaries were instrumental in supporting individual (and family) management of funding and payments. • The question of relative costs remains unanswered—the short duration of the projects and vastly changed method of funding required a "ramp up" of costs. Strong evidence exists, however, that individual control makes more efficient use of funding.
30. Tilly & Wiener, 2001 • Comparative analysis of agency and consumer-directed programs for older persons • To be included, states required to have co-existing state and person-directed programs, at least 2,000 beneficiaries, and a minimum two-year program record • States included in the study: CO, KS, ME, MI, OR, WA, WI.	• Interviews with state program officials (most often the Medicaid office or state agency on aging), aging advocates and other gerontology stakeholders, and representatives from the disability community • Focus on stakeholder preferences, consumer capacity to manage services, service quality, and the status of service workers	• Older consumer preferences for program control varied; the authors recommended flexibility in program management options. • The use of fiscal agents substantially reduced paperwork and financial management burden. • Interview data suggested higher quality of care in consumer-directed programs, though states minimized monitoring of quality. • Independent service workers appeared to fare better in their work environments. • The question of relative costs was not addressed.

Table 10-3 (continued)
Illustrative Literature Review

Authors/Date/Sample	Illustrative Instruments	Key Findings
Goal E: To Use Knowledge and Best Practices		
31. Cooper & Allred, 1992 • 171 parents (110 mothers and 61 fathers) of children at or below age 3 in early intervention in one state • 83% European-American, 7% Native American, 3% African-American. • 62% lower two SES strata as measured by Hollingshead's four-factor index	• Survey of Family Needs (Bailey & Simeonsson, 1988)	• Consistent with other research, parents most often cited the need to access information about future child-care services. • Parents also wanted information about teaching their child, services currently available, and the experiences of other parents. • Mothers had a greater need to learn about other families, make friends, and gain more time alone than did fathers; fathers had a greater need for locating a doctor than did mothers.
32. Gowen, et al., 1993 • 367 parents (267 mothers and 100 fathers) of children (birth to age 8) with disabilities • 87% Euro-American • 42% of families with annual income under $29,000, 8% with annual income over $47,000	Mail survey assessing: • Interests • Childrearing problems • Preferences for sources of information	• Parents wanted to access information on child development, parenting, and community resources. • Parents expressed concern about being able to help their child, planning for the future, and gaining community/peer acceptance of their child. • Parents preferred to use different sources of information to learn about different topics. • As educational level increased, family and friends decreased and reading materials increased as preferred sources of information.

Authors/Date/Sample	Illustrative Instruments	Key Findings
33. Sontag & Schacht, 1994 • Face-to-face interviews with 536 parents in one state who had a young child (mean age 2) with developmental problems • 75% Euro-American, 15% Hispanic, 5% Native American, 2% African-American • 39% of the families had incomes less than $20,000	• Questionnaire with close-ended items assessing: 　Information needs, sources of information, and problems in getting information • Parent participation and participation preferences in early intervention	• 50% of parents wanted more information about the availability of services. • 75% of parents cited medical doctors as the source of useful information. • Native American and Hispanic parents reported greater difficulty in obtaining information than did white parents.
34. Lamb-Parker, et al., 2002 • 75 university researchers and 63 Head Start staff members representing 60 Head Start University Research Partnerships • 2 groups: participants in projects with high levels of shared decisionmaking and participants in projects with low levels of shared decisionmaking	• Head Start Research Partnership Questionnaire assessing the amount and quality of the research partnership	• Participants in projects with higher levels of shared decisionmaking had more open expression of values and differences of opinions, more clearly defined roles, and higher levels of sensitivity for cultural issues. • Participants in projects with high levels of shared decisionmaking had greater participation and greater overall satisfaction. • Participants with high levels of decisionmaking found the research findings and products to be of greater value than those with low levels of shared decisionmaking.

Table 10-3 (continued)
Illustrative Literature Review

Authors/Date/Sample	Illustrative Instruments	Key Findings
35. Ruef & Turnbull, 2001 • Face-to-face or telephone focus groups with 63 individuals representing six stakeholder groups (i.e., administrators, families, individuals with mental retardation and/or problem behaviors, their friends, researchers, and teachers) • Purposive sampling to ensure participant diversity in family characteristics, gender, age, geography (urban/rural), and link to disability • 1 family member a native Spanish speaker; 1 family member African-American; 1 African-American individual with disabilities; 8 Euro-Americans with disabilities	• Research question that served as an interview guide and subquestions that explored stakeholder's unique contributions	• The importance of trusting relationships was noted by almost all stakeholder groups. • Stakeholders agreed on the importance of research-based information and called for more research that is relevant to their needs. • All stakeholders agreed that direct provider groups, including families, friends, and teachers, do not have adequate access to research-based information. • Direct provider groups called for different formats for conveying information relevant to their needs and technical assistance in the use of the information given them.
36. Santelli, et al., 1998 • Case study of PAR team consisting of parent leaders and university researchers who collaborated to design, implement, and disseminate research on efficacy of Parent to Parent programs in five states • PAR team increased from five to more than 12 members over three years; team had equal representation of parents and university researchers	• Critical incidents (i.e., incidents reflecting or pivotal in the process) drawn from verbatim notes of all team meetings and telephone conferences for the three years of the project	• A shared vision and role clarification were critical to reconciling diverse perspectives between families and researchers on the PAR team. • Key to the success of PAR were trust in the legitimacy of stakeholders' perspectives in the research process, opportunities to share members' expertise and perspectives, and equitable compensation for all members. • Challenges to the PAR process included time, funding, and the need for research findings to be made more accessible to families.

the goals. The narrative highlights the trends in the research and recommends the kinds of research that we believe will most directly relate to the goals and their attainment on behalf of families, including not only the parents, but also siblings and other caregivers.

Overarching Goal: To enhance quality of life of all families

Overview of the Knowledge Base

Table 10-3 includes six studies and their findings related to supporting caregiving efforts and enhancing family quality of life. Studies 1–3 (Essex, Seltzer, & Krauss, 1999; Hayden & Heller, 1997; Heller, Miller, & Factor, 1997; Krauss, Seltzer, Gordon, & Friedman, 1996) are examples of seminal descriptive research focused primarily on older caregivers. A trend in the findings of these studies is a lack of a perceived caregiving burden or psychological distress in older parents. Two factors associated with greater caregiving challenge appear to be problem behavior on the part of the individual with an intellectual disability (ID) and the severity of the disability (Essex, et al., 1999; Heller, et al., 1997; Krauss, et al., 1996).

Although family research has placed its greatest emphasis on assessing the perceptions of the primary caregiver (usually mothers), Krauss, et al. (1996) focused on sibling perceptions related to future role expectations for caregiving. It is noteworthy that the individual with ID does not always only receive caregiving from other family members, but rather, also provides supportive activities to their parents, making parental caregiving easier (Heller, et al., 1997).

Gender and life-span factors are evident in the key findings in Table 10-3. Younger caregivers reported significantly more unmet service needs and rated them significantly more as a critical or emergency need (Hayden & Heller, 1997). Younger parents are more likely to be accustomed to having services and therefore have higher expectations for the service system.

Although family researchers have tended over time to focus primarily on negative outcomes for families (i.e., caregiver burden, stress), family theorists and researchers are now trying to look at outcomes that do not have a negative or pathological bias (Antonovsky & Sourani, 1988; Helff & Glidden, 1998; Turnbull, Patterson, Behr, Murphy, Marquis, & Blue-Banning, 1993). Study 4, which had a random assignment experimental design, used two groups to compare positive outcomes for parents who obtained support from Parent to Parent programs (Singer, Marquis, Powers, Blanchard, DiVenere, Santelli, et al., 1999). Results indicate that Parent to Parent support increased mothers' sense of coping efficacy, acceptance, and positive appraisal of their children with disabilities. This kind of traditional experimental research reveals how supports and services foster positive outcomes.

Studies 5 and 6 build on the significant progress already made in envisioning quality of life for individuals with ID (Schalock, Brown, Brown, Cummins, Felce, Matikka, et al., 2002). These studies report the first stage of two long-term research programs devoted to developing new ways of seeing and measuring family quality of life. Park, Hoffman, Marquis, Turnbull, Poston, Mannan, et al. (2003) described the development of a quantitative family quality of life scale consisting of five domains and focusing on families of children from birth to early adulthood. This study is unique in its focus on securing responses from *all* family members and in using a national random sample with over-sampling for families from culturally and linguistically diverse backgrounds and families who experience poverty. Brown, Isaacs, McCormack, Baum, and Renwick (2004) reported their progress in developing and using a qualitative interview protocol for family quality of life consisting of nine domains and focusing, in this study, on families who have children ranging in age from 10 to 36. Both of these research teams plan to develop tools for use by family support programs in (a) tailoring individual supports to families and (b) evaluating their overall service program.

Recommendations for Research

In light of the importance of this overarching goal and the current research to date, we recommend research on the following questions:

1. How and to what extent can we improve the quality of life for caregiving families by supporting the processes that help them adapt to their situation and perceive it in a positive light across the life-span?
2. What policy changes consistent with the overarching goal do families recommend, and what will be the specific impact of policy on family quality of life outcomes?
3. How can family quality of life outcomes most effectively be used as criteria for monitoring and evaluating agencies that provide services and supports to families?
4. How does family quality of life differ across families with varying characteristics, including marital status, racial/ethnic background, income, and community type?
5. What are the most advantageous ways of determining individual family preferences for services and supports that can enhance family quality of life outcomes?
6. What alternative approaches are most appropriate to use in combining the responses of individual family members on outcome measures into a composite family score? How does a composite family score differ from the individual scores of the primary caregiver?
7. What is the relationship between caregiver satisfaction, caregiver burden, and satisfaction with family quality of life for families across the life-span?

Goal A: To partner for control of destiny

Overview of the Knowledge Base

The seventh and eighth selections in Table 10-3 exemplify foundational work related to family-professional partnership. Turnbull, Turbiville, and Turnbull (2000) addressed changing historical models and propose a new framework for empowering relationships between families and parents. McBride, Brotherson, Joanning, Whiddon, and Demitt (1993) provided empirical evidence about emerging partnerships and the destiny-control consequences of those partnerships for families. They studied parents' and professionals' divergent and convergent perceptions of family-centered early intervention practices. Together, these two papers help to define what is meant by parent-professional partnerships, the degree to which models of professional dominance must give way to power sharing, and the ways that families perceive benefits from mutually supportive relationships.

Any effort to promote family-professional partnerships must address the increasing ethnic diversity and social-class divide in America. Studies 9 and 10 examined these issues. Unquestioned ethnocentric ideas and actions, along with taken-for-granted social privilege, can lead to family disempowerment and to professional control over services for families from culturally and linguistically diverse backgrounds (Harry, Kalyanpur, & Day, 1999). Harry, Allen, and McLaughlin (1995b) examined specific professional and organizational constraints in the public schools to partnerships between middle class Euro-American professionals and low-income African-American parents. These studies reveal two themes: (a) the extent to which many families from culturally and socioeconomically diverse backgrounds feel devalued and misunderstood because of ethnocentric assumptions and (b) the extent to which professional organizations and institutions control power and resources. Inflexibility in public school systems sets up a barrier to genuine partnerships.

Researchers are only now beginning to conduct empirical research that demonstrates the applied value of family-professional partnerships for improved family outcomes. Studies 11 and 12 are empirical investigations of the implementation and outcomes of family-centered early intervention and person-centered planning. Romer and Umbreit (1998) conducted controlled intervention research on the implementation of family-centered practices in early intervention programs. Everson and Zhang (2000) used qualitative analysis of transcripts of a focus group interview to examine the experiences of five person-centered planning teams. These studies lend clarity to two key constructs in parent-professional partnerships: family-centered services and person-centered planning. They also demonstrate measurable benefits of these approaches.

Recommendations for Research

A research agenda on family-professional partnerships that enables families to control their destiny must be congruent with the values of self-determination, autonomy, and empowerment. It needs to provide practical guidance on the skills, attitudes, and behaviors that all stakeholders must have in order to create productive reciprocal partnerships in a multicultural society. It also needs to reveal the changes that organizations and interlocking systems of organizations must make to create the environments necessary for partnerships. Finally, research and demonstration projects need to reveal the practices that enable parents to partner in developing public policy that authorizes agency activities. We recommend research on the following questions:

1. What public policies promote and impede family-professional partnerships?
2. What organizational, interorganizational, and intra-agency policies and practices promote and impede partnerships among families and professionals and even among professionals themselves?
3. What additional attitudes, knowledge, and skills do professionals need to enter into partnerships with families, especially those from culturally and linguistically diverse backgrounds?
4. What knowledge, skills, and attitudes do family members, especially those from culturally and linguistically diverse backgrounds, need to enter into equal partnerships with professionals?

5. What are the characteristics of agencies and other organizations that effectively promote family-professional partnerships?
6. How can mutually empowering family-professional partnerships be measured?
7. What are the benefits of partnerships to families and professionals?
8. Are service providers that have partnership philosophies actually implementing them? To what end, and how are they implementing them?
9. What constitutes effective preservice and in-service education for professionals so that they can develop and implement mutually empowering partnerships?

Goal B: To participate fully in communities of choice
Overview of the Knowledge Base

Studies 13–15 (Kraemer & Blacher, 2001; Romer, Richardson, Nahom, Aigbe, & Porter, 2002; Soodak & Erwin, 2000) addressed the participation and perceptions of families of children with disabilities and the supports and services they received. Selections 16 and 17 (Duhaney & Salend, 2000; Erwin, Soodak, Winton, & Turnbull, 2001) are syntheses that examined the experiences and perspectives of families (representing early childhood to adult life cycle stages) regarding inclusive placements. Study 18 (Pretti-Frontczak, Gialloutakis, Janas, & Hayes, 2002) was unique in its attempt to address the need for high-quality, family-centered practices in personnel preparation.

Four trends emerge from these syntheses and studies. One is that families favor inclusive opportunities for their children, particularly in light of the perceived social benefits. Access to individualized instruction, effective support, and qualified personnel, however, remains a serious concern (Duhaney & Salend, 2000; Erwin, et al., 2001; Soodak & Erwin, 2000). Interestingly, professionals who were trusting, flexible, knowledgeable, and supportive of family decisionmaking played a key role in families' positive school and community experiences (Erwin, et al., 2001; Romer, et al., 2002; Soodak & Erwin, 2000).

A second trend is that parents lack inclusive options for their children with disabilities beginning in the child's preschool years and continuing into his or her adulthood (Kraemer & Blacher, 2001; Soodak & Erwin, 2000). Many families continue to assume primary responsibility, often with few or no resources, for creating desirable inclusive environments for their children.

A third trend is the desire for greater representation of diverse populations in research. Three studies include parents from non-European backgrounds, and approximately 25% of the parent participants in two of the studies came from single-parent families. Although progress has been made to include families from diverse backgrounds, the literature still does not reflect adequately the population being served. Families from low-income or nontraditional backgrounds (e.g., families with foster, adoptive, or same-sex parents) are still largely underrepresented in the research, and families of non-European descent have participated in only a small fraction of the samples.

A fourth and final trend is the lack of qualified personnel to provide quality, inclusive, and culturally responsive services and supports. However, when systematic efforts have focused on creating quality, family-centered support to families, positive outcomes occur. For example, when community guides effectively provided personalized support to families, those families achieved a high level of satisfaction and increased access to resources

(Romer, et al., 2002). Similarly, evidence has suggested that when a preparation program for early childhood special education personnel includes a family-centered curriculum, graduate students are satisfied with their training and feel more capable of partnering with families to address the families' priorities related to supports and services (Pretti-Frontczak, et al., 2002).

Recommendations for Research

Although researchers and practitioners have learned much about family supports and services for community participation, many families still do not have high-quality, easily accessible, community-based, inclusive options, and the research community still does not adequately incorporate the nation's population in research studies. We recommend research on the following questions:

1. How can families experience a seamless system of service delivery that provides inclusive, culturally responsive, and family-centered services throughout the life-span?
2. How can families and professionals partner to promote effective change to systems to enhance full participation in families' own communities?
3. What new models of supports and services will appropriately address the needs of families from culturally and linguistically diverse backgrounds and families with nontraditional structures? What are the most effective ways of implementing these new models of supports and services?
4. How do families' preferences for community participation vary across demographic characteristics of the family, nature and extent of disability, and life-span? Given the variations in families, how can models of community participation be best matched with families' priorities?
5. How can personnel preparation programs better train prospective practitioners to partner meaningfully with parents to ensure that the child with the disability can participate in the community the families choose? How can they ensure that the family can participate in its community of choice? How can we make sure the family has the service supports necessary for success?
6. How can federal, state, and local initiatives support new models for research that create significant and sustainable services and supports leading to community participation for families?
7. How can professionals be better prepared to support individual and family self-determination so that supports and services are personally and culturally relevant?
8. What new policies do human services systems need to ensure that families fully participate in communities, and how can the government and the disability community most effectively implement and monitor the policies?

Goal C: To receive services and supports

Overview of the Knowledge Base

Each of the "five A's"—availability, accessibility, appropriateness, affordability, and accountability—embedded in this service and support goal represents a basic challenge emerging as systems try to meet democratic expectations of equity and effectiveness while dealing with severe resource constraints.

Study 19 by Wang, Mannan, Poston, Turnbull, and Summers (2004) examined parents' perceptions about their own advocacy. Despite the substantial growth in special education programs in public schools and a much smaller effort in the states to provide family support, many parents find that they must advocate for services. Advocacy has both costs and benefits to these parents. It can lead to improved services and can enhance a sense of coping efficacy, but at the same time, it can involve adversarial relationships with service providers.

Most of the existing research is centered on the question of what constitutes appropriate services. To begin to address the question of appropriateness, researchers must assess the needs of families and evaluate parent satisfaction. Study 20 by Bailey, Skinner, Correa, Arcia, Reyes-Blanes, Rodriguez, et al. (1999) examined Latino parents' perceptions of need in six areas of support. Study 21 by Westling (1996) reviewed 25 studies examining parents' perceived educational needs for their school-aged children with moderate and severe disabilities. A common theme emerging from these studies is that, although parents generally are satisfied with early intervention and special education services, many family needs are unmet, particularly from the perspectives of the Latino parents in the Bailey, et al. (1999) study.

Studies of accessibility have focused on the challenges faced by underserved communities, usually people from culturally and linguistically diverse backgrounds who live near or below the poverty line. Study 22 by Denney, Singer, Singer, Brenner, Okamoto, & Fredeen (2001) documented the difficulties that non-English-speaking immigrant parents have in making sense of high-technology medical care for high-risk infants when Spanish-speaking personnel are unavailable. In study 23, Zoints, Zoints, Harrison, and Bellinger (2003) interviewed predominantly middle-class African-American parents about their experiences with special education programs. The picture that emerges from these studies is that service organizations, such as hospitals and public schools, have great difficulty in working with traditionally excluded groups of citizens. Consequently, the very systems meant to afford support can become a source of stress for families from culturally and linguistically diverse backgrounds.

In terms of appropriateness, study 23 by Ainbinder, Blanchard, Singer, Sullivan, Powers, Marquis, et al. (1998) used interviewing and qualitative analysis to examine why parent-to-parent programs are effective in providing assistance. A theme emerging from the study is that parents are able to provide a unique form of emotional and informational support that professionals do not afford them.

Study 25 by Johnson and Duffet (2002) examined the question of appropriateness in regard to the special education system by surveying a representative sample of 500 parents. The findings are complex. Although a majority of parents are satisfied with their children's services, one in three is not, and many of these parents are angry about weaknesses in public school programs. A theme emerging from this survey is the urgent need to improve services in order to reduce parent/school distrust and conflict. Research related to affordability will be addressed in the next section. An important research direction for the future is to determine empirically based ways for services to be accountable to families and for families to rely on the accountability system.

Recommendations for Research

Research needs to address many critical questions to ensure effective implementation of goal C:

1. What changes in public policy will make state-level family support services widely available at a sufficient intensity to improve family quality of life?
2. What changes in public policy and in organizational practices will provide intensive services to all families, with a special emphasis on families from culturally and linguistically diverse backgrounds?
3. How can public schools become more flexible and responsive to parent concerns?
4. How can public schools reduce conflict with parents?
5. How can parent self-help organizations become a major part of the array of family support services on a wide scale?
6. What organizational practices and resources will maximize the benefits of parent-to-parent support programs?
7. Do family support services require trained professionals? If so, what should be the content of their training?
8. What are the most feasible and efficient accountability systems that can ensure that individuals with disabilities and their families have available, accessible, appropriate, and affordable services?
9. What are the benefits and drawbacks for families engaging in intensive advocacy to hold the system accountable, and how can professionals take a stronger role in ensuring accountability?

Goal D: To receive and direct funding

Overview of the Knowledge Base

In a goal as potentially inclusive as "funding," we need to establish conceptual boundaries. The boundary we laid down asserts that family support, as an alternative to the present service system, will thrive only if federal and state funding streams permit families to direct the use of those funds to control their family's destiny. In a nutshell, federal and state policy makers must choose between two fiscal strategies, or choose both: (a) new sources of support for families or (b) reallocation of resources toward families and away from traditionally structured services.

Table 10-3 summarizes selected studies related to three topics: (a) evaluations of the use and outcomes associated with consumer-controlled support programs (studies 26 and 27); (b) studies that described the status of family support in the context of current service systems (study 28); and (c) evaluations that considered how family- or consumer-directed programs might affect the administration of state service systems (studies 29 and 30). Human service systems are inherently complex—programs and persons do not operate independently of larger networks of services. How family support programs are managed within these systems is of special interest.

Studies 26 and 27 summarized evaluations of the state-initiated cash subsidy programs that emerged in the 1980s (e.g., Agosta, Knoll, Freud, & Raab, 1992; Heller, Factor, Hsieh, & Hahn, 1998; Herman, 1991; Herman & Hazel, 1991; Melda & Agosta, 1994, 1995; Melda, Agosta, & Smith, 1995; Meyers & Marcenko, 1989; Zimmerman, 1984). They also reviewed the more recent self-determination initiatives launched by the Robert Wood Johnson Foundation (Brown & Foster, 2000; Conroy & Yuskauskas, 1996; Foster, Brown, Carlson, Phillips, & Schore, 2000). The studies consistently reported high levels of satisfaction, increased quality of life, and use of direct cash supports for basic household needs. Whether these support programs reduce out-of-home placement—one of the most common economic justifications for family support—has yet to be directly tested. Family support is evaluated on the basis of reported intent rather than actual placement decisions over an extended time period.

The *State of the States* studies by Braddock, Hemp, Rizzolo, Parish, and Pomeranz (study 28) (2002) has represented the only ongoing national profile of family support and family-directed funding. The studies have tracked a steady expansion of family initiatives since the 1980s. The national profile of ID/DD services spending underscores the relatively minor share of funds devoted to specialized family programs (3.6%). Medicaid, widely discussed as a mechanism for expansion of family support (Agosta, 2002; Cooper, 2002; Gettings & Smith, 1998), currently accounts for approximately one-half of all family support funding (Braddock, 2003).

Bradley, Agosta, Smith, Taub, Ashbaugh, Silver, et al. (2001) and Tilly and Wiener (2001) described large-scale evaluations of family- or consumer-directed programs across multiple state systems (studies 29 and 30). The Bradley, et al. (2001) report summarized an evaluation of the Robert Wood Johnson Foundation Self-Determination Initiative, in which states implemented self-directed services and funding demonstration projects. Tilly and Wiener (2001) selected seven states that had fielded large-scale consumer-directed services programs for older adults. The Bradley, et al. (2001) and Tilly and Wiener (2001) evaluations directly considered the funding and financial management challenges that emerged as a result of a modified service delivery system. These challenges included, among others, (a) developing flexible rate-setting methodologies, (b) involving fiscal agents for management of funds, and (c) monitoring service quality in a decentralized management system.

Recommendations for Research

Policy makers do not add new resources or reallocate present resources unless they are convinced that the goals and expected outcomes are worthwhile and attainable. Future research should inform these policy choices by (a) articulating the goals and desired outcomes of an expanded system of family-directed services, (b) understanding the fiscal demands family goals will impose on service systems, and (c) evaluating *systems-wide* costs and benefits relative to the current methods of services and support. Research needs to tell policy makers what is gained—programmatically and fiscally—through family-controlled funding. Accordingly, four lines of research will address the goals and expected outcomes of increased investment in family support. The first line frames the broader research questions in terms of budgetary implications. It asks, "What should be the intent of expanded policy initiatives? How should the related outcomes be measured?"

The second line investigates the systemic consequences of moving towards family and consumer control in terms of costs, fiscal management, and the way different elements of the service system interact. A number of thoughtful analyses have anticipated the challenges in restructuring systems of funding toward self-direction and consumer control (Hayes, Lipoff, & Danegger, 1995; Nerney, 2001a), but researchers need to provide hard data based on actual programs.

The third line acknowledges that, although some data exist on the system as is, more research is necessary. Studies have provided descriptive data on the structure and financing of state systems and a limited amount of data on specialized family support initiatives. However, researchers and professionals in this field do not have a systematic and broad-based understanding of the nature and extent of family supports already embedded in current state systems, nor do they understand the role that different models of public financing systems play in these services. To what extent do families access existing services as "supports" beyond those formally labeled as "family" programs? To what extent are families disengaged from formal systems?

The fourth and final line recognizes that no systems-level studies have directly evaluated and compared costs and benefits across service models; direct comparisons of benefits and efficiencies will be essential to raising the priority.

The seminal literature has yet to be developed. We recommend research on the following questions:

1. What are the goals of publicly funded programs supporting families, and how should the expected outcomes be measured?
2. To what extent do existing state service systems address these goals for families? What services do families receive beyond targeted family support programs? What is the aggregate funding devoted to supports beyond targeted family support programs?
3. To what extent and in what manner are systems of services as currently structured incapable of meeting family support goals?
4. What are the relative cost efficiencies or benefits of reconfiguring services away from program-centered funding to family-directed funding?
5. What structural changes are required for shifting funding to consumer and family control?

Goal E: To use knowledge and best practices

Overview of the Knowledge Base

Six studies pertain to families' access to, and use of, state-of-art knowledge and best practice. Studies 31–33 exemplify research on families' perspectives on their needs for information and on the way they want to receive information. These studies revealed that information is not effectively reaching all families. Mothers and fathers of children with disabilities continued to report unmet needs (Cooper & Allred, 1992; Gowen, Christy, & Sparling, 1993; Sontag & Schacht, 1994), particularly related to service delivery options, community resources, legal rights, child development, and parenting. Two factors associated with parents' needs are ethnicity (Sontag & Schacht, 1994) and gender

(Cooper and Allred, 1992). For example, families from culturally and linguistically diverse backgrounds have the greatest difficulty in accessing information (Sontag & Schacht, 1994). Similarly, parents' preferences for sources of information differ based on their educational level (Gowen, et al., 1993), ethnicity (Sontag & Schacht, 1994), and gender (Cooper & Allred, 1992).

Research methodology changed between the time of studies 24–27, published in the early 1990s, and studies 28–30, published more recently. Studies 24–27 involved both mothers and fathers of children with disabilities from birth to age eight who were predominately Euro-American. These studies reveal little about the informational needs of parents of older children or those from diverse family backgrounds. In contrast, studies 34–36 (Lamb-Parker, Greenfield, Fantuzzo, Clark, & Coolahan, 2002; Ruef & Turnbull, 2001; Santelli, Singer, DiVenere, Ginsberg, & Powers, 1998) obtained the perspectives of multiple and diverse stakeholder groups. For example, Ruef and Turnbull (2001) incorporated the perceptions of families, individuals with mental retardation and/or problem behavior, their friends, teachers, administrators, and policy makers to identify products that would be useful to each stakeholder group in supporting individuals with mental retardation who had behavioral challenges and to increase quality of life for families.

Studies 34 and 36 reflected a major advance in bridging the research-to-practice gap for families of children with ID. Two studies reported on the efficacy of the collaborative process involved in participatory action research (Lamb-Parker, et al., 2002; Santelli, et al., 1998). These studies reflected the beginning of a paradigm shift that moved from conducting research *about* parents to collaborating *with* families in the research process. This partnership (a) enhances authenticity and validity throughout the research process and (b) ensures desired outcomes for the intended beneficiaries. A trend in the findings of these studies is that information is more useful and relevant to families and is more effectively shared when researchers and families develop partnerships characterized by trust, mutual decision making, shared vision, and parity in roles and resources.

Recommendations for Research

Relevant, research-based information is not yet readily available to families of children with ID, particularly those from diverse backgrounds. However, promising practices, such as participatory action research, are emerging to enhance the utility and availability of information. We recommend research on the following questions:

1. What systemic changes will ensure that all families from culturally and linguistically diverse backgrounds are full partners in developing, implementing, and utilizing research?

2. How can research be funded, designed, implemented, and disseminated to ensure that it effectively serves its intended beneficiaries, i.e., children and adults with disabilities and their families?

3. What supports will build meaningful research partnerships with families? How and by whom will these supports be provided to ensure participation of all stakeholders and beneficiaries of the research?

4. How can researchers become more accountable for producing research that addresses the desired outcomes for families?

5. How can researchers become more accountable and enhance outcomes for children and families by ensuring that professionals and families are aware of and use research findings?

6. How can funding and policy initiatives best support family-professional partnerships such as participatory action research? How can implementation of these initiatives be expedited so as to have an immediate impact for families?

7. What methods and models of dissemination of research findings are effective in expanding access to families, particularly families who have traditionally experienced limited access to information?

USING KNOWLEDGE TO SHAPE OUR NATIONAL AGENDA

Undoubtedly, conducting and reporting research are fundamental activities, but they are not ends in and of themselves; the end is use of research by six different constituencies: (a) people with developmental disabilities of all ages; (b) family members; (c) practitioners; (d) local and state level systems administrators; (e) federal and state policy makers; and (f) faculty in institutions of higher education, especially those in cross-disciplinary training and research programs. It is essential to get information to these individuals in formats they can use. Each has unique, yet sometimes overlapping, needs. The information offered to any constituency must be relevant to day-to-day applications, but also packaged to be easily understood and accommodate diverse languages and cultures. Clearly, these constituencies would benefit if the research community would work in partnership with them to develop empirically based best practices (i.e., those that are time- and cost-efficient) that are easily available and therefore used (Soodak, Erwin, Winton, Brotherson, Turnbull, Hanson, et al., 2002). In an era when policy makers are requiring even more evidence-based information about what works and what is merely believed to work to support families, the research community must give heightened attention to getting the information out for use in the policy making arena.

To meet the requirements of all of these constituencies, we recommend that the research community pursue five lines of work, each of which will extend our current knowledge and improve policy and practice:

1. Researchers must compile the current knowledge base related to best practices in family support, make it accessible, and then extend it. For over 30 years, state policy makers and practitioners have worked to establish and administer initiatives to support families. In this time, targeted research was undertaken, and a great number of policy inquiries and evaluations were completed to document and assess the progress made. No one, however, documented these actions within national research journals or vigorously disseminated information across states. As a result, the existing research base on family support awaits serious analysis. Researchers and policymakers should systematically analyze this information to assess the lessons learned in states and to consider these findings under the standards of evidence-based practice.

2. Policy makers must translate the resulting knowledge base into a series of performance expectations that reflect the most promising evidence-based practices

related to family support. After reviewing the current research base, researchers may develop a series of performance standards to reflect and extend best practices and policy related to family support. These standards may become benchmarks used to examine current activities in states to support families, inform advocacy efforts to improve services, and ultimately establish policy to promote more effective practice.

3. Researchers and faculty in professional development programs should take the lead in promoting the utilization of information related to family support practice and policy. Plentiful information means nothing unless it is usable and accessible. To reach the varied constituencies, the information must likewise be packaged and distributed within varied formats, including the following:

- **Technology-based media.** Technology offers at least a range of options for dissemination and use. One option is an Internet-based clearinghouse/literature base related specifically to family support policy and practice. All clearinghouses have a place for information that is based on single-subject designed research, on qualitative and legal-policy-economics methodologies, and on information that derives from narratives and personal accounts. "Evidence-based" clearinghouses should not be restricted to traditional randomized group-designed research. A large body of data exist, based on evaluations of family support programs at state and local levels, that stakeholders should analyze and include in any clearinghouse. Researchers can make their findings accessible through Web site postings and specialty listservs that permit interchanges of ideas and information. A second option is audio-teleconferencing. Current telephone technology enables participants from multiple states to receive information on family support without having to travel long distances to attend meetings or conferences.

- **Easily understood written materials.** These include policy briefs, guidebooks, curricula, or other printed copy.

- **Journal articles.** Research and evaluation related to family support must appear more frequently within the mainstream research literature. Much of the current research base is state-specific and not widely known. This circumstance must change to ensure that researchers across states can more easily review each others' findings and advance a systematic research agenda.

- **Targeted symposia and meetings.** Stakeholders can convene or participate in symposia or meetings on family support, although these meetings require more effort and expense. These symposia meetings can be convened using a participatory action research model. In this way, all people expected to benefit from the research can work together from the outset to plan a research agenda. They can then carry out the agenda in ways that will enhance the ultimate benefit of the knowledge produced.

- **Materials (written or in other formats) for neighborhood distribution.** Information should be available in neighborhood venues such as family-directed or family-centered service agencies and offices of practitioners to put into the hands of ultimate beneficiaries.

4. Direct training and technical assistance related to family support practice and policy must be available. Direct training and technical assistance directly imparts knowledge and understanding and increases skill development related to family support. Direct training, using a variety of instructional formats and forums, can be designed to accommodate the information needs of each state and the relative skill levels of the training participants. By contrast, technical assistance serves primarily as a problem solving activity to address specific informational needs or issues encountered by participants.

5. The research community and the ultimate beneficiaries (families and practitioners) should use the PAR—participatory action research—model to involve both parties in research from initiation to completion. This method assures relevance without compromising elegance, and it especially makes research useful to traditionally unserved and underserved families.

Anticipating the Changes of the Future

It is now appropriate to put the discussions about the overarching goal and five associated goals and the research related to each into an historical context and then to anticipate that the five issues we address below will be among the most important factors influencing families and research concerning them.

The past two decades have seen significant progress at the federal and state levels in establishing comprehensive systems for supporting families. Underpinning and guiding much of this progress is an enduring belief that families and people with developmental disabilities must be the principal decisionmakers in their lives so they can control their destiny. Family support practices have long reflected this primary principle. Proponents rally around phrases such as "family-directed" or "family-centered" to reflect the level of empowerment sought. More recently, policies surrounding adults with disabilities have embraced this principle as well. Whether or not the individual resides at home with parents, the idea is to promote and honor self-determined lives. Here phrases such as "self-directed" and "person-centered" illustrate the empowered role that families and their members with disabilities should play in controlling their own lives. As we move forward, this fundamental expectation among families and individuals—to play a leading role in determining the substance of one's life—will significantly influence policy and practice.

This said, stakeholders still have much to consider about the present and likely future policy environment and its formidable challenges to policy makers in supporting families. To move forward, we believe that the research community must address at least five related issues:

1. **Problematic federal and state economies.** At the federal level, tax reform and war are the two factors that, above all others, have turned the federal budget surplus into a budget deficit, and proposals to reform the federal tax code, Social Security retirement system, and Medicaid very well may restrict the number of beneficiaries of federal-state programs and the amount each beneficiary receives. Nearly every state is experiencing substantial budget shortfalls and most are targeting health, social services, and education for hold-the-line appropriations. The likelihood of any federal, state, or combined federal-state increase in services

is low. As a result, individuals with disabilities and their families increasingly are being placed at risk of being denied eligibility for services, being cut from services, or having the services they receive altered to encourage government savings. Moreover, the federal fiscal condition makes it unlikely that there will be any large increases in federal funding of research related to disability issues.

2. **Increasing demand for services.** In part because of advances in medical care coupled with the demographics of an aging population, the demand for disabilities services will continue to increase. People with disabilities are living longer. The parents of many adults with disabilities are growing too old to continue to provide care at home. Middle-aged baby boomers are finding that their children with disabilities are now aging into the adult system. Consequently, the pressures on the long-term supports system for children and adults with disabilities can only grow over the next several years. As budget growth slows, however, the outcome will be that more and more people and families will spill over onto waiting lists; there is great peril that the community of people and families increasingly will be divided between the "haves" and the "have nots." Without action, the goal of serving all who need help will become less and less attainable.

3. **Increasing cultural diversity.** Almost one-third of the U.S. population is from racially, ethnically, and culturally diverse groups. These population groups are expected to grow steadily. More than 10.5 million U.S. residents report they speak little or no English, up from 6.5 million in 1990. It is evident that human services systems—including developmental disabilities—have not responded well to our nation's changing demographics by fostering culturally competent services. Many of our nation's citizens are excluded from service systems or find that systems are not flexible enough to accommodate diverse cultures.

4. **Concerns over the workforce.** For many years, it has been a struggle to recruit and retain a stable, skilled workforce to support people with developmental disabilities. This struggle continues and could be even more challenging in the future as many industries chase a shrinking pool of workers. It is well known that one of the root causes of this problem is that wages and benefits are too low. Until this problem is overcome, it will be hard to expand services, and service quality will suffer.

5. **Need for improved interagency collaboration.** It has become obvious that effective responses to human needs often cut across multiple public agencies. Moreover, all stakeholders are becoming increasingly aware that the array of services developed over the past two decades lacks cohesion and has created a patchwork of fragmented services. This outcome is generally viewed as fiscally inefficient by policy makers and unsatisfactory to individual service users. An effective response that takes full advantage of all available resources will require teamwork among state agencies. The service systems most frequently called upon to participate in these collaborations are education, health and mental health, child welfare, developmental disabilities, and juvenile justice. As a result, policy makers and researchers alike must focus on the need to breach the gaps among

categorical programs, combine funding streams, and coordinate teams across administratively separate agencies.

These five challenges place formidable obstacles before families and people with developmental disabilities. Times are changing and growing more difficult. Accepting this reality, however, does not mean that families should become its victims. Research can prevent victimization. Change, after all, imposes choice—either to adapt and accommodate or to seize the opportunity to move the system forward. The latter course challenges all constituencies, especially the research community, to take a hard look at every dimension of the current systems to ensure that scarce resources are put to best use. At the same time, these constituencies must canvas new opportunities and look outside the system to support people and families. Inevitably, the research community will participate with others in redesigning systems to work more efficiently to achieve purposeful outcomes. But that work will proceed with limited, slow-growing budgets.

Among the opportunities available, President Bush's New Freedom Initiative promises to tear "down the barriers to equality that face many of the 54 million Americans with disabilities" (Executive Order 13217). Nested within the initiative are provisions to (a) increase access to community life through technology, (b) expand educational opportunity for youth with disabilities, (c) integrate Americans with disabilities into the workforce, and (d) promote full access to community life. Noted specifically are plans to implement 10-year demonstrations pertaining to respite for families of adults and children with disabilities.

Consistent with this initiative, the Centers for Medicare and Medicaid Services (CMS) has announced a new Medicaid demonstration called *Independence Plus: A Demonstration Program for Family and Individual Directed Community Services.* This initiative is intended to expedite the ability of states to offer individuals who require long-term services and supports and/or their families greater opportunities to take charge of their own health and direct their own services. Two new template versions are available to enable states to tailor the program to their preferences: the § 1115 Demonstration Template and the § 1915(c) Home and Community-Based Waiver Template. Because Medicaid is the chief financing mechanism for supports to individuals with disabilities and their families, Independence Plus brings significant opportunity to states and to the research community.

Opportunities like these are welcome news, yet family and disability advocates also observe emerging policy battles related to the reauthorization of federal legislation such as IDEA and Temporary Assistance for Needy Families (TANF). In face of a troubled economy coupled with other policy concerns, continuing pressure exists to dilute the nation's commitment to families and individuals with disabilities. In response, researchers, in partnership with self-advocates, families, advocates, service providers, federal and state officials, and federal and state legislators, must grapple with new and seemingly more intractable problems of policy, service delivery, and research related to these problems.

ENHANCING REAL LIVES

Jerome's transition to adulthood did not depend entirely on his mother Elizabeth, his father Charles, and his sister Danielle, nor did it end with his commitment to a state institution or the criminal justice system. That tragic trajectory was averted for Jerome, although it is common for so many other 16-year old students with problem behavior in a school system that values discipline over education and that is "free at last" (in the words of a school board member) of the "restrictions" of the Individuals with Disabilities Education Act (IDEA). Instead, Jerome's teachers, prodded by his sister Danielle, decided to challenge the "old paradigm" and to adopt the "new paradigm" of disability—the one that says that the world has to change to accommodate Jerome, even as he learns how to fit into his home community.

In challenging the status quo, these courageous teachers—the "advocrats," they called themselves—were joined by Elizabeth, Charles, Danielle, and a host of family members and friends of the family. Among the most important reliable allies were the directors and staff of a community-based parent resource center. "We're into empowerment and leadership development," said the co-directors of that center. "We know where families want to be and what the outcomes of policy and services should be, but we didn't know exactly how to get there because we didn't have the information we needed about the behavior of Jerome and other students like him. The answer, thankfully, is that we became partners with a consortium of universities that conducted research on positive behavior support and that partnered us in their research, from the very beginning. We provided the 'living laboratory'—the students, families, and schools—and they provided the research power—systematic procedures. And neither we nor the researchers could have made much of a difference without the 'advocrats.'" The result of that multimember partnership was remarkable.

Instead of offering special education alone, Charles' teachers secured his effective participation in the general curriculum of his school. In place of punishment and exclusion, they used positive behavior support, and they enlisted his family and members of his home community in using that approach, too. Instead of just "dropping" Charles at the doorstep of the local developmental disabilities service agency, his teachers and his family and their friends became partners in a long-term, person- and family-centered planning process.

The plan's ultimate goal was for Jerome to receive "self-determination" funding under the Independence Plus Medicaid option. All partners kept uppermost in their minds Jerome's oft-repeated statement, "Momma, I don't want to be a baby anymore. I want to be my own man." Subsidiary goals included his work for the local veterinarian, a job that pleased Charles because he delighted in taking care of the small and large animals. It also provided him with health insurance that, when combined with his Medicaid funding, reimbursed all of his therapies and medications.

A strange thing happened to Jerome on his way to adulthood. One of the other assistants at the veterinarian's—an older man partially disabled by toxic fumes in the first Gulf War—became Jerome's mentor. Through this new friend, Jerome connected with the independent-living movement in their city and his family linked with a political-action organization concerned with not just disability issues, but also with neighborhood revitalization and citizen control of public services.

By the time Jerome left school at the age of 21, services at school and in the adult agency and independent living movement targeted not just him, but also his family and its support needs. Jerome was enrolled in the self-determination option under the Medicaid Independence Plus option, lived in his own apartment near his family's home, and was elected to the governing board of the local family-directed community-based parent resource center.

His mother, Elizabeth, had secured an appointment to the staff of the city councilman from her district, and his father had been appointed to the state special education advisory committee. Moreover, both Jerome and his parents had received computers—a gift of the local disabled-veterans' organization—to use at home so they could stay current on the research about family support and independent living and also constantly monitor and lobby their elected and appointed federal and state representatives.

Jerome's "I don't want to be a baby anymore" is now replaced by "Momma, I'm a full citizen now," to which his father Charles adds, "Yes, and so are we all."

But it is Elizabeth, ever the dissatisfied member of the family, who has the last word. Speaking about the partnership among her family, Jerome's providers, the community-based parent resource center, and the research consortium, Elizabeth stated "our lesson" in less than the proverbial 25 words: "Knowledge is power only if the knowledgeable act powerfully and the powerful act knowledgeably."

* * *

The Manley family—especially Moira's brother Devvie and sister Sallie—committed to learning about state-of-the-art options for supporting Moira while assuring that her siblings and cousins would have their own lives, too. "Independence for Moira and for us, and support for her and us, too" is how Sallie put it. Through a Web site operated by a family-research center at a major university, they learned about the principle and the means for practicing self-determination; about community integration through formal service systems and informal networks, such as Moira's church; about public funding and family resources; and about how to stay up to speed as ideologies and state-of-the-art services change. They were informed by what they learned from the research briefs on the Web site; they were inspired by what they learned from the stories about families and professionals who wanted to go in the same direction as they did; and they were driven to action by Web-casting with other families who also used that research center's Web site.

Realizing that they needed to be partners with professionals and also that they needed to secure the reliable alliances of all of Moira's family members, Devvie and Sallie, with Moira's participation, adopted a person- and family-centered planning and action system. They modeled that system on one that they learned about from the research center's Web site. They invited the community-services coordinator at the local adult service provider agency, Moira's psychiatrist, the director of volunteer services at Moira's church, the chairperson of a group of amateur and published poets (Moira writes poetry), and Moira's cousins to participate in group action planning. All accepted and all agreed to check the research center's Web site from time to time for new ideas and approaches, relieving the Manleys of that duty. "In my busy practice," said the psychiatrist, "I don't have too much time for meetings, but I can access the Web site at any time. Now, how about a listserv for all of us involved with Moira? What we learn for her we can practice for others."

The members of this support circle agreed that Moira's HCBS funds can be used to support her to live on her own; hire a job coach; and pay for her food, clothing, and transportation. They also agreed that her HCBS self-determination life care plan and associated budget can be used for her psychiatric and other medical evaluations and treatments, for her wellness program, and for payments to individuals who provide those and other Medicaid reimbursable services.

They identified an apartment in a complex near one of the married staff in the local provider agency and also near two of Moira's cousins and rented it through a lease signed by her, but guaranteed by her brother and sister. They then created a group action plan that allocated home-visit, recreation, and transportation responsibilities for members of the family and agency staff.

Moira's adult-agency case manager and vocational rehabilitation specialist arranged for her to enter a vocational rehabilitation program that prepares her for competitive work of the kind she enjoys. They made it possible for her to secure a 20-hour per week job, to have weekly advice from the human resources personnel at the job, and to have the manager of the local branch of the Manleys' bank to manage her HCBS money and her earnings. Finally, the members of the action group guided the Manley family into various family-support networks and, through them, into service-delivery networks that, now and in the future, would assure that Moira and her family have the partnerships and services that they need.

From his wheelchair, Moira's father, Peter—as though summing up his case before a jury—reminded the family at his last Christmas with them, "I tell my new associates at the law firm, and I tell you all the time, you've got to do your research. Use the technology available to you. If you've got the law and facts on your side, it's amazing what control you can have over your own destiny. And if you don't have the law and facts, then you've got to scream like hell, as we had to do in a land of ignorance and prejudice, before everything begins to change and before the researchers begin to relate to our problems in a practical way."

CHAPTER 11

Self-Advocacy, Self-Determination, and Social Freedom and Opportunity

LAURIE POWERS, ROBERT DINERSTEIN, AND STEVE HOLMES
with
Ric Crowley, Curtis Decker, Marian Frattarola-Saulino,
Dennis Harkins, Mike Head, Mike Hoenig, Dennis Mithaug,
Teresa Moore, Chas Moseley, Tia Nelis, Essie Pederson, Paul Saulino,
Robert Schalock, John Shea, Gary Smith, Michael Smull,
Vicki Turnage, Nancy Ward, Michael Wehmeyer, and Betty Williams

REAL LIVES

Some people with disabilities who live in programs have lost their ability to dream.
They don't know they have choices, which is really too bad because if you can dream it,
you can do it.

—Tony Phillips

Tony Phillips is a 45-year-old man from New York City. He's a member of
AmeriCorps, a promoter of gospel music, a Deacon at his local church, an inspir-
ing speaker, a person with cerebral palsy, an active member of the National Action
Network, and leader of the self-advocacy movement in New York. For many years
Tony received supports from the "system" in traditional day and residential services. He decided that was not for him and began his personal self-determination
plan. He moved into his own apartment in lower Manhattan, left his day habilitation program, and pursued his dreams. He developed a circle of support to, in
his words, "help me out, but not tell me what to do," and invited the
Commissioner of New York State's Office of Mental Retardation/Developmental
Disabilities to join his circle.

Tony still chooses some supports from the system, including help from a
service coordinator, "who works for me," several home care attendants, some
day supports to help him organize his many activities, and tune-ups for his
walker and dental and medical services. But Tony's life revolves around his chosen pursuits, and he has a wealth of friends and associations. Recently, Tony

257

added co-producer to his list of accomplishments when he worked on a film about the aftermath of 9/11 on the lives of people with disabilities, "We Watch the City." As his quote says, he dreams it and he does it.

* * *

Dan was one of the most fortunate persons I've ever known. He was born into a family who believed that, although he had Down syndrome, he should participate fully in his home community. He attended his local public school, where his many accomplishments included managing the high school football team. As an adult, he lived in his own apartment, held down a job, and knew almost everyone in town. He was the first person with Down syndrome to testify before the U.S. Congress, helping to convince lawmakers to pass the Americans with Disabilities Act. His circle of support included many family members, friends, and advocates such as Senator Tom Harkin, who paid tribute to him during his 2002 victory speech.

Dan passed away in the autumn of 2002 as the result of injuries sustained in an auto-pedestrian accident. Some unenlightened opponents of self-determination dared to say, "He should never have been allowed to be out on his own." A quick word with Dan's friends at the video store, a coach at Ankeny High School, or any member of Congress who heard Dan's testimony would quickly dispel that notion. If all persons with disabilities had the opportunities for self-determination afforded to Dan, this discussion would no longer be necessary.

—Steve Holmes

INTRODUCTION

The last 15 years have been a time of significant change in the lives of persons with intellectual and developmental disabilities (ID/DD); institutions are rapidly downsizing and closing, community supports have expanded, and family leadership and self-advocacy have emerged (Braddock, Hemp, Parish, Westrich, & Park, 1998; Powers, Ward, Ward, Nelis, Ferris, Heller, et al., 2002; Prouty, Smith, & Lakin, 2004). Although the "system" has gradually shifted from "caregiving" to supporting the capacities of individuals and their families to determine and direct their lives, the impact of this new thinking has been largely limited. The developmental disability community has seen modest changes in attitudes and local demonstrations of new support models based on principles of self-determination. In addition, language in some legislation and judicial decisions now conveys a deepened spirit of commitment to freedom and opportunity for people with disabilities. But broad-based systems change that truly supports the rights of people to exercise self-determination, self-advocacy, and social freedom has been limited. Moreover, much legislation and many judicial decisions do not reinforce these areas.

Thus, the promise of self-determination, self-advocacy, and social freedom has yet to be realized. Rather than asking, "To what extent is our nation delivering on the promise of self-determination, self-advocacy, and social freedom," this chapter explores the evolving nature of this promise and what is left to achieve.

Definition of Self-Determination

The term "self-determination" has several definitions derived from personal, social, and rights perspectives. For example, Wehmeyer (1996) defined self-determination as "acting as the primary causal agent in one's life and making choices and decisions regarding one's quality of life free from undue external influence or interference" (p. 22). Powers, Sowers, Turner, Nesbitt, Knowles, and Ellison (1996) defined self-determination as "self-directed action to achieve personally valued goals" (p. 292). From this perspective, self-determination means having the power to make decisions, to direct one's actions, to dream and take risks, and to exercise rights and responsibilities at the individual and collective level (Powers, 2002). Nerney and Shumway (1996) identified four key principles underlying self-determination: freedom, authority, responsibility, and support. Likewise, the Alliance for Self-Determination defined self-determination as the ability of individuals to control their lives, to achieve self-defined goals, and to participate fully in society (Mouth Magazine, 2001).

These definitions affirm self-determination as the power of people with disabilities to control their lives and underscore the vital need for both individual expression of self-determination and access to opportunities to realize it. Self-determination is an outcome of having power over one's life, and self-advocacy is instrumental in reaching this outcome. Social freedom and opportunity are expressions of self-determination often ignored and/or restricted for people with developmental disabilities.

More than 800 self-advocacy groups exist in the U.S. with more than 17,000 leaders with a developmental disability (Dybwad & Bersani, 1996). The self-advocacy movement, as a collective political movement engaging persons with ID/DD, has spurred deinstitutionalization, fostered the growth of individual control in community supports, and promoted important provisions in key legislation, such as the Developmental Disabilities Assistance and Bill of Rights Act of 2000.

International Perspectives

Self-determination has been affirmed in important international human rights doctrines. In 1960, the UN General Assembly used the self-determination claim to justify independence for colonized peoples of the world. Adopted in 1948, the Universal Declaration of Human Rights recognized the values of human freedom. Article 1 stated that "All human beings are born free and equal in dignity and rights; they are endowed with reason and conscience and should act toward one another in a spirit of brotherhood." And Article 2 affirmed that "Everyone is entitled to all the rights and freedoms set forth in this Declaration, without distinction of any kind, such as race, colour, sex, language, religion, political or other opinion, national or social origin, property, birth or other status" (Degener & Koster-Dreese, 1995, p. 278). Further reference to self-determination appears in Article 1 of the International Covenant on Civil and Political Rights (ICCPR), adopted by the UN General Assembly, which states, "All peoples have the right to self-determination. By virtue of that right they freely determine their political status and freely pursue their economic, social, and cultural development" (Degener & Koster-Dreese, 1995, p 160). Unfortunately, this treaty and the Universal Declaration, for the most part, have not been applied to people with disabilities, and disability-specific instruments such as the Standard Rules on the Equalization of Opportunities for Persons with Disabilities (Degener & Koster-Deese, p. 285) are not binding; thus, advocates and a number of countries are seeking a UN disability-specific convention that would have the force of law.

Self-advocacy is a powerful influence for advancing self-determination and improving policies and services for people with disabilities (Mouth Magazine, 2001; Shapiro, 1993). Self-advocacy involves individually or collectively advocating on one's own behalf, as well as working together through coalitions for justice (Hayden & Nelis, 2002). Self-advocacy teaches a person how to make decisions and choices about his or her rights and responsibilities and how people need to support one another (Self-Advocates Becoming Empowered, 2001).

Many professionals, policy makers, and family leaders now recognize that policies and services for people with disabilities cannot and should not be designed or implemented without the full participation and engaged leadership of people with disabilities (Nothing About Us Without Us!).

Focus of this Chapter

In the following sections, we discuss the nature of our evolving national promises of self-determination, self-advocacy and social freedom and opportunity. We identify what must be done to commit to and achieve these promises. Heretofore, the focus has been to create visions, develop tools and models, and clarify and debate the implications of these promises. Our commitments and achievements fall short of our rhetoric. There are gaps between what we say, commit to, and actually do. Our aim is to identify priorities for making self-determination, self-advocacy, and social freedom a reality for citizens with ID/DD.

GOALS AND SOURCES

This section describes the national commitments that have been made to the self-determination and social freedom of individuals with ID/DD in major national policy. These include key legislation and judicial decisions. The commitments contained in these documents have been synthesized into six major national goals for self-determination, self-advocacy, and social freedom. Outcomes and indicators for each goal underscore the real changes required to realize these promises.

The Sources of Our National Goals

Language in a number of federal statutes, regulations, Executive Orders, and court decisions provides impressive support for the national goals of self-advocacy, self-determination, and social freedom and opportunity. Although this language does not always establish legally enforceable requirements, it clearly and consistently establishes that Congress, the Executive Branch, and the courts believe that self-determination should be integrated into all policies affecting people with ID/DD and other disabilities.

The Rehabilitation Act

In the Rehabilitation Act of 1973, as amended, Congress found that individuals with disabilities have the right to live independently, express self-determination, make choices, contribute to society, pursue meaningful careers, and enjoy full inclusion and integration in the economic, political, social, cultural, and educational mainstream of American society. Furthermore, "the goals of the Nation properly include the goal of providing individuals with disabilities with the tools necessary to make informed choices and decisions" (Rehabilitation Act, 1973, § 701(a)(6)(A)). Congress has declared that it is the policy of the United States that Rehabilitation Act programs and activities should be implemented consistently with, among other things, respect for the self-determination, informed choice, full participation, and support for individual and systematic advocacy and community involvement of people with disabilities. The ultimate goal is for people with disabilities to achieve "equality of opportunity, full inclusion and integration in society, employment, independent living, and economic and social self-sufficiency" (Rehabilitation Act, 1973, § 701(a)(6)(B)).

The Developmental Disabilities Assistance and Bill of Rights Act

The Developmental Disabilities Assistance and Bill of Rights Act (DD Act) provides additional support for the goals of self-determination and informed choice. With regard to self-advocacy, in the DD Act, Congress stated that

> the goals of the Nation properly include a goal of providing individuals with developmental disabilities with the information, skills, opportunities, and support to make informed choices and decisions about their lives; live in homes and communities in which such individuals can exercise their full rights and responsibilities as citizens; pursue meaningful and productive lives; contribute to their families, communities, and States, and the Nation; have interdependent friendships and relationships with other persons; live free of abuse, neglect, financial and sexual exploitation, and violations of their legal and human rights; and achieve full integration and inclusion in society, in an individualized manner, consistent with the unique strengths, resources, priorities, concerns, abilities, and capabilities of each individual. (Developmental Disabilities Assistance and Bill of Rights Act, 2000, § 15001(a)(16))

The Developmental Disabilities Assistance and Bill of Rights Act, as amended in 2000, requires Developmental Disabilities Councils to work in partnership with self-advocacy organizations to reach the following goals:

- Support opportunities for individuals with developmental disabilities who are considered leaders to provide leadership training to individuals with developmental disabilities who may become leaders (42 USC Sec. 15024(c)(4)(A)(ii)(II) [2003])
- Establish or strengthen a program for the direct funding of state self-advocacy organizations led by individuals with developmental disabilities (42 USC Sec. 15024(c)(4)(A)(ii)(I) [2003])
- Support and expand participation of individuals with developmental disabilities in cross-disability and culturally diverse leadership coalitions (42 USC Sec. 15024(c)(4)(A)(ii)(III)[2003])

Individuals With Disabilities Education Act

The Individuals with Disabilities Education Act (IDEA) acknowledged that "disability is a natural part of the human experience and in no way diminishes the right of individuals to participate in or contribute to society" (IDEA, 1990, § 1400(c)(1)). IDEA recognized that "improving educational results for children" is essential to "ensur[e] equality of opportunity, full participation, independent living, and economic self-sufficiency for individuals with disabilities" (IDEA, 1990, Id.).

The Americans With Disabilities Act of 1990

The Americans with Disabilities Act of 1990 (ADA) extended the requirement of nondiscrimination toward people with disabilities to a broad range of activities of social life, including employment (both public and private), public services (including transportation), public accommodations, and communications. In the ADA, Congress sought "(1) to provide a clear and comprehensive national mandate for the elimination of discrimination against individuals with disabilities; (2) to provide clear, strong, consistent, enforceable standards addressing discrimination against individuals with disabilities; [and] (3) to ensure that the Federal Government plays a central role in enforcing the standards established in this Act on behalf of individuals with disabilities" (ADA, 1990, § 12101(b)(1)–(3)).

In that regard, Congress found that "individuals with disabilities continually encounter various forms of discrimination, including...overprotective rules and policies, failure to make modifications to existing facilities and practices...and relegation to lesser services, programs, activities, benefits, jobs or other opportunities" (ADA, 1990, § 12101(a)(5)). Such discrimination is at odds with "the Nation's proper goals regarding individuals with disabilities [which] are to assure equality of opportunity, full participation, independent living, and economic self-sufficiency for such individuals" (ADA, 1990, § 12101(a)(8)).

Federal regulations interpreting the ADA have reinforced the focus on integrating people with disabilities into community life. For example, the preamble to the Department of Justice's ADA Title II regulations (on public services) defines "the most integrated setting appropriate to the needs of qualified individuals with disabilities" to mean "a setting that enables individuals with disabilities to interact with non-disabled persons to the fullest extent possible" (28 C.F.R. § 35.130(d) (integration regulation) Nondiscrimination on the Basis of Disability in State and Local Government Services, Section-by-Section Analysis, 56 Fed. Reg. 35705, 1991)).

Olmstead Decision

In 1999's *Olmstead v. L.C., et al.,* the Supreme Court endorsed the ADA findings that unjustified segregation in institutions is a form of discrimination against people with disabilities. The court stated, "institutional placement of persons who can handle and benefit from community settings perpetuates unwarranted assumptions that persons so isolated are incapable or unworthy of participating in community life." Moreover, "confinement in an institution severely diminishes the everyday life activities of individuals, including family relations, social contacts, work options, economic independence, educational advancement, and cultural enrichment" (Olmstead, 527 U.S. at 601). Both the

Clinton and Bush Administrations have moved aggressively to encourage the states to implement the Olmstead decision (Bush, 2001; E.O. 13217). Lower-court cases, interpreting federal and state-based protections, also have recognized the importance of self-determination, choice, and full participation in community life for children and adults with disabilities.[1]

Executive Orders

The Executive Branch, through Executive Orders and policy statements, has clearly emphasized the importance of self-determination for people with disabilities. For example, E.O. 12994, reauthorizing the President's Committee on Mental Retardation, stresses the importance of autonomy and self-determination (with appropriate supports, where needed) for people with intellectual disabilities and seeks to "promote...[their] independence, self-determination, and participation as productive members of society" (E.O. 12994, Preamble, § 6). President Bush's New Freedom Initiative acknowledges the ability of all people, regardless of disability, to participate fully in community life and urges the proliferation (and, in some cases, supports funding) of assistive technology, transportation, and home ownership options to enhance that participation (New Freedom Initiative, 2001).

National Goals for Self-Determination, Self-Advocacy, and Social Freedom

Six major national goals spring from the national commitments:

1. People with disabilities are equal partners in research, training, and dissemination.
2. People with disabilities make informed decisions about their lives.
3. People with disabilities have the opportunity to build their knowledge, skill, and resources, to control their lives and to contribute to their communities.
4. People with disabilities have control over their resources, such as their funding and supports.
5. People with disabilities have meaningful opportunity and support to advocate and demonstrate leadership.
6. People with disabilities have the freedom and opportunity to participate in social activities and social relationships as they desire.

Goal A: People with disabilities are equal partners in research, training, and dissemination

Overview

Historically, most research related to persons with disabilities has been conducted by professionals with little input or involvement by individuals with disabilities. Many persons

---

1. See, e.g., *Ricci v. Okin*, 573 F. Supp. 817 (D. Mass. 1982) ("the right of self-determination and freedom of choice to the person's fullest capacity is now a matter of Massachusetts regulation and...the state is bound to uphold and improve these rights"); *Superintendent of Belchertown v. Saikewicz*, 370 N.E. 2d 417 (Mass. 1977) (right of person with mental retardation to have substituted judgment decision made for him regarding whether to receive medical treatment); *Mills v. Bd. of Education of the District of Columbia*, 348 F. Supp. 866 (D.D. C. 1972) (exclusion of children from public schools).

with disabilities are reluctant to become involved in research because they are concerned that:

1. Much current research does not reflect their priorities for identifying knowledge that could significantly contribute to the lives of people with disabilities.
2. Methods used in conducting research will not yield accurate findings (e.g., in some cases, individuals with disabilities may not provide accurate information to researchers without disabilities, or instruments may word questions in confusing ways).
3. Findings may be interpreted or applied inappropriately (e.g., findings about abuse of people with disabilities in the community may be used to support returning them to institutions rather than to providing community supports that enable people to maintain their safety).

Traditional gateways for involvement in research, training, and dissemination also have been closed to most people with developmental disabilities. For example, universities often have educational requirements that place research positions out of reach for persons with cognitive disabilities, and little value is given to life experience that may make individuals with disabilities ideally suited to define and conduct research. Idiosyncratic language used by researchers and academics further isolates their work from people with disabilities. It conveys the message that one has to be exceptionally intelligent to be involved in research because mastery of complex language is essential.

Government agencies and private foundations reinforce this bias by publishing requests for grant proposals that are difficult for all but the most seasoned researchers to understand. Traditional "expert" and medical models do not make room for people with disabilities to be both the focus of research or instruction and the purveyors of knowledge. After all, one can't be both the person "victimized" by disability and the competent expert. Although these preconceptions are weakening, they still predominate in many research and teaching fields.

Because individuals with disabilities often are not involved in research, training, or dissemination, they may be distrustful or unaware of how these activities could benefit them. Yet high-quality research, training, and dissemination require the involvement of people with disabilities at all levels. Researchers must partner with people with disabilities, learn to be respectful, and communicate about how research can be helpful. They should work directly with advocacy organizations such as People First, whose constituents are directly affected by the research topic. The following outcomes and indicators describe a world in which research teams have reached this goal.

Outcomes and Indicators

Progress in establishing equal partnerships with people with disabilities will be evident when the following goals are met:

- People with disabilities are included at all levels of research (e.g., as principal investigators and co-investigators and in research design; data collection; and analysis, interpretation, and dissemination of findings). The targets or goals identify the involvement of people with ID/DD and measurement of their achievement.

- Requests for proposals are worded in straightforward language that is understandable to the majority of the public, including those with developmental disabilities.
- Partnerships exist among agencies, foundations, researchers, and persons with disabilities that foster individuals' knowledge about accessing, reading, and understanding requests for proposals and writing grants. These skills will be available through workshops, mentoring opportunities, college courses, and practicums.
- Internships and fellowships are available and accessible to leaders with ID/DD within state and federal agencies, foundations, and universities.
- Those selecting people to participate in research, training, and dissemination, value the life experience of people with disabilities as much as they do formal education.
- Individuals with ID/DD will have the opportunity to obtain a college education, take classes, and participate in practicums that will prepare them to assist with research, training, and the dissemination of information.

Goal B: People with disabilities make informed decisions about their lives

Overview

Informed decisionmaking is based on the concept of consent, which presupposes the existence of three elements in the decisionmaker: capacity, information (or knowledge), and "voluntariness" (Dinerstein, Herr, & O'Sullivan, 1999, p. 2). The person must have the understanding, communication skills, and educational capacity (not necessarily the background) to make the decision; the knowledge or information regarding the decision; and the ability to make the decision in a voluntary way, free of coercive influence. Furthermore, the person must be able to communicate the decision (verbally or otherwise) to another person. Capacity is inevitably contextual and interactive in nature; that is, one's decision-making capacity can vary with the nature of the decision sought and the level of explanation and support provided.

Although the law presumes that all adults, including adults with ID/DD, are competent to make decisions until a court determines otherwise, in practice they are often wrongly presumed to be incapable of decisionmaking. Just like people without apparent disabilities, people with disabilities go through life making good judgments about some things and poor judgments about others. The difference between the two groups is that those who do not have disabilities are presumed to be able to make all decisions concerning their affairs, but people with disabilities are frequently assumed to require assistance from others in making most decisions.

According to Dinerstein, et al. (1999):

> State laws provide for surrogates (often called guardians or conservators) to make decisions on behalf of individuals deemed incapable of making decisions for themselves. Some laws (and best practices) require that the surrogate decision-maker use a "substituted judgment" standard for decisionmaking—the decision

that the person him or herself would make if he or she had the capacity to do so—rather than deciding what is in the person's "best interest" (or worse, what the surrogate would decide for him or herself, irrespective of the individual's own values). (p. 3)

In practice, the decision-making authority that people with disabilities exercise becomes a matter of negotiation between the person receiving support and the individual providing the support.

A system that supports individual choice and decisionmaking must allocate authority among the individuals using support, the surrogate (if any), the provider(s), and the state. Each needs to understand its rights to make controlling decisions regarding exposure to risk, participation in the community and at work, and the exercise of basic rights, responsibilities, and free choice. As Dinerstein, et al. (1999) state:

Any interference with the decision-making authority of the person with disability must be the least restrictive intervention possible. As the decision in question increases in level of risk, or becomes more inconsistent with the person's known interests and values, the level of scrutiny given to that decision (and the possible need for formal appointment of a surrogate) rises. (p. 4)

The authority to make decisions regarding the wide range of life activities in which an individual participates, including those that involve risk, most appropriately rests with the individual. Although other parties may share an interest, the person must be the primary authority for judging the appropriateness of those aspects of his or her life that are beyond the experience of the state or the provider to assess.

The use of substitute decisionmakers or guardianship has significant ramifications for a person's future ability to make decisions independently. Even where guardianship is warranted, limited guardianship is preferred to plenary guardianship. There also must be avenues for assisting the person to be as active as possible in the decision-making process.

Outcomes and Indicators

Part of determining if a person is making "informed" decisions is discerning the degree to which the person has authority over his or her decisions and is held responsible for them. Advocates of self-determination must ask whether people (a) make decisions concerning their supports and the lives they lead, (b) make *informed* choices that reflect a knowledge of the alternatives and implications of their decisions, and (c) take an active role in managing their day-to-day lives. All measures, subjective and objective, should reflect a focus on the outcomes of the action and the perspectives of the individuals involved. The following indicators provide the foundation for informed decisionmaking:

- Unless deemed incompetent by a court, individuals with disabilities will make life decisions without interference. They will receive information, opportunities, and support as they desire to help them reach their full capacities for self-direction.
- A process will be in place to offer graduated assistance in decisionmaking and minimize the need to establish guardianship.

- Individuals with ID/DD and members of their formal and informal support network will clearly understand each party's decision-making authority and responsibility. Each goal and activity in the person's support plan will identify the individual or group that (a) holds the authority for decisionmaking or approval, (b) is responsible for action, (c) is accountable for results, and (d) assumes liability for problems that may occur as a result of the decisions. All parties to the plan will demonstrate that they understand how the individual receiving support holds authority for decisionmaking and shares it with various people. Everyone will recognize the conditions necessary for each person to use that authority.

- Although final decision-making authority for particular issues may not rest with the person receiving services, he or she will be actively involved, with or without assistance, in developing and enforcing regulations, overseeing providers, constructing policy and practice guidelines, introducing laws, and establishing and assessing contracts.

- Standards, outcomes, and criteria for successfully fulfilling plans and activities will be personalized, with goals and activities selected by or with the full participation of the individual. The process will be assessed from the perspective of the person receiving support for how well it meets the need to make decisions independently or with assistance. Standards will include a process for resolution of disputes regarding whether a particular choice is informed and reflects the involvement of the person receiving support.

- Individuals will participate as actively as possible in evaluating the quality of their lives, the goals they have and have not achieved, the chosen activities in which they have participated, and the quality of support they receive. Indicators will address aspects of living and/or service provision that only the individual receiving support knows and experiences.

- A person-centered plan will identify how the individual is empowered and encouraged to assume increasing levels of risk and independence. The person's circle of support will know the person's perspective on his or her living and working situation.

- People will be supported to take risks to gain the skills needed to assume responsibility for their decisions and to increase independence and accountability for their actions. Policies, procedures, or plans will be in place to support the growing ability of the individual to assume increasing levels of risk and responsibility. Agreements will be developed to support informed decision making by identifying risks, establishing accountability, and limiting liability (Sabatini & Hughes, 2003).

Goal C: People with disabilities have the opportunity to build their knowledge, skill, and resources, to control their lives and to contribute to their communities

Overview

Many people with disabilities have limited opportunities to grow and develop new knowledge, skills, and interests throughout their lives. Opportunities are still limited, despite the ADA and 40 years of progressive development of community supports;

physical accommodations; assistive technology; rights to education, habilitation, and rehabilitation; and promises of community membership and self-determination.

Most people with ID/DD live in poverty. Control and options in simple and critical life decisions such as where to live, with whom to live, what to do and whom to do it with, and who will provide essential day-to-day support are often denied. Despite promises of inclusion, society continues to view people with disabilities primarily as individuals who need support, not as friends and neighbors who have something to contribute. For this reason, information that promotes capacities to self-direct or contribute or that teaches the skills people with ID/DD need to control their lives (e.g., self-advocacy, management of support providers, financial planning) are of low priority. An important aspect of the articulated national goals for people with ID/DD of all ages is simply to remove the barriers that limit the *opportunity* for each person to be "all that he or she can be." Providing opportunity requires commitment to the following goals:

1. To support the ongoing growth (e.g., knowledge, skills, interests) of people with ID/DD throughout their lives
2. To support opportunities for people with ID/DD to obtain financial wealth, property, and other resources
3. To support the desire of those with ID/DD to control their lives and contribute to their communities

The *capacity* to self-determine includes all factors under a person's control that are likely to allow the person to engage in self-determined pursuits. It includes, for example, (a) the person's *understanding or awareness of his or her needs, interests, and abilities*, (b) the *resources* (or assets) needed to pursue those ends that are consistent with the person's needs, interests, and abilities, and (c) the *ability to manage* those resources to sustain engagement in self-defined pursuits. These capacity components include all of the person's tangible and intangible personal, social, economic, and/or technical resources. Intangible assets include human capital (e.g., education, experience, knowledge, skill, health, hope, vision); social capital (e.g., family, friends, contacts, connections); cultural capital (e.g., knowledge of culture and traditions, ability to cope with social situations and formal bureaucracies); and power and influence.

Outcomes and Indicators

If capacity and opportunity factors are present, the following key outcomes will be possible:

*   Individuals will participate in knowledge and skill development related to their interests and goals at the same level as other citizens. They will learn about and access, as desired, options for capacity-building and necessary supports.
*   Individuals will acquire tangible and intangible resources at the same level as other citizens.
*   Policy and practice barriers to individuals acquiring knowledge, skills, and resources will be removed.
*   Individuals will use their knowledge, skills, and resources, as desired, to direct their lives and contribute to their communities.

Goal D: People with disabilities have control over their resources, such as their funding and supports

Overview

The philosophy of person-directed services recognizes the capacity of individuals to "assess their own needs, determine how and by whom these needs should be met, and monitor the quality of services they receive" (National Institute on Consumer-Directed Long-Term Services, 1996, p. 4). The emergence of person-directed services reflects, in part, a societal shift from social benevolence toward people with disabilities and their families to a growing acknowledgment of, and respect for, their capabilities, autonomy, and personal rights (Powers, 1996).

Compared to attitudes towards individuals with physical disabilities, this shift has been more subtle for older adults and individuals of all ages with intellectual disabilities, who are often perceived as incompetent, passive recipients of help who need protection from abuse (Scala & Mayberry, 1997). The service system for these individuals has generally been designed to address the most dependent, many of whom are perceived to be incapable of directing their services. Case managers also perceive trade-offs between autonomy and safety (Micco, Hamilton, Martin, & McEwan, 1995; Scala, Mayberry, & Kunkel, 1996).

Access to person-directed services, nonetheless, is increasing among adults with significant intellectual disabilities as the boundaries for expressing autonomy have expanded to include shared decisionmaking with trusted others. These approaches allow service users to participate in aspects of service direction, as desired and feasible, and to delegate other service direction responsibilities to their personal allies.

Outcomes and Indicators

If people with disabilities and their families are actually in control of their supports, then the following indicators will be present:

- Individuals and their families will not be merely customers, but rather agents in determining and directing their supports and funding.
- Individuals and their families will be satisfied with the supports they are purchasing or will change "providers" when dissatisfied.
- The power of the service bureaucracy will be diminished, and individuals and their families will access formal services more directly for equal or lower cost.
- Competition and "trying and telling" will promote innovations in support and funding approaches (O'Brien, 2001).
- The "system" will be more adaptable, reliable, and responsive because it is market-driven.

Goal E: People with disabilities have meaningful opportunities and support to advocate and demonstrate leadership

Overview

Williams and Shoultz (1982) defined self-advocacy as people with ID/DD speaking or acting on behalf of themselves or others or on behalf of issues that affect people with disabilities. Williams and Shoultz (1982) pointed out that the self-advocacy movement is an international civil rights movement that originated in Sweden in the 1960s. It is led by, and developed for, people with developmental disabilities as part of the broader disability rights and independent living movement. Self Advocates Becoming Empowered (SABE), the national self-advocacy organization formed after the second North American People First Conference held in Nashville in 1991, affirmed:

> We believe that people with disabilities should be treated as equals. That means that people should be given the same decisions, choices, rights, responsibilities and chances to speak up to empower themselves as well as to make new friendships and renew old friendships just like everyone else. They should also be able to learn from their mistakes like everyone else. (Shoultz & Ward, 1996, p. 221)

Core goals of self-advocacy are to facilitate or assist individuals to recognize their leadership capabilities and to develop future leaders. As self-advocacy leader Nancy Ward (personal communication, February 19, 2004) noted, "It's my responsibility to encourage new leaders and to help them gain confidence in themselves so they can realize their full potential in whatever they choose to do. Seeing the awesome sight of personal growth as people with disabilities realize that they can do what they set out to do makes my job worthwhile."

Self-advocacy also provides a critical vehicle for personal development through peer-based education and support:

> Self-advocacy groups typically give people [with intellectual] and other developmental disabilities their first and most consistent opportunities to develop membership and leadership skills. Within the group, members can learn about their rights and responsibilities, develop confidence about their abilities, practice the skills of speaking in public and studying an issue, learn about voting and group decisionmaking, exercise problem-solving techniques, and develop assertiveness skills. They can also give and receive personal support from people who have had experiences like their own. Even group members who do not communicate verbally can and do participate in the support and learn ways of advocating for themselves and others (Shoultz & Ward, 1996).

Outcomes and Indicators
Key indicators for demonstrating that people with ID/DD have meaningful opportunities and support to advocate and demonstrate leadership include the following:

- People with developmental and intellectual disabilities have the opportunity to learn leadership and self-advocacy skills and to use those skills to influence policy and practice at local, state, and national levels.
- Americans are aware of the self-advocacy movement and the potential of self-advocates to lead productive lives and contribute to their communities (SABE's goal is that 75% of Americans know about self-advocacy).
- People with ID/DD are equal partners in making decisions about resources, policies, and practices that impact their lives and the lives of others with disabilities.
- Self-advocacy groups across the country have equal access to monetary and

other resources allocated for monitoring support systems and influencing policy and practice.

- Students with disabilities learn self-advocacy skills when they are in school and have the opportunity to exercise those skills in educational planning and decisionmaking, particularly during the high school to adult life transition years.

Goal F: People with disabilities have the freedom and opportunity to participate in social activities and relationships as they desire

Overview

In the current context of disability, topics such as employment, education, community living, and related services and supports are typically emphasized. Yet, for most people, opportunities for social involvements most often define quality of life, being part of one's community, having friends, and forming intimate relationships. Many people with ID/DD lack these opportunities because others do not consider their community participation important or attainable or fear that they might be abused or mistreated (Griffiths & Lunsky, 2002; Jordan & Dunlap, 2001). People with ID/DD who manage to date, marry, and have children often face family disapproval and practical barriers as a result of insufficient support and misguided public policy. Despite more enlightened social attitudes than those that once led to forced sterilization, many still do not acknowledge that sexuality is as much a natural part of life for people with disabilities as for everyone else (Brantlinger, 1992; McCabe, 1993).

Social relationships serve a number of reciprocal functions for all people, including companionship, intimacy, continuity, social development, and practical help. Social networks link individuals to many life opportunities, including employment and community participation. Life without social connection is isolating and a major factor in the separation of people with disabilities from the rest of society.

Outcomes and Indicators

Citizens with ID/DD have the right to experience full lives that include friendship, intimate partnership, and parenthood. Key indicators or outcomes that indicate that such rights are recognized include the following:

- People with ID/DD have reciprocal friendships and social connections.
- Family and community members accept that people with disabilities have the rights and abilities to form relationships, marry, and have children.
- Young people with disabilities are provided with information about social relationships, sexuality, reproductive health, marriage, and parenting and learn about the supports and accommodations they may need to function successfully in these roles.
- People with disabilities freely choose their friends and partners, and they have support that fosters their connections with chosen friends and partners.
- Support provided to married people and parents with disabilities emphasizes building their skills, expanding their social networks, and connecting them to resources that will increase their success and ability to manage problems.
- Public policy barriers to social freedom are removed, and people with disabilities have equal opportunity to live full lives that include friendship, marriage, and

parenthood. In particular, people with disabilities are no longer subjected to forced sterilization or arbitrarily restricted from marrying or becoming parents.

REVIEW OF KNOWLEDGE AND RECOMMENDATIONS

This section summarizes our current knowledge and lays out essential areas for future research related to self-determination, self-advocacy, and social freedom.[2] As noted, the quality and scope of research of these topics has been limited. In contrast to extensive research in areas such as special education and long-term services and supports, relatively little research has been conducted on self-determination, self-advocacy, and social freedom, and most of the research has not been obtained directly from individuals with ID/DD. Improving on the status of knowledge on these topics is vitally important to achieving national goals. In doing so, it will be important to develop consensus standards and protocols for conducting research and evaluation on these topics, with sufficient attention to model fidelity. All stakeholders need to establish a recognized set of outcomes against which to conduct research and evaluation. Indicators detailed earlier in this chapter provide a foundation in defining such outcomes. The research agenda needed to address the inadequacies and future needs for research in this area will require federal and private sponsorship of substantial, in-depth, focused research programs. In the past, such commitments have been minimal, and this situation should be corrected.

Goal A: People with disabilities are equal partners in research, training, and dissemination

Overview of the Knowledge Base

Traditionally, most research has been conducted by professionals with little involvement by constituents other than as "subjects" in the research. Researchers are increasingly recognizing participatory action research (PAR) as a valued and effective approach for collaboratively studying and addressing community needs (Minkler, Blackwell, Thompson, & Tamir, 2003). For example, the Institute of Medicine, in its report on educating health professionals for the twenty-first century, included community-based participatory action as one of the eight new areas for development (Rosenstock & Hernandez, 2002).

PAR is an important approach for bolstering the quality and relevance of research. When those who are the subjects of research also are active in designing, implementing, analyzing, and publicizing the research, the likelihood increases that the research will address the most important questions and follow the most appropriate methods.

---

2 See, e.g., *Ricci v. Okin,* 573 F. Supp. 817 (D. Mass. 1982) ("the right of self-determination and freedom of choice to the person's fullest capacity is now a matter of Massachusetts regulation and…the state is bound to uphold and improve these rights"); *Superintendent of Belchertown v. Saikewicz,* 370 N.E. 2d 417 (Mass. 1977) (right of person with mental retardation to have substituted judgment decision made for him regarding whether to receive medical treatment); *Mills v. Bd. of Education of the District of Columbia,* 348 F. Supp. 866 (D.D.C. 1972) (exclusion of children from public schools).

The individuals will also ensure that findings will be clearly interpreted and that new knowledge will be appropriately communicated to the most critical audiences. These benefits were demonstrated in a national study using PAR approaches to investigate the efficacy of parent-to-parent support (Santelli, Singer, DiVenere, Ginsberg, & Powers, 1998). Parent leaders guided the identification of relevant questions, selected methods that parent-to-parent programs could realistically implement, and transformed the findings into tools that have been widely adopted for program improvement.

In addition to improving the quality of research, PAR offers opportunities for participants to develop knowledge and skills that provide a foundation for social action. As expressed by Gaventa, "In the process, research is seen not only as a process of creating knowledge, but simultaneously as education and development of consciousness, and of mobilization for action" (1988, p. 19). Taken to the next level, PAR research and evaluation approaches can be used within an empowerment model that will help participants to recognize their strengths and resources and to gain control over their lives (Fetterman, Kaftarian, & Wandersman, 1996; Small, 1995). Studies using PAR empowerment research with marginalized groups, such as persons of color and individuals with disabilities, have demonstrated the increase in skill development, self-reliance, empowerment, and social and policy change that results (Suarez de Balcazar, Fawcett, & Balcazar, 1998; Stewart & Bhagwanjee, 1999; Powers, Garner, Couture, Dertinger, Lawson, Squire, et al., 2004; Walsh, 1997).

PAR has increased in popularity and credibility; however, researchers continue to have greater difficulty in obtaining funding for PAR in comparison to other research (Israel, Schultz, Parker, & Becker, 2001; Green, George, Daniel, Frankish, Herbert, Bowie, et al., 1995). Specific requirements for successfully carrying out participatory research include the following:

1. Investing in building community linkages and the fiduciary capacities of collaborating organizations so they can function as full partners and promote sustainability
2. Providing adequate information, training, and support that maximizes the capabilities of individuals to be actively involved
3. Adjusting research time schedules to provide opportunities for participants to genuinely influence the direction and implementation of research
4. Acknowledging participant contributions by paying for their time and covering other expenses, such as personal assistance, transportation, meals, and child care (Minkler, et al., 2003)

Despite a growing body of evidence that documents the benefits of PAR, individuals with ID/DD have had limited opportunity to be involved as equal partners. However, preliminary findings are encouraging. For example, a pilot evaluation of individuals with ID/DD functioning as service quality reviewers demonstrated that these reviewers participated effectively with training and accommodations (Bonham, Basehart, Schalock, Kirchner, & Rumenap, 2004). Powers, et al. (2004) conducted a youth-directed research project involving young leaders with diverse disabilities, such as autism and Down syndrome, who successfully participated in designing studies, collecting and analyzing data, and dissminating the results. A PAR evaluation project currently underway in Maryland entitled *ASK ME!* is successfully involving trained individuals who receive ID/DD services in reviewing questions and interviewing peers about services received (Bonham, et al., 2004). Findings suggest that the evaluation and the response rate have improved because researchers with disabilities have participated. Moreover, both the interviewers and those interviewed have more faith in the study.

Recommendations for Research

To more clearly understand and promote the involvement of individuals with ID/DD in research, researchers need to address the following major questions:

1. What opportunities do individuals with ID/DD have to participate in the direction, design, data analysis, and dissemination of research? How do other researchers treat them? How are their contributions acknowledged (e.g., as authors, presenters)?

2. What opportunities are currently available for individuals with ID/DD to learn about grants and research (e.g., reading requests for proposals [RFPs], participating in writing grant applications, discussing and interpreting data, writing and editing manuscripts, promoting the use of findings)?

3. What classes and practicum experiences, in colleges and other settings, are available to individuals with ID/DD to learn about research, applying for and managing grants, conducting research, and disseminating findings? Can individuals with disabilities participate and gain the target skills to receive college credit for their experiences?

4. What is the impact of involving individuals with ID/DD in the focus, design, dissemination, and use of research on the research and on members of the research team?

5. How can participatory action research be designed and conducted so that it involves individuals with ID/DD at all levels? What are the most effective ways for researchers with and without developmental disabilities to work together?

6. What are the most effective models for preparing individuals with ID/DD to actively participate meaningfully in research?

Goal B: People with disabilities make informed decisions about their lives

Overview of the Knowledge Base

The literature on informed decisionmaking and intellectual disability highlights a paradox—it sets the traditional method of protecting vulnerable citizens by making decisions for them against the emerging information about the capacities of individuals to make informed decisions. Historically, informed decisionmaking and intellectual disability have been discussed in the context of informed consent for medical procedures and participation in research (Iacono & Murray, 2003). This focus emerged, in part, in response to the past exploitation of individuals with disabilities, as in the Willowbrook study (Beecher, 1966).

Although some research has identified factors associated with capacity to give consent (Arscott, Dagman, & Stenfert Kroese, 1998; Morris, Niederbuhl, & Mahr, 1993), no consensus exists about what standards should be used to evaluate a person's decision-making capacity. Nor has anyone resolved how to determine a person's capacity to decide in general or with respect to a particular situation (Iacono & Murray, 2003). Many argue that, to determine threshold levels of performance necessary for informed consent, they need normative data on capacity to make decisions (Appelbaum, 1997). With this lack of consensus, subjective impressions are frequently what determines capacity (Rogers, 1999).

Although guardianship is a major issue in the lives of people with ID/DD, little research has focused on proxy consent. One study by Warren, Sobal, Tenney, Hoopes, Damron, Levenson, et al. (1986) found that almost half of the proxy decisionmakers for individuals in nursing homes sought the advice of another person, usually a medical provider, presumably to investigate whether participating in a procedure was in the individual's best interest. Forty-six percent of the proxies did not consent to the procedure for a variety of reasons, including the belief that it would disturb the person, that the person had already been through too much, that the person would not have consented, or that the proxy would not have consented if he or she were the participant. Seventeen percent of the proxies who gave consent said they thought the individual would not have consented if it were his or her choice. Sachs, Stocking, Stern, Cox, Hougham, and Sparage Sachs (1994) found that proxy decisionmakers for people with dementia were protective; they often refused consent for procedures patients were likely to consent to, whether they had dementia or not. In both studies, proxy decisions often were not guided by substituted consideration of what the person would have wanted if he or she were able to make the decision. Proxies frequently did not consider the desires of individuals because of the presumed difficulty of identifying the individual's preferences (Freedman, 2001).

Much of the current knowledge about the impact of informed decisionmaking on the lives of individuals with disabilities comes from the educational literature. For example, several studies show the positive effect of making decisions, expressing preferences, and setting goals on educational and behavioral outcomes (e.g., Dunlap, DePerczel, Clarke, Wilson, Wright, White, et al., 1994; German, Huber Marshall, & Martin, 1997; Kennedy & Haring, 1993; Newton, Ard, & Horner, 1993; Powers, Turner, Ellison, Matuszewski, Wilson, Phillips, et al., 2001; Schunk, 1985). German, et al. (1997) demonstrated that students with cognitive disabilities achieved more of their daily goals when they participated in a goal-setting curriculum. Findings further document the impact of environment on choice-making opportunities. Wehmeyer and Bolding (1999) found that adults with developmental disabilities in typical community settings had more opportunity for choicemaking and higher self-determination than those in congregate community settings (e.g., group homes, sheltered workshops).

Recommendations for Research

A substantial research commitment is needed to understand the nature and extent of informed decisionmaking by individuals with intellectual disabilities, the impact of conditions such as guardianship, and strategies for promoting informed decisionmaking. Key research questions include the following:

1. What are the essential criteria for informed decisionmaking? (What does it look like?) Under what conditions does informed decisionmaking occur for anyone?
2. How, and to what extent, do individuals with disabilities have opportunities to make informed decisions about their lives? How do opportunities for informed decisionmaking vary by factors such as setting, circle of support, severity of disability, involvement in the service system, culture, and participation in self-advocacy?
3. What impact does informed decisionmaking have on people's lives? What are the differences in quality of life for people who make the decisions that shape their lives and supports?
4. What strategies have been effectively employed to reduce or remove these barriers preventing people with ID/DD, including those individuals with severe disabilities, from making informed decisions?
5. What impact does guardianship have on informed decisionmaking within and outside of the areas of a person's life to which it was intended to apply?
6. What have been successful strategies for changing the attitudes and practices of systems, policy makers, and family members to assure that people with disabilities have opportunities to make informed decisions? What kind of organizational structures, management styles, and training for decisionmakers do organizations need to advance acceptance of informed decisionmaking by people with ID/DD?
7. What approaches will educate people with disabilities and the public about the rights and abilities of people with disabilities to make informed decisions?

Goal C: People with disabilities have the opportunity to build their knowledge, skill, and resources, to control their lives and to contribute to their communities

Overview of the Knowledge Base

Many individuals with developmental disabilities live in two realities: they are supported by service systems that are resource-rich while leading personal lives that are distinguished by poverty (Nerney, 2001b). Given this dichotomy, most of the knowledge and resources available to assist individuals have been held by systems and service providers and are focused on "helping" with limited opportunity for "capacity transfer" to individuals and trusted others in their lives.

Although extensive research, much of it described in this volume, has been conducted on the nature and effects of specialized, professional-directed programs in education, employment, and community living for individuals with ID/DD, much less research has focused on how individuals build their own knowledge, skills, and resources and gain entrée to life opportunities. As such, the disability community knows a lot more about taking care of people than it knows about increasing individuals' capacities to take care of themselves.

What has been learned is promising. Various approaches have successfully demonstrated how to support individuals with disabilities and their families in becoming involved in defining and controlling their lives. These approaches include person-centered planning (Holburn & Vietze, 2002), circles of support (Perske, 1988), and self-directed support corporations or microboards (Golden, 2003). Some research has investigated factors associated with individuals with disabilities taking the lead as change agents in their lives. For instance, Sands, Bassett, Lehmann, and Spencer (1998) studied factors that predicted whether students could or would direct their transition planning. These critical factors included participation in general education classes; opportunity to plan, work toward goals, and evaluate progress; and teacher and family support for student involvement. Wehmeyer and Schwartz (1997) found that, one year following high school, students with high levels of self-determination were more likely to be employed than those with low levels of self-determination.

Other research has highlighted successful processes and outcomes associated with student-directed transition planning. Powers, et al. (2001) demonstrated that young people who received coaching to identify, communicate, and achieve their goals, along with peer-support, mentoring opportunities, and peer support for their families, had significantly more success in reaching their goals. Moreover, they showed greater increases in empowerment, transition awareness, and level of participation in transition-planning meetings than did youth in a wait-listed comparison group. Innovative practices also have been documented that help adults and young people with disabilities with person-directed career planning, resource leveraging, and employment and self-employment in their chosen careers (Griffin & Hammis, 2003; Sowers, Cotton, & Malloy, 1994; Sowers, McLean, & Owens, 2002; Sowers, Milliken, Cotton, Sousa, & Dwyer, 2000). Sowers, McAllister, and Cotton (1996) developed strategies for guiding person-centered planning directed as much as possible by the student; assisting students and their families to identify, use, and expand their personal connections to find jobs; and involving students in activities to seek and keep jobs.

Griffin and Hammis (2003) provided numerous case studies of the benefits of self-employment for individuals with disabilities who have started their own businesses. Outcomes associated with the self-employment initiatives were individuals' greater self-confidence that they can achieve their employment goals, increased likelihood that they will find jobs in chosen career areas, and increased ability to draw on expanded personal and community resources.

With regard to community service, people with disabilities have been historically stereotyped as the recipients of support. Society has not recognized their capabilities and responsibilities for community service have not been recognized; yet community service is an important way for persons with disabilities to break down societal misconceptions and to build their personal skill and experience. The involvement of citizens with disabilities is an important priority of the National and Community Services Act of 1990, as amended. Section 120(d)(5)(C) of the act sets aside funds to ensure that persons with disabilities are aware of service opportunities and receive necessary accommodations to help them participate. The act also requires that programs affirmatively recruit and retain individuals with disabilities.

Despite this legislative endorsement, a survey of 208 AmeriCorps programs revealed that 95 programs were involving 873 persons with disabilities, whereas 70 programs reported they had no members with disabilities (Lowery, 1999). Few programs reported that they were actively recruiting members with disabilities; program directors expressed concerns about finances, community resources, and accommodations. Likewise, a subsequent survey of the involvement of individuals with disabilities in AmeriCorps in the Western U.S. revealed that they comprised 0% to 2.5% of AmeriCorps members (Westwood & Powers, 2003). Companion data collected from 130 consumer-controlled disability organizations (e.g., self-advocacy groups, independent living centers) indicated that 85% of the organizations had little to no awareness of national and community service programs. Major barriers to the involvement of individuals with disabilities included lack of referral or recruitment, perceived difficulty in addressing training and accommodation needs, and concern that participants would loose their disability benefits.

Recommendations for Research

Many questions remain unanswered regarding promotion of the capacities, resources, and opportunities that individuals with ID/DD need to direct their lives and serve their communities. Key questions for future research include the following:

1. What knowledge, skills, opportunities, and resources do people with disabilities currently have that enable them to control their lives and contribute to their communities? In what ways do these differ from people without disabilities? How do these vary according to culture, involvement in service system, community characteristics, financial resources, severity of disability, support system, gender, and other factors?

2. What knowledge, skills, opportunities, and resources do people with disabilities want to develop so that they can control their lives and contribute to their communities? How do these vary according to culture, involvement in service system, community characteristics, financial resources, severity of disability, support system, gender, and other factors?

3. What types of experiences and risks are people with disabilities permitted and denied in comparison to people without disabilities? What is the relationship between higher and lower control over one's life and safety and life satisfaction?

4. What are the barriers faced by people with ID/DD in building their knowledge, skills, and resources for controlling their lives and participating in their communities? What strategies are effective in reducing or removing these barriers?

5. To what extent are people with disabilities involved in and exerting control over their person-centered planning (e.g., understanding the purpose, writing the plan, asking questions, gathering information, and carrying out the plan)? In what ways do plans vary based on the extent to which individuals are involved in their planning? What types of approaches are most effective in developing capacities to control their planning?

6   What is the impact on the lives of people with ID/DD and on the lives of others in the community when people have increased capacities, resources, and opportunities to control their lives and contribute to their communities?

7. What approaches can be effectively used to increase the knowledge, skills, and resources of people with ID/DD for controlling their lives and contributing to their communities? How should approaches change as individuals express different levels of involvement and leadership in the phases of their lives? What do others need if they are going to assist people with disabilities effectively?

Goal D: People with disabilities have control over their resources, such as their funding and supports

Overview of the Knowledge Base

At least 29 state developmental disabilities programs took part in a self-determination-based systems-change effort through an initiative sponsored by the Robert Wood Johnson Foundation (Moseley, 2001). In addition, several states are currently implementing cash and counseling or direct cash payment demonstrations with elders and persons with diverse disabilities (Mahoney, Simone, & Simon-Rusinowitz, 2000).

Most agree that promoting self-determination requires that people control funds and services at the level they desire and that an array of supports are provided that will maximize their self-direction capabilities (Flanagan, Green, & Eustis, 1996; Scala & Mayberry, 1997). Such supports include giving individuals adequate information about service options and providers, involving them intimately in the service planning process, and assisting them in recruiting, selecting, training, and supervising their providers (Eustis & Fischer, 1992).

Studies to evaluate the efficacy of self-determined services have varied in their methodological rigor. However, taken as a whole, findings to date suggest self-determination-based services may have benefits for many individuals. For example, Benjamin, Matthias, Franke, Mills, Hasenfeld, Matras, et al. (1998) conducted an interview study of 1,095 users of person-directed and professionally directed personal care programs in California. The users of person-directed services reported significantly higher levels of empowerment over their services and satisfaction with the technical and interpersonal aspects of their services and the service quality than did users of professionally directed services. They also told of significantly higher levels of safety with their assistants, assurance of back-up assistance, and ease of arranging services. Finally, they reported greater emotional, social, and physical well-being as well as fewer unmet needs.

Similar findings were obtained from a study comparing agency-directed and person-directed services for individuals with developmental disabilities (Conroy & Yuskauskas, 1996). The recipients of person-directed services demonstrated significant increases in their control over decisions and quality of life, even though the person-directed services were provided at 12% lower cost. In the evaluation of customer outcomes associated with participation in the Robert Wood Johnson Foundation-funded self-determination initiative, Conroy, Fullerton, Brown, and Garrow (2002) obtained pre- and post-participation data for 800 individuals in nine states. Their findings indicated that participants shifted much of their care from professionals to family and friends. Participants and those closest to them reported significant improvements in participant quality of life in all 14 life areas examined. The cost of customer participation in self-determination-based services was lower than for a comparison group of individuals receiving traditional services. Heller, Factor, Hsieh, and Hahn (1998) also found that families and their adult members with developmental disabilities who received person-directed support reported fewer unmet needs, higher satisfaction with services, and greater self-efficacy than a control group. Caregivers were significantly less likely to desire out-of-home placement than caregivers in the control group. Furthermore, participants with developmental disabilities earned significantly higher wages and were more integrated in the community than were the individuals in the control group.

The Cash and Counseling initiative currently underway in the U.S. is yielding some preliminary findings related to the types of services used and satisfaction with services among participants. Participants have been randomly assigned to receive either cash payments for services they choose or traditional Medicaid-funded personal assistance services (Foster, Brown, Carlson, Phillips, & Schore, 2001; Foster, Brown, Phillips, Schore, & Carlson, 2003). Surveys conducted with participants in Arkansas and New Jersey found that cash payment participants were likely to (a) hire family members or friends to provide their support, (b) use a variety of supports, including home modifications and equipment, (c) use bookkeeping services for the financial management of their service payments, (d) report they are satisfied with the services they receive and the flexibility and control afforded them, and (e) recommend the program options to others (more than 85% said they would).

Similar service preference findings were obtained by Simon-Rusinowitz, Mahoney, Shoop, Desmond, Squillace, and Sowers (2001). Of 378 individuals with ID/DD and surrogate respondents interviewed, 44% of the individuals and 45% of surrogates indicated interest in direct cash payments. Interest was highest among persons with the most severe disabilities who were dissatisfied with their current services and who wanted more control over their services. Interest in cash payments did not vary by age, gender, educational level, living arrangement, experience in managing support providers, overall health status, services received, or cost of services. The majority of respondents also said that they would want assistance or training to learn how to manage a cash option.

A survey of families of children with ID/DD in Florida supported these findings (Simon-Rusinowitz, Mahoney, Shoop, Desmond, Squillace, Fay, et al., in press). Overall, family members showed higher levels of interest in the cash option, especially among those willing to pay a worker directly, those who desired more involvement with services, and those dissatisfied with their current services.

Finally, evaluations of family support programs for families of children with ID/DD also highlight the benefits of providing family-driven flexible supports and cash payments (Agosta & Melda, 1995, May; Allard, Gottlieb, & Hart, 1993; Yuan, Baker-McCue, & Witkin, 1996). Flexible funding that included cash payments was associated with increased efficiency and cost savings in purchasing by families (Yuan, et al., 1996) and greater self-efficacy and empowerment over time (Allard, et al., 1993). Families generally reported their preference for having a knowledgeable service coordinator who could help them find supports and cash payments that they could use flexibly to purchase their supports.

Recommendations for Research

Although existing findings related to the benefits of person-directed services are very promising, the reality is that a relatively small proportion of individuals with ID/DD have access to this option. Moreover, researchers need additional information to adequately understand and document the most effective ways to enable individuals to control their supports and service funding. They can obtain some information by carefully analyzing existing data sets, but they also must gather new data, particularly through longitudinal studies, that can accurately determine the long-term impact on people's lives and on the evolution of the service system when individuals control their supports and funding. Key questions needing further investigation include the following:

1. What control do people really have over resources such as funding and supports from the perspective of the individual and from the perspective of the professional? Is what Medicaid promises in their waivers concerning the support of self-determination actually reflected in state practices? How well are their promises reflected in state practices?

2. What changes within service systems have implemented essential elements of self-determination-based services, (e.g., individualized funding, person-centered planning, fiscal intermediaries)? What approaches appear to have the greatest efficacy in increasing self-determination and for whom?

3. What are the most important factors in a person's successful control over his or her resources? How is the practice/absence of these factors best fostered? What are effective practices for promoting control over resources by people with diverse disabilities, cultural backgrounds, and support networks? How do individual support plans promote and impede individual control over resources and how can plans be changed to increase individual control?

4. What is the relationship between the natural supports people receive and the amount of control they believe they have? What are effective ways of increasing the availability of natural supports and generic services? How well do generic resource planning approaches meet the needs of people with disabilities (e.g., retirement planning, financial planning)?

5. What are effective approaches for individuals to hire, supervise, retain, and fire their support providers directly? How do researchers identify, design, and evaluate promising approaches?

6. How are people with ID/DD outside of the current service system achieving success? How are they accessing and managing resources?

Goal E: People with disabilities have meaningful opportunity and support to advocate and demonstrate leadership

Overview of the Knowledge Base

Self-advocacy also involves advocating with coalitions working together for justice (Hayden & Nelis, 2002). Self-advocacy teaches people with ID/DD how to make decisions and choices about their own rights and responsibilities and how to support others (Self-Advocates Becoming Empowered, 2001). The self-advocacy movement has grown rapidly in the United States in the 30 years since a group of Oregon advocates attended a conference on self-advocacy in England and returned to establish the People First movement (Shapiro, 1993). Virtually every state in the nation now has self-advocacy groups; most have statewide organizations (Dybwad & Bersani, 1996).

Self-Advocates Becoming Empowered (SABE) has established itself as a visible force for influencing national policy and for providing direction for state and local self-advocacy organizations. Most professional and parent organizations, like The Arc and the American

Association on Mental Retardation, have embraced self-advocacy and provide support to groups and individuals. Self-advocates have made recommendations to governmental agencies, such as the Administration on Developmental Disabilities, and served on site-visit teams and as grant reviewers. Self-advocacy leaders regularly testify in state and national hearings and before state and national legislative bodies and influence policy. Self-advocates are vocal proponents for enhancing self-determination and implementing supports emphasizing personal choice and control. Increasing collaboration also is taking place among self-advocacy leaders and leaders from other disability groups (Powers, et al., 2002).

Despite these historical achievements, little research has been conducted on self-advocacy and leadership in developmental disabilities. A study by Pederson, Oldendick, and Nelis (1997) explored the skills that help individuals with developmental disabilities become effective leaders as well as the types of supports leaders need. Self-advocacy leaders said that some of the most difficult skills for people with ID/DD to learn are (a) participating as an equal member of a group, (b) helping others to develop their leadership potential so they can assume leadership roles, (c) knowing their role in the group, (d) knowing how to be a good group facilitator, and (e) being able to run a committee meeting.

Leaders reported that it was most difficult to get support to help them review written materials and learn the processes of a board and the structure of an organization. It also was difficult to find someone that they could talk to who would not tell them what to do or take over their role and who had confidence that people with disabilities could do what they set their minds to do. Self-advocates reported the qualities they deemed most important in support persons. These included (a) treating people with developmental disabilities with respect, (b) believing that people with developmental disabilities can be leaders, (c) being a good listener, and (d) knowing when to step in and when to stay out of a situation.

Powers, Ward, Ferris, Ward, Nelis, Wieck, et al. (1999) surveyed the leadership opportunities available to people with disabilities in Developmental Disabilities Councils and University Centers of Excellence in Developmental Disabilities. Their findings suggested that modest numbers of individuals with disabilities were involved in leadership roles and many were in volunteer or hourly positions. Barriers to involving individuals with disabilities in leadership roles included language and communication problems, lack of leadership opportunities, limited knowledge of leadership development methods and resources, difficulty assessing and providing accommodations and supports, and administrative barriers, such as hiring constraints. The study identified several strategies to increase leadership by individuals with disabilities, including expanding training opportunities; hiring more staff with disabilities; involving individuals with disabilities more directly in training, planning, and policy development; improving accessibility; and collaborating with other agencies and self-advocacy groups.

A related survey of the directors of state developmental disabilities services agencies examined the extent to which these agencies support state self-advocacy organizations (Ward, Ward, Ferris, & Powers, 2000). Forty-two percent of the agencies that responded to the survey indicated they provided in-kind or direct financial support to self-advocacy organizations. All but one said they would consider providing support to self-advocacy organizations in their states. Obstacles to supporting self-advocacy organizations identified by state agencies included difficulty navigating state purchasing and contracting rules, the potential conflict of interest related to funding an organization that may advocate for issues affecting the state, and lack of awareness of self-advocacy organizations and their activities. Agencies emphasized the importance of building long-term relationships with self-advocacy organizations and providing funding to help them hire their own staff.

Recommendations for Research

It would be inappropriate to recommend a broad research agenda in self-advocacy without its being spearheaded by self-advocacy leaders. However, preliminary consideration suggests that there is a need for research on the role of self-advocates in systems and social change, on the impact of self-advocacy on people's lives, and on adult learner models and ways that self-advocates effectively teach based on life experience. Key research questions include the following:

1. What is the role of self-advocacy and self-advocacy leaders in systems change and social change? In states where self-advocacy groups are active, what systems change and development has occurred compared to states without self-advocacy groups? How have these states fostered leadership development among persons with disabilities?

2. What are the experiences and effective practices of successful self-advocacy in policy change and development; in increasing community resources, supports, and opportunities for participation; and in education and training?

3. How does involvement in self-advocacy impact people's lives; for example, how does it impact their personal goal achievement, development, self-esteem, social connection, safety, quality of life, involvement in community, and access to supports and resources? To what extent are people treated positively or negatively when they advocate?

4. How have self-advocacy groups started and received funding? Has the mandate in the DD Act actually made any difference in funding and access to leadership development opportunities?

5. To what extent are self-advocates and self-advocacy groups equal partners in decisionmaking? What barriers exist, and what strategies are effective in addressing them?

6. To what extent is self-advocacy being developed in schools? How are these activities organized and led?

7. What is the involvement of self-advocates in, and their impact on, community volunteerism? What is the importance of reciprocity in receiving from, and giving to, the community?

Goal F: People with disabilities have the freedom and opportunity to participate in social activities and social relationships as they desire

Overview of the Knowledge Base

Historically, people with ID/DD have had very little opportunity for social freedom. Limited research has been conducted in this area, except for studies related to promoting social connection in school and community settings, where the benefits of social participation have been extensively documented for persons with disabilities and community members. Studies have identified a number of strategies, including cooperative learning groups, environmental restructuring, changes in game rules, circles of friends, peer buddies, and social guides for promoting social connection (e.g., Bernabe & Block, 1994; Haring, Breen, Pitts-Conway, Lee, & Gaylord-Ross, 1987; Newton & Horner, 1993; Kamps, Royer, Dugan, Kravitz, Gonzalez-Lopez, Garcia, et al., 2002; O'Brien & Lyle O'Brien, 1993; Schleien, 1993; Schleien, Fahnstock, Green, & Rynders, 1990; Werner, Horner, & Newton, 1998). Some research has also demonstrated the impact of self-management on inclusion (e.g., Koegel, Harrower, & Koegel, 1999).

Although some information is available on marriage and parenting by persons with disabilities, little research has focused on parents with ID/DD. A national study of parents with diverse disabilities revealed several barriers that parents have encountered, among them lack of transportation; negative attitudes, including discrimination; pressure to have a tubal ligation or abortion; health providers' lack of disability expertise during prenatal and birthing care; attempts to have their children removed; and interference with adopting a child (Toms-Barker & Maralani, 1997). Findings from surveys of clinicians, staff, and family members suggest that attitudes about dating by people with developmental disabilities may be improving; however, these groups appear to consider marriage less important and express concern about exploitation and abuse (Griffiths & Lunsky, 2002).

Some attention has focused on sexuality education, including ways to appropriately express physical affection, stranger awareness and ways to stay safe, and the rights and responsibilities of parenthood (American Academy of Pediatrics, 1996; Shaughnessy, Glover, Greene, & Choy, 1999). However, this education has emphasized learning "appropriate" behavior and self-protection, which reflects the assumption that people with disabilities generally behave inappropriately and are vulnerable to exploitation; therefore, corrective and protective education should be provided.

Recommendations for Research

Much additional research is needed for the disability community to further understand the opportunities for, and experiences of, people with intellectual disabilities in expressing social freedom. Key questions for study include the following:

1. To what extent are people with ID/DD becoming involved in their communities, establishing reciprocal friendships, marrying, and raising children?
2. How and to what extent are friendships supported outside the "program" setting?
3. What barriers exist to keep people with ID/DD from forming friendships, marrying, and raising children?
4. What practices and policies can effectively support community belonging, friendship, and love by people with ID/DD? What resources, including education and supports, are currently available to them?
5. What are the best experiences of families supporting people with ID/DD in (a) developing friendships with people with and without disabilities, (b) making connections and enjoying hospitality, (c) getting around their community, (d) understanding sexuality, and (e) supporting marriage and parenthood?

USING KNOWLEDGE TO SHAPE OUR NATIONAL AGENDA

We have highlighted a number of areas where further research is needed to strengthen our national promise to individuals with disabilities so that they can determine and direct their lives and participate as full citizens. To be useful, new findings must make a genuine difference in increasing opportunities for persons with ID/DD and in improving policies and practices. It is important to acknowledge that research most often provides ammunition for supporting initiatives that are already happening rather than leading the way in shaping public policy. Thus, the lack of rigorous research evidence should not be used as a rationale for reversing or holding back the progress of initiatives that make sense and show promise. Rather, researchers must do a better job of keeping up with advocate's and policy maker's priorities, and researchers need additional resources to conduct research while new approaches are developing.

Besides a pressing need for further research, well-established research findings could be more effectively applied to policy and practice improvement. Important areas of application include person-directed services, peer education, and self-advocacy. This information should be used to improve the Medicaid program, which is the principal source of funding for long-term care services and supports for people with developmental disabilities. Medicaid policy continues to be dominated by congregate care models that undermine the fundamental principles of individual choice and control and are at odds with the expressed national goals for persons with ID/DD as conveyed in the Olmstead decision, the ADA, and major legislative and judicial sources.

To be true to the promises made to persons with ID/DD, federal Medicaid law must be thoroughly revamped to embrace self-determination, choice, and control and to establish that individuals and families have the right to determine and direct their own services and supports to the extent that they wish. It must encourage and support practices that promote individual and family control of services, including the use of such devices as financial intermediaries. It should permit resource allocations, with appropriate accountability safeguards, to individual recipients. Equally important, federal Medicaid law should affirmatively provide for states' direct funding of recognized self-advocacy and parent networks to provide training and technical assistance in self-determination and self-direction. If federal Medicaid policy and self-determination are not in alignment, then all the promises made by the national Congress, federal courts, and the President are empty.

Researchers must become much more sophisticated and participatory in their dissemination and training efforts if policy makers and constituent groups are to use the knowledge gained effectively. Key goals for responsive dissemination and training include the following:

1. Package information in ways that policy makers and constituent groups can use directly. Despite the increasing emphasis on the value of empirical rigor and evidence-based practices, it remains the case that policy makers and disability groups still value information that responds to their immediate needs and puts a personal face on data. They want and need findings presented in brief formats

using straightforward language and anecdotal stories that illustrate the meaning of results.

2. Foster ongoing relationships with self-advocacy and family leaders and with policy makers. Such partnerships are essential if research is to become more relevant and valued by those who are in the position to use it to foster change.

3. Support people with disabilities and family members to be the major information outlets and training resources. Researchers must use participatory action approaches that involve individuals with disabilities in all aspects of research. Strategies should include (a) allowing individuals with disabilities and researchers co-present findings, (b) involving individuals with disabilities in writing and editing publications as paid staff and consultants, and (c) developing briefs, newsletters, and other materials that self-advocacy groups and family leaders can effectively use with peer and professional audiences.

Anticipating the Changes of the Future

Policy makers and disability professionals have promised persons with disabilities expanding opportunities for self-determination, self-advocacy, and social freedom. Gains have been made, but much work remains. Individuals with ID/DD and their families rightfully are expecting more. Ironically, the issues of self-determination, self-advocacy, and social freedom have largely been partitioned into discrete arenas for study. For example, there are researchers who focus on person-directed services and others who focus on adolescent transition. Yet fundamental issues of self-determination cut across all areas of life-education, employment, housing, technology, health care, family support, and so forth. Promoting deep changes in policies and practices through research requires that research integrates concepts of self-determination, self-advocacy, and social freedom as core considerations in all areas of life.

Given the aging of our population, it is also critical that we clarify the meaning and expression of self-determination by elders and ways they want to be supported. To understand this issue, we will need to know more about how to support the relationships between individuals with disabilities and their aging family members who provide their support. Finally, because so much of the attention has been focused on individuals who receive services and on service systems, human services know relatively little about how to develop and strengthen communities so that people with ID/DD inside and outside of the formal service system can access opportunities, resources, and supports. If individuals with ID/DD truly are going to assume their place as full citizens, we must focus first on how people with disabilities establish full lives in their communities and second on how we can assist them with systems and formal supports.

Enhancing Real Lives

Tony and Dan are examples of people who fulfilled their dreams through their personal determination and will to live a life of their own design. Through their persistence and dogged determination, each found the help they needed to do the things he wanted to do. Tony, for example, is driven by his belief that "if you can dream it, you can do it."

So how do we relate these stories to the world that would result if we made even partial headway toward the goals discussed in this document? Maybe it would not take someone like Tony 20 years to reach some of his or her goals. Perhaps, in the future, no one would use the tragic accident that caused Dan's death to buttress an argument against full community participation for people with disabilities.

Unlike Tony and Dan, literally thousands of people with similar disabilities in this country have not had succeeded in making their dreams come true; they cannot get the help they need to advance a plan that includes supports outside a system menu. In a world where people are valued for the potential and actual contributions they can make for their communities, where person-centered—not system-centered—priorities are the norm, and where money follows the person and his or her life vision, perhaps many, many more people will have an opportunity to live their dreams. This is the hope for making our national promises real.

CHAPTER 12

Emerging Technologies

MARY RIZZOLO, DAVID BRADDOCK, RODNEY BELL, AMY HEWITT,
AND CARRIE BROWN
with
Cathy Bodine, Diane Nelson Bryen, Daniel Davies, Frank DeRuyter,
Amy Goldman, Elbert Johns, David O'Hara, Missy Perrott,
Olivia Raynor, Mary Ann Romski, Joey Wallace, and Bob Williams

REAL LIVES

Technology and access to information play a central role in the lives of all people in our society. Technology is becoming more important in the lives of persons with intellectual and developmental disabilities (ID/DD) as well. A convergence of fundamental advances in microelectronics, computer science, communications, and the health and rehabilitative sciences has created tremendous potential over the next decade and beyond to develop new technology-based applications for this underserved group. The following two vignettes in educational and employment settings illustrate how technology can positively influence the lives of persons with intellectual and developmental disabilities.

In the Classroom*

TE is a 12-year-old young man with a primary diagnosis of severe mental retardation accompanied by mild cerebral palsy and significant problem behaviors. At the onset of his participation in a project we will describe, he primarily communicated via unintelligible vocalizations and gestures. Although he had a cardboard communication system with a few pictures on it, he was not making progress toward spontaneous functional communication. Initially, the goal was to determine if TE could benefit from a high-technology device with speech output and learn to use it for spontaneous communicative interaction.

TE began to participate in an experimental project and research study at the Language Research Center (LRC) at Georgia State University in Atlanta, GA,

---

* Reprinted with permission from Romski, M. A. & Sevcik, R. A. (1996). *Breaking the speech barrier: Language development through augmented means.* Baltimore: Paul H. Brookes.

where he was provided with a speech-output communication device. The technology was modified by LRC staff to permit TE to access it via pointing to symbols on a touch-sensitive display. Prior to the introduction of the device, his family and teachers participated in a series of instructional sessions during which they learned how to operate the device and use it for communication.

TE was successful! He quickly learned to use the device to communicate a variety of messages. He acquired a vocabulary of more than 75 symbols that he used singly or in combination to express greetings and basic wants and needs as well as to answer questions and interact with unfamiliar partners. After two years of experience with the device, TE was given an opportunity to move into a higher functioning classroom. He interacted and developed friendships with general education peers. At home, TE's behavior improved as well. His family reported increased sociability that permitted them to feel more comfortable with TE's presence in the community and made it easier to live with him on a day-to-day basis. In addition, his attention to educational tasks improved significantly so that strangers could understand some of his words. TE made a smooth transition from the elementary school to the junior high school setting and now has a sight-reading vocabulary of 25 words.

On the Job

In 1997, AbleLink[1] Technologies in Colorado Springs received a call from the Colorado School District's transition office. Sarah, a student-employee with an intellectual disability, was having problems with her warehouse job at a Target department store. She had difficulty remembering the things she had to do and was afraid she would lose her job. The transition job coach provided Sarah with AbleLink's Pocket Coach, recorded instructions for the eight different tasks required for the warehouse position, and set the Coach to play back an audio and visual "to do" list. In three weeks, Sarah was able to repeat verbatim each of the eight task instructions and did not need her Pocket Coach any more. The store also gave Sarah her first raise.

The Pocket Coach is a personal digital assistant (PDA) with a software program than runs on the Windows operating system. The Coach provides an easy-to-use interface for recording and retrieving a series of step-by-step audio and video instructions guiding individuals at their jobs, in performing activities of daily living, or in prompting for other tasks. AbleLink's newly available and more advanced product—the Visual Assistant—is a PDA with an integrated PC-slot digital camera. Staff or caretakers digitally photograph—and narrate—the steps in a task. Persons with cognitive disabilities use the touch screen and verbal instructions and images guide them through the steps. The Visual Assistant is being used in a new application specifically for health promotion in a new research and development project to assist in the improvement of oral hygiene for adults with cognitive disabilities. The research is being carried out by the

---

1. Information on the Visual Assistant and Pocket Coach is available online at http://www.ablelink tech.com/ or by phone at (719) 592-0347.

Westchester Institute for Human Development[2] (Valhalla, New York), AbleLink Technologies, and the Joseph P. Kennedy Foundation.

INTRODUCTION

Technology and access to information play a critical and growing role in the lives of people with and without disabilities. However, people with intellectual and developmental disabilities lag substantially behind all other groups in our society in the utilization of technology. Technology can promote independence, productivity, and quality of life for virtually all persons, but attitudinal barriers often exist in our society that create low expectations of the benefit of technology for persons with ID/DD.

The term "assistive technology device" is defined in the Technology-Related Assistance for Individuals with Disabilities Act of 1988 and the Assistive Technology Act of 1998 as "any item, piece of equipment, or product system, whether acquired commercially, modified or customized, that is used to increase, maintain, or improve functional capabilities of individuals with disabilities" (Title 29, Chapter 31, § 3002(a)(3)). The term "assistive technology service" is defined in these acts as "any service that directly assists an individual with a disability in the selection, acquisition, or use, of an assistive technology device" (Title 29, Chapter 31, § 3002(a)(4)).

Many persons with intellectual and developmental disabilities utilize assistive technologies to enhance functioning in activities of daily living, control of the environment, positioning and seating, vision, hearing, recreation, mobility, reading, learning and studying, math, motor aspects of writing, composition of written material, communication, and computer access. Technologies used range from low-tech devices, such as pictorial communication boards or adapted eating utensils, to high-tech devices, including adapted software and voice output devices with speech synthesis (Technology and Media Division, 2003).

Much progress has been made in assistive technology (AT), but "service providers, policymakers, and payers have generally been incapable of keeping up with the advances" (DeRuyter, 1997, p. 95). This often leads to communication problems between manufacturers, service providers, state/federal agencies, and consumers, which subsequently results in inconsistencies in the quality and effectiveness of the developed technologies (DeRuyter, 1997). This breakdown in communication, coupled with a lack of infrastructure, results in technology access problems for numerous persons with disabilities.

There is also a growing digital divide in computer access between persons with and without disabilities (Kaye, 2000). Although access to computers and the Internet is increasing for most individuals in the U.S., this is not the case for persons with disabilities. Almost 60% of persons with disabilities have never used a computer compared to less than 25% of persons without disabilities (Abramson, 2000). Less than 10% of persons with disabilities have access to the Internet compared to 38% of persons without disabilities. This discrepancy also exists in computer ownership. Less than 24% of people

---

2. Contact the Westchester Institute for Human Development at (914) 493-8202.

with disabilities own a computer compared to over 50% of persons without disabilities (Kaye, 2000).

People with cognitive disabilities—such as ID/DD—are extremely underserved in accessing assistive technologies, not only compared to nondisabled citizens, but also compared to persons with physical and sensory disabilities, themselves an underserved group (Braddock, Rizzolo, Thompson, & Bell, 2004). In excess of 7% of the U.S population has a significant cognitive disability, and the number of such individuals is expected to increase rapidly as the nation's population ages (see Figure 12-1). Cognitive disability is a substantial limitation in one's capacity to think, including conceptualizing, planning, and sequencing thoughts and actions; remembering; interpreting subtle social cues; and manipulating numbers and symbols (Braddock, Rizzolo, Thompson, & Bell, 2004).

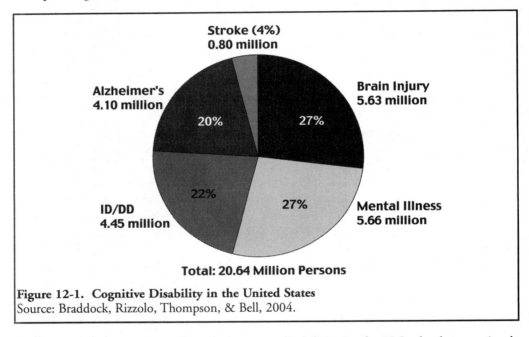

Figure 12-1. Cognitive Disability in the United States
Source: Braddock, Rizzolo, Thompson, & Bell, 2004.

Approximately 22% of people with cognitive disabilities in the U.S. also have an intellectual or developmental disability.

Cognitive disabilities include cerebral palsy, brain injury, Alzheimer's disease and other dementias, severe and persistent mental illness, and, in 4% of the cases, stroke (see Figure 12-1) (Braddock, Rizzolo, Thompson, & Bell, 2004). In 2001, over 20 million persons in the United States had a cognitive disability, and 4.5 million of these individuals had ID/DD. This chapter will focus on individuals with ID/DD.

GOALS AND SOURCES

Participants in The Arc's National Goals Conference held in Washington, DC, on January 6–8, 2003, agreed upon a series of goals regarding technology and persons with ID/DD. The four goals are presented in this chapter along with a discussion of the policy sources which support each goal.

1. To promote research, evaluation, and demonstration projects on technology for persons with ID/DD
2. To promote the dissemination and utilization of information on technology for persons with ID/DD
3. To promote training on technology for persons with ID/DD
4. To promote public policy which supports the use of technology by persons with ID/DD

During the past two decades, several public policy sources have addressed the issue of technology and persons with disabilities. These include the establishment in 1982 of the Bioengineering Program in the Department of Research and Program Services of The Arc of the United States; The Arc's 1997 Position Statement on Assistive Technology; the Technology-Related Assistance for Individuals with Disabilities Act of 1988 and its subsequent amendments and iterations; the Americans with Disabilities Act (ADA) of 1990; the Individuals with Disabilities Education Act (IDEA) of 1990; § 508 of the Rehabilitation Act; § 255 of the Telecommunications Act of 1996; President Bush's New Freedom Initiative (2001, January 20); and most recently, President Bush's Interagency Working Group on Assistive Technology Mobility Devices. A brief overview follows for these initiatives, including discussion of how they addressed the role of technology for persons with disabilities.

The Arc's Leadership

The Arc is a national organization of and for people with developmental disabilities and their families. There are currently chapters in 49 of the 50 states and the District of Columbia and over 140,000 members. The Arc is "devoted to promoting and improving supports and services for people with mental retardation and their families" and has been doing so since the 1950s (The Arc of the United States, 2001).

In 1982, under the leadership of Executive Director Phillip Roos, The Arc established its Bioengineering Program. The mission of this program was to explore the potential of technology to provide solutions for challenges faced by people with intellectual disabilities. This resulted in the development of innovative experimental AT prototype devices, such as adapted dining devices, adapted software, and technologies to improve communication and activities of daily living (ADL) functioning.

The Arc Bioengineering Program emphasized research for people with significant needs (Cavalier, Mineo, & Brown, 1986; Cavalier, 1987; Brown, Mineo, & Cavalier, 1987). The program also developed training strategies to help teachers and caregivers to use and teach others to use technology.

The Arc Bioengineering Program provided important policy leadership at the national level. For example, in testimony before the Subcommittee on the Handicapped of the Committee on Labor and Human Resources of the U.S. Senate in 1988, the Director of the program stated:

> The applications of technology, however, have thus far discriminated against a large number of American citizens. Our technological advances have not been designed with sufficient creativity and flexibility to incorporate the needs of

many people who are mentally retarded....It is the belief of the Association for Retarded Citizens of the United States that these advances will not occur without strong leadership from our federal government (Cavalier, 1988, p. 1)....There is a prevailing belief among many of the leaders in the field of assistive technology that people with mental retardation are not appropriate consumers of assistive technology....People with mental retardation should be named as a "traditionally underrepresented group" with regard to assistive technology and related services; otherwise it will become a further means of discrimination against this group. (Cavalier, 1988, p. 9)

A critical issue that confronted the Bioengineering Program was the widely held notion at the time that technology applications were not "cost-effective" for people with intellectual disabilities due to their relatively small numbers, poverty status, and the high expense of research and development. Unfortunately, The Arc Bioengineering Program was discontinued in 1992.

More than a decade later, The Arc continues to advocate for access to technology by persons with ID/DD. On November 9, 2002, The Arc's Congress of Delegates adopted a position statement on personal supports for persons with mental retardation and closely related developmental disabilities.

Our constituents must receive the supports necessary to lead a meaningful life in the community. These supports should be available based upon functional needs, not eligibility criteria such as diagnosis or income. Common areas of individual support include:

Assistive technology. People must have access to devices, services, and training that improve independence, mobility, communication, environmental control, and self-determination. Designers, manufacturers, service providers, educators, and our constituents with their families should be educated about the benefits of technology...

Supports must be individually planned and applied according to the principles of person-centered planning, self-determination and individual outcomes, and team collaboration. The individual supports must be independently and regularly monitored for quality, safety, and effectiveness. (The Arc of the United States, 2002)

Technology-Related Assistance for Individuals With Disabilities Act of 1988 and Its Subsequent Amendments

The Technology-Related Assistance for Individuals with Disabilities Act of 1988, or "Tech Act," provided funding to AT projects in Arkansas, Colorado, Illinois, Kentucky, Maine, Maryland, Minnesota, Nebraska, and Utah in 1989; to 14 additional states in 1990; to 19 states in 1991; to 7 states and the District of Columbia in 1993; and to Arizona in 1994. (Tech Act funding was provided to the U.S. territories in 1993 and 1994.) The Tech Act called for the development of consumer-responsive comprehensive programs of technology-related assistance for individuals with disabilities. The Tech Act also asked the federal government to identify policies and barriers that impeded the provision of, and payment for, AT.

Reauthorization language in 1993 (the Tech Act Amendments of 1994) stressed major systemic change in the states, focusing on five priority areas, including coordination of activities among state agencies; development and implementation of strategies to address barriers in access and funding; development and implementation of strategies to empower individuals with disabilities; increased outreach to underrepresented populations; and strategies to ensure timely acquisition of AT (Wallace, Flippo, Barcus, & Behrmann, 1995). In 1998 Congress repealed the original Tech Act, replacing it with the Assistive Technology Act of 1998, or "AT Act." The AT Act focused on four priority activities: public awareness, interagency coordination, technical assistance, and training and outreach. It also created discretionary activities with AT Act funds, such as alternative financing systems to increase AT access.

There are currently 56 State Technology Projects in each of the American states and territories (RESNA Technical Assistance Project, 2002). Each of these projects has a common goal: to increase the use of, and benefit derived from, assistive technologies. Major accomplishments of the state projects over the past decade include the establishment of new or improved AT programs (e.g., lending and equipment recycling), AT dissemination and training activities (preservice and in-service, as well as training for consumers, their families, and the general public), and improved AT policy (RESNA Technical Assistance Project, 2002). The state tech projects resulted in hundreds of thousands of persons with disabilities receiving services and supports. Year by year, funding has continued for all states, although the amounts awarded have decreased substantially. On October 25, 2004, President Bush signed the Assistive Technology Reauthorization Act of 2004 (P. L. 108-364), which extends appropriations through 2010. Since the first act was signed in 1988, states have established the necessary infrastructure to administer AT services to individuals with disabilities. The new legislation mandates that states spend at least 60% of the allocated funds on direct services, including demonstration, funding, and device loan programs.

Other Policies and Initiatives Regarding Technology and Persons with Disabilities
The 1990 passage of the ADA was a watershed event for persons with disabilities. The ADA requires that reasonable accommodations and effective communications, including assistive technologies, be provided by employers and by state and local governments (Wallace, 2002). The ADA prohibits discrimination against people with disabilities in employment, public services, public accommodations, and telecommunications (Parry, 1995).

Also in 1990, the Individuals with Disabilities Education Act was reauthorized as the Individuals with Disabilities Act (IDEA) Amendments of 1997 (Pub. L. 105-17). In 1997, AT received special attention as one of five "special considerations" referenced in the law. The revised legislation contained provisions that schools assess each student's need for AT devices and services for the individualized education program (IEP). The need for AT devices and services must be re-evaluated at each annual IEP (Chambers, 1997). Additionally, "if the IEP team determines that AT is required for home use in order for a student to receive FAPE (free and appropriate education), the technology must be provided to implement the IEP" (Office of Special Education Program's Policy Letters, 1990). Safeguards, including mediation and due process protections, are in place to ensure that children with disabilities receive the services they need, including AT devices and services, to benefit from their educational programs (Wallace, 2002).

The Telecommunications Act of 1996 also recognized the importance of technology to persons with disabilities. Section 255 of the act requires that all telecommunications products and services designed after February 8, 1996, be accessible to persons with disabilities if readily achievable "without much difficulty or expense" (Architectural and Transportation Barriers Compliance Board, 1998). The products covered included telephones, pagers, fax machines, and computers with modems (47 U.S.C. §§ 153, 255).

Another policy which addresses technology and persons with disabilities is the Federal Government Procurement of Accessible Information Technology Act of 1998. This act requires that all electronic and information technology purchased for the federal government's own use be accessible to individuals with disabilities. Similar requirements were passed that same year when Congress amended the Rehabilitation Act, mandating federal agencies to make their electronic and information technology accessible to persons with disabilities. Under § 508 (29 U.S.C. 794d), agencies are required to provide employees with disabilities and members of the general public with access to and use of information that is comparable to that provided to federal employees without disabilities. (For a comprehensive discussion of § 508, please see http://www.section508.gov.) Additionally, in 2001 the federal government made funding available to the Disability and Business Technical Assistance Centers (DBTACs) to promote awareness of the need for accessible electronic and information technology in education settings (inclusive of K–12, vocational, and higher education).

More recently, federal initiatives have addressed the role of technology for persons with disabilities. On February 1, 2001, President Bush issued the New Freedom Initiative (NFI) as part of a national effort to reduce barriers to community access for persons with disabilities. One of the goals of the NFI is to increase access to assistive technologies and promote the development of universal designs (U.S. Department of Health and Human Services, 2002). In his announcement of the NFI, President Bush declared:

> The Administration will provide a major increase in the Rehabilitation Engineering Research Centers' budget for assistive technologies, create a new fund to help bring assistive technologies to market, and better coordinate the Federal effort in prioritizing immediate assistive and universally designed technology needs in the disability community. (Bush, 2001, p. 3)

In February 2003, President Bush authorized the establishment of an interagency working group on AT mobility devices. The purpose was to more effectively coordinate the role of the federal government in providing devices to persons with disabilities, a goal cited in his New Freedom Initiative. This working group is charged with identifying all federal programs which provide assistive technologies for the mobility of persons with disabilities. It also works with states and localities to identify state and local programs and resources that provide access to these devices (Office of the Press Secretary, 2003).

Each of the preceding legislative and policy initiatives addresses the increased importance of providing access to technology for individuals with disabilities. It is clear that promoting access to technology and information is a necessary national policy goal.

However, as Enders (2003) states:

> Technological supports, for the population as a whole, and specifically for people with significant disabilities, add a level of issues that have not yet been effectively dealt with in policy. Disability related policy and implementation is in a transitional period today. Technological supports do not fit within the old paradigm of disability, and new policy has not emerged that incorporates rational mechanisms for ensuring adequate technological supports. (p. 4)

REVIEW OF KNOWLEDGE AND RECOMMENDATIONS

This section will focus on the four priority areas identified by the technology working group during The Arc National Research Goals Conference. As noted, these include (a) research, evaluation, and demonstration; (b) dissemination and utilization; (c) training; and (d) public policy. A brief review of the literature and recommendations for future research are presented for each of the four goals.

Goal A: To promote research, evaluation, and demonstration projects on technology for persons with ID/DD

Illustrative Review of Research

One of the main priorities of a national agenda on technology for persons with ID/DD must be research and evaluation. National research priorities illustrate the lack of national goals relating to technology and persons with ID/DD. Of the 22 Rehabilitation Engineering Research Centers (RERCs) funded by the National Institute on Disability and Rehabilitation Research (NIDRR), only one specializes in technology for persons with intellectual disabilities or closely related developmental disabilities (as contrasted with those that specialize in technology for persons with physical or sensory disabilities). Of the 34 NIDRR-funded Rehabilitation Research and Training Centers (RRTCs), none dedicates a significant portion of its research efforts toward technology and persons with intellectual or developmental disabilities. Of the 62 funded Disability and Rehabilitation Research Projects (DRRPs), 12 address technology for persons with disabilities, although only one specifically addresses technology for persons with ID/DD. A review of the 15 Developmental Disabilities Research Centers Web sites indicates equally modest attention to technology.

Much of the research on assistive technologies for persons with cognitive disabilities has focused on the benefits of augmentative and alternative communication (AAC) aids. "In the broadest sense, the goal of AAC interventions is to assist individuals with severe communication disorders to become communicatively competent today in order to meet their current communication needs and to prepare them to be communicatively competent tomorrow in order to meet their future communication needs" (Mirenda, 2001, p. 142). AAC research has helped disprove the widely held belief that persons with significant levels of cognitive disabilities could not benefit enough from communication devices to justify the cost (Light, Roberts, Dimarco, & Greiner, 1998; McNaughton, Light, & Arnold, 2002; Romski & Sevcik, 1997; Turner, 1986, cited in Romski & Sevcik, 2000). Speech recognition and output technology, in particular, has been shown to greatly enhance the participation of individuals with disabilities in educational and other daily activities (Cavalier & Brown, 1998; Lancioni, O'Reilly, & Basili, 2001; Mechling, Gast, & Langone, 2002; Romski, Sevcik, & Adamson, 1999).

Confluence of Advances in Technology

Although the benefits of assistive technologies have been noted in the literature (Davies, Stock, & Wehmeyer, 2003, 2004; O'Hara, Seagriff-Curtin, Davies, & Stock, 2002), the impact of emerging technologies on the lives of people with ID/DD has largely been overlooked. State-of-the-art technological advances in computer science, engineering, communications, rehabilitative science, and microelectronics have rarely been adapted for people with cognitive disabilities. However, the number of people with cognitive disabilities, including individuals with ID/DD, is expected to increase rapidly in the future. As a result, there is increased interest in developing and marketing new technologies for people with cognitive disabilities. Cognitive technologies have the potential to help persons with cognitive disabilities and those with age-related cognitive decline to achieve greater independence, productivity, and quality of life (Bowles, 2003; Eisenberg, 2002; Hammel, 2000; Hammel, Lai, & Heller, 2002; Merritt 2003).

Product engineering is evolving from stand-alone devices and applications to distributed, connected, integrated, and multi-technology systems (Kurzweil, 1990, 1999, 2002). Electronic products are becoming "smart," and software systems more adaptive and personalized. The movement toward smaller, easier-to-use micro-technologies, with larger-scale integration, increased performance, and reduced price, not only benefits the general population, but also those with intellectual and developmental disabilities. Two arenas of technological advancement have the potential to benefit individuals with intellectual and developmental disabilities: personal support technologies and assisted-care systems technologies.

Personal Support Technologies

Personal support technologies (PST) such as personal digital assistants (PDAs) have the ability to greatly enhance the independence, productivity, and quality of life of persons with ID/DD (Bergman, 2002; Grealy, Johnson, & Rushton, 1999; Hart, Hawkey, & Whyte, 2002). For example, parents or caregivers can preprogram a PDA or desktop software with educational, vocational, or daily living tasks to prompt individuals to perform a wide variety of well-defined vocational and independent living tasks (Davies, Stock, & Wehmeyer, 2002a). Specialized PDA software is currently available to enable individuals with developmental and other cognitive disabilities to manage personal schedules with much greater independence (Davies, Stock, & Wehmeyer, 2002b), to help direct individuals during their work tasks (Davies, Stock, & Wehmeyer, 2002a; Furniss, Lancioni, Rocha, Cunha, Seedhouse, Morato, et al., 2001; Furniss & Ward, 1999), and to assist with activities of daily living (Lancioni, O'Reilly, Seedhouse, Furniss, & Cunha, 2000). PDAs can also interface with wireless communication protocols to track and monitor an individual's daily activities and provide prompts to the individual as needed to complete educational or work tasks (Furniss, et al., 2001; Kautz, Etzioni, Borriello, Fox, Arnstein, Ostendorf, & Logsdon, 2001; O'Hara, et al., 2002). PDA technology has also benefited individuals with traumatic brain injury (Cole, 1999) and communication disorders (McDonough, 2002).

Computer-Assisted Learning and Communication

Other personal support technologies include specialized computer training programs (Davies, Stock, & Wehmeyer, 2003, 2004), voice interfaces (Barker, 2002), picture-based e-mail programs, and adapted Web browsers such as WebTrek (Davies, Stock, & Wehmeyer, 2001). Access to personal support technologies can help individuals to remain on task, remind them of upcoming tasks, and provide access to information on the computer or the Internet. The effectiveness of computer-based learning techniques for students with cognitive disabilities has been well documented (Alcalde, Navarro, Marchena, & Ruiz, 1998; Bernard-Opitz, Sriram, & Nakhoda-Sapuan, 2001; Blischak & Schlosser, 2003; Scruggs & Mastropieri, 1997).

Assisted-Care Systems Technology

Another area of emerging technology for persons with ID/DD is assisted-care systems technology. These technologies are designed to assist caregivers and can range from simple monitoring devices to complex assisted-care systems (ACS) integrated into the infrastructure of a building. These emerging technologies can assist in promoting the independence and health of persons with disabilities, including persons with ID/DD, while maintaining safety.

One example of an assisted-care system is the "smart" home. Smart homes and rooms (Pentland, 1996) combine tracking technology and environmental control to provide prompting, including environmental cues such as adjusted lights (Lancioni & Oliva, 1999) and simplified operation of household systems. Many companies, such as Microsoft, Honeywell, and Intel, and universities such as MIT and Georgia Tech, are researching smart home technology as beneficial examples of ubiquitous computing. One company is already developing and using smart home technology to help care for residents with early-stage Alzheimer's disease in assisted living facilities (Elite Care, 2002). Research at the University of Colorado at Boulder is also underway to apply similar smart-supports technology to community- and family-based settings for persons with ID/DD (J. Taylor, personal communication, January 2003).

Residential assisted-care systems integrate indoor/outdoor tracking systems, biosensors, building automation, databases, computer networks, and eventually learning algorithms. Assisted-care systems could provide numerous benefits for persons with intellectual and developmental disabilities, their families, and caregivers. For example, tracking systems can provide feedback to direct support professionals and relatives on daily living activities (Elite Care, 2002). Pattern-recognition and learning software can be used to alert direct support professionals of impending risks or adverse events, including social isolation and abnormal behavior (Elite Care, 2002). Building automation can simplify or control operation of household systems, including disabling an appliance or unlocking a door when an individual reaches a specific room. Although research has focused on how these systems can promote independence in residential settings, much of the technology has potential applications to other environments, including the workplace and classroom.

Smart Transportation/Tracking Technology

Another example of smart technology is the smart transportation system. This system can assist persons with ID/DD with mass transportation by utilizing wireless technologies and PDAs (Fischer & Sullivan, 2002). Travelers can be alerted when their GPS-equipped bus is arriving, and caregivers can be notified if the traveler has boarded the wrong bus. Problems with transportation have been cited as one of the most pressing barriers to the full integration of persons with disabilities into community life (U.S. Department of Health and Human Services, 2001). The availability of reliable and safe transportation options can be an essential precursor to successful transition from school to work.

Tracking technology is also a potentially useful ACS strategy to address wandering. Over 50% of respondents in a survey by the National Down Syndrome Society (2001) identified wandering as a significant problem, and many indicated that wandering behavior occurred at night. Utilizing GPS or local tracking data, monitoring devices can also alert caregivers in the event of a fall or unusual activity, or help locate persons who wander.

Assisted-care systems can also be used to monitor the health of persons with cognitive disabilities. For example, ACS can integrate data from devices that passively monitor biomedical signs (e.g., smart bedsheets or more conventional vital signs monitors). With novel algorithms to estimate health states (Pavel, 2002), ACS can provide an unobtrusive, continuous picture of an individual's health. Research is also underway involving more focused personal health advisory systems for the home (Fauchet, 2002).

Another priority when establishing a national agenda on technology and persons with ID/DD is evaluation. According to DeRuyter (1997), "although assistive technology is often heralded as the means to improved quality of life for people with disabilities, there is little data to support or refute this claim" (p. 89). DeRuyter stresses the need for the AT community to develop measurement tools to assess the usefulness and efficiency of various technological solutions. Great variability exists in the quality of AT devices and services, and a process for evaluating outcomes must be established (DeRuyter, 1995, 1997, 2002).

Recommendations for Research

1. What are the levels of access to, and utilization of, information technology (including the Internet) across the states? What technologies do people with ID/DD and their families say they need?

2. What are the outcomes and impact of technology use by people with ID/DD and their families (e.g., early intervention, special education, transition from school to work, employment participation, health promotion, wellness and mental health, community living, family involvement, self-determination, biomedical research, specialized support for the aging)?

3. What are the outcomes and impact of technology used by provider agencies, direct support employees, and other key stakeholders in the provision of services to people with ID/DD?

4. What design principles in computer-human interface technology increase usability and enhance functionality of technology for individuals with ID/DD?

5. What emerging technologies for persons with ID/DD (e.g., ubiquitous and pervasive computing, intelligent and evolutionary software, Web technologies) have the potential to increase their independence and quality of life?

Goal B: To promote the dissemination and utilization of information on technology for persons with ID/DD

Illustrative Review of Research

The use of AT by persons with disabilities has increased over the past two decades. Reasons include changes in demographic patterns, such as an increased and an aging population, higher rates of technology use, advances in medicine and technology, and the impact of various public policy initiatives. Data from the 1994 National Health Interview Survey on Disability (NHIS-D) indicate that an estimated 7.4 million Americans use AT devices for mobility impairments, 4.6 million persons for orthopedic impairments, approximately 4.5 million for hearing impairments, and about 500,000 for vision impairments (Russell, Hendershot, LeClere, Howie, & Adler, 1997). It is revealing that data were not provided in this study for persons with intellectual or developmental disabilities.

Utilization of Technology by Persons With Developmental Disabilities

Despite the significant benefits, persons with intellectual and developmental disabilities underutilize assistive technologies (The Arc of the United States, 1997; Kemp & Parette, 2000; Mann, Hurren, Tomita, & Charvat, 1997; Wehmeyer, 1995, 1998). One national survey of adults with mental retardation (Wehmeyer, 1998) revealed that the most frequently used device was the wheelchair (12.7%), followed in frequency by home adaptations, including hand rails and ramps (9.7%); hearing aids (8.9%); environmental devices, including adapted eating utensils (5.5%); and communication devices, including touch or point systems and synthesized speech devices (4.9%).

A study by Wehmeyer (1998) assessed the use of personal computers by adults with mental retardation. Thirty-three percent of families reported a computer in their home. In over 70% of these households (n=284), the individual with mental retardation used the computer for communication, education, budgeting, leisure, and work-related purposes. The majority of families, however (n=872), did not own a personal computer, although many believed their family member could benefit from computer access. Reasons given for not having a computer were cost, lack of training, complexity of the computer, "lack of assessment of technology need," and lack of information on the benefits of a computer (p. 48).

In 2001, the National Down Syndrome Society conducted a survey of all attendees at its annual conference to determine utilization rates of computers and other electronic devices. Over 200 family members and professionals responded. Sixty-six percent indicated that a family member with Down syndrome used a computer. Of those identified as using a computer, only 30 individuals used a Web browser, and only two an adapted browser. Twenty-eight individuals reported using an e-mail program, although none of these programs were specifically adapted for persons with cognitive disabilities. Only five individuals used technology-based prompting systems, such as a PDA, to provide cues at home, school, or work (National Down Syndrome Society, 2001).

Universal design ensures that persons with intellectual and developmental disabilities are able to utilize common technologies available to the general public. With universal design, products such as software and computers provide an interface that is suitable for *all* potential users, including those with disabilities. More intuitive, user-centered computing interfaces can empower persons with intellectual and developmental disabilities to use the Internet and personal computers. Web standards such as User Agent Accessibility Guidelines (Festa, 2002), federal regulations such as § 508, and public/private organization initiatives such as the World Wide Web Accessibility Initiative (WAI) of the W3C promote access to software and the Internet for people with disabilities.

But how does one define accessibility? Elbert Johns, Director of TheArcLink, has recommended that the principal components of accessibility be clearly defined for people with intellectual and developmental disabilities and their use of information technology (personal communication, December 30, 2002). Specifically, he noted that for information to be accessible to a person with an intellectual disability, it must (a) decrease the dependence on rote memory as a tool for recalling information, (b) use as many complementary formats as possible (visual, audio, multigraphic), (c) reduce the need for the recipient to use complex organizational skills for comprehension, and (d) be presented in a vocabulary or reading level that approximates the level of the recipient.

Johns (E. Johns, personal communication, December 30, 2002) also noted the need to develop inclusive strategies to enable people with intellectual and developmental disabilities to use mainstream technologies.

> Technology already exists in the form of xml markup language to customize information that is transmitted over the Internet to the needs of the individual recipient. What is missing is a universal, standardized set of definitions, graphics and supplemental information organized by reading or comprehension level that any Web site sponsor could incorporate in its database. Add the development of accessibility settings for Internet browsers that would allow a person with an intellectual disability to set their reading level, along with other preferences. Then imagine a person with an intellectual disability using a computer and the Internet as real tools to shop online for groceries and other essentials, downloading recipes that s/he can actually use, using the Internet in other ways to negotiate day-to-day living, or even an Internet version of Hemingway's The Old Man and the Sea with as many variant forms as the number of people receiving it.

Barriers to Access and Use of Technology by People With ID/DD
Multiple reasons have been cited for not using AT. Wehmeyer (1998) found that (a) few devices were designed specifically for individuals with developmental disabilities, (b) the procedures involved in using these assistive technologies were too complex for many people with developmental disabilities, and (c) individuals with developmental disabilities and their caretakers were largely unaware of the available technologies. Not surprisingly, many individuals with developmental disabilities abandoned the technology they obtained because of its lack of personalization.

Technology abandonment rates of up to 75% have been reported among persons with disabilities generally (Tewey, Barnicle, & Perr, 1994), and they may be even higher for persons with ID/DD. Some of the major reasons technology is abandoned include a disparity between the technology and the needs of the person with a disability (Batavia & Hammer, 1989; Phillips & Zhao, 1993), lack of consumer involvement in selections (e.g., trial use of identified device and/or alternatives), and lack of training on using the device. One study of individuals with mental retardation in Arkansas found that nearly 45% of consumers were unable to test their technology before purchasing it (Parette & VanBiervliet, 1990). Parette and VanBiervliet note, "While the average citizen in our country typically enjoys the privilege of examining a good prior to purchasing it, persons with mental retardation are more often than not denied such access to their technologies and must rely on the judgments of the professionals involved in selecting the technologies for them" (p. 18).

Additional barriers to using AT cited in the Assistive Technology Act of 1998 include a lack of the following:

1. Resources to pay for AT devices and services
2. Trained personnel to assist individuals with disabilities to use such devices and services
3. Information among targeted individuals about the availability and potential benefit of technology for individuals with disabilities
4 Outreach to underrepresented populations and rural populations
5. Systems that ensure timely acquisition and delivery of AT devices and services
6. Coordination among state human services programs and between such programs and private entities (particularly with respect to transitions between such programs and entities), and capacity in such programs to provide the necessary technology-related assistance (Title 29, Chapter 31, § 3001(a)(6))

Another barrier is the lack of effective dissemination strategies in the AT community. Research on technology and persons with disabilities is often disseminated through conference presentations, white papers, and monographs. Since some of these formats are not included in the main searchable databases and indexes, they cannot be accessed easily through typical library search methods. As a result, much of the research on technology and persons with ID/DD does not reach the very researchers, policymakers, advocates, and key stakeholders who could benefit most from it.

Problems also exist in disseminating information about emerging assistive technologies. As noted, service providers, policymakers, and consumers are generally unable to keep up with advances in the technology field. DeRuyter (1997) notes that "this has often contributed to communication problems between manufacturers, vendors, service providers, payers and state/federal agencies" (p. 95). This can result in such problems as:

(1) turf battles amongst manufacturers, vendors, service providers, and payers; (2) the lack of interagency agreements amongst state and federal agencies; (3) inadequate preparatory training resulting in poor qualifications of the professionals providing services; and (4) consumer shopping when recommendations fall short of expectations. (DeRuyter, 1997, p. 95)

Recommendations for Research

Much research is needed to promote the dissemination and utilization of information on technology for persons with ID/DD. Studies are needed to address the following research questions:

1. What methodologies are most effective for increasing consideration, introduction, and adoption/utilization of technology for persons with ID/DD?
2. What are the most effective means of making information available on potential prototypes that might not make it to the market due to low demand? These prototypes (i.e., "orphan technologies"), may result in positive benefits for persons with ID/DD but may not be produced due to low demand.
3. What are the most effective ways to bring this information to market?

Goal C: To promote training on technology for persons with ID/DD

Illustrative Review of Research

Another priority that a national agenda on technology for persons with ID/DD must include is training. One of the purposes of the Assistive Technology Act of 1998 was to provide funding to states to support "technical assistance and training in the provision or use of assistive technology devices and assistive technology services" (Title 20, Chapter 31, § 3001(b)(3)(A)(iii)). AT services include the "training or technical assistance for an individual with disabilities, or, where appropriate, the family members, guardians, advocates, or authorized representatives of such an individual" (Title 20, Chapter 31, § 3002(a)(4)(E)) and "training or technical assistance for professionals (including individuals providing education and rehabilitation services), employers, or other individuals who provide services to, employ, or are otherwise substantially involved in the major life functions of individuals with disabilities" (Title 20, Chapter 31, § 3002(a)(4)(F)).

One group that is often omitted from AT training is direct support professionals working in community human service settings. In addition to parents and family workers, these individuals provide the greatest amount of hands-on, day-to-day interaction and training with individuals with ID/DD. However, these employees are vastly underpaid (Effective Compensation, Inc, 2001; Hewitt & Lakin, 2001; Lakin, Polister, & Prouty, 2003) and often poorly trained to do their job duties, which include assisting people with ID/DD in obtaining, maintaining, and effectively using AT (Taylor, 2001; Taylor, Bradley, & Warren, 1996). Because of the significant role they play in the lives of persons with ID/DD, direct support professionals are essential to the effective use of AT; yet, providing training to this group remains an unmet need.

Direct support professionals (DSPs) work in geographically dispersed areas and are responsible for providing support 24 hours a day, 7 days a week, 365 days a year. Most direct support professionals have more than one job, and an increasingly large percentage do not speak English as their first language. All of these factors, coupled with difficulties accessing training, make it a significant challenge to provide competency-based AT training to these staff.

One significant barrier is that the organizations that employ direct support professionals rely heavily on classroom-based training as the primary mode of delivery. Sessions are not offered regularly, further limiting access by employees, and much of the training is presented in a didactic format, offering limited opportunities for direct support employees to interact.

An alternative to classroom training is Web-based multimedia interactive instruction. This mode of delivery addresses many of the access barriers mentioned. Employees do not have to adjust their schedules to attend sporadic training sessions. Rather, they can receive training anytime and anywhere, provided they have access to a computer and the Internet. Although Web-based and interactive computer-based training has been used in corporate America for many years, the community human service industry lags far behind in the acquisition and use of computer networks, intranets, and the Internet. This limits opportunities for DSPs to gain access to new and evolving information on AT and other important topics. Organizations also lag behind in their use of information technology. Many providers are unable to adequately describe basic and critical information about their workforce (e.g., vacancy rates, turnover rates, demographics of personnel) because they do not utilize technology. Existing software packages, easy access to hardware and software, and sufficient training to master software could dramatically increase organizational effectiveness (Hewitt, Larson, Sauer, Anderson, & O'Nell, 2001).

Recommendations for Research

Participants in The Arc's National Goals Conference felt the following questions should be addressed in future research on training on technology for persons with ID/DD:

1. What are the necessary core competencies regarding technology and ID/DD for stakeholders involved in the design and use of technologies for persons with ID/DD?
2. How can the core competencies identified be infused into university curriculum and staff training programs?
3. What are the most effective ways to train persons with ID/DD to access and utilize assistive and emerging technologies?
4. What are the most effective ways of training direct support professionals to use technology and facilitate the use of technology for persons with ID/DD?

Goal D: To promote public policy which supports the use of technology by persons with ID/DD

As noted earlier, policies addressing technology use by persons with ID/DD include the Technology-Related Assistance for Individuals with Disabilities Act of 1988 and its subsequent amendments and iterations, the ADA of 1990, the IDEA of 1997, the Federal Government Procurement of Accessible Information Technology, § 508 of the Rehabilitation Act, § 255 of the Telecommunications Act of 1996, and President Bush's New Freedom Initiative (2001).

Recommendations for Research

The following list of questions may guide future research on public policies supporting the use of technology by persons with ID/DD:

1. To what extent are the special needs of individuals with ID/DD being considered in federally funded disability programs addressing technology transfer, research, and service delivery?

2. What are the best practices in coordinating funding for technology for persons with ID/DD?

These findings should be included in a special report to Congress on the status of technology knowledge, access, and use by persons with ID/DD and should be jointly sponsored by NIDRR Tech Act Projects and State Developmental Disabilities Planning Councils.

USING KNOWLEDGE TO SHAPE OUR NATIONAL AGENDA

A national agenda is needed to address technology research, evaluation and demonstration, utilization and dissemination, training, and policy as they pertain to persons with intellectual and developmental disabilities. The following policy and research initiatives should guide future efforts to promote access to, and utilization of, technology by persons with ID/DD.

Research, Evaluation, and Demonstration

1. Identify a national ID/DD research agenda driven by state-by-state studies across the life-span specifically addressing (a) access to information technology (including the Internet), needs, and utilization by individuals with ID/DD, as well as by the service systems with which they interact; and (b) attitudinal and policy barriers to accessing information technology and AT for persons with ID/DD.

2. Conduct technology outcome, impact, and benefit/cost studies (a) to identify outcomes and impact of technology use by people with ID/DD and their families (e.g., early intervention, special education, transition from school to work, employment participation, health promotion and wellness [including mental health], community living, family involvement, self-determination, biomedical research, and specialized support for the aging) and (b) to identify outcomes and impact of technology use by provider agencies, direct support employees, and other key stakeholders in the provision of services to people with ID/DD.

3. Launch research initiatives on design principles in computer-human interface technology relevant to individuals with ID/DD (e.g., access to technology, including universal design) in order to identify those factors that increase usability and enhance functionality of technology for individuals with ID/DD.

4. Conduct robust ongoing research and demonstration projects on emerging technologies (e.g., ubiquitous and pervasive computing, intelligent and evolutionary software, Web technologies) as they are developed for people with and without ID/DD.

5. Through research, identify effective training practices regarding technology access, use, and outcomes.

Utilization and Dissemination

1. Encourage the development of books, publications, training manuals, and other information on technology and ID/DD.

2. Promote the dissemination of information regarding technology and ID/DD to multiple, generic audiences in user-friendly formats utilizing clearinghouse methods.

3. Ensure dissemination of information and materials regarding the potential of AT and accessible information technology for people with ID/DD that are specifically targeted to, and accessible by, people with ID/DD, their families, and support networks. Promote dissemination through new and existing efforts such as TheArcLink, Family Village, the Medicaid Reference Desk, Quality Mall, and the Coleman Institute for Cognitive Disabilities.

4. Evaluate the impact of various dissemination methodologies in practice (e.g., increasing consideration, introduction, adoption/utilization of technology).

5. Collaborate to make information available and to bring to market potential prototypes or "orphan technologies"—emerging and promising products that have low demand but high potential to benefit individuals with intellectual and developmental disabilities).

Training

1. Identify and infuse core competencies regarding technology and ID/DD into university curriculum and staff training programs and provide training based on those competencies for all stakeholders involved in the design and utilization of technology and ID/DD. Training should be transdiciplinary and include technology-related disciplines.

2. Promote the initiation of undergraduate and graduate training programs in technology for persons with ID/DD.

3. Provide training to people with ID/DD on technology access and utilization.

4. Ensure the continuation of a federal role in supporting the national infrastructure for providing training and technical assistance (e.g., such as that provided through state programs under the Assistive Technology Act).

5. Provide mandatory training to direct support professionals and paraprofessionals on technology access, use, and outcomes for people with ID/DD.

Public Policy

1. Propose the creation of a national network of Research Centers on Cognitive Disability, including intellectual and developmental disabilities, and Technology.

2. Establish an interagency task force at the federal level on technology and ID/DD to (a) ensure that the special needs of individuals with ID/DD are considered in all federally funded disability programs addressing technology transfer, research, and service delivery, (b) ensure the coordination of federal sources that may be payment sources for technology for persons with ID/DD; (c) identify federal laws, regulations, and policies that present potential barriers to technology for persons with ID/DD (and conversely, those that facilitate access to technology);

and (d) develop coordinated efforts to improve availability of, and access to, technology for persons with ID/DD.

3. Encourage partnerships between public and private entities regarding initiatives in technology and ID/DD.

4. Produce a 2005 report to Congress on the status of technology knowledge, access, and use by persons with ID/DD, jointly sponsored by NIDRR Tech Act Projects and State Developmental Disabilities Planning Councils.

5. Develop policy that incorporates design standards that make generic technology accessible for people with ID/DD (e.g., incorporate access considerations and standards for persons with intellectual and developmental disabilities into § 508 and the World Wide Web Accessibility Initiative).

By a unanimous vote, the participants in the 2003 Arc Research Conference adopted a resolution to be submitted to the Secretary of the Department of Education and the President. This resolution called upon Congress to support legislation continuing federal funding for state Assistive Technology Projects throughout the United States and territories. The resolution is presented in Figure 12-2.

Whereas, hundreds of thousands of citizens with intellectual and developmental disabilities in each of the states and territories have benefited from services, devices, financial resources, and training made possible by the Technology-Related Assistance for Individuals with Disabilities Act, its amendments, and the Assistive Technology Act, and,

Whereas, State Assistive Technology Projects are vital to achieve the goals of President Bush's New Freedom Initiative; and,

Whereas, termination of the State Assistive Technology Projects according to the sunset provisions of the legislation will deny hundreds of thousands of individuals with intellectual and developmental disabilities access to AT services and devices.

Therefore, be it resolved that The 2003 Arc-U.S. National Research Conference herewith recommends that the Secretary of the Department of Education and the President support legislation to permanently continue authorizing and funding State Assistive Technology Projects throughout the United States and its territories.

The Tech Act was reauthorized on October 25, 2004; appropriations were extended through 2010.

Figure 12-2. Resolution Adopted at 2003 ARC-U.S. Conference on Assistive Technology

---

ANTICIPATING THE CHANGES OF THE FUTURE

Due to continuing advances in microprocessor speed and processing capacity, computing power is progressing at an exponential rate, literally doubling every 12 to 18 months (Kurzweil, 1999). Rapid progress in computing power suggests that personal support technologies, assisted-care technologies, and virtual technologies will advance rapidly over the next decade, becoming substantially more personalized. There are also signs that the AT industry is growing. According to a U.S. Department of Commerce (2003) survey, 359 companies manufacturing assistive technologies reported sales of $2.87 billion in 1999, up 21.8% from 1997 sales. Market projections suggest that emerging neuroscience technologies, like brain-machine interfaces permitting brain control of robot arms or computers, will be a $3.6 billion industry by 2008 (Cavuoto, 2004). Many of these technologies hold exceptional promise to benefit persons with intellectual and developmental disabilities and, with time, may significantly improve function in persons with Alzheimer's, Down syndrome, and Parkinson's disease.

Despite the potential of emerging technologies to assist persons with intellectual and developmental disabilities, significant practical impediments must be overcome in commercialization, consumer abandonment, and the design and development of useful products. For example, existing barriers to widespread commercialization of emerging technologies include regulatory burdens imposed by the FDA and the economically disadvantaged status of many persons with ID/DD combined with limited private insurance and Medicaid/Medicare coverage and payment policies (U.S. Department of Commerce, 2003).

Barriers also exist in the financial and organizational feasibility of specific envisioned products and their limited potential to reach the consumer market. Innovative engineering approaches, effective needs analysis, user-centered design, and rapid evolutionary development are essential to ensure that technically feasible products meet the real needs of persons with ID/DD. The obsolescence of most technological devices after only a few years presents a significant barrier to persons with ID/DD. Efforts must be made by advocates, designers, and manufacturers to promote better integration of future software and hardware systems so that forthcoming iterations of personal support technologies (e.g., PDAs, adapted computer software and hardware) and assisted-care systems technologies (e.g., smart homes and transportation systems) do not quickly become obsolete. They need to operate seamlessly across multiple real-world environments in the home, school, community, and workplace.

A lack of infrastructure for technology and persons with ID/DD exists in the states. One method for coordinating the research, training, dissemination, and policy initiatives in technology for persons with ID/DD would be to create a national network of research centers on cognitive disability and technology.

Proposed Centers on Cognitive Disability and Technology

The proposed centers on cognitive disability and technology would advance the independence and quality of life of individuals with cognitive disabilities, including persons with ID/DD, through technology research and development. The centers also would foster public-private partnerships in the development process and promote commercialization and dissemination of new technologies pertinent to cognitive disabilities. The centers would contribute to the nation's economic productivity while reducing financial dependency and long-term costs to federal and state governments.

A network would be created consisting of approximately 10 Centers of Excellence in Technology and Cognitive Disability, located in multidisciplinary university-based settings. Centers would be linked functionally to commercial enterprises and private foundations interested in technology and cognitive disability. Centers would promote the advancement of graduate and undergraduate training programs that focus on current and emerging technologies in educational settings and would include, but not be limited to, core disciplines such as computer science, electrical and computer engineering, biomedical engineering, psychology, imaging science, rehabilitation science, and special education.

The proposed centers would involve consumers with cognitive disabilities, including ID/DD, and their families, service providers, employers, and schools. The centers' purpose would be to facilitate the development and dissemination of viable new technologies to increase the social, economic, and educational participation of persons with disabilities. Innovations in this arena have the potential to equalize the playing field for children with a range of cognitive disabilities, such as learning disabilities, autism, dyslexia, and mental retardation.

Although centers would receive core administrative and research funding from the federal government, they would also compete for and secure research and development funding and related resources from the National Institutes of Health (NIH); National Institute on Disability and Rehabilitation Research (NIDRR); the U.S. Departments of Education, Labor, and Transportation; the National Science Foundation (NSF); the Administration on Developmental Disabilities (ADD); state governments; private industry and foundations; and other sources.

The centers would coordinate their activities with entities such as existing federal technology laboratories, engineering research centers, Rehabilitation Research and Training Centers (RRTCs), Assistive Technology Act information and technical assistance grantees in the states, the nation's 10 regional Disability and Business Technical Assistance Centers (DBTACs) on the ADA, University Centers of Excellence in Developmental Disabilities (UCEDDs), independent living centers, and federally funded Developmental Disabilities Research Centers (DDRCs).

In 1988, Al Cavalier, director of The Arc Bioengineering Program, acknowledged that applications of technology discriminated against individuals with mental retardation. This assertion holds true today. Persons with ID/DD are still an underrepresented group with regard to technology, and attitudinal barriers still exist that create low expectations of the benefits of technology for them. Without strong leadership from the federal government, individuals with ID/DD will not realize the full potential of technology to promote their independence, productivity, and quality of life.

CHAPTER 13

Healthy Aging and Community Participation

TAMAR HELLER, MATTHEW JANICKI, AND BARBARA HAWKINS
with
Alan Factor, Thomas Buckley, Doreen Croser, Philip Davidson,
Rick Greene, Ray Murphy, and Clifford Poetz

REAL LIVES

Paul is a 65-year-old man with Down syndrome. He is very amicable and social and enjoys being with people, "going places," and interacting with his housemates. Paul enjoys arts and crafts, including needlepoint and ceramics. He likes to share his finished works with people he knows at home, work, and church. During the past two years, he has lived in a group home that offers a range of recreational activities, such as caring for and riding horses and gardening. He enjoys going out to lunch and dinner with his friends and staff members, whom he considers his family. Paul also likes working in a day program when he can and relaxing with his peers, who are also retirees. This is a unique social time he treasures.

Paul lived with his family until 1986 and then moved into a group home. He had always worked in sheltered employment and continued doing so after he moved into his new home. Ten years later, Paul decided he wanted to be more independent and chose to move into an apartment complex run by a local developmental disability agency. Here he had his own apartment, and he very much enjoyed his new independence. He was proud that he could ride the bus back and forth to work and earn the money he needed to be able to travel.

Paul lived in his apartment for three more years until he began to find it more difficult to move and therefore to do housework or ride back and forth to work. After thinking it over, Paul decided to move into his current group home. He liked having more people around him and having someone to assist him with the physical activities that had become more of a challenge. He also found that the environment at the new home fulfilled his social and activity needs, and he enjoyed having access to horses and being able to garden every day. Paul saw this as an opportunity "to be with people a lot."

311

Two years ago, injuries from a van accident limited Paul's mental and physical capacities. He experienced a serious neck injury that began his physical and mental decline. Paul currently has a variety of medical concerns—some age-related—including high cholesterol and triglycerides, possible Alzheimer's-disease-related dementia, hyperthyroidism managed with medication, anemia managed with supplements and followed regularly by a hematology clinic, and depression and asthma managed with medications. These conditions have limited Paul's desire to eat favorite foods and his ability to participate in community activities he had found rewarding.

Despite some diminished capacities, other medical issues, and an overall "slowing down," Paul remains positive, social, creative in his crafts, and involved in some of the home's activities. He has chosen to slow down his work activities to one or two days a week and to spend the rest of this time in "semi-retirement" with his peers in an enrichment program. Paul has chosen to remain as mentally and physically active as he can on a day-to-day basis, and he has good days and some bad days. He still enjoys his home and its activities, stating, "it keeps me young."

* * *

Lena is a 40-year-old woman living in a group home and working in a sheltered workshop. She has cerebral palsy and mild cognitive impairment and uses a wheelchair to get around. On weekends she enjoys hanging out at a local mall where she meets Joe, her friend of 15 years, with whom she has her weekly lunch outing. She has a sister who lives nearby that she talks to regularly and visits for dinner a couple times per month. Her parents live out of state, but her father comes to visit her monthly and her mother visits several times per year. In addition to her small SSI stipend and her modest paycheck, she receives money from her father (through a special needs trust fund) for her extra expenses.

Over the last 10 years, Lena has experienced a number of traumatic events and health challenges. Twice, she was hit by a car. After the first accident she needed to use a walker, and after the second accident she needed to use a wheelchair. Before her second accident, she lived independently in a HUD-funded apartment building for people with physical disabilities. After the accident she required more personal care and support because she could not transfer to the toilet or easily move around; she also became very depressed and angry. The local developmental disability services agency suggested that she move into a nursing home because it was becoming too expensive for the agency to meet her support needs. She languished in a nursing home for months until her sister was able to get her into a group home that could provide the support and personal care she needed. She also received antidepressants that improved her mood.

Further crises occurred as Lena developed diabetes, partially induced by the large amounts of soft drinks she consumed and her lack of physical exercise. Her diabetes resulted in high counts of sugar in her blood, bouts of incontrollable incontinence, bowel obstruction, and vomiting. When it became clear that she needed to self-medicate with insulin, the group home administrator sent her to a nursing home, as the staff at the home did not feel that they could be responsible for giving her insulin shots. Once again, she languished in the nursing home. However, in this case, with prodding by her sister, the nursing home trained Lena to monitor her blood sugar and to give herself insulin shots. Hence, she was now able to self-administer her medication and was allowed to return to her group home.

Though she is living in a group home and has an involved sister living nearby, Lena's parents worry a lot about her future and her father still says, "I pray that she dies a few minutes before I die."

INTRODUCTION

The "aging of America" is the most widely recognized population trend of our time. Projections from the U.S. Administration on Aging predict that the proportion of persons over age 65 will increase from 1 in 12 (35 million persons) in 2000 to 1 in 6 (53 million persons) by 2020. Advances in medicine, better health care, safer environments, and positive changes in lifestyle have all contributed to this longer average life-span. At the same time, the life expectancy for persons with intellectual and developmental disabilities (ID/DD) has increased dramatically. The mean age at death for persons with ID/DD was 66 years in 1993—up from 19 years in the 1930s and 59 years in the 1970s. The rise in life expectancy is even higher for adults with Down syndrome, with average age at death rising from 9 years in the 1920s to 56 years in 1993 (Janicki, Dalton, Henderson, & Davidson, 1999). Using a prevalence rate of 1.4%, Yamaki and Fujiura (2002) estimated that 641,161 adults with ID/DD over the age of 60 years lived in the U.S. in 2000 (U.S. Department of Commerce, Bureau of the Census, 2000). These numbers are projected to increase 90% by 2030 to 1,242,794, as the peak of the baby boom generation enters its 60s.

The aging of America has stimulated a host of research and social planning activities in anticipation of the demands this demographic shift will exert upon national resources. Nonetheless, relatively little attention has been given to the extraordinary demands it will place upon the already overburdened service system supporting persons with ID/DD. Service providers are faced with the challenges of providing supports to these individuals as they age and to their families, who are usually the primary providers of care. The increased longevity of adults with ID/DD and the aging of their caregivers have accounted for the growing demand for assistance with transition planning and for alternative residential supports. It has also increased the likelihood of older persons with ID/DD living on their own into retirement and surviving their parents. This phenomenon has stimulated a growing demand for additional individual, family, and residential supports. As more persons with ID/DD survive into older age, we will need to learn more about ways to (a) promote healthy aging, (b) empower families and persons with disabilities to obtain needed supports, and (c) promote aging- and disability-friendly environments.

Three major premises guide the goals and recommendations presented in this chapter. The first is that aging is a life-long process. A growing body of evidence shows that all forms of aging—whether pathological or normal—are affected by factors and events occurring at younger ages. Secondly, this chapter uses the concept of "aging well," an increasingly popular term in the field of gerontology. The "aging well" concept emphasizes the idea that people can adapt and maintain satisfying lives as they age even when, for some individuals, the circumstances are less than optimal (Johnson, 1995). The aim is to live long, in good health, and with an overall sense of well-being.

In general, "aging well" evolves from exercising the choices that create a successful and productive life (Krain, 1995). It is a dynamic process involving the individual in his or her environment within historical and cultural contexts. Since the individual and the environment are interactive, how well people age depends directly upon how well they adapt to and negotiate their environment (Johnson, 1995). People age differently within the context of their personal lives according to individual characteristics and histories that they bring to older adulthood (Edgerton, 1994). However, older adults with ID/DD are vulnerable to conditions that will make their old age potentially more difficult with an increased possibility for infirmity and dependence. Hence, Edgerton (1994) aptly pleaded for a national research agenda that included a focus on the health and well-being of aging persons with ID/DD.

The third premise is that the aging and developmental disabilities services networks must collaborate. As it stands now, frequent fragmentation and overlap of services in the end prove detrimental to the individuals these two networks purport to serve. This situation is unfortunate, as people with disabilities who require long-term care and their family caregivers share support needs related to their health and living circumstances.

GOALS AND SOURCES

Key federal legislation and initiatives and several major research agenda-setting conferences on aging and/or disability have guided our national goals for promoting healthy aging and community participation. Major federal sources include the President's New Freedom Initiative, the Developmental Disabilities Assistance and Bill of Rights Act of 2000 (DD Act), and the Older Americans Act of 2000 (Pub. L. 106-501). Key national expert panels include the National Institute on Disability and Rehabilitation Research Long-Range Plan, 1998–2003; the 1995 White House Conference on Aging, the Healthy People 2010 objectives, and the Surgeon General's Conference on Health Disparities and Mental Retardation (U.S. Public Health Service, 2002).

In addition to federal sources, three major international research agenda-setting conferences that addressed the needs of persons aging with an ID/DD helped guide the national goals and recommendations of the aging strand group:

- The International Association for the Scientific Study of Intellectual Disabilities and World Health Organization Conference on Healthy Aging and Intellectual Disability (World Health Organization, 2000)
- The Rehabilitation Research and Training Center on Aging with Developmental Disabilities (RRTC-ADD) Invitational Research Symposium on Aging with Developmental Disabilities: Promoting Healthy Aging, Family Support, and Age-Friendly Communities (Heller, Janicki, Hammel, & Factor, 2002), held in conjunction with the 2001 annual meeting of the Gerontological Society of America (GSA) in Chicago
- The Tampa Scientific Conference on Intellectual Disability, Aging, and Health that developed recommendations for future research and defined salient areas for medical concern and surveillance (Davidson, Heller, Janicki, & Hyer, 2003)

Our National Goals

The important legislative, policy and commission documents referred to above have established five major goals and commitments to facilitate the opportunities for individuals with ID/DD to age well. These goals include the following:

A. Communities will be "aging and disability friendly" by instituting universal design, environmental modifications, and technologies that make communities fully accessible to people with disabilities as they age. Among essential areas of full access are (a) transportation to allow moving about with freedom and safety; (b) access to goods, services, supports to accommodate impairments; (c) information access to support choice; (d) collaboration between aging and disability networks; (e) universal design, signage, and "visitability"; and (f) changes to community environments (e.g., residential, service, health care).

B. Older adults with intellectual and developmental disabilities will live in community settings of their choice that provide sufficient supports and material security to make them as independent and interdependent as possible. Thus people will age in place in their "home community" and be assured of transportation and safety, personal assistance, and economic security.

C. As adults with intellectual and developmental disabilities and their caregivers age, the caregivers, often family members, will receive sufficient economic, social, and emotional supports. These include tax credits and better training and education, with special attention to underserved communities.

D. Older adults with intellectual and developmental disabilities will have opportunities for valued social roles and full participation in community life. These include life-long learning, self-determination, self-selected activities, friendships and meaningful relationships, and strong social networks developed and maintained across the life-span.

E. Adults with intellectual and developmental disabilities will have increased longevity with improved mental and physical health. This requires reducing health disparities, advancing knowledge of age-related secondary conditions, adopting a "life-span approach," and improving access to health care.

In the pages that follow, we identify the specific sources of these national goals and commitments. We then review current knowledge about the goal areas and identify the topics of research of highest priority in filling gaps in the current knowledge about how to reach our national goals and fulfill our national commitments to persons with ID/DD as they age.

The Sources of National Goals

Goals A and B: To ensure aging- and disability-friendly environments and community settings and aging in place

The New Freedom Initiative (2001) recognized that, "although progress has been made over the years to improve access to employment, public accommodations, commercial facilities, information technology, telecommunications services, housing, schools, and polling places, significant challenges remain for Americans with disabilities in realizing the dream of equal access to full participation in American society" (p. 2).

Both the New Freedom Initiative and Healthy People 2010 emphasized the importance of increasing access to assistive and universally designed technologies through research and development. The NIDRR Long-Range Plan specifically mentions the needs of persons with cognitive limitations, noting that we need to "assure that new technologies for communication, environmental control, and health maintenance, for example, are accessible to those with cognitive limitations and do not exacerbate their exclusion from mainstream activities" (Chapter 5). Furthermore, it recommends the development of technologies that help people with cognitive limitations perform the activities of daily living. Both the Healthy People 2010 (U.S. Department of Health and Human Services, 2000, Goals 6.10–6.12) and the White House Conference on Aging (1995, resolution 22) target reducing environmental barriers to participating in home, education, work, and community activities. Doing so means providing incentives to encourage design, development, construction, and modification of housing for persons of all ages to make aging in place easier.

The New Freedom Initiative and the White House Conference on Aging both stipulate that more needs to be done to increase access to alternate means of transportation for those who cannot get to buses or other forms of public transportation. Furthermore, the NIDRR Long-Range Plan notes the need to identify and evaluate models that facilitate physical inclusion, including supported housing and transportation models that are consistent with consumer choice.

The RRTC Invitational Research Symposium on Aging and Developmental Disabilities and the Tampa Scientific Conference on Intellectual Disability, Aging, and Health particularly recommend promoting aging- and disability-friendly communities. Recommended research goals include identifying and evaluating the most needed and enabling components of "access ready" communities for adults aging with ID/DD and developing model programs in collaboration with local governments and business to create such communities. Goals also point to the imperative to address the "digital divide" that prevents people from accessing desired technology.

Goal C: To support families and other caregivers

The DD Act of 2000 recognizes that "many service delivery systems and communities are not prepared to meet the impending need of the 479,862 adults with developmental disabilities who are living at home with parents who are 60 years or older and who serve as the primary caregivers of the adults" (§ 101). Noting the importance of providing supports to families, the White House Conference on Aging resolution 28 promotes supporting family caregiving through tax credits and better training and salaries for caregivers. In its emphasis on community integration, the NIDRR Long-Range Plan emphasizes the concept of consumer control of supports families receive.

Healthy People 2010 (U.S. Department of Health and Human Services, 2000, Objective 6.13) recommends public health surveillance of not only the health of persons with disabilities, but also of their caregivers. The RRTC-ADD symposium and the Tampa conference recommended research on family caregiving that addresses the demography and well-being of families, positive as well as stressful aspects of caregiving, and the impact of various syndromes of the adults with ID/DD on the caregiving experience. Conferees also recommended further research on family long-term planning and on the involvement of siblings and grandparents in caregiving.

Goal D: To encourage community participation

The Developmental Disabilities Assistance and Bill of Rights Act of 2000 and Healthy People 2010 (U.S. Department of Health and Human Services, 2000, Objective 6.4) note the importance of increasing the opportunities for adults with disabilities to participate in community life and have social relationships. In regard to people who are aging, the 1995 White House Conference on Aging recommendations advocated supporting a social environment that offers quality, integrated, accessible services and that enhances and encourages community participation. The NIDRR Long-Range Plan also emphasizes the role of each individual's right to exercise control over his or her life, based on an ability and opportunity to make choices in everyday activities.

Goal E: To promote healthy aging

As noted in the Surgeon General's Report on Health Disparities and Mental Retardation (2002), considerable disparities among adults with ID/DD are becoming increasingly apparent, and health promotion has thus become a critical need for this population. The report defined three key goals: (a) to integrate health promotion into community environments; (b) to improve quality of health care; (c) to train health care providers; and (d) to increase sources of health care. Within these general goals, specific objectives referencing aging in this population propose to (a) include "premature aging" when developing standards of care; (b) include "age-related conditions" in curricula when training health care providers; (c) evaluate models of coordinated funding for geriatric care; and (d) expand the use of geriatric nurses, physicians, and other allied health workers in community-based care.

Healthy People 2010 (U.S. Department of Health and Human Services, 2000, Objective 6.1) emphasizes the importance of tracking consistent data regarding people with disabilities and also notes the importance of addressing mental health issues among people with disabilities. The NIDRR Long-Range Plan recommends future research targeting the prevention and treatment of secondary conditions as they interact with aging among people with disabilities. The need for a life-span approach in conducting research on health and in developing health promotion strategies has been highlighted both in the NIH consensus conference on Emotional and Behavioral Health in Persons with Mental Retardation/Developmental Disabilities and in the 1995 White House Conference on Aging. Three international consensus conferences specifically targeting health and intellectual/developmental disabilities (i.e., WHO/IASSID Conference on Promoting Healthy Aging and Intellectual Disabilities; RRTC-ADD Invitational Research Symposium on Aging and Developmental Disabilities; and the Tampa Scientific Conference on Intellectual Disability, Aging, and Health) all include recommendations designed to increase our understanding of the underlying causes of age-related declines and development of secondary conditions, increase physical and mental health surveillance, and develop and test health promotion strategies to increase physical and mental health of this population.

Aging- and Disability-Friendly Environments That Enable Aging in Place and Full Community Participation

Overview of the Knowledge Base

As adults with ID/DD experience age-related declines, assistive technology (AT), environmental interventions (EI), and aging- and disability-friendly environments can play a critical role in helping them "age in place," (continue to live in the community) maintain function, and participate in community life. Although research has shown that AT and EI result in improved adaptive functioning among people with disabilities, often these devices are not designed for people with ID/DD and caregivers. Individuals with ID/DD, moreover, often are not aware of these devices or how to use them (Wehmeyer, 1995). In addition, often funding is unavailable that could pay for such equipment, which can be costly. Neither resources nor interventions have been targeted to their needs (Hammel, Lai, & Heller, 2002).

Many new high-tech, computer-based, information technologies have the potential to help adults with disabilities age in place. Such technologies can include, among many others:

- AT for the home and transportation systems
- Communication devices
- E-mail and Web interfaces for those with cognitive impairment
- Telemedicine and telerehabilitation equipment for interventions at a distance
- "Smart" prompting systems that can be worn and connected with home automation devices
- Monitoring, tracking, and feedback technology that provides prompts, warnings, and directions to aid memory and understanding or to prevent wandering (e.g., for persons with Alzheimer's disease)
- Portable devices that enable individuals with cognitive disabilities to travel within the community

As with the general population, advances in computer technology can help people with disabilities access information on the Internet, communicate with others, and learn new skills. Yet there is a growing "digital divide" as people with disabilities, especially those with ID/DD, are less likely to own or use computers (Abramson, Emanuel, Gaylord, & Hayden, 2000; Wehmeyer, 1998). Universal design, augmentative communication technology, and technology training can help reduce this digital divide. Personalized computer software and adapted Web browsers enable persons with ID/DD to more effectively benefit from information technology.

New and effective strategies are emerging to deliver AT and EI to people who are aging with ID/DD. These programs incorporate several key factors, including: (a) informing family, significant others, caregivers, and community agency staff on how to use and obtain AT and EI; (b) actively involving participants in all phases of the intervention; (c) addressing the "digital divide" that results in persons with ID/DD missing out on information technology available to others; and (d) respecting privacy and choice.

Another approach to increasing aging in place and community living is to target whole communities for improvements in accessibility for people who are aging and who have disabilities. Several projects around the country (e.g., in Alabama, Florida, Illinois, Indiana, and New York) have developed innovative ways to make communities more age-friendly and accessible. For examples we can look to the Access Ready Communities Project in Indiana, the AdvantAge Initiative in eight states, and the Creating an Aging Prepared Community Project in New York (Heller, et al., 2002). These projects incorporate many innovative features including the following:

1. Collaborating with businesses to improve accessibility
2. Redesigning transportation systems
3. Actively involving people aging with ID/DD in the development plan for a housing project using a 3-D physical space modeling software and participatory design workshops
4. Developing Internet work collaborations between legislatures, public/private agencies, health networks, and faith communities to help governmental planners prepare for the growing proportion of elderly and disabled persons in their communities

Besides approaches that target whole communities, accommodations are also necessary in residential settings as people age and experience declines or other age-associated challenges. One critical issue is how to provide sufficient supports in community residential settings (whether they are family-based or small group living programs) as adults with ID/DD develop frailty, terminal illnesses, or dementia. Changes in health, adaptive behaviors, and behavioral control will necessitate more time from caregivers, a change in the intensity of supports, environmental accommodations (e.g., to address wandering), and, potentially, changes in residence. Appropriate accommodations made to community settings, such as building modifications, enhanced staffing, and appropriate education and training of care providers, will likely prevent people with ID/DD from unnecessarily being sent to live in restrictive settings like institutions.

Although since the 1970s most states have greatly decreased their reliance on institutions for persons with ID/DD, in 2000, 116,527 persons with ID/DD still lived in congregate settings, including 34,743 in nursing facilities (Braddock, Hemp, Rizzolo, Parish, & Pomeranz, 2002). This segregation occurs despite findings in the literature of the advantages of community living for this population (Heller, Factor, Hsieh, & Hahn, 1998; Larson & Lakin, 1989). Nursing homes often provide insufficient care and support for individuals with ID/DD because these homes are meant to provide nursing care as opposed to habilitation or active treatment. Studies show that the majority of individuals with ID/DD in nursing homes do not require round-the-clock nursing care (Lakin, Hill, & Anderson, 1991).

In 1987 Congress amended the Medical Assistance statute to ensure that persons with mental retardation (MR) would not be inappropriately placed in nursing facilities. States were required to conduct prescreening of new residents and screening of persons already in the nursing facilities. The primary purpose was to ensure that persons with MR or

ID/DD diagnoses received appropriate services, and nursing facilities, by consensus, were deemed inappropriate for most of these residents. However, nationally, persons with ID/DD in nursing homes still comprise 8% of all persons with ID/DD who receive any type of "residential" services in private and public intermediate care facilities for persons with mental retardation (ICF/MRs), state ID/DD institutions, community settings, or nursing facilities (Prouty, Smith, & Lakin, 2004). With the general belief that community living is a right, as backed by the Olmstead decision and the New Freedom Initiative community focus, the government and the disability community have further impetus to rely less on large congregate settings for adults with ID/DD; instead, they must develop viable community settings for older persons.

Little information exists on why some states decide, and others do not, to use institutional models, such as nursing facilities, as a significant part of their service delivery system. For example, the proportion of each state's residential developmental disabilities service system served in nursing facilities ranges from less than 1% in Alaska, Idaho, and Kansas, to over 20% in Alabama, Georgia, Kentucky, and Oklahoma (Braddock, et al., 2002). A study by Rizzolo (2004) found that use of institutional models in states was related to the state's political culture and to the extent that the state relied on the Medicaid home- and community-based waivers. Rizzolo compared three types of political cultures: traditionalistic (desiring to maintain the status quo); individualistic (driven by pragmatic concerns); and moralistic (promoting the good of the community). States with a moralistic culture were the least likely to use state institutions and nursing homes. All stakeholders need to examine ways to promote community versus institutional systems of residential care for older adults with ID/DD.

Recommendations for Research

Two major research goals promote aging- and disability-friendly communities and enable "aging in place" for adults aging with ID/DD:

1. Studies that identify and evaluate new technologies, user-friendly interfaces, and environmental strategies that promote aging- and disability-friendly communities
2. Research on ways to support "aging in place" for older adults with ID/DD experiencing age-related declines (e.g., dementia)

Specific research questions include the following:

1. How do we make adaptive technologies available and usable by people aging with ID/DD?
2. What is the potential impact of these strategies and devices on privacy and personal control of the people using them?
3. What are the important components of "access ready" communities for people aging with ID/DD?
4. What are the most effective strategies for increasing collaboration with local governments and businesses to design such communities; to meaningfully involve consumers in community development; and to create cross-disciplinary

collaborations with gerontologists, architects, designers, aging and disability communities, and city planners to share ideas?

5. How do we provide "dementia-friendly" residential environments for persons with ID/DD experiencing dementia?

6. What are the roles of advocacy and legislative efforts in promoting community residential settings?

Families and Other Caregivers

Overview of the Knowledge Base

Families are the major providers of care for adults with ID/DD, with over 76% of adults of all ages with ID/DD living at home, as indicated in the National Health Interview Survey of 1994 (Fujiura, 2001). Over 25% of these family caregivers are over the age of 60 years (Fujiura, 1998) and an additional 35% are ages 41 to 59 years. Using the Wisconsin Longitudinal Study, which followed high school graduates over a period of 20 years, Seltzer, Greenberg, Floyd, Pettee, and Hong (2001) found that, compared to the general population, mothers who provided long-term care tended to have reduced maternal employment, more family-work strain, and greater alterations in lifestyles. Moreover, families of adults with ID/DD living at home spent considerable out-of-pocket expenses for their adult relatives with disabilities. In a study of families' cash expenditures, Fujiura, Roccoforte, and Braddock (1994) found that families spent an average of 20% of their pretax annual income on unreimbursed expenses for their adult relative with ID/DD.

Although studies show that the presence of disability and poverty is related (Fujiura & Yamaki, 2000), they have provided little information on the intersection of poverty, minority status, and disability over many years of caregiving. A handful of studies have compared the experience of caregiving among African-American, Latino, and Euro-American caregivers of adults with ID/DD (e.g., Magaña, Seltzer, & Krauss, 2004; Pruchno, Patrick, & Burant, 1997). According to these studies, both African-American and Latino caregivers are severely disadvantaged by low levels of education, inadequate income, and poor health. When controlling for these factors, generally these studies have not shown greater burden and depression among minority caregivers, though one study of Latino families did find higher rates of depression among Latino caregivers than among Euro-American caregivers (Magaña, et al., 2004). However, research comparing families from minority groups to those in the majority culture may over- or underestimate depression by failing to take into account the fact that culture may influence how distress is expressed (Betancort & Lopez, 1993).

Researchers are recognizing more and more that developmental patterns and resultant types of family caregiving experiences over time vary across different conditions, etiologies, and syndromes. For example, groundbreaking research, including 10 years of longitudinal data on lifelong caregiving, found differences in caregiving outcomes for families of persons with autism and those with Down syndrome (Krauss, Greenberg, Seltzer, Chou, & Hong, 2001). The study found that mothers of adults with autism reported less favorable relationships with their children than did mothers of adults with Down syndrome. Researchers have neglected parents who have an adult child with both a developmental disability and severe mental health problems. We have scarce research on the challenges faced by aging families of individuals with both diagnoses, their special service needs, or the extent to which the service system can respond to their needs after their parents can no longer provide or direct care.

Although funding has increased for family support programs in the last 10 years, these programs represent a minor share of spending for ID/DD services, representing only 3.6% of the expenditures (Braddock, et al., 2002), and many of these programs only target children. Only 13% of individuals with ID/DD live out of the home (Fujiura, 2001). Families seeking out-of-home placements often encounter long waiting lists or inadequate alternatives. Over 75,000 persons with ID/DD remain year after year on waiting lists for residential services (Prouty, et al., 2004). As they age, parents become less able to provide care as they deal with the aging of their son or daughter and their own aging. Siblings also need to deal with their own aging, careers, and other caregiving responsibilities. Although planning for the future care of their relative when they can no longer provide care is a critical need, fewer than half of families actually make a plan for the future (Heller & Factor, 1993a). Families often do not include their other children and other family members when planning for these future needs, despite the fact that siblings most often take over the responsibility for caregiving when the parents are no longer alive or cannot provide care anymore. Despite the need for research in this area, researchers have seldom focused on ways to encourage sibling involvement in future planning.

Several initiatives around the country have demonstrated how to help families plan for the future, including the Family Futures Planning Project in Rhode Island (Susa & Clark, 1996), Planned Lifetime Advocacy Network in British Columbia (Etmanski, 1996), Family-to-Family Project in Massachusetts (Griffiths, 1997), and the Rehabilitation Research and Training Center on Aging with Mental Retardation (RRTC) Multicultural Family Future Planning Project (Preston & Heller, 1996). Unfortunately, most of these programs have not been empirically tested and have tended to focus the training and support on families rather than on the person with a disability. Although most of these interventions did not report empirical results, anecdotal information suggests limited success of these projects in stimulating future planning and getting families to progress in the planning process. Generally, these projects reported more success in helping families plan when families received ongoing support from other families. One project that has developed and tested a curriculum and intervention model is "The Future is Now" (DeBrine, Caldwell, Factor, & Heller, 2003). This model, which incorporates peer trainers (including other families and persons with disabilities) and training and support both for families and for persons with disabilities, resulted in greater planning (e.g., developing letters of intent), less caregiving stress, more choicemaking by the person with a disability, and greater participation of the adult with a disability in advocacy groups. However, the disability community still needs to develop better methods of including siblings and grandparents, who play an increasingly important role, and of enhancing the self-determination of the adult with disabilities.

The system is developing new models for delivering supports to families and adults with ID/DD that are more consumer-directed or self-determined (by families or by the person with a disability) than the program-directed models of the past. Several studies have begun to examine the impact of these models for people with ID/DD (Heller, Miller, & Hsieh, 1999; Herman 1991; Meyers & Marchenko, 1989) and for elderly persons (Tilly & Wiener, 2001). Heller, et al. (1999) found that a family-directed cash subsidy program for families caring for an adult with ID/DD resulted in improved service satisfaction, fewer unmet needs, greater caregiver satisfaction, and improved community integration and higher wages for the adult with ID/DD.

Caldwell and Heller (2003) found that increased control over respite/personal assistance services in a consumer-directed family support program was associated with increased service satisfaction, increased employment of mothers, and increased community integration of individuals with ID/DD. Paying family members as caregivers also increased community integration of the adults with ID/DD. Although the program did provide consumer direction as families did control the planning and budget, the families often did not consult the person with a disability.

Recommendations for Research
The overall research goal is to encourage studies of family caregiving to support caregiving capacity and transition planning in later life. Specific research questions include the following:

1. What are the influences of both syndrome-specific aspects of caregiving and sociocultural factors such as poverty and cultural backgrounds on the caregiving experiences?
2. What are the family demographic characteristics and how can we tap into existing local, state, and national databases and utilize longitudinal data sets?
3. How do we increase the involvement of siblings in the process of planning for the future care of their sibling with ID/DD?
4. How do we structure services for adults with ID/DD that provide them with both sufficient supports and autonomy as they age?
5. What is the impact (including health outcomes) of consumer-directed models on individuals with ID/DD and family caregivers, particularly single-parent caregivers and aging caregivers?
6. What are effective strategies for partnering with the Administration on Aging National Family Caregiver Support Program to address the issues of aging caregivers who are caring for family members with disabilities?

Promotion of Healthy Aging
Overview of the Knowledge Base
Adults with ID/DD have a higher risk of developing chronic health problems at younger ages than other adults due to the confluence of biological factors related to syndromes and associated developmental disabilities, access to adequate health care, and lifestyle and environmental issues. Service providers and families are striving to meet the growing needs of these aging adults. However, caregivers are frequently hampered by lack of information on age-related conditions, health care resources, and health promotion programs to provide support.

Studies are beginning to show higher rates of morbidity and mortality for adults with ID/DD in comparison with the general population for a number of conditions, including obesity, dental disease, gastroesophageal reflux and esophagitis, constipation, bowel obstruction and intestinal perforation, and gastrointestinal cancer (Evenhuis, Henderson, Beange, Lennox, & Chicoine, 2000). Other examples include nonatherosclerotic heart disease (Kapell, Nightengale, Rodriguez, Lee, Zigman, & Schupf, 1998; Cooper, 1998), mobility impairment (Kearny, Krishnan, & Londhe, 1993; Evenhuis, 1997), thyroid disease (Kapell, et al., 1998), osteoporosis (Center, Beange, & McElduff, 1998), psychotropic drug polypharmacy (Gowdy, Zarfas, & Phipps, 1987; van Schrojenstein Lantman-de Valk, Akker, Maaskant, Haveman, Urlings, & Kessels, 1997), and pneumonia (O'Brien, Tate, & Zaharia, 1991; Janicki, et al., 1999).

In addition, age-related health problems of women with ID/DD are often overlooked in spite of increased risk in certain areas. Women with ID/DD have higher rates of osteoporosis (for those with Down syndrome, epilepsy, and cerebral palsy), earlier onset of Alzheimer's disease and menopause (for persons with Down syndrome), and higher rates of psychiatric illnesses (Walsh & Heller, 2002). To add to the problem, they receive inadequate screening for breast and cervical cancer and heart disease. Given these issues and potentially life-threatening diseases, health promotion activities and medical interventions are essential to enhance useful functioning, prevent secondary disabling conditions, and increase quality of life for older men and women with ID/DD.

The increased longevity of persons with ID/DD directly results from medical and social advances that have also extended the longevity of the general population. Yet, as reported by the World Health Organization (2000), adults with ID/DD are still generally regarded as a devalued class and are often disadvantaged when they attempt to access or secure social and health services. Much of this is due to (a) inadequate public or private services capable of addressing the aging-related needs of adults with ID/DD and offering needed specialty services; (b) a need for supportive services, health surveillance and provision, and family assistance; (c) special problems facing women, who often find themselves as a disadvantaged class; and (d) health practitioners who generally fail to recognize special problems experienced by persons with lifelong disabilities who are aging.

Physical barriers often constitute a problem for many persons with ID/DD. Older women with cerebral palsy reported difficulties obtaining dental and gynecologic care because of accessibility problems (Turk, Geremski, Rosenbaum, & Weber, 1997). Health care facilities often are not accessible to persons with ID/DD, who may have a variety of physical and sensory impairments. Additionally, adults with ID/DD often experience difficulties with examinations and procedures (McRae, 1997; Lunsky, 1999). For many adults with ID/DD, the most important barrier to effective medical care is case complexity. They encounter a variety of medical subspecialists, dentists, audiologists, mental health providers, and other health care professionals, often without sufficient guidance or the services of health advocates.

For this reason, it is important that primary care physicians and other health care professionals recognize that, in general, adults with ID/DD have the same needs for disease prevention, diagnosis, and treatment as other members of the population. Health care providers can benefit from evidence-based practice standards (for example, the international guidelines for the screening and diagnosis of visual and hearing impairments in persons with ID, developed by the International Association for the Scientific Study of Intellectual Disabilities [IASSID] Special Interest Research Group on Health Issues [Evenhuis & Nagtzaam, 1998]). Health care professionals need to rely on comparable standards for specific interventions, conditions, diseases, and syndromes. Further, given the need for medical specialists with an interest and expertise in ID/DD, more must be done to assemble medical and health-related information on exposure, risk factors, syndrome effects, and epidemiological factors that comprise healthy aging in people with ID/DD.

Syndrome-specific effects in several intellectual and developmental disabilities (e.g., Down syndrome, William's syndrome, autism spectrum disorders, PKU, Smith-Lemli-Opitz syndrome, Prader-Willi syndrome) are linked to special risk factors. As noted in the Tampa conference report (Davidson, et al., 2003), basic scientific studies need to examine these syndromes more fully to find out how aging affects people who have them, especially when the syndrome is associated with increased risk for a specific concern (e.g., Down syndrome and Alzheimer's disease). In addition, clinical studies must evaluate strategies for treating or preventing subsequent morbidity and mortality associated with particular syndromes. For example, among adults with cerebral palsy later-life morbidity and functional declines seem to be related to the long-standing effect of the movement disorder on the musculoskeletal system. Also, recent studies of older persons with autism spectrum disorders suggest that with certain approaches they can, to some extent, maintain health and avoid isolation. Hence, it is important to conduct research that establishes the course of healthy aging in people with ID/DD through both longitudinal and cross-sectional tracking studies that can address specific syndromes, health behaviors, and health statuses.

Health promotion strategies for adults with ID/DD have received scant attention, as aptly noted by the U.S. Surgeon General's Conference on Health Disparities and Mental Retardation (U.S. Public Health Service, 2002). Diet and nutrition and physical activities are key components of health-promoting behaviors. Older persons with ID/DD are a nutritionally vulnerable group because of age-related changes, the presence of chronic diseases prevalent in the aging population, feeding problems, multiple concurrent medications, cognitive and functional declines, and syndrome-specific morbidity and comorbidities.

Adults with ID/DD also have low fitness levels (Fernhall, Tymeson, Millar, & Burkett, 1989; Graham & Reid, 2000; Pitetti, Climstein, Campbell, Barrett, & Jackson, 1992), a high incidence of obesity (Rimmer, 2000; Rimmer, Braddock, & Marks, 1995; Rubin, Rimmer, Chicoine, Braddock, & McGuire, 1998), and a tendency towards sedentary lives (Hoge & Dattilo, 1995). Hence, they are also at a higher risk than the general population of developing secondary conditions and age-related declines at an earlier age (Chicoine, Rubin, & McGuire, 1997; Janicki, Heller, Seltzer, & Hogg, 1996; Pitetti & Campbell, 1991). Despite the well-documented evidence of the benefits of participating in regular physical activity for people without disabilities (e.g., Pate, Pratt, Blair, Haskell, Macera, Bouchard, et al., 1995; U.S. Department of Health and Human Services, 1996), few researchers have focused on interventions to promote increased physical activity of persons with ID/DD.

Only a handful of studies have demonstrated the impact of exercise training on fitness measures (e.g., Millar, Fernhall, & Burkett, 1993; Rimmer, Heller, Wang, & Valerio, 2004). Even fewer have focused on the impact of a physical activity and health education program on the psychosocial well-being of adults with ID/DD (Bluechardt & Shephard, 1995; Schurrer, Weltman, & Brammell, 1985). Studies at the Rehabilitation Research and Training Center on Aging with Developmental Disabilities (RRTC-ADD) have revealed the poor fitness levels of adults with ID/DD (Rimmer, et al., 2004). For this population, the RRTC-ADD developed and empirically tested an innovative fitness and health behavior education program called "Nutrition and Health Behavior Education for Adults with Developmental Disabilities" (Heller, Marks, & Ailey, 2001, 2004). Center-based trials demonstrated its effectiveness in improving physical fitness (Rimmer, et al., 2004) and psychosocial well-being, including more positive attitudes towards exercise, higher life satisfaction, and less depression (Heller, Hsieh, & Rimmer, 2004). Over the long term, however, trial subjects did not generalize the center-based program to their natural settings very well. The next challenge is to develop and test methods of delivering health promotion interventions within individuals' natural settings (e.g., where they live, work, or recreate). To do so, providers would need to learn how to train staff, set up on-site health promotion programs, and use fitness and recreation centers in the community.

Recommendations for Research

The overall research goal is to encourage studies that predict, diagnose, or prevent emerging secondary age-related physical and mental health problems in older individuals with ID/DD. Specific research questions include the following:

1. What are the underlying causes of age-related functional decline and disease onset that occur in some genetic syndromes?
2. What characteristics have the potential to protect against age-related common physical or mental health conditions that certain syndromes may confer?
3. What is the trajectory of healthy aging in people with ID/DD?
4. For persons with ID/DD, what are the barriers and facilitators to participating in health-promoting activities such as engaging in exercise, eating healthful diets, and accessing preventive and regular health care checks?
5. What is the impact of long-term care for a member with ID/DD on the health of their family caregivers?

USING KNOWLEDGE TO SHAPE OUR NATIONAL AGENDA

People with ID/DD will benefit from timely research focused on key questions about the biological, behavioral, and social consequences of aging and the impact of social-environmental supports. With such research, subsequent generations of clinicians, policy makers, families, and people with ID/DD will be able to promote more progressive practices and policies that lead to improved health and greater community participation of adults aging with ID/DD. Like other people, older people with ID/DD may have significant physical and emotional health needs that reflect the social and economic circumstances that have shaped their daily lives. Governments have identified environments that foster healthy social relationships, trust, economic security, sustainable development, and other factors related to the priority of advancing the health and well-being of citizens. Healthier communities with greater social cohesion produce healthier citizens. Furthermore, the effect is cumulative and lifelong—good health in childhood affects and contributes to good health in older age.

Knowledge gained from previous and recommended research should help further the goals outlined in this chapter by focusing on several key areas of practice and policy: (a) improvements in health care and promotion; (b) greater support to families and other caregivers; and (c) promotion of aging- and disability-friendly environments. Furthermore, as researchers attempt to get information out to both the aging and disability networks, they must make sure to target the most appropriate approaches for specific groups so that everyone can carry out the programs effectively.

Health Care and Promotion

Unfortunately, among the developed nations in the world, the United States health care structure leaves much to be desired, certainly as it applies to people with special needs. Our nation's health care systems are often inadequate and do not recognize the special needs of adults with ID/DD, especially as they age. Therefore, health care provision is often sketchy at best, and specialty services for people with ID/DD are unavailable, a situation that further compromises their health and potential longevity. Hence, society in general and the disability community in particular need to promote adequate health care coverage policies. In addition, the lack of a coherent medical system may cause wellness programs for people with ID/DD to suffer; this problem, in addition to sensory and mobility impairments, morbid obesity, poor oral hygiene, risky sexual behavior, and other adverse lifestyle or personal attributes, can contribute to difficulties and compromise healthy aging.

We in the disability community need to increase and maintain health promotion activities and medical interventions to enhance useful functioning, prevent secondary disabling conditions, and add to the quality of life of persons aging with ID/DD. Further, given the need for medical specialists with interest and expertise in ID/DD (e.g., psychiatrists, neurologists, physiatrists, otolaryngologists, ophthalmologists, and other specialists with ID/DD knowledge), we need to take action to assemble medical and health-related information on exposure, risk factors, syndrome effects, and epidemiological factors that comprise healthy aging in people with ID/DD. If quality of life for older adults with ID/DD is to be improved, we must ensure that research in this area receives substantial increases in public and private funding. Secondly, we need to create a health outcomes database and identify workable oversight and assessment guidelines. Furthermore, we need to translate these findings into training of health care professionals, who often receive little training on health issues of adults with ID/DD.

Finding physicians who are willing to provide treatment for multiple medical issues is often problematic, and it can be difficult for adults with ID/DD to adhere to complex medication regimens. Finding information about how to treat a condition is often difficult for health professionals and for the people with ID/DD. Many adults with ID/DD have trouble communicating their medical problems to others and often lack an advocate to help them get appropriate health care. In addition, when they are terminally ill, they often receive poor, if any, end-of-life guidance or care.

Given the need to encourage regular exercise, promote and provide healthful diets, attend to regular health care checks, and seek preventive mental health services, those in the disability community need to do the following:

- Clarify empowerment and self-determination strategies
- Identify effects of health costs (e.g., availability of health insurance)
- Enhance professional knowledge about risk factors for threats to successful aging
- Enhance environmental access to appropriate care
- Develop valid and reliable assessment tools

We need to balance informed choices about health care against competing attitudes and values about evidence-based health promotion practices. Hence, we need to develop and implement community models of health promotion among adults with ID/DD (particularly among women disadvantaged by disparities in access and availability of health services) that will fit in with their ongoing lifestyles and thus be effective.

The field has a critical need to develop new approaches and better resources to train health professionals and direct care workers on issues pertaining to aging adults with ID/DD. We can do this by further involving the University Centers of Excellence and the nation's Geriatric Education Centers as well as enlisting the cooperation of the American Medical Association and the American Association on Mental Retardation.

Support to Families and Other Caregivers

All stakeholders must first ensure that family support services are appropriately funded and coordinated. Right now, these services are woefully underfunded in the developmental disabilities system. Many of the available programs, moreover, use agency-directed models, which offer little choice and flexibility for families. Furthermore, services are fragmented, with little bridging between the aging and disability service systems. We need to educate legislators of the necessity of supporting families and to educate families regarding ways to advocate for these changes. To this end, legislators and families need fact sheets, media articles, and public testimonies that use data collected through research and personal stories that highlight the need for progressive changes.

One avenue for bridging the two systems and providing supports to families is the National Family Caregiver Support Program administered by the Administration on Aging. It addresses caregivers of older adults with ID/DD as well as grandparent caregivers of children with ID/DD. In addition, the program funds several initiatives around the country that specifically target adults with ID/DD and their families-initiatives that include cross-training and joint case coordination between the aging and disability service systems.

Second, we must further address the need to help families plan for their future needs, when parents can no longer provide care. Informational materials and training opportunities need to be provided not only to parents, but also to siblings who often take over guardianship or caregiving. The Arc and the Sib Network are beginning to address these issues through online networking and training workshops for siblings.

Third, we must focus on the needs of minority families, families living in poverty, and families who have never been connected to the formal service system. These families may first become known to providers through the aging network or through health professionals who see a frail, aging parent living with a son or daughter with ID/DD. We need to get the word out to these families by targeting community organizations and religious groups in inner city and rural areas.

In our efforts to target families and persons with ID/DD, we need to develop new ways of distributing material through Web-based technologies as well as through more traditional modes. Many older families and persons with disabilities have little access to computers and the internet. We can also reach and influence greater numbers of people through the general media, including television, radio, and newspapers. Material needs to be packaged in lay language that is understandable to families and accessible to people with disabilities. Also, family and self-advocacy organization can distribute information.

Promotion of Aging- and Disability-Friendly Environments

With the use of new technologies and strategies and with more accommodating environments, older adults with ID/DD can increase or maintain their community participation and age in place. Settings could include the home, workplace, communities, and the information superhighway. Each of these settings requires modifications using universal design concepts, which can provide greater access to all people, including those with cognitive and physical disabilities. We need to develop tools to assess these environments and strategies for improving them. Furthermore, we need to identify ways to address the digital divide that prevents people from accessing desired technology.

Since the advent of the Americans with Disabilities Act (ADA) and the Rehabilitation Act, many initiatives have attempted to make the environment more accessible for adults with long-term disabilities and for aging persons who develop a disability. Yet few of these initiatives collaborate across the aging and disability systems. We need to develop model programs that focus on the environment as the driving force for designing and supporting accessible and inclusive communities. To this aim, we need to form partnerships with local governments and to create cross-disciplinary collaboration with gerontologists, engineers, anthropologists, rehabilitation professionals, architects and designers, aging and disabilities communities, and city planners to share ideas.

Most importantly, we need to promote change in social policy to provide supportive AT and EI resources that help adults stay in their living situations and that improve access to social and other community-based activities. Thus we need policies that fund evaluations, equipment, and training programs.

ANTICIPATING THE CHANGES OF THE FUTURE

National trends and emerging issues clearly demonstrate the imperative of addressing the growing needs of adults aging with ID/DD. They also point to the need for collaboration across the aging and disability systems, across centers and countries, and across multiple disciplines. The key emerging issues affecting the research and policy agenda include (a) the demographic imperative, (b) new knowledge on syndrome-specific life courses, (c) technological advances, and (d) increased need for collaboration between aging and disability groups.

Demographic Imperative

With the growing life expectancy and the aging of the baby boom generation, we anticipate a growing number of older adults with ID/DD in the next 25 years. Because parents are living longer, the period of caregiving is also longer, and the potential for caregiving across multiple generations is greater. Hence, the system will face a pent-up demand for more services for aging adults with ID/DD and their families. States maintain large waiting lists of adults requesting residential services, and this demand will only increase further as states face an unprecedented budget crisis. Many families have begun to take matters into their own hands by financing housing for their relatives themselves or jointly with other families. This trend is likely to continue as families seek more and more creative ways to obtain housing and supports for their relatives with ID/DD.

The other major trend is the rapid rise of minority families in the last 20 years, particularly Hispanics and Asian-Americans. Changes have also occurred in the support systems of minority families, who in the past may have relied on extended families. As more and more women are employed, fewer mothers and siblings are available to provide caregiving to adults with ID/DD. This change will necessitate approaches that are more culturally sensitive and that are geared to needs of employed family members. Another issue faced by many minority families is poverty, which contributes to lack of adequate health care, needed adaptive technologies, and needed personal supports.

Syndrome-Specific Trajectories

One of the outcomes of the Tampa Scientific Conference on Intellectual Disability, Aging, and Health (Davidson, et al., 2003) is the recognition of new and exciting research on how people with syndrome-specific ID/DD develop as they age. This research encompasses risks for specific morbidity as well as protective factors associated with specific syndromes and aging. The relationship between Down syndrome and midlife emergent Dementia of Alzheimer's Type (DAT) has been studied in recent years. There are several other promising directions for this type of research, including potential links between a syndrome of ataxia/dementia in male carriers and premutation of the fragile X gene. These studies can inform us about the early occurrence of DAT in adults with Down syndrome and could also provide important clues to understanding DAT in other people. Research is also emerging on potentially protective characteristics conferred by certain syndromes, such as the lack of solid tumors and possible low rates of arteriosclerosis in adults with Down syndrome.

Second, we are beginning to learn about the impact of health practices in earlier life on morbidity and mortality secondary to particular syndromes later in life. For example, studies of adults with cerebral palsy suggest that physical therapy treatments in childhood may be related to later life functional declines in the musculoskeletal system. Some of these declines may be potentially preventable. Recent studies of older persons with autism spectrum disorders, including Asperger and Rett syndromes, suggest preventable threats to health and social functioning. Researchers are developing an interest in examining later life consequences of many other low-incidence syndromes, including PKU, Prader-Willi syndrome, and Smith-Lemli-Opitz syndrome. Finally, specific syndromes may interact in important ways with nutritional requirements, medication usage, and exposure to environmental neurotoxicants.

Technological Advances

The technological revolution has many implications for improving the health and community participation of older adults with ID/DD. These technologies include not only AT and EIs that promote independent functioning, but also advances in medicine and in information technology. Medical advances, such as stem cell technology and gene therapy, have the potential for prolonging the life of adults with ID/DD. Other technological advances, such as telemedicine, can improve health through better monitoring from a distance.

Information technology has the potential to help adults with ID/DD and their families better connect with other people and with resources. On the other hand, many older persons and those with disabilities may have difficulty accessing computers and more complicated technologies. The challenge is to continually develop various methods that people with disabilities can access. Universal design principals also can improve usability for the general public.

Increased Need for Collaboration Between Aging and Disability Systems

With the increased scarcity of financial resources, the need to bridge the gap between the aging and disability networks is growing. Legislation on long-term care and health care affects both people with long-term disabilities and older adults who develop an illness or disability. The New Freedom Initiative and the Olmstead decision pertain to both of these populations and provide an impetus for collaboration between the two groups. Another program that links these two constituencies is the National Family Caregiver Support Program, which targets older family caregivers, including those caring for older adults with ID/DD.

In both legislative and goal-setting arenas (e.g., the reauthorization of the Older Americans Act and a White House Conference on Aging scheduled for 2005), it is important to ensure that disability-related concerns are incorporated into legislative agendas and national policies. Stakeholders can make this happen by taking part in processes established for such purposes, such as Administration on Aging listening sessions, the mini-White House Conferences on Aging, by providing information to delegates to the national conference, and by speaking directly to elected officials and their staff members.

ENHANCING REAL LIVES

The lives of Paul and Lena offer examples of how those with ID/DD can benefit from research advances and of the limitations in our current knowledge bases and practices. Paul's long life is a testament to the extended life expectancy of adults with Down syndrome, whose average age of death was 9 years in the 1920s. Without improved diagnostic measures and research on Down syndrome and Alzheimer's disease, Paul's cognitive and physical decline in the last two years would be poorly understood. Due to the availability of a gerontology program with some expertise in ID/DD, his hyperthyroidism, anemia, depression, and arthritis have been diagnosed and managed with medication.

More research could reveal ways to prevent or slow down the dementia and the other chronic conditions that he has developed. In many people with Down syndrome, these conditions develop 10 to 20 years earlier than in the general population.

Progressive public policies and research on community supports have enabled Paul to participate in community life despite declining health and mental functioning. He has switched from full-time sheltered employment and independent living to group home living and semi-retired leisure activities. He has been able to maintain meaningful social relationships in his group home. Paul has been fortunate in receiving supportive living services, but a large number of adults with intellectual disabilities do not have access to such supports and languish on long waiting lists for services. Without such supports, adults with ID/DD are more likely to experience more rapid declines and may end up in nursing homes.

* * *

Lena also has experienced health-related declines and has developed secondary conditions. However, the health care system and community services have often failed her. Years of poor health habits, poor nutrition, sedentary behavior, and insufficient medical monitoring have resulted in obesity, incontinence, and concomitant uncontrolled diabetes. Trauma to her knees, mixed with her congenital cerebral palsy and her obesity, resulted in her loss of mobility. Her life has been limited by the paucity of research on aging and cerebral palsy and of knowledge of treatments effective in stemming earlier age-related declines.

Although Lena has benefited from supportive living services and a strong family advocating for her, she has also faced many obstacles to "aging in place." Whenever she develops a medical crisis related to her diabetes, she lands in a nursing home for a long time. Upon returning to the group home, she often does not get adequate support to help her with proper nutritional guidance and monitoring. She would benefit from a health promotion program that would help her realize the importance of healthy behaviors and that would fit with her preferences and lifestyle.

Finally, Lena has been able to participate in community life, in large part because of the ADA, which has required accessibility of public spaces and transportation systems for people with disabilities. She is able to find accessible transportation, enjoy restaurants, and meet her boyfriend weekly at the local mall. Although she has used a computer to play games, she would like to have her own computer and learn to e-mail her friends and family. She would benefit from research on ways to lessen the "digital divide" and improve the accessibility of information technology.

In summary, both Paul and Lena exemplify the many challenges facing adults aging with ID/DD. They also highlight the importance of working toward meeting the national goals of improved health and community participation of aging adults with ID/DD. At the same time, they showcase the myriad ways that these individuals with ID/DD have been able to chart a meaningful and enjoyable life for themselves.

References

Abery, B. (1997). What is social inclusion all about? *IMPACT*, Feature Issue on the Social Inclusion of Adults with Developmental Disabilities, *10*(3).

Abery, B., McBride, M., Pierpoint, J., & Snow, J. (1998). Person-centered planning with youth and adults with developmental disabilities [Entire issue]. *IMPACT, 11*(2).

Abery, B. H. (1994). A conceptual framework for enhancing self-determination. In M. F. Hayden & B. H. Abery (Eds.), *Challenges for a service system in transition: Ensuring quality community experiences for persons with developmental disabilities* (pp. 345–380). Baltimore: Paul H. Brookes.

Abery, B. H., & Fahnestock, M. (1994). Enhancing the social inclusion of persons with developmental disabilities. In M. F. Hayden & B. H. Abery (Eds.), *Challenges for a service system in transition: Ensuring quality community experiences for persons with developmental disabilities* (pp. 83–119). Baltimore: Paul H. Brookes.

Abery, B. H. & Stancliffe, R. (1996). The ecology of self-determination. In D. J. Sands & M. L. Wehmeyer (Eds.), *Self-determination across the life span: Independence and choice for people with disabilities* (pp. 111–145). Baltimore: Paul H. Brookes.

Abramson, R. (2000, October 16). Report: Digital divide widens. *The Industry Standard.* Retrieved November 21, 2004, from http://www.thestandard.com/article/display/0,1151,19429,00.html

Abramson, W., Emanuel, E., Gaylord, V., & Hayden, M. (Fall, 2000). *Impact: Feature issue on violence against women with developmental or other disabilities, 13*(3), [Entire issue]. Minneapolis: University of Minnesota, Institute on Community Integration. Retrieved from http://ici.umn.edu/products/impact/133

Access to Credit (1998). *Small Enterprise, Big Dreams.* Frederick, MD: Access to Credit Media Project. (Videotape).

Agosta, J. (2002). *Family support in the United States: The move to Medicaid.* Tualatin, OR: National Center for Family Support.

Agosta, J., Knoll, J., Freud, E., & Raab, B. (1992). *Four pilot family support programs funded by the Illinois Department of Mental Health and Developmental Disabilities: Evaluation findings update.* Salem, OR: Human Services Research Institute.

Agosta, J., & Melda, K. (1995, May). *Supplemental Security income for children with disabilities: An exploration of child and family needs and the relative merits of the cash benefit program.* Salem, OR: Human Services Research Institute.

Agran, M. (Ed.)(1997). *Student-directed learning: Teaching self-determination skills.* Pacific Grove, CA: Brooks/Cole.

Ainbinder, J., Blanchard, L., Singer, G. H. S., Sullivan, M., Powers, L. K., Marquis, J., et al. (1998). A qualitative study of Parent to Parent support for parents of children with special needs. *Journal of Pediatric Psychology 23,* 99–109.

Albin, J. M., Rhodes, L., & Mank, D. (1994). Realigning organizational culture, resources, and community roles: Changeover to community employment. *Journal of the Association for Persons with Severe Handicaps, 19*(2), 105–115.

Alcalde, C., Navarro, J. I., Marchena, E., & Ruiz, G. (1998). Acquisition of basic concepts by children with intellectual disabilities using a computer-assisted learning approach. *Psychological Reports, 82*(3), 1051–1056.

Algozzine, B., Browder, D., Karvonen, M., Test, D. W., & Wood, W. M. (2001). Effects of interventions to promote self-determination for individuals with disabilities. *Review of Educational Research, 71*(2), 219–277.

Allard, M. A., Gottlieb, A., & Hart, D. (1993). *Impact study of the Family Cash Assistance Project: Year three results.* Waltham, MA: Shriver Center.

Allen, R. I., & Petr, C. G. (1996). Toward developing standards and measurements for family-centered practice in family support programs. In G. H. S. Singer, L. E. Powers, & A. L. Olson (Eds.), *Redefining family support: Innovations in public-private partnerships* (pp. 57–86). Baltimore: Paul H. Brookes.

Alper, J., Ard, C., Asch, A., Beckwith, J., Conrad, P., & Gellar, L. (2002). *The double-edged helix: Social implications of genetics in a diverse society.* Baltimore: Johns Hopkins University Press.

Amado, A. (Ed.). (1993). *Friendships and community connections between people with and without developmental disabilities.* Baltimore: Paul H. Brookes.

Amado, A. N., Conklin, F., & Wells, J. (1990). *Friends, a manual for connecting persons with disabilities and community members.* Cambridge, MA: Human Services Research Institute.

Aman, M. G., & Singh, N. (1986). *Abberant Behavior Checklist.* East Aurora, NY: Slosson Educational Publications.

American Academy of Pediatrics. (1996). Sexuality education of children and adolescents with developmental disabilities. *Journal of the American Academy of Pediatrics, 97*(2), 274–278.

American Academy of Pediatrics. (2001). *Medical homes initiative for children with special needs.* Elk Grove Village, IL: Author.

American Association on Mental Retardation. (2002). *Mental retardation: Definition, classification, and systems of supports* (10th ed.). Washington, DC: Author.

American Network of Community Options and Resources (2001). *Results of ANCOR Staff vacancy/Turnover survey.* Annandale, VA: Author.

Americans with Disabilities Act (ADA) of 1990, Pub. L. 101–336, 42 U.S.C. § 12101 *et seq.* (2000).

Americans with Disabilities Act Title II Regulations, 28 C.F.R. § 35.130 (2000).

Anderson, L., Larson, S., Lakin, K. C., & Kwak, N. (2002). Children with disabilities: Social roles and family impacts in the NHIS-D [Entire issue]. *DD Data Brief, 4*(1).

Antonovsky, A., & Sourani, T. (1988). Family sense of coherence and family adaptation. *Journal of Marriage and the Family, 50*(1), 79–92.

Appelbaum, P..S. (1997). Rethinking the conduct of psychiatric research. *Archives of General Psychiatry, 54,* 117–120.

The Arc of the United States. (1997, November). *Assistive technology.* Position statement #17. Retrieved November 21, 2004, from http://www.thearc.org/posits/astec.html

The Arc of the United States. (1998). *The education of students with mental retardation: Preparation for life in the community.* Retrieved August 25, 2002, from http://www.tash.org/resolutions/R33 INCED.html

The Arc of the United States. (2001, July). *Introduction to The Arc.* Retrieved November 21, 2004, from http://www.thearc.org/about.htm

The Arc of the United States. (2002). *Position statement on individual supports.* Retrieved November 21, 2004, from http://www.thearc.org/posits/indvsuppos.htm

Architectural and Transportation Barriers Compliance Board (Access Board). (1998, February 3). *Telecommunications Act accessibility guidelines.* Retrieved November 21, 2004, from http://www .access-board.gov/telecomm/html/telfinal.htm

Ard, C., & Zucker, D. (2002). The commercialization of genetic technologies: Raising public awareness. In J. S. Apler, C. Ard, A. Asch, J. Beckwith, P. Conrad, & L. Geller. (Eds.), *The double-edged helix: Social implications of genetics in a diverse society* (pp. 227–246). Baltimore: Johns Hopkins University Press.

Arnold, N. (Ed). (1998). *Self employment in Vocational Rehabilitation: Building on Lessons from Rural America.* Missoula, MT: Rural Institute, University of Montana.

Arscott, K., Dagman, D., & Stenfert Kroese, B. (1998). Consent to psychological research by people with an intellectual disability. *Journal of Applied Research in Intellectual Disabilities, 11*, 77–83.

Ashbaugh, J., & Allard, M. A. (1984). *Comparative analysis of the cost of residential, day, and other programs within institutional and community settings.* Boston: Human Services Research Institute.

Assistive Technology Act of 1998, Pub. L. No. 105-394, 20 and 29 U.S.C. (2000).

Assistive Technology Reauthorization Act of 2004, Pub. L. No. 108-364.

Association for Persons with Severe Handicaps (TASH). (2000). TASH resolution on inclusive education. Retrieved August 25, 2002, from http://www.tash.org/resolutions/R33INCED.html

Association for Persons with Severe Handicaps (TASH) (2002, January). *TASH resolution on teacher education.* Retrieved February 14, 2002 from http://www.tash.org/resolution/res02teachered.htm

Bahn, S. Mimmack, M., Ryan, M. Caldwell, M. A., Jauniaux, E., Starkey, M., et al. (2002). Neuronal target genes of the neuron-restrictive silencer factor in neurospheres derived from fetuses with Down syndrome: A gene expression study. *The Lancet, 359*, 310–315.

Bailey, D. (2002). *What can universal prekindergarten learn from special education?* (Working paper series). New York, NY: Foundation for Child Development.

Bailey, D., Hebbeler, K., Scarborough, A., Spiker, D., & Mallik, S. (2004). First experiences with early intervention: A national perspective. *Pediatrics, 113*, 887–896.

Bailey, D. B. (2001). Evaluating parent involvement and family support in early intervention and preschool programs. *Journal of Early Intervention, 24*(1), 1–14.

Bailey, D. B., Blasco, P. M., & Simeonson, R. J. (1992). Needs expressed by mothers and fathers of young children with disabilities. *American Journal on Mental Retardation 97*(1), 1–10.

Bailey, D. B., Skinner, D., Correa, V., Arcia, E., Reyes-Blanes, M. E., Rodriguez, P., et al. (1999). Needs and supports reported by Latino families of young children with developmental disabilities. *American Journal on Mental Retardation, 104*(5), 437-451.

Bailey, D. B., Skinner, D., & Warren, S. F. (in press). Newborn screening and developmental disabilities: Reframing presumptive benefit. *American Journal of Public Health.*

Baines, L., Baines, C., & Masterson, C. (1994). Mainstreaming: One school's reality. *Phi Delta Kappan, 76*(1), 39–40.

Baird, P. A., & Sadovnick, A. D. (1988). Causes of death to age 30 in Down syndrome. *American Journal of Human Genetics, 43*, 239–248.

Baker, B., Landen, S., & Kashima, K. (1991). Effects of parent training on families of children with mental retardation: Increased burden or generalized benefit? *American Journal on Mental Retardation, 96*(2), 127–136.

Baker, B. L. (1989). *Parent training and developmental disabilities.* Washington, DC: American Association on Mental Retardation.

Baker, E. T., Wang, M. C., & Walberg, H. J. (1994). The effects of inclusion on learning. *Educational Leadership, 52*(4), 33–35.

Baladerian, N. (1997). Recognizing abuse and neglect in people with severe cognitive and/or communication impairments. *Journal of Elder Abuse & Neglect, 9*(2), 93–104.

Baladerian, N. J. (1985, May). *Prevention of sexual exploitation of developmentally disabled adults.* Paper presented at the 1985 Association of Post-Secondary Educators of the Disabled Convention, Sacramento, CA.

Ballard, J., & Zettel, J. (1977). Public law 94-142 and section 504: What they say about rights and protections. *Exceptional Children, 44*(3), 177–184.

Bambara, L., & Kern, L. (Eds.) (2005). *Individualized supports for students with problem behavior.* New York: Guilford.

Bardoni, B., Castets, M., Huot, M.-E., Schenck, A., Adinolfi, S., Corbin, F., et al. (2002). 82-FIP, a novel FMRP (Fragile X Mental Retardation Protein) interacting protein, shows a cell cycle-dependent intracellular localization. *Human Molecular Genetics, 12,* 1689–1698.

Barker, G. (2002, December 20). Computers just doing what comes naturally. *Melbourne Age.* Retrieved November 21, 2004, from http://www.theage.com.au/articles/2002/12/20/1040174378191.html

Barnett, W. S. (2000). Economics of early childhood intervention. In J. P. Shonkoff & S. J. Meisels (Eds.), *Handbook of early childhood intervention* (2nd ed., pp. 589–610). New York: Cambridge Printing Press.

Barrera, I. (2000). Honoring difference: Essential features of appropriate ECSE services for young children from diverse sociocultural environments. *Young Exceptional Children, 3*(4), 17–24.

Barrera, I., Corso, R. M., & Macpherson, D. (2003). *Skilled dialogue: Strategies for responding to cultural diversity in early childhood.* Baltimore: Paul H. Brookes.

Batavia, A. I., & Hammer, G. (1989). Consumer criteria for evaluating assistive devices: Implications for technology transfer. In J. J. Presperin (Ed.), *Proceedings of the 12th Annual Conference of Rehabilitation Engineering Society of North America* (pp. 194–195). Washington, DC: RESNA Press.

Bateman, B. D., & Linden, M. A. (1998). *Better IEPs: How to develop legally correct and educationally useful programs* (3rd ed.). Longmont, CO: Sopris West.

Baumgart, D., & Ferguson, D. L. (1991). Personnel preparation: Directions for the next decade. In L. H. Meyer, C. A. Peck, & L. Brown (Eds.), *Critical issues in the lives of people with severe disabilities* (pp. 313–352). Baltimore: Paul H. Brookes.

Beach Center on Disability. (1998). *How to develop self-determination.* Lawrence, KS: University of Kansas.

Beasley, J. B., & Kroll, J. (2002). The START/Sovner Center program in Massachusetts. In R. H. Hanson, N. A. Wieseler, & K. C. Lakin (Eds.), *Crisis prevention & response in the community* (pp. 95–127). Washington, DC: American Association on Mental Retardation.

Beasley, J. B., Kroll, J., & Sovner, R. (1992). Community-based crisis mental health services for persons with developmental disabilities: The START model. *The Habilitative Mental Health Care Newsletter, 11*(9), 55–57.

Bedini, L., Bullock, C., & Driscoll, L. (1993). The effects of leisure education on factors contributing to the successful transition of students with mental retardation from school to adult life. *Therapeutic Recreation Journal, 27*(2), 70–82.

Beecher, H. (1966). Ethics and clinical research. *New England Journal of Medicine, 274,* 1354–1361.

Behr, S. K., Murphy, D. L., & Summers, J. A. (1991). *Kansas Inventory of Parental Perceptions: Measures of perceptions of parents who have children with special needs.* Lawrence, KS: Beach Center on Disability, University of Kansas.

Bell, N. J., Schoenrock, C. J., & Bensberg, G. J. (1981). Change over time in the community: Findings of a longitudinal study. In R. H. Bruininks, C. E. Meyers, B. B. Sigford, & K. C. Lakin (Eds.), *Deinstitutionalization and community adjustment of mentally retarded people* (pp. 195–206). Washington, DC: American Association on Mental Deficiency.

Benjamin, A. E, Matthias, R., Franke, T., Mills, L., Hasenfeld, Y., Matras, L., et al. (1998, September). *Comparing client-directed and agency models for providing supportive services at home. Final report.* Los Angeles: University of California at Los Angeles.

Bennett, F. C., Nickel, R. E., Squires, J., & Woodward, B. J. (1997). Developmental screening/surveillance. In Wallace, H. M., Biehl, R. F., MacQueen, J. C., & Blackman, J. A. (Eds.), *Mosby's resource guide to children with disabilities & chronic illness* (pp. 236–247). St. Louis: Mosby.

Bensberg, G. J., & Smith, J. J. (1984). *Comparative costs of public residential and community residential facilities for the mentally retarded.* Lubbock: Texas Tech University, Research and Training Center in Mental Retardation.

Benz, M. R., Doren, B., & Yovanoff, P. (1998). Crossing the great divide: Predicting productive engagement for young women with disabilities. *Career Development for Exceptional Individuals, 21*(1), 3–16.

Benz, M. R., Johnson, D. K., Mikkelsen, K. S., & Lindstrom, L. E. (1995). Improving collaboration between schools and vocational rehabilitation: Stakeholder identified barriers and strategies. *Career Development for Exceptional Individuals, 18,* 133–144.

Benz, M. R., Lindstrom, L., & Latta, T. (1999). Improving collaboration between schools and vocational rehabilitation: The Youth Transition Program model. *Journal of Vocational Rehabilitation, 13,* 55–63.

Benz, M. R., Lindstrom, L., & Yovanoff, P. (2000). Improving graduation and employment outcomes of students with disabilities: Predictive factors and student factors. *Exceptional Children, 66,* 509–529.

Bercovici, S. M. (1983*). Barriers to normalization: The restrictive management of retarded persons.* Baltimore: University Park Press.

Bergman, M. M. (2002). The benefits of a cognitive orthotic in brain injury rehabilitation. *Journal of Head Trauma Rehabilitation, 17*(5), 431–445.

Bernabe, E. A., & Block, M. E. (1994). Modifying the rules of a regular girls softball league to facilitate the inclusion of a child with severe disabilities. *Journal of the Association for Persons with Severe Handicaps, 19*(1), 24–31.

Bernard-Opitz, V., Sriram, N., & Nakhoda-Sapuan, S. (2001). Enhancing social problem solving in children with autism and normal children through computer-assisted instruction. *Journal of Autism and Developmental Disorders, 31*(4), 377–384.

Betancort, H., & Lopez, S. (1993). The study of culture, ethnicity, and race in American psychology. *American Psychologist, 48,* 629–637.

Birenbaum, A. (2003). The future of Medicaid. Paper presented at the Annual Meeting of the Association of University Centers on Disability, Bethesda, MD, November 15, 2003.

Bishop, M., & Crystal, R. M. (2002). A human resources perspective on counselor retirement and replacement in the state-federal vocational rehabilitation program: A nationwide concern. *Journal of Rehabilitation Administration, 26,* 231–238.

Blacher, J. (2001). The transition to adulthood: Mental retardation, families, and culture. *American Journal of Mental Retardation, 106,* 173–188.

Blacher, J. B. (2002). Autism rising: Delivering services without draining parents and school systems. *Exceptional Parent, 32*(10), 94–97.

Blacher, J., & Baker, B. L. (2002). *The best of AAMR. Families and mental retardation: A collection of notable AAMR journal articles across the 20th century.* Washington, DC: American Association on Mental Retardation.

Blackorby J., & Wagner, M. (1996). Longitudinal postschool outcomes for youth with disabilities: Findings for the National Longitudinal Transition Study. *Exceptional Children, 62,* 399–413.

Blanchard, L., Powers, L., Ginsberg, C., Marquis, J., & Singer, G. H. S. (1996). The Coping Efficacy Inventory: Measuring parents' perceptions of coping with a child with a disability and family problems. Unpublished manuscript. University of North Carolina Medical School, Chapel Hill, NC.

Blancher, J. (1998). Much ado about mortality: Debating the wrong question. *Mental Retardation, 36*(5), 412–415.

Blancher, J., Bader, B. L., & Feinfeld, K. A. (1999). Leaving or launching: Continuing family involvement with children and adolescents in placement. *American Journal on Mental Retardation, 104,* 452–465.

Blanck, P. D. (1998). *The Americans with Disabilities Act and the emerging workforce: Employment of people with mental retardation.* Washington, DC: American Association on Mental Retardation.

Blank, R. M. (2001). An overview of trends in social and economic well-being, by race. In N. J. Smelser, W. J. Wilson, & F. Mitchell (Eds.), *America becoming: Racial trends and their consequences* (Vol. 1, pp. 21–39). Washington, DC: National Academy Press.

Blanton, L. P., Griffin, C. C., Winn, J. A., & Pugach, M. C. (Eds.) (1997). *Teacher education in transition: Collaborative programs to prepare general and special educators.* Denver: Love.

Blischak, D. M., & Schlosser, R. W. (2003). Use of technology to support independent spelling by students with autism. *Topics in Language Disorders, 23*(4), 293–304.

Bluechardt, M. H., & Shephard, R. J. (1995). Using an extracurricular physical activity program to enhance social skills. *Journal of Learning Disability, 28*(3), 160–169.

Board of Education of Hendrick Hudson Central School District v. Rowley, 458 US 176 (1982).

Bogdan, R. (1995). Singing for an inclusive community: The community choir. In S. Taylor, R. Bogdan & Z. Lutfiyya (Eds.), *The variety of community experience: Qualitative studies of family and community life* (pp. 141–154). Baltimore: Paul H. Brookes.

Bogdan, R., & Taylor, S. J. (1987a). Conclusion: The next wave. In S. J. Taylor, D. Biklen, & J. Knoll (Eds.), *Community integration for people with severe disabilities* (pp. 209–220). New York: Teachers College Press.

Bogdan, R. & Taylor, S. J. (1987b). Toward a sociology of acceptance: The other side of the study of deviance. *Social Policy, 18*(2), 34–39.

Bogdan, R. & Taylor, S. J. (1989). Relationships with severely disabled people: The social construction of humanness. *Social Problems, 36*(2), 135–148.

Bogdan, R. & Taylor, S. J. (1990). Looking at the bright side: A positive approach to qualitative research. *Qualitative Sociology, 13*(2), 183–192.

Bogdan, R., & Taylor, S. J. (2001). Building stronger communities for all: Thoughts about community participation for individuals with developmental disabilities. In A. Tymchuk, K. C. Lakin, & R. Luckasson (Eds.), *The forgotten generation: The status and challenges of adults with mild cognitive limitations* (pp. 191–202). Baltimore: Paul H. Brookes.

Bonham, G. S., Basehart, S., Schalock, R. L., Kirchner, N., & Rumenap, J. M. (2004). Consumer based quality of life assessment: The Maryland Ask Me! Project. *Mental Retardation, 42*(5), 338-355.

Boo, K. (1999, March 14). Forest Haven is gone, but the agony remains. *The Washington Post,* p. A01.

Booth, T., Simons, K., & Booth, W. (1990). *Outward bound: Relocation and community care for people with learning difficulties.* Milton Keyes, England: Open University Press.

Borthwick, S. (1988). Maladaptive behavior among the mentally retarded: The need for reliable data. In J. Stark, F. Menolascino, M. Albarelli, & V. Gray (Eds.), *Mental retardation and mental health: Classification, diagnosis, treatment services* (pp. 30–40). New York: Springer-Verlag.

Bott, E. (1971). *Family and social network.* New York: Free Press.

Bowles, C. (2003, March 12). World's first brain prosthesis. NewScientist.com. Retrieved November 21, 2004, from http://www.eurekalert.org/pub_releases/2003-03/ns-twf031203.php

Braddock, D. (1999). Aging and developmental disabilities: Demographic and policy issues affecting American families. *Mental Retardation, 37,* 155–161.

Braddock, D. (2003). *The State of the States in Developmental Disabilities Project.* Boulder: University of Colorado, Department of Psychiatry.

Braddock, D., Hemp, R., Parish, S., Westrich, J., & Park, H. (1998). *The state of the states in developmental disabilities* (5th ed.). Washington, DC: AAMR.

Braddock, D., Hemp, R., Rizzolo, M. C., Parish, S., & Pomeranz, A. (2002). *The state of the states in developmental disabilities: 2002 study summary.* Boulder: University of Colorado, Coleman Institute for Cognitive Disabilities and Department of Psychiatry.

Braddock, D., & Mitchell, D. (1992). *Residential services for persons with developmental disabilities in the United States: A national study of staff compensation, turnover and related issues.* Washington, DC: American Association on Mental Retardation.

Braddock, D., Rizzolo, M., & Hemp, R. (2004). Most employment services growth in developmental disabilities during 1988–2002 was in segregated settings. *Mental Retardation, 42*(4), 317–320.

Braddock, D., Rizzolo, M. C., Thompson, M., & Bell, R. (2004). Emerging technologies and cognitive disability. *Journal of Special Education Technology, 19*(4), 49–56.

Bradley, V., Agosta, J., Smith, G., Taub, S., Ashbaugh, J., Silver, J., et al. (2001). *The Robert Wood Johnson Foundation Self-Determination Initiative: Final impact assessment report.* Cambridge, MA: HSRI.

Bradley, V., Ashbaugh, J., & Blaney, B. (1994). *Creating individual supports for persons with disabilities: A mandate for change on many levels.* Baltimore: Paul H. Brookes.

Bradley, V. J., & Kimmich, M. H. (2003). *Quality enhancement in developmental disabilities: Challenges and opportunities in a changing world.* Baltimore: Paul H. Brookes.

Brantlinger, E. (1985). Mildly mentally retarded secondary students' information about the attitudes toward sexuality education. *Education and Training of the Mentally Retarded, 20*(2), 99–108.

Brantlinger, E. (1992). Professionals' attitudes toward the sterilization of people with disabilities. *Journal of the Association for Persons with Severe Handicaps, 17*(1), 4–18.

Bredekamp. S., & Copple, C. (1997). *Developmentally appropriate practice in early childhood programs* (Rev. ed.). Washington, DC: National Association for the Education of Young Children.

Bronfenbrenner, U. (1979). *The ecology of human development: Experiments by nature and design.* Cambridge, MA: Harvard University Press.

Browder, D. (2001). *Curriculum and assessment for students with moderate and severe disabilities.* New York: Guilford Press.

Brown v. Board of Education, 347 U.S. 483 (1954).

Brown, C. C., Mineo, B. A., & Cavalier, A. R. (1987). The overlooked consumer: Technology for persons with severe handicaps. *Proceedings of the American Speech-Language-Hearing Foundation Computer Conference, 5.* Rockville, MD: ASHA.

Brown, I., Isaacs, B., McCormack, B., Baum, N., & Renwick, R. (2004). Family quality of life in Canada. In A. Turnbull, I. Brown, & H. R. Turnbull (Eds.), *Families and people with mental retardation and quality of life: International perspectives* (pp. 183–220). Washington DC: American Association on Mental Retardation.

Brown, L., Nietupski, J., & Hamre-Nietupski, S. (1976). The criterion of ultimate functioning and public school services for severely handicapped students. In L. Brown, N. Certo, & T. Crowner (Eds.), *Papers and programs related to public school services for secondary age severely handicapped students, Vol. VI., Part 1* (pp. 1–13). Madison, WI: MMSD.

Brown, L., Udvari-Solner, A., Temple, J., Kluth, P., Suomi, J., & Ross, C. (2000). *Generating meaningful experiences for a student with significant disabilities in regular education settings.* Manchester: University of New Hampshire, Institute on Disability.

Brown, R. & Foster, L. (2000). *Cash and counseling: Early experiences in Arkansas.* Washington, DC: Mathematica Policy Research.

Brown, W. T. (2002). *Aging-related health effects: Down, Fragile X, and Williams syndromes.* Paper presented at the Tampa Scientific Conference on Intellectual Disability, Aging, and Health. Tampa, FL, December 6–9, 2002.

Brownell, M. T, Ross, D. D., Colon, E. P., & McCallum, C. L. (2002). *Critical features of special education teacher preparation: A comparison with exemplary practices in general education (Draft).* Gainesville, FL: Center on Personnel Studies in Special Education. Retrieved November 20, 2002 from the Center on Personnel Studies in Special Education Web site, http://www.coe.ufl.edu

Browning, P., Thorin, E., & Rhoades, C. (1984). A national profile of self-help/self-advocacy groups of people with mental retardation. *Mental Retardation, 22*(5), 226–230.

Bruininks, R. H., & Lakin, K. C. (Eds.). (1985). *Living and learning in the least restrictive alternative.* Baltimore: Paul H. Brookes.

Bruininks, R. H., Thurlow, M., Lewis, D., & Larson, N. W. (1988). *Postschool outcomes for special education students one to eight years after high school.* Minneapolis, MN: University of Minnesota, Institute on Community Integration.

Bruininks, R. H., Woodcock, R. W., Weatherman, R. F., & Hill, B. K. (1996). *Scales of Independent Behavior-Revised (SIB-R).* Chicago: Riverside.

Budde, J. F., & Bachelder, J. L. (1986). Independent living: The concept, model, and methodology. *Journal of the Association for Persons with Severe Handicaps, 11*(4), 240–245.

Buehler, B. A., Bick, D., & Delimont, D. (1993). Prenatal prediction of risk of the fetal hydantoin syndrome. *New England Journal of Medicine, 329,* 1660–1661.

Burchard, S. N., Hasazi, J. E., Gordon, Yoe, J. (1991). An examination of lifestyle and adjustment in three community residential alternatives. *Research in Developmental Disabilities, 12,* 127–142.

Bureau of Labor Statistics (BLS) (2001). *BLS releases 2000–2010 employment projections* (USDL Publication No. 01-443). Washington, DC: Author.

Burt, D. B., & Alyward, E. H. (1999). Assessment methods for the diagnosis of dementia. In M. P. Janicki & A. J. Dalton (Eds), *Dementia, aging, and intellectual disabilities: A handbook* (pp. 141–156). Philadelphia: Taylor and Francis.

Bush, G. W. (2001, January 20). Announcement of New Freedom Initiative. Retrieved November 21, 2004, from http://www.whitehouse.gov/news/freedominitiative/freedominitiative.html

Butterworth, J. & Fesko, S. (1998). *Conversion to integrated employment: Case studies of organizational change.* Boston: Institute for Community Inclusion.

Butterworth, J., & Hagner, D. (1993). *More like a dance: Whole life planning for people with disabilities.* Augustine, FL: TRN, Inc.

Butterworth, J., Hagner, D., & Helm, D. (2000). Workplace culture, social interactions, and supports for transition-aged young adults. *Mental Retardation, 38*(4), 342–353.

Buysse, V., Wesley, P. W., & Able-Boone, H. (2001). Innovations in professional development: Creating communities of practice to support inclusion. In Guralnick, M. J. (Ed.), *Early childhood inclusion: Focus on change* (pp. 179–200). Baltimore: Paul H. Brookes.

Caldwell, J., & Heller, T. (2003). Management of respite and personal assistance services in a consumer-directed family support programme. *Journal of Intellectual Disability Research, 47*(4/5), 352–366.

Callahan, M. (Aug. 9, 2002). Presentation to SSA and State Partnership Directors on Customized Employment. Annapolis, Maryland.

Callahan, M. J., & Garner, J. B. (1997). *Keys to the workplace: Skills and supports for people with disabilities.* Baltimore: Paul H. Brookes.

Campbell, E. M., & Smith, G. A. (1989, March). *Predictors of service costs for people with developmental disabilities.* Paper presented at the Pacific Rim Conference on Quality of Life for Persons with Disabilities, Honolulu, HI.

Campbell, M., & Malone, R. (1991). Mental retardation and psychiatric disorders. *Hospital and Community Psychiatry, 42,* 374–379.

Campbell, P. C., Campbell, C. R., & Brady, M. P. (1998). Team Environmental Assessment Mapping System: A method for selecting curriculum goals for students with disabilities. *Education and Treatment in Mental Retardation and Developmental Disabilities, 33,* 264–272.

Cantwell, D. P. (1996). Classification of child and adolescent psychopathology. *Journal of Child Psychology and Psychiatry, 17*(1), 3–12.

Capone, A. M. & DiVenere, N. (1996). The evolution of a personnel preparation program: Preparation of family-centered practitioners. *Journal of Early Intervention, 20*(3), 222–231.

Carr, E. G. (1977). The motivation of self-injurious behavior: A review of some hypotheses. *Psychological Bulletin, 84,* 800–816.

Carr, E. G., Dunlap, G., Horner, R. H., Koegel, R. L., Turnbull, A. P., Sailor, W., et al. (2002). Positive behavior support: Evolution of an applied science. *Journal of Positive Behavior Interventions, 4*(1), 4–16, 20.

Carr, E. G., & Durand, V. M. (1985). Reducing behavior problems through functional communication training. *Journal of Applied Behavior Analysis, 18,* 111–126.

Carr, E. G., Horner, R. H., Turnbull, A. P., Marquis, J. G., Magito McLaughlin, D., McAtee, M. L., et al. (1999). *Positive behavior support for people with developmental disabilities: A research synthesis.* Washington DC: American Association on Mental Retardation.

Carr, E. G., Levin, L., McConnachie, G., Carlson, J. I., Kemp, D. C., & Smith, C. E. (1994). *Communication-based intervention for problem behavior. A user's guide for producing positive change.* Baltimore: Paul H. Brookes.

Carta, J. J. (2002). An early childhood special education research agenda in a culture of accountability for results. *Journal of Early Intervention, 25,* 102–104.

Carter, E. A., & McGoldrick, M. (1999). *Changing family life cycle: Individual, family, and social perspectives* (3rd ed.). Boston: Allyn & Bacon.

Carver, C. S., Scheier, M. F., & Weintraub, J. K. (1989). Assessing coping strategies: A theoretically based approach. *Journal of Personality and Social Psychology, 56,* 267–283

Casey, W., Jones, D., Kugler, B., & Watkins, B. (1988) Integration of Down's syndrome children in the primary school: A longitudinal study of cognitive development and academic attainments. *British Journal of Educational Psychology, 58,* 279–286.

Casto, G., & Mastropieri, M. A. (1986). The efficacy of early intervention programs: A meta-analysis. *Exceptional Children, 52,* 417–424.

Catalano, R. F., Berglund, M. L., Ryan, J. A. M., Lonczak, H. S., & Hawkins, J. D. (1998). *Positive youth development in the United States: Research findings on evaluations of positive youth development programs.* Retrieved December 8, 2004, from http://aspe.hhs.gov/hsp/PositiveYouthDev99/

Cavalier, A. (1987). The application of technology in the classroom and workplace: Unvoiced premises and ethical issues. In A. Gartner & T. Joe (Eds.), *Images of the Disabled/Disabled Images* (pp. 129–142). New York: Praeger.

Cavalier, A. R. (1988, May 19). Assistive technology for children and adults with mental retardation or other cognitive impairments. Testimony to the subcommittee on the handicapped of the committee on labor and human resources of the United States Senate. The Bioengineering Program, Department of Research and Program Services, Association for Retarded Citizens of the United States.

Cavalier, A. R., & Brown, C. C. (1998). From passivity to participation: The transformational possibilities of speech-recognition technology. *Teaching Exceptional Children, 30*(6), 60–65.

Cavalier, A. R., Mineo, B. A., & Brown, C. C. (1986). Technological steps towards increased independence for persons with developmental disabilities. In J. L. Levy (Ed.), *Model programs and new technologies for people with developmental disabilities* (pp. 34–35). New York: Young Adult Institute.

Cavuoto, J. (2004, April). Neural engineering's image problem. *IEEE Spectrum,* 32–37.

Center, J., Beange, H., & McElduff, A. (1998). People with mental retardation have an increased incidence of osteoporosis: A population study. *American Journal on Mental Retardation, 99,* 595–604.

Center on Human Policy (2002). *Community participation and social networks: An information package.* Syracuse, NY: Syracuse University, Center on Human Policy.

Certo, N., Schleien, S., & Hunter, D. (1983). An ecological assessment inventory to facilitate community recreation participation by severely disabled individuals. *Therapeutic Recreation Journal, 17*(3), 29–38.

Chadsey, J., Linneman, D., Rusch, F., & Camera, R. (1997). The impact of social integration interventions and job coaches in work settings. *Education and Training in Mental Retardation and Developmental Disabilities, 3*(2), 281–292.

Chambers, A. C. (1997). *Has technology been considered? A guide for IEP teams.* Reston, VA: Council of Administrators of Special Education and Technology of Media Division of the Council for Exceptional Children.

Chambers, B., Abrami, P. C., Massue, F. M., & Morrison, S. (1998). Success for all: Evaluating an early-intervention program for children at risk of school failure. *Canadian Journal of Education, 23*(4), 357–372.

Chao, E. (2002, September). *The direct support workforce crisis.* Presentation at the Annual Government Affairs Conference of the American Network of Community Options and Resources, Washington, DC.

Charlot, L. R. (2002). Mission impossible: Developing an accurate classification of psychiatric disorders in individuals with developmental disabilities. *Mental Health Aspects of Developmental Disabilities, 6*(1), 26–36.

Charlot, L. R., Arbend, S., Silka, V. R., Kuropatkin, B. B., Garcia, O., Bolduc, M., et al. (2002). A short stay inpatient psychiatric unit for adults with developmental disabilities. In J. W. Jacobson, J. A. Mulick, & S. C. Holburn (Eds.), *Contemporary dual diagnosis MH/MR service models, volume 1: Residential and day services* (pp. 35–55). Kingston, NY: NADD.

Chen, D., McLean, M. E., Corso, R. M., & Bruns, D. (2005). Working together in early intervention: Cultural considerations in helping relationships and service utilization. In R. M. Corso, S. A. Fowler, & R. M. Santos (Eds.), *Building healthy relationships with families* (pp. 39–55). Longmont, CO: Sopris West.

Chenoweth, L. (1996). Violence and women with disabilities: Silence and paradox. *Violence Against Women, 2*(4), 391–414.

Chicoine, B., Rubin, S., McGuire, D. (1997). *Health and psychosocial findings of the Adult Mental Retardation Center.* Presentation at the International Roundtable on Aging and Intellectual Disability, Chicago, Illinois.

Child Abuse Prevention and Treatment Act, Pub. L. No. 93-247 (1978), as ammended by Pub, L. No. 108-36 (2003), 42 U.S.C. § 5101 (2000).

Child Health Act of 2000, Pub. L. No. 106-310, 42 U.S.C. §§ 290bb–39 *et seq.* (2000).

Christenson, S. (2002, December). *Check and connect: A model to enhance student engagement and prevent dropout.* Presentation before the National Dropout Forum, Washington, DC: U. S. Department of Education, Office of Special Education Programs.

Cleveland, L., Triest, L., & Luckasson, R. (May 19, 2003). Letter to Jacquelyn C. Jackson, Acting Director, Student Achievement and School Accountability Programs, Office of Elementary and Secondary Education, U.S. Department of Education.

Clyde K. v. Puyallup School District, 35 F.3d 1396 (9th Cir. 1994).

Cole, D., & Meyer, L. H. (1991). Social integration and severe disabilities: A longitudinal analysis of child outcomes. *Journal of Special Education, 25,* 340–351.

Cole, E. (1999). Cognitive prosthetics: An overview to a method of treatment. *Neurorehabilitation, 12,* 39–51.

Colond, J. S., & Weisler, N. A. (1995). Preventing restrictive placements through community support services. *American Journal of Mental Retardation, 100,* 201–206.

Committee on Children with Disabilities (2001). Developmental surveillance and screening of infants and young children. *Journal of Pediatrics, 108,* 192–196.

Committee for Economic Development (2002). *Preschool for all: Investing in a productive and just society.* Washington, DC: Author.

Condeluci, A. (1991). *Interdependence: The route to community.* Delray Beach, FL: St. Lucie Press.

Conroy, J., Spreat, S., Yuskauskas, A., & Elks, M. (2003). The Hissom Closure Outcomes Study: A report on six years of movement to supported living. *Mental Retardation, 41*(4), 263–275.

Conroy, J. W. (1996). The small ICF/MR program: Dimensions of quality and cost. *Mental Retardation, 34*(1), 13–26.

Conroy, J. W. (1998). *On interviewing people with cognitive disabilities: Challenges and best practices.* Narberth, PA: Center for Outcome Analysis.

Conroy, J. W., & Bradley, V. J. (1985). *The Pennhurst longitudinal study: A report of five years of research and analysis.* Philadelphia: Temple University Developmental Disabilities Center.

Conroy, J. W., Fullerton, A., Brown, M., & Garrow, J. (2002). *Outcomes of the Robert Wood Johnson Foundation's national initiative on self-determination for persons with developmental disabilities.* Narberth, PA: Center for Outcome Analysis.

Conroy, J. W., & Yuskauskas, A. (1996). *Independent evaluation of the Monadnock Self-Determination Project.* Ardmore, PA: Center on Outcome Analysis.

Cooper, C. S., & Allred, K. W. (1992). A comparison of mothers' versus fathers' needs for support in caring for a young child with special needs. *Infant-Toddler Intervention, 2*(2), 205–221.

Cooper, R. L. (2002). *Family support and the move to Medicaid.* Presentation at the Family Support in the New Economy Conference, Chicago: National Center for Family Support.

Cooper, S. A. (1998). Clinical study of the effects of age on the physical health of adults with mental retardation. *American Journal on Mental Retardation, 106,* 582–89.

Corcoran, K., & Fahy, J. (2000, June 18). Painful lessons: Lives hung in the balance as firm moved mentally disabled into communities. As problems grew, the state failed to intervene. *The Indianapolis Star,* p. A1.

Coulter, D.L. (2003a). A vision for health. Paper presented at the Annual Meeting of the American Association on Mental Retardation, Chicago, IL, May 22, 2003.

Coulter, D.L. (2003b). A new vision for health: The community health supports model. Paper presented at the Regional Meeting of Region V, American Association on Mental Retardation, New Orleans, LA, August 6, 2003.

Council for Exceptional Children. (2000). *What every special educator must know: The standards for the preparation and licensure of special educators.* Ballston, VA: Author.

Council for Exceptional Children (2001). *Bright futures for exceptional learners: An agenda to achieve.* Ballston, VA: Author.

Council on Quality and Leadership, (1993). *Outcome-based performance measures.* Towson, MD: Author.

Council on Quality and Leadership (2000). *The Council's outcome data base.* Towson, MD: Author.

Craig, E. M., & McCarver, R. (1984). Community placement and adjustment of deinstitutionalized clients: Issues and findings. In N. W. Bray & N. Ellis (Eds.), *International review of research in mental retardation* (vol. 12, pp. 95–122). Orlando: Academic Press.

Crapps, J., Langione, & Swaim, S. (1985). Quantity and quality of participation in community environments by mentally retarded adults. *Education and Training of the Mentally Retarded, 20*(2), 123–129.

Crawford, D. B., & Carnine, D. (2000). Comparing the effects of textbooks in eighth-grade U.S. history: Does conceptual organization help? *Education and Treatment of Children, 23,* 387–422.

Crocker, A.C. (1999). The medical model: A mostly historical discussion. In H. Bersani (Eds.), *Responding to the challenge: Current trends and international issues in developmental disabilities: Essays in honor of Gunnar Dybwad* (pp. 3-9). Cambridge, MA: Brookline Books.

Cronbach, L. J. (1957). The two disciplines of scientific psychology. *American Psychologist, 12,* 671–684.

Cronbach, L. J. (1975). Beyond the two disciplines of scientific psychology. *American Psychologist, 30,* 116–127.

Cross, T. L. (1998). Services to minority populations: Cultural competence continuum. *Focal Point, 3*(1), 1–4.

Crudden, A., McBroom, L. W., Skinner, A. L., & Moore, J. E. (1998). *Comprehensive examination of barriers to employment among persons who are blind or visually impaired.* Mississippi State, MS: RRTC on Blindness and Low Vision.

Cruzan v. Director, 497 U.S. 261 (1990).

Curry, M. A., Hassouneh-Phillips, D. & Johnson-Silverberg, A. (2001). Abuse of women with disabilities: An ecological model and review. *Violence Against Women, 7*(1), 60–79.

Czerlinsky, T., & Chandler, S. (1993). Effective consumer-service provider interactions in vocational rehabilitation. *OSERS News in Print, 5*(4), 39–43.

Dalgleish, M. (1983). Assessments of residential environments for mentally retarded adults in Britain. *Mental Retardation, 21*(5), 275–281.

Danaher, J., & Armijo, C. (Eds.) (2004). Part C updates. Chapel Hill: The University of North Carolina, FPG Child Development Institute, National Early Childhood Technical Assistance Center.

Daniel R. R. v. State Board of Education, 874 F.2d 1036 (5th Cir. 1989).

Daniels, R. (1996). Inside and out. *IMPACT, 9*(1), 10–11.

Darling-Hammond, L., & Young, P. (2002). Defining "highly qualified teachers": What does "scientifi-cally-based research" actually tell us? *Educational Researcher, 31*(9), 13–25.

Data Research. (1997). *Students with disabilities and special education* (14th ed.). Rosemount, MN: Author.

Davidson, P., Cain, N., Sloane-Reeves, J., Giesow, V., Quijano, L., & Houser K. (1996). Factors predict-ing re-referral following crisis intervention for community-based persons with developmental disabili-ties and behavioral and psychiatric disorders. *American Journal on Mental Retardation, 101*(2), 109–118.

Davidson, P. W., Heller, T., Janicki, M. P., Hyer, K. (2003). *The Tampa Scientific Conference on Intellectual Disability, Aging, and Health.* Chicago: University of Illinois at Chicago, RRTC on Aging with Developmental Disabilities.

Davies, D. K., Stock, S. E., & Wehmeyer, M. L. (2001). Enhancing independent Internet access for indi-viduals with mental retardation through the use of a specialized web browser: A pilot study. *Education and Training in Mental Retardation and Developmental Disabilities, 36,* 107–113.

Davies, D. K., Stock, S. E., & Wehmeyer, M. L. (2002a). Enhancing independent task performance for individuals with mental retardation through use of a handheld self-directed visual and audio prompt-ing system. *Education and Training in Mental Retardation and Developmental Disabilities, 37*(2), 209–218.

Davies, D. K., Stock, S. E., & Wehmeyer, M. L. (2002b). Enhancing independent time-management skills of individuals with mental retardation using a Palmtop personal computer. *Mental Retardation, 40*(5), 358–365.

Davies, D. K., Stock, S. E., & Wehmeyer, M. L. (2003). Utilization of computer technology to facilitate money management by individuals with mental retardation. *Education and Training in Mental Retardation and Developmental Disabilities, 38*(1), 106–112.

Davies, D. K., Stock, S. E., & Wehmeyer, M. L. (2004). Computer-mediated, self-directed computer training and skill assessment for individuals with mental retardation. *Journal of Development and Physical Disabilities, 16*(1), 95–105.

Davis, S. A. (1995). *People with mental retardation in the criminal justice system.* Silver Spring, MD: The Arc of the United States.

Deardorff, K., & Hollman, F. (1997). *U.S. population estimates by age, sex, race, and Hispanic origin: 1990 to 1996.* Washington, DC: U.S. Government Printing Office.

DeBrine, E., Caldwell, J., Factor, A., & Heller, T. (2003). *The future is now: A future planning training curriculum for families and their adult relatives with developmental disabilities.* Chicago: University of Illinois at Chicago, Rehabilitation Research and Training Center on Aging with Developmental Disabilities.

DeFur, S. H., & Taymans, J. M. (1995). Competencies needed for transition specialists in vocational rehabilitation, vocational education, and special education. *Exceptional Children, 6*(21), 38–51.

Degener, T., & Koster-Dreese, Y. (Eds.). (1995). *Human rights and disabled persons: Essay and relevant human rights instruments.* Kluwer Academic Publishers.

Denney, M. K., Singer, G. H. S., Singer, J., Brenner, M. E., Okamoto, Y., & Fredeen, R. M. (2001). Mexican immigrant families' beliefs and goals for their infants in the neonatal intensive care unit. *Journal of the Association for Persons with Severe Handicaps. 26*(3) 148–157.

DeRuyter, F. (1995). Evaluating outcomes in assistive technology: Do we understand the commitment? *Assistive Technology, 7,* 3–15.

DeRuyter, F. (1997). The importance of outcome measures for assistive technology service delivery sys-tems. *Technology and Disability, 6,* 89–104.

DeRuyter, F. (2002). Outcomes and performance monitoring. In D. A. Olson and F. DeRuyter (Eds.), *Clinician's guide to assistive technology* (pp. 67–74). St. Louis: Mosby.

Deshler, D. D., Schumaker, J. B., Lenz, B. K., Bulgren, J. A., Hock, M. F., Knight, J., et al. (2001). Ensuring content-area learning by secondary students with learning disabilities. *Learning Disabilities Research & Practice, 16*, 96–108.

DeStefano, L., Heck, D., Hasazi, S., & Furney, K. (1999). Enhancing the implementation of the transition requirements of IDEA: A report on the policy forum on transition. *Career Development for Exceptional Individuals, 22*(1), 65–100.

Developmental Disabilities Assistance and Bill of Rights Act of 2000, Pub. L. No. 106-402, 42 U.S.C. § 15001, 15002, *et seq.* (2000).

Dew, D. W., & Peters, S. (2002). Survey of master's level rehabilitation counselor programs: Relationship to public vocational rehabilitation recruitment and retention of state vocational rehabilitation counselors. *Rehabilitation Education, 16*, 61–66.

Dinerstein, R., Herr, S., & O'Sullivan, J. (Eds.). (1999). *A guide to consent.* Washington DC: American Association on Mental Retardation.

Dobson, J. C., Williamson, M. L., Azen, C., & Koch, R. (1977). Intellectual assessment of 111 four-year-old children with phenylketonuria. *Pediatrics, 60*, 822.

Doe v. Arlington County, 41 F.Supp. 599 (ED. Va. 1999)

Donabedian, A. (1966). Evaluating the quality of medical care. *Milbank Memorial Fund Quarterly, 44*, 166–206.

Donnellan, A. M., Mirenda, P., Mesaros, R. A., & Fassbender, L. L. (1984). Analyzing the communicative functions of behavior. *Journal of the Association for Persons with Severe Handicaps, 9*, 201–212.

Dosen, A. (1993). Diagnosis and treatment of psychiatric and behavioral disorders in mentally retarded individuals: The state of the art. *Journal of Intellectual Disability Research, 37*(1), 1–7.

Douvanis, G., & Hulsey, D. (2002, August). *The Least Restrictive Environment Mandate: How has it been defined by the courts?* Arlington, VA: Council for Exceptional Children, ERIC Clearninghouse on Disabilities and Gifted Education.

Ducharme, G., Beeman, P., DeMarasse, R., & Ludlum, C. (1995). Building community one person at a time. In V. Bradley, J. Ashbaugh, & B. Blaney (Eds.), *Creating individual supports for people with developmental disabilities* (pp. 347–360). Baltimore: Paul H. Brookes.

Duhaney, L. M. G., & Salend, S. J. (2000). Parental perceptions of inclusive educational placements. *Remedial and Special Education, 21*(2), 121–128.

Dunlap, G., DePerczel, M., Clarke, S., Wilson, D., Wright, S., White, R., et al. (1994). Choice making to promote adaptive behavior for students with emotional and behavioral challenges. *Journal of Applied Behavior Analysis, 27*, 505–518.

Dunlap, G., & Kincaid, D. (2001). The widening world of functional assessment: Comments on four manuals and beyond. *Journal of Applied Behavior Analysis 34*(3), 365–377.

Dunst, C. J., & Rheingrover, R. (1981). An analysis of the efficacy of infant intervention programs with organically handicapped children. *Evaluation and Program Planning, 4*, 287–383.

Dunst, C. J., Trivette, C. M., & Cutspec, P. A. (2002, September). Toward an operational definition of evidence-based practices. *Centerscope, 1*, 1–10.

Dunst, C. Trivette, C., & Deal, A. (1988). *Enabling and empowering families: Principles and guidelines for practice.* Cambridge, MA: Brookline Books.

Dupont, A., Vaeth, M., & Videbeck, P. (1987). Mortality, life expectancy, and causes of death of mildly mentally retarded in Denmark. *Upsala Journal of Medical Sciences, Supplement, 44*, 76–82.

Durand, V. M. (1990). *Functional communication training: An intervention program for severe behavior problems.* New York: Guilford.

Durand, V. M. (1999). Functional communication training using assistive devices: Recruiting natural communities or reinforcement. *Journal of Applied Behavior Analysis 32*(3), 247–267.

Dybwad, G., & Bersani, H. A. (1996). *New voices: Self-advocacy by people with disabilities.* Cambridge, MA: Brookline Publishers.

Dykens, E., Hodapp, R., & Finucane, B. (2000). *Genetics and mental retardation syndromes: A new look at behavior and interventions.* Baltimore: Paul H. Brookes.

Dynarski, M., & Gleason, P. (2002). How can we help? What we have learned from recent federal dropout prevention evaluations. *Journal of Education for Students Placed at Risk, 7*(1), 43–69.

Early Childhood Outcomes Center. (2004, April). Considerations related to developing a system for measuring outcomes for young children with disabilities and their families. Retrieved August 18, 2004, from http://www.fpg.unc.edu/~eco/pages/publications.cfm

Early, D. M. & Winton, P. J. (2001). Preparing the workforce: Early childhood teacher preparation at 2– and 4–year institutions of higher education. *Early Childhood Research Quarterly, 16,* 285–306.

Edgerton, R. (1994). Quality of life issues: "Some people know how to be old." In M. M. Seltzer, M. W. Krauss, & M. Janicki (Eds.), *Life course perspectives on adulthood and old age* (pp. 53–66). Washington, DC: American Association on Mental Retardation.

Edgerton, R. B. (1981). Crime, deviance, and normalization: Reconsidered. In R. H. Bruininks, C. E. Meyers, B. B. Sigford, & K. C. Lakin (Eds.), *Deinstitutionalization and community adjustment of mentally retarded people* (pp. 146–166). Washington, DC: American Association on Mental Retardation.

Edmondson, B. (1988). Disability and sexual adjustment. In V. B. Van Hasselt, P. S. Strain, & M. Hersen (Eds.), *Handbook of developmental and physical disabilities* (pp. 91–106). Oxford, UK: Persimmon Press.

Education for All Handicapped Children Act of 1975, Pub. L. No. 94-142, 20 U.S.C. SS 1401 *et seq.* (2000).

Effective Compensation, Inc. (2001). Report for Colorado Department of Human Services, Developmental Disabilities Services, Staffing Stability Survey.

Eisenberg, A. (2002, June 20). A chip that mimics neurons, firing up the memory. *New York Times.* Retrieved November 21, 2004, from http://www.nytimes.com/2002/06/20/technology/circuits/20NEXT.html?ex=1025813651&ei=1&en=21f59dded2f9fad5

Eiserman, W. D., Weber, C., & McCoun, M. (1995). Parent and professional roles in early intervention: A longitudinal comparison of the effects of two intervention configurations. *Journal of Special Education, 29*(1), 20–44.

Elite Care. (2002). *Extended family residences, an alternative to assisted living: Oatfield Estates.* Retrieved November 21, 2004, from http://www.elite-care.com/oatfield.html

Elliott, J. L., & Thurlow, M. L. (2000). *Improving test performance of students with disabilities in district and state assessments.* Thousand Oaks, CA: Corwin Press.

Emergency Medical Treatment and Active Labor Act, 42 U.S.C. § 1395dd (2000).

Emerson, E., Robertson, J., Gregory, N., Kessissoglou, S., Hatton, C., Hallam, A., et al. (2000). The quality and costs of village communities, residential campuses and community-based residential supports in the UK. *American Journal on Mental Retardation, 105*(1), 81–102.

Emerson, E., Robertson, J., Hatton, C., Knapp, M., Walsh, P. N., & Hallam, A. (2005). Costs and outcomes of community residential supports in England. In R. Stancliffe & K. C. Lakin (Eds.), *Costs and outcomes of community services for persons with intellectual disabilities* (pp. 151–174). Baltimore: Paul H. Brookes.

Emerson, F., Moss, S., & Kiernan, C. (1999). The relationship between challenging behavior and psychiatric disorders in developmental disabilities and mental retardation. In N. Bouras (Ed.), *Psychiatric and behavioral disorders in developmental disabilities and mental retardation* (pp. 38–48). Cambridge, UK: Cambridge University Press.

Enders, A. (2003). *Technology and the employment of persons with disabilities.* Washington, DC: U.S. Department of Labor.

Epps, R. E., Pittelkow, M. R., & Su, W. P. (1995). TORCH syndrome. *Seminars in Dermatology, 14,* 179–86.

Erwin, E. J., Soodak, L. C., Winton, P. J., & Turnbull, A. P. (2001). "I wish it wouldn't all depend on me": Research on families and early childhood inclusion. In M. J. Guralnick (Ed.), *Early childhood inclusion: Focus on change* (pp. 127–158). Baltimore: Paul H. Brookes.

Essex, E. L., Seltzer, M. M., & Krauss, M. W. (1999). Differences in coping effectiveness and well-being among aging mothers and fathers of adults with retardation. *American Journal of Mental Retardation, 104*(6), 545–563.

Etmanski, A. (1996). *Safe and secure: Six steps to creating a personal future plan for people with disabilities.* Burnaby: British Columbia Planned Lifetime Advocacy Network.

European Association of Intellectual Disability Medicine. (2003). *The European manifesto: Basic standards of health care for people with intellectual disabilities.* Appeldoorn, Netherlands: Author.

Eustis, N. N., & Fischer, L. R. (1992). Common needs, different solutions? Younger and older home care clients. *Generations, 16,* 17–22.

Evans, G., Todd, S., Beyer, S., Felce, D., & Perry, J. (1994). Assessing the impact of the All Wales Mental Handicap Strategy: A survey of four districts. *Journal of Intellectual Disability Research, 38*(2), 109–133.

Evenhuis H. M. (1997). Medical aspects of ageing in a population with intellectual disabilities: III. Mobility, internal conditions and cancer. *Journal of Intellectual Disability Research, 41,* 8–18.

Evenhuis, H., Henderson, C. M., Beange, H., Lennox, N., & Chicoine, B. (2000). *Healthy aging. Adults with intellectual disabilities: Physical health issues.* Geneva: World Health Organization.

Evenhuis, H. M. & Nagtzaam, L. M. D. (Eds.), (1998). Early identification of hearing and visual impairment in children and adults with an intellectual disability. IASSID International Consensus Statement. SIRG Health Issues.

Everson, J. M., & Reid, D. H. (1999). *Person-centered planning and outcome management: Maximizing organizational effectiveness in supporting quality lifestyles among people with disabilities.* Morganton, NC: Habilitative Management Consultants, Inc.

Everson, J. M., & Zhang, D. (2000). Person-centered planning: Characteristics, inhibitors, and supports. *Education and Training in Mental Retardation and Developmental Disabilities, 35*(1), 36–43.

Executive Order 12994, Continuing the President's Committee on Mental Retardation and Its Membership and Responsibilities, March 21, 1996 (available at 1996 WL 133273).

Family Education Rights and Privacy Act of 1974, Pub .L. No. 93-380, 513, 20 U.S.C. § 1232g (2000).

Family and Medical Leave Act, 29 U.S.C. §§ 2601 *et seq.* (2000).

Farran, D. C. (1990). Effects of intervention with disadvantaged and disabled children: A decade review. In S. J. Meisels & J. P. Shonkoff (Eds.), *Handbook of early childhood intervention* (pp. 501–539). New York: Cambridge University Press.

Farran, D. C. (2000). Another decade of intervention for children who are low income or disabled: What do we know now? In J. P. Shonkoff & S .J. Meisels (Eds.), *Handbook of early childhood intervention* (2nd ed., pp. 510–548). New York: Cambridge University Press.

Farrell, E. (1990). *Hanging in and dropping out: Voices of at-risk high school students.* New York: Teachers College Press.

Fauchet, P. (2002, August). *Behavioral and biological sensing for aging in place at home.* Intel Conference on Computing, Cognition, and Caring for Future Elders.

Federal Government Procurement of Accessible Information Technology Act of 1998, Pub. L. No. 105-220 (2000).

Federal Register (January 22, 2001). *66* 14, 7249-7258. 34 CFR 361.

Feinstein C. S., & Caruso, G. (2003). Independent monitoring for quality: The Pennsylvania experience. In V. Bradley & M. Kimmich (Eds.), *Quality enhancement in developmental disabilities* (pp. 179–196). Baltimore: Paul H. Brookes.

Feinstein, C. S., Lemanowicz, J. A., & Conroy, J. W. (1988). *A survey of family satisfaction with regional treatment centers and community services to persons with mental retardation in Minnesota,* Welsch v. Gardebring *class members.* Philadelphia: Conroy & Feinstein Associates.

Felce, D., de Kock, U., & Repp, A. C. (1986). An eco-behavioral analysis of small community-based houses and traditional large hospitals for severely and profoundly mentally handicapped adults. *Applied Research in Mental Retardation, 7,* 393–408.

Felce, D., & Emerson, E. (2005). Community living costs outcomes and economies of scale: Findings from U.K. research. In R. Stancliffe & K. C. Lakin (Eds.), *Costs and outcomes of community services for persons with intellectual disabilities* (pp. 45–62). Baltimore: Paul H. Brookes.

Felce, D., Lowe, K., & Jones, E. (2002). Association between the provision characteristics and operation of supported housing services and resident outcomes. *Journal of Applied Research in Intellectual Disabilities, 15,* 404–418.

Fenton, J., Batavia, A., & Roody, D. (1993). *Constituency-oriented research and dissemination.* Washington, DC: National Institute on Disability and Rehabilitation Research.

Fernald, W. (1919). After care study of the patients discharged from Waverley for a period of twenty-five years. *Ungraded, 5*(1), 25–31.

Fernhall, B., Tymeson, G., Millar, A. L., & Burkett, L. N. (1989). Cardiovascular fitness testing and fitness levels of adolescents and adults with mental retardation including Down syndrome. *Education and Training in Mental Retardation, 24,* 133–138.

Festa, P. (2002, December 17). W3C Finalizes Disability Guidelines. *ZDNet.* Retrieved November 21, 2004, from http://zdnet.com.com/2100-1104-978272.html

Fetterman, D. M., Kaftarian, S. J., & Wandersman, A., (Eds.). (1996). *Empowerment evaluation: Knowledge and tools for self-assessment and accountability.* Thousand Oaks, CA: Sage.

Fichten, C. S., Barile, M., & Asuncion, J. V. (1999). *Learning technologies: adaptech project: Students with disabilities in postsecondary education.* Montreal, Quebec, Canada: Dawson College, Office of Learning Technologies Human Resources Development.

Field, S., Martin, J., Miller, R., Ward, M., & Wehmeyer, M. (1998). *A practical guide to teaching self-determination.* Austin, TX: PRO-ED.

Fields, T., Lakin, K. C., Seltzer, B., Backman, G., Sprague, D., Hinze, M., et al. (2000). *A guidebook on consumer controlled housing for Minnesotans with developmental disabilities.* St. Paul, MN: The Arc of Minnesota.

Finlay, W., & Lyons, E. (2002). Acquiescence in interviews with people who have mental retardation. *Mental Retardation, 40*(1), 14–29.

Fischer, G., & Sullivan, J. (2002). *Human-centered public transportation systems for persons with cognitive disabilities—Challenges and insights for participatory design.* Paper presented at the Participatory Design Conference (PDC'02), Malmö University, Sweden. Retrieved November 21, 2004, from http://www.cs.colorado.edu/~l3d/clever/assets/pdf/gf-pdc2002-mfa.pdf

Fisher, M., & Meyer, L. H. (2002). Development and social competence after two years for students enrolled in inclusive and self-contained educational programs. *Research & Practice for Persons with Severe Disabilities, 27*(3), 165–174.

Flanagan, S. A., Green, P. S., & Eustis, N. (1996, November). *Facilitating consumer-directed personal assistance services (CD-PAS) through the use of intermediary service models: Eleven states' experiences.* Paper presented at the annual meeting of the Gerontological Society of America, Washington, DC.

Fletcher, R. (1993). Mental illness and mental retardation in the United States: Policy and treatment challenges. *Journal of Intellectual Disability Research, 37*(1), 25–33.

Flower, D. (1994). Legal guardianship: The implications of law, procedure, and policy for the lives of persons with developmental disabilities. In M. F. Hayden & B. H. Abery (Eds.), *Challenges for a service system in transition: Ensuring quality community experiences for persons with developmental disabilities* (pp. 427–447). Baltimore: Paul H. Brookes.

Ford, A., Davern, L., & Schnorr, R. (2001). Learners with significant disabilities: Curricular relevance in an era of standards-based reform. *Remedial and Special Education, 22,* 214–222.

Forrester, A. (1996). Beyond job placement: The self employment boom. In N. Arnold (Ed.), *Self employment in vocational rehabilitation: Building on lessons from rural America* (pp. 1–5). Missoula: Rural Institute, University of Montana.

Foster, L., Brown, R., Carlson, B., Phillips, B., & Schore, J. (2001, June). *Cash and counseling: Customers' early experience in Arkansas and New Jersey.* Paper presented at the Independent Choices National Symposium on Consumer Direction and Self-Determination, Washington, DC.

Foster, L., Brown, R., Carlson, B., Phillips, B., & Schore, J. (2002). *Cash and counseling: Consumers' early experiences in Florida.* Washington, DC: Mathematical Policy Research.

Foster, L., Brown, R., Phillips, B., Schore, J., & Carlson, B. L. (2003, March 26). Improving the quality of Medicaid personal assistance through consumer direction. *Health Affairs,* 163–175, Retrieved May 15, 2005, from http://content.healthaffairs.org/cgi/content/abstract/hlthaff.w3.162v1

Fox, L., & Williams, D. G. (1992). Preparing teachers of students with severe disabilities. *Teacher Education and Special Education, 15,* 97–107.

Foxx, R. M., Faw, G. D., Taylor, S., Davis, P. K., & Fulia, R. (1993). "Would I be able to"? Teaching clients to assess the availability of their community living life style preferences. *American Journal on Mental Retardation, 98*(2), 235–248.

Frank, K. & Wade, P. (1993). Disabled student services in postsecondary education: Who's responsible for what? *Journal of College Student Development, 34,* 26–30.

Freedman, R., Griffiths, S., Krauss, M. W., & Seltzer, M. (1999). Patterns of respite use by aging mothers of adults with mental retardation. *Mental Retardation, 37*(2), 93–102.

Freedman, R. I. (2001). Ethical challenges in the conduct of research involving persons with mental retardation. *Mental Retardation, 39,* 130–141.

Frey, W., Brown, S.C., Rooney, R., & Brauen, M. (2003, June). *International classification of functioning, disability, and health (ICF): Implications for an early intervention data handbook.* Paper presented at the 9th North American Collaborating Conference on ICF, St Louis, MO.

Friedman, S. (1996). *Forming your own Limited Liability Company.* Chicago: Upstart Publishing Company.

Fujiura, G. T. (1998). Demography of family households. *American Journal on Mental Retardation, 103,* 225–235.

Fujiura, G. T. (2000). The implications of emerging demographics: A commentary on the meaning of race and income inequity to disability policy. *Journal of Disability Policy Studies, 11,* 66–75.

Fujiura, G. T. (2001). *Family demography: Emerging policy challenges.* Paper presented at the Invitational Research Symposium on Aging with Developmental Disabilities: Promoting Health Aging, Family Support, and Age-Friendly Communities, Chicago.

Fujiura, G. T., Fitzsimons, N., Marks, B., & Chicoine, B. (1997). Predictors of BMI among adults with Down syndrome: The social context of health promotion. *Research in Developmental Disabilities, 19,* 261–274.

Fujiura, G. T., Roccoforte, J. A., & Braddock, D. (1994). Costs of family care for adults with mental retardation and related developmental disabilities. *American Journal on Mental Retardation, 99*(3), 250–261.

Fujiura, G. T., & Yamaki, K. (2000). Trends in demography of childhood poverty and disability. *Exceptional Children, 66,* 187–199.

Furney, K. S., Hasazi, S. B., & DeStefano, L. (1997). Transition policies, practices, and promises: Lessons from three states. *Exceptional Children, 63*(3), 343–355.

Furniss, F., Lancioni, G., Rocha, N., Cunha, B., Seedhouse, P., Morato, P., et al. (2001). VICAID: Development and evaluation of a palmtop-based job aid for workers with severe developmental disabilities. *British Journal of Educational Technology, 32*(3), 277–287.

Furniss, F., & Ward, A. (1999). A palmtop-based job aid for workers with severe intellectual disabilities. *Technology and Disability, 10*(1), 53–67.

Gajar, A. (1992). University-based models for students with learning disabilities: The Pennsylvania State University in mode. In F. R. Rusch, L. DeStefano, J. G. Chadsey-Rusch, L. A. Phelps, & E. Szymanski (Eds.), *Transition from school in adult life: Models, linkages, and policy* (pp. 51–70). Sycamore, IL: Sycamore Publishing.

Galaburda, A. M. (1991). Neuropathologic correlates of learning disabilities. *Seminars in Neurology, 11,* 20–27.

Gallivan-Fenlon, A. (1994). Their senior year: Family and service provider perspectives on the transition from school to adult life for young adults with disabilities. *Journal of the Association for Persons with Severe Handicaps, 19*(1), 11–23.

Gardner, J. F., & Nudler, S. (Eds.) (1998). *Quality performance in human services: Leadership, values and vision.* Baltimore: Paul H. Brookes.

Gardner, W. I. (1998). Methods of gathering assessment information. In D. M. Griffiths, W. I. Gardner, & J. A. Nugent (Eds.), *Individual centered interventions: A multimodal functional approach* (pp. 67–76). Kingston, NY: NADD.

Gardner, W. I. (2002). *Aggression and other disruptive behavioral challenges: Biomedical and psychosocial assessment and treatment.* Kingston, NY: NADD Press.

Gardner, W. I., & Cole, C. L.(1987). Behavior treatment, behavior management and behavior control: Needed distinctions. *Behavior Residential Treatment, 2,* 37–53.

Gaventa, B., Simon, S. R., Norman-McNaney, R., & Amado, A. N. (2002). Faith communities and persons with developmental disabilities [Entire issue]. *IMPACT, 14*(3).

Gaventa, J. (1988). Participatory research in North America. *Convergence, 24,* 19–28.

Geenen, S., Powers, L., & Lopez-Vasquez, A. (2001). Multicultural aspects of parent involvement in transition planning. *Exceptional Children, 67*(2), 265–268.

George, M. J., & Baumeister, A. A. (1981). Employee withdrawl and job satisfaction in community residential facilities for mentally retarded persons. *American Journal on Mental Deficiency, 85,* 639–647.

German, S. L., Huber Marshall, L., & Martin, J. E. (1997). *Goal attainment through using the Take Action curriculum.* Colorado Springs: University of Colorado, Center for Self-Determination.

Gersten, R. (1998). Recent advances in instructional research for students with learning disabilities: An overview. *Learning Disabilities Practice, 13*(3), 162–170.

Gettings, R. (2003, January 5–8). *Integrating public policy and research on the outcomes of public policy.* Unpublished presentation at the Keeping the Promises Conference on National Goals, State of Knowledge, and Research Agenda for Persons with Intellectual and Developmental Disabilities, Washington, DC (quotation cited in The Arc of the U.S. [2003], *Keeping the promises: Findings and recommendations.* Silver Spring, MD: Author).

Gettings, R. M., & Smith, G. A. (1998). *Medicaid and systems change: Finding the fit.* Alexandria, VA: NASDDDS.

Getzel, L., & Wehman, P. (in press). *Going to college: Expanding opportunities for people with disabilities.* Baltimore: Paul H. Brookes.

Gilmore, D., & Butterworth, J. (1996). Work status trends for people with mental retardation. Boston: Institute for Community Inclusion (UAP), Children's Hospital.

Gilmore, D., & Butterworth, J. (2001). State trends in employment services for people with developmental disabilities. Retrieved from http://www.communityinclusion.org/programs/research/add/statetrends/about.htm

Gilson, S. F. (1996). Students with disabilities: An increasing voice and presence on college campuses. *Journal of Vocational Rehabilitation, 6,* 263–272.

Glasser, I. (1978). Prisoners of benevolence. In W. Gaylin, I. Glasser, S. Marcus, & D. Rothman (Eds.), *Doing good: The limits of benevolence* (pp. 97–170). New York: Pantheon Books.

Golden, J. (2003). *Self-directed support corporations (microboards).* Retrieved January 10, 2004, from http://www.self-determination.com/publications/microboard.html

Gomez, O. (2001). *Facilitating social interactions of adults with developmental disabilities in the community.* Unpublished doctoral dissertation, Lehigh University at Bethlehem, PA.

Good Start, Grow Smart: The Bush administration's early childhood initiative. (n.d.). Retrieved August 15, 2003 from http://www.whitehouse.gov/infocus/earlychildhood/earlychildhood.pdf

Gottlieb, B. (1998). Support groups. In H. S. Friedman (Ed.), *Encyclopedia of mental health* (vol. 3 pp. 635–648). San Francisco: Academic Press.

Gowdy, W. C., Zarfas, D. E. & Phipps, S. (1987). Audit of psychoactive drug prescriptions in group homes. *Mental Retardation, 25,* 331–334.

Gowen, J. W., Christy, D. S., & Sparling, J. (1993). Informational needs of parents of young children with special needs. *Journal of Early Intervention, 17*(2), 194–210.

Graham, A., & Reid, A. (2000). Physical fitness of adults with an intellectual disability: A 13-year follow-up study. *Research Quarterly for Exercise and Sport, 71,* 152–161.

Grealy, M. A., Johnson, D. A., & Rushton, S. K. (1999). Improving cognitive function after brain injury: The use of exercise and virtual reality. *Archives of Physical Medicine and Rehabilitation, 80*(6), 661–667.

Green, L. W., George, M. A., Daniel, M. Frankish, C. J., Herbert, C. J., Bowie, W. R., et al. (1995). *Study of participatory research in health promotion: Review and recommendations for the development of participatory research in health promotion in Canada.* Ottawa, Ontario: Royal Society of Canada.

Greer v. Rome City School District, 950 F.2d 688 (11th Cir. 1991).

Gretz, S. & Ploof, D. (Eds.) (1999). *The common thread: A collection of writings about friendships, relationships and community life.* Harrisburg: Pennsylvania Developmental Disabilities Council.

Griffin, C., & Hammis, D. (2003). *Making self-employment work for people with disabilities.* Baltimore: Paul H. Brookes.

Griffin, C. C. (1999a). Rural routes: Promising supported employment practices in America's frontier. In G. Revell, K. J. Inge, D. Mank, & P. Wehman (Eds.), *The impact of supported employment for people with significant disabilities* (pp. 38–56). Richmond: Virginia Commonwealth University, Rehabilitation Research and Training Center on Workplace Supports.

Griffin, C. C. (1999b). *Working Better, Working Smarter: Building Responsive Rehabilitation Programs.* St. Augustine, FL: TRN, Inc.

Griffiths, D. (1997). Waiting in the wings: Full report on a survey of caregivers with family members on the waiting list for residential services from the Massachusetts Department of Mental Retardation. Waltham, MA: Family to Family. Technical support provided by the Starr Center for Mental Retardation, Heller Graduate School, Brandeis University.

Griffiths, D. M., & Gardner, W. I. (2002a). Programs and intervention approaches for the treatment of persons with dual diagnosis: A summary. In J. W. Jacobson, S. Holburn, & J. A. Mulick (Eds.), *Contemporary dual diagnosis: MH/MR. Service Models. Vol. II: Partial and supportive services* (pp. 141–149). Kingston, NY: NADD.

Griffiths, D. M., & Gardner, W. I. (2002b). Residential and day programs for persons with dual diagnosis: A summary. In J. W. Jacobson, S. Holburn, & J. A. Mulick (Eds.), *Contemporary dual diagnosis: MH/MR. Service models. Vol. I: Residential and day programs* (pp. 123–139). Kingston, NY: NADD.

Griffiths, D. M., & Lunsky, Y. (2002). Changing attitudes towards the nature of socio-sexual assessment and education for persons with developmental disabilities: A twenty year comparison. *Journal on Developmental Disabilities, 71*(1), 16–33.

Grigal, M., Test, D. W., Beattie, J., & Wood, W. M. (1997). An evaluation of transition components of individualized education programs. *Exceptional Children, 63,* 357–372.

Guess, D., Benson, H. H., & Siegel-Causey, E. (1985). Concepts and issues related to choice-making and autonomy among persons with severe disabilities. *Journal of the Association for Persons with Severe Handicaps, 10*(2), 79–86.

Guralnick, M. J., & Groom, J. M. (1988). Peer interaction in mainstreamed and specialized classrooms: A comparative analysis. *Exceptional Children, 54*(5), 415–425.

Guralnick, M. J. (1997). Introduction: Directions for second-generation research. In M. J. Guralnick (Ed.), *The effectiveness of early intervention* (pp. xv–xvi). Baltimore: Paul H. Brookes.

Guralnick, M. J. (2002). Model service systems as research priorities in early intervention. *Journal of Early Intervention, 25,* 100–101.

Guthrie, R., & Susi, A. (1963). A simple phenylalanine method for detecting phenylketonuria in large populations of newborn infants. *Pediatrics, 32,* 338.

Guy, B., Goldberg, M., McDonald S., & Flom, R. (1997). Parental participation in transition systems change. *Career Development for Exceptional Individuals, 20*(2), 165–177.

Hacein-Bey-Abina, S., Le Deist, F., Carlier, F., Bouneaud, C., Hue, C., & De Villartay, J. P., et al. (2002). Sustained correction of X-linked severe combined immunodeficiency by ex vivo gene therapy. *New England Journal of Medicine, 346,* 1185–93.

Hagerman, R. J. (1999). *Neurodevelopmental disorders: Diagnosis and treatment.* Oxford University Press, New York.

Halpern, A. S. (1985). Transition: A look at the foundations. *Exceptional Children, 51,* 479–486.

Halpern, A. S., Close, D. W., & Nelson, D. J. (1986). *On my own: The impact of semi-independent living programs for adults with mental retardation.* Baltimore: Paul H. Brookes.

Hamblin-Wilson, C., & Thurman, S. K. (1990). The transition from early intervention to kindergarten: Parental satisfaction and involvement. *Journal of Early Intervention, 14*(1), 55–61.

Hammel, J. (2000). Assistive technology and environmental intervention (AT-EI) impact on the activity and life roles of aging adults with developmental disabilities: Findings and implications for practice. *Physical & Occupational Therapy in Geriatrics, 18*(1), 37–58.

Hammel, J., Lai, J., & Heller, T. (2002). Impact of assistive technology and environmental interventions on function and living situation status for people who are aging with developmental disabilities. *Disability and Rehabilitation, 24*(1–3), 93–105.

Hammis, D. & Griffin, C. C. (2002). *Social Security Considerations for Entrepreneurs with Significant Disabilities.* Florence, MT: Griffin-Hammis Associates, LLC.

Hamre-Nietupski, S., Nietupski, J., & Strathe, M. (1992). Functional life skills, academic skills, and friendship/social relationship development: What do parents of students with moderate/severe/profound disabilities value? *Journal of the Association for Persons with Severe Handicaps, 17*(1), 53–58.

Hanson, M. J., & Carta, J. J. (1995). Addressing the challenges of families with multiple risks. *Exceptional Children, 62*(3), 201–212.

Hanson, M. J., & Lynch, E. W. (2004). *Understanding families: Approaches to diversity, disability, and risk.* Baltimore: Paul H. Brookes.

Hanson, R. H., & Wieseler, N. A. (2002). The challenge of providing behavior supports and crisis response in the community. In R. H. Hanson, N. A. Wieseler, & K. C. Lakin (Eds.), *Crisis prevention and response in the community* (pp. 33–47). Washington DC: AAMR.

Harbin, G., Rous, B., & McLean, M. (2004, August). *Issues in defining state accountability systems.* Chapel Hill, NC: University of North Carolina, FPG Child Development Institute.

Hard, S. (1986 September). *Sexual abuse of the developmentally disabled: A case study.* Paper presented at the National Conference of Executives of Associations for Retarded Citizens, Omaha, NE.

Haring, T., Breen, C., Pitts-Conway, V., Lee, M., & Gaylord-Ross, R. (1987). Adolescent peer tutoring and special friend experiences. *Journal of the Association for Persons with Severe Handicaps, 12,* 280–286.

Harlan-Simmons, J., Holtz, P., Todd, J., & Mooney, M. (2001). Building social relationships through valued roles: Three older adults and the Community Membership Project. *Mental Retardation, 39*(3), 171–180.

Harniss, M. K., Dickson, S. V., Kinder, D., & Hollenbeck, K. L. (2001). Textual problems and instructional solutions: Strategies for enhancing learning from published history textbooks. *Reading and Writing Quarterly, 17,* 127–151.

Harry, B. (1992). *Cultural diversity, families, and the special education system: Communication and empowerment*. New York: Teachers College Press.

Harry, B., Allen, N., & McLaughlin, M. (1995a). Communication versus compliance: African-American parents' involvement in special education. *Exceptional Children, 61*, 364–377.

Harry, B., Allen, N., & McLaughlin, M. (1995b). *Communication versus reciprocity with families: Case studies in special education*. Baltimore: Paul H. Brookes.

Harry, B., Kalyanpur, M., and Day, M. (1999). *Building cultural reciprocity with families: Case studies in special education*. Baltimore: Paul H. Brookes.

Harry, B., Rueda, R., & Kalyanpur, M. (1999). Cultural reciprocity in sociocultural perspective: Adapting the normalization principle for family collaboration. *Exceptional Children, 66*(1), 123–136.

Hart, D. (2002). *Status of postsecondary education and persons with mental retardation*. National Center for the Study of Postsecondary Education Supports (NCSPES). Honolulu: University of Hawaii.

Hart, T., Hawkey, K., & Whyte, J. (2002). Use of a portable voice organizer to remember therapy goals in traumatic brain injury rehabilitation: A within subjects trial. *Journal of Head Trauma Rehabilitation, 17*(6), 556–570.

Hartmann v. Loudoun County Board of Education (4th Cir. 1997). Available from http://www.law.emory.edu/4circuit/july97/962809.p.html

Hasle, H., Clemmensen, I. H., & Mikkelsen, M. (2000). Risks of leukemia and solid tumors in individuals with Down syndrome. *Lancet, 355,* 165–169.

Hasazi, S., Gordon, L., & Roe, C. (1985). Factors associated with the employment status of handicapped youth exiting high school from 1979 to 1983. *Exceptional Children*, 51, 456–469.

Hasazi, S. B., Furney, K. S., & DeStefano, L. (1999). Implementing the IDEA transition mandates. *Exceptional Child, 65*(4), 555–566.

Hasazi, S. B., Gordon, L. R., & Roe, C. A. (1985). Factors associated with the employment status of handicapped youth exiting high school from 1979–1983. *Exceptional Children, 51*, 455–469.

Hayden, M., & Abery, B. (Eds.). (1994). *Challenges for a service system in transition*. Baltimore: Paul H. Brookes.

Hayden, M. F., & Heller, T. (1997). Support, problem-solving/coping ability, and personal burden of younger and older caregivers of adults with mental retardation. *Mental Retardation, 35*, 364–372.

Hayden, M., Lakin, K. C., Hill, B., Bruininks, R. H., & Chen, T. H. (1992). Social and leisure integration of people with mental retardation who reside in foster homes and small group homes. *Education and Training in Mental Retardation, 30*(2), 53–62.

Hayden, M. F., & Nelis, T. (2002). Self-advocacy. In R. L. Schalock, P. S. Baker, & M. D. Croser (Eds.), *Embarking on a new century: Mental retardation at the end of the 20th century* (pp. 221–234). Washington, DC: American Association on Mental Retardation.

Hayden, M. F. & Senese, D. (1996). *Self-advocacy groups: 1996 Directory for North America*. Minneapolis, MN: University of Minnesota, Research and Training Center on Community Living, Institute on Community Integration.

Hayes, C. D., Lipoff, E., & Danegger, A. E. (1995). *Compendium of comprehesnive, community-based initiatiaves: A look at costs, benefits, and financing strategies*. Washington, DC: The Finance Report.

Hayward, B., & Schmidt-Davis, H. (2000). A longitudinal study of the vocational rehabilitation service program. *Rehabilitation Services Administration, U.S. Department of Education, Fourth Interim Report: Characteristics and outcomes of transitional youth in vocational rehabilitation*. Washington, DC: Research Triangle Institute.

Health Care Financing Administration (1998). Management review of California Home and Community Based Waiver Program for persons with mental retardation and developmental disabilities. San Francisco: HCFA Regional IX Office.

Health Insurance Portability and Accountability Act, Pub. L. No. 104-191, 29 U.S.C. §§ 1181 *et seq.* and 42 U.S.C. §§ 300gg-5 *et seq.*(2000).

Helff, C. M., & Glidden, L. M. (1998). More positive or less negative? Trends in research on adjustment of families rearing children with developmental disabilities. *Mental Retardation, 36*(6), 457–464.

Heller, T. & Factor, A. (1993a). Aging family caregivers: Changes in burden and placement desire. American Journal on Mental Retardation, 98, 417–426.

Heller, T., & Factor, A. (1993b). Support systems, well-being, and placement decision-making among older parents and their adult children with developmental disabilities. In F. Sutton, A. Factor, B. Hawkins, T. Heller, & G. Seltzer (Eds.), *Older adults with developmental disabilities: Optimizing choice and change* (pp. 107–122). Baltimore: Paul H. Brookes.

Heller, T., Factor, A. R., Hsieh, K., & Hahn, J. E. (1998). The impact of age and transitions out of nursing homes for adults with developmental disabilities. *American Journal on Mental Retardation, 103,* 236–248.

Heller, T., Hsieh, K., & Rimmer, J. (2004). Attitudinal and psychological outcomes of a fitness and health education program on adults with Down syndrome. *American Journal on Mental Retardation, 109*(2), 175–185.

Heller, T., Janicki, M., Hammel, J., & Factor, A. (2002). Promoting healthy aging, family support, and age-friendly communities for persons aging with developmental disabilities: Report of the 2001 Invitational Research Symposium on Aging with Developmental Disabilities. Chicago, IL: University of Illinois at Chicago, RRTC on Aging and Developmental Disabilities.

Heller, T., Marks, B., & Ailey, S. (2004). Exercise and Nutrition Health Education Curriculum for Adults with Developmental Disabilities. Chicago: University of Illinois at Chicago, Rehabilitation Research and Training Center on Aging with Developmental Disabilities.

Heller, T., Miller, A. B., & Factor, A. (1997). Adults with mental retardation as supports to their parents: Effects on parental caregiving appraisal. *Mental Retardation, 35,* 338–346.

Heller, T., Miller, A. B., & Hsieh, K. (1999). Impact of a consumer-directed family support program on adults with disabilities. *Family Relations, 48,* 419–427.

Heller, T., Ruch-Ross, H., & Kopnick, N. (1995). *The Illinois Home Based Support Services Program evaluation report.* (Public Policy Monograph Series). Chicago: University of Illinois at Chicago, Institute on Disability and Human Development.

Helmstetter, E., Curry, C. A., Brennan, M., & Sampson-Saul, M. (1998). Comparison of general and special education classrooms of students with severe disabilities. *Education and Treatment in Mental Retardation and Developmental Disabilities, 33*(3), 216–227.

Hemmeter, M. L. (2000). Classroom-based interventions: Evaluating the past and looking toward the future. *Topics in Early Childhood Special Education, 20,* 56–61.

Hemmeter, M. L., Santos, R. M., & Ostrosky, M. M. (2004, December). *Faculty and practitioners' assessment of current practice and training needs related to young children's social emotional development and challenging behavior.* Paper presented at the Annual Conference of the Division for Early Childhood, Chicago, IL.

Henderson, C. M. (2002). *Syndrome-specific health compromises: Framing the questions for research.* Paper presented at the Tampa Scientific Conference on Intellectual Disability, Aging, and Health. Tampa, FL, December 6–9, 2002.

Herman, S. E. (1991). Use and impact of a cash subsidy program. *Mental Retardation, 29,* 253–258.

Herman, S. E., & Hazel, K. L. (1991). Evaluation of family support services: Changes in availability and accessibility. *Mental Retardation, 29,* 351–357.

Hewitt, A., & Lakin, K. C. (2001). Issues in the direct support workforce and their connections to the growth, sustainability, and quality of community supports. Manuscript prepared for the Health Care Financing Administration and the National Project on Self-Determination for People with Developmental Disabilities. Baltimore, MD.

Hewitt, A., & Larson, A. (2004). *Kansas Mobilizing for Change Final Report.* Topeka, KS: Kansas Council on Developmental Disabilities.

Hewitt, A., Larson, S. A., & Lakin, K. C. (2000). *An independent evaluation of the quality of services and system performance of Minnesota's Medicaid Home and Community Based Services for persons with mental retardation and related conditions: Technical report.* Minneapolis, MN: University of Minnesota, Research and Training Center on Community Living.

Hewitt, A., Larson, S. A., O'Nell, S., Sauer, J., & Sedlezky, L (1998). *The Minnesota frontline supervisor competencies and performance indicators: A tool for agencies providing community services.* Minneapolis, MN: University of Minnesota, Research and Training Center on Community Living.

Hewitt, A., Larson, S., Sauer, J., Anderson, L., & O'Nell, S. (2001). *Partnerships for success: Retaining incumbent community support human service workers by upgrading their skills and strengthening partnerships among workforce centers, educational programs, and private businesses.* Minneapolis, MN: University of Minnesota: Research and Training Center on Community Living.

Hill, B. K., Lakin, K. C., Bruininks, R. H., Amado, A. N., Anderson, D. J., & Copher, J. I. (1989). *Living in the community: A comparative study of foster homes and small group homes for people with mental retardation.* Minneapolis, MN: University of Minnesota, Research and Training Center Community Living.

Hoffman, A., & Field, S. (1995). Promoting self-determination through effective curriculum development. *Intervention in School and Clinic, 30*(2), 134–141.

Hoge, G., & Dattilo, J. (1995). Recreation participation of adults with and without mental retardation. *Education and Training in Mental Retardation and Developmental Disabilities, 30,* 283–298.

Holburn, S., & Vietze, P. M. (Eds.) (2002). *Person-centered planning: Research, planning and future directions.* Baltimore: Paul H. Brookes.

Holman, J., & Bruininks, R. (1985). Assessing and training adaptive behaviors. In K. C. Lakin & R. Bruininks (Eds.), *Strategies for achieving community integration of developmentally disabled citizens* (pp. 73–104). Baltimore: Paul H. Brookes.

Holroyd, J. (1987). *Questionnaire on Resources and Stress for Families with Chronically Ill or Handicapped Members.* Brandon, VT: Clinical Psychology.

Horn, R., & Berktold, J. (1999). Students with disabilities in postsecondary education: A profile of preparation, participation, and outcomes. National Center on Education Statistics, U.S. Department of Education, Statistical Analysis Report No. 199-187. Washington, DC: U.S. Government Printing Office.

Horner, R. H. (1990). Ideology, technology and typical community settings: The use of severe aversive stimuli. *American Journal of Mental Retardation, 28*(4), 166–168.

Horner, R. H. (2000). Positive behavior supports. *Focus on Autism and Other Developmental Disabilities, 15*(2), 97–105.

Horner, R. H., & Carr, E. G. (1997). Behavioral support for students with severe disabilities: Functional assessment and comprehensive intervention. *Journal of Special Education, 31*(1), 84–104.

Horner, R. H., Stoner, S. K., & Ferguson, D. L. (1988). *An activity-based analysis of deinstitutionalization: The effects of community re-entry on the lives of residents leaving Oregon's Fairview Training Center.* Eugene, OR: University of Oregon, Specialized Training Program, Center on Human Development.

Horowitz, S. M., Kerker, B. D., Owens, P. L., & Zigler, E. (2000). *The health status of individuals with mental retardation.* New Haven: Yale University Press.

Hosak, K., & Malkmus, D. (1992). Vocational rehabilitation of persons with disabilities: Family inclusion. *Journal of Vocational Rehabilitation, 2*(3), 11–17.

Houghton, J., Bronicki, G. J. B., & Guess, D. (1987). Opportunities to express preferences and make choices among students with severe disabilities in classroom settings. *Journal of the Association for Persons with Severe Handicaps, 12*(1), 18–27.

Houtenville, A. J. (2004). "Disability Statistics in the United States." Ithaca, NY: Cornell University Rehabilitation Research and Training Center, www.disabilitystatistics.org. Posted May 15, 2003. Accessed December 9, 2004.

Houtenville, A. J. C. (2001). *Disability and employment in the USA: National overview based on 2000 Census*. Ithica, NY: Cornell University, Rehabilitation Research and Training Center for Economic Research on Employment Policy for Persons with Disabilities.

Hoyert, D. L., & Seltzer, M. M. (1992). Factors related to the well-being and life activities of family caregivers. *Family Relations, 41*(1), 74–81.

Hunt, P., Farron-Davis, F., Beckstead, S., Curtis, D., & Goertz, L. (1994). Evaluating the effects of placement of students with severe disabilities in general education versus special classes. *Journal of the Association for Persons with Severe Handicaps, 19*(3), 200–214.

Hunt, P., Farron-Davis, F., Wrenn, M., Hirose-Hatae, A., & Goetz, L. (1997). Promoting interactive partnerships in inclusive educational settings. *Journal of the Association for Persons with Severe Handicaps, 22*(3), 127–137.

Hurley, A. D. (1996). Vocational rehabilitation approaches to support adults with mental retardation. *Habilitative Mental Healthcare Newsletter, 15*(2), 29–33.

Hutchison, P. (1990). *Making friends: Developing relationships between people with a disability and other members of the community*. Toronto, Canada: Roeher Institute.

Hyson, M. (Ed.) (2003). *Preparing early childhood professionals: NAEYC's standards for programs*. Washington, DC: NAEYC.

Iacono, T., & Murray, V. (2003). Issues of informed consent in conducting medical research involving people with intellectual disability. *Journal of Applied Research in Intellectual Disabilities, 16*, 41–51.

Indian Child Welfare Act, Pub. L. No. 95-608, 25 U.S.C. §§ 1901 *et seq.* (2000).

Individuals with Disabilities Education Act (IDEA) of 1990, Pub. L. No. 101-476, 20 U.S.C. §§ 1400 *et seq.* (2000).

Individuals with Disabilities Education Act Amendments of 1997, Pub. L. No. 105-17, 20 U.S.C. §§ 651, 1400, 1401. (2000).

Individuals with Disabilities Education Improvement Act of 2004, Pub. L. No. 108-466. (2000).

Institute on Rehabilitation Issues. (2001). *Succession planning: Building a successful organization in a dynamic environment*. Menomonie, WI: University of Wisconsin-Stout Vocational Rehabilitation Institute.

Irvin, L. K., Thorin, E., & Singer, G. H. (1993). Family related roles and considerations: Transition to adulthood by youth with developmental disabilities. *Journal of Vocational Rehabilitation, 3*(2), 38–46.

Israel, B., Schultz, A. J., Parker, E. A., & Becker, A. B. (2001). Review of community-based research: Assessing partnership approaches to improve public health. *Annual Review of Public Health, 19*, 173–202.

Ittenbach, R. F., Abery, B. H., Larson, S. A., Spiegel, A. N., & Prouty, R. W. (1994). Community adjustment of young adults with mental retardation: Overcoming barriers to inclusion. *Palaestra, 10*(2), 32–42.

Ittenbach, R. F., Larson, S. A., Speigel, A. N., Abery, B. H., & Prouty, R. W. (1993). Community adjustment of young adults with mental retardation: A developmental perspective. *Palaestra, 9*(4), 19–24.

Iwata, B. A., Dorsey. M. Slifer, K. J., Bauman, K. E., & Richman, G. S. (1982). Toward a functional analysis of self-injury. *Analysis and Intervention in Developmental Disabilities, 2*, 3–20. Reprinted 1994 in *Journal of Applied Behavior Analysis, 27*, 197–209.

Iwata, B. A., Pace, G. M., Dorsey, M. F., Zarcone, J. R., Vollmer, T. R., Smith, R. G., et al. (1994). The functions of self-injurious behavior: An experimental-epidemiological analysis. *Journal of Applied Behavior Analysis, 27*, 215–240.

Izzo, M., & Lamb, P. (2002). *Self-determination and career development: Skills for successful transition to postsecondary education and employment*. A white paper developed for the National Center on Postsecondary Education Supports, University of Hawaii at Manoa.

Jacobson, J. W. (1996). Rehabilitation services for people with mental retardation and psychiatric disabilities: Dilemmas and solutions for public policy. *Journal of Rehabilitation, 62*, 11–22.

Jacobson, J. W., & Ackerman, L. J. (1988). An appraisal of services for persons with mental retardation and psychiatric impairments. *Mental Retardation, 26,* 377–380.

Janney, R., Snell, M., & Elliot, J. (2000). *Behavioral support.* Baltimore: Paul H. Brookes.

Janicki, M. P., Dalton, A. J., Henderson, C. M., & Davidson, P. W. (1999). Mortality and morbidity among older adults with intellectual disability: Health services considerations. *Disability and Rehabilitation, 21,* 284–294.

Janicki, M. P., Heller, T., Seltzer, G., & Hogg, J. (1996). Practice guidelines for the clinical assessment and care management of Alzheimer's disease and other dementias among adults with intellectual disability. *Journal of Intellectual Disability Research, 40,* 374–382.

Jaskulski, T., Lakin, K. C., & Zierman, S. A. (1995). *Journey to inclusion: A resource for state policy makers.* Washington, DC: President's Committee on Mental Retardation.

Job Accommodation Network (JAN) (1995). *Job Accommodation Network annual report: October 1, 1992 through September 30, 1993.* Morgantown, WV: Author.

Job Training Partnership Act (JTPA) of 1982, Pub. L. No. 97-300, 29 U.S.C. §§ 1501, *et seq.* (2000).

Johnson, D. R., Bruininks, R. H., & Thurlow, M. L. (1987). Meeting the challenge of transition service planning through improved interagency cooperation. *Exceptional Children, 53,* 522–530.

Johnson, D. R., & Sharpe, M. N. (2000). Results of a national survey on the implementation of transition service requirements of IDEA. *Journal of Special Education Leadership, 13*(2), 15–26.

Johnson, D. R., Stodden, R., Emanuel, E., Luecking, R., & Mack, M. (2002). Current challenges facing secondary education and transition services: What research tells us. *Exceptional Children, 68*(4), 19–53.

Johnson, J. & Duffett, A. (2002). *When it's your own child: A report on special education from families who use it.* New York: Public Agenda.

Johnson, K., Andrew, R., & Topp, V. (1998). *Silent Victims: A study of people with intellectual disabilities as victims of crime.* Victoria, Canada: Office of the Public Advocate.

Johnson, T. F. (1995). Aging well in contemporary society: Introduction. American Behavioral Scientist, *39*(2), 120–130.

Johnson, V. A., Greenwood, R., & Schriner, K. F. (1988). Work performance and work personality: Employer concerns about workers with disabilities. *Rehabilitation Counseling Bulletin, 32,* 50–57.

Jones, P., Conroy, J., Feinstein, C., & Lemancowicz, J. (1983). A matched comparison study of cost-effectiveness: Institutionalized and deinstitutionalized people. *Journal of the Association for Persons with Severe Handicaps, 9,* 304–313.

Jordan, B., & Dunlap, G. (2001). Construction of adulthood and disability. *Mental Retardation, 39*(4), 286–296.

Kaiser, A. P., & McWhorter, C. M. (Eds.). (1990). *Preparing personnel to work with persons with severe disabilities.* Baltimore: Paul H. Brookes.

Kalachnik, J. E. (1999). Monitoring psychotropic medication: Neurobehavioral mechanisms of drug action. In N. A. Wieseler & R. H. Hanson (Eds.), *Challenging behaviors of persons with mental health disorders and severe developmental disabilities* (pp. 151–204). Washington, DC: AAMR.

Kalyanpur, M. & Harry, B. (1999). *Culture in special education: Building reciprocal family-professional relationships.* Baltimore: Paul H. Brookes.

Kame'enui, E. J., & Carnine, D. (1998). *Effective teaching strategies that accommodate diverse learners.* Upper Saddle River, NJ: Prentice-Hall.

Kamps, D., Royer, J., Dugan, E., Kravitz, T., Gonzalez-Lopez, A., Garcia, J., et al. (2002). Peer training to facilitate social interaction for elementary students with autism and their peers. *Exceptional Children, 68*(2), 173–187.

Kapell, D., Nightengale, B., Rodriguez, A., Lee, J. H., Zigman, W. B. & Schupf, N. (1998). Prevalence of chronic medical conditions in adults with mental retardation: Comparison with the general population. *Mental Retardation, 36,* 269–279.

Kaufmann, W. E., & Galaburda, A. M. (1989). Cerebrocortical microdysgenesis in neurologically normal subjects: A histopathologic study. *Neurology, 39*(2, Pt. 1), 238–44.

Kaufmann, W. E., & Worley, P. F. (1999). Neural activity and immediate early gene expression in the cerebral cortex. *Mental Retardation and Developmental Disabilities Research Reviews, 5,* 41–50.

Kautz, H., Etzioni, O., Borriello, G., Fox, D., Arnstein, L., Ostendorf, M., & Logsdon, R. (2001). *Assisted cognition: Computer aids for people with Alzheimer's Disease.* Unpublished manuscript. Seattle, WA.

Kaye, H. S. (2000). Computer and internet use among people with disabilities. *Disability Statistics Report* (13). Washington, DC: U.S. Department of Education, National Institute on Disability and Rehabilitation Research.

Kearny, G. M., Krishnan, V. H. R., & Londhe, R. L. (1993). Characteristics of elderly people with a mental handicap living in a mental handicap hospital: A descriptive study. *British Journal of Developmental Disability, 76,* 31–50.

Kemp, C. E., & Parette, H. P. (2000). Barriers to minority family involvement in assistive technology decision-making processes. *Education and Training in Mental Retardation, 35*(4), 384–392.

Kempton, W. & Stanfield, J. (Producers). (1998). *Speaking of sex...and persons with special needs* [video-recording]. Santa Monica, CA: James Stanfield and Company.

Kennedy, C., & Haring, T. (1993). Teaching choice making during social interactions to students with profound multiple disabilities. *Journal of Applied Behavior Analysis, 26,* 63–76.

Kim, S., Larson, S., & Lakin, K. C. (2001). Behavioral outcomes of deinstitutionalization of people with intellectual disabilities: A review of U.S. studies conducted between 1980 and 1999. *Journal of Intellectual and Developmental Disabilities, 26*(1), 35–50.

Kimmich, M. (2003). Trends in quality assurance and outcome monitoring. In V. Bradley & M. Kimmich (Eds.), *Quality enhancement in developmental disabilities* (pp. 19–28). Baltimore: Paul H. Brookes.

Kincaid, D., & Fox, L. (2002). Person-centered planning and positive behavior support. In S. Holburn & P. Vietze (Eds.), *Research and practice in person-centered planning* (pp. 29–50). Baltimore: Paul H. Brookes.

Kishi, G. S., & Meyer, L. H. (1994). What children report and remember: A six-year follow-up of the effects of social contact between peers with and without severe disabilities. *Journal of the Association for Persons with Severe Handicaps, 19,* 277–289.

Kishi, G., Teelucksingh, B., Zollers, N., Park-Lee, S., & Meyer, L. (1988). Daily decision-making in community residences: A social comparison of adults with and without mental retardation. *American Journal of Mental Retardation, 92*(5), 430–435.

Kleinert, H. J., Kearns, J. F., Costello, K., Nowak- Drabik, K., Garrett, M., Horvath, L., et al. (1999). *Research on the impact of alternate assessments: Practical implications for teachers.* Louisville, KY: University of Kentucky.

Kleinert, H. L., & Kearns, J. F. (2001). *Alternate assessment: Measuring outcomes and supports for students with disabilities.* Baltimore: Paul H. Brookes.

Kleinert, H. L., Kennedy, S., & Kearns, J. F. (1999). The impact of alternate assessments: A statewide teacher survey. *The Journal of Special Education, 3*(2), 93–102.

Klintsova, A. Y., Goodlett, C. R., & Greenough, W. T. (2000). Therapeutic motor training ameliorates cerebellar effects of postnatal binge alcohol. *Neurotoxicol Teratol., 22,* 125–132.

Knobbe, C. A., Carey, S., Rhodes, L., & Horner, R. (1995). Benefit-cost analysis of community residential versus institutional services for adults with severe mental retardation and challenging behavior. *American Journal on Mental Retardation, 99*(5), 533–541.

Kochanek, T. T. & Buka, S. L. (1998). Influential factors in the utilization of early intervention services. *Journal of Early Intervention, 21,* 323–338.

Koegel, L., Harrower, J. K., & Koegel, R. L. (1999). Support for children with developmental disabilities in full inclusion classrooms through self-management. *Journal of Positive Behavioral Interventions, 1*(1), 126–134.

Koegel, L. K., & Koegel, R. L. (1995). Motivating communication in children with autism. In E. Schopler & G. B. Mesibov (Eds.), *Learning and cognition in autism* (pp. 73–87). New York: Plenum.

Koegel, L. K., Koegel, R. L., & Dunlap, G. (Eds.) (1996). *Positive behavioral support: Including people with difficult behavior in the community.* Baltimore: Paul H. Brookes.

Kohler, P. D. (1993). Best practices in transition: Substantiated or implied? *Career Development for Exceptional Individuals, 16,* 107–121.

Komissar, C., Hart, D., & Friedlander, R. (1996). *Utilizing all your resources: Individuals with and without disabilities volunteering together.* Boston: Institute for Community Inclusion.

Komissar, C., Hart, D., Friedlander, R., Paiewonsky, M., & Tufts, S. (1997). *Don't forget the fun.* Boston: Institute for Community Inclusion.

Koren, P. E., DeChillo, N., & Friesen, B. (1992). Measuring empowerment in families whose children have emotional disabilities: A brief questionnaire. *Rehabilitation Psychology, 37*(4), 305–321.

Kraemer, B. R., & Blacher, J. (2001). Transition for young adults with severe mental retardation: School preparation, parent expectations, and family involvement. *Mental Retardation, 39*(6), 423–435.

Krain, M. A. (1995). Policy implications for a society aging well: Employment, retirement, education, and leisure policies for the 21st century. *American Behavioral Scientist, 39*(2), 131–151.

Krauss, M. J., Greenberg, J. S., Seltzer, M. M., Chou, R. J., & Hong, J. (2001). Caregiver well-being among mothers of adults with disabilities. Paper presented at the Invitational Research Symposium on Aging with Developmental Disabilities: Promoting healthy aging, family support, and age-friendly communities. Chicago: University of Illinois at Chicago, RRTC on Aging with Developmental Disabilities.

Krauss, M. W., & Erickson, M. E. (1988). Informal support networks among aging mentally retarded persons: Results from a pilot study. *Mental Retardation, 26*(4), 197–201.

Krauss, M. W., & Seltzer, M. M. (1986). Comparison of elderly and adult mentally retarded persons in community and institutional settings. *American Journal of Mental Deficiency, 91*(3), 237–243.

Krauss, M. W., & Seltzer, M. M. (1993). Current well-being and future plans of older caregiving mothers. *Irish Journal of Psychology, 14*(1), 48–63.

Krauss, M. W., Seltzer, M. M, & Goodman, S. (1992). Social support networks for adults with retardation who live at home. *American Journal on Mental Retardation, 96*(4), 432–441.

Krauss, M. W., Seltzer, M. M., Gordon, R., & Friedman, D. H. (1996). Binding ties: The roles of adult siblings of persons with mental retardation. *Mental Retardation, 34*(2), 83–93.

Kregel, J. & Dean, D. H. (2002). Sheltered work vs. supported employment: A direct comparison of long-term earnings outcomes for individuals with cognitive disabilities. In J. Kregel, D. H. Dean, & P. Wehman (Eds.), *Achievements and challenges in employment services for people with disabilities: The longitudinal impact of workplace supports* (pp. 63–83). Richmond: Virginia Commonwealth University, Rehabilitation Research and Training Center on Workplace Supports.

Kretzman, J. & McKnight, L. (1993). *Building communities from the inside out: A path toward finding and mobilizing a community's assets.* Evanston, IL: Northwestern University, Institute on Policy Research.

Kumpfer, K. L., & Alvarado, R. (1998, November). Effective family strengthening interventions. *Juvenile Justice Bulletin.*

Kurzweil, R. (1990). *The age of intelligent machines.* Cambridge, MA: MIT Press.

Kurzweil, R. (1999). *The age of spiritual machines: When computers exceed human intelligence.* New York: Viking.

Kurzweil, R. (2002, November 7). The intelligent universe. *The Edge.* Retrieved November 21, 2004, from http://www.edge.org/3rd_culture/kurzweil02/kurzweil02_print.html

Lakin, K. C., Anderson, L., & Prouty, B. K. (1998). Decreases continue in out-of-home residential placement of children and youth with mental retardation. *Mental Retardation, 36*(2), 165–168.

Lakin, K. C., & Bruininks, R. H. (1981). *Occupational stability of direct care staff in residential services for mentally retarded people.* Minneapolis, MN: University of Minnesota, Research and Training Center on Community Living.

Lakin, K. C., Bruininks, R. H., Hill, B. K., & Hauber, F. (1982). Turnover of direct care staff in a national sample of residential facilities for mentally retarded people. *American Journal of Mental Deficiency, 87*(1), 69–72.

Lakin, K. C., Burwell, B. O., Hayden, M. F., & Jackson, M. E. (1992). *An independent assessment of Minnesota's Medicaid Home and Community Based Services waiver program.* Minneapolis, MN: University of Minnesota, Research and Training Center on Community Living.

Lakin, K. C., Hill, B. K., & Anderson, D. J. (1991). Persons with mental retardation in nursing homes in 1977 and 1985. *Mental Retardation, 29*(1), 25–33.

Lakin, K. C., Polister, B., & Prouty, R. W. (2003). Wages of non-state direct-support professionals lag far behind those of public direct-support professionals and the general workforce. *Mental Retardation, 41*(2), 141–146.

Lakin, K. C., Prouty, R., & Smith, G. (1993). Quality assurance in developmental disabilities [Entire issue]. *IMPACT, 6*(2).

Lakin, K. C., Smith, J., Prouty, R., & Polister, B. (2001). State institutions during the 1990s: Changes in the number of facilities, average daily populations, and expenditures between fiscal years 1991 and 2000. *Mental Retardation, 39*(1), 72–75.

Lakin, K. C., & Smull, M. (1995). Supported living [Entire issue]. *IMPACT, 8*(4).

Lamb-Parker, F., Greenfield, D. B., Fantuzzo, J. W., Clark, C., & Coolahan, K. C. (2002). Shared decision making in early childhood research: A foundation for successful community-university partnerships. In F. Lamb-Parker & C. G. Powell (Eds.), *NHSA Dialog: A Research-to-Practice Journal for the Early Intervention Field, 5*(2 & 3), 356–377.

Lancioni, G. E., & Oliva, D. (1999). Using an orientation system for indoor travel and activity with persons with multiple disabilities. *Disability & Rehabilitation, 21*(3), 124–127.

Lancioni, G. E., O'Reilly, M. F., & Basili, G. (2001). An overview of technological resources used in rehabilitation research with people with severe/profound and multiple disabilities. *Disability & Rehabilitation, 23*(12), 501–508.

Lancioni G. E., O'Reilly, M. F., Seedhouse, P., Furniss, F., & Cunha B. (2000). Promoting independent task performance by persons with severe developmental disabilities through a new computer-aided system. *Behavior Modification, 24*(5), 698–716.

Lankard, B. A. (1993). *Parents and the school-to-work transition of special needs youth.* (ERIC Digest No. 142). Retrieved December 9, 2004, from http://www.ericdigests.org/1994/parents.htm

Larson, S. A., Coucouvanis, K., & Prouty, R. W. (2003). Staffing patterns, characteristics and outcomes in large state residential facilities in 2002. In R. W. Prouty, G. Smith, & K. C. Lakin (Eds.), *Residential services for persons with developmental disabilities: Status and trends through 2002* (pp. 47–59). Minneapolis: University of Minnesota, Research and Training Center on Community Living.

Larson, S. A., & Hewitt, A. S. (2005). *Staff recruitment, retention and training strategies for community human services organizations.* Baltimore: Paul H. Brookes.

Larson, S. A., Hewitt, A., Anderson, L., Sauer, J., & O'Nell, S. (2000). *Minnesota review and analysis of trends in agency maltreatment reports.* Minneapolis: University of Minnesota, Research and Training Center on Community Living.

Larson, S. A., Hewitt, A. S., & Knobloch, B. (2005). Recruitment, retention, and training challenges in community human services: A review of literature. In S. A. Larson & A. Hewitt (Eds.), *Staff recruitment, retention and training strategies for community human services organizations* (pp. 21–40). Baltimore: Paul H. Brookes.

Larson, S. A., Hewitt, A. S., & Lakin, K. C. (2004). A multi-perspective analysis of the effects of recruitment and retention challenges on outcomes for persons with intellectual and developmental disabilities and their families. *American Journal on Mental Retardation, 109*, 481–500.

Larson, S., & Lakin, K. C. (1989). Deinstitutionalization of persons with mental retardation: The impact on daily living skills. *Policy Research Brief, 1*(1), 1–5.

Larson, S. A., & Lakin, K. C. (1991). Parental attitudes about residential placement before and after deinstitutionalization: A research synthesis. *Journal of the Association for Persons with Severe Handicaps, 16*, 25–38.

Larson, S. A., & Lakin, K. C. (1992). Direct care staff stability in a national sample of small group homes. *Mental Retardation, 30*, 13–22.

Larson, S., Lakin, C., Anderson, L., & Kwak, N. (2001). Characteristics of and service use by persons with MR/DD living in their own homes or with family members: NHIS-D analysis. *Mental Retardation and Developmental Disabilities Data Brief, 3*, 1–11.

Larson, S. A., Lakin, K. C., Anderson, L. L., Kwak, N., Lee, J. H., & Anderson, D. (2001). Prevalence of mental retardation and developmental disabilities: Estimates from the National Health Interview Survey disability supplement. *American Journal on Mental Retardation, 106*(3), 231–252.

Larson, S. A., Lakin, K. C., & Bruininks, R. H. (1998). *Staff recruitment and retention: Study results and intervention strategies*. Washington, DC: American Association on Mental Retardation.

Larson, S. A., Lakin, K. C., & Hewitt, A. S. (2002). Direct support professionals: 1975–2000. In D. Croser, P. Paker, & R. Schalock (Eds.), *Embarking on a new century* (pp. 203–219). Washington, DC: American Association on Mental Retardation.

Laws, G., Byrne, A., & Buckley, S. (2000). Language and memory development in children with Down Syndrome at mainstream schools and special schools: A comparison. *Educational Psychology: An International Journal of Experimental Educational Psychology, 20*(4), 447–457.

Laxova, R., Ridler, M. A. C., & Bowen-Bravery, M. (1977). An etiological survey of the severely retarded Hertfordshire children who were born between January 1, 1965 and December 31, 1967. *American Journal of Medical and Genetics, 1*, 75–86.

Legal Information Institute (2002). *Olmstead v. L.C., et al.* (98-536). [Online]. Retrieved from http://supct.law.cornell.edu/supct/html/98-536.ZS.html

Lehr, C. A., Hansen, A., Sinclair, M. F., & Christensen, S. L. (2002). *An integrative review of data based interventions: Moving beyond dropout towards school completion*. Minneapolis: University of Minnesota, Institute on Community Integration.

Lehr, C. A., Johnson, D. R., Bremer, C. D., Cosio, A., & Thompson, M. (2004). *Increasing rates of school completion: Moving from policy and research to practice: A manual for policymakers, administrators, and educators*. Retrieved December 8, 2004, from http://www.ncset.org/publications/essentialtools/dropout/

LeLaurin, K., & Wolery, M. (1992). Research standards in early intervention: Defining, describing, and measuring the independent variable. *Journal of Early Intervention, 16*, 275–287.

Leung, P. (1992). Cross-cultural issues in training and employment. In J. Fischer (Ed.), *East-West directions: Social work practice, traditions and change* (pp. 71–82). Honolulu: University of Hawaii Press.

Levine, E. L., & Wexler, E. M. (1981). *PL 94-142: An act of Congress*. New York: McMillan.

Levy, J. M., Jessop, D. J., Rimmerman, A., Francis, F., & Levy, P. H. (1993). Determinants of attitudes of New York State employees towards the employment of persons with severe handicaps. *Journal of Rehabilitation, 59*, 49–54.

Levy, J. M., Jessop, D. J., Rimmerman, A., & Levy, P. H. (1992). Attitudes and practices regarding the employment of persons with disabilities in Fortune 500 corporations: A national study. *Mental Retardation, 50*(2), 67–75.

Lewis, D. & Bruininks, R. (1994). Costs of community-based residential and related services to persons with mental retardation and other developmental disabilities. In M. Hayden & B. Abery (Eds.), *Challenges for a service system in transition* (pp. 231–264). Baltimore: Paul H. Brookes.

Lewis, D. R., & Johnson, D. R. (2005). Costs of family care for individuals with developmental disabilities. In R. J. Stancliffe & K. C. Lakin (Eds.), *Costs and outcomes of community services for people with intellectual disabilities* (pp. 63–89). Baltimore: Paul H. Brookes.

Lewis, M. A., Lewis, C. E., Leake, B., King, B. H., & Lindemann, R. (2002). The quality of health care for adults with developmental disabilities. *Public Health Reports, 117*, 174–184.

Lian, M., & Fantanez-Phelan, S. (2001). Perceptions of Latino parents regarding cultural and linguistic issues and advocacy for children with disabilities. *Journal of the Association for Persons with Severe Handicaps, 26*(3), 189–194.

Light v. Parkway 41 F. 3rd 1223 (8th Cir. 1994)

Light, J., Roberts, B., Dimarco, R., & Greiner, N. (1998). Augmentative and alternative communication to support receptive and expressive communication for people with autism. *Journal of Communication Disorders, 31*, 153–180.

Lindsey, P. (1994). Assessing the ability of adults with mental retardation to give direct consent for residential placements: A follow-up study for the Consent Screening Interview. *Education and Training in Mental Retardation and Developmental Disabilities, 29*(2), 155–164 .

Lipsky, D. K., & Gartner, A. (1996). Inclusion, school restructuring, and the remaking of American society. *Harvard Educational Review, 66*(4), 762–796.

Livermore, G. A., Stapleton, D. C., Nowak, M. W., Wittenburg, D. C., & Eiseman, E. D. (March 2000). "The economics of policies and programs affecting the employment of persons with disabilities." Rehabilitation Research and Training Center for Economic Research on Employment Policy for Persons with Disabilities, Cornell University. Retrieved from http://www.ilr.cornell.edu

Logan, K., Jacobs, H., Gast, D., Streu, M. A., Daino, K., & Skala, C. (1998). The impact of typical peers on the perceived happiness of students with profound multiple disabilities. *Journal of the Association for Persons with Severe Handicaps 23*(4), 309–318.

Longhurst, N. A. (1994). *The self-advocacy movement: A demographic study and directory.* Washington, DC: American Association on Mental Retardation.

Lord, C., & McGee, W. (2001). *Educating children with autism.* Committee on Educational Interventions for Children with Autism. Division of Behavioral and Social Sciences and Education. Washington, DC: National Academy Press.

Lowe, K. & de Paiva, S. (1991). Clients' community and social contacts: Results of a 5-year longitudinal study. *Journal of Mental Deficiency Research, 35*(4), 308–323.

Lowery, H. (1999). *Introspection, values, action, reality, inclusion: An activity guide to inclusion of people with disabilities.* Washington, DC: Corporation for National Service.

Lowry, M. (1998). Assessment and treatment of mood disorders in persons with developmental disabilities. *Journal of Developmental and Physical Disabilities,104*, 387–406.

Lowry, M., & Charlot, L. (1992). Depression and associated aggression and self injury. *NADD Newsletter, 13*, 1–5.

Luckasson, R., Borthwick-Duffy, S., Buntinx, W. H. E., Coulter, D. L., Craig, E. M., Reeve, A., et al. (2002). *Mental retardation: Definition, classification and systems of supports* (10th Ed.). Washington, DC: American Association on Mental Retardation.

Luckasson, R., Coulter, D. L., Polloway, E. A., Reiss, S., Schalock, R. L., Snell, M. E., et al. (1992). *Mental retardation: Definition, classification, and systems of supports* (9th ed.). Washington, DC: American Association on Mental Retardation.

Lucyshyn, J. M., Dunlap, G., & Albin, R. W. (Eds.) (2002). *Families and positive behavior support: Addressing problem behavior in family contexts.* Baltimore: Paul H. Brookes.

Ludi, D. C., & Martin, L. (1995). The road to personal freedom: Self-determination. *Intervention in School and Clinic, 30*(3), 170–179.

Luecking, R., & Certo, N. (2002). *Integrating service systems at the point of transition for youth with significant disabilities: A model that works.* Minneapolis: University of Minnesota, National Center on Secondary Education and Transition.

Luecking, R., & Crane, K. (2002). Addressing the transition needs of youth with disabilities through the WIA system. *National Center on Secondary Education and Transition Information Brief, 1*(6). Minneapolis: University of Minnesota.

Luiselli, J. K., & Cameron, M. J. (Eds.) (1998). *Antecedent control: Innovative approaches to behavioral support*. Baltimore: Paul H. Brookes.

Lumley, V. & Miltenberger, R. (1997). Sexual abuse prevention for persons with mental retardation. *American Journal on Mental Retardation, 101*(5), 459–472.

Lunsky, Y. (1999). Women with developmental disabilities: Collaborative strategies for providing GYN care. *Abstract of Proceedings: AAMR 123rd Annual Meeting*, New Orleans, May 1999.

Lynch, E. W., & Hanson, J. M. (Eds.). (1992). *Developing cross-cultural competence: A guide for working with young children and their families*. Baltimore: Paul H. Brookes.

Magaña, S., Seltzer, M., & Krauss, W. (2004). The cultural context of caregiving: Differences in depression between Puerto Rican and non-Latina White mothers of adults with mental retardation. *Mental Retardation, 42*(1), 1–11.

Mahon, M. J., Mactavish, J., & Bockstael, E. (2000). Making friends through recreation: Social integration, leisure, and individuals with intellectual disability. *Parks and Recreation, 35*, 25–40.

Malin, N. A. (1982). Group homes for mentally handicapped adults: Residents' view on contacts and support. *British Journal of Mental Subnormality, 28*(1), 29–34.

Mahoney, K. J., Simone, K., & Simon-Rusinowitz, L. (2000). Early lessons from the cash and counseling demonstration and evaluation. *Generations, 24*(111), 41–46.

Malony, M., (1999). Dare to dream. *IMPACT, 12*(1), 6–7.

Malmgren, K., Edgar, E., & Neel, R. S. (1998). Postschool status of youth with behavioral disorders. *Behavioral Disorders, 23*, 257–263.

Mank, D. (1994). The underachievement of supported employment: A call for reinvestment. *Journal of Disability Policy Studies, 5*(2), 1–24.

Mank, D., Cioffi, A., & Yovanoff, P. (1997). An analysis of the typicalness of supported employment jobs, natural supports, and wage and integration outcomes. *Mental Retardation, 35*(3), 185–197.

Mank, D., Cioffi, A., & Yovanoff, P. (2000). Direct support in supported employment and its relation to job typicalness, coworker involvement, and employment outcomes. *Mental Retardation, 38*(6), 506–516.

Mann, W., Hurren, D., Tomita, M., & Charvat, B. (1997). Comparison of the UB-RERC-Aging Consumer Assessments Study with the 1986 NHIS and the 1987 NMES. *Topics in Geriatric Rehabilitation 13*(2), 32–41.

Manning, S., Madsen, J., & Jennings, R. (2000). Pathophysiology, prevention, and potential treatment of neural tube defects. *Mental Retardation and Developmental Disabilities Research Reviews, 6*, 6–14.

Mansell, S., Sobsey, D., & Moskal, R. (1998). Clinical findings among sexually abused children with and without developmental disabilities. *Mental Retardation, 36*(1), 12–22.

Mansell, S., Sobsey, D., Wilgosh, L., & Zawallich, A. (1997). The sexual abuse of young people with disabilities. *International Journal for the Advancement of Counseling, 19*, 293–302.

Marcos, L., Gil, R., & Vasquez, K. (1986). Who will treat psychiatrically disturbed developmentally disabled patients? A healthcare nightmare. *Hospital and Community Psychiatry, 37*, 171–174.

Markey, U., & Markey, D. J. (2003, January 5–8). Extending the benefits of research to all. Unpublished presentation at the Keeping the Promises Conference on National Goals, State of Knowledge, and Research Agenda for Persons with Intellectual and Developmental Disabilities, Washington, DC (quotation cited in The Arc of the U.S. [2003], *Keeping the promises: Findings and recommendations*. Silver Spring, MD: Author).

Marrone, J., Helm, E. T., & Van Gelder, M. (1997). *Families as resources: Putting positive practices into context*. Boston: Institute for Community Inclusion.

Martin, J. E., & Marshall, L. H. (1995). ChoiceMaker: A comprehensive self-determination transition program. *Intervention in School and Clinic, 30*(3), 147–156.

Martin, J. E., & Marshall, L. H. (1996). Infusing self-determination instruction into the IEP and transition process. In D. J. Sands & M. L. Wehmeyer (Eds.), *Self-determination across the life span: Independence and choice for people with disabilities* (pp. 215–236). Baltimore: Paul H. Brookes.

McBride, S. L., Brotherson, M. J., Joanning, H., Whiddon, D., & Demitt, A. (1993). Implementation of family-centered services: Perceptions of families and professionals. *Journal of Early Intervention. 17*(4), 14–430.

McCabe, M. P. (1993). Sex education programs for people with intellectual disabilities: Are they necessary? *Mental Retardation, 31*, 377–387.

McCaughrin, W., Ellis, W., Rusch, F., & Heal, L. (1993). Cost-effectiveness of supported employment. *Mental Retardation, 31*(1), 41–48.

McConnell, S. R. (2000). Assessment in early intervention and early childhood special education: Building on the past to project into our future. *Topics in Early Childhood Special Education, 20,* 43–48.

McCracken, J. T., McGough, J., Shah, B., Cronin, P., et al. (2002). Risperidone in children with autism and serious behavioral problems. *New England Journal of Medicine, 347*(5), 314–321.

McCubbin, H. I., Olson, D. H., & Larsen, S. S. (1981). F-COPES: Family Crisis Oriented Personal Evaluation Scales. In H. I. McCubbin & A. I. Thompson (Eds.), *Family assessment inventories for research and practice* (pp. 201–216). Madison: University of Wisconsin, Family Stress Coping and Health Project.

McDonnell, J., Hardman, M. L., & McDonnell, A. P. (2003). *An introduction to persons with moderate and severe disabilities: Educational and social issues* (2nd Ed.). Boston: Allyn & Bacon.

McDonnell, J. Mathot-Buckner, C., & Ferguson, B. (1992). Transition from school to work for students with severe disabilities. In F. R. Rusch, L. Destefano, J. Chadsey-Rusch, L. A. Phelps, and E. Symanski (Eds.), *Transition from school-to-work for youth and adults with disabilities* (pp. 33–50) Sycamore, IL: Sycamore Press.

McDonnell, L. M., McLaughlin, M. J., & Morison, P. (1997). *Educating one and all: Students with disabilities and standards-based reform.* Washington, DC: National Academy Press.

McDonough, B. (2002, April 24). Wearable tech helps disabled students. *NewsFactor Network.* Retrieved November 21, 2004, from http://sci.newsfactor.com/perl/story/17419.html

McEnroe, P. (2001, October 25). Voiceless and vulnerable. Minneapolis Star Tribune, p. A1-A2.

McFarlin, D. B., Song, J., & Sonntag, M. (1991), Integrating the disabled into the workforce: A survey of Fortune 500 company attitudes and practices. *Employee Responsibilities and Rights Journal, 4*(2), 107–123.

McGaughey, M. J., Kiernan, W. E., McNally, L. C., Gilmore, D. S. & Keith, G. R. (1994). *Beyond the workshop: National perspectives on integrated employment.* Boston: Children's Hospital, Institute for Community Inclusion.

McGregor, G., & Vogelsberg, R. T. (1998). *Inclusive schooling practices: Pedagogical and research foundations: A synthesis of the literature that informs best practices about inclusive schooling.* Baltimore: Paul H. Brookes.

McGrew, K. S., Bruininks, R. H., Thurlow, M. L., & Lewis, D. R. (1992). Empirical analysis of multidimensional measures of community adjustment for young adults with mental retardation. *American Journal on Mental Retardation, 96*(5), 475–487.

McGrew, K. S., Thurlow, M. L., & Spiegel, A. (1993). An investigation of the exclusion of students with disabilities in national data collection programs. *Educational Evaluation and Policy Analysis, 15*(3), 339–352.

McIntosh, R., Vaughn, S., Schumm, J., Haager, D., & Lee, O. (1993). Observations of students with learning disabilities in general education classrooms. *Exceptional Children, 60*(3), 249–261.

McLaughlin, M. J., & Embler, S. (in press). High stakes accountability and students with disabilities: The good, the bad, and the ugly. In. P. Wehman (Ed.), *Life beyond the classroom* (4th ed.). Baltimore: Paul H. Brookes.

McLaughlin, M. J., Fuchs, L., & Hardman, M. (2000). Individual rights and students with disabilities: Some lessons from US policy. In P. Garner & H. Daniels (Eds.), *The 1999 World Yearbook of Special Education* (pp. 24–35). London: Kogan Page.

McLaughlin, M. J., & Nagle, K. M. (2004). Leaving no child behind: Accountability reform and students with disabilities. In S. Mathison & E. W. Ross (Eds.), *Defending public schools volume 4: The nature and limits of standards based reform and assessment* (pp. 107–119). Westport, CT: Praeger.

McLean, M. (1999). Assessing young children for whom English is a second language. *Young Exceptional Children, 1*(3), 20–26.

McMahon, B., Wehman, P., Brooke, V., Habeck, R. Green, H. Fraser, R. (2004). *Business, disability and employment: Corporate models of success: A collection of successful approaches reported from 20 employers.* Monograph. Richmond: Rehabilitation Research and Training Center on Workplace Supports.

McNaughton, D., Light, J., & Arnold, K. B. (2002). "Getting your wheel in the door": Successful full-time employment experiences of individuals with cerebal palsy who use augmentative and alternative communication. *Augmentative and Alternative Communication, 18*(2), 59–76.

McRae, D. (1997). Health care for women with learning disabilities. *Nursing Times, 93*(15), 58–59.

Mechanic, D. (1989). *Mental health and social policy.* Englewood, NJ: Prentice Hall

Mechling, L. C., Gast, D. L., & Langone, J. (2002). Computer-based video instruction to teach persons with moderate intellectual disabilities to read grocery aisle signs and locate items. *Journal of Special Education, 35*(4), 224–240.

Medawar, P. B. (1977). Unnatural science. *New York Review of Books, 24*(1), 13–18.

Melda, K., & Agosta, J. (1994a). *Family support services in Louisiana: A summary of survey results.* Salem, OR: Human Services Research Institute.

Melda, K., & Agosta, J. (1994b). *Family support services in Rhode Island: A summary of survey results.* Salem, OR: Human Services Research Institute.

Melda, K., & Agosta, J. (1995). *Family support services in South Dakota: A summary of survey results.* Salem, OR: Human Services Research Institute.

Melda, K., Agosta, J., & Smith, F. (1995). *Family support services in Utah: Striving to make a difference.* Salem, OR: Human Services Research Institute.

Mercer, J. R. (1973). *Labeling the mentally retarded: Clinical and social system perspectives on mental retardation.* Berkeley, CA: University of California Press.

Merritt, R. (2003, March 19). Nerves of silicon: Neural chips eyed for brain repair. *EE Times.* Retrieved November 21, 2004, from http://www.eetimes.com/story/OEG20030317S0013

Meyer, L. H., Peck, C. A., & Brown, L. (Eds.). (1991). *Critical issues in the lives of people with severe disabilities.* Baltimore: Paul H. Brookes.

Meyer v. Nebraska, 262 U.S. 390 (1923).

Meyers, J. C., & Marcenko, M. O. (1989). Impact of a cash subsidy program for families of children with severe developmental disabilities. *Mental Retardation, 27*(6), 383–387.

Miano, M., Nalvin, E., & Hoff, D. (1996). The pachysandra project: A public-private initiative in supported employment at the Prudential Insurance Company of America. *Journal of Vocational Rehabilitation, 6,* 107–118.

Micco, A., Hamilton, A. C. S., Martin, M. J., & McEwan, K. L. (1995). Case manager attitudes toward client-directed care. *Journal of Case Management, 4,* 95–101.

Miedel, W. T., & Reynolds, A. J. (1999). Parent involvement in early intervention for disadvantaged children: Does it matter? *Journal of School Psychology, 37*(4), 379–405.

Millar, A. L., Fernhall, B., & Burkett, L. N. (1993). Effects of aerobic training in adolescents with Down syndrome. *Medicine and Science in Sports and Exercise, 25,* 270–274.

Miller, P., Fader, L., & Vincent, L. J. (2000). Preparing early childhood educators to work with children who have exceptional needs. In U.S. Department of Education (Ed.), *New teachers for a new century: the future of early childhood professional preparation* (pp. 91–122). Washington, DC: Editor.

Miller, R., Lombard, R., & Hazelkorn, M. (2000). *Teacher attitudes and practices regarding the inclusions of students with disabilities in school-to-work and technical preparation programs: Strategies for inclusion and policy implications.* Minneapolis, MN: University of Minnesota, Institute on Community Integration.

Minkler, M., Blackwell, A. G., Thompson, M., & Tamir, H. (2003). Community-based participatory research: Implications for public health funding. *American Journal of Public Health, 93*(8), 1210–1213.

Minnesota Department of Children Families & Learning. (1998). *Information and training needs survey: Report on the statewide information and training needs of parents with children with disabilities.* St. Paul, MN: Author.

Mirenda, P. (2001), Autism, augmentative communication, and assistive technology: What do we really know? *Focus on Autism and Other Developmental Disabilities, 16*(3), 141–151.

Mississippi Band v. Holyfield, 490 U.S. 30 (1989).

Mithaug, D. E., Horiuchi, C. N., & Fanning, P. N. (1985). A report on the Colorado statewide follow-up survey of special education students. *Exceptional Children, 51,* 397–404.

Mooney, M., & Crane, K. (2002). *Connecting employers, schools, and youth through intermediaries.* Minneapolis: University of Minnesota, Institute on Community Integration, National Center on Secondary Education and Transition.

Moore, C. (1998). *Educating students with disabilities in general education classrooms: A summary of research* [Monograph]. Eugene, OR: Western Regional Resource Center.

Morningstar, M. E., Turnbull, A. P., & Turnbull, H. R. (1995). What do students with disabilities tell us about the importance of family involvement in the transition from school to adult life? *Exceptional Children, 62,* 249–260.

Morris, C. D., Niederbuhl, J. M., & Mahr, J. M. (1993). Determining the capability of individuals with mental retardation to give informed consent. *American Journal on Mental Retardation, 98,* 263–272.

Morris, M., Ritchie, H., & Clay, L. (2002). *Section 14C Of the fair labor standard act: Framing policy issues.* Boston: National Center on Workforce and Disability Institute for Community Inclusion.

Morrison, S. J. (2001). Neuronal differentiation: Proneural genes inhibit gliogenesis. *Current Biology, 11,* R349–351.

Moseley, C. (2001). *Self-determination for persons with developmental disability: Final and summative program report.* Durham, NH: University of New Hampshire, Institute on Disability, University of New Hampshire.

Moseley, C., Gettings, R., & Cooper, R. (2003). *Having it your way: Understanding state individual budgeting strategies.* Alexandria, VA: National Association of State Directors of Developmental Disabilities Services.

Mount, B., & Zwernik, K. (1988). *It's never too early, it's never too late. A booklet about personal futures planning.* Minneapolis: Metropolitan Council.

Mouth Magazine. (2001, January & February). *History is not a spectators sport,* pp. 8–11.

Mulick J. A., & Butter, E. M. (2002). Educational advocacy for children with autism. *Behavioral intervention, 17,* 57–74.

Murphy, S. & Rogan, P. (1995). *Closing the shop: Conversion from sheltered to integrated work.* Baltimore: Paul H. Brookes.

Muzzio, T. C. (2000). Undergraduate rehabilitation education: The need for graduates from the perspective of the public rehabilitation program. *Rehabilitation Education, 14,* 89–96.

National Association of State Boards of Education (1992, October). *Winners all: A call for inclusive schools.* Alexandria, VA: Author.

National Center on Birth Defects and Developmental Disabilities (2003). *Healthy People 2010: Disability and Secondary Conditions.* Atlanta: Centers for Disease Control and Prevention.

National Center for the Dissemination of Disability Research. (1999). *Disability, diversity and dissemination: A review of the literature on topics related to increasing the utilization of rehabilitation research outcomes among diverse consumer groups.* Retrieved December 8, 2004, from http://www.ncddr.org/du/researchexchange/v04n02/systems.html

National Center for the Study of Postsecondary Educational Supports. (2000a). *Technical report: National survey of educational support provision to students with disabilities in postsecondary education settings.* Honolulu: University of Hawaii at Manoa.

National Center for the Study of Postsecondary Educational Supports. (2000b). *Technical report: Postsecondary education and employment for students with disabilities: Focus group discussions on supports and barriers to lifelong learning.* Honolulu: University of Hawaii at Manoa.

National Commission on Excellence in Education. (1983). *A nation at risk.* Washington, DC: U.S. Department of Education.

National Commission on Teaching and America's Future. (1996). *What matters most: Teaching for America's future: Summary report.* Washington, DC: Author.

National Conference on Self-Determination (1989). *Recommendations from the conference participants.* Minneapolis: University of Minnesota, Institute on Community Integration.

National Council on Disability. (2000). *Transition and postschool outcomes for youth with disabilities: Closing the gaps to post-secondary education and employment.* Retrieved December 8, 2004, from http://www.ncd.gov/newsroom/publications/2000/transition_11-01-00.htm

National Down Syndrome Society. (2001). Down Syndrome Research Survey—2001. Survey given to participants of the 2001 National Down Syndrome Society. San Diego, CA.

National Down Syndrome Society. (2002). *Shaping the vision for the 21st Century.* Washington, DC: Author.

National Institute on Consumer-Directed Long-Term Services. (1996). *Principles of consumer-directed home and community-based services.* Washington, DC: The National Council on the Aging.

National Institutes of Health. (2001). *Emotional and behavioral health in persons with mental retardation/developmental disabilities: Research challenges and opportunities.* Bethesda, MD: Author.

National Organization on Disability. (2000). *2000 N.O.D./Harris survey of Americans with disabilities.* Washington, DC: Louis Harris & Associates.

National Research Council. (2000). How children learn. In M. S. Donovan, J. D. Bransford, & J. W. Pellegrino (Eds.), *How people learn: Brain, mind experience, and school* (pp. 79–113). Washington, DC: National Academy Press.

National Research Council (2001a). *Eager to learn: Educating our preschoolers.* Committee on Early Childhood Pedagogy. B.T. Bowman, M.S. Donovan, & M.S. Burns (Eds.). Commission on Behavioral and Social Sciences and Education. Washington, DC: National Academy Press.

National Research Council (2001b). *Educating children with autism.* Committee on Educational Interventions for Children with Autism. C. Lord & J.P. McGee (Eds.). Division of Behavioral and Social Sciences and Education. Washington, DC: National Academy Press.

National Research Council. (2002a). *Minority students in special and gifted education.* Washington, DC: National Academy Press.

National Research Council (2002b). *Scientific research in education.* Committee on Scientific Principles for Education Research. R.J. Shavelson & L. Towne, (Eds.). Center for Education. Division of Behavioral and Social Sciences and Education. Washington, DC: National Academy Press.

National Research Council and Institute of Medicine. (2000). *From neurons to neighborhoods: The science of early childhood development.* Committee on Integrating the Science of Early Childhood Development. J. P. Shonkoff & D. A. Phillips (Eds.). Board on Children, Youth, and Families, Commission on Behavioral and Social Sciences and Education. Washington, DC: National Academy Press.

National Transition Alliance. (1996). Family involvement. *Alliance, 1*(3), 1–5.

Nehring, W. (2005). *Core curriculum for specializing in intellectual and developmental disability: A resource for nurses and other health care professionals.* Sudbury, MA: Jones and Bartlett.

Nelson, J. R., Roberts, M., Mathur, S., & Rutherford, R. B. (1999). Has public policy exceeded our knowledge base? A review of functional assessment literature. *Behavioral Disorders, 24,* 169–179.

Nerney, T. (2001a). *Filthy lucre: Creating better value in long term supports.* Durham, NH: University of New Hampshire Institute on Disability.

Nerney, T. (2001b). *The poverty of human services.* Retrieved February 17, 2004, from http://www.self-determination.com/publications/poverty1.html

Nerney, T., & Shumway, D. (1996). *Beyond managed care: Self-determination for people with developmental disabilities.* Concord, NH: University of New Hampshire, Institute on Disability.

New Freedom Initiative. (2001, February 1). Retrieved May 15, 2005, from http://www.whitehouse.gov/news/freedominitiative/freedominitiative.html

Newman, C. G. (1986). The thalidomide syndrome: Risks of exposure and spectrum of malformations. *Clinics Perinatology, 13,* 555–573.

Newton, J., Ard, W., & Horner, R. (1993). Validating predicted activity preferences of individuals with severe disabilities. *Journal of Applied Behavior Analysis, 26,* 239–245.

Newton, J., Olson, D., & Horner, R. (1995). Factors contributing to the stability of social relationships between individuals with mental retardation and other community members. *Mental Retardation, 33*(6), 383–393.

Newton, J. S., & Horner, R. H. (1993). Using a social guide to social relationships of persons with severe disabilities. *Journal of the Association for Persons with Severe Handicaps, 18*(1), 36–45.

Nieto, M., Schuurmans, C., Britz, O., & Guillemot, F. (2001). Neural bHLH genes control the neuronal versus glial fate decision in cortical progenitors. *Neurontology, 29,* 401–413.

Nietupski, J., Hamre-Nietupski, S., VanderHart, N. S., & Fishback, K. (1996). Employer perceptions of the benefits and concerns of supported employment. *Education and Training in Mental Retardation and Developmental Disabilities, 31,* 310–323.

NIH Consensus Statement (2001). *PKU: Screening and Management.* NICHD: Washington, DC.

Nisbet, J. (Ed.). (1992). *Natural supports in school, at work, and in the community for people with severe disabilities.* Baltimore: Paul H. Brookes.

No Child Left Behind Act. *Reauthorization of the Elementary and Secondary Education Act.* Pub. L. 107-110 §2102(4) (2000).

Nolet, V., & McLaughlin, M. J. (2000). *Accessing the general curriculum: Including students with disabilities in standards-based reform.* Thousand Oaks, CA: Corwin Press.

Northrup, H., & Volcik, K. A. (2000). Spina bifida and other neural tube defects. *Current Problems in Pediatrics, 30,* 313–332.

Nosek, M. A. (1996). Sexual abuse of with physical disabilities. In Krotoski, D. M., Nosek, M. A., & Tuck, M. (Eds.), *Women with physical disabilities: Achieving and maintaining health and wellbeing* (pp. 153–173). Baltimore: Paul H. Brookes.

Oberti v. Board of Education of the Borough of Clementon School District, 995 F.2d 1204 (3rd Cir. 1993)

O'Brien, D., & McCabe, E. (1981). Metabolic evaluation. In W. K. Frankenburg, S. M. Thornton, & M. E. Cohrs (Eds.), *Pediatric developmental diagnosis* (pp. 144–155). New York: Thieme-Stratton, Inc.

O'Brien, J. (1987a). A guide to life-style planning: Using the Activities Catalog to integrate services and natural support systems. In B. Wilcox & G. T. Bellamy (Eds.), *A comprehensive guide to the activities catalog: An alternative curriculum for youth and adults with severe disabilities* (pp. 175–189). Baltimore: Paul H. Brookes.

O'Brien, J. (1987b). A guide to personal futures planning. In B. Wilcox & G. T. Bellamy (Eds.), *The activities catalog: A community programming guide for youth and adults with severe disabilities* (pp. 104–110). Baltimore: Paul H. Brookes.

O'Brien, J. (2001). *Paying customers are not enough: The dynamics of individualized funding.* Retrieved May 15, 2005, from http://soeweb.syr.edu/thechp/ifdynamics.pdf

O'Brien, J., & Lyle O'Brien, C. (1993). Unlikely alliances: Friendships and people with developmental disabilities. In A. N. Amando (Ed.), *Friendships and community connections between people with and without disabilities* (pp. 9–40). Baltimore: Paul H. Brookes.

O'Brien, K. F., Tate, K., & Zaharia, E. S. (1991). Mortality in a large southeastern facility for persons with mental retardation. *American Journal on Mental Retardation, 95,* 397–403.

Ochocka, J., & Lord, J. (1998). Support clusters: A social network approach for people with complex needs. *Journal of Leisurability, 25*(4), 313.

O'Connor, S. (1993). "I'm not Indian anymore": The challenge of providing culturally sensitive services to American Indians. In J. A. Racino, P. Walker, S. O'Connor, & S. J. Taylor (Eds.), *Housing, support, and community: Choices and strategies for adults with disabilities* (pp. 313–331). Baltimore: Paul H. Brookes.

Odom, S. L., & Strain, P. S. (2002). Evidence-based practice in early intervention/early childhood special education: Single-subject design research. *Journal of Early Intervention, 25,* 151–160.

Office of the Press Secretary. (2003, January 12). *Memorandum for the Secretary of Education, Health and Human Services, Labor, and the Commissioner of Social Security on Interagency Working Group on Assistive Technology Mobility Devices.* Retrieved November 21, 2004, from http://www.whitehouse .gov/news/releases/2003/02/20030212-12.html

Office of Special Education and Rehabilitative Services. (2002). *A new era: Revitalizing special education for children and their families.* Washington, DC: Author.

Office of Special Education Program's Policy Letters. (1990, August*). The right to have assistive technology included in the IEP.* Retrieved November 21, 2004, from http://www.uchsc.edu/atp/library/ fastfacts/osep_policy.htm

O'Hara, D., Seagriff-Curtin, P., Davies, D., & Stock, S. (2002, October). Innovation in health education and communication: A research project to demonstrate the effectiveness of personal support technology for improving the oral health of adults with mental retardation. Poster presentation at the inaugural conference of the National Center for Birth Defects and Developmental Disabilities, Atlanta, GA.

Olmsted et al. v. L. C. et al. 527 U.S. 581, 119 S. Ct. 2176 (1999).

Olson, D., Cioffi, M. A., Yovanoff, P., & Mank, D. (2001). Employers' perceptions of employees with mental retardation. *Journal of Vocational Rehabilitation, 16*(2), 125–133.

Ong, W. M. A. (1993). *Asian American cultural dimensions in rehabilitation counseling.* San Diego, CA: Rehabilitation Continuing Education Program Consortium.

O'Neil, J., Brown, M., Gordon, W., Schonhorn, R., & Green, E. (1981). Activity patterns of mentally retarded adults in institutions and communities: A longitudinal study. *Applied Research in Mental Retardation, 2,* 267–379.

O'Neill, L. M., & Dalton, B. (2002) Thinking readers part II: Supporting beginning reading in children with cognitive disabilities through technology. *Exceptional Parent, 32*(6), 40–43.

O'Neill, R. E., Horner, R. H., Albin, R. W., Sprague, J. R., Storey, K., & Newton, J. S. (1997). *Functional assessment and program development for problem behavior: A practical handbook* (2nd ed.). Pacific Grove, CA: Brookes/Cole.

O'Nell, S., & Hewitt, A. (2005). Linking training and performance through competency-based training. In S. A. Larson & A. Hewitt (Eds.), *Staff recruitment, retention and training strategies for community human service organizations* (pp. 125–154). Baltimore: Paul H. Brookes.

Organization for Economic Cooperation and Development (2001). *Starting strong. Early childhood education and care.* Paris, France: OECD.

Orkwis, R., & McLane, K. (1998). *A curriculum every student can use: Design principles for student access.* ERIC/OSEP Topical Brief. Retrieved December 8, 2004, from http://www.cec.sped.org/osep/ udesign.html

Orr, M. T. (1987). *Keeping students in school.* San Francisco: Jossey Bass.

Oswald, D. P., Coutinho, M., Best, A., & Singh, N. (1999). Ethnic representation in special education: The influence of school-related economic and demographic variables. *Journal of Special Education, 32*(3), 194–206.

Parette, H. P., & VanBiervliet, A. (1990). *Persons with mental retardation and technology use patterns and needs*. Little Rock: Center for Research on Teaching and Learning.

Parham v. J.R., 442 U.S. 584 (1979).

Parish, S., Pomeranz, A., & Braddock, D. (2003). Spending trends in family support in the United States. *Mental Retardation, 41*, 174–187.

Parish, S. L., Pomeranz, A., Hemp, R., Rizzolo, M. C., & Braddock, D. (2001) Family support for persons with developmental disabilities in the US: Status and trends. Policy Research Brief, 12(2). Minneapolis, MN: University of Minnesota, Institute on Community Integration.

Parish, S., Seltzer, M., Greenberg, J., & Floyd, F. (2004). Economic implications of caregiving at midlife. *Mental Retardation, 42*(6), 413–426.

Park, J., Hoffman, L., Marquis, J., Turnbull, A. P., Poston, D., Mannan, H., et al. (2003). Toward assessing family outcomes of service delivery: Validation of a family quality of life survey. *Journal of Intellectual Disability Research, 47*(4/5), 367–384.

Park, J., Turnbull, A. P., & Turnbull, H. R. (2002). Impacts of poverty on quality of life in families of children with disabilities. *Exceptional Children, 68*(2), 151–170.

Parker, R. M. & Schaller, J. L. (1996). Issues in vocational assessment and disability. In E. M. Szymanski & R. M. Parker (Eds.), *Work and disability: Issues and strategies in career development and job placement* (pp. 127–164). Austin, TX: PRO-ED, Inc.

Parry, J. (1995). Mental disability law: A primer (5th ed.). Washington, DC: American Bar Association.

Pasternack, R. (April 2002). *High schools and transition into the workforce*. Statement of Robert H. Pasternack, Assistant Secretary for Special Education and Rehabilitative Services before the House Subcommittee on Labor/ HHS/ Education Appropriations, Washington, DC.

Pate, R. R., Pratt, M., Blair, S. N., Haskell, W. L., Macera, C. A., Bouchard, C., et al. (1995). Physical activity and public health: A recommendation from the Centers for Disease Control and Prevention and the American College of Sports Medicine. *JAMA, 273*(5), 402–407.

Patterson, M. M., Higgins, M., & Dyck, D. (1995). A collaborative approach to reduce hospitalization of developmentally disabled clients with mental illness. *Psychiatric Services, 46*(3), 243–247.

Patton, J. R., Cronin, M. E., Polloway, E. A., Hutchinson, D., & Robinson, G. A. (1989). Curricular considerations: A life skills orientation. In G. A. Robinson, J. R. Patton, E. A. Polloway, & L. R. Sargent (Eds.), *Best practices in mild mental retardation*. Reston, VA: Council for Exceptional Children, MR.

Pavel, M. (2002, August). *Unobtrusive health state estimation*. Intel Conference on Computing, Cognition, and Caring for Future Elders.

Peck, C. A., Donaldsson, J., & Pezzoli, M. (1990). Some benefits nonhandicapped adolescents perceive for themselves from their social relationships with peers who have severe handicaps. *Journal of the Association for Persons with Severe Handicaps, 15*(4), 241–249.

Pederson, E., Oldendick, R. W., & Nelis, T. (1997). *A new approach to developing leaders: Relationships among members*. Cincinnati: Capabilities Unlimited.

Pentland, A. (1996). Smart rooms. *Scientific American, 274*(4), 68–76.

Perlmutter, L. C., & Monty, R. A. (1997). The importance of perceived control: Fact or fantasy? *American Scientist, 65*, 759–765.

Perske, R. (1988). *Circles of friends: People with disabilities and their friends enrich the lives of one another*. Nashville: Abingdon Press.

Petersilia, J. (2001). Crime victims with developmental disabilities. *Criminal Justice and Behavior, 28*(6), 655–694.

Petersilia, J., Foote, J., & Crowell, N. A. (Eds.). (2001). *Crime victims with developmental disabilities: Report of a workshop*. Washington, DC: National Academy Press.

Petrij, F., Giles, R. H., Dauwerse, H. G., Saris, J. J., Hennekam, R. C., Masuno, M., et al. (1995). Rubinstein-Taybi syndrome caused by mutations in the transcriptional co-activator CBP. *Nature, 376*, 348–351.

Pfeifer, A., & Verma, I. M. (2001). Gene therapy: promises and problems. *Annual Review of Genomics and Human Genetics, 2,* 177–211.

Phillips, B., & Zhao, H. (1993). Predictors of assistive technology abandonment. *Assistive Technology, 5,* 36–45.

Phillips, I., & Williams, N. (1975). Psychopathology and mental retardation: A study of 100 mentally retarded children. *American Journal of Psychiatry, 132,* 139–145.

Pianta, R. C., & Cox, M. J. (1999). *The transition to kindergarten.* Baltimore: Paul H. Brookes.

Pianta, R. C., Kraft-Sayre, M. Rimm-Kaufman, S., Gercke, N., & Higgins, T. (2001). Collaboration in building partnerships between families and schools: The National Center for Early Development and Learning's transition intervention. *Early Childhood Research Quarterly, 16,* 117–132.

Pitetti, K. H., & Campbell, K. D. (1991). Mentally retarded individuals—a population at risk? *Medical Sciences and Sports Exercise, 23,* 586–593.

Pitetti, K. H., Climstein, M., Campbell, K. D., Barrett, P. J., & Jackson, J. A. (1992). The cardiovascular capacities of adults with Down syndrome: A comparative study. *Medicine and Science in Sports and Exercise, 24,* 13–19.

Pierangelo, R., & Crane, R. (1997). *Complete guide to special education transition services.* West Nyack, NY: Center for Applied Research in Education.

Pierce v. Society of Sisters, 268 U.S. 510 (1925).

Pledger, C. (2003). Discourse on disability and rehabilitation issues: Opportunities for psychology. *American Psychologist, 58,* 279–284.

Polister, B., Lakin, K. C., & Prouty, R. W. (2003). Wages of direct support professionals serving persons with intellectual and developmental disabilities. *Policy Research Brief, 14*(2). Minneapolis, MN: University of Minnesota, Research and Training Center on Community Living.

Poston, D., Turnbull, A., Park, J., Mannan, H., Marquis, J., & Wang, M. (2003). Family quality of life: A qualitative inquiry. *Mental Retardation, 41*(4/5), 313–328.

Powers, L. E. (1996). Family and consumer activism in disability policy. In G. H. S. Singer, L. E. Powers, & A. L. Olson (Eds.), *Redefining family support: Innovations in public-private partnerships* (pp. 413–433). Baltimore: Paul H. Brookes.

Powers, L. E. (2002). Introduction to the special issue. *Journal of Disability Policy Studies, 13*(2), 66.

Powers, L. E., Garner, T., Couture, T., Dertinger, R., Lawson, L., Squire, P., et al. (2004). *Building a successful adult life: Findings from youth-directed research.* Portland, OR: Oregon Health and Science University, Center on Self-Determination, Oregon Health and Science University.

Powers, L. E., Sowers, J., Turner, A., Nesbitt, M., Knowles, E., & Ellison, R. (1996). Take charge: A model for promoting self-determination among adolescents with challenges. In L. E. Powers, G. H. S. Singer & J. Sowers (Eds.), *On the road to autonomy: Promoting self-competence for children and youth with disabilities* (pp. 291–322). Baltimore: Paul H. Brookes.

Powers, L. E., Turner, A., Ellison, R., Matuszewski, J., Wilson, R., Phillips, A., et al. (2001). Take Charge Field Test: A multi-component intervention to promote adolescent self-determination. *Journal of Rehabilitation, 67* (4), 13–19.

Powers, L. E., Ward, M., Ferris, L., Ward, N., Nelis, T., Wieck, C., et al. (1999). *Surveys of the involvement of people with disabilities in University Affiliated Programs and Developmental Disabilities Councils.* Portland, OR: Oregon Health and Science University, National Center for Self-Determination and 21st Century Leadership.

Powers, L. E., Ward, N., Ward, M., Nelis, T., Ferris, L., Heller, T., et al. (2002). Leadership by people with disabilities in self-determination-based systems change. *Journal of Disability Policy Studies, 13*(2) 125–133.

President's Commission on Excellence in Special Education (2002). From http://www.ed.gov/inits/commissionsboards/whspecialeducation/index.html

President's Commission on Mental Health. (1988). *Report of Liaison Task Panel on Mental Retardation.* Washington, DC: Author.

Preston, L. & Heller, T. (1996, October) *Working partnerships to individualize future planning for older families from diverse groups.* The Sixth Lexington Conference on Aging and Developmental Disabilities. Lexington, KY.

Pretti-Frontczak, K., Gialloutakis, A., Janas, D., & Hayes, A. (2002). Using a family-centered preservice curriculum to prepare early intervention and early childhood special education personnel. *Teacher Education and Special Education, 25*, 291–297.

Price, J. L. (1977). *The study of turnover.* Ames, IA: Iowa State University Press.

Prince v. Massachusetts, 321 U.S. 158 (1944).

Prouty, R., & Lakin, K. C. (2004). States' initial response to the President's New Freedom Initiative: Lowest rates of deinstitutionalization in 30 years. *Mental Retardation, 42*(3), 241–244.

Prouty, R., Smith, G., & Lakin, K. C. (Eds.). (2004). *Residential services for persons with developmental disabilities: Status and trends through 2003.* Minneapolis: University of Minnesota, Research and Training Center on Community Living/Institute on Community Integration.

Prouty, R. W., Smith, G., & Lakin, K. C. (2003). *Residential services for persons with developmental disabilities: Status and trends through 2002.* Minneapolis: University of Minnesota, Research and Training Center on Community Living.

Pruchno, R., Patrick, J., & Burant, C., (1997). African American and White mothers of adults with chronic disabilities: Caregiving burden and satisfaction. *Family Relations, 46*, 335–346.

Pueschel, S. M. (1990). Clinical aspects of Down syndrome from infancy to adulthood. *American Journal of Genetics, Supplement, 7*, 52–56.

Pueschel, S. M. (1998). Should children with Down syndrome be screened for atlantoaxial instability? *Archives of Pediatric Adolescent Medicine, 152*, 123–125.

Putnam, J. W., Werder, J. K., & Schleien, S. J. (1985). Leisure and recreation services for handicapped persons. In K. C. Lakin & R. H. Bruininks (Eds.), *Strategies for achieving community integration of developmentally disabled citizens* (pp. 23–273). Baltimore: Paul H. Brookes.

Quilloin v. Walcott, 434 U.S. 246 (1978).

Racino, J. A. (2002). Community integration and statewide systems change: Qualitative evaluation research in community life and disability. *Journal of Health and Social Policy, 14*(3), 1–25.

Radloff, L. (1977). The CES-D scale: A self-report depression scale for research in the general population. *Applied Psychological Measurement, 1*, 385–401.

Raynes, N. V., Sumpton, R. C., & Flynn, M. (1987). Homes for mentally handicapped people. London: Tavistock.

Reidy, D. (1993). Friendships and community associations. In A. N. Amado (Ed.), *Friendships and community connections between people with and without developmental disabilities* (pp. 351–371). Baltimore: Paul H. Brookes.

Rehabilitation Act of 1973, Pub. L. No. 93-112, 29 U.S.C. §§ 701 *et seq.* (2000).

Rehabilitation Act of 1973, as amended (Rehabilitation Act), Pub. L. No. 93-112, 29 U.S.C. §§ 701(a)(3), (a)(6)(A), (B), (a)(8), 703(c), 796 (2000).

Rehabilitation Act Amendments of 1998, Pub. L. No. 105-220, 29 U.S.C. § 701 *et seq.* (2000).

Rehabilitation Engineering and Assistive Technology Society of North America (RESNA) Technical Assistance Project. (2002). Unpublished notes from National Summit on Technology and Disability, Providence, RI, October 7, 2002. Arlington, VA: Author.

Reichle, J., & Wacker, D. (Eds.) (1993). *Communicative alternatives to challenging behavior: Integrating functional assessment and intervention strategies.* Baltimore: Paul H. Brookes.

Reis, S., Neu, T., & McGuire, J. M. (1997). Case studies of high-ability students with learning disabilities who have achieved. *Exceptional Children, 63*, 463–479.

Reiss, D., & Neiderhiser, J. E. (2000). The interplay of genetic influences and social processes in developmental theory: Specific mechanisms are coming into view. *Development and Psychopathology, 12*, 357–374.

Reiss, S. (1990). Prevalence of dual diagnosis in community-based day programs in the Chicago metropolitan area. *American Journal on Mental Retardation, 94*(6) 578–585.

Reiss, S. (1994). *Handbook of challenging behavior: Mental health aspects of mental retardation.* Worthington, OH: International Diagnostic Publishing.

Reiss, S., & Aman, M. G. (Eds.). (1998). *The international consensus handbook: Psychotropic medications and developmental disabilities.* Columbus: Ohio State University, Nisonger Center.

Repp, A. C., & Horner, R. H. (1999). *Functional analysis of problem behavior: From effective assessment to effective support.* Belmont, CA: Wadsworth Publishing.

Reskin, B., & Roos, P. (1990). *Job queues. Gender queues.* Philadelphia: Temple University Press.

Resources for Community Living, Inc. (1997). *Moretown: Vermont Crisis Network.* Unpublished program description.

Ricci v. Okin, 573 F. Supp. 817 (D. Mass. 1982).

Ridington, J. (1989). *Beating the "odds": Violence and women with disabilities* (Position Paper 2). Vancouver, Canada: DisAbled Women's Network.

Rimmer, J. (2000). *Achieving a beneficial fitness: A program and a philosophy in mental retardation: Contemporary issues in health, Volume 1.* Washington, DC: American Association on Mental Retardation.

Rimmer, J. H., Braddock, D., & Fujiura, G. (1994). Cardiovascular risk factor levels in adults with MR. *American Journal of Mental Retardation, 98*, 510–518.

Rimmer, J. H., Braddock, D., & Marks, B. (1995). Health characteristics and behaviors of adults with mental retardation residing in three living arrangements. *Research in Developmental Disabilities, 16*, 489–499.

Rimmer, J. H., Heller, T., Wang, E., & Valerio, I. (2004). Improvements in physical fitness in adults with Down syndrome. *American Journal on Mental Retardation, 109*(2), 165–174.

Rizzolo, M. C., Hemp, R., Braddock, D., & Pomeranz-Essley, A. (2004). *The state of the states in developmental disabilities.* Boulder: University of Colorado, Coleman Institute for Cognitive Disabilities.

Rizzolo, M. K. (2004). *Predictors of use of nursing homes and state institutions for persons with developmental disabilities.* Chicago: Rehabilitation Research and Training Center on Aging with Developmental Disabilities, University of Illinois at Chicago.

Rodgers, R. H., & White, J. M. (1993). Family development theory. In P. J. Boss, W. J. Doherty, R. LaRossa, W. R. Schumm, & S. K. Steinmetz (Eds.), *Sources of family theories and methods: A contextual approach* (pp. 225–254). New York: Plenum.

Roberto, K. A. (1993). Family caregivers of aging adults with disabilities: A review of caregiving literature. In K. A. Roberto (Ed.), *The elderly caregiver: Caring for adults with developmental disabilities* (pp. 3–18). Newbury Park, CA: Sage.

Rogers, J. (1999). Trying to get it right. Undertaking research involving people with learning difficulties. *Disability and Society, 14*, 421–433.

Roeher Institute (1994). *Violence and people with disabilities: A review of the literature.* Ottawa: Roeher Institute.

Rogan, P., Held, M., & Rinne, S. (1999). *A national study of conversion from segregated to community-based employment services.* Institute on Disability and Community.

Rogan, P., Held, M., & Rinne, S. (2001). Organizational change from sheltered to integrated employment for adults with disabilities. In P. Wehman (Ed.), *Supported employment in business: Expanding the capacity of workers with disabilities.* St. Augustine, FL: Training Resource Network, Inc.

Rojahn, J., Borthwick-Duffy, S. A., & Jacobson, J. W. (1993). The association between psychiatric diagnosis and severe behavior problems in mental retardation. *Annals of Clinical Psychiatry, 5*, 163–170.

Romer, L. T., Richardson, M. L., Nahom, D., Aigbe, E., & Porter, A. (2002). Providing family support through community guides. *Mental Retardation, 40*(3),191–200.

Romer, E. F., & Umbreit, J. (1998). The effects of family-centered service coordination: A social validation study. *Journal of Early Intervention, 21*(2), 95–110.

Romski, M. A., & Sevcik, R. A. (1996). *Breaking the speech barrier: Language development through augmented means.* Baltimore: Paul H. Brookes.

Romski, M. A., & Sevcik, R. A. (1997). Augmentative and alternative communication for children with developmental disabilities. *Mental Retardation and Developmental Disabilities Research Reviews, 3*(4), 363–368.

Romski, M. A., & Sevcik, R. A. (2000). Communication, technology, and disability. In M. Wehmeyer & J. R. Patton (Eds.), *Mental retardation in the 21st century* (pp. 299–313). Austin, TX: Pro-Ed.

Romski, M. A., Sevcik, R. A., Adamson, L. B. (1999). Communication patterns of youth with mental retardation with and without their speech-output communication devices. *American Journal on Mental Retardation, 104*(3), 249–259.

Roncker v. Walter, 700 F.2d 1058 (6th Cir. 1983).

Rose, D., & Meyer, A. (2000). Universal design for individual differences. *Educational Leadership, 58*(3), 39–43.

Rosen, J. W., & Burchard, S. N. (1990). Community activities and social support networks: A social comparison of adults with and adults without mental retardation. *Education & Training in Mental Retardation. 25(2),* 193–204.

Rosen, M., Floor, L., & Sizfein, L. (1974). Investigating the phenomenon of acquiescence in the mentally handicapped: 1. Theoretical model test development and normative data. *British Journal of Mental Subnormality, 20*(1), 58–68.

Rosenstock, G. K., & Hernandez, L. M. (2002). *Who will keep the public healthy? Educating public health professionals for the 21st century.* Washington, DC: Institute of Medicine, National Academy of Sciences.

Rotegard, L., Hill, B., & Bruininks, R. H. (1982*). Environmental characteristics of residential facilities for mentally retarded people.* Minneapolis: University of Minnesota, Research and Training Center on Community Living/Institute on Community Integration.

Rubin, I. L., & Crocker, A. C. (Eds.). (1989). *Developmental disabilities: Delivery of medical care for children and adults.* Philadelphia: Lea and Febiger.

Rubin, S. S., Rimmer, J. H., Chicoine, B., Braddock, D., & McGuire, D. E. (1998). Overweight prevalence in persons with Down syndrome. *Mental Retardation. 36*(3), 175–181.

Rudolph, C., Lakin, C., Oslund, J. M., & Larson, W. (1998). Evaluation of outcomes and cost-effectiveness of a community behavioral support and crisis response demonstration project. *Mental Retardation. 36*(3) 187–197.

Ruef, M. B., & Turnbull, A. P. (2001). Stakeholder opinions on accessible informational products helpful in building positive, practical solutions to behavioral challenges of individuals with mental retardation and/or autism. *Education and Training in Mental Retardation and Developmental Disabilities, 36*(4), 441–456.

Rush, A. J., & Frances, A. (2000). Expert consensus guidelines on the treatment of psychiatric and behavioral problems in mental retardation. *American Journal on Mental Retardation, 105,* 1592-28.

Russell, J. N., Hendershot, G. E., LeClere, F., Howie, L. J., & Adler, M. (1997). *Trends and differential use of assistive technology devices: United States, 1994.* Advance data from vital and health statistics; no. 292. Hyattsville, MD: National Center for Health Statistics.

Rutherford, R. B., Nelson, C. M., & Wolford, B. I. (1986). Special education programming in juvenile corrections. *Remedial and Special Education, 7,* 27–33.

Rutter, J. (2002). Nature, nurture, and development: From evangelism through science toward policy and practice. *Child Development, 73*(1), 1–21.

Ryerson, E. (1984). Sexual abuse and self-protection education for developmentally disabled youth: A priority need. *SIECUS Report, 13,* 6–7.

Ryndak, D. L., & Kennedy, C. H. (2000). Meeting the needs of students with severe disabilities: Issues and practices in teacher education. *Journal of the Association for Persons with Severe Handicaps, 25,* 69–71.

Sabatini, C. P., & Hughes, S. L. (2003). *Addressing liability issues in consumer-directed personal assistance services (CDPAS): The National Cash and Counseling Demonstration and selected other models.* Boston: Boston College Graduate School of Social Work.

Sachs, G. A., Stocking, C. B., Stern, R., Cox, D. M., Hougham, G., & Sparage Sachs, R. (1994). Ethical aspects of dementia research. Informed consent and proxy consent. *Clinical Research, 42,* 403–412.

Sacramento v. Rachel H., 14 F.3d 1398 (9th Cir. 1994)

Saint-Laurent, L., & Lessard, J. (1991). Comparison of three educational programs for students with moderate mental retardation integrated in regular schools: Primary results. *Education and Training in Mental Retardation, 26*(4), 370–380.

Salembier, G., & Furney, K. (1997). Facilitating participation: Parents' perceptions of their involvement in the IEP/transition planning process. *Career Development for Exceptional Individuals, 20*(1), 29–42.

Sandall, S. Hemmeter, M. L., Smith, B. J., & McLean, M. E. (Eds.) (2005). *DEC recommended practices: A comprehensive guide for practical application in early intervention/early childhood special education.* Longmont, CO: Sopris West.

Sandall, S., McLean, M., Santos, R. M., & Smith, B. J. (2005). DEC's recommended practices: The context for change. In S. Sandall, M. L. Hemmeter, B. J. Smith, & M. E. McLean (Eds.), *DEC recommended practices: A comprehensive guide for practical application in early intervention/early childhood special education* (pp. 19–26). Longmont, CO: Sopris West.

Sands, D. J., Bassett, D. S., Lehmann, J., & Spencer, K. C. (1998). Factors contributing to and implications for student involvement in transition-related planning, decision making, an instruction. In M. L. Wehmeyer and D. J. Sands (Eds.), *Making it happen: Student involvement in education planning, decision making and instruction* (pp. 25–44). Baltimore: Paul H. Brookes.

Sands, D. J., & Wehmeyer, M. L. (Eds.) (1996). *Self-determination across the life span: Independence and choice for people with disabilities.* Baltimore: Paul H. Brookes.

Sanes, D. H., Reh, T. A., & Harris, W. A. (Eds.). (2000). *Development of central mervous system.* San Diego: Academic Press.

Santelli, B., Singer, G. H. S., DiVenere, N., Ginsberg, C., & Powers, L. E. (1998). Participatory action research: Reflections on critical incidents in a PAR project. *The Journal of the Association for Persons with Severe Handicaps, 23*(3), 211–222.

Santosky v. Kramer, 455 U.S. 745 (1982).

Sarnat, H. B. (1998). Normal Development of the nervous system. In Coffey, E. & Brumback, R. A. (Eds.), *Textbook of pediatric neuropsychiatry* (pp. 9–42). American Psychiatric Press, Inc.

Satir, V. (1972). *Peoplemaking.* Palo Alto: Science and Behavior Books.

Scala, M. A., Mayberry, P. S. (1997, July). *Consumer-directed home services: Issues and models.* Oxford, OH: Miami University, Ohio Long-Term Care Research Project.

Scala, M. A., Mayberry, P. S., & Kunkel, S. R. (1996). Consumer-directed home care: Client profiles and service challenges. *Journal of Case Management, 5*(3), 91–98.

Schaller, J., & Fieberg, J. L. (1998). Issues of abuse for women with disabilities and implications for rehabilitation counseling. *Journal of Applied Rehabilitation Counseling, 29*(1), 9–17.

Schalock, R. L. (1996). Reconsidering the conceptualization and measurement of quality of life. In R. L. Schalock (Ed.), *Quality of life volume I: Conceptualization and measurement* (pp. 123–139). Washington, DC: American Association on Mental Retardation.

Schalock, R. L., & Alonso, M. A. V. (2002). *Handbook on quality of life for human service practitioners.* Washington, DC: American Association on Mental Retardation.

Schalock, R. L., Baker, P. C., & Croser, M. (2002). *Embarking on a new century: Mental retardation at the end of the 20th century.* Washington DC: American Association on Mental Retardation.

Schalock, R. L., Brown, I., Brown, R., Cummins, R. A., Felce, D., Matikka, L., et al. (2002). Conceptualization, measurement, and application of quality of life for persons with intellectual disabilities: Report of an international panel of experts. *Mental Retardation, 40*(6), 457–470.

Schalock, M., & Fredericks, H. D. (1990). Comparative costs for institutional services and services and services for selected populations in the community. *Behavioral Residential Treatment, 5*(4), 271–286.

Schiller, E., & Malouf, D. (2000). Research syntheses: Implications for research and practice. In R. Gersten, E. Schiller, & S. Vaughn (Eds.), *Contemporary special education research* (pp. 251–262). Mahwah, NJ: Lawrence Erlbaum Associates.

Schindler, H. K., & Horner, R. H. (2005). Generalized reduction of problem behaviors performed by young children with autism: Building a technology of trans-situational interventions. *American Journal on Mental Retardation, 110*(1), 36–47.

Schleien, S., Green, F., & Stone, C. (2002). Making friends within inclusive community recreation programs. *TASH Connections, 26*(3) 16–23.

Schleien, S., Hornfeldt, D., & McAvoy, L. (1994). Integration and environmental/outdoor education: The impact of integrating students with severe developmental disabilities on the academic performance of peers without disabilities. *Therapeutic Recreation Journal, 28*(1) 25–34.

Schleien, S., Ray, M., & Green, R. (1996). *Community recreation and persons with disabilities: Strategies for inclusion.* Baltimore: Paul H. Brookes.

Schleien, S. J. (1993). Access and inclusion in community leisure services. *Parks and Recreation, 28*(4), 66–72.

Schleien, S. J., Fahnstock, M., Green, R., & Rynders, J. E. (1990). Building positive social networks through environmental intervention in integrated recreation programs. *Therapeutic Recreation Journal, 24*(4), 42–52.

Schleien, S. J., Ray, M. T., & Green, F. P. (1997). *Community recreation and people with disabilities: Strategies for inclusion* (2nd ed.). Baltimore: Paul H. Brooks.

Schunk, D. H. (1985). Participation in goal setting: Effects of self-efficacy and skills of learning-disabled children. *Journal of Special Education, 19,* 307–317.

Schurrer, R., Weltman, & Brammell, H. (1985). Effects of physical training on cardiovascular fitness and behavior patterns of mentally retarded adults. *American Journal on Mental Deficiency, 90,* 167–170.

Schwartz, C. (1995). Assessing levels of personal autonomy among Israeli adults with intellectual disabilities living in group homes and apartment settings. *Australia and New Zealand Journal of Developmental Disabilities, 20,* 41–50.

Schweinhart, L. J., & Weikart, D. P. (1998). High/Scope Perry preschool program effects at age twenty-seven. In J. Crane (Ed.), *Social programs that work* (pp. 148–162). New York: Russell Sage Foundation.

Scruggs, T. E., & Mastropieri, M. A. (1997). Can computers teach problem-solving strategies to students with mild mental retardation? A case study. *Remedial and Special Education, 18*(3), 157–165.

Self-Advocates Becoming Empowered. (2001). Mission Statement. New Fairfield, CT: Author.

Seltzer, G. B. (1981). Community residential adjustment: The relationship among environments, performance and satisfaction. *American Journal of Mental Deficiency, 85,* 624–630.

Seltzer, M. M. (1985). Informal supports for aging mentally retarded persons. *American Journal of Mental Deficiency, 90,* 259–265.

Seltzer, M. M., Greenberg, J. S., Floyd, F. J., Pettee, Y., & Hong, J. (2001). Life course impacts of parenting a child with a disability. *American Journal on Mental Retardation, 106,* 282–303.

Seltzer M. M., Krauss, M. W., Hong, J., & Orsmond, G. I. (2001). Continuity or discontinuing of family involvement following residential transitions of adults with mental retardation. *Mental Retardation, 39,* 181–194.

Seltzer, M. M., Krauss, M. W., Shattuck, P. T., Orsmond, G., Swe, A., & Lord, C. (2003). The symptoms of autism spectrum disorders in adolescence and adulthood. *Journal of Autism and Developmental Disorders, 33,* 565–581.

Senn, C. Y. (1988). *Vulnerable: Sexual abuse and people with an intellectual handicap.* Toronto: Roeher Institute.

Serna, L., & Lau-Smith, J. (January 1, 1995). Learning with purpose: Self-determination skills for students who are at risk for school and community failure. *Intervention in School and Clinic, 30*(3), 142–146.

Shapiro, J. P. (1993). *No pity: People with disabilities forging a new civil rights movement.* New York: Times Books.

Shapiro, J., Monzo, L. D., Rueda, R., Gomez, J., & Blacher, J. (2004). Alienated advocacy: Perspectives of Latina mothers of young adult children with developmental disabilities on service delivery systems. *Mental Retardation, 42,* 37–54.

Shaughnessy, M. F., Glover, T., Greene, M, & Choy, R. Y. L. (1999). Teaching the mentally retarded parenting skills: International perspectives. In P. Retish & S. Reiter (Eds.), *Adults with disabilities: International perspectives in the community* (pp. 145–157). Hillsdale, NJ: Lawrence Erlbaum Associates.

Shevell, M., Ashwal, S., Donley, D., Flint J., Gingold, M. Hirtz, D., et al. (2003). Practice parameter: Evaluation of the child with global developmental delay. *Neurology, 60,* 367–380.

Shevin, M. & Klein, N. (1984). The importance of choice-making skills for students with severe disabilities. *Journal of the Association of Persons with Severe Handicaps, 9*(3), 159–166.

Shonkoff, J. P. (n.d.). *Closing the science-policy gap: A conversation with council chair Jack P. Shonkoff.* Retrieved December 12, 2004, from http://www.developingchild.net/papers/article_1.pdf

Shonkoff, J. P. (2002). A call to pour new wine into old bottles. *Journal of Early Intervention, 25,* 105–107.

Shriner, J. G., Gilman, C. J., Thurlow, M. L., & Ysseldyke, J. E. (1994/95). Trends in state assessment of educational outcomes. *Diagnostique, 20,* 101–119.

Shriner, J. G., Kim, D., Thurlow, M. L., & Ysseldyke, J. E. (1993). *IEPs and standards: What they say for students with disabilities* (Technical Report 5). Minneapolis: University of Minnesota, National Center on Educational Outcomes.

Shoultz, B., & Ward, N. (1996). Self-Advocates Becoming Empowered: The birth of a national organization in the U.S. In G. Dybwad & H. Bersani, Jr., (Eds.), *New voices: Self-advocacy by people with disabilities* (pp. 216–234). Cambridge, MA: Brookline Books.

Sigelman, C. K., Schoenrock, C. J., Winer, J. L., Spanhel, C. L., Hromas, S. G., Martin, P. W., et al. (1981). Issues in interviewing mentally retarded persons: An empirical study. In R. H. Bruininks, C. E. Meyers, B. B. Sigford, & K. C. Lakin (Eds.), *Deinstitutionalization and community adjustment of mentally retarded persons* (pp. 114–132). Washington, DC: American Association on Mental Deficiency.

Sileo, T. W., & Prater, M. A. (1998). Preparing professionals for partnerships with parents of students with disabilities: Textbook consideration regarding cultural diversity. *Exceptional Children, 64*(4), 513–528.

Simon-Rusinowitz, L., Mahoney, K. J., Shoop, D. M., Desmond, S. M., Squillace, M. A., Fay, B. S., et al. (in press). Consumer preferences for a cash option versus traditional services: Florida children and adolescents with developmental disabilities telephone survey. *Journal of Disability Policy Studies.*

Simon-Rusinowitz, L., Mahoney, K. J., Shoop, D. M., Desmond, S. M., Squillace, M. R., & Sowers, J. A. (2001). Consumer and surrogate preferences for a cash option versus traditional services: Florida adults with developmental disabilities. *Mental Retardation, 39*(2), 87–103.

Sinclair, M. F., Christenson, S. L., Evelo, D. L., & Hurley, C. M. (1999). Dropout prevention for youth with disabilities: Efficacy of a sustained school engagement procedure. *Exceptional Children, 65*(1), 7–21.

Singer, G. H. S., Marquis, J., Powers, L., Blanchard, L., DiVenere, N., Santelli, B., et al. (1999). A multisite evaluation of Parent to Parent programs for parents of children with disabilities. *Journal of Early Intervention, 22*(3), 217–229.

Singh, N. N., Sood, A., Somenkler, N., & Ellis, A. (1998). Assessment and diagnosis of mental illness in persons with mental retardation: Methods and measures. *Behavior Modification, 15*(3), 419–443.

Sirolli, E. (1999). Ripples from the Zambezi. Gabriola Island, British Columbia: New Society Publishers.

Skinner, D., Rodriguez, P., & Bailey, D. B. (1999). Qualitative analysis of Latino parents' religious interpretations of their child's disability. *Journal of Early Intervention, 22*(4), 271–285.

Skinner, J. H. (2002). *Cultural and ethnic influences on healthy aging.* Paper presented at the Tampa Scientific Conference on Intellectual Disability, Aging, and Health. Tampa, FL, December 6–9, 2002.

Slavin, R. E., Madden, N. A., Karweit, N. L., Dolan, L. J., & Wasik, B. A. (1992). *Success for all: A relentless approach to prevention and early intervention in elementary schools.* Arlington, VA: Educational Research Service.

Small, S. A. (1995). Action-oriented research: Models and methods. *Journal of Marriage & Family, 57*(4), 941–955.

Smink, J. (2002, December). *Effective strategies for increasing graduation rates.* Presentation before the National Dropout Forum. Washington, DC: U.S. Department of Education, Office of Special Education Programs.

Smith, B. J., McLean, M. E., Sandall, S., Snyder, P., & Broudy, A. (2004). DEC recommended practices: The procedures and evidence base used to establish them. In S. Sandall, M. L. Hemmeter, B. J. Smith, & M. E. McLean (Eds.), *DEC recommended practices: A comprehensive guide for practical application in early intervention/early childhood special education* (pp. 27–39). Longmont, CO: Sopris West.

Smith, D. D., Pion, G., Tyler, N. C., Sindelar, P., & Rosenberg, M. (2001). *The shortage of special education faculty. Why it is happening, why it matters, and what we can do about it.* Washington, DC: U.S. Department of Education, Office of Special Education Programs.

Smith, G. C., Tobin, S. S., & Fullmer, E. M. (1995). Assisting older families of adults with lifelong disabilities. In G. Smith, S. Tobin, E. Robertson-Tchabo, & P. Power (Eds.), *Strengthening aging families: Diversity in practice and policy* (pp. 80–98). Newbury Park, CA: Sage.

Smith, J. D. (Spring, 2002). Abandoning the myth of mental retardation: Carefully constructing developmental disabilities. *MRDD Express, 12*(3), 1, 7.

Smith, S. W., & Brownell, M. T. (1995). Individualized education program: Considering the broad context of reform. *Focus on Exceptional Children, 28*(1), 1–10, 12.

Snell, M. E., & Brown, F. (2000). *Instruction of students with severe disabilities* (5th ed.). Upper Saddle, NJ: Merrill.

Smull, M. W. (1988). Systems issues in meeting the mental health needs of persons with mental retardation. In J. A. Stark, F. J. Menolascino, M. H. Albarelli, & V. C. Gray (Eds.), *Mental retardation and mental health: Classification, diagnosis, treatment services* (pp. 394–398). New York: Springer-Verlag.

Snyder, P., Thompson, B., McLean, M. E., & Smith, B. J. (2002). Examination of quantitative methods used in early intervention research: Linkages with recommended practices. *Journal of Early Intervention, 25,* 137–150.

Sobsey, D. (1994). *Violence and abuse in the lives of people with disabilities: The end of silent acceptance?* Baltimore: Paul H. Brookes.

Sobsey, D. & Doe, T. (1991). Patterns of sexual abuse and assault. *Sexuality and Disability, 9*(3), 243–259.

Sobsey, D., & Varnhage, C. (1991). Sexual abuse and exploitation of disabled individuals. In C. R. Bagley & R. J. Thomlinson (Eds.), *Child sexual abuse: Critical perspectives on prevention, intervention, and treatment* (pp. 121–139). Toronto: Wall & Emerson, Inc.

Social Security Act (including Titles V, XVI, XVIII, XIX, XX, XXI, and Katie Beckett Waiver, 42 U.S.C. Secs. 1381 *et seq.*), 20 U.S.C. (2000).

Social Security Administration (2001). Annual statistical supplement to the Social Security Bulletin. Baltimore: Social Security Administration, Office of Research, Evaluation and Statistics.

Sontag, J. C., & Schacht, R. (1994). An ethnic comparison of parent participation and information needs in early intervention. *Exceptional Children, 60*(5), 422–433.

Soodak, L. C., & Erwin, E. J. (2000). Valued member or tolerated participant: Parents' experiences in inclusive early childhood settings. *Journal of the Association for Persons with Severe Handicaps, 25*(1), 29–41.

Soodak, L. C., Erwin, E. J., Winton, P., Brotherson, M. J., Turnbull, A. P., Hanson, M. J., et al. (2002). Implementing inclusive early childhood education: A call for professional empowerment. *TECSE, 22*(2), 91–102.

Sovner, R. (1986). Limiting factors in the use of DSMIII criteria with mentally ill/mentally retarded persons. *Psychopharmacology Bulletin, 22*, 1055–1059.

Sovner, R., & Hurley, A. D. (1982). Do the mentally retarded suffer from affective illness? *Archives in General Psychiatry, 40*, 61–67.

Sovner, R., & Hurley, A. D. (1990). Assessment tools which facilitate psychiatric evaluation and treatment. *Habilitative Mental Health Care Newsletter, 9*, 91–98.

Sowers, J., Cotton, P., & Malloy, J. (1994). Expanding the job and career options for people with significant disabilities. *Developmental Disabilities Bulletin, 22*(2), 53–62.

Sowers, J., McAllister, R., & Cotton, P. (1996). Strategies to enhance the control of the employment process by individuals with severe disabilities. In L. E. Powers, G. H. S. Singer, & J. Sowers (Eds.), *On the road to autonomy: Promoting self-competence for children and youth with disabilities* (pp. 325–346). Baltimore: Paul H. Brookes.

Sowers, J., McLean, D., &, Owens, C. (2002). Self-directed employment for people with developmental disabilities: Issues, characteristics, and illustration. *Journal of Disability Policy Studies, 13*(2), 96–103.

Sowers, J., Milliken, K., Cotton, P., Sousa, S., Dwyer, L., & Kouwenhoven, K. (2000). A multi-element approach to creating change in a state employment system. In J. Nisbet & D. Hagner (Eds.), *A part of the community: Strategies for including everyone* (pp. 203–236). Baltimore: Paul H. Brookes.

Sparrow, S. S., Balla, D. A., & Cicchetti, D. V. (1984). *Vineland Adaptive Behavior Scales.* Circle Pine, MN: American Guidance Services.

SPeNSE. (2002). *Study of personnel needs in special education.* Retrieved December 8, 2004, from http://ferdig.coe.ufl.edu/spense/

Stancliffe, R., Abery, B., & Smith, J. (2000). Personal control and the ecology of community living settings: Beyond living-unit size and type. *American Journal on Mental Retardation, 105*, 431–454.

Stancliffe, R. J. (1994, October). *Guardianship, behavior management and people with intellectual disability: Policy and practice in Australia.* Paper presented at the National Guardianship Association Conference, Fort Worth, TX.

Stancliffe, R. J. (1997). Community living unit size, staff presence and resident's choice-making. *Mental Retardation, 35*(1), 1–9.

Stancliffe, R. J., & Lakin, K. C. (1998). Analysis of expenditures and outcomes of residential alternatives for persons with developmental disabilities. *American Journal on Mental Retardation, 103*(6), 552–568.

Stancliffe, R. J., & Lakin, K. C. (2005). Context and issues in research on expenditures and outcomes of community supports. In R. J. Stancliffe & K. C. Lakin (Eds.), *Costs and outcomes of community services for people with intellectual disabilities* (pp. 1–23). Baltimore: Paul H. Brookes.

Stancliffe, R. J., Hayden, M., Larson, S., & Lakin, K. C. (2002). Longitudinal study of the adaptive and challenging behavior of deinstitutionalized adults with mental retardation. *American Journal on Mental Retardation, 107*(4), 302–320.

Stancliffe, R. J., & Lakin, K. C. (1999). A longitudinal comparison of day program services and outcomes of people who left institutions and those who stayed. *Journal of The Association for Persons with Severe Handicaps, 24*(1), 44–57.

Stancliffe, R. J., Lakin, K. C., Shea, J. R., Prouty, R. W., & Coucouvanis, K. (2005). The economics of deinstitutionalization. In R. J. Stancliffe & K. C. Lakin (Eds.), *Costs and outcomes of community services for people with intellectual disabilities* (pp. 289–312). Baltimore: Paul H. Brookes.

Stanley v. Illinois, 405 U.S. 645 (1972).

Stewart, R., & Bhagwanjee, A. (1999). Promoting group empowerment and self-reliance through participatory research: A case study of people with physical disability. *Disability and Rehabilitation, 21*(7), 338–345.

Stodden, R., & Jones, M. (2002). *Supporting youth with disabilities to access and succeed in postsecondary education: Essentials for educators in secondary schools.* Minneapolis: University of Minnesota, National Center on Secondary Education and Transition.

Stodden, R. A., & Conway, M. A. (2003). Supporting individuals with disabilities in postsecondary education. *American Rehabilitation 27*(1), 24–33.

Stodden, R. A., & Dowrick, P. (2000a). The present and future of postsecondary education for adults with disabilities. *IMPACT, 13*(1), 4–5. Minneapolis: University of Minnesota, Institute on Community Integration.

Stodden R. A. & Dowrick, P. W. (2000b). Postsecondary and employment of adults with disabilities. *American Rehabilitation, 25*(3), 19–23.

Stodden, R. A., Whelley, T., Chang, C., & Harding, T. (2001). Current status of educational support provision to students with disabilities in postsecondary education. *Journal of Vocational Rehabilitation, 16,* 189–198.

Stomsness, M. M. (1993). Sexually abused women with mental retardation: Hidden victims, absent resources. *Women and Therapy, 14,* 139–152.

Stoneman, Z., & Crapps, J. M. (1990). Mentally retarded individuals in family care homes: Relationships with the family of origin. *American Journal on Mental Retardation, 94*(4), 420–430.

Storms, J., O'Leary, E., & Williams, J. (2000). *The Individuals with Disabilities Education Act of 1997 Transition Requirements: A guide for states, districts, schools, universities and families.* Western Regional Resource Center.

Strauss, W. L., Unis, A. S., Cowan, C., Dawson, G., & Dager, S. R. (2002). Fluorine magnetic resonance spectroscopy measurement of brain fluvoxamine and fluoxetine in pediatric patients treated for pervasive developmental disorders. *American Journal of Psychiatry, 159,* 755–760.

Strohman, R. (2002). Maneuvering in the complex path from genotype to phenotype. *Science, 296,* 701–703.

Strully, J., & Strully, C. (1985). Friendship and our children. *Journal of the Association for Persons with Severe Handicaps, 10*(4), 224–227.

Suarez de Balcazar, Y., Fawcett, S. B., & Balcazar, F. E. (1998). Effects of environmental design and police enforcement on violations of a handicapped parking ordinance. *Journal of Applied Behavior Analysis, 21,* 291–298.

Sugai, G., Horner, R. H., Dunlap, G, Hieneman, M., Lewis, T. J., Nelson, C. M., et al. (2000). Applying positive behavioral support and functional behavioral assessment in schools. *Journal of Positive Behavioral Interventions, 2,* 131–143.

Summers, C. (1987). *Strong and able: An abuse prevention program for children with disabilities.* San Pablo, CA: Rape Crisis of West Contra Costa.

Susa, C., & Clark, P. (1996). *Drafting a blueprint for change: The coordinators manual.* Kingston, RI: University of Rhode Island.

Swanson, J. M., Flodman, P., Kennedy, J., Spence, M. A., Moyzis, R., Schuck, S., et al. (2000). Dopamine genes and ADHD. *Neuroscience Biobehavior Review, 24,* 21–25.

Tarantal, A. F., O'Rourke, J. P., Case, S. S., Newbound, G. C., Li, J., Lee, C. I., et al. (2001). Rhesus monkey model for fetal gene transfer: studies with retroviral-based vector systems. *Molecular Therapy, 3,* 128–138.

Tate, D. G., & Pledger, C. (2003). An integrative conceptual framework of disability: New directions for research. *American Psychologist, 58,* 289–295.

Taub, S., Smith, G., & Bradley, V. (2003). National core indicators project: Monitoring the performance of state developmental disabilities agencies. In V. Bradley & M. Kimmich (Eds.), *Quality enhancement in developmental disabilities* (pp. 259–276). Baltimore: Paul H. Brookes.

Taylor, J. & Wacker, W. (1997). *The 500 Year Delta.* NY: Harper Business.

Taylor, M. (2001). The direct support odyssey. Presentation at the ANCOR conference. Phoenix, AZ.

Taylor, M., Bradley, V., & Warren, R. Jr., (1996). *The community support skill standards: Tools for managing change and achieving outcomes.* Cambridge, MA: Human Services Research Institute.

Taylor, S., Biklin, D., & Knoll, J. (1987). *Community integration of people with severe disabilities.* New York: Teachers College Press.

Taylor, S. J., & Bogdan, R. (1989). On accepting relationships between people with disabilities and non-disabled people: Toward understanding of acceptance. *Disability, Handicap and Society, 4*(1), 21–36.

Taylor, S. J., Bogdan, R., & Lutfiyya, Z. M. (Eds.) (1995). *The variety of community experience: Qualitative studies of family and community life.* Baltimore: Paul H. Brookes.

Taylor, S. J., Bogdan, R., & Racino, J. (1991). *Life in the community: Case studies of organizations supporting people with disabilities.* Baltimore: Paul H. Brookes.

Taylor, S., Racino, J., Knoll, J., & Lutfiyya, Z. (1987a). Down home: Community integration for people with the most severe disabilities. In S. Taylor, D. Biklen, & J. Knoll (Eds.), *Community integration for people with severe disabilities* (pp. 36–63). New York: Teachers College Press.

Taylor, S. J., Racino, J. A., Knoll, J. A., & Lutfiyya, Z. (1987b). *The nonrestrictive environment: On community integration for people with the most severe disabilities.* Syracuse: Human Policy Press.

Taymans, J. M., Corbey, S., & Dodge, L. (1995). A national perspective of state level implementation of transition policy. *Journal for Vocational Special Needs Education, 17,* 98–102.

Technology and Media Division (TAM) of the Council for Exceptional Children and the Wisconsin Assistive Technology Initiative (2003). *Assistive technology consideration.* Retrieved November 21, 2004, from http://www.ideapractices.org/resources/tam/index.html

Technology-Related Assistance for Individuals With Disabilities Act of 1988, Pub. L. No. 100-407 (2000).

Temple University Developmental Disabilities Center (1990). *The final report on the 1990 National Consumer Survey of people with developmental disabilities and their families.* Philadelphia: Authors.

Terkelson, K. G. (1980). Toward a theory of family life cycle. In E. Carter & M. McGoldrick (Eds.), *The family life cycle: A framework of family therapy* (pp. 21–52). New York: Gardner.

Tewey, B. P., Barnicle, K., & Perr, A. (1994). The wrong stuff. *Mainstream, 19*(2), 19–23.

Tharinger, D., Horton, C., & Millea, S. (1993). Sexual abuse and exploitation of children and adults with mental retardation and other handicaps. In M. Nagler (Ed.), *Perspectives on disability* (pp. 247–263). Palo Alto, CA: Health Markets Research.

Thoma, C. A., Rogan, P., & Baker, S. R. (2001). Student involvement in transition planning: Unheard voices. *Education and Training in Mental Retardation and Developmental Disabilities, 36*(1), 16–29.

Thompson, S. J., Johnstone, C., & Thurlow, M. L. (2002). *Universal design applied to large-scale assessment* (Synthesis Report 44). Minneapolis: University of Minnesota, National Center on Educational Outcomes.

Thompson, T. (2002, May 9). HHS announces steps to xfacilitate state programs to foster community integration. Retrieved from http://www.hhs.gov/news/press/2002press/20020509a.html

Thompson, T. (2003, February 12). A review of the Administration FY 2004 health care priorities: Testimony of the Secretary, U.S. Department of Health and Human Services. Washington, DC: U.S. House of Representatives, Full Committee on Energy and Commerce.

Thorin, E., & Irvin, L. (1992). Family stress associated with transition to adulthood of young people with severe disabilities. *Journal of the Association for Persons with Severe Handicaps, 17*(1), 31–39.

Thurlow, M. L., Elliott, J. L., & Ysseldyke, J. E. (1998). *Testing students with disabilities: Practical strategies for complying with district and state requirements.* Thousand Oaks, CA: Corwin Press.

Thurlow, M. L., & Johnson, D. R. (2000). High stakes testing for students with disabilities. *Journal of Teacher Education, 51*(4), 289–298.

Thurlow, M. L., Sinclair, M. F., & Johnson, D. R. (2002). *Issue brief: Students with disabilities who drop out of school—implications for policy and practice.* Minneapolis, MN: University of Minnesota, Institute on Community Integration, National Center on Secondary Education and Transition.

Ticket to Work and Work Incentives Improvement Act (TWWIIA) of 1999, Pub. L. No. 106-170, 42 U.S.C. SS 1305 *et seq.* (2000).

Tilly, J., & Wiener, J. M. (2001). *Consumer-directed home and community services: Policy issues.* Washington, DC: Urban Institute.

Timmons, J. C., Schuster J., & Moloney, M. (2001). Stories of success: Using networking and mentoring relationships in career planning for students with disabilities and their families. *Tools for Inclusion, 9*(2).Boston: Institute for Community Inclusion. Retreived from http://www.community inclusion.org/publications/text/to12text.html

Tomlinson, C. (1999). *The differentiated classroom: Responding to the needs of all learners.* Alexandria, VA: Association for Supervision and Curriculum Development.

Toms-Barker, L. & Maralani, V. (1997). *Challenges and strategies of disabled parents: Findings from a national survey of parents with disabilities.* Berkeley: Through the Looking Glass.

Tossebro, J. (1995). Impact of size revisited: Relation of number of residents to self-determination and deprivatization. *American Journal on Mental Retardation, 100*(1), 59–67.

Touche Ross & Co. (1980). *Cost study of the community based mental retardation regions and the Beatrice State Developmental Center.* Kansas City, MO: Author.

Traustadottir, R., Lutfiyya, Z. M., & Shoultz, B. (1994). Community living: A multicultural perspective. In M. Hayden & B. Abery (Eds.), *Challenges for a service system in transition: Ensuring quality community experiences for persons with developmental disabilities* (pp. 405–426). Baltimore: Paul H. Brookes.

Trembath, D., Sherbondy, A. L., Vandyke, D. C., Shaw, G. M., Todoroff, K., Lammer, E. J., et al. (1999). Analysis of select folate pathway genes, PAX3, and human T in a Midwestern neural tube defect population. *Teratology, 59*, 331–341.

Troxel v. Granville, 530 U.S. 57 (2000).

Turk, M. A., Geremski, C. A., Rosenbaum, P. F., & Weber, R. J. (1997). The health status of women with cerebral palsy. *Archives of Physical Medicine & Rehabilitation, 78*, S10–17.

Turnbull, A. P., Patterson, J. M., Behr, S. K., Murphy, D. L., Marquis, J. G., & Blue-Banning, M. J. (1993). *Cognitive coping, families, & disability.* Baltimore: Paul H. Brookes.

Turnbull, A. P., Turbiville, V., & Turnbull, H. R. (2000). Evolution of family-professional partnerships: Collective empowerment as the model for the early twenty-first century. In J. P. Shonkoff & S. J. Meisels (Eds.), *Handbook of early childhood intervention* (2nd ed., pp. 630–650). New York: Cambridge Printing Press.

Turnbull, A. P., & Turnbull, H. R. (2000*). Families, professionals, and exceptionality: A special partnership.* Columbus, OH: Merrill Publishing Company.

Turnbull, A. P., & Turnbull, H. R. (2001). *Families, professionals, and exceptionality: Collaborating for empowerment* (4th ed.). Upper Saddle River, NJ: Merrill/Prentice Hall.

Turnbull, A. P., Turnbull, H. R., Erwin, E., & Soodak, L. (2006). *Families, professionals, and exceptionality: Positive outcomes through partnerships and trust* (5th ed.). Upper Saddle River, NJ: Merrill/Prentice Hall.

Turnbull, H. R., Beegle, G., Stowe, M. S. (2001). The core concepts of disability policy affecting families who have children with disabilities. *Journal of Disability Policy Studies, 12*(3), 133–143.

Turnbull, H. R., Wilcox, B. L., Stowe, M. J., & Umbarger, G. T. (2001). Matrix of federal statutes and federal and state court decisions reflecting the core concepts of disability policy. *Journal of Disability Policy Studies,12*(3), 144–176.

Twenty-Sixth Institute on Rehabilitation Issues. (2000). *The family as a critical partner in the achievement of a successful employment outcome.* Hot Springs, AK: University of Arkansas: Region 6 Rehabilitation Continuing Education Program.

Tymchuk, A. J., Andron, L., & Rahbar, B. (1988). Effective decision-making/problem solving training with mothers who have mental retardation. *American Journal on Mental Retardation, 92*(6), 510–516.

Unger, D. D. (2002a). Employers' attitudes towards people with disabilities in the workforce: Myths or realities? In D. Unger, J. Kregel, P. Wehman, & V. Brooke (Eds.), *Employers' views of workplace supports: Virginia Commonwealth University Charter Business Roundtable's national study of employers' experiences with workers with disabilities* (pp. 1–12). Richmond, VA: Virginia Commonwealth University, Rehabilitation Research and Training Center.

Unger, D. D. (2002b). How do front-line supervisors in business perceive the performance of workers with disabilities? In D. Unger, J. Kregel, P. Wehman, & V. Brooke (Eds.), *Employers' views of workplace supports: Virginia Commonwealth University Charter Business Roundtable's national study of employers' experiences with workers with disabilities* (pp. 33–46). Richmond, VA: Virginia Commonwealth University, Rehabilitation Research and Training Center.

U.S. Bureau of the Census (2000). Retrieved from http://www.census.gov

U.S. Bureau of the Census (2001). *Statistical Abstract of the United States: 2001* (121st Edition). Washington, DC: Author. Retrieved from http://www.census.gov/prod/www/statistical-abstract-04.html

U.S. Department of Commerce. (2003). *Technology assessment of the U.S. assistive technology industry.* Washington, DC: Bureau of Industry and Security, Office of Strategic Industries and Economic Security, Strategic Analysis Division.

U.S. Department of Commerce, Bureau of the Census. (2000). Census of population and housing (United States): Census tract relationship files (CTRF) (Computer file). Washington, DC: U.S. Department of Commerce, Bureau of the Census (producer), 2001. Ann Arbor, MI: Inter-university Consortium for Political and Social Research (distributor), 2002.

U.S. Department of Education (1995). *Seventeenth annual report to Congress on the implementation of the Individuals with Disabilities Education Act.* Washington, DC: Author.

U.S. Department of Education. (1996). *To assure the free appropriate public education of all children with disabilities: Twentieth annual report to Congress on the implementation of the Individuals with Disabilities Education Act.* Washington, DC: Author.

U.S. Department of Education. (1999). *To assure a free and appropriate public education of all children with disabilities: 21st annual report to Congress on the implementation of the Individuals with Disabilities Education Act.* Washington, DC: Author.

U.S. Department of Education. (2001). *Twenty-third annual report to Congress on the implementation of the Individuals with Disabilities Education Act.* Washington, DC: Author.

U.S. Department of Education. (2002). *No Child Left Behind: A desktop reference.* Washington, DC: Author, Office of the Under Secretary.

U.S. Department of Health and Human Services. (1996). *Physical activity and health: A report of the Surgeon General.* Atlanta: Centers for Disease Control and Prevention, National Center for Chronic Disease Prevention and Health Promotion.

U.S. Department of Health and Human Services. (2000). *Healthy People 2010* (2nd ed.). Washington, DC: U.S. Government Printing Office.

U.S. Department of Health and Human Services. (2001). *Olmstead update no. 5* (SMDL #01-007). Baltimore: Author.

U.S. Department of Health and Human Services. (2002, June 10). *The New Freedom Initiative.* Retrieved November 21, 2004, from http://www.hhs.gov/newfreedom/init.html

U.S. Department of Health and Human Services, Administration for Children and Families (2001). *Head Start Performance Standards on Services for Children with Disabilities.* Retrieved December 22, 2004, from http://www.acf.hhs.gov/programs/hsb/performance/1308/1308_a.htm

U.S. Department of Justice. (2003). Education and correctional populations. Retrieved December 8, 2004, from http://www.ojp.usdoj.gov/bjs/abstract/ecp.htm

U.S. Department of Justice, Nondiscrimination on the Basis of Disability in State and Local Government Services, Section-by-Section Analysis, 56 Fed. Reg. 35705 (July 26, 1991).

U.S. Department of Labor. (1991). The Secretary's commission on achieving necessary skills. Retrieved December 8, 2004, from http://www.wdr.doleta.gov/SCANS/scansorder.cfm

U.S. Department of Labor, Bureau of Census, Employment status of persons with disabilities, November 6, 2004.

U.S. General Accounting Office (2001, September). Report to Congressional Requesters. *Special Minimum Wage Program.* [Online] Retrieved from http://www.gao.gov/new.items/d01886.pdf

U.S. General Accounting Office. (2003, July). *Special education: Federal actions can assist states in improving postsecondary outcomes for youth.* Retrieved December 8, 2004, from http://www.gao.gov/new.items/d03773.pdf

U.S. Public Health Service. (2002). *Closing the gap: A national blueprint for improving the health of individuals with mental retardation.* Report of the Surgeon General's Conference on Health Disparities and Mental Retardation. February 2002. Washington, DC.

U.S. Senate (2003). S. Con. Res. 21 Direct Support Professional Recognition Resolution, Congressional Record, 149, October 22, S13062.

U.S. Social Security Administration, Office of Policy (2001). SSI Annual Statistical Report, 2001. Retrieved from www.ssa.gov/statistics/ssi_annual_stat/2001/index.html

Vandercook, T., York, J., & Forest, M. (1989). The McGill Action Planning System (MAPS): A strategy for building the vision. *Journal of the Association for Persons with Severe Handicaps, 14,* 205–215.

van Schrojenstein Lantman-de Valk, H. M. J., Akker, M., Maaskant, M. A., Haveman, M. J., Urlings, H. F. J., & Kessels, A. G. H. (1997). Prevalence and incidence of health problems in people with intellectual disability. *Journal of Intellectual Disability Research, 41,* 42–51.

Vescovi, A. L., Galli, R., & Gritti, A. (2001). The neural stem cells and their transdifferentiation capacity. *Biomedicine and Pharmacotherapy, 55,* 201–205.

Volpe, J. J. (2001). Neural tube formation and prosencephalic development. In J. Volpe (Ed.), *Neurology of Newborn* (4th ed., pp. 3–44). Philadelphia: W. B. Saunders.

Wagner, M., & Blackorby, J. (1996). Transition from high school to work or college: How special education students fare. *The Future of Children: Special Education for Students with Disabilities, 6*(1), 103–120.

Wagner, M., Cameto, R., & Newman, L. (2003). *Youth with disabilities: A changing population.* A Special Topic Report of Findings from the National Longitudinal Transition Study-2 (NLTS2). Menlo Park, CA: SRI International.

Walker, H., Colvin, G., & Ramsey, E. (1995). *Antisocial behavior in public school: Strategies and best practices.* Pacific Grove, CA: Brookes/Cole.

Walker, H. M., Horner, R. H., Sugai, G., Bullis, M., Sprague, J. R., Bricker, D., et al. (1996). Integrated approaches to preventing antisocial behavior patterns among school-age children and youth. *Journal of Emotional and Behavioral Disorders, 4,* 193–256.

Walker, P. (1999). From community presence to a sence of place: Community experience of adults with developmental disabilities. *Journal of the Association for Persons with Severe Disabilities, 24*(1), 23–32.

Walker, P., & Edinger, B. (1988). The kid from cabin 17. *The Camping Magazine, 60*(7), 18–21.

Wallace, J. F. (2002). Assistive technology and developmental disabilities. In W. I. Cohen, L. Nadel, & M. E. Madnick (Eds.), *Down syndrome: Visions for the 21st century* (pp. 381–391). New York: Wiley-Liss, Inc.

Wallace, J. F., Flippo, K. F., Barcus, J. M., & Behrmann, M. M. (1995). Legislative foundation of assistive technology policy in the United States. In K. F. Flippo, K. J. Inge, and J. M. Barcus (Eds.), *Assistive technology: A resource for school, work, and community* (pp. 1–21). Baltimore: Paul H. Brookes.

Walsh, J. (1997). *Stories of renewal: Community building and the future of urban America.* New York: Rockefeller Foundation.

Walsh, K. K., Kastner, K., & Green, R. G. (2003). Cost comparisons of community and institutional residential settings: Historical review of selected research. *Mental Retardation, 41*(2), 103–122.

Walsh, K. K., & Kastner, T. A. (1999). Quality of health care for people with developmental disabilities: The challenge of managed care. *Mental Retardation, 37,* 1–15.

Walsh, P. N., & Heller, T. (Eds.) (2002). *Health of women with intellectual disabilities* (pp. 59–75). Oxford, UK: Blackwell.

Walsh, P. N., Heller, T., Schupf, N., & Lantman-de Valk, H. (2000). Healthy ageing-adults with intellectual disabilities: Women's health and related issues. *Journal of Applied Research in Intellectual Disabilities, 14,* 195–217.

Wang, M., Mannan, H., Poston, D., Turnbull, A. P., & Summers, J. A. (2004). Parents' perceptions of advocacy activities and their impact on family quality of life. *Journal of Research and Practice in Severe Disabilities, 29*(2), 144–155.

Ward, M. J. (1988). The many facets of self-determination. *Transition Summary,* National Information Center for Children and Youth with Handicaps, *5*(1), 2–3.

Ward, N., Ward, M., Ferris, L., & Powers, L. E. (2000). *Survey of support for self-advocacy organizations by developmental disabilities agencies.* Portland, OR: Oregon Health and Science University, National Center for Self-Determination and 21st Century Leadership.

Warren, J. W., Sobal, J., Tenney, J. H., Hoopes, J. M., Damron, D., Levenson, S., et al. (1986). Informed consent by proxy: An issue in research with elderly patients. *New England Journal of Medicine, 315,* 1124–1128.

Warren, S. F. (2002). Genes, brains, and behavior: The road ahead. *Mental Retardation, 40*(6), 471–477.

Watkins, M. L. (1998). Efficacy of folic acid prophylaxis for the prevention of neural tube defects. *Mental Retardation and Developmental Disabilities Research Reviews, 4,* 282–291.

Way, W., & Rossmann, M. M. (1996). *Lessons from life's first teacher: The role of the family in adolescent and adult readiness for school-to-work transition.* Berkeley, CA: National Center for Research in Vocational Education.

Wehman, P. (1993). *The ADA mandate for social change.* Baltimore: Paul H. Brookes.

Wehman, P. (2001). *Supported employment in business: Expanding the capacity of workers with disabilities.* St. Augustine, Fl.: Training Resource Network, Inc.

Wehman, P. (2002). *Strategies and resources for supporting transition-age adolescents with disabilities.* Baltimore: Paul H. Brookes.

Wehman, P., Everson, J., & Reid, D. H. (2001). Beyond programs and placements: Using person-centered practices to individualize the transition process and outcomes. In P. Wehman (Ed.), *Life beyond the classroom: Transition strategies for young people with disabilities* (pp. 91–124). Baltimore: Paul H. Brookes.

Wehman, P., Kregel, J., & Barcus, M. (1985). From school to work: A vocational transition model for handicapped students. *Exceptional Children, 52*(1), 25–37.

Wehman, P., Revell, W. G., & Brooke, V. (2003). Competitive employment: Has it become the "first choice" yet? *Journal of Disability Policy Studies, 14*(3), 163–173.

Wehman, P., Revell, W. G., & Brooke, V., & Inge, K. (in press). *Inclusive employment: Persons with disabilities going to work.* Baltimore: Paul H. Brookes.

Wehman, P., Revell, G. & Kregel. J. (1998). Supported employment: A decade of rapid growth and impact. *American Rehabilitation, 24*(1), 31–43.

Wehmeyer, M. L. (1995). The use of assistive technology by people with mental retardation and barriers to this outcome: A pilot study. *Technology and Disability, 4,* 195–204.

Wehmeyer, M. L. (1996). Self-determination for youth with significant cognitive disabilities: From theory to practice. In L. E. Powers, G. H. S. Singer, & J. Sowers (Eds.), *On the road to autonomy: Promoting self-competence for children and youth with disabilities* (pp. 115–133). Baltimore: Paul H. Brookes.

Wehmeyer, M. L. (1998). National survey of the use of assistive technology by adults with mental retardation. *Mental Retardation, 36*(1), 44–51.

Wehmeyer, M. L. (2001). Self-determination and transition. In P. Wehman (Ed.), *Life beyond the classroom: Transition strategies for young people with disabilities* (pp. 35–60). Baltimore: Paul H. Brookes.

Wehmeyer, M. L. (2002). The confluence of person-centered planning and self-determination. In S. Holburn & P. M. Vietze (Eds), *Person-centered planning: Research, practice, and future directions* (pp. 51–69). Baltimore: Paul H. Brookes.

Wehmeyer, M. L. (in press). Self-determination, student involvement, and leadership development. In P. Wehman (Ed.), *Life beyond the classroom: Transition strategies for young people with disabilities* (4th ed.). Baltimore: Paul H. Brookes.

Wehmeyer, M. L., Agran, M., & Hughes, C. (1998). *Teaching self-determination to students with disabilities: Basic skills for successful transition.* Baltimore: Paul H. Brookes.

Wehmeyer, M. L., & Bolding, N. (1999). Self-determination across living and working environments: A matched-samples study of adults with mental retardation. *Mental Retardation, 37*(5), 353–363.

Wehmeyer, M. L., Gragoudas, S., & Shogren, K. (in press). Self-determination, student involvement, and leadership development. In P. Wehman (Ed.), *Life beyond the classroom: Transition strategies for young people with disabilities.* Baltimore: Paul H. Brookes.

Wehmeyer, M. L., Kelchner, K., & Richards, S. (1996). Essential characteristics of self-determined behavior of individuals with mental retardation. *American Journal on Mental Retardation, 100*(6), 632–642.

Wehmeyer, M. L. & Lawrence, M. (1995). Whose future is it anyway? Promoting student involvement in transition planning. *Career Development for Exceptional Individuals, 18*(2), 68–84.

Wehmeyer, M. L. & Metzler, C. A. (1995). How self-determined are people with mental retardation? *Mental Retardation, 33*(2), 111–119.

Wehmeyer, M. L., Palmer, S. B., Agran, M., Mithaug, D. E., & Martin, J. E. (2000). Promoting causal agency: The self-determined learning model of instruction. *Exceptional Children, 66*(4), 439–453.

Wehmeyer, M. L., & Schwartz, M. (1997). Self-determination and positive adult outcomes: A follow-up study of youth with mental retardation or learning disabilities. *Exceptional Children, 63*, 245–256.

Wehmeyer, M., & Schwartz, M. (1998). The self-determination focus of transition goals for students with mental retardation. *Career Development for Exceptional Individuals, 21*(1), 75–86.

Wehmeyer, M. L., & Stancliffe, R. J. (2003). Self-determination across the life span. In M. Wehmeyer, B. Abery, D. Mithaug, & R. Stancliffe (Eds.), *Theory in self-determination: Foundations for educational practice* (pp. 229–311). Springfield, IL: Charles C. Thomas.

Weiner, J. S., & Zivolich, S. (1998). Universal access: A natural support corporate initiative at Universal Studios Hollywood. *Journal of Vocational Rehabilitation, 10*(1), 5–14.

Weinshilboum, R. (2003). Inheritance and drug response. *New England Journal of Medicine, 348*, 529–537.

Weissman, I. L., Anderson, D. J., & Gage, F. (2001). Stem and progenitor cells: Origins, phenotypes, lineage commitments, and transdifferentiations. *Annual Review of Cell Developmental Biology, 17*, 387–403.

Wenglinksy, H. (2000, October). *How teaching matters: Bringing the classroom back into discussions of teacher quality.* Princeton, NJ: Educational Testing Service, Policy Information Center. (ERIC Document Reproduction Service No. ED447128).

Werner, K., Horner, R. H., & Newton, J. S. (1998). Reducing barriers to improve the social life of three adults with severe disabilities. *Journal of the Association for Persons with Severe Handicaps, 22*(3) 138–150.

West, M., Hill, J., Revell, G., Smith, G., Kregel, J. & Campbell, L. (2002). Medicaid HCB Waivers and supported employment: Pre- and post-Balanced Budget Act of 1997. *Mental Retardation, 40*(2), 142–147.

Westling, D. L. (1996). What do parents of children with moderate and severe disabilities want? *Education and Training in Mental Retardation and Developmental Disabilities, 32*(2), 86–114.

Westwood, D., & Powers, L. E. (2003). *Survey of AmeriCorps participation by individuals with disabilities.* Portland, OR: Oregon Health & Science University, Center on Self-Determination, Oregon Health & Science University.

White House Conference on Aging Adopted Resolutions (1995). Washington DC: University of Illinois at Chicago.

Whitechurch, G. G., & Constantine, L. L. (1993). Systems theory. In P. J. Boss, W. J. Doherty, R. LaRossa, W. R. Schumm, & S. K. Steinmetz (Eds.), *Sourcebook of family theories and methods: A contextual approach* (pp. 325–352). New York: Plenum Press.

Whyte, W. F. (Ed.) (1991). *Participatory action research.* Newbury Park, CA: Sage.

Wilcox, B., & Bellamy, G. T. (1982). *Design of high school programs for severely handicapped students.* Baltimore: Paul H. Brookes.

Will, M. (1984). *OSERS programming for the transition of youth with disabilities: Bridges from school to working life.* Washington, DC: Office of Special Education and Rehabilitative Services.

Willer, B., & Intagliata, J. (1980). *Deinstitutionalization of mentally retarded persons in New York state.* Buffalo: State University of New York at Buffalo, Research Foundation.

Willer, B., & Intagliata, J. (1984). *Promises and realities for mentally retarded citizens: Life in the community.* Baltimore: University Park Press.

Williams, P., & Shoultz, B. (1982). *We can speak for ourselves.* Bloomington: Indiana University Press.

Wilson, C. & Brewer, N. (1992). The incidence of criminal victimization of individuals with an intellectual disability. *Australian Psychologist, 27*(2), 114–117.

Winton, P. J. (2000). Early childhood intervention personnel preparation: Backwards mapping for future planning. *Topics in Early Childhood Special Education, 20*(2), 87–94.

Winton, P. J., & DiVenere, N. (1995). Family-professional partnerships in early intervention personnel preparation: Guidelines and strategies. *Topics in Early Childhood Special Education, 15*(1), 296–313.

Winton, P. J., McCollum, J., & Catlett, C. (1997). *Reforming personnel preparation in early intervention: Issues, models, and practical strategies.* Baltimore: Paul H. Brookes.

Wisconsin v. Yoder, 406 U.S. 205 (1972).

Wolery, M., & Bailey, D. B. (2002). Early childhood special education research. *Journal of Early Intervention, 25,* 88–99.

Wood, J. W., Johnson, K. G., & Omori, Y. (1967). In utero exposure to the Hiroshima atomic bomb. An evaluation of head size and mental retardation: Twenty years later. *Pediatrics, 39,* 385–392.

Wood, W., & Test, D. W. (2001). *Final performance report: Self-determination synthesis project.* Retrieved December 8, 2004, from http://www.uncc.edu/sdsp/home.asp

Woolley, M. (2003, January, 5–8). *The role of research in social progress.* Unpublished presentation at the Keeping the Promises Conference on National Goals, State of Knowledge, and Research Agenda for Persons with Intellectual and Developmental Disabilities, Washington, DC (quotation cited in The Arc of the U.S. [2003], *Keeping the promises: Findings and recommendations.* Silver Spring, MD: Author).

Workforce Investment Act (WIA) of 1998, Pub. L. No. 105-220, 29 U.S.C. SS 2801 *et seq.* (2000).

World Health Organization. (2000). *Healthy aging—Adults with intellectual disabilities: Summative Report.* Geneva: Author.

World Health Organization (2001a). *International Classification of Functioning, Disability and Health.* Geneva, Switzerland: Author.

World Health Organization (2001b). *World Health Organization: International Classification of Functioning, Disability, and Health.* Retrieved December 20, 2004, from http://www.who.int/research/en/

Worton, R. (2001). Presidential address. *American Journal of Human Genetics, 68,* 819–825.

Wyden, R. (Chair)(1993). Growth of small, residential living programs for the mentally retarded and developmentally disabled. Hearing before the Subcommittee on Regulation, Business Opportunities, and Technology, Committee on Small Business, U.S. House of Representatives, March 29, 1993. (Serial No. 103-8). Washington, DC: U.S. Government Printing Office.

Yamaki, K., & Fujiura, G. (2002). Employment and income status of adults with developmental disabilities living in the community. *Mental Retardation, 40,* 132–141.

Yelin, E., & Katz, P. (1994). Labor force trends of persons with and without disabilities. *Monthly Labor Review, 117,* 36–42.

Young, I., Sigafoos, J., Suttie, J., Ashman, A., & Grevell, P. (1998). Deinstitutionalization of persons with intellectual disabilities: A review of Australian studies. *Journal of Intellectual and Developmental Disabilities, 23*(2), 155–170.

Young, M., Nosek, M., Howland, C., Chanpong, G., & Rintala, D. (1997, December). Prevalence of abuse of women with physical disabilities. *Archives of Physical Medicine and Rehabilitation,* 78, Supplement 5, S32-S38.

Yuan, S., Baker-McCue, T., & Witkin, K. (1996). Coalitions for family support and the creation of two flexible funding programs. In G. H. S. Singer, L. E. Powers, & A. L. Olson (Eds.), *Redefining family support: Innovations in public-private partnerships* (pp. 357–385). Baltimore: Paul H. Brookes.

Zarit, S., Reever, K., & Bach-Peterson, J. (1980). Relatives of the impaired elderly: Correlates of feelings of burden. *Gerontologist, 20,* 649–655.

Zettel, J. J. (1982). Implementing the right to a free appropriate public education. In J. Ballard, B. A. Ramirez, & F. J. Weintraub (Eds.), *Special education in America: Its legal and government foundations* (pp. 23–40). Reston, VA: Council for Exceptional Children.

Zigman, W., Schupf, N., Sersen, E., & Silverman, W. (1996). Prevalence of dementia in adults with and without Down syndrome. *American Journal on Mental Retardation, 100,* 403–412.

Zigmond, N. & Baker, J. (1995). Concluding comments: Current and future practices in inclusive schooling. *Journal of Special Education, 29*(2), 245–250.

Zimmerman, S. L. (1984). The mental retardation family subsidy program: Its effects on families with a mentally handicapped child. *Family Relations, 33*(2), 105–118.

Zoints, L. T., Zoints, P., Harrison, S., & Bellinger, O. (2003). Urban African American family's perceptions of cultural sensitivity within the Special Education system. *Focus on Autism and Other Developmental Disabilities, 18*(1) 41–50.

Praise for *National Goals*

The *National Goals and Research for People with Intellectual and Developmental Disabilities* is by far the most comprehensive view of the field of intellectual and developmental disabilities. Recognizing the life span issues and the complexities of assuring full community membership for people with intellectual and developmental disabilities, this book provides a platform for reform for the next decade. Building upon the knowledge base of the past, this book projects a vision for that future that responds to the concerns of many about where are we going and what needs to be done. The focus on research and the clear implementation recommendations for the future are all within this one text. This book will serve as the road map for the coming decade for people with intellectual and developmental disabilities in all of the major life domains.

William E. Kiernan, Director
Institute for Community Inclusion, University of Massachusetts Boston

National Goals and Research for People with Intellectual and Developmental Disabilities provides much needed guidance for the formulation of public policy and future action that will benefit people with intellectual disabilities in the United States and, as such, this publication challenges us all to take those actions.

Nancy Thaler
Director for Quality Improvement Strategies for
Home and Community Based Services
Centers for Medicare & Medicaid Services

Many federal agencies and much federal legislation call on diverse stakeholders to work together on issues of importance to persons with disabilities. The national goals conference and *National Goals and Research for People with Intellectual and Developmental Disabilities* derived from it, is an exceptional example of the wisdom of such expectations. The many federal and state government, professional, advocacy, and academic organizations that supported this effort should take pride in the product of their commitments and contributions. Most importantly, in that same spirit, they should continue to work together to fulfill the recommendations and achieve the goals outlined in this book.

Robert (Bobby) Silverstein
Center for the Study and Advancement of Disability Policy

This is an important monograph that outlines a clear agenda for future goals and research for people with intellectual and developmental disabilities. With contributions from leading researchers, self-advocates, family members, and other influential persons, it is a 'must read' for policymakers, researchers, and others committed to the participation of people with disabilities in society.

Steve Taylor, Editor, Mental Retardation
Director, Center on Human Policy, Syracuse University

National Goals and Research for People with Intellectual and Developmental Disabilities does something not done anywhere else. In one place, with a coherent structure, all the major issues impacting people with intellectual disabilities across the lifespan are addressed by some of the leading researchers and practitioners in the field. This is an indispensable volume for students, researchers, and practitioners.

Steven M. Eidelman
Robert Edelsohn Professor of Individual and Family Studies
University of Delaware

For the first time, every policy goal related to intellectual disability is collected in this book and accompanied by explanatory descriptions of the data supporting each goal. The book is extremely comprehensive in its scope. It should be read by everyone interested in creating a better future for persons with intellectual disabilities, especially policymakers, administrators, and public officials with responsibility in this area.

David L. Coulter
Harvard Medical School

Most practitioners and professionals would see this title and think this book is just for researchers. They would be wrong. One definition of a true professional is someone who knows what he or she does not know. This book, and the conference on which it was based, represents the best of the professional spirit. It brings together experts in many fields, but also involves and listens to families and people with intellectual and developmental disabilities whose expertise has come from living their lives with dreams and goals, often struggling to find good information. The book summarizes what we do know, raises key questions for exploration and discovery as both practitioners and researchers, and invites us both to listen to the people we serve in order to understand what is most important and to speak in ways that can be understood. Read it. You might be surprised by what you know, and realize you have something to contribute to the key research questions in the field. If it helps us all keep the promises of effective help implicit in the word "professional," everyone learns, and everyone wins.

William Gaventa, Associate Professor
Director, Community and Congregational Supports
The Elizabeth M. Boggs Center on Developmental Disabilities
UMDNJ-Robert Wood Johnson Medical School

As a health services researcher in the field of intellectual disability, I commend the process and product of *National Goals and Research for People with Intellectual and Developmental Disabilities*. It is an important framework for directing model programs development and research in the next decade. The chapters provide thorough reviews and recommendations for inquiry in a broad array of topics that will impact the lives of individuals with developmental disabilities.

Suzanne McDermott, Professor
Department of Family and Preventive Medicine
University of South Carolina School of Medicine Family Practice Center

The ARC of the US and the American Association on Mental Retardation have produced an exquisite piece of scholarship that chronicles the current knowledge-base in the field, as well as articulating the research goals for the future. The work was achieved through the enormous wisdom and skills of a diverse group of stakeholders including family members, people with intellectual and developmental disabilities, scholars and policymakers. It will no doubt serve as the seminal resource in the field and will guide research and practice well into the next decade.

Susan Hasazi
Stafford Distinguished Professor of Leadership and Special Education
University of Vermont

The book is the blueprint for the future of supports for individuals with disabilities and their families. It details everything from research, best practices, public policy, and future direction. Every professional in this field must have this book as a resource on their desk.

Cathy Ficker Terrill, President and CEO
Ray Graham Association

This text provides the 21st century blueprint for improving the lives of children and adults with intellectual and developmental disabilities at home, school, the community, and workplace. An all-encompassing document, this material is evidence based yet highly practical for policymakers and practitioners at all levels. This book brings together the best and brightest minds in the field of intellectual and developmental disabilities with the challenge to implement these cutting edge goals as soon as possible.

Paul Wehman, Professor
Director, Rehabilitation Research and Training Center
Virginia Commonwealth University

This book reports the findings of an extraordinary meeting of over 250 national leaders in developmental disabilities policy, research, advocacy, and service provision who came together to carefully examine the critical role research plays in accomplishing national policy goals. Chapter authors offer insightful in-depth analyses of the challenges and opportunities in today's turbulent policy environment and the need for a new research focus on the real-life priorities of people receiving support, the conversion of what we *know* to what we *do* and on ways of introducing innovative ideas into existing public policy and practice. The book provides a comprehensive description of the key "research to practice" issues that must be addressed if current national policy goals are to be met, and a clear roadmap for all those interested in "keeping the promises" that have been made to Americans with intellectual and developmental disabilities.

Charles R. Moseley, Director of Special Projects
National Association of State Directors of Developmental Services